The Blue Guides

D0519658

Israel and the Palestinian Territories

Kay Prag

BLUE GUIDE

A&C Black • London
WW Norton • New York

1st edition
Published by A & C Black Publishers Limited
37 Soho Square, London W1D 3QZ

© Kay Prag 2002
Maps and plans drawn by Robert Smith © A & C Black.
'Blue Guides' is a registered trade mark

All photographs in this guide are reproduced with kind permission of Kay Prag.

A CIP catalogue record of this book
is available from the British Library.

ISBN 0–7136–4844–9

Published in the United States of America by
WW Norton and Company, Inc
500 Fifth Avenue, New York, NY 10110

Published simultaneously in Canada by
Penguin Books Canada Limited
10 Alcorn Avenue, Toronto, Ontario M4V 3B2

ISBN 0–393–32249–1 USA

Kay Prag studied archaeology at the universities of Sydney, London and Oxford, and has excavated on many sites in the Near and Middle East, beginning in the Old City of Jerusalem in 1963. She is currently working on the publication of those excavations in Jerusalem, and of more recent work at Tell Iktanu in Jordan.

A&C Black uses paper produced with elemental chlorine-free pulp, harvested from managed sustainable forests.

Cover picture: the Dome of the Rock, the Two Domes, © Antoine Simmenauer, courtesy of Robert Harding.com
Frontispiece: the entrance to the Qubba Nahwiyya in the Haram, Jerusalem

Printed and bound in Great Britain by Butler and Tanner Ltd, Frome and London.

Contents

Maps and plans

Introduction

This guide covers all the land on the southern half of the eastern coast of the Mediterranean that is currently directly accessible from Israel. It comprises a most varied landscape of considerable beauty and drama, despite its relatively small scale (the maximum distance between Lebanon in the north and Egypt in the south is 420km, between the Mediterranean coast and the Jordan River just 110km). The heights may be hills rather than mountains, but the landscape includes the lowest spot on the surface of the globe: the Dead Sea. The cliffs and valleys as much as the separate regions into which the guide is divided, provide a diversity hardly to be matched elsewhere.

The independent state of Israel was declared in May 1948 in Tel Aviv. Israel has an elected president, and is governed by an elected prime minister and representatives in the Knesset (parliament), which sits in Jerusalem. Israel is a place of rapid growth, with a population expanding by birth and immigration from a total of just over a million in 1949 to just under six million in 1997. The population in 1997 was approximately 4.7 million Jews, 868,000 Muslims, 126,000 Christians, and 96,000 Druze.

The Palestinian Territories are located in the Gaza Strip (until 1967 under Egyptian jurisdiction) and the West Bank of the Jordan River (until 1967 under Jordanian jurisdiction) and are the subject of ongoing negotiations. Responsibility for the internal administration has rested with the Palestine National Authority since 1994, led since its inauguration by Chairman (from 1996 President) Yasser Arafat, with an elected Palestinian Legislative Council, and ministries based in Gaza. Approximately three million Arabs live in the West Bank area and the Gaza Strip, of whom 3 per cent are Christian and the rest Sunni Muslim; many Palestinians living abroad also have residency rights.

The focus of the region is Jerusalem, and for good reason much of the guide is devoted to it. Its significance for Eastern as well as Western culture can hardly be overstated; it is one of the great cities of the world, deeply lodged in the hearts of Jew, Christian and Muslim. It was rarely of material significance, just a small town in the hills, and the wonderful buildings and care lavished on it derived not from its own wealth but from the religious significance it held for its possessors. The capital cities of the region usually lay in the fertile coastal plains and valleys, on the great strategic and commercial routes: materially rich places such as the Canaanites' Hazor and Megiddo, the Egyptians' Gaza, Herod the Great's and the Romans' Caesarea, Ramla of the early Islamic caliphs, and the capital of the first state of Israel at Tel Aviv.

The region was also the great land bridge between Asia and Africa, with a coast open to Mediterranean commerce and to invasion from Egypt, Asia and Europe. Its political history, as well as its ethnic and linguistic makeup, is a reflection of all this. The guide too reflects the diversity of the region: the coastal plain with its combination of alluvial soils and sand dunes, the wooded hills of Galilee in the north, the natural beauty still preserved in the central hills, the desert scenery of the Negev, and the ancient richness and importance of the Jordan Valley. It attempts to introduce the traveller to the changes through the long millennia of archaeology and history, including the environmental and political changes. The intention is to give priority to information which may not be readily available on the site; and the emphasis is on the history and the archaeology, rather than on modern politics, art and popular culture. These can change so rapidly that information is best sought in the vast array of tourist literature, newspapers and websites now available, which can be more quickly updated than a guide book. Independent visitors are advised to check these resources before travelling, as border crossing rules are volatile. For such travellers, awareness of local customs and manners can disproportionately increase the pleasures of travel in the area. For those with more limited time, there are many good tour companies that can make appropriate arrangements.

Acknowledgements

In the years that have passed since *Blue Guide Jerusalem* was published I have continued to be grateful to all those then acknowledged. In the compilation of this guide, I am particularly indebted to the latest edition of Edmund Bosworth's *The New Islamic Dynasties*, to Denys Pringle's volumes on the Crusader monuments; to the Israel Tourist Board and the Israel Nature and National Parks Protection Authority for their information; to Dani Bahat, Roni Reich, Emmanuel Eisenberg, Shimon Gibson for information on their work and other help; for on-the-spot help from Elaine Myers, Joanne Clark and Yuval Yekutieli; to Andrew Petersen for information on some of the Islamic buildings; to Stephen Day and the Palestine Exploration Fund who provided the opportunity to visit Bethlehem; to Jonathan Prag for his photography and company in visiting sites, and to John Prag for his patience during the whole process. The British School of Archaeology in Jerusalem (latterly the Council for British Research in the Levant) again provided the base and the invaluable library background for visits to the region. I would again like to thank the Palestine Exploration Fund and the John Rylands Library of the University of Manchester for access to their splendid libraries. In the end, it is the libraries, as much as the sites, which provide the resources and the pleasures behind producing a guide book. Finally, I wish to record my debt to Denys Pringle who read the text and saved me from a number of errors.

How to use the guide

Background information is provided in the first section, including practical and historical details. The guide to Jerusalem forms the second section. The final section covers the rest of the country, divided geographically (partly reflecting political borders) into six zones. It is prefaced by some information on the flora and fauna for which the region is remarkable and which emphasises how great is the need for conservation measures there. The Palestinian territories, except for Gaza and Jericho, are mainly in the central hills zone. It is not useful to offer routes, as each traveller's agenda will be different, and governed by available time and interests. Many routes will involve more than one geographical zone, as distances are generally short. By putting the sites into geographical zones it is hoped that the descriptions will benefit from the contextual historical and environmental information; also, if time permits after a visit to one site, you will be aware of what else can be seen in the vicinity, or along your particular route.

Generally within each zone the sites are listed in order from north to south, with rough priority from west to east. In such an arrangement, the index is of course of major importance. The variant spellings of site names is a great problem; made worse by there usually being Hebrew, Arabic or historical (biblical or Crusader or other) variants. Generally the guide attempts to give priority to the most popular place name in English-speaking usage, but usually lists the Hebrew and Arabic variants in some consistent transliteration. Be aware that transliteration varies widely—the variants are not necessarily incorrect, just bewildering.

Highlights

The guide uses a system of stars for the major sites and monuments recommended as priorities for the visitor. In Jerusalem, the 7C AD Dome of the Rock on the 1C BC–AD Temple platform, the 12C Church of the Holy Sepulchre and the 16C city walls must be on the itinerary of every visitor. It is impossible to list all the sites that can be visited in the regions. For a rounded view of the long history of the country, the following are suggested:

Neolithic	The great tower at Jericho
Chalcolithic	The Nahal Mishar hoard in the Israel Museum
Early Bronze Age	The town at Arad
Middle Bronze Age	The great mudbrick ramparts and gates at Ashkelon and Dan; the newly discovered towers protecting the Gihon spring in Jerusalem
Late Bronze Age	The palace at Hazor and the basalt sculptures found on the site are now dispersed between the local museum and the Israel Museum
Iron Age	Megiddo with its gates and water system
Hellenistic period	The towers at Samaria
Herod the Great	The enclosure of the mosque at Hebron, and Herodion
Later Roman period	The Dionysus mosaic at Zippori
Byzantine period	The town of Caesarea
Early Islamic period	The palace at Khirbat al-Mafjar, and its decoration in the Rockefeller Museum
Crusader period	Acre and Nimrod's Castle
Later Islamic period	The medieval walls of Jerusalem and the town at Acre

To draw all this together, visit the Israel Museum and the Islamic Museum in the Haram, in Jerusalem.

Abbreviations

The following abbreviations are used in this guide.

Abbreviations

A.   Arabic
H.   Hebrew

Books of the Bible

Gen.   Genesis
Levit.   Leviticus
Num.   Numbers
Deut.   Deuteronomy
Jos.   Joshua
Jud.   Judges
I Sam.   1st Book of Samuel
II Sam.   2nd Book of Samuel
I Chron.   1st Book of Chronicles
II Chron.   2nd Book of Chronicles
Neh.   Nehemiah
Ps.   Psalms
Jer.   Jeremiah
Zech.   Zechariah

Apocryphal books

Macc.   Maccabees

Symbols used in the guide

☎   telephone
▤   fax
▨   web site/e-mail address

PRACTICAL INFORMATION

 Planning your trip

When to go

In general, the region has a Mediterranean climate, which means that nearly all rain falls in the winter and spring, and the rest of the year is hot and dry. However, the climate varies noticeably from one area to another: the hill country is colder (possibly around 6°C in January) and has occasional snow in winter (November to March); the coast is both warmer, and more humid in summer (June to September). The Jordan Valley and Dead Sea have their own climate, very dry and with very hot summers (around 40°C in August), but the mild winters make Elat and Jericho ideal winter resorts. The Negev is arid, hot in summer, cold in winter and at night. To visit sites, spring and autumn are generally the best times; to avoid rain, go in summer and autumn; for swimming, in summer; for flowers and birds, in March to May. The nights tend to be cool in the hills even in summer, so bring a light jacket; warm clothes and rain gear are necessary for the winter; and in all regions, you will need comfortable, strong shoes, or sandals in the summer, both with good soles. If you visit in summer, a hat, sun protection cream and sunglasses are essential.

National Tourist Boards/Organisations

Israel Government Tourist Offices (IGTO) abroad

Contact the following offices for updated lists of hotels, bed and breakfasts, kibbutz hotel and guest houses, kibbutz fly-drive holidays, self-catering accommodation and campsites; information on holidays, kibbutz work, archaeological participation, bus and train services, ferries, border crossing regulations, road regulations and local tour operators. Useful **web sites** include www.infotour. co.il and www.goisrael.com

UK: 180 Oxford St, London W1N 0EL (☎ 020 7299 1111, 🖷 020 7299 1112); the Israel Information Centre, 142 Bury Old Rd, Manchester M8 6HD (☎ 0161 721 4344), and also Birmingham, ☎ 0121 643 2688; Scotland, ☎ 0141 577 8240, 🖷 0141 577 8241; Wales ☎/🖷 029 2046 1780.

USA: 800 Second Avenue, New York. NY 10017 (☎ 212/499 5650, 🖷 212 499 5655); 5 South Wabash Ave, Chicago, Illinois 60603 (☎ 312/782 4306, 🖷 312/782 1243); 5151 Belt Line Road, Suite 1280, Dallas, Texas 75240 (☎ 800/472 6364, 972/991 9097/8, 🖷 972/392 3521); 6380 Wilshire Boulevard #1718, Los Angeles, California 90048 (☎ 213/658 7462/3, 🖷 213/658 6543)

Canada: 180 Bloor St West, Suite 700, Toronto, Ontario M5S 2V6 (☎ 800/669 2369, 416/64 3784, 🖷 416 /964 2420)

Australia: Australia-Israel Chamber of Commerce, Tourism Department, 395 New South Head Road, Double Bay, Sydney, NSW 2028 (☎ 29326 1700; 🖷 29326 1676).

Netherlands: Stadhouderskad 2, 1054 ES Amsterdam. ☎ 020 612 8850.

Palestinian Territories
Information is available from the following organisations:
Palestinian Ministry of Tourism and Antiquities in Gaza, ☎ 07 282 9461/2, ✉ www.visit-palestine.com/
PASSIA (The Palestinian Academic Society for the Study of International Affairs), ✉ www.passia.org which has information on travel, accommodation and guided tours
The Palestinian Association for Cultural Exchange (PACE), 20 Jerusalem-Nablus Road, POB 841, Ramallah and ✉ www.planet.edu/~pace/ offers maps, guide books and lists of guides to the Palestinian Territories
Bir Zeit University, ✉ www.birzeit.edu/

Formalities
It should be stressed that the first resort for information for all independent travellers should be the Israeli Consulate, which is usually located in the capital city of countries that maintain diplomatic relations with Israel; some addresses, telephone and websites are listed below.

UK: Israel Embassy, Consular Department, 15a Old Court Palace, London W8 4QB,☎ 020 7957 9500/visa enquiries 9517, ▤ 020 7957 9577; ✉ www.israel-embassy.org.uk/london. Open Mon–Thur 10.00–13.30, Fri 10.00–12.30.

USA: Embassy of Israel, 3514 International Drive, NW, Washington DC 20008, ☎ 202/364 5500; ✉ www.israelemb.org/; Consular Department ☎ 202/364 5557. There are nine other consular departments through the USA which serve their respective regions, at Atlanta, Boston, Chicago, Houston, Los Angeles, Miami, New York, Philadelphia and San Francisco.

Canada: 50 O'Connor Street, Suite 1005, Ontario K1P 6L2, Ottawa, ☎ 613/567 6450.

Australia: 6 Turrana Street, Yarralumla, Canberra, ACT 2600, ☎ 02 6273 1309.

Netherlands: Buitenhof 47, 2513 AH, Den-haag, ☎ 070 376 0500.

Republic of Ireland: Carrisbrook House, 122 Pembroke Road, Ballsbridge, Dublin ☎ 4 01 668 0303.

Passports and visas
All tourists to Israel are required to have full passports which should be valid for a minimum six months from date of entry, and to be in possession of a return ticket. UK, US, Canadian and many other nationals can be issued visitor visas free of charge at point of entry but this should be checked before travelling. The Israeli tourist visa is valid for three months, and must be retained until departure from Israel. For information on longer stays, or non-holiday visits, the relevant consulates should be consulted. There are no vaccination requirements for entry to Israel. There are no additional visa formalities for visiting the Palestinian Territories, but passports should be carried at all times and may need to be presented at crossing points to areas under the Palestinian Authority. It is possible to travel to and from Israel via Jordan and Egypt but careful enquiry concerning current border crossing regulations, times, exit/entry charges and visas should be made at the relevant embassies prior to booking/travelling.

Those intending to visit an Arab or African country which does **not** have diplomatic connections with Israel can request to have their Israeli entry form rather than their passport stamped on arrival (at discretion of the Israel authorities), as passports with Israeli visas or entry stamps are not accepted in those countries. Note that Jordanian and Egyptian departure stamps at land crossing entry points to Israel are also an indication of a visit to Israel. Passports will also be stamped if an extension of stay in Israel is obtained from the Ministry of the Interior, the offices of which can be found in most major Israeli towns.

These regulations apply to visitors arriving by air at Ben Gurion Airport, which is open 24 hours daily. The same regulations apply to land crossings from Egypt and Jordan but the arrangements are more complex (see below), more subject to change and should be checked before travelling. If visas are required, they must generally be obtained in advance.

Border crossings to/from Egypt Tourist visas for Egypt (necessary for all nationalities except South African) must be obtained in advance from the Egyptian consulates in Elat and Tel Aviv, or abroad. Tourist visas restricted to the Sinai coast and St Katherines are issued free at Taba for a stay of up to seven days but visitors must return via Taba; check for updates on costs and regulations with the consular section of the Egyptian Embassy in your country (in London, 2 Lowndes St, Knightsbridge, ☎ 020 7235 9777); for other information, contact your local Egypt Tourist Office. Tourists are admitted with Israeli stamps in their passports, but cannot proceed to other Arab and African countries which do not have diplomatic connections with Israel (see above).

The **Rafiah (Rafah) border crossing** is open 09.00–17.00. Rafiah lies 50km southwest of Ashkelon. *Metzada Tours* (☎ 03 544 4454) and *Pullman Tours* (☎ 03 527 0474/5/6; ▤ 03 527 0477) provide 10 and 12-hour bus rides to Cairo, the first from Tel Aviv, the latter from Tel Aviv and Jerusalem. Check for updated prices of tickets and border exit tax.

The **Nitzana border crossing** is open 08.00–16.00. It is 60km southwest of Ashkelon.

The **Taba border crossing** is open 24 hours, closed on Yom Kippur and Id al-Adha (☎ 07 637 2104). Taba lies 7km south of the centre of Elat, and is served by a frequent, regular bus service (no. 15) from the Central Bus Station in Elat (note that the bus stops running at 16.30 on Friday). The border crossing may take up to two to three hours depending on how many are in the queue. Exit tax from Israel 66NIS (no exit tax if going to Taba only); border tax to Egypt is about 17EP.

Transport: note that (at the time of writing) occasional buses run to Nuwaiba only; otherwise hire cars or very expensive taxis are available on the Egyptian side of the border. Private cars only (not pick-ups, diesel, 4 x 4 etc, or rental) may cross the frontier subject to restrictions and insurance.

Border crossings to/from Jordan Visa regulations should be checked in advance with the Jordan Consulate in your country (in London ☎ 020 7937 3685) or in Tel Aviv (☎ 03 751 7722). You may cross as a tourist with an Israeli stamp in your passport, but cannot proceed to other Arab and African countries that do not have diplomatic connections with Israel (see above). Only privately owned vehicles (not taxis or rented cars) with appropriate documentation, which are not registered in Israel or Jordan, may cross the border.

The Beth Shan border crossing (Shaikh Hussain Bridge) is the main crossing for tourism, and may be used by individuals requiring a Jordanian visa on the border. It is located on the Jordan River 23km south of the Sea of Galilee. Open Sun–Thur 06.30–22.00, Fri–Sat 08.00–20.00, closed on Yom Kippur and Islamic New Year. ☎ 06 658 6422 (Jordan ☎ 00962 6 37524). Departure tax NIS 53.

Transport: regular bus services from Tel Aviv, Haifa and Nazareth to Amman go by this bridge; it is advisable to book in advance via Dan Information (☎ 03 639 4444), New Central Bus Station, Tel Aviv, open Sun–Thur 06.00–15.00. Bus departs 07.00, arrives Amman 14.00. Jordanian visa must be obtained in advance if you are travelling by bus.

The Allenby Bridge border crossing (in Jordan, the King Hussain Bridge), ☎ 02 994 2626, the principal crossing for Palestinians, is located on the Jordan River 12km north of the Dead Sea, east of Jericho. Open 08.00–24.00; Fri 08.00–15.00, closed Sat and Jewish holidays. It is necessary to arrive at least 90 minutes before the bridge closes. Departure tax NIS 102. Jordanian visa should be obtained in advance.

Transport: service taxis (set rate for a seat) from Jerusalem (Damascus Gate) and local bus from Jericho.

The Arava border crossing is 4km north of the town of Elat. Open Sun–Thur 06.30–0.00, Fri–Sat 08.00–08.00, closed Yom Kippur and Id al-Adha. ☎ 07 633 6811. Departure tax NIS 53 (NIS 18 if you are returning the same day and using public transport).

Transport: *Egged* bus no. 16 from Elat Central Bus Station; taxi to Aqaba.

Customs
Video equipment and personal computers must be declared by visitors to Israel and deposits paid against duty and taxes, which will be refunded when re-exported on departure. More detailed information is available through the consulates.

Tour operators
A current list of many companies offering tours, holidays and travel arrangements to visit Israel is available from the tourist information services and from travel agents. Among those available in the UK are Andante Travels, Israel Travel Service, Peltours and Thomson Holidays; in the USA, AAA Travel and Carlson Wagonlit Travel. Many pilgrimage tours are available through church and other organisations.

Money and currency regulations
The unit of currency throughout Israel and the Palestinian Territories is the **New Israeli Shekel** (NIS) which is divided into 100 **agorot**. Shekels are available as paper notes for values of NIS 200, 100, 50 and 10, and as coins for NIS 10, 5, 1 and for 50 (NIS 0.5), 10 and 5 agorot. Jordan dinars are also accepted in Palestinian areas. The most usually cited and accepted currency for hotels, car hire and many goods is the US$. Other currencies can be changed in banks and post offices or at money changers who can easily be found in the areas of the Damascus Gate, Jaffa Gate and Salah al-Din Street in Jerusalem. Travellers' cheques (dollar and sterling) are exchangeable; and cash machines accepting various international credit cards (American Express, Mastercard, Visa) are

widely accessible in Israel. Taxis, buses etc require local currency, and it is advisable to obtain some currency in small denominations before arrival for these purposes, though exchange services are available at the airport.

There are no restrictions on the amount of local and foreign currency brought into the country; but the amount of NIS which can be exchanged for foreign currency on departure at Ben Gurion or Haifa is limited to US$500 without a bank receipt as evidence of original exchange. Payment in foreign currency exempts tourists from paying Value Added Tax on accommodation bills and some purchases, including package holidays paid abroad. Elat offers duty free shopping.

Health

No vaccinations are legally required, but bear in mind the type of holiday you are planning—whether camping or luxury hotel—and the areas to be visited (check with your doctor). Most upset stomachs are due to change in diet, and it is recommended that some medication be carried and instructions followed carefully. Sun is a far more potent factor than anticipated by many visitors from northern climates, and protection for skin, eyes, and head (including the back of the neck) is important; sunburn is dangerous, but so also is sunstroke. To avoid dehydration, drink plenty of non-alcoholic fluids and have a reasonable salt intake. Mosquito repellents will be needed in the summer. It is sensible to have a small pack of immediate remedies and travel/medical insurance. The medical facilities are generally good.

 Getting there

By air

The main airport is the **Ben Gurion International Airport** (☎ 00972 3 972 3344) immediately north of Lod on the coastal plain, 18km southeast of Tel Aviv and 51km northwest of Jerusalem. It is served by 24 international airlines. Smaller international airports (mainly charter) are located in the south of the country at Ovda and at Elat. The national carrier is *El Al*; it operates direct flights from London, Manchester, New York, Los Angeles, Baltimore, Washington, Miami and from Canada (Toronto). As flights out of Ben Gurion are often early in the day, and there is usually a three-hour check-in requirement, an advance check-in service is available the previous evening (not Friday or a holiday eve) in Jerusalem, Tel Aviv, Haifa and Elat. *TWA*, *Tower Air* and *Air Canada* also operate direct flights from North America. Return flights should be reconfirmed not less than 72 hours before departure. There are also regular charter flights from European countries, see travel agents. There is an information office at the airport, ☎ 03 971 1485.

The **Gaza International Airport**, south of Gaza City (☎ 07 213 5696) currently serves charter flights from many countries.

Travelling on

A shuttle bus (no. 222) operates hourly from the airport to Tel Aviv between

â

04.00 and midnight. *Egged* buses operate every 15 minutes from 05.00 to 22.00 for Tel Aviv, every 30 minutes from 06.30 to 20.00 for Jerusalem, every 40 minutes from 06.30 to 20.30 for Haifa.

The journey to Jerusalem takes up to one hour; intending travellers should check availability of transport on the eve of Jewish religious holidays and on major holidays. Transport by sharut or service taxis (set rate for a seat in a taxi), and by ordinary taxi is also available. *Nesher Taxi Service* (21 King George St, Jerusalem, ☎ 02 625 7227) offers a 24-hour shared taxi (usually a nine-seater minibus) service from your door to the airport at fixed fares, but requires at least 24 hours' advance booking.

By train

There are no international train connections to Israel. The railways built in the earlier 20C only operate internally.

By bus

Coach connections to Egypt and Jordan provide regular services to the border crossing points (see border crossing information above). For times and costs, check locally.

By car

Questions about rules and regulations concerning cars, caravans and permits should be addressed to the *Israel Automobile Club*, POB 36144, Tel Aviv, Israel. Cars can be imported by foreign visitors for up to one year, and without duty for up to three months. Private cars with the appropriate documents and insurance may be taken across the Jordan and Egyptian border crossings, but not rented cars or taxis.

By sea

The main passenger port is Haifa which is served by car ferries mainly from Italy, Greece, Rhodes, Turkey and Cyprus. The *Adriatica* and *Hellenic Mediterranean* lines operate services to Israel. Check at travel agents for details. The ferry from Piraeus to Haifa via Cyprus, Rhodes or Crete takes about 58 hours. Information on prices, timetables, routes, customs and other formalities can be obtained from tourist offices; a branch of the Israel Government Tourist Office is located at Haifa Port. Information on cruise companies which include Israel may also be obtained from Tourist Information offices and travel agents.

 # Where to stay

With a range of hotels, kibbutz country hotels and guest houses, holiday villages, youth hostels, field schools, hospices, self-catering rooms and apartments, and campsites, there is a huge range of accommodation from which to choose. Prices vary seasonally, with Easter, other religious holidays and summer as high season, and are generally higher in Israel than in the Palestinian Territories. Package holidays of various kinds offer flexibility, especially in fly/drive arrangements and cheaper access to luxury hotels. Lists of available accommodation can be obtained from Israel Tourist Offices. For up-to-date listings, rates and booking internet deals, see also ✉ www.inisrael.com/hotels and http://tourism.yellow-pages.co.il/. Other organisations to contact include:

Israel Youth Hostels Association, 1 Shazar Street, Jerusalem 91060, ☎ 02 655 8400, 📠 02 655 8401.

Society for the Protection of Nature in Israel, SPNI Tourist Service, 4 Hashefela St, Tel Aviv 66183, ☎ 03 6388666, 📠 03 687 7695.

Israel Camping Association, 112 Moshav, Mishmar Hashiva, Israel, 50297, ☎ 03 960 4524 or 03 960 4350; 📠 03 960 4712.

Christian Information Center, ☎ 02 627 2692; 📠 02 628 6417.

Jerusalem Media and Communication Center, POB 25047, #7 Nablus Rd, East Jerusalem 97300, Israel, ✉ www.jmcc.org.

Food and drink

Food

Food is generally very good, well and cleanly prepared and locally produced. At the simplest level, salads of tomatoes, cucumbers and other local produce, including yogurt, cheese and eggs, are a staple diet, especially at breakfast. In most areas the main meal is taken at midday. It is sensible to restrict the intake of uncooked food, vegetables and fruits during your first few days in the country; also to wash fruit carefully and to avoid street stalls or anywhere that appears to offer less than the cleanest kitchens. The range of backgrounds in Israel's population results in a wide variety of food; thanks to Jews of East European origin you can find bagels, latkes, blintzes, bortsch, goulash, schnitzel, steak and gefilte fish, strudels—and excellent cake and coffee shops; North African Jews may offer chicken dishes with rich sauces.

Arab cooking is mainly available in East Jerusalem, old Acre and Palestinian towns such as Ramallah and Jericho, where restaurants feature *mezze* (vegetable or meat starters with 25 or more varieties), kebabs and chicken dishes. Arab cooking usually reflects that of the old Ottoman world, modified by local resources, and has deeply influenced the cuisine of modern Israel.

Some local cheap and characteristic foods widely available include **falafel** (deep fried balls of seasoned ground chickpeas), **humous** (creamy purée of chickpeas, sesame paste, oil and lemon), **tahina** (sesame cream purée), and many salads with egg-plant and tomatoes, all usually offered with or in pitta bread or wrapped in flat unleavened bread with a variety of sauces; **kebabs** (lamb, minced or cut, or chicken, grilled on a skewer) often with rice; and **shawarma** (sliced lamb or chicken cooked on a spit). If buying at a street stall choose one that is clearly popular and has a rapid turnover with freshly cooked food, usually at midday. Apart from the pitta bread, *kayik* (the rings of bread covered with sesame seeds) are very good; among the Arabs bread is often eaten with seasoning of herbs, spices and oil, and bread sellers will often have small por tions of such seasoning available. A few old-style bread bakeries still exist. Confectionery includes many of the pastries familiar within the old Ottoman world, such as *baklava* (thin, flaky pasty enclosing chopped nuts and covered with syrup or honey) and *kanafe* (trays of orange pastry dough covering soft white cheese, in syrup—best served hot); and also fat plaits of gum-like grape-juice sweets.

Beef, chicken and fish dishes are the foundation of most restaurant menus, particularly grilled or minced. In Arab restaurants grilled chicken or lamb kebabs, frequently with rice, aubergine, lentil or beans (*ful*) are good; stuffed vegetables; *magloubah* (layers of aubergine, chicken and rice, served 'upside-down'); musakhan (chicken baked smothered in olive oil and onions, served with sumak spice on bread); *mansaf* (lamb or chicken in a yogurt sauce on rice and bread) and a huge variety of salads including normally humous (chick pea and tahini paste), *labaneh* (thick yogurt-style cheese), *mutabal* (aubergine purée), tabouleh (cracked wheat with parsley, mint and lemon) and *kibbeh* (pounded cracked wheat shell with meat and nut stuffing, usually fried). In the varied cuisines in restaurants in Israel an international range of dishes is available, but grilled steak or fish is often listed, liver in a variety of styles, stuffed meats and poultry, sometimes with fruit or vegetable sauces; pasta dishes; meatballs with varied sauces; schnitzels (thin veal or turkey steaks coated with matsos crumbs); sweet and sour dishes; *cholent* (beans and other vegetables stewed slowly usually with beef); characteristic starters in East European Jewish restaurants may include blintzes (small pancakes, often stuffed with sweet cheese) or gefilte fish (marinated, jellied, minced or stuffed); or beetroot soup (bortsch) or chicken and dumpling soup. Both Israeli and Palestinian restaurants may offer more adventurous meat cuts, such as spleen and heart.

Drink

All tap water is drinkable and chlorinated. However, it is wise to introduce your system gradually to the local tap water; bottled water is widely available, as are excellent fresh fruit juices, as well as the usual range of cans and bottles of fizzy drinks. In restaurants, coffee is served in various ways, from filter to Nescafé, and espresso to 'Turkish'. In cafés it will probably come out of a machine. Particularly in Arab areas, tea, possibly with mint, is still sometimes served in a glass; it usually comes with sugar so remember to ask for no sugar if so required.

Wines, beers and spirits, both imported and local, are widely available for tourists. The local varieties of beer include *Taybah* (fairly sweet, German process), *Gold Star* and *Maccabee* and are generally cheaper than imported varieties. The local wines include *Cremisan* and *Latroun*, which have been produced for many years by Christian communities living south and west of Jerusalem; and extensive Israeli production particularly in the Carmel area. The local production of spirits includes brandy, *arak* (aniseed flavour) and various liqueurs.

Restaurants

Many restaurants advertise in the tourist information newspapers. They vary widely, according to location and purpose, from expensive to cheap, from high-quality restaurants to roadside cafés and sandwich bars. Jewish restaurants often reflect the origin of the owner; most are kosher, which indicates that the food has been prepared according to religious dietary laws, with meat correctly slaughtered and prepared, no prohibited foods such as pork, shellfish, game etc., as proscribed in the Bible (e.g. Levit. 11 and Deut. 14). Strictly applied this means also a refusal to serve meat and dairy products at the same meal—e.g. no milk in coffee for about five hours after eating meat—and closure on Shabbat.

Other typical Jewish eating places are dairy restaurants (milk, cream and egg dishes, pancakes and blintzes, ice cream and salads), delis (hamburger, pastrami, sandwiches, salads, fries etc.), fish, vegetarian and health food restaurants (vegetarian quiches, casseroles and pies, tofu, grains, fruit juices).

International styles of cookery abound: there are Chinese, French, Hungarian, Indian, Italian, Japanese, Kurdish, Mexican, Romanian, South African, Thai and other restaurants, which are sometimes also kosher.

A 10 per cent service charge may be added to your bill; hotels usually include a 15 per cent service charge.

 Getting around

By rail

A train service operates between Tel Aviv, Haifa and Nahariyya (2 hrs and 45 mins); Tel Aviv, Rehovot, Netanya (limited service Fri, Sat, holiday eves or holiday). Sadly the railway line built in Ottoman times between Jerusalem and Tel Aviv is currently closed, requiring major renovation. Much of the old Ottoman and Mandate railway system (to Cairo and Damascus) was closed in 1948; surviving sections operate mainly for freight.

By bus

Israeli bus services are excellent, run to time, are reasonably frequent and are not expensive, but do not run from Friday eve to Saturday eve, or on holiday eves. The main operator is the *Egged Bus Cooperative* (☎ 03 694 8888 for National Information Center). Bus stations serving the regional buses exist in most of the major towns, usually a short distance from the centre. Timetables (written in Hebrew; explained in English at larger centres) and information on costs are available from the ticket offices, where tickets need to be bought before boarding the bus. For location of bus stations, see the relevant towns in the guide, but consult Tourist Information Offices for up-to-date information at the time of your journey. Booking systems are operated on longer journeys, which can (and in some cases, such as Elat to Tel Aviv or Jerusalem, should) be booked in advance with numbered seats. In the larger bus stations the stands are numbered and destinations are shown in English as well as Hebrew. On long journeys, stops are made for food and toilet facilities. Extensive networks of buses exist in Jerusalem (excellent plan of network available), Tel Aviv and Haifa for which timetables can be obtained.

A variety of special fares are available: monthly tickets; books of tickets, which can be bought on local buses, usually providing 11 journeys for the cost of 10; student discounts with International Student Card; 'Israbus' passes valid on all

Egged services for overseas visitors; discount tickets for local and intercity buses are available at bus stations. Otherwise set rates apply to be paid on entering at the front of the bus; exit at middle.

In the underfunded Palestinian Territories the buses are very cheap but usually also very old. They run between the Jordan Border Crossing and Jericho; and between Jerusalem (East Jerusalem bus stations) and various towns in the West Bank including Bethlehem.

By car

Driving is generally good outside Jerusalem and Tel Aviv, which have very heavy traffic and one-way systems. Signposts on most major roads are in English as well as Hebrew script. Delays on motorways around Tel Aviv are not unusual.

Car hire

Numerous car hire firms operate in Israel with offices in major cities and at Ben Gurion Airport; international companies with offices at Ben Gurion airport include *Avis* (☎ 03 971 1919), *Budget* (☎ 03 971 1504), *Eldan* (☎ 03 639 4343 and ✉ www.eldan.co.il/); *Europcar* (☎ 03 972 1097), *Hertz* (☎ 03 971 1165). You should make advance bookings directly in your home country, or through travel agents, who generally require a minimum of 6–7 working days to process the booking (they also offer fly/drive holidays). There are many local car hire firms who generally offer cheaper rates. Requirements are an international credit card; a valid international driving licence is preferred, but a valid national driving licence may be acceptable for nationals whose countries have a relevant ageement with Israel; drivers should be over 21 (sometimes 25) with a clean licence.

Some car hire firms will not offer insurance in the Palestinian Territories—hopefully this is improving, but check in advance. Palestinian car hire firms include *Petra* (☎ 02 582 3735) in East Jerusalem; car hire is also available in major towns in the West Bank.

Rules of the road

Driving is on the right. Speed limits are 50km in built up areas, 80km on open roads, 96km on authorised roads, but they vary under local requirements. Seat belts should be worn (fines apply). Motorcycle and scooter riders and their passengers should wear safety helmets. **Parking** in major towns is usually difficult; parking is prohibited where curbs are painted red or red and white; if painted blue, parking is permitted on purchase of a permit at book stores and news stands; fines are imposed. Petrol stations are often closed at night, and on Saturdays and Jewish holidays.

By air

There are a number of domestic airports. Jerusalem's is at Atarot (Qalandia) c 10km north of the centre of Jerusalem. It serves some international charter flights, but mainly domestic flights to Tel Aviv, Haifa, Rosh Pinna and Elat.

By bicycle

Avoid mid-summer and mid-winter; traffic on main roads is a hazard. Cyclists can contact the *Jerusalem Cyclists Club*, POB 7281, Jerusalem, ☎ 02 624 8238.

By taxi

There are numerous taxi firms. **Israeli taxis** have yellow plates; they may be unwilling to enter the West Bank and Gaza Strip. Taxis in the **West Bank** have blue and green licence plates and are not permitted to enter Jerusalem. All urban taxis by law have electronic meters which must be displayed and activated at the start of journeys. Taxis are available during Shabbat. There are fixed tariffs for journeys within and between cities. Surcharges operate between 21.00 and 05.30. Tipping is optional. The sharut or service taxis, which run on fairly set routes in and mainly beyond the city, are inexpensive and usually quicker and more comfortable than buses and cost little more; tipping in service taxis is not customary. You pay for an individual seat in the sharut; usually on longer journeys the service waits until it is full. Between cities, seats can be booked in advance through a travel agent. Local advice is necessary for costs, routes, points of departure etc. Palestinian taxis are orange-yellow in colour; fares are negotiable.

 Language

The official languages of the State of Israel are modern Hebrew and Arabic. English is the most commonly used other language: information for tourists and most main and tourist road signs are also given in English. Russian is widely spoken.

Modern Hebrew is distinct from classical or biblical Hebrew, although based on the same alphabet of 22 letters and written from right to left. Classical Hebrew is used for liturgical purposes. The development of a language suited to the needs of the modern world took place from the 19C, particularly under the instigation of Eliezer ben-Yehuda (1852–1922) who emigrated to Israel in 1881 and compiled the first modern Hebrew dictionary. Hebrew was recognised as an official language under the Mandate Government before 1948. The Academy of the Hebrew Language was established in 1953.

Some Jews still speak the forms of Hebrew developed in medieval times: Yiddish, which is basically a mixture of German and Hebrew and is spoken by Ashkenazi groups; and Ladino, which incorporates much Spanish and is spoken by some Sephardi communities. Owing to the very high percentage of Jewish immigrants from all over the world, many Israelis speak at least one other language.

Arabic, like Hebrew, is a Semitic language, related to the older Aramaic and adopted widely since the Islamic conquest in the 7C. It has 28 letters and is also written from right to left. Arabic is the language of the Muslim and Christian Arab communities.

Useful words and phrases

English	Hebrew	Arabic
Hello	*shalom*	*marhaba (salaam alaikum)*
How are you?	*ma shlomka(m), shlomek(f)*	*kif halak(m), kif halik(f)*
Goodbye	*shalom*	*hatrak(m), hatrik(f)*
		ma salama (response)
Thank you	*toda raba*	*shukran*
Please	*bevakasha*	*min fadlak(m), min fadlik(f)*

Sorry	*slika*	*mit asif(m) mit asifa(f)*
Yes/no	*en/lo*	*aywa (nam)/la (shukran)*
Where is ...	*eifo yesh ...*	*wain fi ...*
toilet	*ha bait shimush*	*al bait moya*
left	*smol*	*ash-shimal*
right	*yemin*	*al-yamin*
straight ahead	*yashar*	*dogri*
street	*rehov*	*tarik*
today	*ha-yom*	*al-yom*
tomorrow	*makhar*	*bukra*
kilo	*kilo*	*kilo*
half (kilo)	*khetzi*	*nus*
quarter (kilo)	*reva*	*ruba*
Sunday	*yom rishon*	*yom al-ahad*
Monday	*yom shaini*	*yom al-itnain*
Tuesday	*yom shlishi*	*yom at-tlata*
Wednesday	*yom reva*	*yom al-arba*
Thursday	*yom khamishi*	*yom al-khamis*
Friday	*yom shishi*	*yom al-juma*
Saturday	*shabbat*	*yom as-sabt*

Numbers

	Hebrew	Arabic			
1	*ekhad*	*wahid*	6	*shaysh*	*sitta*
2	*shtayim*	*itnain*	7	*sheva*	*saba*
3	*shalosh*	*tlata*	8	*shmoneh*	*tmana*
4	*arba*	*arba*	9	*taysha*	*tisa*
5	*khamaysh*	*khamsa*	10	*eser*	*ashara*

Major religious festivals and public holidays

Because of the varied ethnic and religious communities in the Holy Land the number, date and variety of religious festivals is very complex. Because different calendars (solar and lunar) are employed by the different communities, the dates of the festivals vary slightly from year to year and the intending traveller is well advised to check the dates of major holidays when making travel plans, both to avoid travelling when many services are closed, and because Jerusalem in particular can be very crowded at Easter and Passover. Current calendars are available on a number of the websites listed above.

Jewish holidays

The Hebrew calendar is lunar and adapted by leap years to a solar cycle so that religious holidays based on seasonal events fall at the right time of year. The Hebrew year dates from the Traditional Year of the Creation c 3761 BC, so that AD 1998 = the Jewish Year 5758/59.

Tu Be Shevat (Feast of the Trees, spring, tree-planting) January/February.

Purim (Festival of Queen Esther who thwarted a massacre of Persian Jews in the 5C BC) February/March.

Pesach (Passover, Feast of the Unleavened Bread, the Israelites spared before the Exodus from Egypt) March/April, six days, with a public holiday at beginning and end.

Holocaust Memorial Day May.

Memorial Day for the fallen in Israel's Wars May.

Independence Day (foundation of the State of Israel; a public holiday) April/May.

Lag BeOmer (commemorates no deaths on the 33rd day of a 1C epidemic); April/May.

Jerusalem Day (Capture of West Jerusalem) May/June.

Shavuot (Feast of Weeks, ends the period of mourning after Passover; a public holiday) May/June.

Tish B'av (Mourning for the destruction of the Temple in 587 BC and AD 70; a public holiday) July/August.

Rosh Hashana (New Year is the start of a ten-day fast; Jews visit the Pool of Siloam in Jerusalem where sins are symbolically cast into the water; a two-day public holiday) September/October.

Yom Kippur (the most important holiday, on the ancient Day of Atonement—Exodus 30:10—ends the ten-day New Year fast; a public holiday) September/October.

Sukkot (The Feast of Tabernacles, a harvest festival; the building of booths and tents in gardens commemorates the wanderings of the Exodus) September/October, seven days of which the first is a public holiday.

Simhat Torah (Rejoicing for the law—the Torah—at the end of Succoth; a public holiday) September/October.

Hanukkah (The Festival of Lights, celebrates the Maccabean capture of Jerusalem from the Seleucids in 164 BC) November/December.

Muslim holidays

The Muslim calendar is lunar but not adapted to the solar calendar so that the years recede by 10 or 11 days annually. The festivals are not linked to the seasons. The Muslim year dates from AD 622 when Muhammad moved from Mecca to Medina. In the Muslim calendar AD 1998 = the year 1418/19 of the Hegira (Flight).

New Year

Maulid (Muhammad's birthday).

Beginning of Ramadan (the ninth month is a month of fasting when Muslims may not eat, drink or smoke between dawn and dusk).

Lailat al-Kadr (26th day of Ramadan, Koran given to mankind).

Id al-Fitr (last three days of Ramadan).

Id al-Adha (sacrifician celebration).

Christian festivals

Based on a 365-day year adjusted by a leap year every four years, the calendar is calculated from the traditional birthdate of Christ. Lent, Easter, Ascension, Pentecost and some other feasts are moveable, being calculated according to the old calendar. For information, the *Christian Information Centre*, opposite the Jaffa Gate, Old City, Jerusalem; POB 14308, Jerusalem 91142, Israel (☎ 02 627 2692, 🖷 02 628 6417, ✉ http://198.62.75.1/www1/ofm/cic).

Christmas (birth of Christ) Western churches, 24/25 December; Eastern Churches, 7 January.
New Year Western Churches, 1 January; Eastern Churches, 14 January.
Easter (Resurrection of Christ) March/April.

Sports

Activities available around the country include boating, canoeing (especially in the north), hiking, trekking, horse and camel riding, skiing on the Hermon slopes in winter (the *Hermon Ski Resort*, ☎ 06 698 1337), and camping. Information on spectator and participatory sports can be obtained from the various regional tourist information offices. The *Society for the Protection of Nature in Israel* (☒ www.spni.org) organises walks; many private tour firms organise trekking and riding. Camp sites are often available at the National Parks; for further information on camping, see the leaflet available from branches of the *Israel Government Tourist Office*, or contact the *Israel Camping Association*, 112 Moshav, Mishmar Hashiva 50297, Israel, the *Israel Diving Federation* in Tel Aviv, ☎ 03 523 6436 or 03 960 4524.

Water sports are widely catered for at the Mediterranean and Red Sea resorts and beaches. For information on **diving**, contact the *Israel Diving Federation* (see above). Note the safety regulations for swimming (coast, inland lakes, Dead Sea); it is permitted only at authorised beaches with colour coded flags—white = safe, red= dangerous, black = forbidden. Swimming pools and tennis courts are usually available at large hotels and holiday resorts, although many pools are open only in the summer (July to September).

Golf is available only at the *Hotel Dan Caesarea—Caesarea Golf Club*, ☎ 06 636 1172. For **tennis**, the *Israel Tennis Centre* is located at Ramat Hasharon near Tel Aviv, and in the Qatamon quarter in Jerusalem, ☎ 02 413 866; for tennis in the Galilee area, ☎ 06 673 1564; for further information contact the *Israel Tennis Association*, 79 Maze Street, Tel Aviv.

Entertainment

For current lists of cultural activities, see the *Jerusalem Post*, *Helloisrael* (free weekly guide to Israel published by the *Ministry of the Interior*, Jerusalem), and *Israel Today* (published free by the *Israel Government Tourist Office*).

You can attend **concerts** at all levels, from the Israel Philharmonic, the Jerusalem Symphony Orchestra, the Haifa Symphony Orchestra to open air pop concerts in the summer. **Theatre** is popular, usually in Hebrew, though simultaneous translation facilities may be available. There are English programmes on Israeli **radio** and **television**. The TV news in English on Channel 1 is at 18.15.

Additional information

Access for the disabled
There are some facilities available at Ben Gurion Airport, public institutions, hotels and campsites (ramps, adapted lavatories, telephones etc.). Enquiries can be made at the *Advisory Centre for the Disabled* (*Milbat*) at the Sheba Medical Centre in Tel Aviv (☎ 00972 3 530 3739).

Buying antiquities
If you are buying antiquities, the legal safeguard and guarantee against fakes is to buy at shops displaying the sign of two figures carrying a bunch of grapes (which indicates that it is licensed by the Ministry of Tourism), but an export permit is required and there is a fee of 10 per cent of the purchase price. Otherwise the export of antiquities (defined as objects fashioned by man pre-dating AD 1700) is strictly prohibited.

Crime and personal security
The situation is generally good, but theft from careless tourists in crowded areas or individuals camping on beaches etc. is a problem. It is worthwhile using the safes or safe deposits generally provided by hotels and not carrying more valuables than necessary. Carry money, documents etc in secure and sensible ways.

Electrical current
220 volts AC, single phase, 50 Hertz. Sockets are usually three pronged but many can accept two-prong plugs.

Embassies, Legations and Consulates in Israel
UK Embassy: 192 Hayarkon St, Tel Aviv 63405, ☎ 03 510 0497/0166; emergency (after hours) ☎ 03 524 9171. **Consulate-General**: Tower House, Harakevet St, West Jerusalem, ☎ 02 671 7724; Shaikh Jarrah, East Jerusalem, ☎ 02 628 2481.
Republic of Ireland Consulate: 10 Miriam, Herzliya, ☎ 09 950 9055 or ☎ 03 696 4166.
US Embassy: 71 Hayarkon St, Tel Aviv, ☎ 03 519 7575. **Consulate-General**: 18 Agron St, West Jerusalem, ☎ 02 623 4271; Nablus Rd, East Jerusalem, ☎ 02 622 7230.
Canadian Embassy: 220 Hayarkon St, Tel Aviv, ☎ 03 636 3300.
Australian Embassy: 185 Hayarkon St, Tel Aviv, ☎ 03 695 0451.
Netherlands Consulate: 4 Weizmann, Tel Aviv, ☎ 03 695 7377.

Emergency telephone numbers
Emergency Medical Care ☎ 101 in most urban areas.
Police ☎ 100.
Fire ☎ 102 (Jerusalem, Tel Aviv, Haifa).

Opening hours

Shops are normally open 08.00–13.00, 16.00–19.00, urban shopping malls 08.00–22.00, but times can vary. Jewish shops are closed Friday afternoon and Saturday; Muslim shops may be closed on Friday; Christian shops are closed on Sunday.

Banks Normal opening times are Sun, Tues, Thur 08.30–12.30, 16.00–17.30, Mon 08.30–12.30, Wed and Fri 08.30–12.00; closed Sat and Jewish religious holidays.

Post offices Most post offices are open Sun, Mon, Tues, Thur 08.00–12.30, 15.30–18.30; Wed 08.00–13.30, Fri and hol. eves 08.00–12.00; closed Sat and major holidays. There is a toll-free number for further information ☎ 177 022 2121. Postal services are marked by a sign with a white stag on a blue ground. Stamps can also be bought from bookstalls, some shops serving tourism and big hotels. Magnetic phone cards for public telephones are also available from post offices.

Internet services

These are available in major hotels, and there are various internet cafés in Tel Aviv and Jerusalem (e.g. *Strudel The Internet Bar*, 11 Monbaz St, Russian Compound, Jerusalem, Sun–Fri 10.00–02.00, Sat 15.00–02.00; ✉ http://home.palnet.com/strudel).

Local customs

In general Israelis are informal, wear standard European casual clothing appropriate to the time of year (in summer shorts, sleeveless tops, and swimming costumes on the beach). Stricter religious communities may retain a variety of traditional dress and expect visitors to be modestly dressed. The main local customs to note relate to religious observances. In Israel most public services cease sometime during Friday afternoon for Shabbat (the Sabbath) and resume late on Saturday or Sunday morning. In very Orthodox Jewish areas, such as Mea She'arim in Jerusalem, where religious laws relating to Shabbat are strictly observed, modest dress must be worn by tourists and no cars can be driven during this time—the relevant roads/areas are normally closed by barriers. Men should wear a head cover in synagogues.

In Muslim areas generally, as for religious sites of all dominations, modest dress (not shorts, some sleeves) should be worn. Traditional headdress and even occasionally traditional costumes are retained in some of the more rural areas. Alcohol is not usually available in strictly Muslim areas and tourists are advised to respect local customs. The principal weekly observance for Muslims is the mosque in the late morning on Friday, when the sermon may be relayed over loudspeakers, as is the call to prayer made five times daily. Modest dress is required for the holy sites of all religions.

National Parks

Most of the major archaeological sites in Israel have been made into national parks with opening hours, entrance charges and good facilities, including excellent brochures included in the ticket price. A Green Card, available at all National Parks, gives admission to six sites over 14 days at a cost of 70 NIS or to all the parks over 14 days at a cost of 102 NIS. Individual entrance fees vary for adults, children and groups from site to site. More than 58 parks and nature reserves cover the whole country. The parks are open April to September 08.00–17.00; October to March 08.00 to 16.00; some reserves have extended hours. Note that on Friday and eves of holidays, sites usually close 1 hour or more earlier; on eves of Rosh Hashana, Passover and Yom Kippur sites close 2 hours earlier; on Yom Kippur all sites are closed. Israel Parks Authority, 3 Am Ve Alamo St, Givat Shaul, Jerusalem 95463, ☎ 02 500 5474, 🖷 02 500 5471, ✉ www.parks.org.il.

Newspapers
The principal English language newspaper in Israel is the *Jerusalem Post* (see also ✉ www.jpost.com/). The *Jerusalem Times* serves the same purpose for the Palestinian view. Many foreign (especially US) newspapers are available.

Public toilets
Well maintained toilets are available at main bus stations for a small charge.

Telephone and postal services
Card operated public phones provide access to local and international calls; cards are widely available in newsagents and other shops (NIS 18 plus). A full range of postal services is available, mail, fax, telegrams and currency exchange in post offices; Eurocheques can be cashed. Postal services are marked by a sign with a white stag on a blue ground. Stamps can be obtained from bookstalls etc. and big hotels.

A brief history of Israel and the Palestinian Territories

Earliest prehistory

Evidence for early hominids and the making of stone tools probably dates back about one million years and early sites are widely distributed through the region. Important remains of Neanderthal man and of *Homo sapiens* have been excavated in caves especially around Mount Carmel and the upper Jordan Valley. The development from the old (Palaeolithic) to the middle (Mesolithic) stone ages was a long and uneven process, with the transition taking place around 15,000 BC. Then the process of change increased greatly, with the first evidence for food processing, settlements, art and ritual. A culture termed Natufian (from the Wadi al-Natuf in the Bethlehem region where it was first discovered) characterises the south Levant at this time. Complex tools, domestication of the dog and a hunter-gatherer society were features marking cultural changes.

The Neolithic period

Within the period 9000–5500 BC such great and rapid changes took place they have long been referred to as 'The Neolithic Revolution'. The southern section of the Fertile Crescent (a region of relatively high rainfall that arcs from the Zagros Mountains of Iran in the east, westwards across north Syria and down the east coast of the Mediterranean Sea), with suitable climate, indigenous plants and animals, was one of the earliest Neolithic zones. The domestication of plants such as wheat and barley, of animals such as sheep, goats, cattle and pigs took place over just a few millennia and underpinned the development of modern civilisation: of farming, village life, pastoralism, architecture, art, complex and permanent societies with ritual and some technological complexity. The period has been divided into early 'Pre-pottery' or 'Aceramic' phases, and later 'Pottery Neolithic' phases. In the early part of the period, sites are relatively sparse. The most sophisticated site is the small village at the Jericho oasis, with a remarkable stone-built tower and wall. Here, and elsewhere in increasingly larger villages, is evidence for the practice of burying the dead beneath the floor, often removing the head, in a rite probably involving ancestor worship. This practice developed in the later Pre-pottery Neolithic phase into the making of plastered skulls and large (around half life-size) plaster figures of men and women. Plaster was also widely employed for floors. It was an expensive commodity, and was sometimes painted with red patterns.

Pottery, a major technical accomplishment, began to appear around 6000 BC and was used not just to make small containers, but increasingly large storage jars, important for protecting food supplies against damp and rodents.

The Chalcolithic period

As its name implies ('the copper/stone period'), the major technological steps forward from c 5500 to 3600 BC involved metalworking, and the development of long-distance exchange mechanisms for raw materials such as copper, shells, and a variety of stones such as haematite (a kind of iron ore). It is clear that at this time also society became more complex, with specialised craftsmen more highly dependent on a diversified agricultural and pastoralist economy, and more regional in its nature. The grape, the olive and the date were all in cultivation. Village settlements were still quite small, and there seems to have been a low level of social diversity. However, buildings identified as temples, wall paintings depicting processions, and more complex burial rituals indicate sophisticated cultural processes. The Nahal Mishmar treasure from the Dead Sea area reveals the complex technology of casting copper using the lost-wax process and the mining, circulation and recycling of metals to produce fine ceremonial artefacts. Archaeology also reveals high quality weaving of linen cloth and reed matting, of leather working, and the use of a well-made olive-wood bow and reed arrows. Sites have been excavated throughout the region, but are best illustrated in museum collections.

The Early Bronze Age

Artefacts of bronze (an alloy of copper and a small percentage of tin, ideally around 10 per cent) do not begin to appear until near the end of the Early Bronze Age (c 2000 BC), and for most of the period, copper, flint and wood were still the major materials used for tools and weapons. The period from 3600 to 2000 BC is marked by the appearance and the disappearance of densely built up, fortified towns. Although the basis of the economy remained the same, the political economy changed radically. It may be that it was based on intense cultivation of the olive and grape and a trade in the oil and wine and other goods produced; pastoralism was important in the economy, but the luxuries may have been obtained from the intensification of agriculture and horticulture.

It seems likely that internal relationships between and within towns and external relations between Palestine and Egypt altered under economic pressures. Demographic change and intensity appears, and may have been fuelled by Egyptian exploitation. The critical role of Egypt in the affairs of the south Levant is clear by the end of the fourth millennium BC when some Egyptian colonies or settlements appear in the southeast. At the beginning of the period the settlement pattern appears to be of very many unfortified settlements which ranged from large to quite small. By c 2800 the population appears to be more concentrated in fewer towns which were usually surrounded by stone and brick fortifications with towers and gates; by c 2500 the fortification systems can be 8 metres or more wide, and enclose towns up to 16 hectares in size. Within the towns there is evidence for communal structures, identified as palaces, temples, public granaries and reservoirs, suggesting hierarchical, well-organised societies.

Unlike the contemporary societies of Egypt and Mesopotamia, there is no real evidence for a literate society—no more than the pictographs based on seal impressions on pottery. We know little about the language and ethnicity of the population. The skeletal evidence suggests it was generally but not exclusively of gracile (slender) Mediterranean type, and it is assumed on broader linguistic grounds that the indigenous language was an old Semitic variant, and ancestral to the West Semitic language 'Amorite' for which there is evidence a little later in the region. That Early Bronze Age society was not stable is indicated by the destruction and abandonment of towns at different times, and around 2350 BC virtually all fortified towns appear to have been destroyed or simply abandoned in favour of more ephemeral, unfortified but sometimes large settlements and a society based on a more flexible, less intensive agro-pastoralism and very little trade. The period of urban decline also coincides with the First Intermediate Period in Egypt, and the virtual disappearance of the Egyptian trade. It is a period of unstable urbanism in Syria which may have affected the south.

The Middle Bronze Age

Between 2000 and 1800 BC, starting with the coastal plain and the north Jordan Valley, the urbanisation of Palestine really began, a phenomenon associated with the growth of city states in both the north and south Levant, and often identified with the **Canaanites**. There is no evidence to prove that the inhabitants were called, or thought of themselves, as Canaanite, or indeed Amorite, but the designation has been pushed backwards from the second half of the second millennium because there is considerable continuity visible in the material remains between 2000 and 1200 BC. Major sites were surrounded by great earthern banks, capped by walls, enclosing up to 60 hectares at Ashkelon, and at Hazor some 180 hectares. Complex, arched, city gateways of brick; palatial buildings; the development of foreign trade, harbours and seafaring; all illustrate the growth of wealth at this time. The profits derived from the import of tin for the manufacture of bronze was a factor in the soaring wealth of the town of Hazor.

The impact of northern ('Syrian') culture is clear at this time, and there is some evidence for the development of literacy. A few clay tablets inscribed in the cuneiform script of the north, testify to at least a scribal contact with Syria; and rare items illustrate the development of a local alphabetic script; indeed it seems likely that the earliest true alphabetic script, the proto-Sinaitic or proto-Canaanite, the primal ancestor of the alphabet in which this book is written, developed in this area from around 1800 BC. It seems to have been inspired by the interaction of the Egyptian hieroglyphic script and the local Semitic language. The cultural impetus extended as far as Egypt, where a 'Canaanite' dynasty using south Levantine artefacts ruled at Avaris following the conquest of the Delta. The resurgence of Egypt under a native dynasty c 1550 BC is commonly thought to bring the period to a close, with evidence for the massive destruction of many towns.

The Late Bronze Age

Fluctuations in Egyptian power dominated the second half of the second millennium BC in the south Levant, a time when the cultural influence of **Egypt** was deeply impressed on that of Palestine. Long periods of Egyptian control of resources may be the cause of an intense decline in urban settlement in the region, despite a brisk international trade around the eastern end of the Mediterranean Sea. The campaigns of the Pharaohs of the Eighteenth Dynasty probably inhibited the political redevelopment of the local city states. Places such as Jaffa and Beth Shean witness the presence of Egyptian garrisons; the centre of the Egyptian administration in the south Levant was at Gaza, and garrisons and granaries mark Egyptian control. There is evidence of wealth in these centres, but less in the countryside generally.

The Egyptian royal archives discovered at Tell al-Amarna (the Amarna Letters, c 1350 BC, the state archives of the Pharaoh Akhenaten, Dynasty XVIII in Egypt) provide important information about the rulers and activities of the small kingdoms of southern Canaan. The Canaanites worshipped a pantheon of Semitic deities, the most important of whom was Ba'al, in many local forms. Our knowledge of these, however, is still largely based on texts discovered elsewhere, at Ras Shamra in Syria for example, as very few survive from the southern Levant. It may be that the Canaanites of the south wrote mainly on perishable leather or papyrus, and only those documents inscribed on clay in cuneiform survived. Political stability deteriorated with the arrival from the north and west of the 'Sea Peoples' in the southeast Mediterranean, first as mercenaries, then as invading settlers. Between the late 13C and early 12C most of the Canaanite culture of the towns of the south Levant was destroyed in a complex series of events, reflected in the whole eastern Mediterranean zone.

The Iron Age and later ~ c 1175–63 BC

The area of greatest prosperity in the following two centuries were the settlements of these '**Sea Peoples**' (the Sherden, Tjekker, Philistines) who established a rich territory in the southwest coastal plain and foothills, which was controlled by a federation of five principal cities, known to us as the Philistine Pentapolis. Evidence for public buildings and strong artisan capacity has been excavated, iron working was known early, and iron was increasingly in use there for tools and jewellery. The artefacts, especially the pottery, illustrate cultural continuity as well as novelty between the 13C and the 10C. The Old Testament describes the battles between the Philistines and the Israelites. By the 10C the hill country and the northern regions were also in process of recovery, and the development of Megiddo and Hazor as well as Gezer and Jerusalem is attributed in the Old Testament to Solomon's development of the Israelite kingdom which had been politically united by David. This source also refers to a raid by the Egyptian Pharaoh Sheshonq c 925 BC. The archaeological evidence clearly shows a pattern of growth by the 9C–8C into the small nation states of Israel and Judah, and their neighbouring states of Philistia, Phoenicia, Aram, Ammon, Moab and Edom. The Old Testament gives an account of alliances and more frequent warfare between them.

The region having always been under the influence of Egypt, now became increasingly dominated by **Assyria**. In 841 Jehu paid tribute to Shalmaneser III of Assyria, and in the 8C the expanding military power of the Assyrian Empire finally reached the south Levant. Destructive campaigns included those of Tiglath-Pileser III in 734 which reached as far south as Gaza and Ascalon; in 732 BC he annexed part of the northern kingdom. Sargon II in 722/1 sacked Samaria, and Assyrian control in the region was firmly established; the famous campaign of Sennacherib took place in 701 BC when he laid siege to Jerusalem. The northern kingdom of Israel had been turned into an Assyrian province by late in the 8C, and at the beginning of the 6C the Babylonians who captured and sacked Jerusalem in 587 BC had turned the whole region into a Babylonian province. Both conquests were followed by significant population exchanges with distant regions.

Assyrians, Babylonians and Persians in turn ruled the area as distant provinces of their empires. The Persian empire extended religious tolerance to the province of Judah and permitted the rebuilding of the Temple in Jerusalem (537 BC) and the building of a temple on Mt Gerizim in the 6C–4C BC. In particular the coastal cities continued to thrive until the conquest of **Alexander the Great** in 332 BC.

> ### Early writing
> Relatively little has survived to illustrate the early Hebrew script, which developed along with those of the neighbouring kingdoms, such as Phoenician, Aramaean and Moabite (which are all related Semitic languages). Short inscriptions on small objects, some *ostraka* (inscribed potsherds), and fragments of a monumental inscription provide a background for the text of the Old Testament, the oldest surviving fragments of which date to the last centuries BC.

Under this first great (Greek) wave of Western conquest, Alexander imported many of his followers, army veterans and Macedonians, to settle the new pagan cities which he (re)established. Greek came to be the language of culture, with Aramaic that of the countryside, with related Hebrew and Syriac versions. Following Alexander's death in 323 BC, Palestine was in turns the property of the Hellenistic Ptolemaic and Seleucid dynasties founded by Alexander's generals, which succeeded to the Greek Empire of Alexander, and which continued to encourage the adoption of Hellenistic culture, language and architecture in the region.

Jewish antipathy to pagan institutions and rule developed over the following years and led to the Hasmonean Revolt in 167 BC. The revolt was led by Mattathias and his five sons, whose family became known as the Hasmoneans. One of the sons, Judas Maccabeus, recaptured Jerusalem from the Seleucids in 164 BC (commemorated at Hannukah, the Jewish Festival of Lights). The conquests of the Hasmonean king Alexander Jannaeus in the late 2C/early 1C BC did not relieve increasing social and religious schisms in the 1C BC. There was bitter religious dissent between the Pharisees (a sect of Judaism concerned particularly with the interpretation of religious law and strict observance of ritual purity) and the more conservative Sadducee sect (the party of the High Priests, supporting the Hasmonean rulers and holding views at variance with those of the Pharisees. They rejected, among other ideas, a belief in the resurrection of the body. The name Sadducee derives from Zadok, David's High Priest).

The Roman period ~ 63 BC–AD 324
Pompey annexed the Seleucid territory to Rome in 64 BC. He broke up the Hasmonean kingdom into a series of petty states, confirmed Hyrcanus II (a Hasmonean) as High Priest in Jerusalem, but entrusted the administration of the kingdom to **Antipater the Idumean**. Idumeans were Edomites who moved westwards into Judah following its depopulation by the Babylonians. Antipater, under Roman favour, became the client ruler of most of the former Hasmonean territory. He made his elder son, Phasael, governor of Jerusalem, and his younger son, Herod, governor of Galilee. After Antipater's murder in 43 BC the two sons became rulers of Judaea. Surviving various revolts by his Jewish citizens, who

disliked both his foreign origins and his extermination of the Hasmonean dynasty, **Herod the Great** became sole ruler by 37 BC.

The kingdom under Herod and the Herodian dynasty he established, was at first virtually autonomous, then from AD 6 in practice under the rule of Roman governors (of whom Pontius Pilate, AD 26–36, was one) with headquarters at Caesarea Maritima. Herod built splendid palaces for his own use, magnificent pagan cities (such as Caesarea and Sebaste) as well as the greatest monument of Judaism, the rebuilt Temple in Jerusalem, and fostered the Graeco-Roman culture of the time. Latin became the language of law and administration, but existed in addition to Greek, Hebrew and Aramaic. **Jesus of Nazareth** was born (often said c 4 BC) into a period of increasing Roman power, and lived through a period of prosperity but increasing Jewish religious and political schism, fear and resentment. The Crucifixion is generally dated c 29/30. The **First Jewish Revolt** (AD 66–73) affected virtually the whole country, and culminated in the total destruction of Jerusalem in AD 70. The capital of the Roman and Byzantine administration was for the next 600 years at the port city of Caesarea Maritima; Jerusalem became a Roman garrison city. When the **Second Jewish Revolt** (AD 131/2–135) against Rome was crushed, Hadrian built the city of Aelia Capitolina on the site of Jerusalem.

During this second (Roman) wave of Western conquest, many Roman veterans were settled in Caesarea, Jerusalem and Emmaus. The province of Palestine was the home of pagans, Jews and Christians, both the latter groups suffering periods of great persecution especially under the Roman emperors Nero, Decian and Diocletian. In 313 the Imperial Edict of Milan made Christianity a legitimate religion within the empire, and in 324 Constantine brought Palestine within the Christian Eastern Roman Empire.

The Byzantine Period ~ c 324–634

This was a period of tremendous demographic growth fuelled by a development of the agricultural landscape during a long period of relative political stability. The **Emperor Constantine** inaugurated a period of immense change in the region. By 335 a great shrine and basilica over the sites of the tomb of Christ and the place of the Crucifixion had been built in Jerusalem, and others elsewhere in Palestine. As conversion spread, the pagan temples of the Roman period gradually went out of use and were destroyed in the 4C–5C; their sites were often taken by the new churches. The area of Jewish settlement lay particularly in Galilee and to some extent this geographical separation relieved difficulties between communities. A period of Christian pilgrimage began and reached its apogee in the 5C–6C, particularly in the time of Justinian, with very widespread building of churches. Jerusalem became the centre of a patriarchate in 451. Schisms and debates within the Eastern church were intense in Syria, but were less marked in contemporary Palestine which became one of the great centres of monasticism. Bitter religious conflicts developed between Judaism and Christianity however, and reached a peak at the time of the Samaritan Revolts in the 6C, which were crushed with great cruelty. The increasing weakness of the Byzantine Empire by the 7C was revealed by the Sassanian conquest of 614, which was short-lived, but devastated large areas. Although the Emperor Heraclius eventually negotiated a peace, the end was in sight.

The Early Islamic Period ~ c 634–1099

The **Prophet Muhammad** died in 632, his teachings accepted throughout most of Arabia. The sanctity of Jerusalem was subsequently ensured by the traditional identification of the 'furthest place of prayer' of the Koran with the Aqsa mosque in Jerusalem. His successors, the 'orthodox' caliphs, four elected leaders all related by marriage to the Prophet, carried on the spread of Islam. Under brilliant military leadership, the Arab armies, usually in extended Bedouin-like raids, sometimes in set battles, cut with incredible speed through the divided and weakened Byzantine and Sassanian empires. Persia, Iraq, Syria, Palestine and Egypt fell to them in the first 20 years after Muhammad's death. There appears to have been relatively little change initially, with the new conquerors, in relatively small numbers, retaining much of the local Byzantine administration. Arabic became the common language. Under the **Umayyads** (the dynasty from the Meccan clan of Umayya, who succeeded the Orthodox caliphs, and who were supporters of the murdered caliph Uthman), the agricultural landscape was maintained, in some cases extended; and major building projects put in hand especially in Jerusalem and at the new provincial capital, which was built at Ramla on the coastal plain. The Islamic capital, at Damascus, was closer than the old Byzantine centre at Constantinople. The stability is indicated by the fact that some new churches were built, and the service of many maintained; some continued right through to the Crusader period. At least one synagogue of the late 4C/early 5C in the north near Hazor continued in use to the end of the 12C. Widespread damage was caused by the earthquake of 749. When the centre of the Islamic Empire shifted eastwards from Damascus to Raqqa and then to Baghdad under the **Abbasid Dynasty**, there is some evidence for decline, with major routes being maintained by a series of caravanserais (inns).

The Christian world

In Christendom, the balance of power had shifted from the Western capital (Rome) to the Eastern Byzantine capital (Constantinople), particularly following the fall of Rome in 410. Paralleling this political shift there were increasing theological schisms between the Eastern and Western churches in belief and practice, which led to a serious rupture in 863, confirmed in 1064 when a papal bull of excommunication was laid on the altar of Santa Sophia in Constantinople. Increasingly in Muslim-ruled Palestine a need for a protecting power for the Christian population and shrines arose; Charlemagne played a role as protector of Christians in the east in the 9C, but since the 4C Eastern Christians had looked mainly to the Byzantine emperors in Constantinople.

The **Fatimid dynasty** established itself in Cairo in 969 and shortly after included Syria and Palestine in its territory. Though this dynasty was Shiite, most of their subjects in Palestine were of the Sunni persuasion. The Fatimids for the most part showed tolerance to Christians and Jews. The port towns in the west, such as Caesarea and Akko, were still relatively prosperous, but a political and economic decline intensified in the hill country of Palestine, where living conditions were often insecure, with increased raiding by Arab and Turcoman tribes from the north and east. Increasing persecution of Christians culiminated in the destruction of the Church of the Holy Sepulchre in Jerusalem on the orders of the Fatimid caliph al-Hakim in 1009. Major Turcoman and Seljuk raids devastated some areas. The 11C was a period of difficulty for all in the region, and the threats to Christian shrines and peoples in the East served as one of the reasons for the Crusades, as generated by the pope and the Western church, in response to an appeal by the Byzantine emperor in Constantinople.

The Crusader period ~ 1099–1291

The third great wave (especially French, Italian, German) of Western conquest and settlement took place with the establishment of the Latin Kingdom of Jerusalem from 1099. The greater part of the kingdom was lost in 1187, but some foothold was retained up to the destruction of Acre in 1291. The Crusader capital was established at Jerusalem, and several hundred fine churches and chapels mark the religious zeal and purpose of the Crusades, and fine castles the strategic defence of the kingdom. The monuments of Crusader work are to be found throughout the area, particularly on the coast and around Jerusalem, and often survive today in the fabric of Palestinian villages. The kingdom reached its greatest expansion by 1112 and included at that time Jerusalem and all the coastal cities south from Beirut except Ascalon and Tyre, most of Palestine to the Jordan River; it extended east to the great fortress of Krak des Chevaliers in Southern Syria, and included southern Transjordan as far as the Gulf of Aqaba.

The Crusader conquest was difficult to sustain both politically and militarily, being permanently dependent on reinforcements from the West (there were eight Crusades between 1096 and 1270, but lesser campaigns continued into the late 15C), and on the divided and weakened state of the Arab and Turkish Muslim opponents. When Salah al-Din managed to unite a strong Muslim force, the Crusader army proved inadequate at the Battle of the Horns of Hattin in 1187.

Along with the political conquest by the West, the Crusades also reintroduced the Primacy of Rome with the triumph of the Western (Latin) church and the control of the Patriarchate and of the major shrines, some, like the Church of the Holy Sepulchre, being completely rebuilt. The Eastern (Orthodox) church, to which persuasion most of the pre-existing Christian inhabitants belonged, continued in more secure circumstances, sharing in the major shrines, but sharing little of the political success of the Latins and the new Christian settlers. Relations between Eastern and Western Christians worsened following the sack of Constantinople in 1204 by the army of the Fourth Crusade; and the Latins were included in the general expulsion following the Muslim triumph in 1291 (see below).

The Later Islamic period ~ 1187–1917

The last 1000 years have seen a succession of Muslim dynasties ruling Palestine.

The Ayyubid Dynasty (1169–1250 in Egypt). Salah-al-Din (Saladin), as the real founder of this dynasty, ended Fatimid rule in 1171 and captured Jerusalem 16 years later. The dynasty was Sunni Muslim, as were the majority of the Muslim inhabitants of Palestine, and extended toleration to Jews and Christians. They permitted Christian access to many of the holy places, and established many new sites of Islamic pilgrimage. Another major raid, by the Khwarizmian Turks, took place in 1244.

The Bahri Mamluk Dynasty (1250–1390). The Mamluks, the former slave guard of the Ayyubid rulers, came to power in Egypt in 1250. These were mostly of South Russian, Qipchaq Turkish and Mongol origin, converted to the Sunni branch of the Muslim faith. They established good relations with both the West and Byzantium. The most capable soldier and probably the best known ruler was Baybars I (1260–77) who claimed successes against Crusaders and Mongols, and finally drove the Crusaders from Acre in 1291. The Bahri Mamluks invested considerably in the region, and although Mamluk building concentrated on Jerusalem and Gaza, fortresses such as Qala'at Nimrud, and the network of roads and bridges and khans that ensured communications with Egypt and Syria survive as an indication of this investment. There was also extensive cultivation of sugar in the Jordan Valley. The high point of the dynasty came under al-Nasir Muhammad. A widespread commercial network extended to the Far East, and production of ceramics and metalwork flourished. Pilgrimage and Christian activity increased in the 14C, under the sustained efforts of the Franciscan Order. The first Franciscan friars arrived in 1217, followed in 1219 by the visit of their founder St. Francis of Assisi; the Order achieved a series of agreements, including that over the Custody of the Holy Places in 1342, which re-established the presence of the Latin church. Economic difficulties beset all the Christian communities.

The Burji Mamluks (1382–1517 in Palestine, –1811 in Egypt), had a similar background to that of the Bahri Mamluks in that they began as slave guards, but they were mostly of Circassian origins. The 15C was a period of relative social and economic decline following the ravages of the Black Death in the 14C. Agriculture as well as trade shrank, taxation was heavy, and there were greater problems with Bedouin infiltration and lack of security. The dynasty had little continuity, and power was divided among numerous strong amirs.

The Ottoman Dynasty (in Palestine 1517–1917). The dynasty was at its peak in the 16C when Selim the Grim (1512–20) conquered Syria and divided the former territories of the Mamluks into pashaliks of the Ottoman Empire. His successor, Sulaiman the Magnificent, repaired and adorned Jerusalem because of the great Muslim shrines there, but this proved a brief interlude of prosperity. By the 17C weak government, an impoverished countryside, plague, riots and tribal raiding had brought much of Palestine to a low ebb. Under the Ottomans the Greek church was more successful than the Latin, and during the 17C–18C they regained rights to the principal shrines in Jerusalem and Bethlehem; despite pressures from the Latin patriarchate which was re-established in 1847, these rights were confirmed by the sultan in 1862–63, and have become known as the Status Quo.

In the secular world, factions developed and local shaikhs and leaders achieved power. Fakhr al-Din, a Druze amir, was powerful in upper Galilee in the early 17C. Dahir al-Umar (1749–75), a Bedouin shaikh who ousted and replaced the Ottoman governor, rebuilt Akko and ruled the northern region; he was followed by Jazzar Pasha (1775–1804). Napoleon Bonaparte, following his invasion of Egypt, led an army north into Palestine in 1799, up through Ramla and the coastal plain to Akko, which he besieged. Al-Jazzar, with the help of the English fleet under Sir Sidney Smith, successfully defended the city and halted the French. Ibrahim Pasha, based in Cairo and under theoretical Ottoman suzerainty, successfully ruled much of Palestine and Transjordan between 1832 and 1840. The Crimean War, in the middle of the 19C, created more changes in the balance of European power in the Near East. Then the increasing impact of the industrialised West, the coming of the railway and the steamship, increasing Jewish immigration under the stimulus of the Zionist movement, a changing infrastructure and, finally, the First World War, the Arab Revolt, nationalism and the defeat of the Ottoman and German armies by the Arab and British armies in 1917 all changed the face of Palestine.

The British Mandate period ~ 1920–48

A civil administration was set up for Palestine on 1 July 1920 and the League of Nations approved a British Mandate in 1922. The conflict over a national home for the Jews became the principal political focus. A British census of 1922 estimated the population at just over 757,000 of which 11 per cent were Jewish. In 1921 the Jewish National Council and the Muslim Supreme Council were set up, followed in 1929 by the Jewish Agency and in 1936 the Higher Arab Committee, both based in Jerusalem. Increasing Arab anxiety at ever-increasing Jewish immigration, land purchase and nationalistic aspirations led to a state of terrorism and civil war between the Arab and Jewish communities. Proposals for partition considered in 1946–47 were rejected and Britain relinquished the Mandate to the United Nations. The Mandate ended on 15 May 1948, with the departure of the last British troops on the previous day.

Recent times

The foundation of the **state of Israel** was declared in Tel Aviv on 14 May 1948. War between the Arab and Israeli forces began the following day. It led in the ensuing months to a huge exodus of Palestinian refugees (an estimated 726,000), particularly from the villages of the coastal and southern areas, and from among the Bedouin of the Negev, to the West Bank, to Jordan, to Lebanon and world wide. From 1948 to 1967 the country was partitioned under armistice agreements: the north, the coast and the south were administered by Israel, the central hills and central Jordan Valley by Jordan, and the Gaza Strip by Egypt. Jerusalem was declared the capital of the new state of Israel on 5 December 1949. As this status is not formally recognised by the UN (United Nations), most foreign embassies are still located in Tel Aviv. The 'Law of Return' was passed in 1950, granting every Jew from any country the right to entry and full Israeli citizenship. Property of Arab refugees was vested by Israel with a custodian of Absentee Property, and was then sold to the Development Authority. In 1959 Yasser Arafat established the political/military organisation al-Fatah, and in 1963 the Arab League established the Palestine Liberation Organisation (PLO).

During the Six Day War in June 1967, Israel captured Sinai, the West Bank and part of the Golan Heights. Immediately following the war, the Israeli parliament enacted a law bringing East Jerusalem within the confines of West Jerusalem, brought into effect on 28 June 1967. A UN resolution calling on Israel to withdraw from occupied territories was passed in November 1967, but new immigration centres, expropriation of land, building of settlements and industrial projects in East Jerusalem were rapidly developed to inhibit any future separation. The West Bank was placed under military occupation and a process of Jewish settlement inaugurated on expropriated land there, which continues today with a tight curb on the Palestinian economy and education, and regular imposed curfews and closures. In 1969 Arafat became Chairman of the PLO.

In 1978 Israel invaded south Lebanon, and signed the Camp David Accords with Egypt which led to the return of Sinai to Egypt. The increasing destabilisation and civil war in Lebanon and then the massacres in the Palestinian refugee camps in Lebanon took place in 1981/2. In 1985 the PLO and Jordan signed an accord. In December 1987 the Palestinian uprising called *Intifada* began in Gaza and confrontations escalated between Israel and the Arabs in Palestine. In July 1988 King Hussein of Jordan declared Jordanian disengagement from the West Bank. The Palestinian National Council agreed to accept partition and in November 1988 issued a Declaration of Palestinian Independence, calling for a Palestinian state with Jerusalem as its capital. The Madrid Peace Conference followed the Gulf War in 1991, and successful negotiations were concluded in Norway in 1993. These led to the signing of the Oslo Agreements on areas of Palestinian Autonomy, including Gaza from 1994 onwards, and agreements on border crossings. Israeli troops withdrew from Salfit in 1995 and by the end of the year from Palestinian West Bank cities, except Hebron. The 88 seat Palestinian Legislative Council was elected in 1996, with Arafat as President. In 1997 Israeli troops withdrew from 80 per cent of Hebron. In 2000 Israel withdrew from south Lebanon. Talks on implementation of the Oslo agreements foundered, and the Palestinian revolt and its repression continue.

Chronological tables

Archaeological periods in Palestine

Prehistoric

c 700,000–15,000 BC	Palaeolithic (Old Stone Age)
c 15,000–8300	Mesolithic (Middle Stone Age)
c 8300–5000	Neolithic (New Stone Age)
c 5000–3600	Chalcolithic ('Copper Age')

Bronze Age

c 3600–3000	Early Bronze Age I
c 3000–2650	Early Bronze Age II
c 2650–2350	Early Bronze Age III
c 2350–2000	Early Bronze Age IV/Middle Bronze Age I
c 2000–1750	Middle Bronze Age IIA
c 1750–1550	Middle Bronze Age IIB
c 1550–1400	Late Bronze Age I
c 1400–1300	Late Bronze Age IIA
c 1300–1170	Late Bronze Age IIB

Iron Age

c 1170–1000	Iron Age I
c 1000–900	Iron Age IIA
c 900–800	Iron Age IIB
c 800–586	Iron Age IIC

Historical periods in Palestine

586–332	Babylonian and Persian periods
332–152	Hellenistic I
152–37	Hellenistic II (Hasmonaean)
37 BC–AD 70	Roman I (Herodian)
AD 70–180	Roman II
180–324	Roman III
324–451	Byzantine I
451–640	Byzantine II
640–1099	Early Islamic
1099–1291	Crusader
1187–	Later Islamic

Lists of rulers

Kings of Judah and Israel

The united kingdom

c 1020–1004 BC	Saul
c 1004–965	David
c 965–928	Solomon

Judah		Israel	
928–911	Rehoboam	928–907	Jeroboam
911–908	Abijam	907–906	Nadab
908–867	Asa	906–883	Baasha
867–846	Jehoshaphat	883–882	Elah
846–843	Jehoram	882	Zimri
843–842	Ahaziah	882–871	Omri
842–836	Athaliah	871–852	Ahab
836–798	Joash	852–851	Ahaziah
798–769	Amaziah	851–842	Jehoram
769–733	Uzziah	842–814	Jehu
758–743	Jotham	814–800	Jehoahaz
733–727	Ahaz	800–784	Jehoash
727–698	Hezekiah	784–748	Jeroboam
698–642	Manasseh	748	Zechariah
641–640	Amon	748	Shallum

640–609	Josiah		747–737	Menahem
609	Jehoahaz		737–735	Pekahiah
609–598	Jehoiakim		735–733	Pekah
597	Jehoiachin		733–724	Hoshea
596–586	Zedekiah			

Neo-Babylonian

626–605 BC	Nabopolassar
605–562	Nebuchadnezzar II
562–560	Amel-Marduk
560–556	Nergal Sarussur
556–539	Nabunaid

Persian

559–530 BC	Cyrus
530–522	Cambyses
522–486	Darius I
486–464	Xerxes
464–423	Artaxerxes I
423–404	Darius II
404–359	Artaxerxes II
359–338	Artaxerxes III
338–336	Xerxes II
336–331	Darius III

Seleucids

311–281 BC	Seleucus I Nicator
281–261	Antiochus I Soter
261–246	Antiochus II Theos
246–225	Seleucus II Callinicus
225–223	Seleucus III Soter
223–187	Antiochus III the Great
187–175	Seleucus IV Philopator
175–164	Antiochus IV Epiphanes
163–162	Antiochus V Eupator
162–150	Demetrius I Soter
150–145	Alexander Balas
145–140	Demetrius II Nicator
145–138	Antiochus VI Epiphanes
138–129	Antiochus VII Sidetes
129–125	Demetrius II Nicator
126	Cleopatra Thea
125–121	Cleopatra Thea and Antiochus VIII Grypus
125	Seleucus V
121–96	Antiochus VIII Grypus
115–95	Antiochus IX Cyzicenus
96–95	Seleucus VI Epiphanes Nicator
95–88	Demetrius III Philopator
95–83	Antiochus X Eusebes

94	Antiochus XI Philadelphus
94–83	Philip I Philadelphus
87–84	Antiochus XII Dionysus
69–64	Antiochus XIII
67–65	Philip II

Ptolemies

304–282 BC	Ptolemy I Soter
285–246	Ptolemy II Philadelphus
246–221	Ptolemy III Euergetes
221–204	Ptolemy IV Philopator
204–180	Ptolemy V Epiphanes
180–145	Ptolemy VI Philometor
145–144	Ptolemy VII Neos Philopater
145–116	Ptolemy VIII Euergetes II
116–107	Ptolemy IX Soter II
107–88	Ptolemy X Alexander I
88–81	Ptolemy IX Soter II (restored)
80	Ptolemy XI Alexander II
80–51	Ptolemy XII Neos Dionysos
51–30	Cleopatra VII Philopator
51–47	Ptolemy XIII
47–44	Ptolemy XIV
44–30	Ptolemy XV

The Hasmoneans

152–142 BC	Jonathan
142–134	Simeon
134–104	John Hyrcanus
104–103	Aristobulus
103–76	Alexander Jannaeus
76–67	Salome Alexandra
67–63	Aristobulus II
63–40	Hyrcanus II
40–37	Matthias Antigonus

The Herods

37–4 BC	Herod the Great	4 BC–AD 34	Philip
4 BC–AD 6	Archelaus	AD 37–44	Herod Agrippa I
4 BC–AD 39	Herod Antipas	53–100(?)	Agrippa II

Roman Procurators

c AD 6–9	Coponius	46–48	Tiberius Alexander
9–12	M. Ambibulus	48–52	Ventidius Cumanus
12–15	Annius Rufus	52–60	Antonius Felix
15–26	Valerius Gratus	60–62	Porcius Festus
26–36	Pontius Pilatus	62–64	Albinus
36–37	Marcellus	64–66	Gessius Florus
41–46	Cuspius Fadus		

Roman and Byzantine Emperors

27 BC–AD 14	Augustus	268–270	Claudius III
AD 14–37	Tiberius	270–275	Aurelian
37–41	Caligula	275–276	Tacitus
41–54	Claudius	276–282	Probus
54–68	Nero	282–283	Carus
68–69	Galba	283–285	Carinus
69	Otho	283–284	Numerianus
69	Vitellius	284–305	Diocletian
69–79	Vespasian	286–305	Maximianus
79–81	Titus	305–306	Constantius I
81–96	Domitian	305–311	Galerius
96–98	Nerva	306–307	Severus
98–117	Trajan	306–312	Maxentius
117–138	Hadrian	308–324	Licinius
138–161	Antoninus Pius	308–313	Maximinus II
161–180	Marcus Aurelius	307–337	Constantine the Great
161–169	Lucius Verus	337–361	Constantius II
180–192	Commodus	337–350	Constans
193	Pertinax	360–363	Julian
193	Didius Julianus	363–364	Jovian
193–194	Pescennius Niger	364–375	Valentinian I
195–197	Clodius Albinus	367–383	Gratian
193–211	Septimius Severus	375–392	Valentinian II
209–212	Geta	364–378	Valens
198–217	Caracalla	379–395	Theodosius I
217–218	Macrinus	383–408	Arcadius [East]
218	Diadumenian	393–423	Honorius [West]
218–222	Elagabalus	402–450	Theodosius II (and
222–235	Severus Alexander		Eudocia) [East]
235–238	Maximinus I	425–455	Valentinian III [West]
238	Gordian I	450–457	Marcian [East]
238	Gordian II	457–474	Leo I [East]
238	Balbinus	467–472	Anthemius [West]
238	Pupienus	474–491	Zeno [East]
238–244	Gordian III	491–518	Anastasius I
244–249	Philip I	518–527	Justin I
247–249	Philip II	527–565	Justinian I
249–251	Trajan Decius	565–578	Justin II
251–253	Trebonianus Gallus	578–582	Tiberius II
251	Hostilianus	582–602	Mauritius Tiberius
251–253	Volusian	602–610	Phocas
253–260	Valerian	610–641	Heraclius
253–268	Gallienus	641–668	Constans II

Early Islamic Caliphs

Orthodox Caliphs
(AD 632–661; AH 11–40)

632–634	Abu-Bakr	644–656	'Uthman
634–644	'Umar	656–661	Ali

Umayyad Caliphs
(AD 661–750; AH 41–132)

661–680	Mu'awiya	717–720	'Umar
680–683	Yazid I	720–724	Yazid II
683–684	Mu'awiya II	724–743	Hisham
684–685	Marwan I	743–744	al-Walid II
685–705	'Abd al-Malik	744	Yazid III
705–715	al-Walid I	744	Ibrahim
715–717	Sulaiman	744–750	Marwan II al-Himar

Abbasid Caliphs
(in Iraq and Baghdad: AD 749–974; AH 132–363; note: the Dynasty continued to AD 1258; AH 656)

749–754	al-Saffah	862–866	al-Musta'in
754–775	al-Mansur	866–869	al-Mu'tazz
775–785	al-Mahdi	869–870	al-Muhtadi
785–786	al-Hadi	870–892	al-Mu'tamid
786–809	Harun al-Rashid	892–902	al-Mu'tadid
809–813	al-Amin	902–908	al-Muktafi
813/833	al-Ma'mun	908–932	al-Muqtadir
(817–819)	Ibrahim b. al-Mahdi (in Baghdad)	929/932–934	al-Qahir
		934–940	al-Radi
833–842	al-Mu'tasim	940–944	al-Muttaqi
842–847	al-Wathiq	944–946	al-Mustakfi
847–861	al-Mutawakkil	946–974	al-Muti'
861–862	al-Muntasir		

Fatimid Caliphs
(Egypt and Syria: AD 975–1171; AH 365–567; note: the Dynasty commenced in AD 909; AH 297)

975–996	al-'Aziz	1130–31	interregnum; al-Hafiz as Regent
996–1021	al-Hakim		
1021–36	al-Zahir	1131–49	al-Hafiz as Caliph
1036–94	al-Mustansir	1149–54	al-Zafir
1094–1101	al-Musta'li	1154–60	al-Fa'iz
1101–30	al-Amir	1160–71	al-'Adid

Crusader Dynasty (1099–1291)

(sovereignty in Jerusalem ended in 1187)

1099–1100	Godfrey of Bouillon
1100–18	Baldwin I
1118–31	Baldwin II
1131–61	Melisande and Fulk of Anjou
1143–63	Baldwin III
1163–74	Amalric I
1174–85	Baldwin IV
1185–86	Baldwin V
1186–92	Sybil
1192	Isabel and Conrad of Montferrat
1192–97	Isabel and Henry of Champagne
1197–1205	Isabel and Amalric II
1206	Isabel
1206–12	Mary La Marquise
1210–12	John of Brienne
1212–25	John of Brienne (as regent)
1225–28	Frederick II of Hohenstaufen
1228–54	Conrad I
1254–68	Conrad II
1269–84	Hugh I (Hugh III of Cyprus)
1284–85	John I
1285–91	Henry I

Later Islamic rulers

Ayyubid Sultans

(in Egypt; AD 1169–1252; AH 564–650)

1169–93	al-Nasir I Salah-al-Din (Saladin)
1193–98	al-'Aziz 'Imad-al-Din
1198–1200	al-Mansur Nasir-al-Din
1200–18	al-'Adil I Sayf-al-Din
1218–38	al-Kamil I Nasir-al-Din
1238–40	al-'Adil II Sayf-al-Din
1240–49	al-Salih Najm-al-Din Ayyub
1249–50	al-Mu'azzam Turan-Shah
1250–52	al-Ashraf II Muzaffar-al-Din

Ayyubid Sultans

(in Damascus; AD 1186–1260; AH 582–658)

1186–96	al-Afdal Nur-al-Din 'Ali
1196–1218	al-'Adil I Sayf-al-Din
1218–27	al-Mu'azzam Sharaf-al-Din
1227–29	al-Nasir Salah-al-Din Da'ud
1229–37	al-Ashraf I Muzaffar-al-Din
1237–38	al-Salih 'Imad-al-Din (first reign)
1238	al-Kamil I Nasir-al-Din
1238–39	al-'Adil II Sayf-al-Din
1239	al-Salih Najm-al-Din Ayyub (first reign)

1239–45	al-Salih 'Imad-al-Din (second reign)
1245–49	al-Salih Najm-al-Din Ayyub (second reign)
1249–50	al-Mu'azzam Turan-Shah (with Egypt)
1250–60	al-Nasir II Salah-al-Din

Bahri Mamluk Sultans
(in Egypt and Syria; AD 1250–1390; AH 648–792)

1250	Shajar al-Durr
1250–57	al-Mu'izz 'Izz-al-Din Aybak
1257–59	al-Mansur Nur-al-Din 'Ali
1259–60	al-Muzaffar Sayf-al-Din Qutuz
1260–77	al-Zahir Rukn-al-Din Baybars I al-Bunduqdari
1277–80	al-Sa'id Nasir-al-Din Baraka Khan
1279	al-'Adil Badr-al-Din Salamish
1279–90	al-Mansur Sayf-al-Din Qalawun al-Alfi
1290–94	al-Ashraf Salah-al-Din Khalil
1293–95	al-Nasir Nasir-al-Din Muhammad (first reign)
1294–97	al-'Adil Zayn-ad-Din Kitbugha
1296–99	al-Mansur Husam-al-Din Lajin
1299–1309	al-Nasir Nasir-al-Din Muhammad (second reign)
1309	al-Muzaffar Rukn-al-Din Baybars II al-Jashankir
1310–41	al-Nasir Nasir-al-Din Muhammad (third reign)
1341	al-Mansur Sayf-al-Din Abu-Bakr
1341–42	al-Ashraf 'Ala'-al-Din Kujuk
1342	al-Nasir Shihab-al-Din Ahmad
1342–45	al-Salih 'Imad-al-Din Isma'il
1345–46	al-Kamil Sayf-al-Din Sha'ban I
1346–47	al-Muzaffar Sayf-al-Din Hajji I
1347–51	al-Nasir Nasir-al-Din al-Hasan (first reign)
1351–54	al-Salih Salah-al-Din Salih
1354–61	al-Nasir Nasir-al-Din al-Hasan (second reign)
1361–63	al-Mansur Salah-al-Din Muhammad
1363–77	al-Ashraf Nasir-al-Din Sha'ban II
1377–82	al-Mansur 'Ala'-al-Din Ali
1382	al-Salih Salah-al-Din Hajji II (first reign)
1382–89	al-Zahir Sayf al-Din Barquq
1389–90	Hajji II (second reign, with honorific title al-Muzaffar)

Burji Mamluk Sultans
(in Egypt and Syria; AD 1382–1517; AH 784–922)

1382–89	al-Zahir Sayf-al-Din Barquq (first reign)
1389–90	Hajji II (second reign)
1390–99	al-Zahir Sayf-al-Din Barquq (second reign)
1399–1405	al-Nasir Nasir-al-Din Faraj (first reign)
1405	al-Mansur 'Izz-al-Din 'Abd-al-'Aziz
1405–12	al-Nasir Nasir-al-Din Faraj (second reign)
1412	al-'Adil al-Musta'in (Abbasid Caliph, proclaimed Sultan)
1412–21	al-Mu'ayyad Sayf-al-Din Shaikh
1421	al-Muzaffar Ahmad
1421	al-Zahir Sayf-al-Din Tatar

1421–22	al-Salih Nasir-al-Din Muhammad
1422–38	al-Ashraf Sayf-al-Din Barsbay
1438	al-'Aziz Jamal-al-Din Yusuf
1438–53	al-Zahir Sayf-al-Din Jaqmaq
1453	al-Mansur Fakhr-al-Din 'Uthman
1453–61	al-Ashraf Sayf-al-Din Inal
1461	al-Mu'yyad Shihab-al-Din Ahmad
1461–67	al-Zahir Sayf-al-Din Khushqadam
1467	al-Zahir Sayf-al-Din Yalbay
1467–68	al-Zahir Timurbugha
1468–96	al-Ashraf Sayf-al-Din Qa'it Bay
1496–98	al-Nasir Muhammad
1498–1500	al-Zahir Qansuh
1500–01	al-Ashraf Janbulat
1501	al-'Adil Sayf-al-Din Tuman Bay
1501–16	al-Ashraf Qansuh al-Ghawri
1516	al-Ashraf Tuman Bay

Ottoman rulers

(From the conquest of Palestine, AD 1512–1918; AH 918–1336)

1512–20	Salim I Yavuz ('the Grim')	1695–1703	Mustafa II
		1703–30	Ahmad III
1520–66	Sulaiman II Qanuni	1730–54	Mahmud I
1566–74	Salim II	1754–57	'Uthman III
1574–95	Murad III	1757–74	Mustafa III
1595–1603	Muhammad III	1774–89	'Abd al-Hamid I
1603–17	Ahmad I	1789–1807	Salim III
1617–18	Mustafa I (first reign)	1807–08	Mustafa IV
1618–22	'Uthman II	1808–39	Mahmud II
1622–23	Mustafa I (second reign)	1839–61	'Abd al-Majid I
		1861–76	'Abd al-'Aziz
1623–40	Murad IV	1876	Murad V
1640–48	Ibrahim	1876–1909	'Abd al-Hamid II
1648–87	Muhammad IV	1909–18	Muhammad V Rashad
1687–91	Sulaiman III		
1691–95	Ahmad II		

British Mandate

1920–1948

Art and architecture

In a region such as the southern Levant it may be claimed that the external influences are so continuous over the millennia that there is no indigenous art and architecture, and that the whole is eclectic and derivative. Nevertheless, the region's sites and museums are full of the superb creations of local and imported craftsmen, many uncovered by archaeological excavation, and these reveal the country and its past.

Art

Palestine can claim what are probably some of the world's earliest efforts at portraiture in the plastered skulls recovered from the **Neolithic** levels at Jericho (to be seen in the Rockefeller Museum, Jerusalem). Using human skulls (usually without the mandible which affects the proportions), great skill was employed to make (reconstruct?) the features in smooth and sometimes painted plaster, with cowrie shells set in the eyeholes. Modelling of birds and other animals in clay and wax, and production of copper figures employing the lost-wax casting technique, were in vogue in the fourth millennium BC at a number of **Chalcolithic** sites (e.g. Nahal Mishmar; displayed in the Israel Museum). Fine Canaanite jewellery in precious metals and semi-precious stones, and ivory-carving made to decorate small items of furniture, attest to the skills of the craftsman in the **second millennium** and have resonances with the contemporary art of Syria. Many of the motifs on the scarabs are Egyptian in origin. Larger sculptures of the period, frequently carved in basalt (as at Hazor and Beth Shean), often suggest Egyptian and Hittite influence. Figurative art was generally not part of the indigenous tradition of the Iron Age, but small seals attest to the continuity of older traditions at least amongst the rich, as do ivories, which are generally Phoenician, Syrian or Egyptian in style.

From the **Hellenistic** and **Roman periods**, fine jewellery in the Mediterranean-wide classical style can be seen in museums (the Rockefeller Museum in Jerusalem and many others); its introduction presages the appearance of Pompeian style wall-paintings in palaces (e.g. Masada) and expensive houses, such as the Palatial Mansion in Jerusalem, and of mosaics covering both walls and floors. These paintings and mosaics exhibit classical themes and patterns, and in many cases appear to have been carried out by imported craftsmen. Local schools of mosaicists developed in the **Byzantine period**. While still using classical themes and motifs, these schools, are characterised by attractive local themes; there are fewer scenes of the pagan gods, hunting, gladiatorial games and bloodshed, while more of the produce and wildlife of the countryside appear, all laid in coarser, but often charming and lively naive styles (e.g. Zippori). Generally the motifs of the Roman period were employed in the decoration of churches, including marble chancel screens.

Many of the features of Byzantine art, as well as some of the craftsmen themselves, were taken over by the **early Islamic** caliphs; and the fine wooden carved panels in buildings, such as the Aqsa panels in the Rockefeller Museum and the Islamic Museum in the Haram in Jerusalem, often bear a close resemblance in style and motif to those of previous centuries (as in the tie-beams of the Church of the Nativity at Bethlehem). However, these traditional features were also adapted to produce an art style which is distinctive in wall paintings, metalwork and in particular the use of carved stucco (e.g. from the Hisham Palace at Jericho, and in the Rockefeller Museum in Jerusalem). During the **Umayyad period** figurative art was still widespread, but the iconoclasm which affected both Christians and Muslims in the 8C enforced radical departures from older classical styles. Vegetal and geometric designs now increasingly predominated in artistic output. Fine jewellery of the **Fatimid period** has also been found (at Caesarea and now in the Israel Museum).

Much of the surface ornament (particularly the wall painting) of the **Crusader period** has disappeared, but the capitals from the Church of the Annunciation at Nazareth are particularly notable. They are very fine examples of French work of the 12C.

Glass-making has been a longstanding tradition in the region, and some very fine Roman and Islamic glass survives, especially the painted mosque lamps. These traditions form the background to the 19C–20C Hebron glass workshops as well as to modern art glass, which is widely available. Textiles in general reveal fine weaving, but the most ornate survivors are of medieval and recent Islamic date (see some in the Islamic Museum in the Haram in Jerusalem) and ecclesiastical garments, the latter mainly revealing European influence (e.g. in the Greek Orthodox Patriarchate Museum, Jerusalem, and many churches).

Architecture

Jericho still holds the record for the earliest monumental architecture known, in the form of its round tower with stepped interior passage dating to the eighth millennium BC; but as yet it is isolated from any earlier or later architectural parallel. Architectural forms developed slowly but by the fourth and third millennia BC, moderately sophisticated versions of broad-room buildings were built, and complex systems of city walls, gates and towers. The normal building materials of the region were stone and sun-dried mudbrick, and timbers for ceilings which supported a flat thatch and clay roof. Beaten mud or plaster was generally used for flooring, or cobblestone paving in heavily used or wet areas. Architecture was relatively small-scale compared to that of Egypt and Mesopotamia. The finest architectural works of the **Middle and Late Bronze Ages** were the temples and palaces with finely dressed ashlars of basalt lining the lower exterior walls, and their entrances guarded by basalt lion orthostats. At the same time great systems of earth ramparts, passage gates and curtain walls were being developed, which reveal the mastery of brick arches and slope retention.

The surviving architecture of the **first millennium BC** is generally not impressive. Many attempts have been made to match the Old Testament description of the Solomonic temple in Jerusalem with contemporary evidence, for the written description by far exceeds the magnificence of anything revealed by archaeology. The idea of a three-room sanctuary preceded by two columns and an altar is paralleled in earlier Canaanite temples from Hazor and from temples of the 9C and later in north Syria, but no nearer parallels are yet known. Some magnificent ashlar masonry in probable Phoenician style was found at Samaria and Dan in this period, and fine monumental passage gates (as at Megiddo). The entrances to royal enclosures were decorated with massive rectangular pilaster capitals (from Hazor and Jerusalem), probably dating from the 8C–7C BC, which have parallels in Transjordan and in contemporary Syrian and Anatolian architectural ornament. Apart from the water systems (rock-cut tunnels and shafts) and the city walls, few large public structures which pre-date the Roman period are well preserved and relatively little of the Hellenistic period in particular.

In the **Roman period** the situation changed, due to the massive masonry and superb building techniques employed. Herod the Great can be credited with initiating such work in Palestine; his building programmes reflect his political alliances, his wealth and the scale of his ideas. The remains of his great cities and structures survive at Caesarea, Jerusalem and Hebron in particular and reflect these innovations. Herod combined a Hellenistic talent for choosing fine settings in the landscape for his architecture with a Roman capacity to build for eternity. The excellent hard local limestones in the hill country were used, or basalt where this was the local stone, and supplemented by concrete, hydraulic plaster and mosaic floors. Great numbers of massive monolithic granite columns were used, imported from Egypt and Turkey and capped with Ionic, Corinthian or Composite capitals. The quality of his masonry is unsurpassed. Flat lintels and drafted masonry are characteristic, and pilasters exploited the strong light and shade of the Eastern world for maximum dramatic effect. The siting and execution of the North Palace at Masada, and the palaces and pleasure grounds at Herodion and Jericho, provide an Eastern reflection of the luxuries of Rome itself. Fine domes supported by pendentives were also a development of the Roman period. Large timbers being scarce, the dome and the barrel vault were developed in the Near East for roofing. Theatres and amphitheatres were constructed on classical models, the latter particularly associated with military garrisons.

From the Roman period onwards the public basilica, with its pitched and tiled roof, became a regular feature of the architecture of the region, influencing the form of most later synagogues and churches. Roman public basilicas were built more solidly than private structures and have tended to survive longer. The basilicas, together with colonnaded streets and bath houses with domed roofs, provide the basic architectural format for the following centuries.

In the **Byzantine period**, much more building was carried out in fired brick or in rubble masonry sometimes faced with marble veneer on thinner walls; the granite columns and other elements of the Roman period were extensively reused in these buildings. In the courtyard houses of well-to-do citizens it is mostly the stone trimmings that survive. These include a range of marble and limestone capitals, including a 'basket' style, with weave or lattice patterns. The basilica form provided the basic pattern for synagogues and churches. Synagogues varied in orientation, with either the ornamented façade, or a wall with niche or apse opposite the entrance to which the congregation turned, facing towards Jerusalem; whereas churches normally had their altars facing east, except in rare instances such as the basilica in Jerusalem which was oriented westwards towards the Tomb of Christ. Stone was the regular material used in the building of the semi-fortified monasteries of the Byzantine period; many churches and reservoirs tended to be rock-cut. The Byzantine tradition of the octagonal martyrium church/shrine (i.e. one dedicated to a martyr) was the architectural predecessor of the Umayyad Dome of the Rock in Jerusalem, and both also made extensive use of glass mosaic on the walls. The square bell tower of churches influenced the early form of the Islamic square minaret.

In the **Umayyad period** very high quality masonry was once again used for important buildings, such as the palaces in Jerusalem, Jericho and Minya, with large square, flat-dressed ashlars being used in the construction of vast court-yard buildings, and mortar used in foundations and rubble cores. Builders of the Byzantine round arch gradually developed the technique of strengthening it with the joggled voussoir (interlocking keystones), and the same technique was carried through into the slightly pointed arch of the Early Islamic period.

During the **Crusader period**, building in stone, with a distinctive dressing technique and masons' marks, was regular practice for churches, castles and other buildings, and very many survive. The decoration of Frankish churches was much in the European style, but the castles and churches built throughout the region owed much to their local predecessors, Roman and Byzantine. The developed pattern of castles—central keep, lower bailey, with inner and outer lines of curtain walls adapted to site contours, long defensible passage approaches, towers, upper firing platforms, postern gates and ditches—was often adapted to coastal situations, with guarded access to a harbour or anchorage. Sculptural and painted decoration tended to be restricted to the commander's quarters and the chapel. Particular features of public buildings, gates and door-ways, especially churches, are rather stiff-leaved acanthus capitals; some capitals are more elaborate, with figures of saints or Christian symbols such as the lamb. Equally characteristic are the small marble columns, sometimes elaborately twisted but still monolithic, which decorated windows and portals; and the elbow consoles which support the vaulting in large rooms. Pointed ribbed vaulting was common, as was barrel vaulting in storage and working areas.

During **Ayyubid times** similar strong architectural styles were employed, often using strong rough-bossed masonry (with dressed edge and rough, raised-central area), which gradually became more decorative under the **Mamluks**. By the 13C coloured stone was used for public buildings: palaces, schools, hospices and large houses often having façades decorated with alternating horizontal bands of red and white or black masonry (*ablaq*); these colours can also mark the structural features, such as the joggled voussoirs over the entrance, creating elaborate decorative patterns. The vaulting over the entrance often contains sta-lactite or honeycomb (*muqarnas*) decoration, sometimes stucco with inlay, and inscriptions in elaborately stylised calligraphy add to the intensity of ornament. For houses, where the entrance led into simpler, quiet and private courtyards, such decoration was mostly restricted to the façade. Mosques were generally built to a broad-room plan, and the *qibla* wall with the concave niche (the mihrab) is oriented to the southeast, towards Mecca. The courtyard with ablution facilities is an important element. In the 12C–13C the minarets were usually still square, but the upper part became cylindrical during Mamluk times.

Under Ottoman rule foreign investment tended to be more sporadic and court styles more rarely imported. In the **early Ottoman period** building was con-centrated in Jerusalem, where the magnificent city walls reveal that small masonry was characteristic. Streets received fine decorative fountains as public facilities. Tiles rather than mosaic were now more commonly employed as wall ornament: the Dome of the Rock was refaced with tiles. The interiors of bath houses in traditional styles were cased in marble veneer and tiles (e.g. Akko).

Ottoman minarets tended to be thin cylinders. Castles were adapted for gun warfare with round towers and gun-slits (see Yehiam). More ornate styles characterise the **later Ottoman period**, continuing until the 19C, when European influence became overwhelming.

Until recent times the characteristic building material was stone for the well-to-do and in the highland villages, and mudbrick for the rural lowlands, with domed and flat roofs. Much medieval architecture remains incorporated in the later village structures of the highlands.

Further reading

Background reading

Atlas of Israel. Survey of Israel and MacMillan (1985).

Cleave, R. *The Holy Land. A Unique Perspective*. Lion Publishing, Oxford (1993).

Facts About Israel. Israel Information Center, Jerusalem.

Epstein, I. *Judaism: a historical presentation*. Penguin, Harmondsworth (1990).

Healey, J.F. *The Early Alphabet. Reading the Past*. British Museum Publications, London (1990).

Kedar, B.Z. *The Changing Land. Between the Jordan and the Sea. Aerial photographs from 1917 to the present*. Yad Ben-Zvi Press and Mod Publishing House, Jerusalem (1999).

PASSIA Diary. The Palestinian Academic Society for the Study of International Affairs: Jerusalem.

Rogerson, J. *The New Atlas of the Bible*. Macdonald, Oxford (1985).

Schiffman, L.H. *Reclaiming the Dead Sea Scrolls*. Anchor reprints paperback; Jewish Publications hardback. Doubleday, New York (1995)

Strange, J. (ed.) *Bible Atlas*. American Bible Society, New York (1999).

Primary sources

Major sources include of course the *Bible* (often the New English Bible is the edition quoted) and the *Koran*. The *Jewish War* and *Jewish Antiquities* were written in the late 1C AD by the Jewish soldier and historian Flavius Josephus; archaeological evidence tends to verify first hand descriptions of his times. Many pilgrims, travellers, artists, writers, as well as local theologians, historians and geographers who wrote descriptions or histories of the region, as well as other works, are mentioned with the date of their visit or their writings in the Guide. Just a few of these writers include Origen of Alexandria (185–253, theologian, who translated parts of the bible into Greek); Bishop Eusebius of Caesarea (c 260–340); the otherwise unidentified Pilgrim of Bordeaux in 333; Egeria (a nun perhaps from Spain in 384); St Jerome (the translator of the Bible into Latin, c 340–420); the pilgrim Arculf (680) who gave an account of his visit to the Holy Land to the monk Adomnan; the *Commemoratorium de Casis Dei* (a report on the Christian establishments compiled for Charlemagne, c 808); al-Ya'qubi (Muslim historian, 874); al-Muqaddasi (Muslim geographer, c 985); Yahya (a Christian historian from Antioch, 11C); Nasir-i Khusraw (Persian poet and traveller, c 1047);

al-Umari (Mamluk writer, 1347); Niccolas of Poggibonsi (monk, traveller, 1346); Felix Faber (a monk from Ulm in Germany, late 15C); Mujir al-Din (Muslim historian, 1495); Fr Bernadino Amico (Italian writer and illustrator, in Palestine 1593–97, published 1609); Evliya Celebi (Turkish traveller, 1648–1650); Corneille le Bruyn (Cornelius van Bruyn, Dutch artist, 1681); Henry Maundrell (English visitor, 1697).

More about these and the very many other sources can be found in F.E. Peters, *Jerusalem: The Holy City in the Eyes of Chroniclers, Visitors, Pilgrims and Prophets from the Days of Abraham to the Beginnings of Modern Times*. Princeton University Press, Princeton (1985); and in the translations of J. Wilkinson, *Egeria's Travels to the Holy Land* (rev. ed. Ariel, Jerusalem, 1981); and *Jerusalem Pilgrims before the Crusades* (Aris and Philips, Warminster, 1977).

Travel writing

Curzon, R. *Visits to Monasteries in the Levant*. George Newnes, London. (Various editions. First published in 1848).

Kinglake, A.W. *Eothen*. Everyman ed., Dent, London. (Many editions exist, first published in 1844).

Archaeology

References to archaeologists and historians whose work is often integral to the descriptions in this guide have perforce been omitted for lack of space; notably these include among many, E. Pierotti, C. Wilson, C. Warren, C.R. Conder, C. Schick and C. Clermont-Ganneau, all of whom carried out major explorations in 19C Palestine.

Amiran, R. *The Ancient Pottery of the Holy Land*. Massada Press, Jerusalem (1969)

Auld, S. and Hillenbrand, R. (eds) *Ottoman Jerusalem. The Living City 1517–1917* British School of Archaeology in Jerusalem and the World of Islam Festival Trust, London (2000).

Ben-Tor, Amnon (ed.) *The Archaeology of Ancient Israel*. Translated by R. Greenberg. Yale University Press, The Open University of Israel, New Haven and London (1992).

Biddle, M. *The Tomb of Christ*. Sutton Publishing, Gloucestershire (1999).

Boas, A.J. *Crusader Archaeology. The Material Culture of the Latin East*. Routledge, London and New York (1999).

Burgoyne, M.H. with Richards, D. *Mamluk Jerusalem*. World of Islam Festival Trust and British School of Archaeology in Jerusalem, London (1987).

Holum, K.G, Hohlfelder, R.L., Bull, R.J. and Avner, R. *King Herod's Dream. Caesarea on the Sea*. Norton, New York and London (1988).

Kennedy, H. *Crusader Castles*. Cambridge University Press (1994).

Kenyon, K.M. *Digging up Jerusalem*. Benn, London (1974).

Levy, T.E. (ed.) *The Archaeology of Society in the Holy Land*. Leicester University Press (1995).

Petersen, A. *A Gazetteer of Medieval and Ottoman Islamic Buildings in Palestine (Part I; Israel)*. British Academy Monographs in Archaeology, London (2001).

Pringle, D. *The Churches of the Crusader Kingdom of Jerusalem*. Vols. I and II. Cambridge University Press (1993, 1998).

Pringle, D. *Secular Buildings in the Crusader Kingdom of Jerusalem. An Archaeological Gazetteer*. Cambridge University Press (1997).

Stern, E. (ed.) *The New Encyclopedia of Archaeological Excavations in the Holy Land*.

4 vols. IES and Carta. Simon and Schuster, New York and London (1993).

Yadin, Y. *Masada. Herod's Fortress and the Zealots' Last Stand.* Weidenfeld and Nicolson (1966).

Yadin, Y. *Hazor. The Rediscovery of a Great Citadel of the Bible.* Weidenfeld and Nicolson (1975).

History

Bosworth, C.E. *The New Islamic Dynasties. A chronological and geneaological manual.* Edinburgh University Press (1996).

Martin, Gilbert *Jerusalem in the Twentieth Century.* Pimlico, London (1996).

Hourani, A. *A History of the Arab Peoples.* Harvard University Press, Cambridge, Mass. (1991).

Khalidi, Walid (ed.) *Before Their Diaspora. A Photographic History of the Palestinians 1876–948.* Institute for Palestine Studies, Washington DC. USA (1991).

Khalidi, Walid (ed.) *All That Remains. The Palestinian Villages Occupied and Depopulated by Israel in 1948.* Institute for Palestine Studies, Washington DC. USA (1992).

Lewis, B. *The Arabs in History.* New ed., Oxford University Press. First published 1950 (1993).

Maalouf, A. *The Crusades through Arab Eyes.* al-Saki Books, London (1984).

Millar, F. *The Roman Near East, 31BC–AD337.* Harvard University Press (1993).

Riley-Smith, J. (ed.) *The Oxford Illustrated History of the Crusades.* Oxford University Press, Oxford (1995).

Runciman, S. *A History of the Crusades.* 3 vols. Penguin Books (1951).

Said, E. *Orientalism: western conceptions of the Orient.* Penguin, Harmondsworth (1995).

Tessler, M. *A History of the Israeli-Palestinian Conflict.* Indiana Press, Bloomington (1994).

Art and architecture

Creswell, K.A.C. and Allan, J. *A Short Account of Early Muslim Architecture.* Scholar Press (1989).

Ettinghausen, R. and Grabar, O. *The Art and Architecture of Islam 650–1250.* 2nd ed. New Haven CT and Yale University Press (2001).

Food and cookery

Herbst-Krausz, Zorica *Old Jewish Dishes.* Corvina, Budapest (1991).

Roden, Claudia *A Book of Middle Eastern Food.* Penguin, Harmondsworth (1970).

Rose, E. The New Complete International Jewish Cookbook. Robson Books, London (1997).

Costume

Weir, Shelagh *Palestinian Costume.* British Museum, London (1989)

Flora and fauna

Blamey, M. and Grey-Wilson, C. *Mediterranean Wild Flowers.* Harper Collins (1993).

Foggi, B. and Innocenti, A. *Flowers of Israel.* English Edition. Bonechi and Steimatzk. (Undated).

Polunin, O. and Huxley, A. *Flowers of the Mediterranean.* Chatto and Windus, London (1981).

JERUSALEM

Jerusalem (Arabic: al-Quds; Hebrew: Yerushalayim; Greek and Latin: Hierosolyma) is situated c 52km from the Mediterranean Sea at latitude 31° north, longitude 35° east. It lies on the limestone watershed of the hill country, at c 780m above sea level, with ancient agricultural terraces and modern afforestation to the west and north, and the barren hills of the Judaean wilderness to the east and south. Economically and demographically its natural role is that of a small market town in the hills; its significance is primarily religious and political. It has not always been the capital city of the region, but because of its primary importance to Jews, Christians and Muslims, magnificent shrines have been built there for millennia. To Jews it is the focal point of their religion, the site of the Temple built by Solomon in the 10C BC; it is the centre of the Christian world, as the site of the Crucifixion and the Resurrection of Christ in the 1C AD; and to Muslims it is the sacred city of the Prophets and location of the Prophet Muhammad's Night Journey (7C AD), the third holiest city in the Muslim world and the second most important place of pilgrimage after Mecca.

The centres of attention for visitors are the Church of the Holy Sepulchre and the Herodian Temple platform with the Dome of the Rock, the Aqsa Mosque and the Western or Wailing Wall. Between these points, the focus of millions of pilgrims, lies a dense and bewildering mass of buildings and people packed into a small space which can reward weeks rather than days of exploring to begin to uncover the historical, religious, architectural and ethnic layers of this revered place.

Jerusalem is a good centre for touring, having large numbers of hotels, an excellent bus system, and many facilities geared to tourism.

Jerusalem lies on a series of hills or ridges intersected by deep valleys. The ancient city was located on the southeast ridge (c 700m above sea level) because it was adjacent to the only permanent water source, the spring Gihon, and to the gardens in the Kidron Valley. The Temple was located on the high point (c 743m) of the east ridge. It was separated from the higher Western Hill (c 770m above sea level) by a once deep valley, the Central or Tyropoeon (Cheesemakers') Valley, which extended northwards up to the area of the modern Damascus Gate. Occupation spread to the west hill only in the 8C BC, and to the north in Herodian and Roman times. The city is bounded to the west and south by the Hinnom Valley.

The medieval or **Old City** of Jerusalem, covering c 82 hectares, is roughly quadrilateral in shape and is enclosed by walls of local limestone built by Sulaiman the Magnificent in the 16C, much repaired and restored since. The Old City is divided into four quarters based on religious and ethnic factors. Only a part overlies the ancient city. The location of the city shifted in the course of centuries according to the demands of strategy and population growth and decline.

The dominant impression in the unrestored parts of the Old City is of the fine local limestone used for the traditional domed houses and for the narrow stepped streets, the stones of which are polished by centuries of pedestrian traffic. The stone in the Jerusalem area often has a reddish vein, and reflects the changes of light throughout the day, looking fresh and yellow in the early morning, grey-whitish in the harsh midday sunshine, with deeper, subtler shades of gold and pink emerging in the late afternoon and evening. The Old City of Jerusalem has

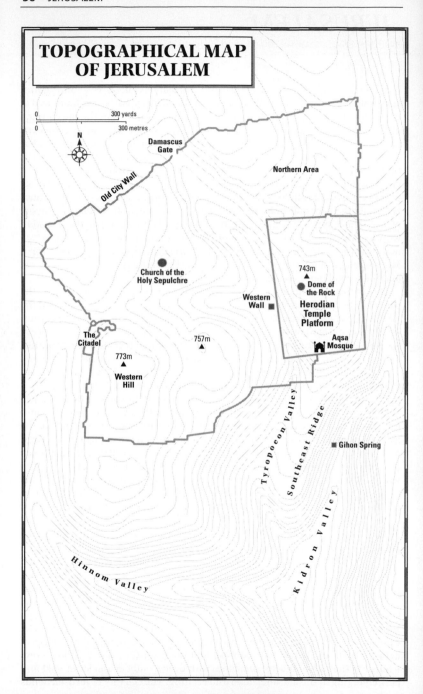

TOPOGRAPHICAL MAP OF JERUSALEM

0   300 yards
0   300 metres

N

Damascus Gate

Northern Area

Old City Wall

Church of the Holy Sepulchre

743m ▲
Dome of the Rock ●

Western Wall ■

Herodian Temple Platform

The Citadel

757m ▲

773m ▲
Western Hill

Aqsa Mosque

Tyropoeon Valley

Southeast Ridge

■ Gihon Spring

Kidron Valley

Hinnom Valley

amazing variety to offer the wanderer at all hours. The mellowness of masonry, which in much of the Muslim Quarter has stood for 500 and sometimes 1000 years, and in some places for as much as 2000 years, gives Jerusalem a timeless visual quality.

The modern city expanded beyond the medieval walls in the second half of the 19C. The new suburbs were built with local stone by custom during the Turkish period, and by law during the British Mandate period, but that by-law had to be set aside to keep pace with housing demands in Israel in later years. Today there is an attempt to continue and preserve this visual image, both in new building and particularly in restoration. The new west city, with its parliament and other civic buildings, is built on modern European and American models.

The city is diverse in character and history. **East Jerusalem**, part of the Hashemite Kingdom of Jordan from 1948 until 1967, but annexed by Israel on 28 June 1967, includes the ancient and medieval cities of Jerusalem with modern suburbs to the north, mostly of 19C and 20C date and contains a mixed Jewish and Arab population. **West Jerusalem**, part of the state of Israel since 1948, consists of modern suburbs dating to the 19C and 20C. It is far larger than the older city and is almost completely Jewish. Since 1967 the integration of the two sections has been shaped by the building of many new highways and suburbs in and around the Old City.

Practical information

Tourist information

The Jerusalem Visitor Center is at Safra Square (☎ 02 625 8844), and there is a Tourist Information Office at the Jaffa Gate (☎ 02 628 0382). Open Sun–Thur 08.30–17.00, Fri and days preceding Jewish holidays 08.30–14.00, Sat and religious holidays closed. Leaflets and maps with tourist information, newspapers with current events, information on tours and guided walks, bus maps and items of general interest are available.

Getting around

Local bus services are frequent and cheap but note that Jewish-owned bus services do not operate on the Sabbath (Friday evening and Saturday); *Egged* provides an excellent route map and street index of the Jerusalem city routes, available from the new Central Bus Station (for western Jerusalem, Mount Scopus and the coast), which is located in the Jaffa (Yafo) Rd, in the western section of the town at Romema; apart from Friday evening or Saturday, most services from here operate at approximately 15-minute intervals 06.00–24.00. Timetables for all routes are available in Hebrew. The Damascus Gate Bus Station serves the Arab community on the east side of the town and areas of the West Bank. These services operate daily.

Where to stay
Hotels

There is a very large choice of accommodation available in Jerusalem, advance booking is usually necessary in high season, which includes Easter, summer and Christmas. The following list includes a selection only from central East and West Jerusalem; for fuller lists of hotels (and restaurants), consult the Israel Government Tourist Offices and websites, Palestinian information sources and local free tourist newspapers. Websites

JERUSALEM CENTRE

Church of St. Stephen

Garden Tomb

PROPHET STREET

NABLUS ROAD

HEL HANDASA

T KHAN AZ-ZAIT

Damascus Gate

SHIITE ISRAEL

JAFFA ROAD

HA-ZANHANIM

City Walls

CHRISTIAN QUARTER

New Gate

St. Saviour

al-Khanqah Mosque

TARIQ AL-KHANQAH

SHLOMZION

Zawiya Kubakiyya

NEW GATE ST.

ST. FRANCIS STREET

CHRISTIAN QUARTER ST.

St. Alexander's Russian Chapel

Church of the Holy Sepulchre

Mamila Pool

Independence Park

Tancred's Tower

Greek Orthodox Patriarchate

Ch. of the Redeemer

NEW BAZAAR

FRED WILLIAM ST.

SUD AL-LAHHAMIN

GERSHON AGRON

Mosque of Umar

Muristan

St. George

JAFFA ROAD

Pool of the Patriarch Bath

St. John the Baptist

KING DAVID

DAVID STREET

ST. MARK'S ST.

Jaffa Gate

Christ Church

HABID STREET

Tower of David

Citadel

St. Mark's Church

Old Yishuv Court Museum

ARMENIAN PATRIARCHATE ROAD

Armenian Convent of St. James

Armenian Garden

ARMENIAN QUARTER

BETHLEHEM ROAD

Convent of the Olive Tree

Tomb of Herod's Family

Zion Gate

Church of the Holy Saviour

KEREN HA-YESSOD

Bloomfield Park

Dormition Church

Montefiore Windmill and Houses

Sultan's Pool

Tomb of David

Mount Zion

GRAPES TOMB, AMMUNITION HILL, GIBEAH OF SAUL,
MOUNT SCOPUS, HEBREW UNIVERSITY, HADASSAH HOSPITAL

Rockefeller
Museum

N

SALAH AC-DIN STREET

Post
Office

SULAIMAN STREET

Stork
Tower

Herod's
Gate

MOSLEM
QUARTER

HARAT AL-SA'DIYYA

A. AL-HINDI

HARAT
AL-MAWLAWIYYA

AQABAT
AL-BISTAMI

SHARI'A BAB AL-ZAHRA

SHARI'A MUHAMMAD DARWISH

St. Anne's
Church

St. Nicodemus
Church

Pools of
Bethesda

Monastery of
the Flagellation

Convent of the
Sisters of Sion

TARIQ BAB SITTI MARYAM

'Umariyya Boys'
School

al-Karimiyya

St. Stephen's Gate

Tomb of the
Virgin Mary

VIA DOLOROSA

Antonia
Fortress

T. KHAN AL-ZAIT

TARIQ AL-WAD

Church of
All Nations

TARIQ AL-SARAY

St. Veronica

T. BAB AL-NAZIR

A. AL-TAKIYYA

Dar al-Sitt
Tunshuq

Maktab
Bairam
Jawish

Ribat
al-Mansuri

AL-WAD

Golden Gate

Cave of
Gethsemane

St. Alexander's
Russian Chapel

Ch of the Redeemer

SUQ AL-'ATTARIN

SUQ AL-LAHHAMIN

Suq al-Qattanin

T. AL-KHALIDIYYA

Western Wall

Haram al-Sharif

Dome of
the Chain

East Wall

Dome of the Rock

SUQ AL-KHAWAJAT

Khan al-Sultan

Jaliqiyya

Wilson's Arch

Gate of the Chain

Tomb of
Jehoshaphat

al-Taziyya

T. BAB AL-SILSILA

HABAD STREET

JEWISH QUARTER LANE

Tashtamuriyya

Israelite Tower

JEWISH
QUARTER

Aqsa Mosque

Islamic
Museum

Tomb of
Absalom

Tomb of
Bene Hezir

Burnt
House

St. Mary of
the Germans

Southern
Archaeological
Zone

Tomb of
Zechariah

Wohl
Museum

Ramban & Hurva
Synagogues

Palatial
Mansion

Dung Gate

Nea Church
of Justinian

Car
Park

City Walls

City of David
Archaeological
Garden

Kidron Valley

BETHANY

Gihon
Spring

SILWAN

St. Peter
in Gallicantu

Pool of
Siloam

0   300 yards

0   300 metres

BIR AYYUB

MOUNT OF OLIVES, CHURCH OF DOMINUS FLEVIT, BETH PHAGE,
CHAPEL OF THE ASCENSION, CHURCH OF THE PATERNOSTER

often offer good package deals.

First class hotels

American Colony Hotel, Nablus Rd. East Jerusalem; ☎ 02 627 9777; 📠 02 627 9779.

King David Hotel, 23 King David St; ☎ 02 620 8888; 📠 02 620 8882.

Hilton Hotel, 7 King David St. ☎ 02 621 1111; 📠 02 621 1000.

Crowne Plaza Jerusalem, Givat Ram; ☎ 02 658 8888; 📠 02 651 4555.

Mt Zion Hotel, 17 Hebron Rd, Jerusalem 93546; ☎ 02 672 2568; 📠 02 673 1425.

Sheraton Jerusalem Plaza, 47 King George St; ☎ 02 629 8666; 📠 02 623 1667.

YMCA Three Arches, King David St; ☎ 02 625 7111.

Middle range hotels

Casa Nova Hospice, between the Jaffa Gate and New Gate in the Old City; ☎ 02 628 2791.

Christ Church Hospice, opposite the Citadel in the Old City; ☎ 02 627 7727

Holyland Hotel, Nezer David St, Bayit Vegan; ☎ 02 643 7777; 📠 02 643 7744.

Jerusalem Hotel, Nablus Rd. East Jerusalem, opposite bus station; ☎ 02 628 3282; 📠 02 628 3282.

A Little House in the Colony, 4a Lloyd George St. in the German Colony in the southern suburbs; ☎ 02 563 7641; 📠 02 563 7645.

Mount Scopus Hotel, Nablus Rd. Shaikh Jarrah, East Jerusalem; ☎ 02 582 8891; 📠 02 582 8825.

Notre Dame Hotel, Hatzanchanim Rd, opposite New Gate of the Old City; ☎ 02 627 9111; 📠 02 627 1995.

St Andrew's Hospice, 1 David Remez St, at St. Andrew's Church of Scotland overlooking the Hinnom Valley; ☎ 02 673 2401.

al-Zahra Hotel, 13 al-Zahra St, East Jerusalem; ☎ 02 628 2447; 📠 02 628 2415.

Seven Arches, Mount of Olives; ☎ 02 627 7555; 📠 02 627 1319.

Hostels

Petra, David St. Old City; ☎ 02 628 2356; internet and e-mail station.

Tabasco, 8 Aqabat al-Taqiya off Suq Khan al-Zait, Old City; ☎ 02 628 3461. Note that hostels in West Jerusalem are generally more expensive and noisier.

 Where to eat

A wide variety are listed or advertised in tourist literature; business lunches in West Jerusalem are good; food is generally cheaper in East Jerusalem and more Arab in character. Alcohol is not served in the Muslim Quarter. Many of the main hotels have excellent food, such as the *American Colony restaurant*, pool café and bar (Nablus Rd). Also in East Jerusalem, the *Askidinya Restaurant* (Shimon ha-Zadik St, ☎ 02 532 4590), *Pasha's* (☎ 02 582 5162), *Antonio's* at the *Ambassador Hotel* (☎ 02 582 8515) and *Kan Zaman* at the *Jerusalem Hotel* (☎ 02 627 1356) all offer excellent food and a good variety of particularly Arab food. The best French restaurant in Jerusalem is at the *Notre Dame Hotel* (☎ 02 627 1995). Vegetarian restaurants in West Jerusalem include *Alumah* (8 YaVetz), *Village Green* (10 Ben Yahuda), *Angelo's* (9 Horkenos) serves fish/vegetarian; *Fink's* (2 haHistradrut, ☎ 02 623 4523; not Fri) offers East European Jewish cooking and a bar.

There are many cafés and sandwich bars in the Old City many of which offer falafel sandwiches, shawarma and similar food to eat in or take away; *Abu Shukhri* (al-Wad St, Old City down towards the Western Wall); *al-Sharq* (150 Aftemos, in the Muristan); and an excellent traditional café just inside the Jaffa Gate on the left. In West Jerusalem, as well as many bars and falafel places, quick lunches are available at *Bonkers Bagels* (Zion Square and 10 King George St); and *Riff-Raff* (19 Hillel). For traditional Arab cakes and sweets, try *Jaffar Sweets* (42 Suq Khan al-Zait, Old City) and *Zalatimo's* (further along Suq Khan al-Zait, Old City at the Holy Sepulchre). Many bars are to be found in the area around Zion Square. Most of the main visitor attractions sell fairly standard refreshments.

Banks

There are several with cash machines in Zion Square; cash machines are fairly common in West Jerusalem.

Post offices

The main post office in West Jerusalem is near the east end of the Jaffa Rd; in East Jerusalem at the corner of Sulaiman and Salah al-Din Streets, opposite Herod's Gate. International Phone Center, 3 Koresh Street (236 Jaffa Road), open Sun–Thur 08.00–21.00, Fri 08.00–14.00.

Churches

For information, the Christian Information Office, opposite the Jaffa Gate, Old City (☎ 02 627 2692).

Principal synagogues

Hekal Shlomo, 58 King George St (☎ 02 563 5212); Sephardic Synagogues, Jewish Quarter, Old City (☎ 02 622 6773).

Principal mosques

Aqsa Mosque, Old City; Khanqah Mosque, Old City; Mosque of 'Umar, Old City; Shaikh Jarrah Mosque, Nablus Rd., East Jerusalem.

Booksellers

There are numerous booksellers in West Jerusalem and a good bookshop in the foyer of the Israel Museum; in East Jerusalem booksellers are mainly located on Salah al-Din St. A biennial Book Fair is held in Jerusalem, and every spring Hebrew Book Week is marked by numerous book markets.

Major hospitals

Hadassa Ein Kerem ☎ 02 677 7111; Hadassah Mt Scopus (☎ 02 584 4111); St. Joseph (☎ 02 582 8188).

Public toilets

These can be found at several places, including the Central Bus Station; in the Old City by the entrance to the Khan al-Sultan at the west end of the Tariq Bab al-Silsila, near the main bazaar; in the northwest corner of the plaza at the Western Wall; there are facilities at most major tourist sites.

History

Chalcolithic and Early Bronze Age The earliest traces of settlement on the ridge above the Gihon spring date to the Chalcolithic period and to Early Bronze Age I, perhaps also Early Bronze Age II (c 5000–3000 BC). As well as these fragmentary remains there are some burials of Early Bronze IB, but nothing of the later Early Bronze Age has as yet been discovered in the town area. A cemetery of c 2000 BC existed on the higher south and east slopes of the Mount of Olives.

Middle Bronze Age The first walled town was built on this ridge c 1800 BC. Only minor traces of houses belonging to the town have been found, but midway down the east slope sections of a stone-built defence wall, 2m–3m in width, has been uncovered and around the spring itself massive walls, towers and a rock-cut reservoir show a highly organised effort to defend and conserve the crucial water supply. A roofed channel led the overflow water of the spring south to the gardens of Silwan. The Execration Texts in which the Egyptians cursed their enemies (c 1850–1810 BC) mention Jerusalem (*Urushalimmu*, meaning 'Shalim has founded'; Shalim may be a Canaanite deity manifest in the evening star), and two rulers named Yaqir-'ammu and

Shayzanu, whose names suggest an Amorite linguistic background. Little is known of the town's history in the succeeding centuries.

Late Bronze Age Jerusalem is mentioned in the Amarna Letters (c 1350 BC, state archives of the pharaoh Akhenaten, Amarna, Egypt), when the ruler of Urushalimmu was Abdi-Khipa ('worshipper of Khipa', a Hurrian goddess venerated especially in Anatolia), whose name might suggest the man was of non-Semitic ethnic origin. Six letters survive in this archive, which were sent to the Egyptian king by Abdi-Khipa. The letters reveal him as a petty hereditary ruler of a small state, confirmed in his office by the Egyptian king, to whom he was vassal and paid tribute. Jerusalem supported an Egyptian garrison of Kashi (Cushite, Sudanese) mercenaries of whose behaviour he complained. Abdi-Khipa would have been subordinate to the Egyptian Resident or Governor in Gaza, at a time when Egyptian officials and messengers travelled between the towns of Canaan. His duties included enforcement of Egyptian policy and the furnishing of porters and escorts for Egyptian caravans. Nonetheless he engaged in disputes with his neighbouring rulers, and was at war with marauding bands of *'apiru*, unsettled peoples or refugees of uncertain origins, who were sometimes employed as mercenaries, and from among whom the Hebrews may in part have originated. He was allied with three other rulers of Canaanite towns in fighting these peoples; one of them sent a contingent of 50 chariots, and they appealed for more help from the Egyptian army. No rulers of Jerusalem are mentioned during the late 14C–13C BC under the strong rule of such Egyptian kings as Seti I and Ramses II, and Egyptian influence over the Jerusalem area may well have continued well into the 12C BC.

Only at the end of this period—of some stability imposed by the Egyptians, and rather limited prosperity—is major rebuilding indicated in Jerusalem. Preserved on the crest of the southeast ridge, directly above the spring, are massive terraces of rubble-filled compartments which raised the surface of the slopes some 10m above bedrock. This massive terracing probably supported a strong and high citadel on the crest above the spring, as it added a flat area of some 200 square metres to the top of the hill. Because so few remains of other structures have been found, it is not clear whether the Middle Bronze Age city wall was still in use surrounding a residential quarter. The date of the terracing and fortress above the spring is disputed, and may not be earlier than the 12C.

For this period, the Old Testament adds considerable interest to our picture of Jerusalem, although its composition and origins are of uncertain date and historical weight. The first reference, Gen. 14:18–19, is the least reliable. It refers to Melchizedek, king of Salem (Shalim) who was 'priest of God Most High', and gave a blessing to Abraham. And there is a reference to Adoni-zedek, King of Jerusalem (Jos. 10:1,3), who led a coalition of five Amorite kings against Gibeon and was defeated by Joshua and the invading Israelites traditionally in the late 13C or 12C. The names of these kings of Jerusalem are again of 'Amorite' type but at a time when the inhabitants of Jerusalem are also described in the Old Testament as Jebusites (Jos. 15:63). Whether or not the Jebusites had links with the Hittites or Hurrians, they are closely allied with the peoples called Amorites and Canaanites.

Iron Age I Although the Old Testament claims Israelite successes against the town and its Jebusite inhabitants in the time of the Israelite conquest, it also states that the Jebusites remained entrenched in their citadel in Jerusalem until it was conquered by David at the beginning of the 10C BC. Various translations of II Sam. 5:8 suggest that entry was gained either by the drain or gutter, or by grappling irons, and according to I Chr. 11:6 Joab was the first to enter the citadel. This has given rise to the theory that the citadel was entered by way of 'Warren's Shaft' (pp 220–221); more recently, and perhaps more plausibly, the much older Middle Bronze Age water system has been suggested. David did not completely drive out the Jebusites, who continued to live alongside the Israelites at Jerusalem (Jos. 15:63; Judges 1:21) but he made it his capital.

Iron Age II The establishment of the town as the religious and political capital of the new united kingdom of Israel edges Jerusalem a little further into the light of history. The choice of a site midway between the northern and southern Israelite tribal territories, neutral but accessible, and on the strategic north–south route through the hill country, was politically astute despite the relative poverty of the agricultural and economic resources of Jerusalem's territory. At all times, Jerusalem's economic importance increased only when it had a significant political or religious role. Undoubtedly much of the old Canaanite town, population and customs survived, and this influence is seen in many aspects of the life of the city in the succeeding centuries.

David is said to have occupied the stronghold of Jerusalem and built the city, starting at the Millo and working inwards (II Sam. 5:9–12). Hiram, King of Tyre, sent cedar logs, carpenters and stonemasons to build David's palace: a sizeable building to accommodate his harem, large court and a picked guard of 30. David brought the Ark of the Covenant to Jerusalem from Kirjath-jearim, housed it in a tented shrine and appointed Abiathar of the Shiloh priesthood and Zadok to be the high priests. All this activity, for which there is no surviving evidence, could only have been funded by David's military success. During his reign he is said to have built an empire covering most of Palestine except for a small Philistine state on the coast. He held all the kingdoms of Transjordan, and for a short time most of south and central Syria as far as the Euphrates river to the northeast, and the boundary with Tyre to the northwest; but these stories of vast success are countered by the fact that the Davidic town at Jerusalem probably covered only about 4.5 hectares.

His successor, **Solomon**, was anointed king by the High Priest Zadok at the spring Gihon. Much of the territory briefly gained by David was lost during Solomon's reign, but his wisdom, administrative capacity and building work became famous. In Jerusalem he built lavishly: the Temple, his palace, the House of the Forest of Lebanon, his Judgement Hall, a palace for the daughter of the Egyptian Pharaoh who was one of his wives, Millo, and the wall of Jerusalem (I Kings 9). He maintained the alliance with the King of Tyre, and also had Phoenician craftsmen to aid in his construction works. The lavish and expensive decoration of his buildings is carefully described (I Kings 6 and 7). He consolidated the Temple as the one legitimate shrine, as the eternal dwelling of the God of Israel, and the focus of Israel's faith and covenant with God for all time. Jerusalem became the central and only legitimate focus of cult and thus played an immensely important role in unifying the Israelite tribes. The Temple and the palace alone took 20 years to build, but virtually nothing of any of his work is known to have survived.

The archaeological evidence indicates that the Jebusite terraces were repaired and rebuilt with a massive stepped revetment. Parts of a casemate wall were found which perhaps mark the Solomonic extension of the city along the ridge to the north. It is assumed that Solomon's new buildings were located in an area called the Ophel, between the old Jebusite fortress and the new Temple on the high point of the east ridge to the north of the town. This increased the size of the town to c 12.8 hectares. To the south there are some traces of occupation in the lower city.

With the death of Solomon c 928 BC, the defection of the northern tribes and thus the loss of all the rich lands and tax of the northern territory, Jerusalem was reduced in economic status, in political status (it was the capital of the southern kingdom of Judah only), and in religious status (the establishment of rival cult centres in the north). Jerusalem survived in this role until 586 BC but took a relatively minor place in history. A list of rulers is given in the Books of the Kings, and their relations with neighbouring states are described. Uzziah, Hezekiah and Manasseh are all credited with improving the fortifications of Jerusalem during this period.

Jerusalem in the 8C–6C BC is, however, rather better preserved than the earlier towns. Two major events affected its growth and shape. The city expanded considerably in the 8C BC, probably after an influx of refugees following the destruction of the northern kingdom of Israel by Sargon II in 722/21 BC. In face of the renewed threat from **Assyria** and the invasion of Judah by Sennacherib in 701 BC, **Hezekiah** took drastic steps to refortify the city. On the southeast ridge, on or near the old Middle Bronze Age wall line, a new east fortification wall was built midway down the slope. A number of large 8C BC houses are preserved, cut into the older terraces above. The ruins include stepped alleys, drainage channels and lavatories. Hezekiah also built a new water system ('Hezekiah's Tunnel'), which took the water of the Gihon spring underground beneath the east ridge to a reservoir in the central valley; and there may well have been additional reservoirs in the lower Tyropoeon Valley.

A population explosion in the 8C BC led to the first settlement of the Western Hill, at first unwalled, and then massively fortified, probably by Hezekiah. Parts of this wall have been found in the Jewish Quarter of the Old City (see Jerusalem, section 7). Most of its line is not precisely determined: some archaeologists hold the view that the whole of the Western Hill and the Tyropoeon Valley were included within the walls that enclosed the Misneh (or Second Quarter) and the Makhtesh (or Commercial Quarter), thus enclosing the reservoirs at the lower end of Hezekiah's Tunnel. This maximalist view would see the size of Jerusalem vastly increased (to c 60 hectares) during the 8C BC. Others believe that this fortification covered only part of the Western Hill, and the Tyropoeon Valley was still not occupied except by a hidden subterranean reservoir and overflow channel or tunnel. Although strategically the maximalist explanation would make better sense (but only if there was manpower to defend such an extended line of wall), no finds of this date have yet been made within the Tyropoeon Valley; and extensive, presumably extramural, quarrying is found around the north and west of the area. The minimalist view could fit Isaiah's description of Hezekiah's actions: 'between the two walls you made a cistern for the waters of the Old Pool' (Isaiah 22:8–11), but the discovery of an outer wall on the east side of the city now provides an alternative location for this pool. A later phase of defensive walls of this period was found in the same area of the Jewish Quarter, perhaps built by Manasseh or just before the Babylonian destruction.The increasing size of the city is indicated by the ring of burials around it.

Jerusalem surrendered to the **Babylonians** in 597 BC and King Jehoiachin, with the queen mother and leading citizens, was exiled, and a great plunder exacted. Nine years later the Babylonian army came again and in January 588 BC Jerusalem came under siege. The city held out for nearly 18 months: in July 587 BC the Babylonians breached the walls, the ruler Zedekiah fled, was captured, and had his sons executed in front of him before he was blinded and taken to Babylon in chains, where he died. Other officials were executed, and further deportations were made. Shortly after the fall of the city, the walls were levelled and the city burnt.

The temple built by Solomon was destroyed by the Babylonians and the rest of its treasures taken. Much of what had originally been placed there by Solomon must have been seriously depleted prior to this event, during the looting by the Egyptian king Sheshonq c 925 BC, and with the high tribute exacted in the time of Ahaz in the later 8C BC, and again in 597 BC.

The Post-Exilic and Persian periods Only a remnant of the population of Jerusalem survived in the ruined city amid a foreign population of deportees brought from other parts of the Babylonian Empire. The leading citizens remained in Babylon after the fall of the Babylonian Empire in 539 BC. Recovery of the city began with the edict of Cyrus in 538 BC when the Persian ruler permitted Sheshbazzar, as ruler of Judah, and Zerubbabel son of Shealtiel, to return to Jerusalem to rebuild the Jewish Temple on the same site as previously (c 537–515 BC). It is possible that part of the present east wall of the temple platform, in a Persian style of masonry, marks this rebuild, though others think it is Seleucid or Herodian, and perhaps even Solomonic. Poverty and schism among the small Jewish population, and pressures from the 'foreign' population meant a slow revival of Jerusalem as part of the Persian province of Yehud, but there was an improvement in the time of Ezra, the priest and scribe, with the return of more exiles (457–428 BC). Under Nehemiah, governor of Yehud c 445 BC, the city walls were rebuilt. These were restricted to a very small area on the crest of the southeast ridge and the temple area. Nehemiah describes the rubble still littering the surface following the Babylonian destruction of 142 years previously, and the co-operative effort lasting 52 days by which the new walls were constructed. Parts of this wall survive at the top of the southeast ridge. The Western Hill was not reoccupied from 587 till the 2C BC.

Early Hellenistic period Jerusalem became part of the Hellenistic world following Alexander the Great's conquest in 332 BC. After Alexander's death, the city was first the possession of the Ptolemies from c 301 BC and then from 198 BC of the Seleucids under Antiochus III. His successor Antiochus IV Epiphanes made a severe and antagonising effort to Hellenise the Jews, which included renaming the city Antiochia, and the desecration of the Temple by building an altar to Zeus and sacrificing a pig on it—the event referred to as 'the abomination of desolation'.

Late Hellenistic period Remains of Hasmonean Jerusalem (c 164–63 BC) reflect the expansion of the kingdom. On the east side of the city there was

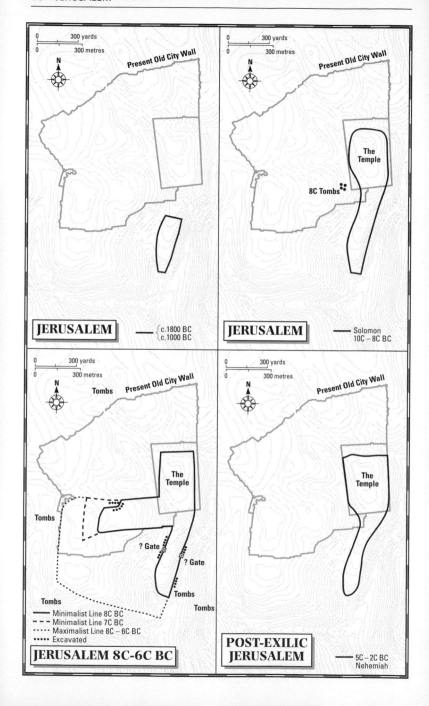

JERUSALEM

c.1800 BC
c.1000 BC

JERUSALEM

Solomon
10C – 8C BC

8C Tombs

The Temple

JERUSALEM 8C-6C BC

Tombs

The Temple

? Gate

? Gate

Tombs

Tombs

Tombs

Tombs

Minimalist Line 8C BC
Minimalist Line 7C BC
Maximalist Line 8C – 6C BC
Excavated

POST-EXILIC JERUSALEM

5C – 2C BC
Nehemiah

The Temple

Present Old City Wall

300 yards
300 metres

N

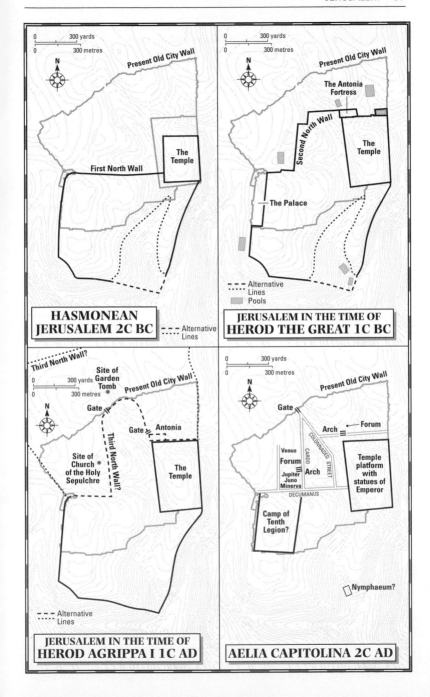

HASMONEAN JERUSALEM 2C BC

0 300 yards
0 300 metres
N
Present Old City Wall
First North Wall
The Temple
--- Alternative Lines

JERUSALEM IN THE TIME OF HEROD THE GREAT 1C BC

0 300 yards
0 300 metres
N
Present Old City Wall
The Antonia Fortress
Second North Wall
The Temple
The Palace
--- Alternative Lines
Pools

JERUSALEM IN THE TIME OF HEROD AGRIPPA I 1C AD

Third North Wall?
Site of Garden Tomb
0 300 yards
0 300 metres
N
Present Old City Wall
Gate
Gate
Antonia
Third North Wall?
Site of Church of the Holy Sepulchre
The Temple
--- Alternative Lines

AELIA CAPITOLINA 2C AD

0 300 yards
0 300 metres
N
Present Old City Wall
Gate
Arch
Forum
COLONNADED STREET
CARDO
Venus
Forum
Jupiter Juno Minerva
Arch
Temple platform with statues of Emperor
DECUMANUS
Camp of Tenth Legion?
Nymphaeum?

little growth, with Nehemiah's wall on the crest of the ridge continuing in use with the addition above Gihon of towers and an earth and gravel glacis to consolidate the steep slopes below. The growth of the city is again shown by the reoccupation of the Western Hill. The wall described by the 1C AD Jewish historian Josephus as the First North Wall of Jerusalem was built during this period, probably towards the end of the 2C BC and along the same line as the broad wall of the 8C BC.

During the 1C BC the main occupation began to shift to the Upper City on the Western Hill, away from the Lower City on the southeast ridge. Impressive tomb monuments began to be constructed beyond the walls, including the Tomb of the Bene Hezir in the Kidron Valley and the Tomb of Jason on the west. The Hasmonean city may have been laid out in a grid plan as devised by Hippodamus of Miletus (5C), and provided with aqueducts and pools.

The Roman Period In 63 BC Pompey besieged and took Jerusalem, and entered but did not destroy the Temple. The favour of Rome and defeat of the Hasmoneans led to the rise of **Herod the Great** (37–4 BC). In Jerusalem he built the great temple platform, a large part of which still survives; he rebuilt Zerubbabel's temple on a grand scale: almost nothing of it remains, but it was undoubtedly on the same site as its Hasmonean predecessor. He built a magnificent palace, full of trees, canals and frescoes, on the Western Hill, with three massive towers to fortify its north end: much of one of these towers survives, though only some foundations and fragments of his palace have been found. And he fortified a new suburb in the north part of the city (enclosed by the Second North Wall of Josephus, which ran from the Gate Gennath to the Antonia).

The Antonia, a strong fortress on the site of the Hasmonean tower Baris, was built, and named for his friend Mark Antony. It stood on the rock at the northwest corner of the Temple enclosure and utilised the water of the adjacent Struthion Pool. He also added to the city's amenities such Hellenistic amusements as a theatre and a hippodrome, the sites of which are lost, though Josephus says the hippodrome was to the south of the temple area.

Undoubtedly there was a considerable increase in the population, with a new suburb and so much building work, and considerable additions to the city's water supply were constructed.

Some impressive tombs of this period and the following century ring the city, including the 'Tomb of Absalom' in the Kidron Valley, and the 'Tombs of the Sanhedrin', and the Tomb of Helena of Adiabene on the north side. Private building also flourished. The ruins of fine villas have been found on the Western Hill, with frescoes, stucco and mosaic decoration. Some credit Herod with the new grid plan for the city.

This was the Jerusalem of the time of Christ, whose lifespan (perhaps 4 BC–AD 29/30) probably fell within the reign of Herod's successor, Herod Antipas (4 BC–AD 39). Herod's Temple was still brand new (indeed not quite finished) and stood in an enlarged and beautified city.

During the reign of the most capable of the later Herods, Herod Agrippa I, more building work was carried out.

With Roman rule growing more severe, and sectarian resentment increasing, with fears especially among the Pharisee and Zealot sects of further acts of desecration in the Temple, events led to the **First Jewish Revolt** AD 66–73, in the reign of Agrippa II and the Procuratorship of Gessius Florus (AD 64–66).

By August 66 Jerusalem was in the hands of the Jews, a government had been set up and silver coinage of the Revolt was being minted. According to Josephus, during the Revolt the Jewish insurgents burnt the Antonia, much of the Upper City and Herod's Palace. In the first attempt to quell the revolt Cestius Gallus pitched camp on Mount Scopus in November 66, set fire to the suburb of Bezetha and very nearly took the Temple from the north before making a disastrous retreat (War II:528–555). By AD 67 the Romans were moving to counter-attack, and had regained Galilee. In AD 68 Vespasian reached Jerusalem. The final assault was organised by his son Titus, who built a siege wall around the city. A detailed account is given by Josephus of the hideous sectarian strife among the Jews within the walls, of the famine and of the preparations for the assault by the Romans. Titus destroyed Jerusalem in AD 70, including the complete demolition of the Herodian Temple. The signs of destruction in the villas on the Western Hill (the Burnt House, see p 206), and in the houses, shops and street in the Tyropoeon Valley are immense; great slabs of masonry were overthrown, the valley was clogged metres deep in ash, rubble and human bones, all giving realism to Josephus' description of the horror of the event. Though the Romans were shocked by the numbers who had died of famine during the siege, yet they showed no mercy to the living, whom they pursued and slew till the lanes of the city ran with blood.

By Roman decree all inhabitants of Jerusalem were taken captive and the city was levelled. The southeast ridge, ancient Jerusalem, never regained its importance. The temple area lay in ruins or as open space until the Islamic conquest in 638. The Tenth Roman Legion (Fretensis) was stationed in Jerusalem, and its camp lay on the Western Hill in the former area of Herod's palace. Very little trace of this camp survives, except for roof tiles, bricks and a few inscriptions.

A Jewish remnant again remained in, or returned to, Jerusalem despite the Roman decree that Jews should no longer live there, and it was these and the Jewish inhabitants of Judaea who mounted the **Second Jewish Revolt** (131/32–35). The cause of this second revolt was in part the Roman plan to set up a colonia (a strategically placed Roman colony populated partly by Roman veterans) on the site of Jerusalem. The rebels forced the retreat of the Tenth Legion from Jerusalem, which again became the Jewish capital for a short period. In Year 4 of the revolt (in the summer of 135) the rebels were forced out of Jerusalem by Hadrian and Septimius Severus.

Hadrian then continued with his plans for the founding of the **Colonia Aelia Capitolina**. The Roman work is marked by extensive levelling of the landscape in the northwest quarter and an almost completely new layout of the city, on which the present plan of the Old City is based. Jews were forbidden to dwell in Aelia, which was a relatively insignificant place, as the capital of the Roman province of Judaea was at Caesarea on the coast. The layout of the city walls is uncertain. There may have been none, apart from the defences of the Legionary camp. The Roman gates at the Damascus Gate and at Ecce Homo were in use, perhaps as triumphal arches like that at the new forum.

The layout of the town was typically Roman, with a *cardo maximus* running south from the present Damascus Gate, on the line of the present Suq Khan al-Zait; and a *decumanus* running east from the modern Jaffa Gate on the line of David St and the Street of the Chain. A column in honour of Hadrian and Antoninus Pius stood just inside the north gate ornamenting the open area at the top of the cardo and the columned street running south-east along the line of the modern Tariq al-Wad. This column was still in existence in Byzantine times and is the origin of the modern Arabic name of the Damascus Gate (Bab al-Amud, the Gate of the Column). In the northwest quarter, most of which was now included within the city, the Tripartite temple of Jupiter Capitolinus, Juno and Minerva, the temple of Venus and the forum with Triumphal Arch were laid out as part of the monumental scheme connected with the cardo another parallel paved road has been found to the west under Christian Quarter St. In the northeast section, as well as a columned street on the line of the Tariq al-Wad, the Triumphal Arch which may have been built as a city gate by Herod Agrippa I (see Ecce Homo, p 146) now stood on a magnificent pavement (the Litho-

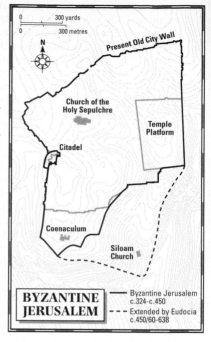

stratos) which covered over the old Hasmonean and Herodian Struthion Pool. The camp of the Tenth Legion and a secondary barracks area were still sited in the southwest quarter, of which little remains. The Legion was eventually posted south to Elath at the end of the 3C. The cardo, at least in monumental form, does not seem to have extended south of the line of the decumanus at this time. The Roman period lasted until 324.

The Byzantine Period Judaean Christians in the early years were a part of the Jewish community participating in synagogal worship. In the first generation the disciples are said to have met in a house at the south end of the Western Hill, and the site of the tomb of Christ was venerated by the community. Gentile conversion began at an early date. Differences in the beliefs of Jews and Jewish Christians increased during the First Revolt, when, not sharing in the Jewish messianic and political aspirations, many Christians moved away from the areas of Zealot fanaticism. According to the 3C–4C bishop, scholar and historian Eusebius, who admits that it was a partly oral tradition, of which he could find no written chronology, there were 15 bishops in Jerusalem before the Second Jewish Revolt, all of whom were short-lived, of Jewish descent and circumcised. The first was James, the brother of the Lord. Not until after the Second Revolt, when Jews were no longer permitted to live within the city of Aelia, were the first Gentile bishops consecrated there. The split widened during the Second Revolt. Many Christians suffered in periods of Roman persecution and a considerable list of martyrs is commemorated. Alexander Flavian came to Jerusalem from Cappadocia as a pilgrim and was persuaded to remain as bishop, c 212–51, dying in prison a martyr in the persecution under the Emperor Decius.

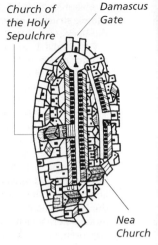

Church of the Holy Sepulchre

Damascus Gate

Nea Church

Madaba Map mid 6C

The acts of the Emperor Constantine from 324 had a lasting impact on Jerusalem. The Church of the Holy Sepulchre was built and at the Council of Chalcedon in 451 the city was raised to the status of a Patriarchate of the Orthodox church. At this time it is clear that Jews were again permitted to live in the city. Precisely when a Jewish community re-established itself in Byzantine Jerusalem is not known.

Jerusalem reached its peak in the Byzantine period under the Emperor Justinian (527–65). The mosaic map of the mid-6C found at Madaba in Jordan depicts the main churches in the city at a time when Theodosius the pilgrim counted another 24 churches on the Mount of Olives. There were three principal stages in the evolution of the city at this period.

Earliest Byzantine Jerusalem (4C) had its walls and street plan on the lines of the Roman Aelia, and contained the Church of the Holy Sepulchre and many other churches, including the 'Mother of all churches' and the Coenaculum on Mount Zion, the sites of which were enclosed within the city wall some time before 333.

Empress Eudocia built the episcopal palace, the churches of Pentecost, and Caiaphas, and of the Virgin at the Siloam Pool, c 450–60. She also extended the city wall to enclose Siloam and the south end of the Tyropoeon Valley. The wall followed the line of the earlier walls on the east side of the southeast ridge.

Justinian's town (6C) lay within the lines of Eudocia's walls, but included a grand layout, with the extension of the cardo in monumental form south to the Nea Church and Gate. The paved streets and stepped roads excavated on the southeast slopes of the Western Hill probably belong to the time of Justinian. It was a large town, with all the amenities of public water supply and drainage.

In 614 Jerusalem fell to the Sassanians (the final dynasty of ancient Persia), despite the efforts of the Patriarch Zacharias to negotiate a surrender. The ensuing massacre and destruction was horrendous, and it is said that 33,000 died. The Emperor Heraclius (610–41) negotiated a peace, but the city was a shadow of its former self: hardly any Christian monument that survived this devastation fails to show the cracks and scars of destruction. In 638 Jerusalem surrendered to the Caliph Umar.

The Early Islamic Period With the arrival of the **Orthodox Caliphs**, under the terms of the surrender of Jerusalem the Christians retained their sanctuaries; Jews and Christians became subject to a poll-tax and to an Arab administration based broadly on the previous Byzantine one. Jerusalem was called Iliya (Aelia).

The Muslim population of Jerusalem immediately following the conquest was small. There were some settlers from Medina and the Yemen. Observing the treaty to respect the Christian sanctuaries, Umar and his successors built on the empty site of the Jewish temple and on the land directly to the south

Abd-al-Malik (685–705) of the **Umayyad Dynasty**, built the first major Islamic structure in Jerusalem, the shrine or place of pilgrimage, the Dome of the Rock (691–92). By this time the Muslim population was increasing, and c 710 Walid I (or possibly Abd-al-Malik) rebuilt the congregational Aqsa Mosque on a grand scale. The city walls were more or less on the present line of the Old City walls, except on the south where the old Eudocia line was probably still the city limit. Pilgrims in the 9C could still discern the line of Eudocia's walls, which were finally pulled down by the Fatimid caliph al-Aziz in 975.

During the **Abbasid Dynasty** Jerusalem was a relatively poor religious centre in the provinces. At the beginning of the 9C, in the time of Harun al-Rashid, negotiations with Charlemagne resulted in some more building and endowment of Christian churches.

The region of Jerusalem was increasingly insecure during the later part of the **Fatimid Dynasty**, which included a brief interlude of anti-Christian fanaticism in the reign of the caliph al-Hakim who destroyed the Church of the Holy Sepulchre in 1009. Numerous buildings to serve the Muslim community were constructed, including hospitals, baths, places of ablution and improvements to the water supply. The mosques and gates of the Haram were beautified with mosaics and other features. The city walls, for the most part on the present line, were improved in 1033 and 1063. The impoverished town, the main exports of which were oil, cheese, cotton and fruit, also suffered from earthquakes. In 1071 the Turcoman warlord Atsiz captured Jerusalem, followed by the Seljuqs in 1078; the Fatimids retook the city after a 40-day bombardment in 1098. Hardly had the Fatimids regained the city than the armies of the First Crusade arrived at Jerusalem in 1099.

The Crusader Period (1099–1291)
The Crusader period left its mark on Jerusalem as elsewhere in the Near East in fine secular and ecclesiastical buildings and in hardened secular and religious attitudes.

The Frankish army arrived before the walls of Jerusalem on 7 June 1099. An attack mounted on 13 June failed and the army set about the construction of siege engines. A solemn procession around the city took place on 8 July; and the final attack began on 13 July. By the evening of the 14th, Raymond of Toulouse's siege tower was up to the walls on the southwest side of Mount Zion, but failed to enter the city. In the morning of the 15th, the siege engine of Godfrey of Bouillon was got up against the northeast wall not far from the present Herod's Gate, where Robert of Normandy and Robert of Flanders were stationed. At midday Godfrey and his brother Eustace of Boulogne reached the top of the wall, followed by Tancred, who went on to take the Haram. The Fatimid governor Iftikar held out in the south until early afternoon, and then retreated to the Tower of David, and sued for terms. Apart from the Fatimid garrison, almost every other Muslim and Jew in the city was slaughtered in the ensuing massacre, which profoundedly shocked even many Christians at the time. Thus in the early 12C the population was entirely Christian, both local Orthodox and Western Latins. The Muslims and Jews had been massacred or expelled, and some (Jacobite, i.e. Syrian Orthodox) Christians had fled to Egypt. This situation was radically changed by the Muslim reconquest. Jerusalem surrendered to Saladin in 1187, was regained by diplomacy in 1229, but was finally lost in 1244.

The Later Islamic Period The **Ayyubid Dynasty** began this phase. When Salah-al-Din (Saladin) regained Jerusalem in 1187, even the Latin Christians were ransomed or sold into slavery rather than massacred immediately following the capture of the city. Many Crusader buildings in Jerusalem were converted to Muslim use and the buildings in the Haram reverted to their original purposes of mosque and shrine. At least 24 buildings of this period survive in and around the Old City. The city wall was rebuilt. In 1219, due to the political instability occasioned by the advent of the Fifth Crusade, al-Mu'azzam decided to dismantle strategic sections of the city walls, in case they should be retaken by the Crusaders. They remained in this condition until 1537. Under the Peace Treaty of 1229 between al-Kamil and Frederick II of Germany, the Crusaders again took possession of Jerusalem, and though the Muslims retained their shrines, Christians were permitted to pray in the Haram. This arrangement was shortlived, for in 1244 the Khwarizmian Turks took the city. Dispossessed of their own homeland by the Mongols, they in turn were defeated in 1246. By 1247 al-Salih Ayyub was in control of Jerusalem. Some damage was sustained during this turbulent period, and very little was built.

During the **Bahri Mamluk Dynasty**, the period that ensued, Jerusalem remained an unwalled city, but a great number of pious Muslim foundations were built all along the western and northern boundaries of the Haram, which today give the Old City much of its character. In particular, tombs of notables were located adjacent to the Haram, within the city walls, where they had not previously been permitted. Fifty-five monuments of the period have been recorded. In 1267 Rabbi Nachmanides described Jerusalem as in a very poor state, with 2000 inhabitants, all Muslim except for 300 Christians and two Jews. It was a flourishing period for the Georgian Christians, who had good relations with rulers coming from the same area. Conditions improved considerably during the 14C. The Franciscans (a Latin Catholic Order), who had withdrawn from Palestine at the fall of Acre in 1291, returned in 1335 and settled in a house on Mount Zion. Their Custodian of the Holy Places cared for the welfare of Latin pilgrims and merchants. With the onset of plague in the mid-14C conditions again declined.

Under the rule of the **Burji Mamluks** (1382–1517 in Palestine), the pattern of building continued in Jerusalem with more caravanserais, palaces, schools and devotional and teaching foundations, completing one of the finest surviving medieval complexes in the Islamic world. Twenty-four monuments of this period have been recorded in Jerusalem, but locally economic conditions continued to worsen: Rabbi Obadiah of Bartenura wrote in 1488 that Jerusalem was desolate, with no walls, and the tiny Jewish community especially wretched.

At the start of the **Ottoman Dynasty** in Jerusalem (1517–1917), Sulaiman II 'the Magnificent' (1520–66) was responsible for a considerable programme of work in Jerusalem, including the rebuilding of the walls of the Old City as we see them today. They are mostly on the same lines as those of the Fatimid period. He also restored and beautified the Haram. Jerusalem became the seat of a Turkish governor of a district or *sanjaq*, but in the 16C and 17C this was a fairly low-grade posting, and only increased in status in the 19C.

Very few Ottoman Turks actually lived in Jerusalem. The early Ottoman archives for 1525/26 record 934 households in Jerusalem, of which 616 were Muslim, 199 were Jewish and 119 were Christian. During the later 17C there was civil unrest owing to a weak government, plague in Jerusalem, riots, and tension among the Christian sects, which was exacerbated by heavy taxation. In 1685 the few remaining Georgian Christians finally departed, under a heavy burden of debt. Local Arab families became prominent in the administration and leadership of the city. From the 16C the Jewish population increased by immigration, but in the mid-19C the total population of the city was still very small, about 15,000, of whom some 7000 were Jewish, 5000 were Muslim and 3000 Christian.

Not all areas within the Ottoman city walls were built up: for example there was an arable field in the Muristan area c 1850. The water supply system in particular had declined by 1860, with aqueducts out of use or in poor repair, and cisterns not regularly cleaned. By the end of each summer fever was endemic in the city. Generally speaking the town was considerably decayed by the later 19C, and contemporary etchings show that the stonework was in a poor state, with cactus, caper bush and other weeds growing in the cracks. From the end of the Crimean War (1856) much greater European interest in the city developed, and many new buildings were constructed outside the walls to the west. By 1912 the population had grown to 70/80,000, but the inhabitants suffered great hardships during the First World War, and their numbers declined sharply through emigration and disease.Thirty-five diverse monuments of the Ottoman period are recorded in Jerusalem. The Ottoman period ended with the Turkish surrender of the city on 10 December 1917 and the entry of General Allenby and the British forces into Jerusalem the next day.

British Mandate Period (1920–48) Not all areas within the city walls were built up, and vegetables were still being cultivated within the northeast quarter of the Old City in 1927. The Mandate Government much improved the supply of piped water to the city, from Solomon's Pools in 1918 and from the springs at Ras al-Ain on the coastal plain in 1934. Both pipelines served the Romema Reservoir in the northwest of the city. The population of Jerusalem increased greatly, and many administrative and service buildings were constructed in the new west suburbs.

Recent times From 1948 to 1967 the city was partitioned, with the western suburbs administered by Israel, and the Old City and the northern suburbs by Jordan; Israel captured East Jerusalem in the Six Day War; the old armistice line is now called the 'Green Line'. On 22 June 1967, following the Six Day War, the Israeli parliament enacted a law bringing East Jerusalem within the confines of West Jerusalem which was brought into effect on 28 June. New immigration centres, expropriation of land, building and industrial projects in East Jerusalem were rapidly developed to inhibit any future separation. The municipal boundaries were extended in 1993. Today the city is ringed by modern Israeli development, new road systems and extensive new housing. In 1987 the population stood at 442,000 of whom 330,000 were Jewish, 100,000 were Muslim and 12,000 were Christian. In 1995 the population was 591,400, of whom 417,000 were Jewish, and 174,000 was the combined total of Arabs and others.

1 • The walls and gates of the Old City

Sulaiman the Magnificent had the walls of the city rebuilt in their present form in 1537–41, and they have been subject to various restorations since. Sections are on the line of those built at earlier periods, which were dismantled by al-Mu'azzam in 1219. The walls embrace a circuit of 4018m, surrounding a roughly quadrilateral space (north = 1281m, west = 875m, south = 1100m, east = 762m) which contained the medieval city, and today have seven gates open to passage. The southwest, west and northwest walls served a defensive purpose in 1948–67 when they formed the Jordanian front line on the Armistice Line of 1948, and still bear scars from the fighting at that time. The walls, of fine local stone of mellow colour, enhance the concept of the medieval city they were built to defend, and enclose the densely packed houses and streets, nearly all of which retain the narrow, stepped crookedness of the medieval town. Cars can only enter where gates and walls have been breached for this purpose at the Jaffa, Zion, Dung, St. Stephen's and New Gates.

A pleasant walk with fine views can be had along part of the top and around the outer footing of the circuit of the walls. The whole circuit of the walls is a green belt in the care of the National Parks Authority, except in the area of the Muslim cemetery along the east wall. Entrance and exit for the Rampart Walk is from the Damascus and Jaffa Gates; exit only at St. Stephen's Gate. Open daily 09.00–16.00 except Fri 09.00–12.00; admission charged (combined tickets available). The distance from St. Stephen's Gate to the Damascus Gate is 1150m; from Damascus Gate to Jaffa Gate is 1000m. The following description of the walls and gates runs south from the Jaffa Gate.

The Jaffa Gate

The Jaffa Gate (H. Sha'ar Yafo, A. Bab al-Khalil or Gate of the Friend—i.e. Abraham, the Friend of God—thus by association also the Hebron Gate leading to the shrine of the Prophet Abraham at Hebron) was built by Sulaiman II in 1538. In Crusader times the Gate of David was located here.

The outer gate retains its early Ottoman form with a curved joggled lintel bearing the builder's inscription, set within a higher pointed arch. The entry contains a left-angled turn; above the gate are restored machicolation and parapet. The original gate is still used for pedestrian entrance, but the curtain wall to the south was demolished and the citadel moat filled in 1898 by order of Sultan Abd-al-Hamid II to allow Kaiser Wilhelm II of Germany to ride into the city in a carriage. It was also the point of entry for Allenby and the British army in December 1917.

Wall: Jaffa to Zion Gate Immediately south of the gate is the Citadel (see p 189), the west wall of which is mostly Mamluk work, but a gate and outer bailey of Sulaiman II are visible. The wall south of the Citadel is a fine stretch of parapeted curtain wall with a series of external rectangular off-sets. It is the work of Sulaiman, and the outer footings have been cleared to bedrock as part of the scheme for the National Park to preserve the character of the Old City. A path for pedestrians to view the remains follows the wall, and parts of the earlier Ayyubid, Crusader and Herodian or Hasmonean city wall foundations can be seen beneath the present wall. Just south of the Citadel, below the walls and behind iron gates fronting the grass, can be seen several 8C BC tombs cut in the bedrock. Note the fine flat-dressed façades recessed in the bedrock, the small entrances and the dressed benches inside on which the dead were disposed. To the west is the Hinnom valley, with the Montefiore Windmill and the modern city. From the rectangular off-set at the southwest angle of the Old City is a fine view of the Church of the Dormition and the Tower of David (see Jerusalem, section 8).

The Zion Gate

The Zion Gate (H. Sha'ar Ziyyon, A. Bab al-Nabi Da'ud—Gate of the Prophet David) was built by Sulaiman II in 1540. It was badly damaged in the fighting in 1948 and a flat concrete lintel replaces the original flat joggled voussoirs with a shallow relieving arch. The entrance is set within a pointed arch with machicolation above, with small gadrooned arches and ornamental panels at the sides. The gate-chamber has a right-angled turn and pedestrians need to be careful of cars. A reused inscription of the Third Roman Legion (Cyrenaica) dedicated to Jupiter Serapis and Trajan (c 115–117) built into the gate was noted in 1894.

Wall: Zion to Dung Gate A fine stretch of wall runs down the hill to the Dung Gate, the outer footings of which have also been cleared and landscaped for the National Park since 1967. The Ottoman wall appears to follow very closely the course of the earlier 11C–13C wall. Following the outer face of the wall down the hill and past the first off-set in the wall, part of a square Ayyubid tower can be seen projecting from the wall footings. Its north side and central pier were discovered against the inside face of the wall. It was built in 1212 and dismantled by order of al-Mu'azzam in 1219. Just inside the wall to the east of the Ayyubid tower a 2.5m-wide stretch of the Crusader wall was uncovered.

Continuing east outside the city wall, the main projection on the outer face of the wall on this stretch of the defences is the Sulphur Tower (A. Burj al-Kibrit), built in 1540 (inscription on south face). Part of an earlier large tower (11C–13C) of mixed masonry projects beneath it. A fragment of the Lower Aqueduct which brought water from Solomon's Pools to the temple area can be seen nearby. It was built in the 2/1C BC and with many repairs, including the insertion of the ceramic pipes now visible, was still in use during the earlier part of the 20C. A small path leads up along the wall face at this point to remains of a 6C hospice(?) built by Justinian, which was probably connected with his great Nea Church (see p 208). A fragment of the southeast apse of the Nea Church is visible just 50m north of the Sulphur Tower. Here four courses of very large drafted blocks with rough bosses preserved to a height of 3m project from beneath the angle of the city wall. The upper course is restored.

Descending from the high path, the next salient in the city wall to the east also has an earlier 11C–13C tower of small masonry projecting beneath its foundations. The adjacent area contains the cuttings of many baths and cisterns of the 1C AD. Just west of the Dung Gate a massive tower in rusticated masonry of 11C–13C date is perhaps to be identified with the fortification adjacent to the Crusader Gate of the Leatherworkers. Steps on the west side lead into the interior of the tower. Note how steeply the rock scarp rises from here to the west. Running south from below the foundations of the tower is a fine stretch of a paved Byzantine road.

The Dung Gate

The Dung Gate (H. Sha'ar ha-Ashpot, A. Bab al-Magharibba—Gate of the Moors, because it gave onto the now destroyed Maghariba quarter) was built in 1540–41, and was probably a small Ottoman postern gate with a pointed arch.

It was enlarged and the long concrete lintel inserted during Jordanian times to permit the entry of motor trafffic after the Jaffa Gate was closed in 1948.

For the wall between the Dung Gate and St. Stephen's Gate, see pp 94–99.

St. Stephen's Gate

Dating to 1538, this has a particularly confusing set of names: A. Bab Sitti Maryam (St. Mary's Gate), as it leads out towards the Church and Tomb of the Virgin Mary in the Valley of Jehoshaphat. In Sulaiman's time, Bab al-Ghor (Gate of the Valley [of Jordan]). In Crusader times this was the Gate of Jehoshaphat, and the north gate was called St. Stephen. After 1187 the name was transferred to the east gate. The Hebrew name Sha'ar ha-'Arayot (Lions' Gate), derives from the confronted lions or panthers carved on either side of the arch, which were the armorial device of the Mamluk sultan Baybars I (1260–77), reused by Sulaiman II.

The Ottoman gate has a curved lintel (restored), with a machicolation above a pointed arch. The angled-gate chamber was removed in Mandate times to allow entry for cars. Bedrock lies c 6.1m below the gate. Just 40m to the northeast of the gate was the **Pool of St. Mary** (Birkat Sitti Maryam). Of uncertain but probably not ancient date, this built stone-lined tank was filled in during 1986. It was supplied by aqueduct and in recent times served the bath house just inside the gate.

Wall: St. Stephen's to Herod's Gate This section of the wall was particularly vulnerable to attack from the high ground to the north and had a deep rock-cut ditch to defend it. The wall has a large number of insets and off-sets in the section leading up to the tower at the northeast angle of the city, called the Stork Tower (A Burj Laqlaq), which dates to 1538–39 and was also built by Sulaiman II (inscription above small pointed arch in upper storey). A sheep market is held each Friday morning adjacent to this tower. The earliest foundations of a city wall on this line were probably not earlier than the 3C or beginning of the 4C. The Crusaders surmounted the walls and entered the city in this section, probably just to the east of Herod's Gate, at noon on 15 July 1099. The rock outcrop of Karm al-Shaikh, opposite on the north, contained many rock-cut tombs, mainly Roman and Byzantine in date.

Herod's Gate

A. Bab al-Zahra (Gate of Flowers, from its decoration), Bab al-Sahira because it led out to the former Muslim cemetery on the hill of al-Sahira opposite, the gate was identified as that of Herod because a medieval house, the Dair al-'Adas (Dair Abu 'Adas, the 'monastery of [the father of] lentils') towards the lower end of Shari'a Muhammad Darwish, near the Convent of the Flagellation, was thought in medieval times to be the Palace of Herod Antipas (Abu 'Adas and Antipas sound alike) who condemned Christ.

The present gate is a small one, with the usual bent axis. The east-facing exterior gateway has ornamental details similar to the 16C gates of Sulaiman II, in particular the rosette panel above the arch compares with that at St. Stephen's Gate, and the relief boss at the apex of the arch compares with those at the Damascus Gate and the Zion Gate; there is a joggled relieving arch above the lintel, and space for a missing inscription.

Wall: Herod's Gate to the Damascus Gate Gardens have been laid out along the base of the wall, which is here built on bedrock. Beneath the second high scarped outcrop east of the Damascus Gate (the 'Hill of Bezetha'), is the modern entrance to **Solomon's Quarries** (signposted from the gardens opposite the bus station in Sulaiman St). Open Sun–Thur 08.00–16.00; Fri 08.00–13.00; admission charged. This is a great cave with galleries—an ancient quarry extending c 200m southeast under the city. The quarry exploited a stratum of *malaki* limestone. It was rediscovered c 1852 or a little earlier, but is noted before the 19C. The date of the quarrying is uncertain, though it is traditionally linked with Solomon's quarry for the building of the Temple (I Kings 5:15–7). The quarry may have been the work of Herod the Great, or Herod Agrippa I, and may be the 'Royal Caverns' mentioned by Josephus (War V:147). In Jewish works from the 3C it appears to be called Zedekiah's Grotto, and this tradition is preserved in the works of al-Muqaddasi (10C) and Mujir al-Din (c 1495). Variants of the Zedekiah legend say the cave extended all the way to Jericho, and was the hidden route by which Zedekiah escaped the besieging Babylonians in 586 BC. The Old Testament account (II Kings 25:4–5; Jer. 52:7–8) describes Zedekiah as fleeing down the Kidron.

Damascus Gate

The Damascus Gate (A. Bab al-'Amud, Gate of the Column) was reconstructed in 1537–38 on Roman foundations. The Hebrew name is Sha'ar Shekhem (leading to the Shechem Rd); in Crusader times it was called the Gate of St. Stephen, as tradition located the stoning of St. Stephen outside this gate. The pilgrim Theodosius in the 6C called it the Galilee Gate.

History

The Arabic name of the Damascus Gate preserves the memory of the column erected in honour of the emperors Hadrian and Antoninus Pius which stood in the open place just inside the Roman gate at the top of the *cardo maximus* in Aelia Capitolina, from c 135. The present gate overlies the ancient gate almost exactly. The area just outside the gate was used for burials in the early part of the 1C AD and was then outside the walls, and a 1C BC date has been claimed for a gate tower beneath the present structure. In AD 40–41 Herod Agrippa I built the Third North Wall of the city which may have been on the present line or further north. Bedrock here is some 8m below the present surface.

The visible east Roman gate was either constructed or reconstructed (both views are proposed) by Hadrian for Aelia Capitolina (inscription above east gate). At that time a round-arched triple gate was flanked by two great towers with internal stairs to the ramparts above. These structures may have reused some of the drafted stones from the Temple destroyed in AD 70. No traces of the contemporary 1C AD walls (if they existed) have yet been found. This gate complex led to a great semicircular paved plaza with honorific column, from which in turn the *cardo maximus* and a second colonnaded street led southwest and southeast respectively. The gate continued in use through the Byzantine period. The Madaba Map of the 6C shows the gate from the interior of the city (p 71), with a single round-arched gate flanked by two high towers and the honorific column still prominent. The lateral gates may therefore have been blocked by this time, and were certainly out of use in the 8C, when the flanking towers were divided into two storeys, and two large Umayyad cisterns were built which blocked the exteriors of the side gates. The east interior staircase to the ramparts was also converted into a cistern and the east guard chamber of the tower into an oil pressing area, which in turn was abandoned in the Fatimid period.

The whole gateway was remodelled in Crusader times, when the tower chamber was sealed, and an angled gate complex with east-facing entrance was thrown out to the north. Two rooms covered the Umayyad cisterns on either side of the gate, that on the west with a fresco of the Virgin Mary was certainly a chapel. This complex was destroyed either by order of al-Mu'azzam in 1219 or in the sack by the Khwarizmian Turks in 1244, when the guard chamber and gateway were filled with earth and stones. Steps were later laid over the rubble of the Crusader gatehouse, and there is little evidence for gate or wall till 1537, when Sulaiman II laid out his newest gate almost precisely over the Roman gate. The lack of a gate between 1219 and 1537 is confirmed by the evidence of Rabbi Obadiah of Bartenura in 1488.

The original paved plaza is preserved in a museum beneath the gate and with access to the City Walls and Rampart Walk, is entered through the old Roman gate. Open daily 09.00–16.00 except Fri 09.00–14.00; admission charged; combined tickets available. The present steps and bridge to the gate are modern, built 1966–67. The bridge was intended as a temporary structure in a larger plan for displaying the archaeological remains. The Ottoman gate can best be viewed from the steps to the north. The smaller masonry used by the Ottomans can easily be distinguished from that of the Roman period beneath. Sulaiman built directly onto the Roman work and the present towers overlie the Roman ones. The Ottoman gate is a fine example of Sulaiman's work, with a flat lintel of joggled blocks, triangular relieving arch and inscription above. The gateway is set back within a pointed arch with decorated voussoirs. There is a wealth of fenestration, crenellation and machicolation variously restored above.

Entering the gate, the passage makes a double bend first to east, then to south through a lofty gate passage before arriving in the Muslim Quarter (see Jerusalem, section 3). The gate passage itself has been the location of money changers' shops for many years. It is the most satisfying way to enter the Old City, as it is always crowded with those passing through to buy and sell in the suqs beyond.

Below the modern bridge the Roman and Crusader remains are visible. Immediately east and below the modern gate level are the east tower and east gate of the triple gate built or rebuilt by Hadrian in AD 135, but perhaps begun by Herod Agrippa I in AD 40–41. The fine masonry, large blocks dressed flat with narrow drafted margins, are probably 1C BC stones in secondary use, but note the fine mouldings of the tower. The inscribed stone above the east arch certainly dates to the time of Hadrian in 135. Some 15m north of the Roman gate the lower courses and threshold of the Crusader gate tower can be seen.

Descending by stairs to the west of the bridge, the remains of the west Roman gate tower, a few fragments of a Crusader chapel, and traces of frescoes still adhering to the walls, can be seen in the lower west area. This chapel was built above an Umayyad cistern. The Crusader roadway runs directly beneath the bridge to enter the city at precisely the same spot as the present entrance, but at a lower level. The central Roman gate, and the Byzantine gate were all located on the same spot but at a lower level. You then turn right and arrive in front of the east Roman gate.

The entrance to the City Walls and Roman remains is through the Roman gate. Entering, turn left into the great east tower chamber of the Roman gate, which served as a guard chamber. It is a large and lofty rectangular chamber. The northwest wall is set obliquely due to the shape of the gate tower. The jumble of masonry used, the rock cuttings, and various alterations are the result of different periods of reuse. A second storey was inserted in the Byzantine period. The equipment for the Umayyad oil press on display indicates one period of reuse, as does the 16C vaulted ceiling. The 44 steep steps of various type and date lead to the top of the Ottoman gate.

Returning to the entrance lobby, turn left to the passage to the south, which leads to the section of the Roman and Byzantine plaza which has been cleared and displayed beneath the present street level. The large polished ancient slabs, some ribbed, which slope gently down from the gateway for about 50m provide a magnificent setting for an interesting photographic display of Jerusalem's later history. You can see parts of a Crusader road and sewer and some Crusader houses built over the plaza and renovated in the Mamluk period. A low annexe to the west allows access to a gaming-board incised on the pavement, similar to those in the Convent of the Sisters of Sion (see p 146). At the south end are some vaults of the Mamluk period.

Walls: Damascus Gate to New Gate This stretch of the Ottoman wall has numerous projections, and towards its west end has a salient extending nearly 50m to the north. Excavations provided evidence that this stretch of the 16C city wall lies on Byzantine foundations which may have been built not earlier than the 3C–4C.

The New Gate

This gate (H. Sha'ar He-Hadash) lies near the northwest angle of the Old City and was cut through the city wall in 1887 by the Ottoman Sultan 'Abd al-Hamid II to provide access to the new suburbs then being built to the northwest. It leads into the Christian Quarter (see Jerusalem, section 4).

Walls: New Gate to Jaffa Gate Inside the most prominent north-facing angle of the city wall, a small 16C mosque, Masjid al-Qaymari, can be seen from the ramparts. At the northwest angle of the walls are the remains of the construction known as **Tancred's Tower**, or the Castle of Goliath (A. Qasr Jalut). Most of the remains are in Christian Brothers' College inside the walls, but parts have been uncovered in excavations just outside the walls. The square tower, with its large blocks of drafted masonry, has sometimes been identified with the Psephinus Tower of Herod Agrippa I, but although much of the masonry is reused from some 1C AD structure, the building is probably Crusader. Attempts to date the fortifications on this line to the Herodian period, or to locate the Psephinus Tower here, cannot be substantiated. Psephinus in any case is described by Josephus as an octagonal tower (War V:160). A 12C Crusader tradition maintained that this was the spot where David slew Goliath. Tancred, after whom the ruined tower is named, played an important role in the taking of Jerusalem in 1099.

The north wall of the tower, and the city wall to the north of it lie outside the line of the present Ottoman city wall. These fortifications were bounded by a tremendous rock-cut ditch, 19m wide and more than 7m deep. The tower may have been destroyed c 1219 by the Ayyubid al-Mu'azzam who ordered the demolition of the fortifications of Jerusalem. The ruins were levelled in the 16C when Sulaiman II built the present city wall over them. Some reused Crusader capitals have been built into the lower part of the city wall.

The Ottoman wall then continues to the Jaffa Gate.

2 • The Haram al-Sharif

**Haram al-Sharif (the Noble Sanctuary), otherwise called Bait al-Maqdis (the Holy House), or in Hebrew Har ha-Moriyya (Mount Moriah), Har ha-Bayit (the Temple Mount) or Beth ha-Maqdas (the Holy House), is the architectural and visual focus of the Holy City of Jerusalem.

The Haram area, raised on a great masonry platform, covers c 14 hectares which is nearly one-sixth of the total area of the Old City. The sacred precinct, with its gem-like central building, its open spaces, its mosques, arcades, trees, light and serenity, is one of the glories of the world. As a focus of two great religions, being the site of the Jewish Temple as well as the second most important place of pilgrimage in the Muslim world, it has symbolic and religious overtones which add to its undoubted impact on the visitor.

The platform is that built by Herod the Great to support the Jewish Temple. It probably covers the site of an earlier platform built by Solomon for the First Temple (c 961/954–586 BC) which was reused by Zerubbabel (for the Second Temple, c 537/515); and was in use until rebuilt by Herod the Great from 20 BC; its superstructure was destroyed by the Romans in AD 70. The present central shrine is the Muslim Dome of the Rock, originally built 691/92 by the Umayyad caliph 'Abd al-Malik. The great Aqsa Mosque to the south, though much restored, is founded on the 8C Umayyad and Abbasid mosque, which probably rests on an earlier mosque of 639/40. The fine buildings and porticoes which surround the Haram are principally Mamluk work of the 13C–15C but include both earlier and later structures. Remarkable survivals of the early Islamic period are housed in the Islamic Museum on the Haram platform.

The dimensions of the platform are: north 310m; west 488.3m, south 281.20m, east 466.65m. Upper platform: north 156.15m, west 167.75m, south 128.10m, east 161.65m.

The ancient topography is largely obscured by monumental building, and exploration has been limited by the very sacredness of the site and attendant fears of desecration. The limestone east ridge of the city climbs steadily from the south to a peak at the exposed limestone bedrock located under the present Dome, approximately 743m above sea level. The surface has been almost completely covered by millennia of construction work, and altered by quarrying, but it is clear that the ridge dropped sharply on the east side to the Kidron Valley, and on the west to the Tyropoeon Valley. To the northeast another deep valley running southeast towards the Kidron cut across the northeast corner of the Haram, but to the northwest the rock rises higher than the Holy Rock to the escarpment on which Herod built the Antonia fortress. This area, like the same ridge further south, may have contained natural caves which in various periods were converted to tombs or cisterns.

• **Admission** The Haram is open daily 08.00–15.00, closed to non-Muslims on Fri and Muslim hols; admission free. Entrance is charged for admission to the mosques and museum, tickets are available from the kiosk inside the Moors' Gate. The mosques are open 08.00–11.30, 12.30–14.00; 07.30–10.00 during Ramadan; closed Fri and Muslim hols. Access for non-Muslims is from the Chain or Moors' Gates only, although visitors may leave by other gates. Special permission is needed to enter some monuments, and some areas especially on the east side are closed at present; security in the Haram is very

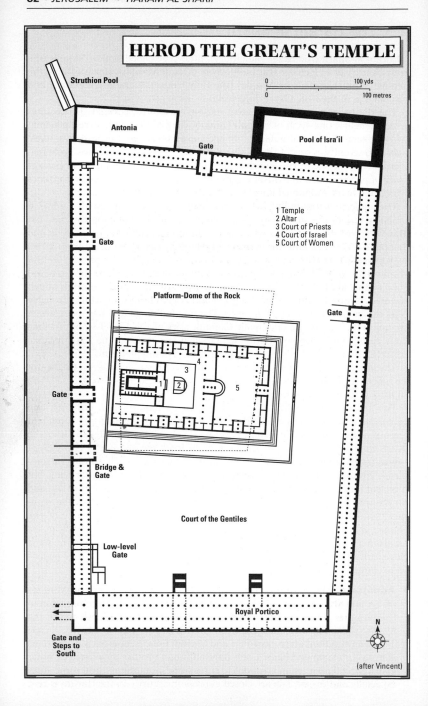

HEROD THE GREAT'S TEMPLE

Struthion Pool

0   100 yds
0   100 metres

Antonia

Gate

Pool of Isra'il

1 Temple
2 Altar
3 Court of Priests
4 Court of Israel
5 Court of Women

Gate

Gate

Platform-Dome of the Rock

Gate

1
2
3
4
5

Gate

Bridge & Gate

Court of the Gentiles

Low-level Gate

Royal Portico

N

Gate and Steps to South

(after Vincent)

strictly observed. It is necessary to dress modestly, and to remove outdoor shoes before entering the Dome of the Rock and the Aqsa Mosque; bags and cameras must also be left outside.

- The best approach to the Haram is on foot from the Jaffa, Damascus or Dung Gates; by Bus 1 or 2 to the Dung Gate, or by the south ring road to a car park near the Dung Gate. Festival or other busy times should be avoided.

- For those with only a short time available, the Dome of the Rock (see p 116), the Aqsa Mosque (see p 125), the Islamic Museum (see p 133) and the areas including the Western (Wailing) Wall (see p 88) and Tunnel (p 91) are the most important sections. Access to the Western Wall and Tunnel needs to be booked in advance.

- The full tour requires at least a whole day and the description which follows the History below has been subdivided into seven sections. The descriptions generally start at the northeast corner of the Haram, and move towards the west, but you can begin the tour at any point.

History

Tradition equates the high point of the ridge with Mount Moriah, where Abraham offered his son Isaac as a sacrifice to God (Gen. 22), and with the site of the threshing floor of Araunah the Jebusite, bought by David c 1000 BC as the site on which to build an altar (II Sam. 24:18–25), and that on which his son Solomon subsequently built the first Jewish Temple.

The Solomonic or First Temple According to the Old Testament (I Kings 5), Solomon began to build the Temple in the fourth year of his reign (c 961 BC) and completed it in his 11th year, with the assistance of the Phoenician king, Hiram of Tyre, who sent cedar, pine and stonemasons to help with the work. No trace of this structure remains, but the biblical description tells us it was a tripartite building, with an inner Holy of Holies in which the Ark of the Covenant was placed. The Temple was of stone and timber construction, and the interior was richly decorated with cedar and gold. The entrance faced east, and in front of the vestibule stood two free-standing columns named, for unknown reasons, Jachin and Boaz (I Kings 7:21). Further east in the court was an altar of unhewn stones for burnt sacrifice. It is debated whether the altar or the Holy of Holies stood over the peak of the rock. The dimensions of the building were 60 cubits long (the cubit being c 0.45m or a little more), 20 cubits wide, 20 to 30 cubits in height, with a vestibule adding another 20 cubits to the front. The two columns were 18 cubits high, and the altar to the east was 20 cubits square and 10 cubits high. The terrace on which the Temple stood was 5 cubits in height. This plan was undoubtedly similar to temple buildings of slightly later date excavated in Syria, and also seems to have had architectural ancestors among Canaanite temples (e.g. Hazor). The Solomonic Temple apparently had side chambers in the north, west and south walls which served as treasuries and storehouses for the offerings made to the Temple. The Temple stood within an inner and an outer court. Due to the narrowness of the ridge Solomon must have built a platform or terrace to support it, a smaller predecessor of the present one, which according to Josephus, extended to the present east wall and had a single portico.

The Temple was looted of many of its treasures by the Egyptian pharaoh Sheshonq c 925 BC (I Kings 14:25–26) and again robbed of its treasure and finally destroyed completely by the Babylonians in 586 BC. During the three and

THE HARAM AL-SHARIF

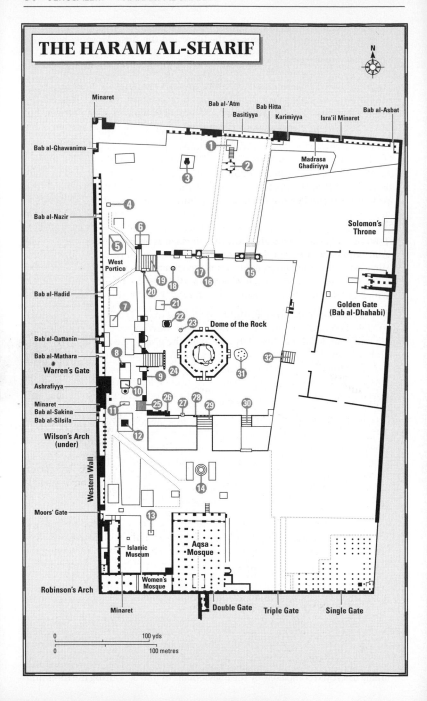

N

Minaret

Bab al-'Atm
Basitiyya
Bab Hitta
Karimiyya
Isra'il Minaret
Bab al-Asbat

Bab al-Ghawanima

Madrasa
Ghadiriyya

Bab al-Nazir

Solomon's
Throne

West
Portico

Bab al-Hadid

Dome of the Rock

Golden Gate
(Bab al-Dhahabi)

Bab al-Qattanin

Bab al-Mathara
Warren's Gate

Ashrafiyya

Minaret
Bab al-Sakina
Bab al-Silsila

Wilson's Arch
(under)

Western Wall

Moors' Gate

Islamic
Museum

Aqsa
Mosque

Women's
Mosque

Robinson's Arch

Minaret

Double Gate
Triple Gate
Single Gate

0   100 yds

0   100 metres

a half centuries of its existence the First Temple was regarded by the Israelites as the sole legitimate shrine of God, though other shrines were built in the northern kingdom of Israel and indeed in Judah. It is frequently mentioned in the Old Testament; most of the kings of Judah were crowned in its court.

The Post-Exilic or Second Temple The temple was rebuilt after the Exile in Babylon by Zerubbabel c 537–515 BC. This building was almost certainly on the same site as its predecessor, and probably built to a similar plan but lacking much of the splendour of the First Temple. The ritual was probably much as before, but the Holy of Holies was empty, for the Ark was lost at the time of the Babylonian destruction and not replaced. This Second Temple was probably improved and more richly adorned during the 3C and 2C BC as the city expanded, but little is known of it.

The Herodian Temple The Temple of Zerubbabel was completely replaced and incorporated into the massive platform and new temple built by Herod the Great, begun c 20–18 BC and completed not long before its destruction in AD 70. The magnificence of the Herodian Temple can be assessed by the remains of the platform that are still visible. The scale and perfection of the masonry of the lower part of this platform can be admired in Jerusalem, while the style of the upper wall surrounding the enclosure can be understood by looking at the smaller but better preserved temenos wall of the mosque in Hebron which was also constructed by Herod (see p 393). Enough survives below ground level on the northwest side of the Haram to show that the same pilastered ornament once decorated the upper enclosure wall in Jerusalem. Nothing survives in its original position of the structures on top of the platform, which were overthrown by the Romans in AD 70; but a fairly detailed account of them survives in the works of Josephus (War V:1–226, and Antiq. XV:380–425), and is supplemented and clarified by fragments found in excavation, or still preserved at foundation or subterranean level.

The Temple enclosure may have had nine gates. There were at least four gates on the west side, two at the courtyard level and two below; the two Hulda Gates on the south side were also below the level of the courtyard; there were probably two on the east side, including the Susa Gate used by the priests for special ceremonies only; and one on the north, the Tadi Gate which was of lesser importance. The lower gates led by way of ramps from the paved streets at ground level adjacent to the platform, up through the subterranean vaults supporting the platform to the temple courts above.

The Herodian Temple courts were surrounded by a portico, that on the south, the Royal Stoa or Portico, being of double width, with 162 monolithic columns with Corinthian capitals in four rows. This structure, occupying the south end of the temple platform, was used for teaching and temple-linked activities, including shops. After the Sanhedrin (the Jewish Council of Elders) was expelled by the Romans from its ancient council chamber (The Chamber of Hewn Stone) in AD 30, it met in this stoa.

The outer court of the temple was the court of the Gentiles. Within it, the sacred area was set at a higher level, surrounded by a fence and approached by stairs. At each gate into this higher area was a notice in Latin or Greek (fragments of two have been discovered) prohibiting entrance to non-Jews on pain of death. Within was first the Court of the Women, then beyond to the west through the Beautiful Gate, that of the men. Further west a fence restricted entry to the Court of the Priests in which lay the altar of sacrifice. Most of the inner gates were plated in gold and silver. To the west, and facing towards the east, was the Temple.

Herod had all the materials prepared in advance to speed the rebuilding of the Temple itself, and the work was completed in 11 or 12 years. It was based on the Solomonic plan, tripartite and with an inner Holy of Holies. The façade was covered with plates of gold, and above the enormous doors (themselves draped with multicoloured hangings) was a golden vine from which hung bunches of grapes the height of a man. The façade was topped by a cornice. The rest of the exterior of the building was of white marble and according to Josephus the effect was of a mountain, blinding in the sunlight and capped by snow. In the main chamber were the altar for incense, the table with the shewbread and the golden candlestick. The inner doors were veiled by a great Babylonian curtain of linen, embroidered with blue, scarlet and purple. Within the inner room, inaccessible and inviolable, was the empty Holy of Holies. Numerous rooms, subterranean cisterns and passages restricted to the use of the priests, and connected with the ritual, lay in and under the adjoining courts and the terraces that supported them. Before the Temple stood the square altar of sacrifice, with corners shaped like horns. At it, Herod sacrificed 300 oxen in the celebrations which concluded the building work, and the people likewise, according to their means.

It is this temple with which Jesus is linked. It was still being built at the time of His presentation; and the money changers and usurers whom He overthrew may have been based in the Royal Stoa.

The Roman destruction The Royal Stoa was damaged in the riots in AD 64–66 and repairs were still under way when the First Jewish Revolt started in AD 66. The complete destruction of the buildings on the platform is recorded by Josephus, and the huge debris of columns, blocks, capitals, and fragments of ornamental masonry—including two sundials, friezes and cornices which lay on the ground beneath the south end of the platform—are mute testimony to the ferocity of the Roman destruction in AD 70.

The Temple area certainly lay in ruins for many years, at least until the founding of the Roman city of Aelia Capitolina after the Second Jewish Revolt. It seems unlikely that Bar Kosiba (Bar Kochba), the Jewish leader in the Second Revolt, had time or resources to do more than plan the rebuilding of the Temple in 132–33. Early writers say Hadrian set up statues in the area of the Temple, variously mentioning statues of Hadrian on foot and on horseback, and a statue of Jupiter. Perhaps the ruins were levelled, the platform itself repaired (or at least tidied) and statues set up, c 135.

In 333 the Bordeaux Pilgrim recorded only that there were two statues of Hadrian in the Temple area, an altar in front of which was a slab with the blood of Zechariah, and not far away a pierced stone at which the Jews lamented the destruction of the Temple. The precise dates at which Jews were able to return to Jerusalem, either to visit the site for pilgrimage and prayer, or to settle, are unknown. Some relaxation of the ban on settlement probably followed the death of Hadrian, either late in the 2C AD or during the 3C AD.

The platform appears not to have been densely built up in Byzantine times but the Madaba Map (see p 71) in the mid-6C seems to show some structures on the perimeter of an open space, perhaps with a chapel in the southeast angle; and at least one pilgrim seems to refer to a chapel or church. The Golden Gate on the east side of the Haram was open, possibly from the 5C and reconstructed in 631 for the solemn procession for the rededication of the fragments of the True Cross regained from the Persians; this led from the Golden Gate across the Temple Mount west to the Church of the Holy Sepulchre. The Temple Mount had no particular significance for Christians but given the size and well-organised civic amenities of Jerusalem in the 5C–6C, it is unlikely that the platform was left in a ruinous state.

The Dome of the Rock and the Aqsa Mosque The full redevelopment of the Temple Mount as a focus of veneration came with the Arab conquest in 638. It was from the first accepted by the Arabs as a sacred site. The building of the Aqsa Mosque from c 639/40, and then the Dome of the Rock in 691/92, began centuries of Muslim construction work in and around the Haram which continues today, and which gave this part of the city its present character.

Considerable destruction was wrought by an earthquake in 749, and rebuilding followed. Another earthquake in 1033 led to the abandonment of the Umayyad structures to the south and the blocking of the south gates.

Changes, but fortunately not destruction, in the Haram area accompanied the conquest of Jerusalem and the setting up of the Crusader Kingdom in 1099–1100. The Dome of the Rock was converted into a Christian church. The Aqsa Mosque first served as the palace of the king, and was later handed over to the Templar Order as their headquarters. Many traces of Crusader work remain especially in the gates of the Haram area and in the remodelling of the Aqsa. An Augustinian convent was built on the north side of the Haram.

After 1187 the area was restored fully to Muslim use, the Augustinian convent was torn down and many mihrabs installed; Christians were prohibited from entering. Many structures in the vicinity of the mosques date to the Ayyubid and Mamluk periods. By the end of the 15C the Haram walls were lined by fine Mamluk buildings, the high point of Mamluk construction being reached under the Sultan al-Nasir Muhammad. Repairs, renovations and extensions were made in the Ottoman period.

After the schools, hospices, fountains and other religious or semi-religious institutions were built and endowed they became the responsibility of a council of the religious and civic Muslim notables, the *'ulama*. The endowments and offerings are still held as a trust which is known by their Arabic name *waqf* (plural *awqaf*) and it is this trust which is responsible for the gathering of revenue and the maintenance and administration of the many public institutions in its care.

During Mandate times there was some further repair to the walls, and in particular repairs to the Aqsa Mosque, which was damaged in the earthquake of 1927. A major restoration of this mosque was made in 1938–43.

Some damage was sustained by mortar bombing in the fighting in 1948. In 1951, King Abdullah I was assassinated in the Haram on his way to the Aqsa. Major renovations of the Dome of the Rock were carried out in the 1960s when the old lead domes of both the Dome of the Rock and the Aqsa Mosque were replaced by anodised aluminium. The minbar of Salah al-Din in the Aqsa Mosque was destroyed by fire on 21 August 1969. The anodised aluminium domes were again replaced with lead in the 1990s, and the Dome of the Chain completely restored.

The Western Wall or Wailing Wall area

The *Western Wall area (H. Ha-Kotel Ha-Ma'aravi) is the focus of Jewish religious activity in the Old City. An enormous space has been cleared in front of this area of the Herodian platform to allow access for prayer and for festivals and celebrations, and the scene is always busy.

History

The foundation and lower courses of the Western Wall formed the lower part of the platform supporting the Jewish Temple built by Herod the Great, commencing c 20/18 BC and completed some 46 years later.

Following the destruction of the Temple by the Romans in July AD 70 and the Roman decree prohibiting Jews to dwell in the city, only traces of bakehouses, baths and other structures serving the Tenth Roman Legion, which garrisoned the city in the succeeding centuries of Roman rule, were found in the excavations in the vicinity. Talmudic and pilgrim accounts suggest that some time after the death of Hadrian in 138, especially in the 3C and 4C Jews began to return to the city and to come annually to lament the destruction of the Temple on 9 Ab (in the month of July). Some went to the site of the destroyed Temple and the Rock, others avoided the desecration of the Holy of Holies and came to the Western Wall. With later relaxation of the prohibition more Jews returned to settle in the city and to come to the Temple area at other pilgrimage festivals. This intermittent pilgrimage to the site continued over the centuries, increasing under favourable conditions, as in the reign of Julian the Apostate (361–63) and for a few years following the Persian Conquest (614) and declining or ceasing completely at others, such as the early Crusader Period from 1099.

After the construction of the Muslim shrines on the platform from 639, access to the Temple site itself was denied to the Jews, and the Western Wall then or later became the focus of pilgrimage. After the Muslim reconquest in 1187, al-Malik al-'Adil (the brother of Salah al-Din) endowed the area adjacent to the Western Wall in favour of the Maghariba community (North African Muslims, Moors) c 1194. The Afdaliyya Madrasa for adherents of the Maliki rite was founded here about 75m west of the Wailing Wall. Further development took place in the Mamluk period, when a zawiya for the Moors was built and endowed in 1303 by Shaikh Umar al-Masmudi, and the Zawiya of Abu Madyan was founded here in 1320.

Resettlement of Jews in Jerusalem began again and a small and impoverished community came regularly to the Wall from the mid-13C/14C; the traditions and feeling of the Jewish community for the Wailing Wall increased in the 16C when the population also increased. Most of the area immediately west of the Haram wall continued to be occupied by the houses, shrine and mosque of the Moors. The area of the Wailing Wall frequented by the Jews was then small but adequate for the needs of a small community; in the early 20C it measured 47.5m in length and less than 4m in width, with five courses of Herodian masonry exposed. Against these stones the Jews leant and prayed, and there wept for the downfall of Jerusalem and their Temple, coming most frequently after 16.00 on Fridays for the beginning of the Sabbath.

In 1877 there were moves by the Jewish community to buy the land around the Wailing Wall, which came to nothing due to internal dissent within the community itself. In 1920 further discussions ended due to lack of funds. In 1930 an international committee of the League of Nations decided that the area of the Wailing Wall, the pavement, and the Magharibi houses and mosque constituted a Muslim Holy Place, but Jews were to have access for religious purposes. With the division of the city after the fighting in 1948, during which the State of Israel was declared independent, the Wailing Wall area was inaccessible from Israel, but was accessible to tourists. On 10 June 1967 the whole impoverished Moors' Quarter, including the mosque and the shrine of Shaikh 'A'id (the 12C Afdaliyya Madrasa), was bulldozed to make way for the present great plaza and mass Israeli access. The official designation of the area was changed to the Western Wall.

The Government Ministry of Religions since 1968 has cleared an underground corridor to the north adjacent to the Western Wall. This is now partly open to tourists and much of archaeological interest is exposed. Extensive archaeological exavations have also taken place since 1968 south of the Moors' Gate of the Haram, where an archaeological park has been created.

There are various ways to access the Western Wall. One is the pedestrian underpass from the Tariq al-Wad to the north. The underpass is closed at night and occasionally at other times—there is a gate and security check. Within the underpass can be seen, from the north, an arch of the 8C–11C; on the right a fragment of the great paved Roman and Byzantine street running from the Damascus Gate to the south of the Dung Gate; and an earlier arch of the 1C BC/AD. The arches support the causeway which today carries the Street of the Chain (Tariq Bab al-Silsila). Other points of entry to the Wall are by the steps in the northwest corner which lead down from the Tariq Bab al-Silsila; by the steps on the west side leading from the Jewish Quarter; by the road in the southwest corner leading down from the Jewish Quarter and the Zion Gate; and through the Dung Gate of the Old City on the south (where there is a security check).

The focus of the area for the Jewish community is the great plaza in front of the Western or Wailing Wall of the Temple enclosure. Since 1967 an expanse of the Herodian masonry 57m in length has been exposed; seven courses are now visible above the pavement, and a further 19 lie below to a depth of 21m. The fine yellow-grey stones with drafted edges are cut with great precision and set without mortar. The average height of the courses is 1m–1.2m but the highest is 1.86m. Stones vary in length from 1m to 3m but many are longer; one stone near the southwest corner of the Haram is nearly 12m long. Blocks weighing up to 100 tons were lifted 9m to 12m in this immense building project. The wall grades outward towards the base which provides stability and visual relief. The foundation courses have narrow drafted margins and rough central bosses which were not meant to be seen, and the upper ones a smoothly dressed flat boss and wider margin which makes the most of the fine colour and texture, strong and beautiful.

At the south end of the Western Wall part of the enormous stone lintel of ***Barclay's Gate** can be seen. Named after its discoverer in the 1850s (J.T. Barclay, an American medical missionary) it is c 82m north of the southwest angle of the platform and at present is mostly hidden by a small prayer room for Jewish women in the angle formed by the ramp leading up to the Moors' Gate. The lintel, a vast single stone, measures 7.5m x 2.1m, of which c 1m can be seen outside, and rather more inside the prayer room. The now blocked gate opening beneath it is 8.76m in height. The threshold, now missing, was probably at Herodian street level, c 722.7m, the lintel at c 731m, the paving of the Temple Court at c 738m, and the pilastered upper wall began at c 741.5m. Originally Barclay's Gate gave access from the stepped paved Herodian street to a passage and ramp leading up to the Temple Courts above. This gate has been identified with the Kiponos Gate mentioned in the Misnah.

Most other remains in the Western Wall area are of later date. The upper 19 courses of the wall itself include four large courses probably of Umayyad date and 15 courses of smaller stones, parts at least of which are Ottoman repairs. The building with four rectangular windows above the northeast corner of the plaza and the arch to the men's prayer hall, is the Tankiziyya, an early 14C Islamic structure built on older foundations (see p 160).

The paving of the plaza is post-1967 and the area against the wall itself is divided according to Jewish Orthodox requirements into separate men's and women's enclosures for prayers and the celebration of festivals. The area is very crowded at these times and sightseeing is best avoided from 15.00 hours on Fridays, all day on Saturdays and at the main religious festivals. The southern end of the plaza is defined by a ramp left in the clearances of 1968 to allow access by the Moors' Gate into the Haram.

Set back within the southwest corner of the Haram is the square shaft of the al-Fakhriyya minaret. The upper structures at the southwest angle of the Haram are of Crusader and later date, and include the Islamic Museum at the southwest angle, with the Fakhriyya Mosque and courtyard (with trees) immediately north (see p 90 and p 108).

One of the main fascinations of this area is to obtain a glimpse of the complex of walls and rock cuttings which survive under the medieval city. The area on the north side of the Western Wall plaza forms part of the Jewish men's prayer room with limited access. For tourists access is from the centre of the north side of the plaza.

Wilson's Arch or the Passageways and Arches area

Open Sun, Tues, Wed 08.30–15.00, Mon, Thur 12.30–15.00, Fri 08.30–12.00; admission charged. Entrance and exit on the Western Wall plaza. The first part of the visit includes the ancient causeway which crossed the Tyropoeon Valley from the Temple platform to the Western Hill (the upper city). This causeway still supports the medieval city above.

History

An earlier causeway was destroyed when supporters of the Hasmonean Aristobulus in the battle against Pompey in 63 BC retreated to the Temple, cutting the causeway behind them (Josephus, War I:143; Antiq. XIV:58). The second causeway was built by Herod the Great and was destroyed in the same way by the Sicarii Zealots during the First Jewish Revolt (AD 66–70). In the Herodian structure, a single arch springing from the Temple wall supported the road above leading to a Temple Gate. The remains of the monumental arch were discovered by C.W. Wilson (Royal Engineer) in the 19C and named after him. To the west the causeway was supported on two tiers of vaults forming a viaduct. The causeway was rebuilt or added to many times. It has been beneath ground level for many centuries (though partly in use for storage and cisterns).

*Wilson's Arch**. The vaulted chambers facing the entrance support the causeway and show many building phases; the chamber on the south is earlier (Hasmonean and Herodian), that on the north for the most part dates to the 8C–11C and carried the Mamluk aqueduct as well as the street above to the Haram. Parts of these arches further to the west can also be seen in the underpass leading from the Tariq al-Wad to the Western Wall plaza.

Continuing to the west, you pass through a maze of Byzantine and Crusader walls and vaults to the modern prayer hall established in front of the Herodian wall. Through the gate which bars tourist access can be seen the same fine masonry with drafted edges as in the plaza, but here in almost pristine condition. Three shafts cut in the floor of the prayer hall (by Warren in 1867) permitted inspection through glass of the unexposed foundation courses of the Herodian wall. The section of the wall visible has 21 courses of drafted stones. The great Wilson's Arch can be seen. This single arch was 22.5m high, today just 7.6m can be seen above the level of the present paving. The lower visible courses and springers of the arch are Herodian in date, the upper courses of smaller masonry are probably an Umayyad reconstruction.

Opposite the prayer room, steps lead down to a complex of vaulted chambers. The most important is the so-called **Masonic Chamber**. It was explored by Warren in 1867, but discovered earlier and used secretly by Masons who connected it with Solomon's works in the adjacent temple. It lies c 26m west of Wilson's Arch. The north–south axis of this chamber is skewed to the Haram wall suggesting it is of different date, but may be Herodian. It is a large rectangular vaulted chamber. Entrance is at the southeast corner through a double door with decorated lintels and jambs. The room has a cornice at shoulder height with Herodian masonry below, and shallow pilasters above, at regular intervals and at the corners. This decoration is preserved to within one course of the top in the northeast corner, where a very weathered volute capital can just be discerned. A broken column stands at the centre of the room, under a vault, which is a later construction, as is the masonry of the south wall.

The Western Wall Heritage, the tunnel

The entrance to the **Western Wall Heritage is in the centre of the north side of the plaza. Open 08.30–18.00; pre-booked groups of not less than 20 may be self-guided, individuals must join a guided tour; to book ☎ 02 627 1333. Admission charged. Exit is in the Via Dolorosa. The Western Wall Tunnel is entered through another gate to the north of Wilson's Arch.

The tour begins in a large Ayyubid/Mamluk vaulted hall with a model of the temple and Herodian work along the Western Wall, through which the successive phases of the history of construction in the area have been visually recreated. A narrow tunnel cut along the Herodian wall cuts through more Mamluk vaulting which supports the structures lining the Haram wall, into which many cisterns were built. Opposite the model are steps down to the Western Wall, where the largest Herodian stone yet discovered can be seen—a monolith 13.6m in length and probably 3.5m–4.5m deep and 3.5m high, occupying the height of three average courses of Herodian masonry. It probably weighs around 570 tons. The faces have projecting knobs, perhaps used to manoeuvre them into position. **Warren's Gate** (named after its 19C discoverer) is another low level gate which pierced the West wall of the Herodian Temple. The blocked gate passage was used as a synagogue in the 11C, and was in use as a cistern in the 19C. It is located c 52m north of Wilson's Arch. Further north the tunnel passes a section of the polished stone balustrade of a Hasmonean pool. Towards the north end, evidence that this quarter was not finished is shown by the remains of quarries and columns with Doric capitals. At the far end, the tunnel enters the impressive deep roofed channel of an older Hasmonean water system which provided water from the Struthion Pool to the Temple area, and which was cut by the Herodian building work. The main part of the pool can be seen in the Convent of the Sisters of Zion (see p 142).

The Southern Archaeological Zone

The archaeological area is entered just inside the Dung Gate and has been laid out with paths for tourist access. Remains of the Herodian and Umayyad periods are of particular interest here. Open daily 08.00–17.30; guided tour at 14.00.

Taking first the path to the north, and looking above and to the right, you see, at 12m north of the corner of the Haram, the springers and lower voussoirs (three courses only remain) of a huge arch jutting from the Herodian masonry called ***Robinson's Arch** in 1835 after its American discoverer (no. 1 on the map on p 94). It had a span of c 12.4m and a width of 15.5m. Until 1968 this arch was virtually at ground level and you can judge the enormous quantity of debris that has been removed in the archaeological excavations by the different patina of the stone on the Haram wall above and below the former surface. It was thought that another causeway, like the one at Wilson's Arch, led across the Tyropoeon Valley from the Upper City to the west to the Royal Stoa of the Herodian Temple, but an alternative view based on Josephus (Antiq. XV:410), that steps led up from the Lower City to the south, has been confirmed by the discovery of the base of a single pier (2) east of the arch from which a series of shorter piers carried the staircase to the south. These piers are visible opposite the arch. In the piers are four Herodian shops with flat lintels of fine drafted masonry and with small round relieving arches above each doorway. The great paving slabs of the adjacent Herodian road were nearly a metre in length. Nearly all of this area has been cleared to the Herodian level, but may be a repaving in the time of Herod Agrippa II. Against the Haram wall the remains of rather poor shops were discovered. Beneath the street is a large partly rock-cut and partly stone-built drain.

The Herodian masonry at the southwest angle of the Haram is particularly well preserved, and contains one of the larger blocks known from the Temple platform, nearly 12m in length. Much fallen Herodian masonry was found in this area, including fragments of an Ionic T-framed doorway below Robinson's Arch, and the southwest corner stone of the Herodian parapet which, according to its inscription, marked the spot where the trumpet (H. *shofar*) was blown to mark the beginning of the Sabbath. On the right a small screen on the Haram wall protects a Hebrew inscription, quoting Isaiah 66:14, which probably dates to the years 361–63 when for a short time the Jews hoped to restore the Temple. To the left the remains of a large Umayyad building were found overlying Byzantine and Roman remains. All along the Haram wall the Herodian roadway has been exposed (3).

Two horizontal channels cut in the Haram masonry at and below the level of the base of Robinson's Arch were probably made in Umayyad times to carry water from the aqueduct to the newly built quarter south of the Haram. The masonry above the arch is a patchwork of various periods. At the southwest angle itself four courses of probable Umayyad work survive above the Herodian. Above are areas which are probably Abbasid and Fatimid repairs, but most of the higher southwest corner is Crusader work, with patches of Ayyubid, Mamluk and Ottoman work further north.

History of the area south of the Haram

A complex history of occupation was revealed in the area adjacent to the south wall of the Haram. It is assumed to be part of the area within which Solomon built his palaces and House of the Forest of Lebanon, but few Iron Age structures have been found. It is the area described by Josephus as Ophlas or Ophel, and in Herodian times a monumental paved road and plaza with steps led along the south face of the Temple platform to two great gates which connected the Temple and the Lower City to the south.

After the Roman destruction the area was extensively quarried and not again occupied until the Byzantine period. From the mid-5C the south boundary of the city was at the south end of the Tyropoeon Valley and this was again a prosperous part of the town.

The whole area was completely redeveloped in Umayyad times when a large complex of buildings was constructed adjacent to the Haram, perhaps by Walid I. Masonry from earlier buildings (including Herodian columns) was reused in the work. Parts of six large buildings were uncovered, all rectangular structures with interior courts. It is recorded that the Umayyads restored the town walls and built a governor's palace or Dar al-Imara. These buildings seem to have been occupied into the 9C but some occupation of the area continued to the 10C–11C. These structures were part of the development of Jerusalem by the Umayyad Dynasty as a Muslim religious centre focused on the shrine and mosque in the Haram.

Most of the masonry visible, including the crossroads adjacent to the southwest angle of the Haram, belongs to the Umayyad palace and other large buildings constructed by the Umayyads for a new quarter of the city. A large building to the west may have been a hospice for wealthy pilgrims. It was rectangular, c 90m wide, with entrances on the east and west sides, of which the jambs and thresholds survive; large piers carried the structure. The Ottoman city wall is built over its south wall. An Ayyubid gate can be seen near its southwest corner. A paved street constructed in the Byzantine period runs parallel to the east wall, and ends at a tower.

The **Umayyad palace** (**4**) lies on the east side of the street, its partly restored and landscaped remains covering the whole area in the angle between the present salient of the City wall and the Haram wall. The palace was 85m x 95m with long halls surrounding a colonnaded central court, two storeys high with the upper storey linked at the mid point of its north wall by a bridge to the Haram platform for direct access to the Aqsa Mosque. Two small projections can be seen high on the masonry of the south wall of the Haram which provided the evidence for the existence of this bridge. The ground floor entrances to the palace were in the centres of the east, north and west walls. The palace was well supplied with piped water and drains. The masonry is a mixture of reused Herodian drafted stones, and flat dressed Umayyad blocks. Herodian and Byzantine

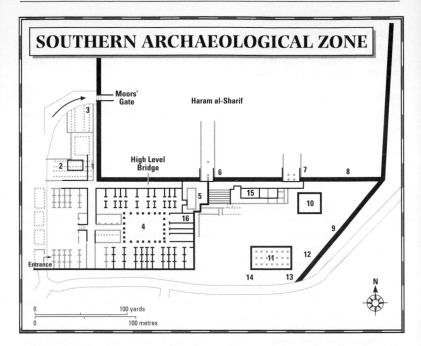

SOUTHERN ARCHAEOLOGICAL ZONE

Moors' Gate

Haram al-Sharif

3

2

1

High Level Bridge

6

7

8

5

15

10

16

4

9

11

12

Entrance

14

13

N

0   100 yards

0   100 metres

columns (one has been restored) and capitals were also reused in the palace. To the south, the present south wall of the city (Ottoman, 16C, small stones) is built on top of the line of the south wall of the 8C Umayyad palace (large stones).

The paved way towards the Umayyad east doorway, blocked in the 16C by the foundations of the Ottoman city wall, now leads to a double-arched entry opened in the city wall during the excavations. Just to the north are the structures (**5**) built against the south end of the Aqsa Mosque. They have the appearance of a rather ruinous double tower, buttressed on the west side by two tall blind arches; the walls may have been built as a tower by the Templars in the 12C, and refurbished by Salah al-Din (inscription of 1191), perhaps also primarily as a tower. Within it the Zawiya al-Khanthaniyya was endowed at the same time. A room for the reader of the Friday sermon, the Dar al-Khitaba was located here in the 15C. The complex was already in a very ruinous state in the 19C. It is possible to go up this tower, and to walk around the city walls as far as the Dung Gate. From this area you may prefer to descend to the Byzantine complex and go beneath the city wall to the lower eastern section of the archaeological garden and reverse the order of the tour.

Pass through the opening in the city wall, round the corner of the tower to the left, and to the north is part of the blocked entrance of the **Double Gate** (**6**) (H. western Hulda Gate, A. Abwab al-Akhmas). About three-quarters of this gate is hidden by the city wall built in front of it. The gate was constructed by Herod the Great and formed one of the main approaches to the Temple from the Lower City. In front of it and the Triple Gate to the east was a paved street 6.4m wide, reached at this point by a flight of 30 monumental steps 65.5m wide with a plaza below to the south. The gate may well have been blocked in Roman times as the Temple area was then little used, and the ramp within may still have been filled with the rubble of the destruction of AD 70; it was cleared and rebuilt in the Umayyad period, but blocked during Fatimid times (c 1033). During the Crusader period, the area south of the Haram was no longer within the city walls, and the gate has remained blocked since that time.

The gate stood c 100m east of the southwest angle of the Haram and was 12.8m wide with a thick pier dividing the entrance passage. The threshold is c 12m below the level of the Haram esplanade. The remaining east section of a decorative archivolt above the gate arch is Umayyad. It contains relief acanthus rosettes reminiscent of carvings on the early wooden tie-beams of the Aqsa Mosque, and on the soffits of the tie-beams in the Justinian church at Bethlehem, all dating between the 6C and 8C. Above is a shallow relieving arch topped by a straight cornice with palmettes and dentils. The archivolt is set in front of, and partially obscures, the Herodian lintels, monoliths c 5.5m x 2m with simple drafted edges. The plan of the gate is closely paralleled by that of the Golden Gate (see below), and compares with probable double Umayyad gates on the west and north walls of the Haram. In the third course above the arch, under the end of the cornice, is a reused statue base with inscription naming Hadrian (2C), which may have belonged to a statue placed in the temple area (TITO AE HADRIANO/ ANTONINO AVGPIO/PPPONTIFAVGVR/DD). The later window in the blocking beneath the cornice gives on to the inner vestibule of the gate.

Adjacent to the gate, the lowest course of masonry is the Herodian master course, 1.67m high and resting on two further courses of Herodian masonry set in the bedrock beneath the paving. The master course continues all the way to the southeast angle of the Haram. The wall above is a patchwork of blocking and rebuilding. Much of the lower fine squarish stone courses may be Umayyad or earlier. The large rectangular window above to the right marks the floor level of the Aqsa Mosque and may be Crusader work, reconstructed in 1330–31 according to an inscription of al-Nasir Muhammad. The eight buttresses and recesses mark the aisles and arcades of the mosque; the central aisle being marked by the large window with round arch flanked by two smaller round arched windows with round windows between. These upper windows probably originate in the design of the third phase of the structural history of the Aqsa, probably 11C, but all the windows have been restored this century. The buttress at the east end is Ottoman, but the recess adjacent contains elements of much earlier work, in particular the lower windows, and may belong to the first period of the structural history of the Aqsa.

The partially restored pavement, steps and broad plaza continue east towards the blocked **Triple Gate** (**7**), (H. eastern Hulda Gate). This was a very large gate, c 15m wide, of which a fragment of the very large Herodian jamb with mouldings survives at ground level on the west side. This is the only original part of the gate to survive in situ and the original plan is uncertain. Its history appears to be similar to that of the Double Gate. The extant triple arch is presumably that of the Umayyad reconstruction, blocked in the 11C. South of the gate are some re-erected marble columns found in the excavations.

Further east another blocked arch, known as the **Single Gate** (**8**), is visible in the south wall of the Haram. This, as is clear from the masonry around it, was not one of the Herodian gates, but was probably constructed as a postern gate in Crusader times and has been blocked since c 1187. It opens onto the sixth gallery of Solomon's Stables. The arch is pointed, and the voussoirs begin at about the level of the surviving Herodian masonry. Beneath the level of this blocked gate the Herodian paved street, which descends eastwards from the area of the Triple Gate towards the edge of the Kidron Valley, was supported on a row of vaulted chambers. Marks of the burning of these vaults can be seen. From one of these chambers, 34m west of the southeast angle of the Haram, a tunnel (not open to visitors) leads north into the substructure of the Haram. It is lined with fine Herodian masonry and ends at a doorway into a vault beneath Solomon's Stables. The purpose of the passage is uncertain.

Continuing east, windows (perhaps also of Crusader date or later) can be seen in the upper courses of smaller masonry, which allowed light and air to penetrate to the vaults beneath the Haram platform. Various repairs to the south wall of the Haram are noted, by the caliph al-Zahir in 1035 (his inscription can be seen on two crenellations near the southeast angle of the Haram wall), and by al-Nasir Muhammad (1294–1340), as well as by Sulaiman II in 1537–41. Arriving at the southeast angle of the Haram Wall, the corner itself is traditionally identified with the Pinnacle of the Temple (Matt. 4:5, Luke 4:9). Here the level of the bedrock drops steeply to the Kidron Valley and there is a fine view. The Herodian wall is founded on bedrock at 695m above sea level at this point and rises to support the Haram esplanade at 738m. Thirty-five courses (c 40m) of magnificent Herodian masonry remain. There were a maximum of 41 courses of masonry in the Herodian platform at this point, of which up to 26 would have showed above ground, the rest being foundations.

The much smaller stones of the Byzantine wall (**9**) abut the southeast angle of the Haram and continue southwest to enclose the Lower City. The Byzantine wall is probably that constructed by the empress Eudocia in the 5C.

The large area southeast of the Haram has all been cleared in the excavations since 1968, and is enclosed within the southern archaeological zone. Just to the southeast of the Triple Gate is a building (**10**) in which was found a staircase with carved stone balustrade. This may originally have been built as a palace for Eudocia in the 5C, and later used as a monastery, described by the historian Theodosius in 530, to accommodate the 600 nuns of an enclosed order, but the evidence is uncertain. A Byzantine street descends to the south where a large Umayyad building of the 8C (**11**) was excavated. Its rectangular plan is marked by massive piers. It is built over Iron Age remains, more of which can be seen to the east in a deep excavation (**12**). These are the oldest features discovered in the area, dating to the 7C–6C BC. They include part of a tower, gate and storerooms of unmortared stones built into the later Byzantine wall. To the south (**13**) is part of a building of the Herodian period, proposed as the palace built by Queen Helena of Adiabene, which is also doubtful. To the southwest are more remains of Byzantine houses (**14**). As you return through the excavation area, the principal remains visible are those of Herodian and Roman quarries, and ablution places (**15**) of which there is quite a number between the stairways leading to the Double and Triple Gates and in the area to the south. People coming to the Temple could wash before entering. Passing again through the entrance in the city wall, on the right are steps that go down to a preserved Byzantine house with mosaic floor (**16**). From here you can descend further to view a fine Herodian cistern.

You have to to return to the Dung Gate and walk round by the road to continue the tour along the outer east side of the Haram area.

The East Wall of the Haram

Most of this area lies within the Muslim cemetery and a special permit may be required to visit it. A good view can be obtained from the road below, or from the Mount of Olives opposite, especially with binoculars.

Standing at the southeast angle of the Haram the Herodian platform seems to tower almost dizzily above you. To the left 13 courses of smoothly dressed small masonry with rubble fill abut the Herodian platform to the right. The wall to the left is that of the Byzantine city, built by Eudocia in the 5C. To the right the weathered courses of drafted Herodian masonry survive to within 7m of the top. Above and to the right there is much evidence for later repairs and rebuildings. In Herod's original platform the interior was not a solid fill of rubble, but—especially at this southeast corner where the bedrock dropped away so steeply—the interior ground level was built up by as many as four tiers of vaults, of which Solomon's Stables were probably the second from the top.

Walking north, at c 20m the springers of another very large Herodian arch can be seen above. This is clearly a parallel feature to Robinson's Arch on the west side of the Temple, and probably supported another flight of monumental stairs leading up from the east or southeast to an eastern entrance to the Herodian Royal Stoa. It also therefore implies that there was an outer line of defence wall to the east at this point. Warren, during his explorations in 1867–68, certainly encountered sections of a rather massive wall 43.5m south of the Golden Gate, and 14m east of the Haram wall. Founded on bedrock, it ran north–south, was more than 1.5m wide, and was built, with mortar, of masonry with marginal drafts and projecting rough bosses. The date is obscure. The Haram wall in this area shows very clearly the strong outward batter of the lower walls stepping down to the massive foundations which are set in a cutting in bedrock.

Just beyond the arch, at c 32m north of the southeast angle of the Haram, is one of the still controversial features of the Haram platform, a straight joint continuing upwards for nearly half the present height of the wall. The later masonry to the left is certainly that of Herod the Great (from c 20 BC); the earlier masonry to the right has a different character, the blocks being within the smaller size range of the Herodian blocks, but differing in drafting and cutting, and in particular with a more projecting and rougher boss. Various explanations for this change have been suggested.

Further north, near the Golden Gate, large, rough, weathered masonry can be seen in the course at ground level. It has been suggested that part of the original Solomonic east wall is to be seen here. Josephus (Antiq. XX:219–22) narrates the events in the time of Agrippa II when work on the construction of the Herodian Temple had finally finished and 18,000 men were unemployed: 'so they persuaded him to rebuild the eastern cloisters. These cloisters belonged to the outer court, and were situated in a deep valley ... and were built of square and very white stones ... This was the work of King Solomon, who first of all built the entire Temple. But King Agrippa, who had the care of the Temple committed to him by Claudius Caesar, considered that it is easy to demolish any building, but hard to build it up again, and that it was particularly hard to do it to those cloisters, which would require a considerable time and great sums of money'; so Agrippa wisely decided the unemployed could pave the streets of the city instead! Peter and the other disciples taught in Solomon's Portico after the Crucifixion (Acts 5:13). The older parts of the east wall may belong to the 5C–4C BC, but it was restored in 961/62 by the Amir 'Ali b. Ikhshid, by al-Zahir in 1035 and by Sulaiman II in the 16C.

A path leads north from this point through the Muslim cemetery which lies adjacent to the whole length of the east wall of the Haram. Approximately 260m north along the wall is a small off-set in the masonry by which is located the blocked Bab al-Jana'iz (the Funeral Gate) or Bab al-Buraq (the Gate of Muhammad's steed). It may have been a Crusader(?) postern; 1.40m high, its flat lintel has a cross set in an elaborate nimbus.

The Golden Gate

A little to the north is the *Golden Gate (A. Bab al-Dhahabi), a double gate (also blocked) whose façade projects from the wall. The south entrance is called the Gate of Mercy (A. Bab al-Rahma); and the north entrance the Gate of Repentance (A. Bab al-Tawba); the central dividing pier is missing. (For the interior of the gate, see p 109.)

History

There are varied references to gates in the east wall of the Herodian and later platform and their location is often uncertain. In Herodian times and presumably deriving from the Persian period, Shushan Habirah (the Gate of Susa the Capital), lay in the east wall and was used by the priests during the Ceremony of the Red Heifer. This was a Jewish purification ritual, in which the High Priest led out a red heifer to be sacrificed and burnt on the Mount of Olives (Numbers 19:1–10). This east gate may also have been used in the Scapegoat Ritual performed annually on the eve of Yom Kippur, the Day of Atonement, when a goat symbolically laden with the sins of the community was driven out of the city to be killed in the wilderness to the east. The location of this Herodian gate is not known but two huge ancient interior jambs on the alignment of the Herodian wall suggest the Herodian gate may also have been on this site.

The present gate is cut through the wall at a height of 12.5m–13m above the bedrock and the threshold is 6.5m below the interior level of the Haram. The date is uncertain: it could be mid-4C or perhaps built by Eudocia in the mid-5C—a gate on the site is depicted on the Madaba Map in the mid-6C. Or it may have been built for the triumph of the Emperor Heraclius in 631. In its present form it is most likely to be Umayyad. Some elements of the decoration (the pilaster capitals supporting the archivolt) appear to be of late Roman style, and is probably reused; much of the remainder supports the attribution to the 7C–8C (the style of the relief work including the rosettes, the early form of joggled voussoirs on the south side of the structure inside the Haram, the unit of measurement employed, which is the same as for the Dome of the Rock). The plan is very similar to that of the Herodian double gates in the south wall, and the monolithic jambs visible in the interior are perhaps Herodian, but the projecting façade implies a rebuilding at a later stage. It may not have been open regularly in the Byzantine or early Islamic period. In the time of the Crusaders (12C) it was opened just twice a year for the solemn procession on Palm Sunday and on the Feast of the Exaltation of the Cross; a Crusader chapel was located at the Porta Aurea. Since that time it has been blocked.

The façade, c 18m wide, has a shallow double arch with elaborate archivolt supported at either end by pilasters with Corinthian capitals of late Roman or Byzantine style probably in reuse. The details are virtually identical with those on the interior façade of the gate. The central pier is missing. Narrow window slits are built in the false windows of the later blocking. Ornamental roundels and recessed panels of later date (16C) ornament the façade below the crenellations which extend all along the east side of the Haram platform.

Traditions

The gate is the setting for many Muslim and Jewish traditions: it is the gate by which the just will enter on the Day of Judgement, hence its popularity as a burial location. Many stories grew up around it from the 8C onwards when its name was confused with that of the Herodian 'Beautiful Gate', the Greek horaia (beautiful), and Latin aurea (gold). It is believed by many Christians that Jesus entered the city by this gate on Palm Sunday and that at the Second Coming He will again enter here. A Muslim tradition holds that a Christian conqueror will ride through the gate.

Structures in or against the inner face of the Haram wall

The inner face of the north wall

At the northeast corner is **Bab al-Asbat** (Gate of the Tribes), in Crusader times the Gate of Paradise. It was restored in 1816–17 with reused Crusader masonry; gate and chamber form a small complex of pointed arches. To the west is the **North Riwaq**, a portico or arcaded ambulatory extending along most of the north wall of the Haram. It is a magnificent row of pointed arches of smoothly dressed masonry built in various stages from the 10C to 1432 on the line of the earlier Herodian north wall of the Temple enclosure, and incorporating Umayyad, Fatimid and Ayyubid work. These arches are mostly walled in and provided with a modern window and door. Further west, the frontage has several notable 13C–15C Mamluk buildings, largely Muslim religious schools containing the tomb of the founder, with Ottoman additions. None of the buildings are open to visitors (some are now used as dwellings), but many of the Haram façades have characteristic Mamluk ornament.

Starting at the first pier west of the Bab al-Asbat, **piers 1–11** are not later than 1345, but they contain no Crusader stones and may possibly be Ikhshidid (c 961–62) or Fatimid (11C) work. Built partly on the 11th pier is the base of the **al-Asbat** or **Isra'il Minaret**, built in 1367/68. Five steps lead to the portal in a pointed arched recess, which gives access to the roof of the portico. Above, a plinth with pyramidal buttresses has entrance on the east side to spiral stairs to the muezzins' gallery. The round shaft has three storeys, with moulded string courses and incised friezes. The shaft may have been reconstructed in the Ottoman period, and the top was completely renewed after the earthquake of 1927. The founder's inscription is on the door lintel, which has red and cream joggled voussoirs, and a tympanum with four tiers of muqarnas (stalactite) vaulting.

Beyond the next three arcades to the west (which date before c 1397) is the small Madrasa Ghadiriyya, built in 1432 by the Amir Muhammad b. Dhulghadir (of a Turcoman Anatolian dynasty). It was originally on two floors, the upper extending slightly to the north of the Haram wall; it hung out c 1.5m over the

Pool of Isra'il and also extended over the four recessed arcades of the portico to the west. Most of this upper floor, which was the major part of the madrasa, has been destroyed. At the west end, above **pier 18**, there is one remaining blocked window with muqarnas ornament. On the ground floor, the recessed entrance portal, of red and cream masonry, with slightly pointed horseshoe arch, has the customary benches and founder's inscription, though the latter is mostly destroyed. The façade, now much neglected, has rectangular windows: one to the west and two to the east of the door, paired with slit windows above. The slits to the east have a larger trilobed window between them. Inside a vestibule and passage with three chambers survive.

The next group of structures which project south beyond **pier 19** contains the Karimiyya, endowed in 1319 as a madrasa by Karim al-Din. This rather dull façade was perhaps originally a conversion of three porticoes on the Haram frontage into an assembly hall. The structures above are Ottoman. Much of the building lies to the north outside the Haram, with the entrance fronting onto the east side of the Tariq Bab Hitta. Adjacent on the west side is the **Bab Hitta** (Gate of Remission) reconstructed in 1220 between **piers 20** and **21**. The gate and porch are part of a two-storey structure. The high, pointed arch with decorated cornice above gives onto a deeply shaded chamber with pointed domed ceiling, and contains some reused Crusader masonry. It is closed by large wooden gates with a small wicket. It may have orginated as a double gate in the Umayyad period, with the second gate passage to the west now incorporated into the tomb chamber of the Awhadiyya.

Bays 21–23 contain much reused Crusader masonry, and date to c 1295–98. Behind the blocked portico is the Awhadiyya (see p 139), with the now inaccessible Tomb of al-Awhad, Superintendent of the Two Harams from 1295. **Bays 24–28** date from between c 1295 and 1345 and were perhaps built at the same time as the Dawadariyya which lies behind them and was completed in 1295 (see p 141). Above the blocked portico, at first floor level, is the façade of the **Basitiyya**. This madrasa or khanqah was endowed in 1431 by 'Abd al-Basit who became inspector of the army under Sultan Tatar. It consists of several elements which lack architectural cohesion. From the west (above pier 28) there is (1) a plain window and a blocked entrance portal with muqarnas arch of reused masonry and benches at the sides, which was originally approached from the Haram by a staircase; (2) a triple line of rectangular windows with grilles which gave onto the main assembly room, with blind triple window above; (3) a double window recessed in a pointed arch with round oculus above, which uses unmatched Crusader marble columns, capitals and bases. (4) Two other small rectangular windows to the east.

Piers 29–38 are Ayyubid, constructed 1213/14, with later alterations. An inscription on pier 31 records the Ayyubid work. Between piers 30 and 31 is the **Bab al-'Atm** (Gate of Darkness), also called Bab al-Malik Faisal (Gate of King Feisal of Iraq), Bab Sharaf al-Anbiya' (Gate of the Glory of the Prophets) and Bab al-Dawadariyya (after the building on the east). A high archway flanked by buttresses leads into a dark vaulted passage closed by wooden doors. It dates to 1213/14 but it has been suggested that the present gate is the west passage of an Umayyad triple gate like that at the south end of the Haram where the scale is smaller but the plan is similar. Above the gate is the upper floor of the **Madrasa**

Aminiyya, dating to 1329/30. It was built by Amin al-Mulk, a state official of Coptic origin in the time of al-Nasir Muhammad, who converted to Islam under Baybars II. This is now approached by an Ottoman outside staircase on the west side of the gate, built when the madrasa was converted to domestic use, and the west window was altered into a door. The original entrance and ground floor lie on the west side of Tariq Bab al-'Atm (see p 141). The elaborate and symmetrical Haram frontage at first floor level has five windows; the middle three above the Bab al-'Atm restored in the 20C. They have red and cream voussoirs supported on six marble columns with Crusader acanthus leaf capitals. The outer windows are set in recessed pointed arches. The high façade on the west is a later addition.

To the west is the **Madrasa Farisiyya** endowed in 1352/53 by Faris al-Din, a Mamluk official who was at one time governor of Gaza. It is built over the portico and entered by stairs under the portico that supports the Almalikiyya to the west. Most of the frontage was rebuilt in Ottoman times. Over piers 35 to 37 is the **Almalikiyya**, a madrasa endowed in 1340 by Almalik al-Jukandar, who started as a slave and rose to become a court official of al-Nasir Muhammad. He was the 'Bearer of the Polo Stick'. The madrasa has survived virtually unchanged, with an assembly hall overlooking the Haram and the founder's inscription which bears his blazon of polo sticks above the piers. New piers were built to support the structure, with buttresses continuing to the top of the façade, and a string course above the piers; at the top is a two-tiered muqarnas cornice. The intervening façade is recessed. Alternate courses of red and cream stone and three windows with round oculus above complete a façade whose symmetry is only marred by an extension beyond the west buttress. To the rear is an open courtyard with two tiers of rooms and a tomb chamber.

Adjacent, to the west, is a fine complex marked by a long, symmetrical façade topped by three domes. This is the **Khanqah** or **Madrasa Is'irdiyya** which is built at first floor level over the portico, **piers 40** to **42** being constructed at the same time. It was built and endowed in 1359 for Majd al-Din al-Is'irdi, perhaps of a merchant family, who came from Siirt southwest of Lake Van in Turkey. It was restored in 1927/28 with some modifications, when it became the Aqsa Library (now in the Ashrafiyya, see below). The central feature in the façade is the curved salient of the back of the mihrab supported on muqarnas corbelling. The façade is an expanded version of the Almalikiyya, with four windows to the assembly room and a dome chamber at both ends. During the restorations various modifications were made to the windows, and the rectangular pediment above added. The east dome was then modified to match the west dome. The large double window of the west dome chamber contained Crusader columns, bases and acanthus capitals which were replaced with modern 'Islamic' muqarnas capitals and bulbous bases. The site is compressed against the rock scarp behind, and the interior of the building is divided into two sections by a massive east–west wall, 4m wide, which may be a surviving part of Herod the Great's Antonia fortress (see p 142). The Mamluk builders had to cut through this to link the assembly room on the south with the court on the north. The court has two storeys of cells on three sides, approached by a spiral staircase in the northeast corner. The façade of the court has pleasingly restrained decoration, with, from the top, a cornice with muqarnas band; a row of small keyhole ventilation windows; a row of rosette windows giving onto a line of upper cells; and a row of square windows to the lower cells which were approached from a rear corridor.

On the south side of the court is an iwan, with a tomb, probably of the founder, on the west. The tomb chamber is finely decorated with a pointed horseshoe arch of black and white voussoirs supported by Crusader marble columns with unmatched capitals which are in excellent condition. There is a fine Mamluk iron grille protecting the chamber. Here the lower 2m of the wall appear to be of Herodian masonry with a section of the upper ornamental pilasters. The court also contains a well.

At the west corner of the Is'irdiyya the portico ends and the Haram wall and rock scarp are set back to the north among trees. The scarp may have been cut in Herodian times as the base for the Antonia fortress. Next to the Is'irdiyya, the scarp is capped by the long two-storey Umariyya Boys' School built in 1923/24, which destroyed or enveloped some Mamluk buildings. A buttress against the west end of the Is'irdiyya is the last fragment of a portico which once contained the access to the **Subaybiyya**, a tomb and madrasa built before 1406 for 'Ala' al-Din 'Ali b. Nasir al-Din Muhammad, the governor of the fortress of Subayba (Castle of Nimrod above Banias, see p 421). About 7.5m above the esplanade, and adjacent to the Is'irdiyya, is a blocked door and two windows of pink and cream masonry. The surviving lintel of the door and the left window are of mottled red granite; at either end of the door lintel are limestone blocks with cup and napkin blazons in lobed medallions. When the school was built above the ruins of the Subaybiyya, the interior became inaccessible. The north side may have included the ruined Mamluk doorway in the south frontage of the Via Dolorosa (Scala Sancta, p 142).

Rising above the modern part of the school to the west is a cluster of buildings. These also have earlier foundations. In the highest domed building, the two top storeys are part of the Ottoman barracks. The third storey from the top is part of the **Jawiliyya**, a madrasa built for Sanjar al-Jawili between 1315 and 1320; its Haram frontage, of red and cream coursed masonry, has a row of five windows, the three central ones belong to the south iwan, and the outer ones to flanking rooms. All have been cut in a massive wall which probably belonged to the Antonia, like the wall in the Is'irdiyya to the east. To the west the **Madrasa Muhaddathiyya** was endowed in 1360 by a scholar from Ardabil. Part of a window with muqarnas decoration can be seen towards the west end of the complex. Cut into the rock scarp c 8.9m above the explanade are several large sockets which probably held the roof beams of the Herodian portico. Traces of porticoes of the Herodian, pre-Mamluk and Mamluk periods have all been found.

In the northwest angle of the Haram is the **al-Ghawanima minaret** built 1298–99 by the superintendent of the Two Harams in the time of Sultan al-Mansur Husam al-Din Lajin. It takes its name from the nearby gate. This Syrian-type square tower minaret, the tallest and largest in the Haram, lends great character to the area, with six storeys rising well above the height of the enclosure wall. At the base blind arcades with columns and decorated stonework are surmounted by a muqarnas cornice; above, the upper storeys are approached from the east; each storey varies, and each is separated by moulded string courses. The second, fourth, fifth and sixth storeys all contain reused Crusader columns, capitals and bases, either in the windows or in the corner nooks. At the sixth storey, the balcony level, Crusader capitals in the blind arcades on the west, north and east sides, though much battered, appear to depict two angels ministering to the seated figure of Jesus. It is thought that these capitals (and a fourth now in the Islamic Museum) were brought from the nearby Crusader Chapel of the Repose (Umariyya School, p 145) from which they were probably removed sometime after 1244. Above, an octagonal lantern is capped by a circular drum and a bulbous dome.

The inner face of the west wall

Just south of the northwest angle of the Haram are steps up to the two pointed archways containing the Bab al-Ghawanima, a gate built 1307/08(?) and named after the Ghanim family, descendants of the man whom Salah al-Din appointed Shaikh of the Salihiyya Madrasa (see p 139). The Crusader Gates of Grief were located here. To the south a group of two-and three-storey structures line the Haram wall, as far as the great West Portico. This has 69 piers supporting an open arcade constructed in various stages from 1307/08 to before 1483 and continuing with few interruptions down most of the west side of the Haram. It is in itself a magnificent structure, giving weight and dignity and an area of coolness to the court. The strong piers and simple cornice contain a splendid vista.

The **first six piers** were constructed between 1345 and 1361, the first two incorporating much Crusader masonry. Standing over the first eight open bays with slightly pointed arches is the **Manjakiyya**, built as a madrasa by Sayf al-Din Manjak al-Yusufi in 1361 but possibly intended as his residence. He was a Mamluk official in the time of al-Nasir Muhammad, and had a chequered career, ending in Cairo, where he died in 1375. He was responsible for much building work in Cairo, Damascus and elsewhere. The endowments for this madrasa are listed in Safad (Upper Galilee), and around Jerusalem. The building now houses the Department of Pious Endowments and Islamic Affairs (the Awqaf). The entrance is from the north side of the Tariq Bab al-Nazir. The Haram frontage contains a domed loggia with a fine double-arched window whose black and white voussoirs spring from three marble columns with reused Crusader capitals and bases on the side columns; the central capital is a Mamluk copy(?). The columns themselves have unusual decoration. The round oculi above have reddish infills of later date. The remaining first-storey windows are rectangular; those at the south end give onto the prayer hall above the Bab al-Nazir. Above, at the second storey, is an unsightly Council Chamber built in 1935. The Mamluk façade is topped by a narrow cornice, and the central area is roofed by an octagonal drum with lights and a high cemented dome.

Continuing south, the **Bab al-Nazir** (Gate of the Inspector or of the Watchman), also called Bab al-Habs (Gate of the Prison, from the prisons which were earlier located in the street outside) leads from the **8th arcade** of the west portico. The original gate may be Umayyad but the voussoirs lack the characteristic chamfering; the restoration of the doors of the gate was noted in 1200; the portal was constructed in 1307–08. On **pier 9** of the portico, a beautiful inscription of 1307/08 with fine calligraphy in a broad and ornate border records the building of the two bays south of the gate, that of the gate itself, and the one to the north. The moulding of the bay in front of the gate ends with a pair of pendant muqarnas stalactites, and the dome in the portico is supported by a fine muqarnas transition zone. The same date is given to all the remaining bays to pier 16.

Piers 17 to 44 are relatively homogeneous, and being a part of the construction of the Bab al Qattanin should date to 1336/37, though bays 23–29 around the

Bab al-Hadid were rebuilt in 1928 after the earthquake of 1927, and bays 39–44 were affected by the building of the Ashrafiyya (see below).

Bab al-Hadid (the Gate of Iron), between piers 24 and 25, was restored on the same dimensions as an earlier gate in 1354–57 by the builder of the adjacent madrasa, and was thus sometimes called Bab Arghun. Behind the portico south of this gate, various rooms have been employed during this century as the tombs of men honoured by burial close to the sanctuary. Immediately south of the gate is **al-Arghuniyya**, a madrasa and tomb completed in 1358 for the Amir Arghun al-Kamili (see p 153). The tomb of the founder is placed in the northeast corner chamber, with a window onto the first bay of the portico south of the gate. It has a cenotaph, with burial vault below. The east iwan was employed as the tomb of King Husain ibn 'Ali who died in Amman in 1931. He was a leader in the cause of Arab Independence during and after the First World War. The large cenotaph is covered by a gold-embroidered green brocade cloth made in 1946/47 in Cairo and can be seen through the ornate window in the second bay of the Haram portico. The third bay contains the present entrance to the Arghuniyya.

To the south **al-Khatuniyya** is a madrasa begun in 1354 by Oghul Khatun, daughter of Shams al-Din Muhammad b. Sayf al-Din of Qazan (from Baghdad, perhaps from a Turkish or Mongol family), and completed in 1380. The original entrance to a large complex is from Tarik Bab al-Hadid (see p 153). The Haram frontage is much altered. The tomb chamber has two cenotaphs: on the south, the smaller cenotaph is presumably that of the founder; on the north is the larger one of 'Abd al-Hamid, a Hashemite leader. The central window and the south door have elaborate funerary inscriptions relating to the five people buried in the assembly hall of the madrasa during this century, including the tomb of the Indian Muslim leader, Muhammad al-Hindi, friend and benefactor of the Arabs of Palestine. He was the first to be buried here in 1930. Also here are the tombs of Musa Kazim Pasha al-Husaini, Chairman of the Arab Higher Executive in Palestine and member of one of the great Palestinian families of Jerusalem, who died in 1933; and of his son, 'Abd al-Qadir Musa Pasha, who died in the battle at Qastal on 8 April 1948 in the Arab struggle for the preservation of Palestine.

Immediately south at pier 32, steps lead down to the **Bab al-Qattanin** (Gate of the Cotton Merchants), built in 1336–37 by the Amir Tankiz al-Nasiri for al-Nasir Muhammad as part of a new commercial complex (Suq al-Qattanin, p 153 It may well have been a new gate to the Haram, not standing on older foundations. The gate is set in a trefoil recess with cream and black voussoirs within a much larger recess with vast semi-dome. The semi-dome rests on five tiers of very fine stalactite corbelling, and has a pointed arch with red and cream voussoirs. The façade is capped by a stepped cornice. The gate itself has fine, carved wooden door panels.

Two bays south of the gate, between piers 34 and 35 is the **Bab al-Mathara** (the Gate of Ablution), which was open in Ayyubid times and restored 1267. The gate leads to the Ablution Place, the siqaya of al-Malik al-'Adil built in 1193. The rather plain archway leads to the Zuqaq Bab al-Mathara. On the right is the **Ribat al-Zamani**, a late Mamluk pilgrim hospice built in 1476/77 by Ibn al-Zamin, who was a merchant and a favoured associate of Sultan Qa'it Bay. The narrow site is squashed in behind the Suq al-Qattanin. The upper floors include three rooms taken from the south lodgings of the suq, and formerly extended over the Haram portico. The hospice has a tall entrance portal, with shallow trefoil arched recess with seven tiers of muqarnas work. Two courses above the door lintel is a joggled string course within a frame moulding. One course higher is the founder's inscription in a sunk panel. To the east of the portal is an elaborately decorated window with its original iron grille. There are four tiers of muqarnas work in the window recess. The work compares with that of the Ashrafiyya (see below), being late Mamluk with Cairene influences.

Opposite on the south side of the road is the entrance to the 'Uthmaniyya (see below). The decorated façade contains two windows to the tomb chamber and a flight of steps to the main portal which has red and cream masonry. It has elaborate detail in the ornamental voussoirs and string courses. Adjacent to the west is an annexe of three storeys, of which the upper may date to 1656. These are built partly above the roof of the Ablution Place.

The **Ablution Place** at the end of the lane, though much altered, is the original water installation or siqaya built in 1193 by al-Malik al-'Adil. It has a cross-vaulted entrance bay with pointed arch with gadrooned voussoirs and brackets supported by elbow consoles. There were latrines for men and women on the south and north sides respectively of the Ablution Place, and on the west a bath house (see Jerusalem, section 3, Hammam al-Shifa'). The east wing of the Ablution Place now serves as a women's lavatory.

Returning to the Haram, behind and above piers 34 to 39 is the **'Uthmaniyya**, a madrasa and tomb of Isfahan Shah Khatun, endowed in 1437, with original entrance on the south side of the Zuqaq Bab al-Mathara. The founder is otherwise unknown, but perhaps came from Turkey and founded the madrasa for the study of religious law and for Sufi devotions. The lower storey has windows from the portico to the founder's tomb chamber (bay next to Bab al-Mathara) and to the assembly room (bay next to al-Ashrafiyya). The upper storey above the portico may once have extended to the north of the Bab al-Qattanin. At the south end of the upper storey is a window with red and cream jambs set in a recess with four tiers of muqarnas corbelling and a fluted conch. Of the six other windows the most elaborate is a large double window or loggia with pointed arches supported by three reused marble columns. Above are roundels with interlocking radial voussoirs. All the rectangular windows have their original Mamluk iron grilles. Near the south end of the roof there remains one small pointed dome on an octagonal drum containing arches with gadrooned voussoirs (view from the Dome platform to the east).

Jutting out from the portico to the south is the ***Ashrafiyya**. A madrasa built in 1482 by the Mamluk Sultan al-Ashraf Sayf-al-Din Qa'it Bay as a Shafi'i institution to house 60 Sufis and law students, it was by the 15C used for public inquiries. It suffered earthquake damage in 1496 and was being plundered for building stones by 1552. Its important upper storey became ruinous, but the ground floor assembly hall now houses the Aqsa Mosque Library. Though only part of this ruined school remains, in its original splendour it was called the third jewel of the Haram. The ornate decoration of its portal is a fine example of late Mamluk work.

The structure was the work of a Coptic architect following two previous attempts in the reign of Sultan Khushqadam in 1470–75 and 1480, which were demolished. The ground floor has an elaborate entrance porch of Cairene type with painted courses simulating coloured masonry. A cruciform panel bearing low relief strapwork with star patterns crowns the vault, with arabesque lozenges to the sides. On the north side is a bench and a grilled window which gives onto the assembly hall. It is set in a recess with muqarnas hood and has a lintel of interlocking stones, carved, with joggled pseudo-relieving arch above, and an oculus of carved voussoirs, coursed in red and cream stone. Among the elaborate decoration of corbelling and tympanum are three circular cartouches of Qa'it Bay. The doorway on the west has a trefoil-arched recess of red, black and cream masonry bedded in lead

Reconstruction of the façade of al-Ashrafiyya (Courtesy of A.G. Walls)

which would originally have outlined the stones in black (also a 15C Cairene technique). The decoration is very elaborate, with mouldings, carvings, and strapwork; six courses above the threshold is the founder's inscription. The lintel is of mottled grey granite. The original doors of walnut, inlaid with pine and bound by inscribed brass bands are now in the Islamic Museum. Muqarnas corner squinches support a shallow semi-dome, of limestone inlaid with patterns in red stone, a black substance and turquoise faience.

The entrance leads into a lofty vestibule, and then to the assembly hall to the north. The assembly hall is built in three bays of the west portico, with three more built against them to the east. It is decorated with red and cream coursed masonry. The three windows in the east wall are modern restorations. The upper floor was more extensive, as it extended over the Baladiyya to the west (see p 160). It consisted of terraces with cells and latrines at a high level around the screened Baladiyya court on the west side; but overlooking the Haram on the east and above the assembly hall was a notable madrasa, the ruined remains of which can be viewed from the Dome platform opposite. Only parts survive of the north, west and south walls of a room formerly 10.5m high, with four iwans. The south iwan was the largest, with a mihrab originally inlaid with marble, porphyry and granite. A Koranic inscription (once gilded) runs round the walls above the windows. There was a loggia window on the east side, with marble columns, gilded capitals and tympana filled with polychrome glass set in plaster tracery. Mujir al-Din describes this madrasa: 'the floor is entirely paved with polychrome marble, and the walls are panelled in marble. The ceiling is of wood covered with gold leaf and azure; it is extremely well-built and beautiful and very high.'

Adjoining the south side of the Ashrafiyya is the west minaret of the Haram, the **Minaret of the Chain**, rebuilt in 1329–30 by the Amir Tankiz. The minaret may stand on the site of an earlier Umayyad minaret, and was damaged in an earthquake in 1496 or 1546. The upper part was probably rebuilt in Ottoman times, the Ottoman spire being removed in 1894 and replaced by an ashlar drum and dome. It was repaired in 1923/24. A traditional square Syrian tower, it has four storeys divided by string courses, the third storey being the most decorative: it has a recess with three tiers of muqarnas corbelling and reused Crusader columns, capitals and bases.

To the south is the most important of the Haram gates, a double gate, with the closed Bab al-Sakina (Gate of the Ark) on the north and the **Bab al-Silsila** (Gate of the Chain) on the south. The gate is set down from the portico within a low pointed arch. It lies at the end of the main street leading down from the Jaffa Gate, the Citadel and the great suqs, and has a minaret above it.

History of the Gate of the Chain

The original gate on the site may have been an Umayyad double gate constructed by 'Abd al-Malik; it was certainly important in Fatimid times when the south entrances to the Haram were blocked. Nasir-i Khusraw (1047) records that it was then elaborately decorated with mosaics, probably ordered by the caliph al-Zahir when he restored the mosaics in the Dome of the Rock (1027/28) and in the Aqsa (1034–36): surviving bonding marks on the outer façade may derive from this decoration. This was one of the principal medieval entrances to the Temple (the Beautiful Gates in Crusader times) and received considerable adornment. Much of this survives on the present gate, despite a rebuilding by the Ayyubids (1187–99).

A small courtyard fronts a double vestibule before the gates. The outer portals have fine sets of Crusader marble columns with acanthus capitals, double sets on the south and triple on the north gate. The upper range has elaborate twisted columns (se p 160), and the capitals also merit a close look, especially those at the north end, where fine carving includes a male figure and two lambs, flowers and foliage. The elaborate pendentives have fluted semi-domes supporting the roof domes. The portals, with wooden doors, have flat joggled lintels and round arches. For other buildings in the vicinity, see Jerusalem, section 3.

Piers 45 to 55 of the West Portico, south from the Gate of the Chain, have been rebuilt and are not uniform. The upper storey of the Tankiziyya (see p 160) was built over this part of the portico in 1328/29 and an inscription indicates these piers were built in 1313/14. The Sufi madrasa and khanqah of the Amir Tankiz al-Nasiri is entered from the Tariq Bab al-Silsila. The ground floor behind the

Haram portico has four windows, and a blocked door which originally led to the madrasa above. The upper storey has been much altered, but includes a pair of arched windows, now partly blocked to take rectangular glazing, with black and white voussoirs supported by reused columns, and elbow brackets from a central pier which replaces an original third column.

Bays 56 to 67 are homogeneous, and date from between 1345 and 1483. The last two piers of the West Portico (of uncertain date between 1332 and 1483) contain the inner porch of the Bab al-Maghariba (the Gate of the Moors), dating to 1314–15(?), which led out to the Moors' Quarter and the Western Wall.

The buildings to the south of the gate now house the Islamic Museum in Crusader and Ayyubid buildings, partly remodelled in 1871. Immediately south of the gate is a north-facing façade with two large pointed arched entrances, respectively the entrances to the al-Maghariba mosque on the east and the Fakhriyya mosque on the west. Neither is now used as a mosque. The entrance portals are mostly constructed of reused Crusader material, including the hood moulds, and in the Maghariba entrance, elbow brackets supporting the lintel. The Maghariba tympanum is now blocked, that of the Fakhriyya partly open. The latter has a smaller pointed arch built inside it, also of largely Crusader materials. Between the two is a late Mamluk or Ottoman mihrab. The al-Maghariba Mosque was built in a large Ayyubid vaulted hall c 1194, for the use of the Maghariba community outside the adjacent Haram gate. The **Fakhriyya Mosque** was the zawiya, khanqah or madrasa of Fakhr al-Din Muhammad, Inspector of the Army in the time of al-Nasir Muhammad. He was a devout Coptic Christian who considered suicide rather than conversion to Islam, but later became a devout Muslim. It was built before 1332 in the ruined remains of an Ayyubid vaulted hall and by the 16C had become a Sufi khanqah. Its assembly hall was probably located in the west end of the Crusader hall to the south. A local family, of Abu al-Su'ud, a member of which was overseer of the mosque in 1556/57, gradually came to own and live in it until recent times, when it was called the Dar Abu al-Su'ud, and was the centre of the Shafi'i sect of which Abu al-Su'ud was mufti. The mosque is now in use as the office of the Islamic Museum. It is a columned hall divided into three aisles by vaults and piers. The piers and upper structure were built in Ottoman times (c 1556?) when the original polychrome patterned marble floor appears to have been badly relaid. The mihrab in the south wall is probably the Mamluk original. It has coloured marble panels flanked by two Crusader columns still retaining their capitals and bases; a loop and roundel at the top is inscribed 'for Allah'. The doorway at the southeast corner also has Crusader columns and capitals in reuse, one standing on a bulbous Mamluk base. Although the Fakhriyya is not accessible, it can be seen from the west from the area south of the Western Wall.

Passing the remodelled east façade of the Maghariba mosque, now the Islamic Museum, we come to the al-Fakhriyya minaret, the southwest minaret of the Haram, and the smallest, built after 1345 but before 1496. It fell before 1546, was rebuilt after 1672 and restored in 1923/24. A Syrian-type square tower with three storeys, it is built over the north wall of the Crusader hall. The upper part, including the muqarnas corbelling, dates to 1923/24, but little is known of its original form.

The inner south and east walls

With the exception of the Aqsa Mosque relatively few structures are built against the south and east walls. The south wall contains the façade of the south wing of the Islamic Museum and the Women's Mosque of the Aqsa, which are contained in a great Crusader hall built, but probably not finished, by the Templars probably in the 1160s. The façade has many 12C masons's marks, five windows and a fine Ayyubid doorway flanked by pairs of Crusader marble columns and capitals. For the Aqsa itself, see pp 125–134.

Currently most of the east side of the Haram is not accessible. Approximately halfway between the Aqsa Mosque and the southeast angle of the Haram is the Mihrab Da'ud, a large open-air mihrab rebuilt by al-Mansur Lajin between 1297–99. Here splendid views combine with a peaceful and serene quality. When accessible, the entrance to Solomon's Stables is in the southeast angle (see p 135) and from here there is a magnificent view from the 'Pinnacle of the Temple' over the Kidron Valley and the village of Silwan. Further north is one of the finest prospects of the Dome of the Rock, the Dome of the Chain and the east arcade.

About three-quarters of the distance along the east wall, you arrive at the inside of the blocked *Golden Gate, or Bab al-Dhahabi (not accessible, but the inner facade can be viewed). For its history, see p 98.

The exterior lies 6.3m below the level of the present court, with the gate complex set in a paved court. The double gate has two shallow round arches with floral relief ornament on the archivolt, similar to those on the outer east façade of the gate. Two free-standing lateral arches extend west from the corners of the gate hall. The north and south sides of the gate chamber have three engaged rectangular pilasters, and at the east end of the south wall is a round-arched lesser entrance. At the east end of the roof are two hemispherical cupolas on high drums which rest on the old pendentives. These probably date to the 12C–13C.

The interior is a large hall, stone paved, with six domes supported on a central east–west axis by two free-standing monolithic marble columns with Byzantine Ionic capitals, and two wall piers with Corinthian capitals. The elaborate decoration includes pilasters (four on both north and south walls) with Corinthian style capitals which have been compared to 5C work. There is a carved cornice above. The decoration, incorporating some reused elements, is thought variously to date between the 6C–8C. The interior door jambs are based on very large stones, respectively 3.40m and 4.50m high, which are aligned on the course of the original wall and could suggest the existence of an original Herodian gate.

Kursi Sulaiman (Solomon's Throne) stands against the east wall of the Haram just to the north of the Golden Gate and is a rectangular structure with two shallow domes. Its name derives from an old Muslim story that when King Solomon died, it was necessary to conceal his death from the demons and thus avert the prophecy that his Temple would be destroyed and his kingdom disintegrate. The dead king was propped on his throne with his staff and not until that decayed and collapsed did the demons discover they had been released from his authority.

References are made to the Throne of Solomon from the 10C, but the building appears to date to c 1600 or later. It seems to be the same as that described by the Turkish traveller, Evliya Celebi in 1648–50. It is just possible that it was built by Sulaiman the Magnificent as part of his building programme in Jerusalem, and in the course of time earlier traditions concerning Solomon accrued to it. Alternatively the structure may have been rebuilt to the same pattern in the 19C, for various late 19C writers refer to it as a modern building. It contains a venerated cenotaph visited by Muslims at the Feast of Bairam. It is possible also that it preserves the tradition of Solomon's portico, which lay on the east side of the Temple and is referred to by Josephus (Antiq. XX:219–222).

Subterranean vaulting supports this part of the esplanade, for in this area the bedrock is at a great depth beneath the present surface. Continuing north you come to the Bab al-Asbat and complete the circuit of the inner Haram wall.

Lesser shrines and structures within the Haram al-Sharif

These structures are numbered in sequence and shown on the accompanying map. Most are fountains, prayer platforms and mihrabs, summer pulpits or decorative structures. They were pious donations for the use of the pilgrims and those who come to pray, teach and learn at the mosque and the sanctuary, added at various times since the Dome of the Rock was built. The fountains and cisterns are now for the most part unused since piped water was brought to the Haram. Some of the cisterns are very old, perhaps originating in the time of the First Temple; some were in use in Hasmonean and Herodian times when they were supplied by aqueducts, some from the pools southwest of Bethlehem. The aqueduct system was repaired up to the 20C; the fountains are mostly of Mamluk and Ottoman date.

The north end of the esplanade

1. Sabil al-Sultan Sulaiman (the Fountain of Sultan Sulaiman), or Sabil Bab al-'Atm. One of the many fountains built in Jerusalem by Sultan Sulaiman II, 'the Magnificent', it dates from 1537. Steps descend on the south side of a simple rectangular structure with an elaborately decorated arch containing a fountain in a recess with inscribed panels and stalactite ornament.

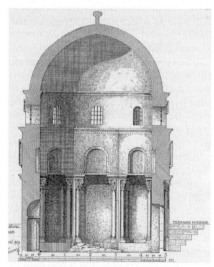

Qubbat Sulaiman, section drawing (H. Vincent and F.-M. Abel, Jérusalem Nouvelle, Vol. II, pl. LXI: Gabalda, Paris, 1922).

2. Directly south of the fountain is the Pavilion of Sultan Mahmud II, built in 1817–18. This is a square structure with heavy corner piers and large, open, pointed arches which support a low octagonal drum and a small steep dome.

3. To the west is **Qubbat Sulaiman** (Solomon's Dome), which may be a late 12C Crusader construction, modified by the Ayyubids c 1200. It is an elegant dome built over a jutting piece of bedrock, around which many traditions have accumulated: one story is that Solomon prayed here when the Temple was completed. The octagonal building with a blocked pointed arch in each façade, has a tall circular drum with eight openings. Above them the hood moulding joins to form a continuous cornice, with another cornice at the top. Steps descend to the entrance on the north side, for the interior floor level is lower. If the archways were originally open, each may have been flanked by three columns with broad-leaved acanthus capitals, but this ornamentation is only certain for the outer two. The mihrab in the south wall is flanked by small columns and capitals. The building has a distinctive charm, and through its rather isolated position has an important landscape role in the Haram.

4. The **Well of Ibrahim al-Rumi**, or Sabil Basiri, was built 1435–36. This was a wellhouse for distributing water to the poor, now disused. The founder's inscription is on the south wall. The small square structure is built over a large, much older rock-cut cistern. It has a door on the east side, and water was distributed through pointed-arched windows in the other three walls. The façade is capped by an ornamental cornice and is roofed by a shallow stone dome. A raised prayer platform, the Mastaba Basiri, constructed 1400, is just to the southeast. It has a rather heavy mihrab with a round arch flanked by columns and capped by a stepped cornice.

5. Just to the southwest is Sabil al-Shaikh Budayr, a fountain of 1740–41. This is a rather small, rectangular building with a high small dome, and open round-arched windows protected by metal grilles between the columns. It stands on a low plinth. It also has a raised prayer platform on the south side.

6. To the east, at the foot of the Dome platform steps, on the north side, is the fountain Sabil Sha'lan, built 1216–17, then restored 1429 and again in 1627–28; the external mihrab dates to 1650–51. It is a rectangular structure with open arches. The dome over the angle of the L-shaped cistern room is one of the few early shallow stone domes remaining on fountains of a type once characteristic in Jerusalem.

West of the Dome Platform

7. The Mihrab 'Ali Pasha, is just northeast of the Cotton Merchants' Gate, and was built in 1637–38.

8. The fountain, ***Sabil Qa'it Bay**, is one of the most attractive small features in the Haram, and is a typically late Mamluk structure with many Cairene influences. It was perhaps built as the final adjunct to the nearby Madrasa Ashrafiyya (also by Sultan Qa'it Bay) in 1482. It was restored in 1883 by 'Abd al-Hamid II as the inscription records, and some repair work was done in the 20C. The inscription also refers to an earlier

Fountain of Qa'it Bay

structure built by Sultan Inal (1453–61) which had a stone dome built over a well, nothing of which seems to remain. The fountain is located on the north-west corner of a small open-air oratory (musalla) with a free-standing mihrab on the south. A large cistern beneath it may have been constructed in part of the ancient Herodian gate passage noted by Warren below the Bab al-Mathara. The overall height of the structure is 13.28m. The rectangular base has windows on the south, west and north sides covered by metal grilles which are at least partly Ottoman in date. The window ledges are supported by typically Mamluk brackets. The joggled decoration on the flat window lintels is not original and probably replaces strapwork with a star pattern. The door lies on the east, placed to one side of an otherwise plain façade. Red and cream stone is employed, and highlights the relief arabesque and strapwork. Each corner has an engaged column with some fine relief work, a Mamluk base and a stalactite capital. A fine calligraphic zone bordered with relief strapwork runs right round the building and records the builder, its restorer, and verses from the Koran. Above, a transition zone with pyramidal buttresses converts the rectangular base to the round dome. This middle zone, with four arched lights, supports a tall stone dome with fine relief arabesques which give distinction to this charming fountain.

Architecturally the structure seems to be patterned on contemporary funerary monuments in Cairo, but to have been influenced by local Jerusalem traditions and workmen. The interior (locked) has water troughs below the windows and cups were once chained to the windows. A well recess is located on the inner east wall. The window lintels are also ornate; above are muqarnas pendentives. On the south side, beneath the window, is a fountain trough made from a Herodian frieze.

9. Hujrat Bir al-Zait (the oilstore) is one of a range of rather domestic-looking buildings on either side of the stairs below the Dome platform. Those to the north of the stairs are of two storeys; this, just east of the fountain of Qa'it Bay, has one storey. These are Ottoman cells for prayer and study.

10. Sabil Bab al-Mahkama and Birka Ghaghanj are an Ottoman fountain and a pool dating to 1527. The fountain is an octagonal structure with a leaded dome and a roofed verandah.

11. The Mastabat al-Tin just to the south is a rectangular raised prayer platform, built in 1760–61.

12. Qubba Musa (Dome of Moses) was built in 1249–50 by al-Malik al-Salih Ayyub. This is a medium-sized dome just inside the Gate of the Chain with a mihrab on the south side of the prayer platform, used as a place where late-comers to the mosque can pray.

South of the Dome Platform

Just inside the Moors' Gate, near the former entrance to the Fakhriyya Mosque, is a small Ottoman fountain, the Sabil Abu al-Su'ud, named for the family who occupied the mosque for some centuries (see p 108).

13. In the space between the Islamic Museum and the Aqsa Mosque is a small domed structure Qubba Yusuf Agha (Dome of Yusuf Agha), built in 1681.

14. In the space between the Aqsa Mosque and the Dome Platform is the great ablutions fountain **al-Kas** (the cup or fountain). Ritual ablution is an important preliminary to prayer at the mosque and the Haram needs a good supply of running water. Here a large stone basin is surrounded by a wrought metal screen, below which are taps and drains for washing. There are several reservoirs or cisterns under the platform to the west, south and east of this fountain, some of which were originally fed by conduit and aqueduct from springs near Hebron, and Solomon's Pools near Bethlehem.

Another large cistern, the Bir al-Waraqa (Well of the Leaf) lies to the south under the Aqsa Mosque. Its name derives from the charming story that one of the Caliph Umar's companions went down to recover the jar he had dropped while filling it at the cistern, and found at the bottom a gate leading into an orchard. He plucked a leaf to show to his friends when he emerged, and as it came from Paradise it never faded.

The Platform of the Dome of the Rock and lesser structures upon it

The **Dome Platform** is set 2.5m to 6m above the esplanade. The platform is approached by eight flights of stairs, two on the north, three on the west, two on the south and one on the east. The platform must date at least to the time of 'Abd al-Malik when the Dome of the Rock was built. In the 10C and probably earlier there were only six staircases; according to Nasir-i Khusraw (1047) there was one each on the east and north, and two each on the west and south sides. At the top of each flight is a graceful arcade, or Qanatir, a series of arches (sometimes called mawazin, or 'scales' from the tradition that scales to weigh the souls of the dead will be suspended from them on the Day of Judgement). These date largely from the 10C to the 15C. There are 16 rooms, most on the north side of the platform, which were used for the 'Servants of the Haram'. They were built at various dates mostly from the 17C to recent times. They have a mixture of marble and built stone columns; the local qualities of their rather humbler architectural style add to the character and charm of the Haram area.

15. The Northeast Qanatir (Mawazin Bab Hitta) was constructed in 1326. Three stilted arches with gadrooned ornament are supported on two columns and two piers. The columns and acanthus capitals are in secondary use. Two inscriptions on the south face record the building of the arcade and the paving of the terrace in the reign of al-Nasir Muhammad. Cells flank either side of the arcade, the group on the west being larger, with a portico at the front.

16. The North Qanatir is further west and was constructed in 1321. This arcade replaced an earlier one perhaps destroyed by the Crusaders. It has three arches on two reused columns and two piers; the marble columns, bases and capitals in Corinthian style are probably Byzantine. There is a saw-tooth motif on the cornice above. An inscription on the south façade records it was built in the reign of al-Nasir Muhammad. These arches are also flanked by cells.

17. On the west side of the North Qanatir is the Cell of Muhammad Agha, a domed structure with arcaded front, built in 1588.

18. The 16C(?) Qubbat al-Arwah (Dome of the Winds, or Spirits), stands on the left just to the west on a shallow plinth. It has eight marble columns capped by unmatched capitals with dosserets of varied heights. These support slightly pointed shallow arches with relief rosettes; an octagonal drum topped by a cornice has a shallow stone dome topped by a finial with crescent.

19. At the northwest angle of the platform is the Northwest Qanatir with four arcades, rebuilt in 1376–77 and restored between 1519 and 1567. The steps are cut into the terrrace. The arcades have inlaid red, black and white roundels, and fine acanthus capitals on white columns.

20. Standing above the south side of the northwest stairs is the Qubbat al-Khadir

(16C?), a very small but elegant dome supported by six little marble pillars and very mixed, rather plain capitals. It is named for St. George or St. Elijah.

21. A short distance to the south is Masjid al-Nabi (1700/01), a stone building with a new dome. There are two windows to each side and a door on the east with inscription above. It is associated with Shaikh al-Khalili from Hebron, thus also called Qubbat al-Khalili.

22. Just to the southeast is a tall domed, octagonal structure, the **Qubbat al-Mi'raj** (Dome of the Ascension of the Prophet). The remarkable series of capitals decorating the interior suggests it was originally the 12C Crusader baptistery, rebuilt or modified by the Ayyubids in 1200–01 (inscription above the door) to mark the place where the Prophet prayed before he ascended to Paradise. Eight arches with columns support a high leaded dome, topped by a small cupola. There is a mihrab in the south wall. The northeast side was damaged in 1948 and repaired by King Abdullah I of Jordan in 1951.

23. The small open dome to the southeast is the Qubbat al-Nabi (Dome of the Prophet or of Gabriel), built in 1538–39 and restored in 1845. It is distinguished by its slender columns and leaded dome.

24. Almost opposite the west door of the Dome of the Rock is the West Qanatir built in 951–52 (builder's signature). Twenty-five steps cut into the terrace lead up to four arches. Slender monolithic columns, three different capitals and high pointed arches combine with some elegance to decorate one of the main approaches to the Dome platform. The ends of the arcade are supported by rectangular piers.

25. At the end of the west side of the platform, the Southwest Qanatir (or Mawazin Bab al-Silsila), built in 1472, has three arches similar in style to the Mamluk arcades on the north side. All the columns, capitals and bases are in reuse, and are probably all Byzantine. The central arch has red and cream voussoirs, the lateral arches are gadrooned. The inscription of the east face records its building by Sultan Qa'it Bay. The building abutting it to the north is Ottoman.

26. Occupying the west end of the south edge of the platform is the Qubba Nahwiyya (Dome of Literature, or Library) built in 1207–08, originally as a Koran school. Later it was used as a small school for literature and a library. The door is flanked by intricately knotted marble columns (see frontispiece).

27. To the east between the library and the pulpit is Qubba Yusuf built in 1681. This is a tall, open, rectangular building, very decorative, with a tiny dome or cupola.

28. Immediately adjacent to the south Qanatir is the **Minbar of Burhan al-Din** ('Summer Pulpit'), added to and restored by 1388 by the Qadi Burhan al-Din, and again restored in 1843 by the Sultan 'Abd al-Majid. Until at least the end of the 17C, prayers on Muslim feast days and prayers for rain were said from here. The original structure consisted of a hexagonal domed pavilion with trefoil arches and a relief fluted dome on an elaborate rectangular base with horseshoe arches, those on the north and south sides being blocked by later additions and abutments. Its purpose is uncertain, but it was built almost entirely of high quality Crusader marble sculpture, perhaps a former 12C ciborium, reused soon after 1187. In 1345 it is noted as a dome (Qubbat al-Mizan, the Dome of the Balance) rather than a pulpit. By 1496 it was certainly in use as a pulpit; it may have been used as an occasional pulpit from the 13C, approached when needed by mobile wooden stairs. Burhan al-Din's work may have been to build the stone stair and balustrade. The 1843 work (recorded above the present entrance) blocked a columned rectangular opening beneath the upper section of the stairs with 19C Ottoman panelling. On the east side is a flat mihrab with marble panelling against the west abutment of the South Qanatir. It has a pointed arch on two reused marble columns and is recorded by 1345. It is structurally later than the adjacent dome.

29. Adjacent is the South Qanatir, Maqam al-Nabi, possibly from the 10C. It has four arches supported on two piers and three monolithic columns, the two outer being of red granite, the inner of marble. On these rest sub-Corinthian capitals with, above, relief rosette roundels and pointed arches. Twenty-one steps descend in the direction of the Aqsa Mosque.

30. Just over 30m to the east is the Southeast Qanatir, Maqam al-Ghuri, on which an inscription on the central spandrels (which may not be in situ) records that it was built in 1030; another inscription on the north spandrel notes a restoration in 1211–12. It has three arches.

31. Perhaps more correctly regarded as an integral part of the Dome of the Rock, is the small dome which lies directly east of the east door of the Dome of the Rock, the ***Dome of the Chain** (A. Qubbat al-Silsila).

History of the Dome of the Chain

Built in 691–92 by 'Abd al-Malik at the same time as the Dome of the Rock itself, and regarded by many as an architect's model for the main building, this dome was probably used as the treasury of the shrine (compare the treasury in the Umayyad Great Mosque in Damascus), and like the Dome of the Rock was probably also covered in polychrome glass mosaic. There are many theories about it, as it lies more or less at the exact centre of the Haram and the Herodian platform. It is possible that it stands on the site of the Herodian (and Solomonic) altar of sacrifice with the Dome of the Rock to the west overlying the site of the Temple. If such traditions were still extant in the 7C at the time the site was selected, such sanctity would further have protected the contents of a treasure deposited there. Nasir-i Khusraw in 1047 notes a beautiful mihrab. In Crusader times it was the Chapel of St. James the Martyr (the Less) with Christian paintings. It was restored by the Muslims in 1199–1200, and remains of a probably early Ayyubid mihrab have been discovered beneath the later 13C work. The mihrab with pointed arch in the south side had marble decoration added in 1261–73 by Sultan Baybars. It has undergone numerous alterations in the course of its 13 centuries, and restoration work in the 1990s involved stripping the whole surface back to the stone, and repaving.

As in the Dome of the Rock, there are two concentric rows of columns, the outer 11 supporting the ambulatory roof and arcade with shallow round arches and the inner six supporting the hexagonal drum and the dome. The columns, of varied marbles, are monolithic, mostly reused Byzantine, and are so placed that all 17 can be seen at one time from any angle. The capitals are of both basket and acanthus types. The exterior was coated with tiles in 1561–62 by Sulaiman II. The marble panelling of the mihrab has been renewed, but some traces of painting and carved rosettes remain on the structure. The dome has a rather outward curve with a fluted knopf on top.

The dome is also called the Mahkamat Da'ud (David's Place of Judgement); stories connected with it say that a chain was once stretched across the entrance or hung from the ceiling, either by Solomon or by God. If this was grasped by a liar a link fell, giving judgement on a witness.

32. The East Qanatir stands above the only stairs on the little used east side of the Dome platform, and may date to the 10C when a staircase is recorded here. Five arcades add a characteristically graceful sense of perspective to the view of the Dome of the Rock from the east. The columns are of light coloured marble, and have acanthus capitals of varied types.

The Dome of the Rock

The **Dome of the Rock (A. Qubbat al-Sakhra) formerly erroneously known as the Mosque of Umar, is the crown of the Haram al-Sharif, built in Byzantine-Syrian architectural style, with innovations marking it as one of the first great buildings of Islamic architecture. It is a shrine of gem-like beauty, once shining with the rich colours of gold and polychrome glass mosaic both inside and out. Built by the fifth Umayyad caliph 'Abd al-Malik, its purpose was threefold: to recognise the sanctity of Jerusalem, and of the Rock associated with the Prophets on which it stood; to mark the consolidation of Islamic rule in Syria when Jerusalem, Damascus and other cities were rivalling Mecca as political and religious capitals; and to balance the great monuments of Byzantine Christianity which had already stood for centuries in the Holy City. The Prophet Muhammad at first prayed in the direction of the Holy City of Jerusalem, but following an inspiration the direction of prayer (qibla) was changed to Mecca. The prayer niche (mihrab) which later marked the direction of prayer, in Jerusalem faces to the south. The Dome of the Rock is the third holiest place in Islam after the Ka'ba at Mecca and the Prophet's Mosque in Medina, and is the second most important place of pilgrimage. When political circumstances allowed, thousands visited the shrine as part of a great annual pilgrimage to Mecca and Jerusalem.

The Dome of the Rock is located over the highest point of the rock on the southeast ridge (c 743m above sea level), rather than centrally to the Haram enclosure, on a platform c 2.5m–6m high, which raises the structure to a dominant situation within the open court. The Dome is not a congregational mosque, but a shrine with ambulatories, intended as a place of pilgrimage and prayer. The empty spaces within reflect the iconoclast and monotheist traditions of Islam, enhanced by the beauty of the floral and geometric decoration which covers nearly the whole surface of the shrine.

The Caliph drew on craftsmen and traditions of the world conquered by the armies of Islam. Greek- and Arabic-speaking Christians, Jews, Egyptians and Persians may have been employed. Though the building belongs in the Syrian-Byzantine tradition, the result reflects a triumphant amalgamation of many elements. The architects are unknown, but a later source recalls that 'Abd al-Malik appointed two overseers, Yazid ibn Sallam and Raja' ibn Haiwa.

The building is of local stone, the lower walls decorated with marble veneer. The upper walls and drum, inside and out, were originally encrusted with gold and polychrome glass mosaics which were replaced and repaired at intervals, and eventually in the 16C the exterior mosaic work was replaced with Kashani tiles, which were renewed in 1958–62 during a complete structural renovation. The dome, constructed with an inner and outer vault of wood, covered in lead and originally gilded, rebuilt and repaired at various times, was replaced in 1961 by a lighter covering of gold-coloured anodised aluminium; this has since been replaced with a gilded lead dome in keeping with the original design. Over the centuries pious donations have seen to the continuous repair and refurbishment of this great and ancient shrine. Its plan has been copied elsewhere, for example in the Temple Church in London built by the Templars in the 12C. It is said to hold up to 3000 people.

History

The Umayyad period Built in 691–92 on the site sacred to the Jewish, Christian and Muslim Holy Books, the Dome is revered for its associations with Mount Moriah, where Abraham offered Isaac as sacrifice, as the site of the threshing floor of Araunah the Jebusite purchased by David, where Solomon built his Temple and where the temples of Zerubbabel and Herod the Great once stood.

Following the Roman destruction of AD 70 the area was in ruins. No structure seems to have stood over the Rock itself between AD 70 and c 691 when the Umayyads started work, though already by 644 Muslims believed it was the site of Muhammad's miraculous Night Journey.

The design of the Dome of the Rock is based on Syrian-Byzantine traditions. The building itself had some contemporary parallels. The Constantinian Church of the Holy Sepulchre in Jerusalem had an immense dome of similar size over a rock in which the tomb of Christ was cut. Justinian's church at Bethlehem was built over a cave in the rock; octagonal shrines existed at Capernaum, Caesarea and Gadara.

The Dome of the Rock is the result of very precise geometrical design, with balanced and harmonious proportions which represent the first great period of Islamic architecture. It is said that the cost of construction was seven years' revenue from the province of Egypt, the money being placed in a model of the projected building (the Dome of the Chain) which was the Treasury of the Shrine. The last of the gold was sufficient for the gilding of the dome. In Umayyad days the cleaning of the shrine was done with water scented with attar of roses, musk and saffron; fragrant wood and incense were burnt on the Rock, and sweet-smelling oils were used in the many lamps. The original dome was a double wooden vault, with wool and hair insulation between the two vaults, and a gilded metal surface for which wool, felt and leather coverings were made to protect it in winter.

The Abbasid period Al-Ma'mun (813–33) repaired the dome, and altered 'Abd al-Malik's founding inscription. He also left inscriptions on the lintels of the doors (831). Muhammad's footprints on the Rock are mentioned by the Muslim historian Ya'qubi in 874.

The Fatimid period The dome collapsed in 1016, and was rebuilt in 1022/23 by al-Zahir. At this time a marble balustrade was placed around the Rock, the floors were covered by silk carpets, and a great silver candelabrum was suspended above the Rock, which fell down c 1060.

The Crusader period The building became the Crusaders' Templum Domini, the Temple of Our Lord, a church served by canons of the Augustinian order. Christian pilgrims began to remove bits of the holy Rock, which were sold as relics, so that the surface had to be paved with marble to preserve it, and a tall and beautiful wrought-iron screen was put up between the columns of the inner arcade. It remained in position until 1960, when it was removed, and part can be seen in the Islamic Museum.

The Ayyubid period Following Salah al-Din's recapture of Jerusalem in 1187 the mosque was restored. The wooden screen now around the Rock was installed by al-'Aziz 'Imad al-Din in 1198/99.

The Mamluk period The mosaics were restored. In 1432 al-Ashraf Saif al-Din Barsbay endowed the shrine with land and property, the revenues of which were to be used for the upkeep of the building, which became the responsibility of the Waqf authority. In 1448 the dome was badly damaged by fire and repaired. Al-Ashraf Qa'it Bay gave four great doors sheathed with decorated copper (now in the Islamic Museum) in 1467/68.

The Ottoman period In 1545–46 Sulaiman II replaced the mosaics on the exterior drum with coloured tiles, and not long after also on the upper walls of the octagon. Craftsmen were imported specially from Kashan (Persia) but may have made the actual tiles in Jerusalem. Abd al-Hamid I brought craftsmen from Damascus to repair the tiles, and further work on them was done by Mahmud II in 1817–18. He again employed craftsmen from Damascus, but tiles of poorer quality and some different designs were used. In 1853 Sultan Abd al-Majid I repaired and strengthened the dome and redecorated the interior. Not long after the Russian-Turkish treaty of 1856 non-Muslims were permitted to enter the Haram al-Sharif for the first time in centuries. In 1874 Sultan Abd al-Aziz made major repairs and placed a crystal chandelier inside the south entrance. Sultan Abd al-Hamid II put the band of Kashan tiles bearing verses of Sura XXXVI from the Koran onto the upper part of the octagon walls, just below the parapet.

The British Mandate period Tile-makers were brought from Kütahya in Turkey in 1919 to repair tiles on the Dome. In 1927 and 1936 Jerusalem was shaken by earthquakes, and during the 1930s it was clear that rising damp and decay were adversely affecting the structure. Repairs were started but hindered by the Second World War and the intensifying civil struggle. Some damage to the structure was sustained during the fighting in 1948.

The Jordanian period In 1952 an appeal was launched by the Supreme Muslim Council for funds for the complete restoration of the shrine. The weight of the lead roof was exacerbating the damage to the structure and foundations caused by earthquake, penetration of water and age. The Arab world donated £525,000, and in 1956 work began under a Saudi Arabian contractor. The Egyptian Government also gave technical services then valued at £70,000; experts in mosaic restoration were brought from Italy, and the late King Muhammad of Morocco gave new carpets for the ambulatories. The foundations were strengthened with concrete, and three pillars, two in the southeast, and one on the north had to be replaced. The outer façade was completely refaced with tiles made specially at Kütahya in Turkey and with marble from Greece, and in 1961/62 the dome was completely resurfaced with a lightweight gold-coloured aluminium shell. The platform was repaved.

Since 1967 the Awqaf administration has continued the work of preservation of this holy place; many fragments of the old structure have been placed in the Islamic Museum. The dome has again been resheathed and gilded.

The exterior

The base is a stone-built octagon c 53.75m in diameter, built of local limestone masonry in courses c 0.8m in height. Each exterior façade is c 20.59m in length. The base of the exterior wall forms a plinth, above which there are seven tall recessed panels or bays in each façade of the octagon. The lower wall is veneered with grey-veined white marble which was restored in 1958–62. The southwest side has a sundial. The original design of the Dome of the Rock also had polished marble covering on the lower walls. Some panels which survived in good condition were used to replace worn panels in the interior. In the centre of the southwest and southeast sides near floor level are rectangular windows protected by metal grilles.

The upper walls of the octagon are faced with predominantly blue, white, green, black and yellow **tiles** made in Kütahya in Turkey and placed on the building in 1958–66, to much the same designs as those previously on the structure but with stronger colours. The patterns are mostly stylised floral motifs. They include the lily and lotus design, tulip patterns, other flowers and stars, and bands and borders of blue-glazed tiles. There are a number of fine panels of blue and white calligraphy which contain verses from the Koran; particularly to be noted is a band of tiles extending right round the façade just below the parapet which contains verses from Sura XXXVI, Ya Sin. This is a copy of the original placed by Sultan 'Abd al-Hamid II in 1876. A selection of the older tiles removed in the restoration work has been preserved in the Islamic Museum.

The eight sides each contain five **windows**, with a blind panel in the recess at either end. The outer faces of these 40 windows are covered by tiled grilles, with similar motifs to those of the adjacent walls, and contain small glazed areas which limit the amount of light penetrating to the interior through a wall 1.3m thick. In 691–92 these windows were built with round arches and probably had

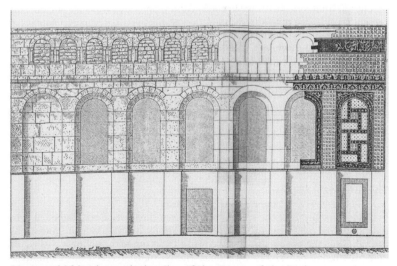

Masonry hidden beneath the tiles of the Dome of the Rock
(C. Clermont-Ganneau, Archaeological Researches in Palestine during the years 1873–1874, *Vol. I, opposite p 180: London, 1899*

marble grilles of the type seen in the Great Mosque in Damascus. In the 16C when the exterior was tiled, the windows were given the then fashionable pointed arch, but the original round-arched masonry still exists beneath the tiling. The height of the façade, including the parapet, is 12.1m. The parapet itself once had 13 small round-arched niches flanked by columns in each façade, covered with mosaic, but these were also hidden by the tiles in the 16C and only rediscovered in the restorations of 1873/74. The fragments of mosaic then uncovered are variously said to be original Umayyad work or dated to a pre-Sulaiman restoration, probably that of Baybars in the 13C.

Behind the parapet, the roof of the ambulatories slopes up to the drum. The drum is circular, with four buttresses which rise from the interior piers, and has 16 tiled windows. The top of the drum has another fine inscribed band in blue and white which quotes the Koran, Sura XVII (the Night Journey). The dome itself, a wooden double dome of 1022, now resheathed in lead, is of fine proportions, notably wide and steeply rounded. At the top is a finial with a crescent. The latter is a modern replacement: two older ones can be seen in the Islamic Museum. The overall height of the building is 35.36m, not including the finial.

There are four **doors** or gates, with flat lintel and arched lunette above, oriented to the cardinal points of the compass and named for them. The North Door is the Bab al-Janna (Gate of Paradise). The West Door (Bab al-Gharb) has a shell-pattern stone grille on the lunette above it which is probably the original Ummayad work. The South Door, marks the direction of prayer, the Bab al-Qibla, and faces the Aqsa Mosque. The East Door is also called the Gate of David (Bab Da'ud), or Gate of the Chain (Bab al-Silsila), because it leads to the Mahkamat Da'ud (David's Place of Judgement), which is the Dome of the Chain.

All the double-leafed doors have been replaced in the recent restorations. The doors are 4.35m high, 2.55m wide and have shallow, tunnel-vaulted tiled porches in front, once with gable roofs. All the porches have been altered. The present south porch differs from the others in having an open porch supported on eight reused monolithic columns with Corinthian capitals. The columns are variously of grey, green and red marble and porphyry. The porch ceiling, of coffered wood, was originally built by Mahmud II in 1817. The arches and vaults are now decorated in blue and white tiles, and in the arcades above the lintels are excerpts from the Koran. The tunnel vault ceilings were originally covered in mosaic, which still remains above the *East Door, where it is perhaps a Fatimid replacement. It has rainbow-coloured scallops and chequerboard patterns. Each lintel has a decorated metal plate on the soffit, with repoussé and studded relief work painted in gilt, black and green, mostly showing vine scrolls and leaves, grapes and acanthus, which probably date to the original structure and compare with the decoration on the tie-beams inside the first ambulatory.

The interior
Leave shoes, bags and cameras at the entrance.

You are first aware of the spacious dimness of the interior, with subdued light reflecting from half-seen golden ornament, before the eye is drawn upwards by the light from the less deeply set windows in the drum to the richness of the gold and red curving patterns in the dome. The partially screened but illuminated mysteries of the Rock, bare and quarried, but marking the ancient and long venerated point of contact between God and man, draw the visitor towards the central area beyond the ambulatories.

The Outer Ambulatory The lower walls are veneered with grey-veined white marble with quartered panels cut to show symmetrical patterns of veining, an original scheme of decoration restored by Salah al-Din c 1189 with later renovations. On the lintels above the doors, and in a dado beneath the windows is a band of fine gilded work in black and gold. Generally what remains of the lower windows is 19C and later renovation. The lunette window over the west door has a stone grille which may be original. The window arches contain grey, red and black voussoirs.

The inner side of the outer ambulatory is defined by eight six-sided piers and 16 columns which support an octagonal arcade. The piers are veneered in grey-veined white marble with red and black inlays, also much restored from the time of Salah al-Din; there are fine marble panels with relief foliage designs and of probable Umayyad origin set in the outer face of the pier of the southeast side. The monolithic columns of red and green marble or porphyry are of varied height and origin, most deriving from the ruins of Roman and Byzantine Jerusalem. The unmatched and uneven bases are encased in marble boxes and collars which level the design. The capitals, in a variety of styles from Corinthian to Composite, are brightly gilded and one formerly showed a cross suggesting its original use had been in a Byzantine church. Above the capitals are grey-veined marble dosserets, which are of different thicknesses to bring the varied lengths of the columns to a uniform height. These support the arcades which are linked by ornate *tie-beams, a fine and original Umayyad feature, the design of which resembles a Corinthian architrave. These are iron and wood beams, encased in bronze sheathing, with marble casing on top, 0.64m deep. The undersides are 6m from the floor, painted black with green borders and with gilded relief work showing bunches of grapes, formalised vine, leaf and tendril designs, and studded bands in 16 different designs. The inner sides are equally ornate, with acanthus and other patterns in bands; the outer sides are plainer, with smaller gilded designs, and a projecting marble cornice above.

The wide and gently pointed **arches** above are covered in gold and polychrome **glass mosaic work**, which, though much restored, dates to the original structure of 691/92. The beautiful designs, with lavish rosette and floral patterns, are worked in shades of blue, green and predominantly gold, and the mosaic cubes themselves are set at projecting angles further to reflect and sparkle in the light. The spandrels each contain a vase with exotic flowers and acanthus-like leaves, which grow upwards, tree-like, and are ornamented with necklaces and pendants. In the half-spandrel adjacent to each pier the design expands downwards from a cornucopia. On the faces of the piers are acanthus plants with magnificent Byzantine jewellery; on the narrower flanks of the piers are either elaborate foliage designs or, on eight of the piers, much more naturalistic trees. On one is a wind-blown date palm laden with fruit, its stem encrusted with medallions, and flanked by two little trees—a design that has been compared with Byzantine mosaics from Ravenna. The Islamic concept of filling the field with decoration, together with an Eastern delight in rich colour, with blue, indigo, gold and silver and added mother-of-pearl, gives this Syrian mosaic school a brilliance of its own. Olive or almond trees are also depicted. The leaves, green shaded with indigo, rest on gold stems, and gold and silver fruits, such as dates, olives, pomegranates, cherries, citrus and grapes are depicted. Shells, winged motifs and rosettes vary the patterns. The borders and soffits of the arches have more stylised rosette patterns and some splendid garlands.

At the top of the mosaic, both sides of the arcade contain the ***founder's inscription** in a single line of Kufic (early Arabic) script in gold on bluish-green mosaic, a full 240m in length, which runs right round the ambulatories and ends with the date 691/92 on the east end of the south outer face of the arcade. The name of 'Abd al-Malik originally inscribed on it was erased by al-Ma'mun (813–30), who inserted his own name instead, but the workman neglected to alter 'Abd al-Malik's earlier date. The original inscription read (in part): 'This dome was built by the servant of God, 'Abd al-Malik Ibn Marwan, the Prince of the Believers, in the year 72. May God accept it and be pleased with him. Amen.' Other sections of this inscription contain verses of the Koran which promulgate the Islamic rejection of Christianity and the Christian dogma of the Trinity. e.g. Sura IV, verses 169: 'O you People of the Book, overstep not bounds in your religion, and of God speak only the truth. The Messiah, Jesus, son of Mary, is only a Messenger of God, and his Word, which he conveyed into Mary, and a Spirit proceeding from him. Believe therefore in God, and his prophets, and say not three. It will be better for you. God is only one God. Far be it from his glory that he should have a son.'

The octagonal arcade supports the roof of the outer ambulatory, the ***ceiling** of which is of very fine gilded and painted plaster. The relief patterns, including arabesque and interlacing star patterns, medallions and intricately interwined foliage, are contained in rectangular and trapezoidal panels with multiple borders. Though much restored, this ceiling may date c 1318/19–1327/28, from the reign of al-Nasir Muhammad. Some of the panels achieve great richness of design, gracefully relieved with light and harmonious colours, in which red, gold, green and blue predominate.

The east door, which leads to the Dome of the Chain, has on its south side an enclosed stairway (not open to the public) which gives access to the roof. A ladder up the outer east side of the drum gives onto a narrow platform with a small doorway leading to the interior gallery. Steps between the inner and outer vault previously led to a trapdoor in the dome from which access to the crescent finial could be had.

Immediately east of the south door, set into the outer wall, is the mihrab which indicates the direction of prayer.

The Inner Ambulatory has a more modern ceiling, also of wood with painted relief stucco designs restored in 1780 and since, and inferior to those in the outer ambulatory.

The circular inner arcade is supported on four piers and 12 columns. The columns are of various sizes, made of marble and porphyry of a variety of shades of grey, green and red. The bases are set at varying heights. The capitals, of Corinthian and Composite type, are older than the shrine, probably of Byzantine date, and heavily gilded. The arches rest directly on them, and are linked by narrow, undecorated tie-beams.

The arches, of grey-veined marble, have alternating black and white voussoirs, and alternate red and black panels inserted in the spandrels on the inner side. The ***spandrels and arches** on the outer side, however, have also retained their original 7C mosaics. There is no inscription, and they appear to have survived in quite good order. This arcade, 1.1m in breadth, supports the drum itself. Just opposite the south door and built against two columns of the inner arcade is a marble pulpit supported on ten pillars. It was given by al-Zahir Barquq in 1387.

The Drum This is 20.44m in diameter and richly decorated. Directly above the arches is a decorative band with running spiral vine pattern in gold. It borders a great quarter-round moulding covered with designs and inscription in gold on a blue-green background. Above the moulding is a panel of mosaic running right round the drum. Though redone by al-Zahir, Salah al-Din and al-Nasir Muhammad in 1027/28, 1189 and 1318 respectively, and again in 1853, 1874 and 1958–62, these magnificent **mosaics appear to follow the original Umayyad designs faithfully. Much remains intact, as is indicated by the small rectangular inscription in the upper border, which records the restoration of the decoration of the dome by al-Zahir in 1027/28. The design on the lower register is uniform, with 16 panels having a total length of 64m and a height of 4m. The central motif of each panel is placed above each of the 16 columns and piers of the inner arcade, and depicts a bulbous vase encrusted with gems and mother-of-pearl, from which an acanthus plant springs. Within the spirals of the foliage are stems bearing leaves, fruit and grapes. Note that the vase above the northeast pier is identical with those in the outer arcade. A cornice marks the upper border of this register of the mosaic.

The upper register contains 16 windows and 16 panels of mosaic. These mosaics have suffered far more from the passage of time but nonetheless retain much of the richness of the original Umayyad work. They were so badly decayed by 1946 that in the renovations of 1958–62 they had to be virtually remade. The preservation varied. Two panels on the southeast, with geometric ornament, are complete replacements of Ottoman(?) date. Other panels have been considerably retouched, but five or six survived virtually intact. These show the original design of a pedimented vase covered with jewels, from which twine jewelled leaves; each panel and window has a rich border. The designs are picked out in many colours and in mother-of-pearl on a gold ground. The richness is enhanced by motifs borrowed from Byzantine imperial jewellery, such as diadems, breastplates and rosettes, perhaps symbolic of the conquest of the Byzantine lands by Islam.

The 16 windows in the drum include six which date to the time of Sulaiman the Magnificent in the 16C; the rest are more recent restorations. The best windows are now in the Islamic Museum. They are made up of an inner window of plaster and coloured glass, an intermediate window of plaster and plain glass, and the outer window of pierced tiles.

Together, these two magnificent registers in the drum make up a total height of 9.4m and are surmounted by another great cornice.

*The Dome The original of 691/92 fell in 1016, was rebuilt in 1022 according to inscriptions still on the ribs of the dome, and restored in 1189, 1318, 1448, 1830 and 1874. The average diameter of 20.44m was clearly based on that of the dome of the Constantinian Church of the Holy Sepulchre which averages 20.46m. Its height at the apex is 35.3m. A painted wooden arcade marks the gallery at the base of the dome, which lies between the two wooden shells of which it is constructed, each containing 32 ribs which meet at a circular plate at the summit. Immediately above the gallery a strapwork band of relief stucco links eight rectangular panels and eight medallions of beautiful calligraphy, which record the work of three restorers of the dome and its decoration. The first is that of Salah al-Din c 1189. His commemorative inscription reads: 'In the name of Allah, the Beneficent and Merciful God, Salah al-Din, our Ruler, Sultan and King, the Victorious Scholar, Just, Vigorous, son of Ayyub, may God rest his soul, ordered the renovation of the decoration of the Holy Dome in the year 586 H.' Another panel records al-Nasir Muhammad: 'This dome was renovated and regilded, and the outer one leaded by order of our Lord, God's shadow on earth, Executor of His commands, Sultan Muhammad, son of the Victorious Martyred Qala'un, may God rest his soul, in the year 718 H' (1318). The third was by Mahmud II in 1818 who also releaded the outside of the dome. Other repaintings and repairs are listed such as that by 'Abd al-Majid I in 1853. The present much restored decoration is said to be based on that of al-Nasir Muhammad. The arabesques, which decrease in size as they move towards the apex subtly increasing the perspective of the height, are painted in gold, red and white on a green background over relief stucco. The effect is of great richness. Towards the centre, a circular inscribed band contains Koran, Sura II, verses 255 and 256 (in part): 'God! There is no God but He; the Living, the Eternal; nor slumber seizeth Him, nor sleep; His, whatsoever is in the Heavens and whatsoever is in the Earth!'

Suspended from the floral medallion at the apex is a heavy chain which once supported a chandelier.

The Rock At the centre of the building beneath the dome and encircled by the ambulatories lies the Holy Rock. It is surrounded by a very fine wooden screen with intricately carved and inlaid panels erected by the Ayyubid al-'Aziz 'Imad al-Din in 1199, according to its inscription. The Rock itself is 18m x 13m and projects c 1.5m above the present paving. At the southwest angle of the Rock is a tall rectangular shrine with gilded grilles, topped by a small but elaborate cupola, which contains relics of the Prophet in a gilded reliquary, including a hair from his head. The base of the shrine is constructed of marble slabs carved with swags of foliage supported on tiny fluted and spiral marble columns through which the Rock can be seen. The marble base may be that of the gilded cupola resting on marble columns 'at the place of the Foot' that was constructed by the Crusaders to venerate what they believed to be the footprint of Christ, and which was recorded by the secretary of Salah al-Din. Here the visitor can touch the rock where Muslim tradition identifies the footprint of Muhammad. A medieval tradition recounts that the Rock tried to follow Muhammad as he ascended, leaving the imprint of his foot at this point, with the hollow cave beneath, while to the west is the impression of the hand of Gabriel, who restrained the Rock from following the Prophet. The rock, cut for various purposes, still shows the traces of the Crusader reshaping.

At the southeast angle of the Rock, adjacent to the southeast pier, a fine marble entrance way of Crusader date leads to the cave beneath the Rock. A later pointed arch is supported by delicate Composite capitals. These and the relief work are gilded. The cave below, reached by 16 new marble steps, is almost square, c 4.5m across and less than 2m high. Near the centre of the ceiling is a shaft 0.46m in diameter which has given rise to suggestions that the cave might have been cut nearly 4000 years ago as a shaft tomb. The cave was certainly recut in Crusader times, and then used as a place of confession. Today there are two small shrines to Abraham and al-Khadir (Elijah) on the north and northwest sides respectively. On either side of the steps are prayer niches of David and Solomon. That to the right as one descends (of Solomon) has a shallow but ornately decorated niche. It may date to the time of 'Abd al-Malik, 691/92. The niche of David to the left (south) as one descends has pairs of small twisted rope marble columns supporting a trefoil arch.

Tales of the Rock

The cave has many traditions associated with it, some deriving from the 12C and 13C, others more recent. Muslim tradition holds that the Rock came from Paradise and was visited by angels long before the creation of Adam; that it is the centre of the world, lying above the bottomless pit, with the waters of Paradise flowing beneath the cave; and that it is supported on a palm tree growing out of the river of Paradise; that here Noah's Ark grounded after the Flood. Here too, the spirits of the dead can be heard awaiting Judgement Day, when the Ka'ba at Mecca will come to the Rock and God's throne will be planted on the Rock; this is why a depression in the floor of the cave is called the Well of Souls (A. Bir al-Arwah). Abraham, Isaac, Jacob and Elijah are all associated with the cave; Muhammad prayed here, and from here was transported to Heaven on the back of his legendary steed, al-Buraq. The impression of Muhammad's head or hand was seen by some on the ceiling of the cave, as well as his footprint on the Rock. The Rock is said to have spoken to Muhammad, and also to have greeted the Caliph Umar after the conquest in 638.

In the Talmud the Rock lies at the centre of the world and covers the abyss in which the waters of the Flood rage. Abraham, Melchizedek and Isaac sacrificed or were almost sacrificed here; Jacob anointed the Rock. It is regarded in some traditions as the spot where the Ark of the Covenant stood; and some held that the Ark of the Covenant was concealed at the time of the destruction of Jerusalem in 587 BC and lies buried here still.

The Aqsa Mosque

The **Aqsa Mosque (A. al-Masjid al-Aqsa al-Mubarak, the 'Furthermost' Blessed Mosque), built against the south wall of the Haram, is the great congregational mosque of Muslim Jerusalem, the place of the Friday midday prayers and sermon, when the suqs of Jerusalem are full of people coming to the mosque. It is the ancient centre of Muslim worship, as opposed to the great pilgrimage shrine to the north, the Dome of the Rock, on the higher platform, which from a distance appears to dominate the Aqsa.

Whether the first mosque in Jerusalem, the mosque of Umar, was built on or near this site shortly after 638 is not certain. The Christian pilgrim Arculf described a mosque in 680 which appears to have been on this site. Certainly a splendid mosque built by 715 by al-Walid I is the basis of the structure visible today, though it has undergone considerable structural alterations in the course of the centuries. The mosque reached its maximum extent with 15 aisles in the 8C under the Abbasids. It was briefly the palace of the Crusader rulers of Jerusalem from 1099 and then the headquarters of the Knights Templar from 1118, both of whom also left their imprint on the building.

The present building, a great basilica consisting of seven aisles oriented to the south or qibla wall and Mecca, has a dome over the central nave in front of the mihrab. It has a magnificent façade with a portico of seven bays, rebuilt and extended between the Crusader period and the 15C. The mosque lies on the same axis as the Dome of the Rock and the great ablution fountain between the two, part of Abd al-Malik's layout for the Haram. The mosque contains interesting Fatimid mosaics, though the dome area has been restored following the disastrous fire in 1969 which destroyed the pulpit given by Salah al-Din. The south end of the building has extensions to east and west; that on the west is called the Women's Mosque (A. Jami' al-Nisa) and that on the east contains three separate places of worship: the Mosque of Umar, the Mosque of the Forty Martyrs, and the Mihrab of Zacharia.

The Aqsa, constructed of local limestone, measures c 80m x 55m (including the porch) and has been the object of major restoration work—in 1924–27 (just before the earthquake of 1927), 1938–43 and since, under the care of the Supreme Muslim Council. The dome has been re-covered with dark grey lead. The mosque can hold up to 5000 worshippers.

History of the Aqsa Mosque

The early history of the Aqsa mosque is complex. The structural history has been variously correlated with the limited historical evidence available. The question of where the first mosque in Jerusalem was built is not resolved. The name, al-Aqsa, was previously applied to the entire Haram area, and only in later centuries was it restricted to the mosque. Some say that the Caliph Umar, following his acceptance of the surrender of Jerusalem in 638, went to the site of the Holy Rock, ordered the cleansing of the site, and built the first mosque on or near the Rock itself. This is one reason why the Dome of the Rock was often called the Mosque of Umar by the Franks. Others think the first mosque was on or near the site of the present Islamic Museum (because of the ancient masonry and the traditions linking this area with the miraculous Night Journey of Muhammad). Another view, and perhaps this is more likely, is that Umar built the mosque in the south area of the present building, where the oldest parts of the present structure were preserved. Apart from the Double Gate with entrance passage beneath the mosque and parts of the platform itself, no traces of Herodian building have been discovered on the site. It is assumed that at least by the time of Umar (and probably in Roman and Byzantine times) the ruins of the Herodian Royal Stoa had been cleared, and the south wall of the Haram built up to near its present level, as the Herodian platform is the foundation of the mosque. The lowest visible repairs to the Herodian south wall are currently dated to the Umayyad period.

Aqsa 1 The earliest mosque, of which traces are preserved, was an aisled structure shorter than the present mosque, c 51m long. Its floor was paved with pale grey marble. The character of the interior decoration is suggested by surviving fragments of marble revetment and painted plaster; mosaic tesserae were significantly absent. Slender dark marble monolithic columns with Byzantine capitals were re-used.

The court outside this mosque (under the present north end) was paved with white and pink flagstones with ornamental drain covers.

This structure was probably the one built by Walid I c 715; alternatively it is identified as the original mosque built by Umar c 639–40, and the structure described in a pejorative fashion by Arculf in 680 as a squarish and fairly roughly constructed building, partly of wood, in the ruins of the Herodian Royal Stoa. It is often assumed that this was a simple building, its roof supported by pillars of a type attested elsewhere at this period, but which was, notably, large enough to hold up to 3000 people and served the Muslim community for about 70 years both before and after the construction of the Dome of the Rock in 691–92. The size of Aqsa 1 would suit a congregation of 3000, the figure given by Arculf for Umar's mosque, and it seems likely that the conqueror of Jerusalem would have availed himself of the skills of local craftsmen to build a first mosque befitting the new rulers of the city.

Aqsa 2 In its next phase, the mosque was extended in length to the present north wall. Dome-bearing arches were built supported on slender, square masonry piers built alongside the monolithic columns, presumably to support the lateral thrust of a newly built dome. The north wall included the three central north doors which still survive and are certainly 8C, probably Umayyad work, and built of hard limestone.

Perhaps Aqsa 2 was the 15-aisled mosque rebuilt by the Abbasid Caliph al-Mahdi (completed c 774) with a wide central aisle bridged by great wooden tie-beams. Alternatively, it was started by the Umayyad Caliph 'Abd al-Malik (685–705) and completed by al-Walid I (705–15) in 709–15. Several features appear to be Umayyad and al-Muqaddasi (985) noted that the dome of the Aqsa was Umayyad. Like the Dome of the Rock, it had mosaic decoration, for al-Walid had gilt glass tesserae brought from Constantinople. In the early years the main entrance to the mosque was by the Double Gate and the passages beneath the mosque, leading up from the Umayyad quarter to the south.

The doors of the Umayyad structure, whether in Aqsa 1 or 2, were covered in gold and silver.

Aqsa 3 In a partial reconstruction of Aqsa 2, the whole structure between the dome and the north wall was demolished and rebuilt employing softer limestone and mortar. What resulted is the basis of the present layout of the mosque. The mosque had a gable roof and a great and beautiful lead-sheathed dome over the central aisle in front of the mihrab. Three central aisles, 52m long north of the dome, were carried on four rows of six columns, each supporting seven arcades (each larger than the 12 they replaced) with slightly pointed, slightly stilted arches. The walls on these arcades supported the gable roof and contained a row of interior windows, with an additional upper row of clerestory windows in the higher walls on either side of the central aisle. The arcades were braced by wooden tie-beams above the capitals. Great cypress beams 13m long formed the ceiling of the central aisle, recycled from the earlier structure when the aisle was wider. They had had carved ornamental soffits or consoles at either end, and more carving decorated the cross beams at the corners (see Islamic and Rockefeller Museums). Virtually the whole of this central area survived intact until 1938.

It seems likely that this structure was built by the Abbasid caliphs al-Mansur and al-Mahdi between 754 and 785. Parts of the mosque fell down in the earthquake of 749. Some reconstruction took place c 758/59 when al-Mansur took the gold and silver from the Umayyad doors to pay for some of the repairs. The mosque was extended 771–80 (after another earthquake in 774 described by al-Muqaddasi), the work being credited to al-Mansur (754–75) and al-Mahdi (775–85). The mosque reached its greatest extent at this period. It consisted of 15 aisles, seven on either side of the central nave. In this mosque the older work still standing around the mihrab 'stood like a beauty spot'. Later a portico with marble pillars was built onto the north façade by 'Abd Allah ibn Tahir, the governor of Syria (820–22).

The Fatimid Period On 10 December 1033 a great earthquake damaged the Aqsa. In the subsequent restoration (c 1034–36) under the Fatimid Caliph al-Zahir (whose inscriptions mention work on the dome), the mosque was reduced in size to suit the increasing impoverishment and probable depopulation of the city. It was most likely a five-aisled structure, as Nasir-i Khusraw in 1047 says it had five doors. The subterranean entrance passage from the south was blocked at this time, following the abandonment of the south quarter, and the main entrance to the Haram was thereafter from the west (see the Gate of the Chain, p 107). The glass mosaic on the north dome-bearing arch is dated by an inscription to al-Zahir (who had also restored the mosaics of the interior of the drum of the Dome of the Rock in 1027/28). Some of the earliest painting on the old tie-beams of the aisle arcades has also been credited to al-Zahir (see Islamic Museum).

The Crusader Period The Haram area was an integral part of the Crusader town from 1099, and Godfrey of Bouillon, ruling with the title of 'Defender of the Holy Sepulchre', made the Aqsa his headquarters; it served briefly as a palace for his successor, Baldwin I, the first Crusader King of Jerusalem. He gave it to the Order of the Knights Templar which was founded in 1118, and they in turn made it their headquarters (the Palatium or Templum Salomonis) and made various structural alterations and extensions to suit its new function. The fine decorations remained undamaged. Various annexes were constructed, including the great Templar Hall (now occupied by the Women's Mosque and the Islamic Museum); halls or tower were built out to the south over the Double Gate, which remained blocked; a great triple portico was contructed in the area of the southeast aisles with an open area to the north in the present northeast aisles; the three central bays of the north porch were constructed between 1099 and 1187.

The Ayyubid Period When Salah al-Din regained the city in 1187 he immediately restored the Aqsa to its previous function and form, removed the cross from the dome, refurbished the interior of the dome, and the floors and walls with marble and mosaics; he also made the mihrab with its mosaics. Salah al-Din also gave a beautiful pulpit of carved, inlaid and gilded cedar wood (which had been made for Nur al-Din Zangi in 1168, who had planned to install it in Jerusalem when he conquered the city). The exterior of the central bays of the north porch were rebuilt in 1217/18 by al-Mu'azzam. He also rebuilt the central dome of the porch. The round window in the east wall above the Mihrab of Zacharia is thought to be 13C, perhaps added when a screen wall was built closing the Crusader portico.

The Mamluk Period Following repairs and re-decoration in the 13C and 14C, in 1350–51 al-Nasir Hasan enlarged the mosque to seven aisles.

The Ottoman Period Sulaiman II made repairs in 1561, and Uthman III replaced some wood and the lead of the dome in 1752. Extensive repairs to the mosque and dome were carried out by Mahmud II in 1817. 'Abd al-'Aziz installed stained-glass windows in 1874. A certain amount of painting and plastering of the interior seems to have preceded the visit of Kaiser William II of Germany in 1898, including some poor paintings by an Italian artist which covered the Fatimid mosaic on the north dome-bearing arch.

Later history In 1924–27 the Supreme Muslim Council carried out major repairs to the mosque, with the supervision of the Turkish architect Kemal al-Din. Three pillars beneath the mosque were strengthened with reinforced concrete. The eight pillars and four arches supporting the dome were replaced, as were the tie-beams. Thirty new stained-glass windows were installed. The painted plaster over the mosaic on the north dome-bearing arch was removed. All the work was faithful to previous designs and an inscription over the prayer niche records the repairs. In 1927 an earthquake damaged the mosque, and another in 1937 left the east aisles in a dangerous condition.

Major excavations and rebuilding followed in 1938–42, carried out by the Supreme Muslim Council under the supervision of Mahmud Pasha Ahmad, and with the Department of Antiquities as observer. The work involved the demolition to the foundations of all the long walls and arcades of the mosque except for those of the two west aisles and the arcades flanking the dome. The reconstruction of the nave and east aisles followed, using monolithic marble columns imported from Italy, with locally carved capitals in Byzantine style; also the reconstruction of the upper part of the north wall of the mosque, and its complete internal refacing, including a partial reconstruction of the jambs and lintels of the central doors. The front five bays of the porch were restored, and the Crusader vaulted annexes to the east were torn down. At this time the roof was replaced with a steel structure. The east and central part of the floor was repaved. The decoration of the ceiling of the central aisle was the gift of King Farouk and the Egyptian government.

A number of bombs hit the mosque between July and December 1948, and repairs were carried out. An anodised aluminium silver-coloured outer shell replaced the old lead covering of the dome in 1967. On 21 August 1969 Salah al-Din's minbar was destroyed by arson and the adjacent walls and ceilings of the mosque damaged. Extensive repairs included the making of a copy of the minbar. The old columns and much of the stonework in the southeast section of the mosque have been replaced or refaced. The dome is newly re-covered in dark grey lead.

Though almost totally restored, the mosque retains the plan and numerous details of its accumulated architectural history since the 7C/8C.

The exterior

The mosque with its porch is essentially a large rectangular building aligned north–south, c 80m long and c 55m wide with extensions at the southeast and the southwest. It has a modern gable roof over the main aisle, modern flat roofs over the lateral aisles, with a recently re-covered 8C–11C dome over the space before the mihrab which is c 26.7m high, plus a crescent finial. The main north façade consists of a portico, with three pointed arches on either side of a larger central arch. The three central bays were originally constructed in the Crusader period and the central arch is somewhat Romanesque in style mostly rebuilt in 1217/18. The two outer bays to east and west were constructed between 1345 and 1350, which is recorded in the inscriptions in the respective spandrels above the east and west piers. The central inscriptions, also set between small ornamental columns, record on the left al-Mu'azzam's 1217/18 rebuilding of the porch mentioned above, and on the right. Sultan Qa'it Bay's contribution of the crenellations and upper border of the façade. Above the porch the wall was rebuilt in 1938–42; the three upper windows with slightly horseshoe-shaped arches are probably the work of the Fatimid al-Mustansir. To the rear of the porch, the bays match the seven rectangular doorways leading to the seven interior aisles. The ***three central doors** are notable, each set in a monumental moulded framework with flat lintels of joggled masonry, topped by very slightly pointed arches containing lunettes; they are variously dated to the Umayyad or the Abbasid period. Stylistically and structurally they are certainly 8C, and probably Umayyad. The upper frame of the great central door is damaged, but the size of the opening is 6.85m x 4.8m and that of the smaller east door is 4.25m x 2.99m. The west door was restored in Crusader times, and again in 1938–43, the others survived better and were only partly renewed in 1938–43. The two outer pairs of doors to east and west with pointed arches above, like their respective porticoes, are probably 14C.

The east façade was completely rebuilt in 1938–42. There is one doorway in the east side, the Gate of Elias (A. Bab Ilyas), also rebuilt in 1938–43. The three structures which project eastwards at the south are respectively the Mihrab of Zacharia, the Mosque of the Forty Martyrs, and the Mosque of Umar. The rear of the Mihrab of Zacharia contains a rectangular window and round relieving arch; above is a 13C round window. The best views of the low drum and high dome of the Aqsa can be had from the southeast corner of the Haram (at present not accessible), or from the Mount of Olives. Just in front of the mosque and to the east of the main entrance are steps leading down to the subterranean Aqsa (normally closed).

The interior

Entrance is by the main door, leaving shoes, bags and cameras outside.

The restorations carried out in the 20C, and the many windows, contribute to the sense of space and light in a vista of columns and rugs. The mosque contains 75 columns and 33 piers in addition to smaller ornamental columns in various places; there are 155 windows, of which 121 containing coloured glass are nearly all 20C replacements. The layout of the mosque developed between the 7C and the 14C, but almost all has been restored in the 20C.

The columns of the central nave and the two rows to the east are of Italian

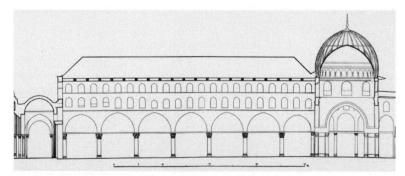

Section through the Aqsa Mosque (R. W. Hamilton, The Structural History of the Aqsa Mosque: *Oxford, 1949)*

marble with limestone capitals in local Byzantine style. They were installed in 1938–43 and conform to the earlier plan. The central aisle is flanked by arcades with pointed arches; above each arch are three slightly pointed small arched openings each in turn paired with 21 clerestory windows to each side. The painted medallions at intervals along the upper wall name friends and relations of the Prophet, including 'Ali and Umar, in ornate calligraphy. The chandeliers and rugs are new. The carved and painted ceiling of the central nave, predominantly blue, white, gold and brown in geometrical and floral designs was given by Farouk I and the Egyptian Government in 1943. It replaces the massive wooden roofbeams whose carvings (7C/8C) are now preserved in the Islamic Museum. The east aisles have a modern coffered ceiling, and first west aisle has a timber ceiling of no great antiquity, the other two aisles to the west have groined stone and plaster ceilings (14C). The tie-beams in the arcades, of gilded metal, are replacements of earlier wooden ones which had c 13C and later paintings (Islamic Museum).

Although the pillars and piers supporting the dome were replaced in 1927, most of the work above is that of al-Zahir in 1034–36. In particular the *mosaics on the north face of the north dome-bearing arch, are of Fatimid date. They are dated by the double row of Kufic inscription at the top, which names al-Zahir. Elaborate acanthus and floral motifs expand upwards from the lower corner of the half-spandrel to the central window above the apex of the arch. Resemblances to the Umayyad style are probably due to the use of the same workmen employed by al-Zahir in 1027/28 to restore the mosaics on the drum of the Dome of the Rock. The style here is much less flexible, and the attempt to fill the field of decoration less successful than in the Umayyad originals. The *dome itself, a double casing of wood and metal resting on a shallow drum, which has seven windows with stained glass, has been renovated on various occasions as its inscriptions record. Its interior apex is 23.5m above the floor. The mosaics on the drum were restored by Salah al-Din in 1189, and contain much gold and green in the designs of vases, trees, flowers, rosettes and leaves reminiscent of the probable Umayyad originals. There are also fine designs on the moulding and pendentives below.

Renovations to the dome were also made by al-Nasir Muhammad in 1327 and Mahmud II (1808–39) as the inscriptions in the panels of the dome record, in exactly the same way as these three rulers recorded their actions in the Dome of the Rock.

In the south wall of the mosque is the *mihrab or prayer niche of Salah al-Din. Six graceful small columns of variously coloured marble flank the niche, with mosaic in the upper part and marble casing below. The inscription, in gold mosaic, reads: 'In the name of merciful and compassionate God, the restoration of this Sacred Mihrab and the entire restoration of the mosque was commanded by the servant of God and his agent Yusuf Ibn Ayyub Abu'l-Muzaffar, the Victorious King, Salah al-Din, when he conquered Jerusalem in the name of God in the year 583 H. He thanks God for this success and may God have mercy on him.' To the right, until its destruction by fire in 1969, stood the beautiful inlaid cedarwood minbar or pulpit also presented to the mosque by Salah al-Din, which was one of the finest surviving wooden minbars of that period. Opposite this minbar is a dikka, or platform for the relayer of the prayers, supported on 14 slender columns with Crusader capitals, built against the northwest pier supporting the dome, which is of later date. Immediately west of the destroyed minbar in the south wall are two small mihrabs, of Moses and of Jesus; the latter traditionally contained the footprint of Jesus said to have been brought here from the Chapel of the Ascension on the Mount of Olives in medieval times; to the right is a doorway leading south into the Dar al-Khitaba, or room for the reader of the Friday sermon and other attendants of the mosque, which was built in the 15C in the earlier Crusader/Ayyubid tower (see p 94). Nearby, two columns stand close together: tradition holds that if the faithful can pass between them they will see the houris of Paradise; if they cannot pass between them, they may not enter Paradise. The gap between the columns is much chipped and worn. The second aisles to east and west of the mihrab contain rectangular windows at floor level probably dating from the 12C/14C.

To the west is the **Women's Mosque** (A. Jami' al-Nisa) or the White Mosque (A. al-Buq'a al-Baida'). This is located in the east part of the great Templar Hall of the 12C. The west end can be seen in the Islamic Museum. The east end of the hall was probably made into a mosque shortly after 1187 by Saladin.

The southeast area of the Aqsa has a more complex history and has been almost totally restored. It is currently closed to the public. This part contained the oldest preserved sections of the mosque, with Byzantine marble columns and capitals dating to the 7C/8C. Restorations of some of these can be seen in the second east aisle.

Immediately adjacent to the south wall on the east side is the **Mosque of Umar** entered by an archway from the main mosque. It is 30m x 8m, constructed of limestone, and has a vaulted roof with pointed arches and three large and three small windows. The prayer niche, between the second and third piers of the south wall, has a twisted column on either side with richly and grotesquely carved capitals of Crusader date. Tradition says it marks the site of Umar's prayers in 638, and according to Mujir al-Din the building is a remnant of the mosque built by Umar in the 7C, hence its present name. Most of the fabric is Ottoman, but much of the exterior south wall is earlier and is perhaps Umayyad.

On the north side of the Mosque of Umar is the **Mosque of the Forty Martyrs** (A. Jami' al-Arba'in). Also restored, it is approached through trefoil arches with red and white voussoirs, and measures 9m x 8m. It contains two windows with coloured glass, the lower walls are cased in polychrome panelled marble, and verses from the Koran form a decorative dado on the walls above, in particular those describing Muhammad's Night Journey. The structure dates to the Crusader and Ayyubid periods.

On the north side of the Mosque of the Forty is the **Mihrab of Zacharia**, standing on the site where he is said to have been slain. The commemoration is perhaps of that Zechariah son of Berachiah (Matt. 23:35), who was killed in the time of the Persian king Darius between the Temple and the altar, but confused with Zechariah, father of John the Baptist, whom tradition held to have been slain by Herod the Great because of the failure of the Massacre of the Innocents to kill John. This tradition is old, for according to the Bordeaux Pilgrim (333) within the ruined Temple enclosure was an altar in front of which was a marble slab with the blood of Zechariah. Nasir-i Khusraw (1047) mentions a mihrab of Zacharia, which might have been destroyed in the Crusader alterations. The south wall has a mihrab with an ornate marble trefoil arch decorated in high relief and supported by two pairs of small pillars with acanthus capitals. High in the east wall is a round window of the 13C, and below is a rectangular window which is flanked by a carved fluted column with acanthus capital on the north, and a squared marble box capped by a non-matching capital on the south. The lower walls have coloured marble facings. The piers on either side of the entrance are probably of the 7C/8C but the rear wall is post-Crusader. North of this mihrab is the east door of the mosque, the Gate of Elias, rebuilt in 1938–42. The east arcades were completely restored in 1938–43.

The Islamic Museum

The **Islamic Museum is located in 12C Crusader and Ayyubid buildings in the southwest corner of the Haram platform, and was established in 1927. It contains a remarkable display, mainly of objects and architectural fragments of the Haram structures removed in the course of restorations which serve almost as much as the buildings themselves to illustrate the magnificence and antiquity of the sacred precinct. Admission charged. Hours of entry as for the mosques.

The court in front of the entrance contains many pieces of stone sculpture which have been collected from the buildings in and around the Haram. They include a variety of capitals, and a sarcophagus, probably of the 1C AD, which has had a varied history. It measures 2.02m x 0.55m, and the front is decorated with five rosettes in relief; two wreaths, one with rosettes, decorate the ends; the back is plain. It was discovered in the dismantling of a fountain which stood outside the north entrance of the Gate of the Chain in 1871. It may have been brought from the Tombs of the Kings (see p 246) by Sultan Qa'it Bay in 1482.

The entrance and domed vestibule of the museum were built as part of a remodelling of the east façade of the al-Maghariba mosque in 1871. To the left, the first three sections of the museum are located in the south part of the mosque in part of an early Ayyubid hall with vaulted roof dating c 1194. At the south end is the remnant of the mihrab which has been cut through to provide access to the south part of the museum. Only the semi-dome at the top, and the flanking reused Crusader marble columns and acanthus capitals remain. The mihrab itself was built in the blocking of the earlier west entrance to the Templar Hall. The display contains objects which illustrate the history of the Haram and Islamic Jerusalem: fine Korans (one is 800 years old), documents, glass mosque lamps including a fine example dating to the early Mamluk period, metalwork and some textiles, including a beautiful multi-coloured robe found in the Baladiyya Madrasa near the Gate of the Chain.

Pass through the door to the **great Templar vaulted hall**, built in the 1160s and probably part of the monastic quarters of the Knights; after 1187 the east end was converted into the Women's Mosque of the Aqsa, and later the west end served as the assembly hall of the Fakhriyya madrasa. Ten pointed vaults are supported by great central piers and wall piers in this half of the hall; the hall serves as a splendid display area for a remarkable collection of structural remains and objects of 7C and later date removed from the buildings in the Haram in the course of various restorations, including fragments of the original mosaics from the Dome of the Rock.

The *Great Doors* of the Dome of the Rock, sheathed in ornamental copper plating, were presented by Sultan Qa'it Bay in 1467–68. Among the most impressive objects in the display, they were removed from the mosque during the restorations. The inscriptions at the top record the restorations of Sulaiman II between 1552 and 1566. Other exhibits include tiles of various periods from the 16C taken from the exterior of the Dome of the Rock; two great gilded finials from the top of the Dome, one removed in the restorations of 1899 and the other in 1961; and the crystal chandelier which was hung over the Rock by 'Abd al-Hamid II in 1876, removed to the Aqsa in 1951 before it came to the museum.

Perhaps the most important objects in the display are the fragments of the mighty ****carved roof beams** from the central aisle of the Aqsa Mosque. Cut from cypress trunks and originally 13m in length, the beams had carved consoles and soffits. The beams were probably originally employed in the Umayyad Mosque (8C), were reused in the Abbasid Mosque (later 8C), and remained in use until removed in 1948. The date of the earliest carving could be as early as the 7C or as late as the 11C, but 6C/7C graffiti discovered on the beams, and the style of the carving, tend to support the earlier date. Their survival in situ into the 20C is remarkable. Some of the painted tie-beams from the arcades of the aisles are also preserved. The earliest painting appears to go back to the time of Salah al-Din or al-Mu'azzam in the 12C–13C, some just possibly to al-Zahir in the 11C, but much is later.

The marble balustrade of Crusader workmanship, which ornamented the mihrab in the Aqsa till the 19C, is also in the museum, as are some fine windows of the 16C and later. Some capitals of various periods are also on display including a white marble capital depicting two angels ministering to the seated figure of Jesus, thought to be the fourth of a set once decorating the Crusader Chapel of the Repose on the site of the Umariyya Boys' School (see p 145). The other three still decorate the gallery of the al-Ghawanima minaret (see p 102). Dating c 1160 they are similar to Crusader sculptures found at Sebastiya (now in the museum in Istanbul) and Nazareth (in the Church of the Annunciation at Nazareth) that belong to a school of sculpture originating in the Bourges district of east central France. There are also the magnificent cauldrons which equipped the charitable kitchen established by Khassaki Sultan, the wife of Sulaiman the Magnificent, in 1552, which was still functioning in the 19C (see p 150).

Subterranean features

Subterranean features only accessible from within the Haram are at present normally closed to visitors. The Haram area as a whole has many cisterns and other underground chambers incorporated in its substructure and underlying bedrock, many of which are ancient, some dating to the Hasmonean and Herodian periods. The construction of the Struthion Pool at the northwest corner of the Haram in 2C–1C BC appears to have cut an earlier channel feeding cisterns in the northwest area of the Haram, and a conduit of the 8C BC leads south towards the temple from the northern Pool of Bethesda. Some Haram cisterns are rock-cut, others are built within the vaulting which supports the platform. Most are purpose-built to provide water for ritual ablution and cleansing within the Haram in the days when water was harvested from rainfall or was brought to the Haram by aqueduct or channels. Piped water supplies have now largely superseded this need, and those cisterns still in use are mostly used for watering the gardens and cleaning. Some are very large, in particular the one called 'The Sea' with 12,000 cubic metres capacity. Other cisterns nearer the Dome of the Rock may utilise rooms and passages once used by the Herodian priesthood.

Beneath the present Moors' Gate lies the blocked Barclay's Gate, a Herodian gate (see p 89). In the original Herodian plan, the low-level gate led into a level passage c 21m long running east under the Temple court to a chamber covered by a well-built dome; it then turned at right angles towards the south and rose at a gradient of 1 in 20 by a ramp or steps to the surface opposite Robinson's Arch. A late Muslim legend claimed that Muhammad tethered his steed, al-Buraq, by the gate before visiting the Aqsa and ascending to Paradise. The gate was afterwards called Bab al-Nabi, the Gate of the Prophet. The inner gate passage was subsequently converted into cisterns and a subterranean mosque, called al-Buraq, now abandoned. Access to the mosque and the inside of Barclay's Gate is by special permission only.

The Subterranean Aqsa

The 'ancient' Aqsa (A. al-Aqsa Qadima) is at present usually closed to tourist access, but interesting remains of Herodian and Umayyad times exist. A flight of steps just in front and to the east of the main entrance to the Aqsa Mosque leads to a ramp which formed part of the original principal entranceway from the Double Gate in Herodian times. Unlike the ramp at Barclay's Gate, which turned at right angles, this was a straight sloping passage. The gate was refurbished and the ramp extended in the 7C/8C and formed the main entrance to the Haram from the Umayyad Quarter to the south. It was probably blocked c 1033 or 1047.

A wide, descending ramp running the whole length of the mosque above gives onto a square vestibule of Herodian masonry in which a massive white marble monolithic column, 1.25m in diameter with flat acanthus leaf capitals, supports four arches and shallow, fluted pendentives capped by flat domes. The ceiling has fine geometric and acanthus relief decoration of probable Herodian date, though Umayyad repairs are possible. In the early 8C the west side was blocked with a heavy mass of masonry which forms a foundation for the mosque above. Necessary structural repairs were made in 1926–27, and reinforced concrete inserted to support the mosque.

Solomon's stables

The whole southeast angle of the Haram is supported by subterranean vaulting, part of which used to be accessible to tourists, though at present it is usually closed. The vaulting was first constructed by Herod the Great, and the springers of two Herodian arches have been recorded. The southeast corner is estimated to have had four levels of vaulting which raised the ground level from c 695m above sea level to about the present level of the platform at 738m. Only one level is accessible, where the columns are generally now thought to be Umayyad work reusing Herodian masonry. The upper parts and arches were reconstructed in Crusader times. The 'stables' were actually used as stables in Crusader times. Their use in Herodian times is unknown, but they may have been used for storage.

When open, access is by the flight of stairs in the southeast angle of the Haram. Beneath the entrance, Muslim tradition locates the Cradle of Jesus, where it is said Mary and the infant Jesus rested before starting the journey to Egypt to escape from Herod. The shrine is constructed from a great block of stone, with a painted semi-dome, supported by four marble pillars. It could be a Roman statue niche, with shell flutings, which may once have contained the small bronze cult statue from the Temple of Jupiter in Aelia Capitolina (which some authorities locate on the Temple platform). It and two others nearby may have been reused in a Byzantine chapel here dedicated to St. James, and a Crusader one dedicated to St. Simeon. Arab tradition identifies the two subsidiary niches as the Mihrabs of Mary and Zacharia.

The area of the stables is impressive, approximately 500 square metres, containing 88 pillars which divide the area into 13 north–south galleries. The piers are rectangular, the lower parts of reused drafted blocks of Herodian masonry. Many still show the rings by which the Crusaders tethered their horses. The arches and ceilings are of smaller Crusader blocks. At the south end of the sixth gallery from the east is the inner side of the blocked Single Gate, a postern and stable exit dating from Crusader times.

3 • The Muslim Quarter

Occupying c 28 hectares, this is the largest but least known quarter in the Old City.

History

The area contains the new suburb enclosed by Herod the Great in the 1C BC between the Gennath Gate and the Antonia fortress, the Antonia itself, and the new quarter of Bezetha enclosed by Herod Agrippa in AD 41–44. The line of the present northeast city walls does not seem to pre-date the 3C–4C. The entire area was within the Christian Byzantine city. In Umayyad times the principal Muslim quarter lay to the south of the Haram, but gates and repairs on the west and north sides of the Haram indicate activity in these quarters also. The west side of the Haram became more important in Fatimid times, but there are also indications of increasing Muslim work along the north side of the Haram. Jews are noted as living in the northeast quarter of the city in Fatimid times when this part was called the Jewish Quarter. It was taken over by the Christians during the 12C and the remains of several churches have been noted. These were mostly converted into Muslim schools and mosques under the Ayyubids and Mamluks, when the north side of the city was developed further and became part of the Muslim Quarter. Several Ayyubid Muslim foundations are known in the areas north and west of the Haram. The areas adjacent to the Haram were developed particularly in Mamluk times for religious schools and tombs (although many of these are now also in domestic use). Along the route of the Via Dolorosa, especially from the 13C, Christian places of memorial developed into churches and hospices, many refurbished in the late 19C or early 20C. In Ottoman times the Antonia escarpment housed the seat of the Ottoman administration with the palace of the governor to the west. Shops, markets and caravanserais were located on the west side of the quarter, adjacent to the old markets. Many of the present structures of the quarter incorporate older foundations and much exploration remains to be done. Despite early Ottoman refurbishment, the quarter has decayed since the 16C.

The area north of the Haram has numerous and varied places of interest, but very few of the Muslim monuments are open to visitors, being in private occupation. Because much of the decoration was lavished on the façade, especially the entrance, many are still well worth visiting. Entering the Old City by St. Stephen's Gate, immediately to the right inside the walls the **Hammam Sitti Maryam** is an old bath-house rebuilt in the 18C, still used in the 1980s. The bath house was fed by conduit from a pool outside the city walls, and was very popular with women. Many of the Arabic names for the monuments and the street in the vicinity of the gate are named after St. Mary because the gate led out to the tomb of the Virgin Mary. A fountain, the Sabil Sitti Maryam, is also just by the gate, and is one of several built by Sulaiman II in 1537. On the left the road leads to the Haram Gate, the Bab al-Asbat.

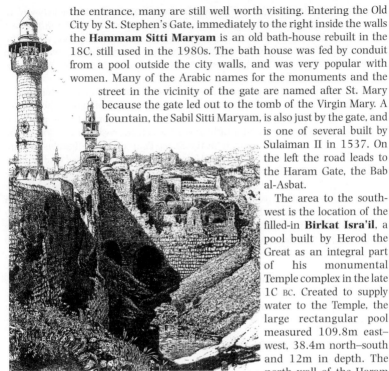

The area to the southwest is the location of the filled-in **Birkat Isra'il**, a pool built by Herod the Great as an integral part of his monumental Temple complex in the late 1C BC. Created to supply water to the Temple, the large rectangular pool measured 109.8m east–west, 38.4m north–south and 12m in depth. The north wall of the Haram formed its south side. The pool seems to have continued in use in Byzantine

The Birkat Isra'il from the east (C.W. Wilson, Picturesque Palestine, Vol. I. p 66: Virtue & Co., London, 1880)

times. Around 1170 the Templars identified this pool with that of Bethesda (since excavated to the north, see below), and this identification was still accepted in the 19C. By then the Birkat Isra'il was out of use and half filled with debris.

The Pools of Bethesda and St. Anne's Church

Continuing to the west along Tariq Bab Sitti Maryam, at c 45m on the right is the entrance to St. Anne's Church, and the monastery of the White Fathers. The church is a fine 12C Crusader monument, converted into a Muslim school (the Salahiyya Madrasa) after 1187, and restored as a Christian church in the 19C. Its stark and fine simplicity make it one of the most peaceful places in Jerusalem. Excavations adjacent revealed the Pools of Bethesda (Latin: *Piscina Probatica*, the Sheep Pool). Open 08.00–12.00, 14.00–17.00; closed Sun.

History

The earliest use of the site was for a reservoir or pool (the north pool), cut in the 8C BC, which fed the First Jewish Temple to the south by channel. The pool was filled by rainwater collected on the slopes to north and west. The first recorded mention of the two pools is in the Seleucid period, when they were called the 'Great Pools', when the southern pool was cut by Simon the Just c 300 BC. The area was developed in Roman times as a healing pool, where the sick, blind, lame and paralysed gathered to await a cure when the waters were disturbed (90 BC–AD 70). It was the site of Jesus' miracle in healing the crippled man (John 5:1–13).

Within the later Roman city of Aelia Capitolina it was associated with a temple or shrine of healing, dedicated to Serapis (Aesculapius). The theologian and writer Origen (231–46) describes four colonnades or porticoes around the four sides, and a fifth across the central rock-cut division of the pools. By the mid-5C a church 'at the Sheep Pool' or 'of the Paralysed Man' had been built and dedicated to St. Mary, whose birth was linked traditionally with the site. The church was built on the east side of the pools, partly overhanging the central division and held on seven arches, and partly built over the earlier healing place. The birthplace of Mary was also linked with Nazareth, but various details of her early life are compatible with a birthplace in Jerusalem. St. Mary's is shown with its portico on the Madaba Map in the 6C (see p 71). This church was probably destroyed by the Persians in 614 and restored by Modestus soon after; some sort of church remained in the 9C, when it is mentioned in the Commemoratorium as 'St. Mary (where she was born at the Probatica) 5 (clergy) and 25 women dedicated to God as anchoresses'. An Arab writer (Abu'l-Fida) says the Muslims had taken over the church before the 12C, possibly after the attack of al-Hakim in 1016. By the end of the 11C only a very poor ruin known as St. Anne's still existed.

In the 12C the site was associated with the birthplace of the Virgin Mary, and the House of St. Anne, her mother, the wife of Joachim. Bethesda and the Arabic Bait Hanna form a play on words meaning House of Grace. In the Crusader period a fine church was built on the present site, and also a chapel on the site of the earlier Byzantine church. These were part of a convent for Benedictine nuns, which was well endowed by Baldwin I. After placing his wife, Arda (an Armenian princess), here in 1104, he married Adelaide of Sicily. The convent endowments included the central great suq of Jerusalem. Joveta, the sister of Queen Melisande, was a novice here in 1130 before becoming head of the convent at Bethany. The church was extended later.

After Salah al-Din's conquest in 1187 the church was turned into a religious school (the Salahiyya Madrasa) for Shafi'ite Muslims. In 1699 it was still regarded by Christians as the house of Joachim and Anne, and although it was Muslim property, the Franciscans were allowed to say Mass there on the Feasts of the Immaculate Conception and the Nativity. The Muslims said it was haunted, and it began to be abandoned. In 1854 it was being used as a stable for the Turkish governor's horse soldiers. The church was granted to Napoleon III in 1856 by the Ottoman Sultan 'Abd al-Majid I in recognition of help rendered by France in the Crimea, by which time it had reached such a state of neglect that rubbish filled it nearly to the roof. Complete restoration followed in the 1860s, which amounted to a virtual rebuilding. The site was excavated in 1888–1900. The Museum of the White Fathers contains remains from the excavations and various other archaeological items; permission is necessary to visit.

Passing through to the court (the medieval cloister), various fragments of masonry and sculpture discovered in the excavations are displayed. On the opposite side of the court is *St. Anne's Church. This 12C building, in classic Romanesque style, has a fine entrance portal, with pointed arch and hood mouldings; in its tympanum, the inscription of Salah al-Din (1192) records the establishment of the Salahiyya Madrasa. The archivolt and cornice are finely carved. The top window in the façade is the most ornate. It has gadrooned voussoirs supported by marble columns with acanthus capitals, and is capped by an elaborately carved archivolt. The interior is a basilica with three naves, tall, dim and austere in style. The fine pointed vaulting is restored. The crypt, to which stairs in the south aisle descend, contains chapels built in some of the caves of the earlier Roman temple. Despite the 19C restoration, the church is the finest example of Romanesque architecture in Jerusalem.

Outside the church, to the north, a noticeboard illustrates the discoveries relating to the **Bethesda Pools**. To the left, parts of two very large, deep, rectangular rock-cuttings can be seen; they continue for an unknown distance under the houses to the west. The north pool (50m x 40m) is said to date originally to the 8C BC; that on the south to the 3C BC. At the east end of the pools are the remains of caves and healing baths of the Roman period, the foundations of the Byzantine church (a basilica with three apses which was partly built on vaulting at the east end of the pool), and a Crusader chapel. Above the ruins on the north side is a Byzantine mosaic.

Returning through the courtyard, in the wall on the right opposite the front of the church is a 12C niche, which was installed here at the time of the restoration of the dome of the Church of the Holy Sepulchre in 1867. It came from a chapel in an upper floor of the Patriarch's palace on the west side of the Church of the Holy Sepulchre, through which a view of the Tomb of Christ could be obtained from above the Rotunda gallery. Further along, a staircase with railing gives access to the southeast corner of the southern pool, which is 13m deep.

Back in the street, turn right, to reach a crossroads at c 80m; on the left the road leads to the Haram gate, the Bab Hitta. At the southwest angle of the junction is the **Ribat al-Maridini**, a hospice built in 1361/62 for pilgrims from Mardin in modern southeastern Turkey. The frontage, on both Tariq Bab Hitta, and Tariq Bab Sitti Maryam, is plain; the lower courses appear to belong to a pre-14C structure, and the upper storey is Ottoman. The entrance portal, on Tariq Bab Hitta, is plain, with a pointed arched recess within which the door has been reduced in size. There is a relieving arch of joggled voussoirs, and space for an inscription in the tympanum. On the same frontage, the central window has a typical Mamluk iron grille; on the north frontage, with plain fenestration, a shop now occupies the west part.

To the south of the Maridini, just before arriving at the Bab Hitta, is the **al-Awhadiyya**, the tomb of al-Malik al-Awhad of 1298 (see p 100). The tomb (and possible hospice and madrasa) of the great-great nephew of Salah al-Din, who was Superintendent of the Two Harams in Mamluk times, is now occupied as private dwellings. The east façade is the principal one, and has at the north end a fine entrance portal with reused Crusader marble columns and capitals, and a cloister vault above with a blazon-like decorative hub. A few metres to the south is a blocked window to the courtyard, which has above it a carved panel of intricate Mamluk work. The blocked window to the tomb chamber is in the gate entrance. The façade has a cornice, and traces of Ayyubid and earlier walls in the lower courses.

The street ends at the Bab Hitta, which has an outer porch of Ayyubid date; it contains some coursed drafted masonry, and a pointed dome.

Opposite the Awhadiyya is **al-Karimiyya** a madrasa built in 1319. Karim was a Copt who became a great Mamluk state official (the Inspector of the Privy Purse in the time of al-Nasir Muhammad) and later converted to Islam. He was eventually disgraced, partly on an accusation of protecting Christians. He built a number of Muslim religious foundations in Cairo and Damascus. The simple entrance portal, with pointed arched recess and stone benches, contains a rectangular doorway with monolithic lintel and is now blocked. Most of the north end of the building behind is Ottoman.

Returning to the crossroads, continue to the left along Tariq Bab Sitti Maryam (or Tariq al-Mujahidin). Beyond the shop in the west end of the Maridini hospice is a straight joint; to the west there is Crusader masonry in the lower courses, and Ottoman above. The wall from here to the corner forms the north frontage of the Sallamiyya Madrasa which is entered from the west frontage. At the east and west ends of this frontage are two blocked Crusader doorways. Continuing on to a vault spanning the road above the entrance to the Tariq Bab al-'Atm, on the right are a ruined minaret, madrasa and mosque, the **Mu'azzamiyya** (or later al-

Mujahidin), which was built as a madrasa by the Ayyubid governor of south Syria and Palestine, al-Mu'azzam Isa, and completed 1217/18). The base only survives of a Syrian-type square tower minaret. The chamber used as the assembly hall of the Ayyubid madrasa fronts the street with three windows, and contains tombs, at least two being 15C. The now missing floor above it contained the mosque, but only part of the mihrab survives. To the north the remains of the courtyard has vaulted chambers on three sides. There are Ottoman and modern additions. The madrasa served the Hanafi community, and its construction meant all four schools of Islamic law then had schools in Jerusalem. The building incorporated much reused earlier rusticated masonry, and a slab with one of the Herodian inscriptions ban-

The Minaret of the Mu'azzamiyya (the Mujahidin Mosque) in Tariq Bab Sitti Maryam (C.W. Wilson, Picturesque Palestine, Vol. I, p 30: Virtue & Co. London, 1880)

ning non-Jews from entering the inner court of the Temple was found in the basement of the madrasa in 1871. The adjacent shop fronts are more recent.

Just beyond on the left is the Tariq Bab al-ʿAtm which leads south to the Haram Gate of that name. This mostly vaulted and thus gloomy street contains some fine Mamluk portals well worth visiting. On the left is a row of three fine Mamluk windows with muqarnas hoods which give onto the assembly hall of the **ʿal-Sallamiyya**, a madrasa built c 1338 by a merchant, al-Majd al-Sallami, who came from south of Mosul on the Tigris in modern Iraq. As well as mercantile activities, he was useful to Sultan al-Nasir Muhammad as a slave merchant and importer of Mamluks, and as a trusted diplomatic negotiator. The main entrance just to the south is very fine Mamluk work. The portal, with benches set in a deep recess, has an unusual muqarnas canopy. The doorway, with red and cream coursed jambs, and a lintel with pseudo-voussoirs resting on three tiers of muqarnas work, still contains the original iron-plated double doors and heavy knockers. The balcony, above and to the south, supported on carved brackets and framed by mouldings, partly covered by later vaulting over the street, is a contemporary feature. This frontage has a number of parallels with Cairene work (Mosque of Almas, Cairo) unique in Jerusalem and may be the work of a team sent from Cairo. The interior (not open) has a vestibule and passage leading to a large court, with cells and a vaulted assembly hall. The upper floors are largely Ottoman.

Adjacent on the south is the **ʿal-Dawadariyya**, the khanqah built in 1295 by ʿAlam al-Din Sanjar al-Dawadari, a Mamluk Amir who served in turn under the Sultans Baybars, Qalaʿun, Khalil, Kitbugha, Lajin and al-Nasir Muhammad, from Aleppo and the north, to Damascus and Egypt in the south. He took part in the assault on Acre in 1291, and finally died and was buried at Krak des Chevaliers in Syria in 1300. This is a large madrasa and khanqah which lies adjacent to the Haram north portico. Because of the gloomy vaulting it is hard to see the splendid entrance portal set in the plain façade. A red and cream coursed masonry recess containing benches has a doorway with monolithic lintel and joggled relieving arch. Above the relieving arch the founder's inscription runs round all three sides of the recess. Above it are three tiers of muqarnas work, and monolithic fluted cupolas. On the street side of these are two pointed trefoil arches, of which the central impost is suspended. The structure and decoration are complex, with parallels in Damascus, especially with the ʿAdiliyya Madrasa. The entrance opens directly into a large open court with cells on the west, north and east sides, and three larger ones on the south side. The cells have typical Mamluk pointed doorways, with slit windows to admit light and air from above. On the south side is the assembly hall, marked by a fine door and two flanking windows in shallow recesses. The entrance recess has a horseshoe arch. Red and cream coursed masonry, joggled relieving arches and rosettes in the tympana are all decorative features which add to the sense of importance. A cornice moulding marks the original height of the walls. This building was richly endowed as a Shafiʿi khanqah; it was converted to a school (Madrasa al-Bakriyya) some time before 1914.

The street ends at the Bab al-ʿAtm (see p 100); within the west end of the south wall of the Dawadariyya are two blocked archways which may be the two east passages of an Umayyad triple gate, with the present Bab al-ʿAtm in the west passage. Opposite the Dawadariyya, on the west side, is the **Aminiyya**, a madrasa or khanqah founded in 1329/30 by Amin al-Malik, a state official of Coptic origin in the time of al-Nasir Muhammad who converted to Islam under Baybars II. The east frontage of this madrasa is obscured by buttresses and later vaulting; it has a plain doorway which contrasts with its ornate frontage onto the Haram (see p 101).

Returning to Tariq Bab Sitti Maryam and turning left, at c 30m the Shari'a Muhammad Darwish (also called the 'Aqabat Dair al-'Adas) on the right leads up to Herod's Gate.

A diversion can be made through the Muslim quarter at this point, up to Herod's Gate (p 77) and returning by Shari'a Bab al-Zahira. There are some rather obscure monuments in this area, which are not open to visitors; the principal rewards of the walk are the streets in the quarter.

Continuing west along Tariq Bab Sitti Maryam, a few metres from this point on the south side of the road, the frontage contains the right jamb of a Mamluk doorway in red and cream coursed masonry set within a moulded frame, with part of a joggled string course inlaid in black. This was the location in the 19C and early 20C of the Second Station of the Cross, the Scala Sancta of the Via Dolorosa of the Christians, believed to be the entrance to Pilate's Praetorium by which Jesus left the Praetorium and outside which he took up the cross. Tradition links a staircase on this site with the 28 marble steps said to have been taken by St. Helena to Rome and installed in front of the Lateran Palace by Pope Sixtus VI in 1589. The doorway may have been the original north entrance of the Subaybiyya, the early 15C madrasa and tomb of a Mamluk official (see p 102) which became inaccessible when the Ottoman barracks and later the school were built on the Antonia.

The Antonia Fortress and associated Christian traditions
On the south side of Tariq Bab Sitti Maryam is the site of the Antonia Fortress of Herod the Great, now occupied by the Umariyya Boys' School. On the north side is first the Monastery of the Flagellation, and further to the west the Convent of the Sisters of Sion. The history of this area is best described as one unit.

History
The high rock peak northwest of the Temple may be the location of the Hananel Tower rebuilt by Nehemiah (Neh. 3:1), located at or near the northwest corner of the ancient city, and which still had a garrison of 500 in Ptolemaic times. Antiochus IV Ephiphanes destroyed it in 167 BC. A new tower, of Baris, was rebuilt perhaps by the Jewish hero Judas Maccabeus, but more likely by the Hasmonean ruler John Hyrcanus I (134–104 BC). It was surrendered to Pompey in 63 BC, and to Herod in 37 BC. The latter rebuilt it probably between 37 and 35 BC and named it Antonia in honour of his friend and patron Mark Antony. In the Hasmonean period a stepped rectangular pool (the Struthion Pool) was cut in the rock northwest of the fortress, and this was filled by rainwater brought by aqueduct and channel from the slopes further to the northwest. The Antonia fortress is described by Josephus (War V:238–45) as set on a precipitous rock, covered with flagstones both decorative and defensive, with a wall with four high corner towers enclosing a main tower. The Herodian north and west porticoes of the Temple were set against the rock scarp below to the south and could be entered from the fortress. The fortress was

probably restricted to the top of the rock scarp, an area today c 120m x 45m. A wall, c 4m in width which runs east–west along the south edge of the scarp as far as the Is'irdiya Khanqah (see p 101), was the south wall of the Herodian fortress. However, the fortress was probably not the Praetorium at which Pontius Pilate condemned Jesus to death; that event is more likely to have been at the old Herodian palace on the site of the present citadel.

After the expulsion of the Roman garrison from the Antonia in AD 66, it was occupied by the Jews during the First Jewish Revolt, and was one of the principal points of attack in the siege laid by Titus in AD 70. After capturing the Third and Second North Walls of the city (War V:302 and 331), Titus raised earthworks opposite the Antonia. These were completed by mid-June and are described by Josephus (War V:466): 'Of the first two, that at Antonia was thrown up by the V Legion over against the middle of the pool called Struthion, the other by the X11 Legion about 20 cubits away'. The Jewish defenders in the Antonia dug a mine right up to the wood and earth siege ramp, and destroyed it by fire. After building a siege wall around the city, Titus had the siege earthworks rebuilt. The second siege ramps were much larger and took 21 days to complete (War V:523; VI:5). The Jewish counter-attack on them in mid-July failed, and Roman siege engines were brought up. At that point the wall of the Antonia collapsed into the mine dug for the first earthworks; and after a few delays, the Romans captured the Antonia on 24 July. Some of the Romans then got into the Temple precinct through the mine. Shortly after, the Antonia was razed (VI:43) to permit an easy approach for the final attack on the Temple itself. The description does not clarify the problem of the location of the Second and Third North Walls of the city, but it is apparent that Titus was already inside them when working against the Antonia.

As the Antonia was razed by the Roman army in AD 70, most of the remains on the site are of a later date. Around 135, as part of Hadrian's new Roman city, a magnificent pavement was laid over the Struthion Pool north-west of the fortress, parts of which can be seen in the Convents of the Flagellation and the Sisters of Sion. It may be the site of a forum. The triple gate of which the Ecce Homo Arch was the centre may have been built as a triumphal arch in Hadrian's city (like the one that stood at the east side of the forum off the *cardo* but it might be earlier).

Numerous later Christian traditions have grown up around this area, based on the supposition that the Antonia was the Praetorium of Pontius Pilate, where the events described in John 18:28–19:16 took place: the flogging and condemnation of Jesus and the start of his walk with the Cross to Golgotha. The Pavement in particular has been associated with the tribunal and the mocking of Jesus by the Roman soldiers.

The Byzantine tradition seems to have placed the Praetorium, and the Church of St. Sophia (of the Holy Wisdom, the House of Pilate) somewhere to the west or south, towards the Tyropoeon Valley. The church was destroyed by the Persians in 614, is mentioned in the 8C, but thereafter seems to have disappeared. The Crusaders then found it difficult to locate the site of Pilate's House, but built a 'Chapel of the Repose' where Jesus spent the night after his arrest, on part of the site of the Antonia. They built the 12C Crusader Churches of the Flagellation and Condemnation of Jesus on the Pavement to the north (see the Monastery of the Flagellation, below), but after the expulsion of the Crusaders in 1187, the Antonia site became inaccessible to Christians; by the 13C the Christian commemoration was entirely at the Church of the Flagellation, and the Via Dolorosa started in this vicinity. The Crusader Chapel of the Repose was converted into an Ayyubid tomb c 1200, and a Mamluk madrasa, the **Jawiliyya**, was built in 1315/20 adjacent to it (see p 102). The complex was renovated in 1469 when the Jawiliyya seems first to have been converted into a government administrative headquarters, whence the Mamluk Governor of Jerusalem gave judgements from his seat in the iwan. The Ottoman governors seem to have retained the arrangement. Amico (1594–97) notes that the building was still being used as a praetorium, just as when Jesus was condemned to death. In 1835, in the time of Ibrahim Pasha, the complex was rebuilt as a barracks for the Ottoman garrison. In 1864 the former Chapel of the Repose was being used as a grain store for the artillery horses. Fifty years later the Ottoman governor was still receiving visitors in the Jawiliyya. In 1923/24 the complex was converted to a school. The dome over the 13C tomb was demolished after the earthquake of 1927.

The Christian traditions focused on the buildings north of the fortress were particularly strong by the 14C. Pilgrims in the 17C say the building on the site of the Flagellation was being used as a stable by the Ottoman Mustafa Bey c 1623–40. He had a room for his harem built above it, and the Christians presumed divine retribution when the building collapsed at once. In 1719 it was being used by a Turkish weaver, and pilgrims were admitted on payment of a candle. The Franciscans were given the site by Ibrahim Pasha in 1838 and, with financial help from Maximilian of Bavaria, restored and enlarged the Chapel of the Flagellation in 1839. It was completely rebuilt in 1927–29 and restored in 1984.

In 1901–04 the remains were excavated of a nearly square, three-aisled 13C chapel in which four columns had supported a dome over the Roman pavement. This was later rebuilt as the Chapel of the Condemnation.

As you enter the court of the **Monastery of the Flagellation**, on the right is the Chapel of the Flagellation, a 12C single-aisled chapel now with a sanctuary covered by a domical vault decorated with the crown of thorns (architect A. Barluzzi, 1927–29). Open 08.00–12.00, 14.00–18.00 (–17.00 in winter).

On the left side of the court is the Chapel of the Condemnation. This early 20C chapel was built on medieval foundations, with four central columns of pink marble, and at the west side has a section of the Pavement of the 2C, the larger part of which can be seen next door in the Convent of the Sisters of Sion. Striated slabs indicate the line of the Roman road. The Chapel is the **First Station of the Cross** in the Franciscan procession (see p 178), marking the place where Pilate condemned Jesus. The **Second Station**, where Jesus took up the Cross, is in the entrance to the court.

The cloister contains various sculpted fragments found in excavations. Opposite the entrance to the court is the Museum of the **Studium Biblicum Franciscanum** (open 09.00–11.00 by appointment only). The important archaeological teaching collection contains materials from Franciscan excavations, and finds encountered during building operations, from all over the country, but particularly from Jerusalem, Capernaum, Nazareth and Herodion. There are displays of scuplture, ceramics, glass, coins and weights as well as small collections of material from Egypt and Mesopotamia. Particularly notable are the restored baptistery font of the Constantinian basilica at the Church of the Holy Sepulchre; the 16 bells of 12C–14C date found in 1863 and 1926, with a set of 221 organ pipes, and several silver and Limoges enamelled candlesticks, all from the Church of the Nativity at Bethlehem. There is a 17C/18C model of the Church of the Nativity made in olive wood inlaid with mother-of-pearl, a magnificent example of one of the traditional crafts of Bethlehem. There is also a very fine collection of 17C–19C apothecary jars and jugs from Savona in Italy, which were part of the Latin monastery's dispensary equipment until brought to the museum in recent years.

You can visit the **Umariyya Boys' School** outside of school hours. On the elevated rocky site of the Antonia fortress, the school is approached by a flight of steps on the south side of the street almost opposite the entrance to the Monastery of the Flagellation. It was an earlier site of the First Station of the Cross. On entering the courtyard of the school, opposite are the oldest remains in this complex which backs onto the Haram. The lower rooms at the west end are pre-Mamluk vaulted structures. Towards the centre is a high arch which was originally the south iwan of the Jawiliyya madrasa, built by Sanjar al-Jawili in 1315–20 (see p 102). He may have been a Kurd, from Diyarbakr in modern southeast Turkey, and was a high Mamluk official. The iwan is flanked by two vaulted chambers, and all the recesses and windows at the back are cut through a massive 4m-wide pre-existing wall, probably that of the Herodian Antonia. The five Mamluk windows with coursed red and cream masonry can be viewed from the Haram. From these windows one can gain a good idea of the way the Antonia fortress controlled the Temple area from above. Above the iwan arch, on the north side, are two heraldic blazons with two lines and a dot incised within a circle, probably those of the founder. The madrasa originally extended to the north, with a court surrounded by cells on the west, north and east sides. It was entered from the north. All that part of the madrasa was destroyed in 1923/24.

Immediately west (or right) of the madrasa are the remains of the 12C **Chapel of the Repose** built c 1160 on the site where it was thought Jesus rested in prison after his arrest in Gethsemane. The small chapel, like the Jawiliyya, is built against the massive Herodian wall, with a curiously angled window cutting through the wall itself. On the north side were a vestibule and a domed chamber. The chapel vestibule was probably the original location of the four capitals showing angels ministering to Jesus which were reused in the nearby al-Ghawanima minaret in the 13C (see p 102). The domed chamber of the chapel was made into the tomb of an Ayyubid Amir, Shaikh Darbas al-Kurdi al-Hakkari c 1200 (several of the Kurdish tribe of the Hakkari fought with Salah al-Din). The large domed porch, with pointed-arched openings and drum, dome and cupola, was demolished after the earthquake of 1927, and only a modern low cenotaph now marks the Shaikh's grave. All the modern buildings on the east side belong to the school (1923/24). The rest of the structures around the complex are mainly Ottoman.

Returning to the street, continue to the next crossroads to see the ***Convent of the Sisters of Sion**. The visitors' entrance is on the east side. The Sisters of Sion founded a convent and orphanage, now a hospice, in 1857. A visitor centre and shop, a small museum and an excellent tour route are provided. Open daily except Sunday 08.30–12.30, 14.00–1700. The Convent contains a large part of the pavement or 'Lithostraton' laid over the Struthion Pool, and the north lateral arch of the Roman 'Ecce Homo', the central arch of which can be seen in the street outside.

The **Struthion Pool** (the 'Sparrow Pool', or the Double Pool) is a rock-cut water cistern with stepped edges, oriented northwest–southeast. It measures 52m x 14m and c 4.5m–5.5m deep, with the floor stepping down towards the southeast, and was originally an open tank or pool, cut in the 2C/1C BC. A channel runs from the southwest corner to the Temple area where it is cut by the Herodian wall. It was fed by channel from the Damascus gate area where rainwater was collected from the higher slopes. The pool was roofed over in the 2C with impressive barrel vaults which add c 8m to the height of the cistern. What can be seen today is only a small part, for the east half of the pool lies beyond the partition wall with round arches on the left of the viewing platform; the wall behind to the north is ancient, blocking off c 10m; and the wall at the far south end, with pointed arch, is modern and blocks off another c 13m. It was emptied of debris in 1934/35 and today is filled by ducts leading rainwater from the roof of the convent in the normal method by which cisterns are filled in the city.

Part of the rock-cut counterscarp of the ditch surrounding the north side of the Antonia fortress may be seen, before you reach the **Pavement** (or *lithostraton* in Greek, *gabbatha* in Aramaic), which is believed by some to be that pavement mentioned in John 19:13 where Pilate took his seat at the tribunal. However, the accepted date of the pavement is later, c 135, when it was laid for a Hadrianic forum on the contemporary vaults over the Struthion pool below.

The Pavement measures c 48m north–south and 32m east–west; rectangular slabs of reddish limestone, often 1m in length and 30–35cm thick, were laid on cement. The area of the street in the south part is striated to prevent horses slipping, but all the slabs are polished by long wear. Channels and drains led rainwater to the cistern below. Incised on the surface are various games, including one described as the 'King's Game' in which the winner lands on a sword—a game likely to have been played by soldiers. The pavement now lies c 2m beneath the present road.

The **Ecce Homo Arch** can be seen as you leave the convent. Tradition holds that it is the place outside the Praetorium where Pilate showed Jesus to the Jews, saying 'Ecce Homo'—'Behold the Man' (John 19:5). The central arch bridges the Tariq Bab Sitti Maryam and has since the 13C been part of the Christian Via Dolorosa. An inscription (medieval) on the west face reads TOLLE TOLLE CRUCIFIGE EUM (Away with him! Away with him! Crucify him!). The north arch was revealed in 1851 during heavy rain when adjacent walls collapsed; it was later incorporated in the chapel of the Sisters of Sion and can be seen at the east end of the church by entering a door off the Tariq Bab Sitti Maryam which leads into a vestibule at the west end of the chapel. The south arch has been destroyed, but the footing was recorded in the Darvish al-Uzbakiyya building opposite. The triple arch has usually been attributed to Hadrian c 135, built as a triumphal arch at his east forum, on the pavement on which it was said to stand; it undoubtedly served this purpose in the 2C. A recent study has maintained that the sober if not severe style, the mouldings, the plan and proportions, which are closely paralleled by the Augustan gate at Aosta in northwest Italy (and also

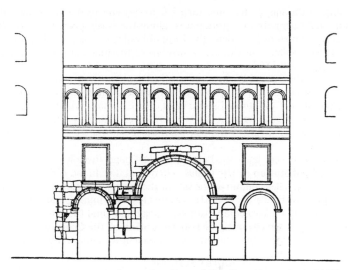

Reconstruction of the Ecce Homo Arch (Y. Blomme, Revue Biblique, 1979, p 260, Fig. 7)

those at Nîmes and Autun in France) indicate that it must have been originally by Herod Agrippa I (AD 41–44) or earlier, and served as the east gate of the city. The footings extend beneath the pavement, and pre-date it. The structures above the arch are later, belonging to the building on the south side of the road.

Returning to the entrance to the Sisters of Sion on the corner of Shari'a Bab al-Zahira, turn left uphill and right into Hosh Bakir, a lane leading east along the north side of the Convent of the Flagellation, at the end of which is the **Greek Orthodox Church of St. Nicodemus**, on a site with numerous late medieval traditions.

History of St. Nicodemus

The church is an old foundation, possibly originally Byzantine. It appears to be a Crusader-period church standing on older foundations with medieval alterations. The lower level of the church had three apses, with a portico and court to the west; the upper level had a domed church. In medieval times it or a nearby house came to be associated with the palace of Herod Antipas to which Jesus was taken after his arrest at Gethsemane. Also in this area, Brother Felix Faber, a Dominican priest from Ulm in Germany who made two pilgrimages to the Holy Land in 1480 and 1483, visited the House of Simon the Pharisee who invited Jesus to eat with him (Luke 7:36). Both stories are reflected in the name Dair Abu 'Adas (Convent of the Father of Lentils; Abu 'Adas is a corruption of the name Antipas). The church has been rebuilt and rededicated to St. Nicodemus, but the old traditions live on in the shape of an ancient pot from which it is said the Patriarch Sophronius (7C) gave lentils to the poor.

Returning to the top of the lane, turn left to descend to the Tariq Bab Sitti Maryam, and turn right to continue west along the street, towards one of the main ancient streets of Jerusalem, the Tariq al-Wad (the Valley Road, following the Tyropoeon Valley). On the north side before the junction is the Austrian Hospice, founded in 1863.

To the right the Tariq al-Wad ascends to the Damascus Gate (see p 77); to the left it continues down the Tyropoeon Valley. Turning left, in the surface of the street some slabs of the striated paved road of the Roman-Byzantine city have been relaid after excavation some 3m below the present surface. This was one of the main porticoed streets of the city from the 2C to the 7C depicted on the Madaba Map.

Immediately on your left is the Polish Catholic Chapel (usually closed), which marks the **Third Station of the Cross**, where Jesus fell. In the 19C this station was marked by a fallen column at the side of the street against the façade of the ruined bath house built c 1557, the Hammam al-Sultan. Immediately south of it is the entrance to the Armenian Catholic Patriarchate and the Church of Our Lady of the Spasm, which marks the **Fourth Station of the Cross**, where Mary met Jesus. This and the other stations, are marked by a plaque on the wall.

History of the Third and Fourth Stations

In the 19C most of the ruins on this site were those of the Hammam al-Sultan. The east section of the ruins was used as a stable by the Pasha. In 1864 the one Armenian Catholic monk in Jerusalem purchased the land, as the traditional sites of the Third and Fourth Stations of the Cross. Excavations revealed mosaics 5.75m beneath the surface. The remains associated with the mosaics appeared to be those of a three-aisled Crusader cruciform church, possibly of the 13C. In the south apse was a patch of fine 5C/6C mosaic, blackened by fire and depicting two sandals. The motif of two sandals is known elsewhere in Byzantine contexts which are not necessarily Christian or ecclesiatical, including almost identical mosaic sandals in a tomb near the Church of St. Peter in Gallicantu (see p 216) and some in a bath house at Timgad in Tunisia. It is possible the site is that of a Byzantine bath house. Tradition holds that these footprints mark those of Mary, and the commemoration on the site seems to have started by at least the 13C/14C; at the end of the 16C Amico locates the place where Jesus met his mother near this site. The modern Church of Our Lady of the Spasm was built in 1881 on the older remains.

The streets that lead east and west off the Tariq al-Wad contain much of interest, in particular numerous Mamluk foundations. The first street to the left is the Daraj al-Saray, leading to one of the Haram gates, the Bab al-Ghawanima (see p 103) and the site of the Old Saray (palace of the governor). At c 80m on the left is the Zawiyat al-Afghanistaniyya, dating from 1630/31.

Follow the first turning to the right (or west) off the Tariq al-Wad, the Tariq al-Alam or al-Saray, and continue the route of the Via Dolorosa. Immediately on the left is the modern **Fifth Station of the Cross**, where Simon of Cyrene took up the Cross. This station was previously located further south down Tariq al-Wad, at the site known as the House of the Rich Man. This (and the nearby House of the Poor Man) are dwellings built in the 14C. Continuing along Tariq al-Alam, at c 50m on the left is the Zawiya Zahiriyya(?) of the 15C(?).

A little more than halfway up the hill, just beyond a turning to the left and where a vault covers the street, is, on the left, the **Church of the Holy Face and St. Veronica** which marks the **Sixth Station of the Cross**.

> ### The holy face
> The tradition that St. Veronica gave her handkerchief to the Lord and received it back with the imprint of his face goes back to the mid-14C. The story has varied much in the course of the centuries. In the 3C–4C it was believed that a drop of Jesus' blood fell from his head; in the 12C the story developed and included the handkerchief used to wipe his face. By the 13C the story included the imprint of his face on the handkerchief.

The site seems to be associated with a Byzantine church known as the 'House of Cosmas and Damian', the *Anarguri* or 'penniless' twin brothers, physicians, who charged no fee, martyred in the 4C. Their birthplace is mentioned in the Commemoratorium in the early 9C and may be the same place as their 12C house (which was located between Golgotha and the present Church of the Spasm). The likelihood of the identification is increased by the finding of a damaged inscription on this site which mentions 'the holy A . . .' possibly the 'Anarguri'. The present church thus marks the site of an old church and a medieval tradition.

At the top of the street and at the northwest angle of the junction with Khan al-Zait St is the **Seventh Station of the Cross**, the Porta Judicaria (Gate of Judgement), where tradition holds that the sentence of death was posted. This station was included in the route of the Via Dolorosa in the 14C to prove to confused pilgrims that the place of Crucifixion and burial lay outside the city (see p 167). This is one of the busiest parts of the suq. (For the remainder of the Via Dolorosa, see Jerusalem, section 4.) Turning left (south), continue for c 55m along Khan al-Zait St and take the next left turning, into the 'Aqabat al-Takiyya. In the southeast angle of the junction lies the Khan al-Zait, a large vaulted hall with four aisles divided by two rows of four pillars. The pillars, with rather poor capitals, extend below the present floor level to the base of rock-cut cisterns. Probably originally a market, the khan was later a soap factory and the cisterns were used for storing olive oil. Shops line the west side, and a number of columns in the vicinity probably derive from the Roman-Byzantine *cardo maximus*.

Continuing east down the 'Aqabat al-Takiyya, at c 110m on the right is one of the most important Mamluk monuments in Jerusalem, the ***Dar al-Sitt Tunshuq**, a palace built by the Lady Tunshuq in 1388.

History of the Dar al-Sitt Tunshuq

> Little is known of Sitt Tunshuq, a lady living in Jerusalem by 1391/92 and buried in her mausoleum opposite, for the building has no founder's inscription. It is possible that she was a princess of the Muzaffarid dynasty in Persia, a refugee from the invasion of Timur. According to Mujir al-Din, the street was called Market St before the palace was built. In 1552, Khassaki Sultan, the favourite wife of the Ottoman Sultan Sulaiman II established a charitable foundation in the complex, which included a Sufi convent, a soup kitchen for the poor, a caravanserai and stables. It retained its charitable function into modern times. Because of this charitable association, 19C Christians identified

the place as the 4C Hospital of St. Helena. In the late 19C, part of the building became the residence of the Ottoman governor. In the 20C, an orphanage for 150 boys was established here, the entrance to which is from the south.

The building is not open to visitors, but the façade is of interest. The main part consists of three portals. The central portal is the widest and least impressive. It has an unusual cinquefoil arch of red, black and cream masonry, and was intended as the entrance to the ground-floor stables. The tall west portal is now blocked, but is finely decorated. It has a moulded frame, red and cream masonry and a joggled string course. There is a rectangular window with inlaid star-pattern border above the door, which includes turquoise faience inlay. The inscription is from the Koran, Sura XV:46–55. This was the most important entrance, leading to a great reception hall and other chambers on an upper floor. The large circular window between the two doors gives onto the main hall. To the east is a third ornate portal, also blocked, which leads to an open yard. It is the most impressive entrance, with a deep recess, red and cream masonry framed by a red band and mouldings, with a joggled string course above the lintel. Above this are four tiers of muqarnas supporting a colourful semi-dome. Between these elements is an elaborate inlaid panel. Although it is a less important door, the decorative emphasis has been placed here to balance the ornate doorway of the mausoleum opposite. This is the only Mamluk palace known in Jerusalem.

The **Mausoleum of Sitt Tunshuq** opposite the east portal on the north side of the street was completed before 1398 when the lady died. It was converted to domestic use between 1720 and 1920, when a new doorway was cut on the west side of the original portal. The portal contains red, black and cream masonry and the doorway has a monolithic lintel with an undercut joggled string course. The inlaid strapwork in the tympanum compares with that on the palace opposite. The domed tomb chamber (not open) lies on the right side. It has a pair of windows with marble lintels, joggled relieving arches and marble inlay, with joggled string course above. The façade is capped by a parapet of finials. The dome, whose apex is 11.94m above the floor of the tomb chamber, is supported on a drum with 12 pointed-arched windows. The interior of the tomb chamber has a cenotaph on the floor and tomb beneath; a mihrab in the south wall has reused Crusader capitals and a joggled pointed arch of rare marbles, with marble strapwork in the spandrels. The conch (and until 1935 other parts of the walls) has rare carved stuccowork of probably eastern Islamic inspiration.

Adjacent to the east side of the east portal of the palace, a fourth portal, with an Ottoman trefoil arch, led to part of the Khassaki Sultan's charitable foundation. In the 1860s granaries, horse-turned flour-mills, ovens and kitchens in the complex still produced free food for the poor, and the great cauldrons from its kitchen are now in the Islamic Museum in the Haram (see p 134).

At the east end of the 'Aqabat Takiyya, on the south side, is the **Maktab Bairam Jawish**, or the Madrasa Rasasiyya, of 1540. This is an early Ottoman structure which retains many Mamluk features. It was built as a school and dwelling house by the Amir Bairam Jawish, and named 'Rasasiyya' because of the use of lead to bond the masonry. The façade has red and cream coursed masonry, with a central course of basalt. A compact façade set in a moulded frame surrounds a shallow portal recess. The doorway has a joggled relieving arch; the façade has three grilled windows. The central and most interesting feature is the pointed arch with chevron mouldings above, which is typical of the early Ottoman style in Jerusalem, especially that of Sulaiman II. The arch contains a fluted conch. The main room on the upper floor, now a classroom in the present school, was a mosque and contains a mihrab with polychrome panelling. The dome is set on muqarnas pendentives.

After crossing the Tariq al-Wad, follow the street leading ahead to the east, the Tariq Bab al-Nazir or Ala al-Din; note on the corner to the left the fountain built by Sulaiman II in 1537, the Sabil Tariq Bab al-Nazir or Sabil al-Haram. A heavy cornice surmounts the elaborate pointed arch, with corner columns topped by muqarnas capitals, and inner small columns with grotesquely twisted shafts. At c 50m on the left is the Hasaniyya, the Madrasa of Husam al-Din al-Hasan, of 1434. He was the Superintendent of the Two Harams and a governor of Jerusalem. The rooms are all at first floor level in a rather plain façade. Near the east end is a window which retains some of its original gadrooned voussoirs and gives onto the assembly hall of the madrasa, containing a very fine marble dado and mihrab (not open).

Adjacent on the east side but at ground floor level, is the entrance to the **Ribat of Ala al-Din**, a hospice for poor pilgrims built 1267/68 by Ala al-Din Aydughdi al-Basir, a Mamluk of the Ayyubid Sultan al-Salih Ayyub, and then of Baybars. He became blind, and took the office of Superintendent of the Two Harams under Baybars and Qala'un. By 1537 he was referred to as a wali (saint) and a shaikh. The building had a lively history, for in Ottoman times it was given as dwelling to the Sudanese Muslims who served as Haram guards. Later it became a prison for those who had been sentenced (hence the modern name Habs al-Dam, Prison of Blood), until the prison was moved to the Russian Compound (see p 264) in Mandate times. It is now inhabited by the African community.

The façade is heterogeneous, including a doorway with an Ottoman lintel. On the east, the rectangular window of the founder's tomb chamber has its original iron grille. The interior (not open) was converted into a mosque for the African community in 1971.

Beside it to the east is the **Manjakiyya**, the madrasa (1361) of Manjak al-Yusufi an official of al-Nasir Muhammad who had a rather chequered career and died in Cairo in 1375. He did much building work in Cairo, Damascus and elsewhere as well as this madrasa in Jerusalem. Built partly above the West Portico of the Haram (see p 103), the Manjakiyya had reached a ruinous state early in the 20C; it was reconstructed in 1921/22 and now houses the Awqaf Department of Endowments and Islamic Affairs, which is entered by a modern portal from the north side of the gate chamber of the Bab al-Nazir. The original entrance is adjacent on the west. It has corner columns with muqarnas capitals and three tiers of muqarnas corbelling supporting the dome above.

The outer porch of the Haram gate, Bab al-Nazir, has a semicircular frontal arch rebuilt c 1204 but with traces of earlier springing which may be Umayyad. The inscription on the wooden door indicates that it was renewed c 1204. On the south side of the gate is the Wafa'iyya, the zawiya of the Abu'l-Wafa family, of 1380/81, much of which is possibly Ayyubid, a complex of probably pre-existing rooms bought by the family in the late 14C. The narrow frontage includes the shop in the outer gate porch, and the adjacent window and door. The upper part of the plain frontage is Ottoman.

Much of the south side of Tariq Bab al-Nazir is occupied by the **Ribat al-**

Mansuri, a pilgrim hospice built by the Sultan Qala'un in 1282/83 for poor Sufis and pilgrims. He also built a hospice and hospital in Hebron. Like the Ribat of Ala al-Din opposite, in Ottoman times the hospice housed the Sudanese Haram guards, then became a prison for those awaiting sentence (modern name Habs al-Ribat, the Prison Hospice). It housed the African community, but has been restored.

The long façade contains reused Crusader materials. Various sources refer to a Crusader church dedicated to St. Michael or to St. John the Evangelist in this area. According to Mujir al-Din, a Byzantine church was occupied by two madrasas to the west of the hospice (the Yunusiyya and the Jarakisiyya). It seems likely that a Crusader church in the vicinity may have provided *spolia* for Ayyubid and Mamluk construction work. The Mamluk work includes two fine windows at the east end of the ground floor. A wide pointed arch with red and cream voussoirs fronts the deep entrance porch with the founder's inscription at the rear. The pointed arch with chevron ornament and a rosette in the tympanum in the upper west façade is typical of the time of Sulaiman II.

Returning to the Tariq al-Wad, turn left to continue south. The next turning to the left is the twisting Tariq Bab al-Hadid, which leads to the Haram gate of the same name. It contains six more monuments of the Mamluk period. At c 45m on the right at a junction of the lane leading south to the Suq al-Qattanin, the southwest side is occupied by the entrance to the Hanbaliyya, the madrasa of Baidamur al-Khwarizmi, 1380. He was a Mamluk official who was several times imprisoned and finally arrested as implicated in a plot against Sultan Barquq. The complex, a spacious Mamluk complex with cells around a court with a fine iwan and mihrab is now occupied by small houses. The entrance portal with a pointed-arched recess, has benches, and the doorway has a monolithic lintel with a flat relieving arch of red and black joggled voussoirs.

Continuing almost to the Bab al-Hadid, where the lane ends, the left side of the lane is occupied by two Mamluk pilgrim hospices. The largest frontage is that of the **Jawhariyya madrasa and ribat** built by Jawhar al-Qunuqbayi in 1440. He was an Abyssinian eunuch who rose to power under Sultan al-Ashraf Barsbay as Treasurer, then as Steward of the Royal Harem under al-Malik al-Zahir Jaqmaq. His hospice and school is built on two levels, the upper extending east over the adjoining hospice and the west portico and gate of the Haram. The lower façade, including the founder's inscription above the door, was damaged before 1914; the building was further damaged by subsidence due to tunnelling in the sub-structure in 1971 (the Western Wall Tunnel, see p 91); and restored in 1982/83. It now houses the Department of Islamic Archaeology. The recessed entrance portal, with red and cream masonry framed by moulding, has two windows to the main hall on the right side. The most interesting parts of the remaining façade are those of the upper level to the east which contains three rectangular windows; that on the east is plain, the central and west windows have roundels of carved chevron work above them; the central window also has three tiers of muqarnas work at the top; the west window has an incised diaper-work frame. The assembly hall of the madrasa above the Haram gate and portico has been demolished, but above the gate porch a blocked window remains, with a pointed arch with chevron voussoirs and its original iron grille. The intervening ground floor façade adjacent to the gate is that of the Ribat Kurt, built 1293/94 by Sayf al-Din Kurt, a brave soldier and a good Amir of Sultans Lajin and al-Nasir

Muhammad, who died fighting the Mongols in 1299. This hospice is the oldest structure adjacent to the gate, and it may be that its foundation was the reason the gate was placed here. The gate (the Bab al-Hadid) and the twisted street, which is not on the alignment of the older city grid, may both belong to this period.

The south side of the street contains two other Mamluk foundations. Adjacent to the Haram is the Arghuniyya, the madrasa and tomb of Arghun al-Kamili, a former governor of Damascus, who completed the building in 1358. He was a court official who became the Master of the Robes as is indicated by the blazon on his inscription. The endowments for the madrasa include dues from near Krak des Chevaliers in Syria. The façade is symmetrical except for the entrance doorway to the Khatuniyya on the right. It has coursed red and cream masonry framed by a moulding and contains a tall entrance portal which has the founder's inscription running right round the recess with blazons showing a napkin in the middle of a shield with three fields. Above the lintel is a marble inlaid representation of a joggled relieving arch; and above, a frieze of joggling which extends around the façade. The windows on either side have the same delicate mouldings, and inlaid marble interlocking trefoils above. The east window, into the tomb chamber, has its original iron grille; the west window has been converted into a door.

On the west side is the simple pointed-arched entry to the Khatuniyya Madrasa of 1354–80.

On the west of the Khatuniyya portal is the façade of the **Muzhiriyya Madrasa** built by Abu Bakr b. Muzhir in 1480/81, a Mamluk official perhaps of a family from Nablus; it was later used as a domestic residence and is now rather ruinous. The façade has a tall portal in a framed red and cream panel. The trefoil-arched recess has eight tiers of muqarnas corbelling; above the door lintel is a string course with black and yellow joggling. To either side above is an identical pair of double windows with pointed horseshoe arches divided by a marble shaft. Below on the east side a fine pair of rectangular windows with grilles have four tiers of muqarnas work above and greyish marble lintels. The relieving arches above the lintels have light arabesque tracery on alternate yellow stone voussoirs, also to be seen two courses above.

Suq al-Qattanin

Returning to the Tariq al-Wad, turn left and continue south for c 65m; on the left is the entrance to the *Suq al-Qattanin (the Market of the Cotton Merchants). This is a splendid Mamluk bazaar completed in 1336/37, built by Tankiz al-Nasiri for the Sultan al-Nasir Muhammad. Extensively restored by the Awqaf in 1974. As well as a long covered market street with shops on either side and fine gates at both ends, there are living quarters above the shops, two bath houses and a caravanserai. It is an interesting place to stop for a glass of tea or some coffee.

The west portal has a pointed-arched recess containing a flat lintel with seven interlocking voussoirs, with relieving arch and circular oculus in the tympanum. The four lower courses of masonry may be earlier Crusader work. It is a much less ornate gate than that at the east end (for which see p 104). Inside, the covered street is 95m long, with vaulted roof and 30 pairs of side bays most of which contain shops on the ground floor and living or storage space above. The west end shows different construction to the east and may originally have been a Crusader market extended to the east by Tankiz. On the north exterior side, approached by stairs from bay 16, is a corridor providing access to the living accommodation. On the ground floor to the north of bays 6–10 is a vaulted hall which may have been part of a caravanserai (the Khan al-Qattanin) founded by Zaynab al-Khassakiyya, the wife of Sultan Inal (1453–61). To the northeast is the Khatuniyya Madrasa (see above).

Steps at bay 29 lead up to the elaborate gate at the Haram end of the suq, which has two inscriptions on the west face of the original wooden doors.

There are numerous structures on the south side of the suq which are an integral part of the layout. Leading to the south off bay 21 is an entrance to the Ablutions Place of the Haram built by al-'Adil in 1193 (see p 104). The south side of the adjacent bays 20 to 17 contain the frontage (a blocked wide porch) of the **Hammam al-Shifa'**, a bath house built by 1330 with a curious alignment which may indicate it had an older predecessor. It is built on the traditional Roman-Byzantine bath house model, with the entrance leading to a changing room, and cold, warm and hot rooms served by a furnace or boiler. The bathing rooms are lit by domes with small glazed shafts. The main changing room has a marble floor, and a central octagonal oculus above a tank with a fountain made from a Byzantine basket capital which still retains its CHI-RHO monogram. In the northwest of the bath house a well-shaft descends through accumulated debris for 26m to a water source, with a rock-cut passage to a deeper pool. This rather poor and bad-tasting source of water was investigated in the 19C. The water seeps from a subterranean source in the Tyropoeon Valley.

A broad arch at the south side of bays 8–9 leads to the **Khan Tankiz**, a caravanserai. In the early 20C the khan contained a flour mill, and was a farm in the 1960s. It is now very ruinous. A wide passage flanked by four bays (shops) leads to the doorway, which is 2.7m wide with a monolithic lintel and a relieving arch containing three very large stones. The founder's inscription is carved on the keystone of the relieving arch, on the lintel and on the corbels which support it. The blazon of Tankiz is carved on the lintel and the corbels, showing a cup on a circular field. Inside little remains of the original squarish court.

Immediately adjacent to bays 1–3 at the west end is the **Hammam al-'Ain**, built before 1330. Leaving the suq, turn left and the bath house entrance is in the Tariq al-Wad. It was restored by the Department of Islamic Archaeology in 1984. A fairly modern porch and steps lead down to the changing room roofed by a dome on pendentives. It also has a central tank with fountain, and raised alcoves around the walls for changing. It was originally paved with coloured marble, only a small fragment of which survives in a west subsidiary room of the warm room. A large tank in the southwest of the bath house served the fountain against the outer wall of the bath house, the Sabil Tariq al-Wad, built by Sulaiman II in 1536. This can be seen on the left about 20m south of the bath house entrance. A pointed-arched recess with archivolt supported by built columns and acanthus-style capitals has three tiers of muqarnas corbelling in the semi-dome, and the founder's inscription beneath. An ancient sarcophagus with three roundels, probably dating to the 1C AD, has been employed as the water trough.

Almost opposite the entrance to the Suq al-Qattanin, 'Aqabat al-Khalidiyya leads west. At c 20m on the right a blacksmith's workshop occupies a well-preserved 12C Crusader church, uncertainly identified as that of St. Julian or of St. John the

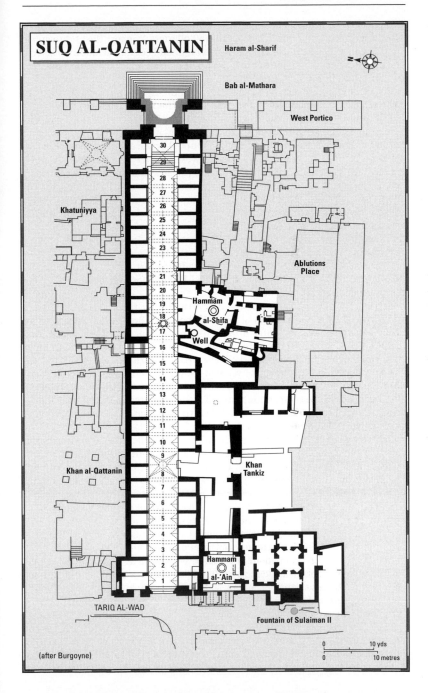

SUQ AL-QATTANIN

Haram al-Sharif

Bab al-Mathara

West Portico

Khatuniyya

Ablutions Place

Hammam al-Shifa

Well

Khan al-Qattanin

Khan Tankiz

Hammam al-'Ain

TARIQ AL-WAD

Fountain of Sulaiman II

0   10 yds
0   10 metres

(after Burgoyne)

Evangelist. A three-aisled basilica with three apses, it has two rows of three piers, all with cornice mouldings. These, with wall pilasters, support the groin-vaulted roof. The north and central apses are preserved, and contain windows. The central apse has a rectangular exterior chevet. The plan is similar to those of St. Mary of the Latins and St. Mary the Great in the Muristan (see Jerusalem, section 4).

Continuing to the west, passing a turning to the right, and at c 120m a turning to the left, we arrive at the Tariq al-Qirimi (Hakkari St). In the angle on the left is the **Madrasa al-Lu'lu'iyya** founded in 1373/74 by Badr al-Din Lu'lu' Ghazi, a freedman of Sultan al-Ashraf (whose zawiya is now a mosque adjacent to the Damascus Gate). The façade, now disrupted by the addition of modern buttresses, occupies approximately the southwest quarter of the street. It had a rather fine if severe frontage, with both the upper and lower storeys defined by cornices. Part of the building, and the lower three courses of the façade, are older than the madrasa. The main portal, with simple pointed-arched recess, has red and cream voussoirs and employs reused marble imposts. The upper storey contains a fine reception hall which may have formed part of the residence of the founder. In 1854 the madrasa was called the 'German Inn'. The lower floor was restored in 1983 and the upper floor is a private dwelling.

Adjacent on the north is the Madrasa Badriyya, an Ayyubid foundation of 1213/14, built by Badr al-Din Muhammad al-Hakkari for the Shafi'i sect. A plain entrance leads to an open court.

Continuing north just beyond the Badriyya and on the opposite side of the road is the Zawiya al-Qirimiyya. It was built before 1386 by an amir who was a disciple of the ascetic Shafi'i Shaikh Shams al-Din Muhammad al-Qirimi (1321–86) who, with some of his descendants, was buried here. The frontage has been much rebuilt and buttressed. The shallow entrance recess with pointed horseshoe arch has a doorway of red and cream masonry with carved borders; above the lintel are joggled voussoirs with a simple but attractive pattern and a small window in the tympanum. The hall inside has now been converted into a mosque; partitioned off on the north side is the founder's tomb chamber which is lit by two grilled windows from the street.

Returning down the street past the Lu'lu'iyya, turn left and take the turning on the right which leads south to the Tariq Bab al-Silsila; turn right into this main street and walk almost to the main bazaar. At c 55m on the right an entrance leads into the **Khan al-Sultan* or al-Wakala, a Crusader caravanserai restored in 1386/87 by Sultan Barquq, the revenues from which then went to the upkeep of the Haram. This is a remarkably preserved dependency of the great bazaars to the west, which illustrates further the role of Jerusalem as a prosperous medieval commercial centre under the earlier Mamluks. It was a place to which merchants brought goods for retail distribution, and was probably intended in particular for valuable goods, to serve as a bonded warehouse where taxes would be levied (perhaps a system established by Frederick II, c 1229). It provided lodgings for merchants and pilgrims on the upper floor, stabling for animals, and storage space for goods on the ground floor. The stable was used for donkeys until recently, and the complex now contains small industrial workshops.

The entrance passage leads past shops (and public toilets), and to the left a covered market street, which are at least as early as the Crusader period. On the north side it leads to a market hall, an almost intact Crusader edifice with splendid corbelled cornices. Two tiers of cells on either side are reached by galleries. In the middle of the west side is the entrance to the stable. To the north is a court-yard complex added by Barquq. Some of the cells on the east and central west sides are Mamluk, but most of the remainder are later additions. Original stair-cases in the southwest and southeast corners led up to the upper floor, parts of which are Ottoman. The inscription on the north wall records a fountain of 1763/64 which no longer exists.

Tariq Bab al-Silsila

Leaving the Khan al-Sultan, turn left and begin a walk down the full length of the Tariq Bab al-Silsila. This is one of the main streets of the city, which is partly founded on the great Hasmonean/Herodian/Mamluk vaulted causeway which crossed the deep Tyropoeon Valley, and linked the Upper City to the Temple Platform. It was one of the principal cross streets of the Hadrianic city, the Street of the Temple in Crusader times, and remains one of the main links between the east and west sides of the town.

The street is partly vaulted. At c 110m on the southeast corner of the first turning to the right (A. Harat Maydan or H. Misgav Ladakh St), is the Mamluk **Tashtamuriyya**, established by Sayf al-Din Tashtamur in 1382/83. At the peak of his career he was the First Secretary of State of Sultan Sha'ban (1370–77), but later was permitted to resign and live in Jerusalem, where he built this combined residence, tomb and religious school with charitable adjuncts, cultivated his interest in religious sciences, poetry and music, died, and was buried in the tomb chamber on the ground floor. The main façade on Tariq Bab al-Silsila has an elaborate portal in a frame just west of centre. It has a trefoil recess with muqarnas hood; below is a joggled string course, and a doorway set in red and cream coursed masonry flanked by benches. To the right is the façade of the large domed tomb chamber. Here two fine rectangular windows with iron grilles, fine marble mosaic paving on the sills, and monolithic lintels beneath the founder's inscription set in a panel bordered by joggled motifs, are also enclosed within a moulding. The decoration of the windows is designed to draw attention to them as the site of readings from the Koran. Inside the tomb chamber are two cenotaphs, probably those of the founder and his son. There is a mihrab in the south wall; and a fine door with the original decorative bronze knockers leads from the vestibule on the east side.

At the west end of the façade is a fountain, and above it a room built partly on projecting brackets which was intended as a place for the care and teaching of orphans. The east side of the frontage contains three shops on the ground floor, possibly part of a pre-existing market. The reception hall and roof court were built on the top floor, and residential quarters occupied the middle floor. Parts of the building are in private occupation.

Opposite the Tashtamuriyya are the remains of Crusader vaulted market halls containing limestone columns with simple capitals. The upper storey is probably Ottoman, and a wooden oriel window obscures an arch with gadrooned voussoirs. On the east side of the halls, dating to sometime after 1352, is **al-Kilaniyya**, the tomb of Jamal al-Din Pahlavan (who came from Gilan in the Caspian area). The tomb complex, though not the tomb chamber itself, was remodelled for domestic use and became a family sinecure in the 18C. The symmetrical façade of the Kilaniyya is topped by a rectangular pediment and cavetto moulding. The recessed entrance portal has a three-tiered muqarnas hood, with a set of three windows above. To either side are pairs of rectangular windows (those on the east are blocked) set in moulded frames. The windows and door have an undercut relieving course above the lintels, and blank panels above were perhaps originally intended for an inscription. Above each is a single window with muqarnas hood, and each of the three units of the façade is topped by a dome. The original iron-plated wooden doors remain, as do the original grilles and shutters on the west windows.

Still on the north side of the street, and to the east of the Kilaniyya, is **al-Taziya**, the memorial madrasa of Sayf al-Din Taz, c 1361. He was a Mamluk official (Cup-bearer) of the Sultan al-Nasir Muhammad, whose career ended miserably: after being blinded, he died and was buried in Damascus. It has a modest façade, with a large rectangular window with red and cream masonry, grille, and monolithic lintel with a dedicatory inscription which includes the founder's blazon of a cup in a circular shield at either end. There is joggled panelling above. On the upper floor is a typical Ottoman oriel timber window set in the Mamluk façade with small Mamluk windows on either side. The building had two tomb chambers on the ground floor; the remaining chambers seem to have been residential, including a private bath house. It was probably occupied by the descendants of Taz. Much of the upper floor is 18C Ottoman. The ground floor tomb chambers now contain a shop with raised floor level.

Opposite the Taziya, on the south side of the street at the corner with 'Aqabat Abu Madyan, is the **Turba (Tomb) of Baraka Khan**, built between 1265 and 1280, extended in 1390 and now the Khalidi Library. Only the façade remains, the interior having been almost completely rebuilt in the 19C. Its principal feature is a remarkable early Mamluk doorway built in Romanesque style. Baraka Khan was one of the four chiefs of the Khwarizmian bands invading Syria and Palestine in the 1230–40s, whose power ended in a battle south of Homs in 1246, following which it was said Baraka Khan's head was displayed on the citadel gate at Aleppo. The tomb was built sometime after his death by a member of his family. He was married to a half-sister of an Ayyubid Sultan, his daughter married the Mamluk Sultan Baybars I, and a grandson became Sultan al-Sa'id Nasir al-Din Baraka. A son of Baraka Khan died in Damascus in 1279, and his body was transferred to Jerusalem in 1280 and buried here with his father.

The building has a complex history. The lowest projecting courses may be part of the vaults of the 8C–11C reconstruction of the ancient causeway. The three tallest pointed blocked arches visible in the east part of the façade may be the remains of early 13C Crusader shops, bought in the later 13C by the family of Baraka Khan. At this stage the fine door to a tomb chamber on the west end was added. It has outer gadrooned voussoirs and an inner chevron-decorated arch. The hoodmoulds and imposts appear to be Mamluk. The doorway was converted into a window to the present library by 1920. In 1390 extensive alterations were made, the high Crusader arches were blocked, and a typical Mamluk doorway and window were constructed inside them. The portal has a pointed horseshoe arch, and had imitation gadrooned decoration to copy the door to the west. The door jambs are of red and cream masonry. A niche on the right side contains a drinking trough and it also was gadrooned. The window in the arcade to the west is very ornate, with red and cream masonry; the lintel has an inscription and two blazons (perhaps the tribal badge of the family) with polychrome marble veneer above. The inscription in the tympanum recording the burial of Baraka Khan is not in situ, and above is an oculus. The Khalidi library of some 12,000 books and manuscripts was created here in 1900, with a reading room on the west side of a courtyard.

A few metres further east is the Dar al-Qur'an al-Sallamiyya, the Koran School of Siraj al-Din Umar al-Sallami, endowed in 1360, in a 13C building. A single barrel-vaulted chamber was blocked in the 13C, leaving a small window. A later door was added to the right. It became a Koran school in 1360, and has been a *waqf* of the Khalidi family since 1788/89. The upper two storeys are later additions; the stairs across the frontage were added in 1811 and replaced in 1983. The ground floor was used c 1836 for the burial of a Shaikh al-Khalidi.

Opposite, on the north side of the street and on the west side of the steps (Daraj al-'Ain or the Aqueduct Steps) descending to the Tariq al-Wad is the Tomb of Baybars al-Jaliq, the **Jaliqiyya**, dating to 1307. He was a Mamluk of the Ayyubid Sultan al-Malik al-Salih Ayyub, one of the 'men of the wardrobe', who was an amir under Baybars, fought against the Mongols in the battle of Homs in 1281, and died outside Ramla. The building consists of a domed tomb chamber at the corner, with an antechamber to the north originally entered from the Daraj al-'Ain (now blocked).

The Jaliqiyya stands on earlier foundations which rest on the vaults of the ancient causeway. On the spandrel of the east arch of the south façade is an inscription recording Sultan Qa'it Bay's restoration of the Haram aqueduct which ran across the causeway. The south façade of the Jaliqiyya has a window giving onto the tomb chamber, with inscription above. The chamber contains a cenotaph of the founder(?), and another smaller one of an unknown person. The upper storey is Ottoman.

Continuing east towards the Bab al-Silsila, at c 45m on the left is the **Turba of Turkan Khatun**, of 1352/53, another lady about whom little is known, but perhaps again, like Lady Tunshuq (see p 150), of eastern Islamic origin. The tomb contains two chambers: that on the street is the original tomb, but when the room was employed for domestic uses the cenotaph was moved to the north. The façade is elaborately carved. The window jambs are of alternate blocks of red and cream masonry, but the rest of the masonry is plain limestone. Above each of the window lintels is a large elaborately carved stone, with slight undercutting to relieve pressure on the lintel. The carving has a pattern of stars and palmettes. Another recessed carved panel sits above each window, and a smaller one on the central pier. A later parapet obscures the dome, which is set on an octagonal drum with eight pointed recesses, four containing windows. The interior of the tomb chamber also has panels of low relief carving in the tympana. The original entrance was on the west side. When it was blocked, the west window was converted into a door.

At c 35m further east we arrive at the little courtyard before the Bab al-Silsila. On the entrance corner on the north side is al-Sa'diyya, the **tomb of Sa'd al-Din Mas'ud**, Chamberlain in Damascus in the time of al-Nasir Muhammad. It was endowed in 1311. The modern name is the Dar al-Khalidi. It has a tomb chamber on the east with two windows with grilles, a vaulted hall on the west, and an entrance between them with an early muqarnas portal. The doorway is set in red and brownish coursed masonry. Above the door is a frieze of inlaid strapwork, in which the inlay seems to be of mortar coloured red with crushed pottery, and black with charcoal.

As you enter the little square, on your left against the east wall of the Sa'diyya is an ornate Ottoman fountain (Sabil Bab al-Silsila) installed by Sulaiman II in 1537. It is built with much reused Crusader stonework, including a fine wheel window which may have come from a nearby church; the trough below also has a fine Crusader frieze. An earlier paving level is also exposed. On the north side of the square, and extending over the Sa'diyya, is the Ribat al-Nisa, a Women's

Columns at the Bab al-Sakina, north side

Hospice endowed in 1330, which was founded by the Amir Tankiz. It has a high trefoil-arched portal recess.

Tucked away in the east corner of the north wall is the entrance to the **Baladiyya**, the funerary madrasa of Manklibugha al-Ahmadi, c 1380. It is now partly incorporated in the Aqsa Library, and partly privately occupied. The present small door is not the original entrance to the complex, which lay c 3.23m to the north. The inscription (not in situ) above the door records the mausoleum of Manklibugha, but he may not be buried here. Another inscription higher up over three windows is that recording the first building stage of the Ashrafiyya in 1470 (see p 105). A Crusader church of St. Giles may have stood on the site. The sculpture still ornamenting the fountain on the west side of the square and the gate on the east side could have come from such a church. This is the important double gate, the Bab al-Sakina and Bab al-Silsila, the Gate of the Chain, see p 107.

On the south side of the gate is one of the most important of the buildings of medieval Jerusalem, **al-Tankiziyya**, the madrasa and khanqah of Tankiz al-Nasiri, of 1328/29.

History of the Tankiziyya

The Tankiziyya is built on the earlier substructures associated with the ancient causeway beneath it, of Herodian, Roman, Umayyad and later date. Tankiz was a Mamluk slave who rose to prominence under al-Nasir Muhammad, became the governor of Damascus in 1312, and effective ruler of all Syria until he fell from power in 1340, was imprisoned and put to death in Alexandria. Tankiz was eventually buried in Damascus in 1343. He is known to have carried out various works in Damascus and Jerusalem (see above, Suq al-Qattanin). The building was used as a tribunal in the time of Sultan Qa'it Bay, becoming the regular seat of the Qadi in 1483. Probably during the 19C it became a law court (al-Mahkama), continuing to be used as such during the early years of the Mandate period, and then became the residence of the head of the Supreme Muslim Council, Amin al-Husaini. Restorations were carried out in the 1920s. Since 1967 it has been an Israeli army post. Various traditions have clung to this area over the centuries. The ancient Council Chamber of the Sanhedrin (Jewish religious court) was located somewhere in the vicinity. It may have been this recollection which led to the location of the Byzantine Church of the Holy Wisdom, or St. Sophia, on the site of the Praetorium, (linked with the condemnation of Jesus by the Jewish High Priests and elders of the Sanhedrin) on an unidentified site in the Tyropoeon Valley between the 4C and the 6C. The tradition had disappeared by the 12C, and eventually in medieval times the Praetorium was identified with the site of the Antonia (see above). Whether such traditions influenced the choice of the Tankiziyya as a law court is unclear, and latterly it has been suggested that the site of the Byzantine 'Praetorium' lay at the Palatial Building excavated beneath the Yeshivat HaKotel in the Jewish Quarter (see p 205).

Only the façades of the Tankiziyya can be viewed, as the building is not open to visitors. The main feature of the façade is the portal which abuts the Ayyubid outer arch of the Bab al-Silsila. The portal has three tiers of muqarnas work in a deep recess, supporting a pointed semi-dome with chevron fluting. The doorway has a monolithic lintel, with joggled inlay above. The founder's inscription runs right round the recess in the course above, and contains three depictions of the founder's blazon, a chalice on a circular field, one above the door, the others on either side of the recess. Above is another joggled course. The portal has close parallels with that of the mosque built by Tankiz in Damascus. The four shops to the west (or right) of the entrance are part of the original endowment.

The ground floor interior contains a cruciform madrasa with four iwans, with central octagonal oculus. Under the oculus in the court is an octagonal stone basin with fountain, in former times supplied from the aqueduct. The mihrab has marble panelling probably laid by Syrian craftsmen and contains two Crusader columns and capitals, and Damascus glass mosaic in the conch. A splendid enamelled glass lamp inscribed 'madrasa of Tankiz' is now in the Islamic Museum. The south elevation of the building can be seen from the plaza at the Western Wall.

You can return through the city either to the Damascus or Jaffa Gates, or exit to the south by the Dung Gate.

4 • The Christian Quarter

The northwest quarter of the Old City is occupied by the Christian communities, excluding the Armenians who have their own quarter to the southwest (see Jerusalem, section 6). It covers c 18 hectares. The Christian community expanded during the Byzantine and Crusader periods, but was greatly reduced in 1187 when the Latin Christians either paid ransom to leave, or went into slavery. A small community remained, mainly Orthodox and Jacobite (a secessionist Orthodox group, see p 195), in the vicinity of the Church of the Holy Sepulchre and a few other Christian monuments. Today the quarter is bounded on the east by Khan al-Zait St (on the line of the Byzantine *cardo maximus*, the main north–south road) and on the south by David St (the old *decumanus*, east–west). This area was probably not inside the city until it was rebuilt as Aelia Capitolina (135).

The principal points of interest are the Church of the Holy Sepulchre, the markets, the Pool of the Patriarch's Bath, the Church of St. John the Baptist, and the Muristan. Much of the quarter is occupied by patriarchates, schools, churches, hospices and convents belonging to the various Greek and Latin communities. David St and Christian Quarter St are the main shopping streets for tourists and specialise in local embroidery, glass, pottery, olive-wood carving, antiquities and copies of antiquities. The food-selling areas are along the main streets between

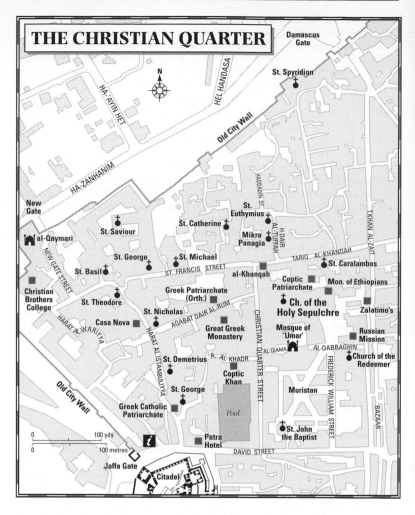

THE CHRISTIAN QUARTER

Damascus Gate

HEL HANDASA

HA-'AYIN HET

HA-ZANHANIM

Old City Wall

St. Spyridion

New Gate

al-Qaymari

St. Saviour

St. Catherine

St. Euthymius

Mikra Panagia

H.DAIR AL-TUFAH

HADDADIN ST.

AL-DAIR

TKHAN AL-ZAIT

St. George

St. Michael

ST. FRANCIS STREET

TARIQ AL-KHANQAH

St. Caralambos

St. Basil

al-Khanqah

Coptic Patriarchate

Mon. of Ethiopians

NEW GATE STREET

Christian Brothers College

St. Theodore

Greek Patriarchate (Orth.)

Ch. of the Holy Sepulchre

Zalatimo's

HARAT AL-WARIYA

Casa Nova

St. Nicholas

AQABAT DAIR AL-RUM

Great Greek Monastery

Mosque of 'Umar

Russian Mission

CHRISTIAN QUARTER STREET

AL-QIAMA

AL-DABBAGHIN

Church of the Redeemer

HARAT AL ISTANBULIYA

St. Demetrius

A. AL KHADR

Coptic Khan

FREDERICK WILLIAM STREET

BAZAAR

Old City Wall

St. George

Greek Catholic Patriarchate

Pool

Muristan

0   100 yds

0   100 metres

Petra Hotel

St. John the Baptist

DAVID STREET

Jaffa Gate

Citadel

the Christian and Muslim Quarters: Khan Al-Zait St with mixed goods, fruit and vegetables, confectionery, spices, nuts and herbs; the three great central markets where meat, hardware, metal and textiles are sold in the former Crusader markets built over the Byzantine *cardo maximus*. A walk here provides an insight into the city and its people. Country people also bring their produce to sell along the streets leading from the Damascus Gate to the Muristan. Nearly always crowded, the shallow stepped streets, graded for pedestrians and for loaded baggage animals, are partly roofed to protect people and goods from the hot sun and winter rain. Even narrower and often steeper, more private streets lead away from them to the dwellings.

As you enter the Old City by the Jaffa Gate, the **Tourist Information Centre** is located a few metres inside on the left. A few metres further is the Franciscan book shop. On the right is the Citadel (Jerusalem, section 5). Information on times of services at the various churches can be had from the **Christian Information Centre** opposite the Jaffa Gate, in Armenian Patriarchate Rd (open 08.30–13.00; closed Sun). ✉ http://198.62.75.1/www1/ofm/cic/CICmain.html.

Continuing straight ahead to the beginning of David St, on the left is the Petra Hostel. The best view of the ***Pool of the Patriarch's Bath** (A. Birkat Hammam al-Batrak), or the Pool of Hezekiah, can usually be obtained from the roof here for a small payment.

History of the Pool

The original date of the open pool has not been properly established, although tradition ascribes it to Hezekiah (king of Judah 727–698 BC). Quarries of the 7C BC existed in this area, and it is possible that a rain-fed pool existed from that time, just north of the line of the 8C–7C city wall. It could also be part of a Hasmonean or Herodian quarry or water storage system. It is probably the pool Josephus (War V:468) calls the Amygdalon or Tower Pool, where Titus built siege ramps in AD 70. It was probably connected with the Upper Aqueduct from Solomon's Pools, constructed by the Tenth Roman Legion to provide water for the Legionary camp in Jerusalem after AD 70. Thereafter the pool was in virtually continuous use. Charters of 1137 and 1167 indicate that the pool then belonged to the Latin Patriarch, whose palace lay adjacent to the Church of the Holy Sepulchre. The water was used by him and the occupants of neighbouring houses, who paid him for the water. Salah al-Din transferred these rights to the mosque which he founded in the Patriarch's palace after 1187. In more recent times it was fed by a channel from the Mamilla Pool to the west, and the waters were used for the bath house to the east in Christian Quarter St. The pool now contains water only after rain when it is a splendid sight; at other times it is unsightly due to the rubbish which almost fills it.

Viewed from above, the pool has changed little in appearance since the 19C. The large slightly irregular rectangle (nearly 72m x 44m and c 7m deep) is surrounded by houses. The north side is occupied by the plain two-storey façade of the Coptic Khan, behind which rise the truncated bell tower and the grey dome of the Church of the Holy Sepulchre, one of the few places from which a good prospect of these structures can be obtained. On the east is a range of domed buildings characteristic of Jerusalem with rooms jutting out over the pool. Above them is a fine view over the east side of the Old City, with the tower of the Church of the Redeemer to the northeast, and to the east, in the foreground the silver dome of the Church of St. John the Baptist (see below), in the distance the golden Dome of the Rock (see Jerusalem, section 2) and the Mount of Olives.

Continuing down David St with its many small shops, turn left into Christian Quarter St and almost immediately on the right is the entrance to the little courtyard containing the Greek Orthodox ***Church of St. John the Baptist** or Prodromos, the Forerunner, and adjacent monastery (see **no. 3** on plan of the Muristan).

History of the Church of St. John the Baptist

St. John the Baptist was beheaded at Machaerus in Transjordan by order of Herod Antipas (Mark 6:28); his followers were permitted to remove his body for burial, which traditionally took place at Samaria-Sebastiya. This tomb was pillaged by pagans in 362, but some relics were rescued and sent to various other cities, including Jerusalem (to a 4C monastery on the Mount of Olives). Another story says the head was sent to the palace of Herod Antipas in Jerusalem. There is no 4C tradition of a church of St. John the Baptist in Jerusalem, but the presence of the relics may account for the construction of a church on this spot in the 5C, most likely in the time of the empress Eudocia c 450–60. The existence of such a church is noted c 500. The present crypt and foundations date to the 5C and the door on the south side, and the old cisterns, suggest there may have been a monastery attached. It was destroyed, and many Christians massacred, in the Persian attack of 614. It was rebuilt by St. John Almoner (Eleimon), Patriarch of Alexandria, who is particularly commemorated for the aid he rendered to the Christian community of Jerusalem after the Persian devastations. After the Crusader conquest the church became the chapel of the Order of the Hospital of St. John of Jerusalem.

The crypt of the present church seems to have been been filled with debris and largely abandoned in 1187, after which the upper storey only (the present church) remained in use probably served by the Greek Orthodox. By 1347, according to the pilgrim Nicolas of Poggibonsi, there was a tradition that this church was the site of the house, not of Zechariah the father of St. John the Baptist, but of Zebedee, father of St. John the Evangelist. In 1483 Felix Faber notes there was a mosque near the Church of the House of Zebedee, and in 1596 Amico relates that the upper church of Prodromos was a mosque. However, it certainly came back into Greek ownership at this period, and in 1660 a large hospice for Christian pilgrims was built adjacent. In 1674 a Latin claim that the church had been dedicated to St. John the Evangelist was rejected.

The crypt was cleared out in the 19C and a splendid reliquary (now in the Greek Orthodox Patriarchate Museum, see below) was discovered hidden in the masonry of the altar. The excavations revealed various decorative architectural fragments of Byzantine and Crusader origin.

A pleasant small courtyard with trees and with a balcony at an upper level greets the visitor. If the church is locked, you will need to find the priest. The façade has a small modern belfry, and various fragments of reused frieze and pilaster built into it. Faint inscriptions can be seen on the façade and belfry. The present church is of the 11C with renovations, and is a trefoil shape with three apses built to north, east and south of a central square (5.56m) where four pillars or piers support the dome. The drum contains eight windows; the exterior of the high dome is painted silver. The plan is based on the 5C church, which is partly visible in the crypt, lying c 6.5m below the modern road level. The approach to it is from the south, where steps descend to the narthex. In the crypt the central area is roofed by groined vaulting, and the side apses have been much rebuilt. The wrought-iron grille over the altar may be 12C. The exterior east side of the church may be seen from the central square in the Muristan, including the modern window cut in the upper wall of the east apse.

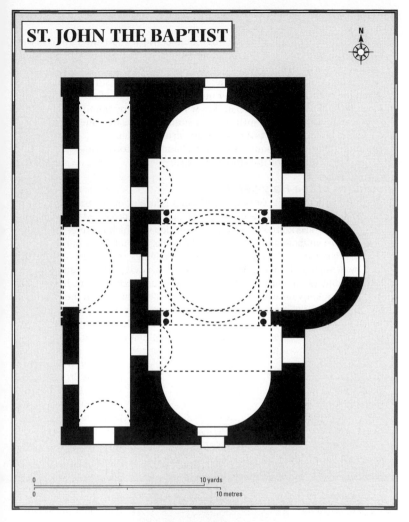

ST. JOHN THE BAPTIST

N

0   10 yards
0   10 metres

Continuing along Christian Quarter St, 90m to the north on the right a covered street, the Qantarat al-Qiama, leads down to the Church of the Holy Sepulchre. You descend the steps, past shops selling candles, incense, olive wood and pictures as suitable mementos of a visit to the holy places, and immediately ahead is the entrance to the so-called **Mosque of Umar**, originally the Mosque of Afdal Ali, in Ottoman times of Umar b. al-Khattab. This is a place of prayer for Muslims rather than a tourist site, but the history of the mosque is of interest. It was built in 1193 by Afdal Ali, the son of Salah al-Din, on the northwest corner of the property of the Knights of St. John. The popular name derives from the story that in 638 the Caliph Umar went outside the Church of the Holy Sepulchre to pray: in fact he went to the entrance portico at the east end of the church and a 10C/11C mosque later marked that site, which Christians were forbidden to enter.

The outer entrance to the mosque was rebuilt between 1839 and 1861. On the east side of the courtyard is a tall minaret rebuilt before 1465. This has a Syrian-type square tower with shaft divided by mouldings into three storeys. The base contains much Crusader masonry, some of which may be in situ remains of the 12C Hospital of the Knights (see **no. 4** on Muristan plan). The first storey has slit windows set in pointed horseshoe arches with Koranic inscriptions on the tympana. Above the one on the south side is a sundial. Above the muezzin's gallery an octagonal lantern supports a small round drum and dome.

Continuing past the mosque, a sharp left and right turn brings you to the courtyard of the Church of the Holy Sepulchre.

The church of the Holy Sepulchre

This is the focal point of the Christian church. It is located on the traditional sites of the Crucifixion, burial and Resurrection of Christ. First dedicated in 335, it has had a dramatic and continuous history, illustration of which is preserved in the fabric of the present building. Despite its great dome, the building is hardly distinguishable architecturally among the massed buildings of the city around it. Divided ownership and the continuous stream of services, pilgrims and tourists make this a difficult building for the hasty visitor to appreciate. It is, however, a church which greatly rewards time given to it. Deeply imbued with the weight of its own history, and above all by the faith of the millions of pilgrims who have prayed at and venerated this site for more than 16 centuries, the church is one of the great monuments of Jerusalem despite the loss of many of its ancient glories.

The roof of the Church of the Holy Sepulchre, from the east

A major restoration of the church was carried out from 1959, which, in removing partitions as well as performing vital structural repairs, revealed the church as a coherent monument of the 12C. Many of these partitions have since been reintroduced, but the recent restoration of the great dome permits more light to enter.

- The church is open 04.00–20.00; 04.00–21.00 in high summer; 04.00–19.00 in winter. Visitors of both sexes should wear modest dress. A list of the times and dates of the services and the principal ceremonies during the Easter period and at other times is usually available from the Christian Information Centre (see p 163).

History

Archaeological investigations have shown that this site was outside the city until the Roman Aelia Capitolina was built in the 2C. The location is c 230m north of the line of the First North Wall of the city, and perhaps 120m west of the line of the Second North Wall (although the position of this is uncertain). The earliest remains found beneath the church seem to be quarrying and tombs of the 8C–6C BC and the 1C AD on a rocky hillside on which 2C buildings of Aelia Capitolina were built. It is therefore possible that it could have been the Place of the Skull (Golgotha) used c AD 30 for the Crucifixion and burial of Jesus as described in the Gospels (Matt. 27:32–3; 28:11; John 19:17, 41–42), when Joseph of Arimathea gave his nearby tomb for the burial. All the closest companions and followers of Jesus saw the site in a garden close outside the city, so there is the basis for the development of a positive tradition. This lends weight to the early (4C) tradition which maintained that the first Christians immediately following the death of Jesus venerated the site of his tomb on this spot. The tradition is said to have been sufficiently strong to survive the turbulent events which intervened, perhaps partly due to an oral tradition of a continuous succession of bishops in Jerusalem beginning with St. James the Less (who was martyred c AD 62). These events included the departure of the Christian population of Jerusalem to Pella in the Jordan Valley c AD 66 and the destruction of Jerusalem in AD 70. The site was built over by Hadrian in 135. Following the departure of the Romans in 324 and inclusion of Palestine within the Eastern Roman Empire, the tradition provided sufficient basis for the Roman building to be torn down in 326 in the search for the tomb buried beneath it. The description of the search and the successful outcome are given by Bishop Eusebius of Caesarea in his *Life of Constantine* (c 337–40). The rock-cut tomb was found in 326/27, where the tradition had dictated, by Bishop Makarios of Jerusalem, the direct episcopal successor of St. James the Less.

The Emperor Constantine gave orders for the building of a great church, and the basilica or Martyrium at Golgotha was dedicated on 17 September 335. It is thought that the great Rotunda of Constantine over the Tomb itself took longer to complete and was not finished until sometime after 340. A great deal of rock had to be quarried and levelled, to leave the tomb standing free of its original hillside. At first the Tomb was covered by a small columned edicule in a court surrounded by porticoes. Eusebius does not record the story that Empress Helena, the mother of Constantine, discovered the fragments of the True Cross in a cistern adjacent to the rock of the Crucifixion. This tradition is first mentioned c 351.

The Church of Constantine This was much the largest church to stand on the site and its plan has been restored from fragments still existing in the present structure and in adjoining buildings. It consisted of two main elements: the Basilica of Constantine, then also called the Martyrium or place of witness, marking the site of the Crucifixion; and the Rotunda over the Tomb which was called the Anastasis or Church of the Resurrection. Between and around the two main buildings were courts and subsidiary buildings. Descriptions of the church and its services have survived in the accounts of the Pilgrim of Bordeaux (333) and Egeria (384).

The basilica itself was entered from the east from the *cardo maximus* by a propylaeum with three doorways. This led to a large, slightly irregular atrium with porticoes and exedra; thence by three or five doors to the basilica itself which was oriented west towards the Tomb. It was a five-aisled church, the central aisle being the widest. The lateral aisles contained an upper and lower gallery, supported by large columns in the front row with square pillars in the back row. The height of the roof of the central aisle was perhaps 22m with clerestory windows. The apse at the west end is described as having 12 columns capped by huge silver urns. According to Eusebius, the exterior was covered with fine polished stone, the interior with multi-coloured marble. The basilica had a lead roof, and inside the coffered ceiling was covered with brilliant gold which sparkled and 'which, like some great ocean, covered the whole basilica with its endless swell'.

The north and east walls of the basilica, and the south wall of the atrium may be reused elements of Hadrian's civic basilica or of the Temple of Venus. Access to the great porticoed court to the west was by doorways at the head of the lateral naves. The west side of the court was formed by the façade of the church of the **Anastasis** over the Tomb of Christ. The dome of the Rotunda had a diameter of 20.44–48m. The depiction of the Constantinian buildings on the mosaic in the apse of St. Pudenziana at Rome shows a rather low dome, presumably built of wood with a lead covering. The semicircular back wall contained three apses oriented north, west and south. The dome was supported by 12 columns and eight piers, the latter set in pairs at the cardinal points. The columns were tall and slender and gave a sense of lightness as well as providing more space for circulation than heavy piers would allow. The Tomb itself was beneath the dome, on the central axis but slightly north of centre. Egeria describes the liturgy celebrated in the Anastasis in 384, and how the Bishop went inside a screen to enter the cave tomb to pray. The Stone moved by the Angel from in front of the Tomb is mentioned by 348. The edicule over the Tomb was adorned with columns and had its roof decorated with gold and silver. Daily prayers at night, morning, noon, afternoon and evening were said in the Anastasis. Egeria describes also the decoration, of mosaic, gold, jewels, and silk with gold stripes for curtains and hangings; at night candles and great glass lanterns gave bright illumination.

The Anastasis has parallels with Roman mausolea (e.g. the Mausoleum of Constantia at Rome, which is smaller) but the greater use of wood and more slender columns employed here must have created an increased sense of light and spaciousness. It was intended as a monument to the glory and triumph of the Resurrection rather than a memorial to the dead.

The Anastasis was set in walled courts lined by monastic cells on the north and west sides. To the south of the Constantinian complex lay a court and the baptistery. On the site of Calvary, where today the almost vertical pillar of rock rises 4.75m from the surrounding quarried bedrock, the remains are less certain. Egeria refers to a Cross, and to services conducted both before and behind it. The chapel behind the Cross seems to have been part of the Martyrium, at the west end of the south aisle. The Church of Golgotha may have been built after the restoration by Modestus in the 7C (see below).

Fire damaged some areas near the Rotunda early in its history, and the original wooden floors were replaced by vaulting, perhaps in the time of Justinian.

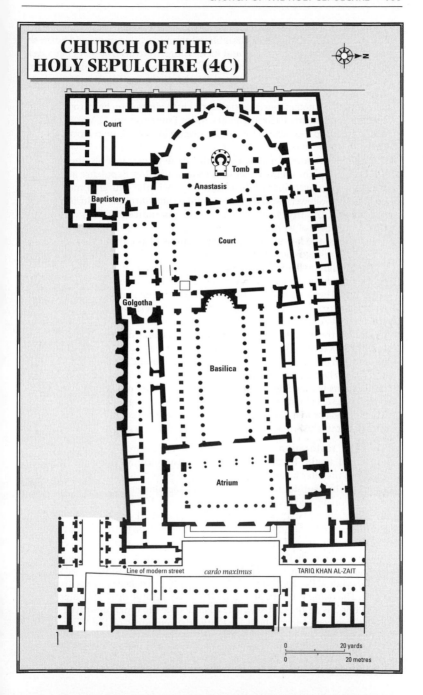

CHURCH OF THE HOLY SEPULCHRE (4C)

Court

Tomb

Anastasis

Baptistery

Court

Golgotha

Basilica

Atrium

Line of modern street   *cardo maximus*   TARIQ KHAN AL-ZAIT

0   20 yards
0   20 metres

On 6 May 614 the Sassanian (Persian) army reached Jerusalem, seized the fragments of the True Cross, slaughtered many of the monks, and burnt the church. The roof, decorations and furnishings were destroyed. Repairs were carried out by Modestus, Abbot of St. Theodosius in the Judaean desert, whose work is still commemorated by the Orthodox church. The pilgrim Arculf in 680 says that in his time the Stone moved by the Angel had been split into two unequal parts, and squared into altars. The Emperor Heraclius retrieved and returned the fragments of the True Cross on 21 March 631, but as the threat to the eastern Byzantine empire increased, he removed them to Constantinople in 633.

On the surrender of Jerusalem to the Arab armies in 638, the Patriarch Sophronius led the Caliph Umar on a tour of the Holy Sepulchre and when it was time for prayers invited the Caliph to pray in the church. Umar declined because his followers would otherwise take the church as a Muslim place of prayer, and the treaty of surrender had guaranteed the sanctity of the Christian places of worship in the city.

By at least the late 9C the annual ceremony of the miraculous descent of the Holy Fire was celebrated.

The Muslims in the 10C were more aggressive, and in 938 had rioted, burned the south doors and half the portico, and devastated Golgotha and the Anastasis. They took part of the east entrance to the Holy Sepulchre and built a mosque to mark the site of Umar's prayers. An inscribed stone (probably of al-Hakim or al-Zahir in the early 11C) forbidding entrance to Christians was found in 1897 in the southeast area of the basilica, and may derive from this mosque.

On 18 October 1009, on the orders of the Fatimid Caliph al-Hakim, the church and the Tomb were destroyed in an act of anti-Christian fanaticism. The work, described by the Christian Arab chronicler Yahya, was devastating. The basilica was left a complete ruin; the tomb of Christ itself, though cut in the bedrock, is said to have been demolished with pickaxes and virtually obliterated. The Rotunda proved more resistant, and although the columns and superstructure were overthrown, much of the lower exterior wall survived in the ruins.

The 11C restoration The restoration of the church was, until recently, attributed to the Byzantine Emperor Constantine Monomachos in 1048 (because the later historian William of Tyre records it as his work). Now it is thought that substantial repairs were made almost immediately after the destruction by al-Hakim, between 1012 and 1023, and were completed under Michael IV Paphlagon c 1040. This work was restricted to the Rotunda, and to the adjacent courts and chapels. The Rotunda was rebuilt on the surviving stubs of the Constantinian walls. The columns were cut in half and re-erected. They thus had rather clumsy proportions, with large rough capitals, and supported slightly pointed arches and an upper gallery instead of the original flat architrave. Some fine Umayyad carving was reused in this work. The dome was rebuilt as a timber cone. A large apse with a great arch was built out on the east side. The edicule over the much destroyed rock-cut Tomb was completely rebuilt enclosing the remnants of the 'Chapel of the Angel' and the Tomb. The site of the bench on which the body of Jesus had been laid was clad with the marble slab still there today.

The Crusader church The Crusaders may have made few structural alterations initially, but in July 1149 they dedicated new chapels decorated with mosaics on Golgotha. By 1153 they had built the new five storey bell-tower, but work on the great new church was probably not completed for some years (c 1150–80). This church, with little alteration, forms the structure that we see today. It used the Rotunda, with its 11C form almost intact, but the 11C east apse was demolished and the Crusader church was extended over the west end of the Constantinian basilica. It was built in the style of the Romanesque galleried churches of contemporary France; its altar and apses were placed to the east, and it was entered from the west through the great arch (the Arch of the Emperor) which had supported the 11C apse. However despite building in this European style, the Crusaders made their work harmonize with the pre-existing buildings. Thus they built on the same two levels as their predecessors. A new façade with the same proportions and alignment as previously was constructed in 12C style. This survives and leads into what originally was a typical transept of a 12C Romanesque church. Crusader kings were buried in the church.

Under the terms of the treaty of 1187 Salah al-Din spared the church, though he took off the cross, broke the bells and locked the doors. A Sufi convent occupied the Latin Patriarch's palace. Orthodox and Jacobite Christians were allowed to remain in the city, but the Latins were expelled until 1192, when two priests and two deacons were allowed to return and pilgrim access was restored. Despite Byzantine pressure to restore to the Orthodox the sole rights they had enjoyed under the Fatimids, Salah al-Din refused to allow any one sect to control the church and Muslims retained the keys to the edicule. Following the treaty of 1229, when Jerusalem was restored to the Franks, Frederick II of Germany crowned himself Emperor in the church. In 1244 the Khwarizmian Turks sacked the church, massacring the Christians inside, and pillaged the Crusader royal tombs.

After the Crusaders In the 14C, Greeks, Latins, Georgians, Armenians, Jacobites, Copts and Ethiopians all had rights in the church, and to avoid dissent the keys to the main doors were held by Muslims. The Franciscans, who returned to Palestine in 1335, had probably gained a foothold in the church by 1345. By the 15C the edicule over the Tomb and its keys were in their hands. The Armenians had by then been supplanted by the Georgians on Calvary and the Jacobites owned the Chapel of Helena. In 1555 the edicule over the tomb was rebuilt by Boniface of Ragusa (then the Franciscan Custos). Conditions in the 15C and 16C were difficult, and tension grew between the communities in the church. Territorially the Greek and Armenian churches were the most successful. In 1644 the Georgians were unable to pay the Ottoman taxes; the Ethiopians met the same difficulties, sold much of their property to the Copts to meet their debts, and retreated to the ruined cloister. For a short period the Copts left, and on their return in the 16C the Sultan gave them the ruins of the cloister of the Latin Canons where they built the present convent and church. In 1632 Sandys described the Easter ceremony of the Holy Fire as 'fitting better the solemnities of Bacchus'. By 1685 the Georgians had left Jerusalem, crippled by debt and declining numbers; most of their churches and convents were taken over by the Greeks. By 1699 only the Greeks, Latins and Armenians could afford to pay the Ottoman taxes and still said mass in the church.

Repairs to the Dome of the Holy Sepulchre were carried out in 1719 by the Greeks and Latins; the height of the bell tower, by now rather unsafe, was also reduced. The Armenians acquired the Chapel of Helena from the Jacobites, and laid a new floor there.

On 12 October 1808 fire broke out in one of the chapels of the Rotunda and spread through the whole building. The Rotunda in particular was badly damaged, seven of the ten surviving 4C/11C columns disintegrated and two-thirds of the building collapsed including most of the west end of the church. Numerous problems and intrigues arose over the restoration, in the course of which the Greek Orthodox secured rights over more of the church, as also did the Armenian Orthodox, who contributed substantially to the cost of repairs. In the restoration of 1809–10, the Greek architect Nikolaos Komnenos of Mitylene (1770–1821) rebuilt much of the complex. The present building with heavy cupola was built over the Tomb. Also at this time the tombs of Godfrey of Bouillon, Baldwin I and Baldwin V, which had stood as monuments of the Latin Kingdom of Jerusalem just inside the entrance to the Chapel of Adam, were broken up and removed by the Greeks, as were other Crusader tombs near the Stone of Unction.

Horrific scenes occurred in the Rotunda during the Easter ceremony of the Miracle of the Holy Fire in 1834. Seventeen thousand pilgrims were estimated to be in the city, of whom a good number were in the Sepulchre for the ceremony. The crowds and numbers of candles were such that the smoke rolled in great volumes out of the aperture at the top of the dome. Hysterical frenzy was followed by a panic to get out and it was estimated that 300 were crushed to death in the struggle.

A restoration to the dome was carried out in 1867/68 at the joint expense of France and Russia. Other work was done on the west tower. In 1927 an earthquake shook the building and the 12C dome over the crossing in the Greek cathedral had to be taken down and reconstructed; the south façade was encased in steel scaffolding and buttresses, as was the Rotunda. In 1947 the edicule over the Tomb also had to be supported. A new dome was installed in the Rotunda in 1935. In 1959 a plan for repair and restoration was at last agreed by the various communities. The redecoration of the Rotunda was completed in 1997 in time for the millennial celebrations.

The exterior

The forecourt or **Parvis**, has the remains of an arcade constructed in the 11C/12C near the south end. The entrance to the church is on the north side of the court; the *****Crusader façade** constructed before 1180 is the most prominent feature. A double arcade with frieze at both ground and first-storey level are each surmounted by a cornice. The upper cornice is reused 2C Roman work; the lower cornice is a 12C copy. The pointed arches are of typical Romanesque-Gothic type with gadrooned voussoirs. A hoodmould of finely carved rosettes surmounts the gadrooned arches of the portals. The entrance doors (the right entrance was blocked after 1187) are flanked by marble triple columns with capitals and imposts carved in floral designs which support flat modern lintels. The carved originals are in the Rockefeller Museum. The left tympanum bears the impression of the mosaic which once adorned it and perhaps depicted the Resurrection. The ladder on the façade gives access to the window ledge which is Armenian property.

Just in front of the central columned jamb beneath boards, is the tomb of Philip d'Aubigny, an English Crusader who died 1236. He was one of the councillors of King John at the time of Magna Carta, Governor of the Channel Islands and Tutor to Henry III. He made several pilgrimages to the Holy Land, including one in 1222 when he travelled by Damietta and Acre. The tomb has a trapezoid slab with bevelled edges, with a three-line epitaph in 13C lettering: HIC IACET PHILIPPVS DE AVBINGNI CVIVS ANIMA REQVIESCAT IN PACE. AMEN. The tomb was preserved under a bench, and discovered during the bench's removal in 1867. Above the façade can be seen the dome over the crossing, reconstructed after the earthquake of 1927. The modillions on the drum have characteristic 12C carving.

The **west wall of the Parvis** contains the rectilinear chevets of the 11C chapels built on the site of the Constantinian baptistery. They belong to the Greek Orthodox community. The south chapel is that of St. James the Less, the brother of Christ (now the church of the Arab Orthodox community); the central chapel was originally the Chapel of the Trinity, later of the Forty Martyrs, and was used for marriages and baptisms; and the north chapel is dedicated to St. John the Baptist but has also been associated with the Monastery of the Trinity where formerly the Patriarchs of Jerusalem were buried. The Crusader bell tower above it was built by 1153. It had five storeys, but the height was reduced by nearly half in 1719. That it was subsequent to the original design of the façade is indicated by the destroyed symmetry of the main façade, including a blocked window above and to the west of the entrance, which can just be seen.

The **east wall of the Parvis** has, adjacent to the church, a small domed structure which was once the 12C Crusader entrance to the Church on Calvary, afterwards converted to the *__Chapel of the Franks__.

The area in the vicinity of Calvary was particularly richly decorated by the Crusaders. Externally, the small marble columns and ornamental carving of cornice and window arches are well preserved. The 12C door has a fine carved relief tympanum with twined foliage and bunches of grapes; the 12C capitals have acanthus leaves and volutes, and the imposts have foliage. There is a frieze of birds in a vine over the window and an agreeable pair of confronted lions at the southeast corner of the cornice. Inside it has the Greek Chapel of St. Mary of Egypt (ground level) and the Latin Chapel of the Agony of the Virgin (above); both are closed. The former marks the spot where the 6C ikon of the Theotokos prevented Mary the Egyptian from entering the church. The latter can be seen through a window from the Chapels on Calvary.

Of the other buildings with entrances in the east wall of the Parvis, the first is the Coptic Chapel of St. Michael, with a painting of St. Michael weighing souls; from this a staircase leads to the Chapel of the Ethiopians and the Coptic convent to the northeast; the next entrance to the south leads to the Armenian Chapel of St. James; and near the southeast corner of the court, the Greek Monastery of Abraham.

The interior

As you enter the Church of the Holy Sepulchre, it is as well to remember that the entire structure is divided between six sects of the Christian church: principally the Latin Catholics, Greek Orthodox and Armenian Orthodox, to a lesser extent the Jacobites (Syrians), Copts and Ethiopians all of whom guard their rights to various parts of the building jealously.

We enter the south transept of the 12C church, truncated at a short distance by the restored wall of the present Greek cathedral, with a bright, modern two-tier gallery constructed across it. To the left of the entrance was formerly the high bench, or diwan, where the hereditary Muslim doorkeeper sat. He held the keys of the church to prevent disputes arising among the various Christian sects. The steep stairs to the right behind the blocked east doorway (early 13C) lead up to **Calvary** or **Golgotha**, meaning the place of the skull, the traditional site of the Crucifixion of Christ and the two thieves, and associated also with the burial place of Adam. At the top of the stairs are two chapels. On the south is first the Latin Chapel of the Nailing to the Cross, with attractive 12C mosaic ceiling depicting an inhabited vine scroll, including Adam and Eve and the Ascension; there are shell and other patterns in the voussoirs, with the Cross flanked by white doves in the apse. Here, at the **Tenth** and **Eleventh Stations of the Cross**, Jesus was disrobed and nailed to the Cross. Through a window in the south wall the Chapel of the Agony of the Virgin can be seen. On the north side is the Greek Chapel of the Exaltation or Raising of the Cross with its many gold and silver plated icons, which marks the **Twelfth Station of the Cross**. The slot cut for the cross is shown in the east apse along with those of the two thieves. The top of the rock, here nearly 2x2m and 4.75m above the adjacent quarried surface, can be touched under the altar of the Greek chapel and also seen through glass in the Chapel of Adam below.

The site has been venerated as that of the Crucifixion since the 4C, and a church has existed probably since the 7C. It was incorporated in the lateral aisle of the Crusader church and the present four arches probably form part of the older ciborium. Between the two chapels is the Latin 'Stabat altar' the **Thirteenth Station** where Mary received the body on its removal from the Cross.

At the bottom of the steps, beneath Calvary is the Chapel of Adam. The chapel of the Skull (of Adam) was located here against the face of the rock of Golgotha in the original 4C Constantinian layout, for it was early associated with the tradition which said that Adam was buried at Golgotha (Origen, AD 185–253). Part of Calvary can be seen under glass in this chapel, with a fault in the rock said to have been caused by an earthquake at the time of the Crucifixion, but probably an original flaw, which caused the workmen to abandon this section of the old quarry. Near the entrance were the now missing tombs of Godfrey of Bouillon and Baldwin I, the two first Crusader rulers (see above). Fragments of the tomb of Baldwin V, which was also here, are now displayed in the Greek Orthodox Patriarchate Museum (see below). The tombs had already been disturbed during the invasion of the Khwarizmian Turks in 1244.

Just beyond the entrance to the chapel is the Stone of Unction where, according to tradition, the body of Jesus was anointed by Nicodemus after being taken down from the Cross (John 19:38–40). This low slab of limestone replaced a 12C slab destroyed in 1808. The location and ownership of the slab has varied in the course of the centuries, and now the many lamps over it are variously owned by Armenians, Copts, Greeks and Latins.

Continuing to the left, past the end of the restored wall of the Greek Catholicon, you come straight to the restored ***Rotunda** or **Anastasis**, the Church of the Resurrection built by Constantine, and under it, the site of the Tomb of Christ. Only slightly displaced, the present piers and columns mark the location of the original 12 columns and eight pillars of the 4C Rotunda. The dome, completed in the 1960s, is decorated (1997) with a 12-pointed star whose rays symbolise the outreach of the 12 apostles. The diameter of the dome is 20.44–48m and the height is c 34m.

Now walled in by the partitions of storerooms, the ambulatory behind the columns is divided by cross vaulting into two storeys. The rear wall, though not visible within the church, is still largely 4C and preserved to a height of 11m, to just below the level of the original cornice. The 4C exedras to north, west and south survive. The south exedra is not accessible to the public, but the *Syrian Chapel is located in the west exedra. Entered through a hole in the masonry on the south side of the chapel is a dark, rock-cut tomb typical of the 1C BC/AD, part of which was cut away when the rock around the Tomb of Christ was removed in the 4C. A 16C tradition located the tombs of Joseph of Arimathea and Nicodemus here. The antechamber of the original tomb may have lain to the east, and the tomb chamber may have contained ten kokhim (burial places) with an ossuary in the floor; the ossuary and several kokhim are still visible. This tomb and others, reinforce the evidence that the Tomb of Christ was part of a cemetery outside the walls in the 1C BC/AD.

Most of the north exedra of Constantine can also be seen. A later passage cut through the 4C wall leads to a small court with Constantinian cells against the north wall, each having a door with flat lintel and shallow relieving arch, and a small window.

The site of the Tomb and Resurrection of Christ, 36m from Golgotha, is covered by an ugly small chapel dating to 1810. The original tomb venerated in the 4C was demolished on the orders of al-Hakim in 1009. That was certainly the tomb, probably of 1C BC/AD date, discovered by Makarios in 326 and which tradition then held was that of Jesus, in which he was laid on the eve of the Sabbath and from which he rose on the Easter Sunday morning. There is a possibility but no certainty that this really was the tomb of Christ, but its importance lies more in the faith, prayers and veneration surrounding it than in any material remains. Many descriptions of the edicule and Tomb exist from the 4C. The present apsidal marble structure conforms in general layout to the earlier edicule, in part dates from 1555, may contain earlier elements within its structure, and is approached from the east. The entrance is flanked by benches and massive candelabra: the stone dates to 1810, the bronze to 1877. Within are two tiny chambers served by the Greeks, Latins, Armenians and Copts. The first chamber is the Chapel of the Angel. In the centre is the small altar formed from part of the large stone said to have been rolled away from the mouth of the tomb by the Angel. In the wall by the entrance steps ascend to the roof. A low door gives entry to the **Chapel of the Holy Sepulchre** which is the **Fourteenth Station of the Cross**. Inside the door of the marble-lined chamber is an inscription naming Komnenos, the Greek architect of the restorations of 1810. Three bas reliefs in white marble represent the Resurrection; a bench covered with a marble slab lies against the north wall. It marks the empty burial place of Christ.

At the west end of the edicule is the Coptic chapel, which is said to preserve a tiny rock-cut remnant of the original tomb that survived al-Hakim's destruction in 1009. The Copts have maintained this chapel probably since the 16C.

To the north of the Rotunda is the **Chapel of St. Mary** where legend relates that Christ appeared to Mary, his mother, after the Resurrection. Built in the 11C it was only a little altered by the Crusaders in the 12C, when it was approached from the street to the west by an impressive entrance portal with gadrooned voussoirs resting on fine acanthus capitals (see Christian Quarter St below). It is now the most important Franciscan chapel. To the right of the entrance, a relic said to be a fragment of the Column of the Scourging is displayed. To the north is the Franciscan Convent. To the east is the Latin Sacristy where sword, spurs and cross said to be those of Godfrey of Bouillon were preserved. These formed part of the investiture regalia of the Order of the Holy Sepulchre, an order with Crusader origins conferred on illustrious pilgrims in later centuries. Here steps led up to the Latin parts of the galleries.

Returning towards the Tomb, opposite it to the east is the great arch—**the Arch of the Emperor**—which was constructed in the 11C to support the new apse. Short twin columns were built up with heavy bases and capitals which contained reused Umayyad elements. Monogramed capitals of Justinian formed great imposts to support the springing of the arch. The apse itself was removed in the 12C by the Crusaders, who employed the arch as entrance to their new church. The 12C west piers are built adjacent to the great arch. Through the arch we enter the Greek **Catholicon**, which occupies the crossing of the Crusader church. It is separated from the Crusader transepts by later partition walls, once necessary as supports but since the recent restorations no longer functional apart from their capacity to bear ornament. An early tradition associated the Centre of the World with the site of the Crucifixion and Resurrection, and by the 10C it was marked by an omphalos, now located in the west end of the cathedral. Most of the Catholicon lies over the Constantinian and 11C courtyard; the remnants of the 4C apse (which was at the west end of the Constantinian basilica facing towards the tomb) were uncovered a few years ago partly under the south side of the present choir. The present Greek semicircular choir contains two episcopal thrones, that on the north for the Patriarch of Antioch, that on the south for the Patriarch of Jerusalem.

The 12C **Crusader church** can be seen both inside and outside the Catholicon. Completed by c 1180, it consisted of a nave and side aisles, with ambulatory and semicircular apse facing towards the east. Much restored from 1959, it has the character of a Romanesque-transitional Gothic galleried church, with vaulted upper galleries over the side aisles. The use of vaults on ogival transept crossings was also imported from the West. The pointed arches are characteristic, but much of the sculpture has an Eastern character as also does the cupola resting on drum resting on pendentives over the transept crossing. Five Umayyad capitals were reused in the north transept and the crossing. Returning through the great arch and walking round to the right to the north aisle, the massive piers and columns of the 12C cathedral and the narrow round arches of the portico in the 11C courtyard or 'Holy Garden' sit side by side. The latter are called the 'Seven Arches of the Virgin' and contain a remarkable jumble of recycled and restored elements including Byzantine basket capitals at the west end.

At the east end of the north aisle is the chapel called the Prison of Christ, which according to 12C tradition housed Jesus and the two thieves before the Crucifixion. Epiphanius the Monk mentions the Prison of Christ in the 8C. The chapel probably originated as a liturgical station where the Passion and Death of Christ were commemorated.

Continuing into the ambulatory or retro-choir of the Crusader church there are three chapels located in the three apses in the outer wall probably also remodelled from the 11C court. The northeast chapel is the Greek Chapel of St. Longinus. A 5C tradition claims he was the Roman soldier who pierced Jesus' side with a spear (John 19:34). He was blind in one eye, but on being cured by the water and blood which spurted forth, he repented and was converted. The central east apse contains the Armenian Chapel of the Parting of the Raiment. The third chapel in the southeast apse is the Greek Chapel of the Derision or the Crowning with Thorns. A relic, the Column of Derison, stands near the centre but may not be of particular antiquity.

Between the first and second of these chapels is an ornate 12C doorway which led to the Canons' Monastery. Between the second and third chapels, 29 steps lead down to the large *Chapel of St. Helena, 5.3m below the level of the church. This is the Armenian Chapel of St. Krikor (Gregory). Many crosses have been carved on the walls by medieval pilgrims. The chapel consists of three aisles and two apses. The north and south walls are the foundations of the Constantinian church—it is thought the crypt did not exist in the 4C, but was built by the Crusaders in the early 12C, when older monolithic columns were reused to support the dome. The pointed vaulting dates to the 12C. A tradition that the columns shed tears is attributed by some to the marble sweating in subterranean humidity. The north apse is dedicated to the Penitent Thief, the south apse to the Empress Helena (mother of Constantine). A seat in the southeast corner is said to have been occupied by the Empress during the search she instituted for the True Cross, a story first mentioned c 351. Thirteen more steps descend in the southeast corner to the Chapel of the Invention or Finding of the Cross. The Greeks have the right side, the Latins the left of the chapel. A life-sized statue of Helena holding the cross has been placed here. The chapel is part of a larger cave walled off in antiquity. A section of the larger cave to the north was investigated in the 1970s and after clearance is now the Armenian Chapel of St. Vartan and the Armenian Martyrs. The whole underground cutting (c 25m long and 6.5m to 13m in height) is part of a cave-quarry probably of the 8C–6C BC. The ceiling consists of a harder stratum of limestone, where the remains of quarrying can also be seen. Quantities of Iron Age sherds were recovered, and remnants of walls built by Hadrian in the 2C. One of these contains a reused stone, perhaps of the 1C BC, with a drawing of a merchant ship and inscription DOMINE IVIMVS ('Lord we shall go'). The Hadrianic walls were cut by those of Constantine, and rectangular cisterns to north and south of the Chapel of St. Helena may also be of Constantinian date because they are on the same alignment as the 4C walls. These may be the Constantinian cisterns mentioned by the Bordeaux Pilgrim in 333, but another deep cistern known as the Cistern of St. Helena lies to the north, under the Coptic Monastery. At least 12 cisterns are known under the Church of the Holy Sepulchre.

Returning to the main church and continuing along the south Crusader aisle, you pass on the left a flight of steps up to Calvary, and further on to the left arrive again at the main entrance. Other fragments of the Constantinian Holy Sepulchre can be seen in adjoining buildings (see below, the Russian Chapel and Zalatimo's shop).

Leaving the Parvis by the small doorway at the southeast corner one enters the Harat al-Dabbaghin. At c 70m on the left is **St. Alexander's Russian Chapel**, once the Alexandrovsky Hospice of the Russian Palestine Society, built following

The modern route of the Via Dolorosa and the Stations of the Cross

This is a summary of the route. For descriptions of Stations 1–7, see Jerusalem, section 3; for Stations 10–14, see above; for Stations 8–9, see below.

The original route depends on the location of the site of the Praetorium, which tradition locates at the Umariyya School on the site of the Antonia fortress to the east, but which is more likely to have been on the site of the present Citadel to the west. The beginnings of this act of pious remembrance are described by Egeria c 384 when it began at the place of Jesus' arrest at the foot of the Mount of Olives, and proceeded with hymns through the east gate of the city to Calvary, arriving by dawn on Good Friday. The pious rite became very popular in the 13C, when it started at the House of Pilate and the Chapel of the Flagellation. The present locations are largely those established by the 17C. The buildings at each station are of various periods, all later than the time of Christ. The pilgrim route is regularly performed and starts near the west end of the Tariq Bab Sitti Maryam, at the Umariyya School (see p 145), crosses the centre of the Old City and ends at the Holy Sepulchre. The Franciscan pilgrims' procession starts from the Chapel of the Flagellation every Friday at 15.00.

Station 1, the Praetorium where Christ was condemned, at the Umariyya School on the site of the Antonia Fortress or at the Chapel of the Flagellation.

Station 2, in the entrance to the Monastery of the Flagellation (Franciscan); formerly in the street, where the 'Scala Sancta' marked the place outside the Praetorium where Jesus took up the Cross. The route then passes beneath the Ecce Homo Arch.

Station 3, where Christ fell, just opposite the Austrian Hospice at the junction with the Tariq al-Wad at the Polish Catholic Church.

Station 4, just down the Tariq al-Wad on the left, at the Armenian Catholic Church of the Spasm, where Christ met the Virgin Mary. Before taking the next turning to the right, the House of the Rich Man can be seen, built over the road to the south; next to it was the House of the Poor Man. Both are part of the tradition from the 14C, and where the 5th Station used to be located.

Station 5, at the first turning to the right into Tariq al-Saray, on the left, where Jesus fell for the second time and Simon of Cyrene took up the Cross. A modern chapel.

Station 6, continuing up the hill, to the Church of the Holy Face and St. Veronica, midway up on the left. Since the 13C, tradition located this as the place where St. Veronica offered her handkerchief to Jesus, and received it back with the imprint of his face.

Station 7, at the top of the ascent at the intersection with Khan al-Zait St, the Porta Judicaria. This station, at which legend relates the decree of death was posted on the city gate, was introduced in the 13C to prove that the Holy Sepulchre was outside the city in the time of Jesus.

Station 8 at the Monastery of St. Caralambos, where Christ addressed the women who accompanied him: 'Daughters of Jerusalem, weep not for me.' This is marked by a plaque on the left of the street up the hill opposite. This station has moved quite often. Return to the main street, turn right (south) and continue a short distance to steps ascending to the left; at the top,

continue along the street to the west to
Station 9, at the entrance to the Coptic Convent, where Christ fell for the
third time. In the 13C this station was located in the Parvis.
Stations 10, 11, 12 and **13** are on Calvary in the Church of the Holy
Sepulchre (see above).
Station 14 is at the Tomb.

the visit of the Grand Duke Sergei Alexandrovitch in 1881 (see also Jerusalem, section 12, Russian Compound). Open Mon–Thur 09.00–13.00, 15.00–17.00; closed Sun and holidays.

Archaeologically interesting remains were discovered and preserved during the construction of the present building. The rather destroyed fragments are carefully preserved in the basement. They include complex fragments of buildings of Hadrianic Jerusalem reused in the time of Constantine (see the plan of Constantine's Church of the Holy Sepulchre, p 172).

As you descend the stairs, on the right is a column of the time of Michael IV (1037/41) with a plain cushioned capital and cross carved on the shaft. It was constructed on the site of the triple-arched east entrance to the principal forum of Hadrian (AD 135), of which a part of the north bay is preserved. Two Corinthian capitals survive, with acanthus leaves surmounted by two birds flanking a knot. The higher capital to the left is still in situ; the one to the right has been incorporated into the later Byzantine arch. Descend through the arch and turn left; on the left, the sill at the top of another flight of stairs marks the level of the Hadrianic podium or of the Constantinian south cloister. In front are the remains of the walls of the Hadrianic basilica or temple platform which were reused by Constantine for the Church of the Holy Sepulchre. The entrance may have been part of the Hadrianic arch, but was employed in the Constantinian layout as an entrance to the south cloister; tradition holds that it is the entrance by which Jesus was led out of the city on the way to his crucifixion. On the right are the remains of two shattered and blackened columns which derive from the portico of the Hadrianic and Constantinian *cardo maximus*. Remains of others have been noted nearby. To the left are the remains of the southern entrance in the east façade of the basilica of the Holy Sepulchre cut in the Roman wall by Constantine; the remains of the principal central entrance of the east façade exist in a shop to the north (see below, Zalatimo's Sweetshop). Constantine had the Roman wall veneered with marble, and the pitting visible in its surface is to key the plaster used in this process. Two other doors on the south side may also have been cut by Constantine as entrances from the south cloister to the atrium of the basilica. At the top of the stairs is a modern chapel; just above floor level on the north side drafted Roman masonry is visible. Through the doorway is a small museum which displays objects found in the excavations. The 11C inscription prohibiting non-Muslims from entering the Mosque of Umar built at the entrance to the Church of the Holy Sepulchre, was found in these excavations. To the left of the museum entrance is a medieval archway which led to the Canons' Cloister.

After you leave the Russian Chapel, continue to the end of Harat al-Dabbaghin, and turn left into Khan al-Zait St. At c 50m on the left, tucked into the angle beyond the steps, is *Zalatimo's Sweet Shop*. Ask the owner for permission to visit a storeroom containing the massive remnants of the 4C central doorway between the propylaea and east atrium of the Constantinian basilica (better preserved than the south doorway seen in the Russian Chapel). The wall in which it was inserted is probably also part of the Hadrianic basilica of 135. This central door still stands nearly 4m high.

Ascending the adjacent steps brings you to various other remains associated with the Church of the Holy Sepulchre. At the top of the steps, continue along the Aqabat Dair al-Sultan, pass the small doorway into the courtyard, turn left and continue to the end of the lane. Straight ahead is the entrance to the Coptic Patriarchate. To the right is the Queen Helen Coptic Church. Inside the entrance at the back of the church is a deep, angled flight of 43 uneven steps which descends into the old 'Cistern of St. Helena', of uncertain date but a good example of the few large ancient subterranean cisterns to be found in Jerusalem currently accessible.

In the 16C the Sultan gave the Copts the ruins of the 12C Latin cloister, where they built the bishop's house, a hospice for pilgrims, and a church (now restored); this has given the complex its local name, Dair al-Sultan. The column shaft to the left of the entrance to the Patriarchate marks the **Ninth Station of the Cross**. The entrance on the left side of the passage leads to the **Ethiopian Monastery** on the roof above the Chapel of St. Helena. Through heavy Ottoman taxation and debt the Ethiopian community lost its ownership of various parts of the Church of the Holy Sepulchre (the Chapel of St. Mary the Egyptian, of St. Michael and of the Apostles in the Parvis were taken over by the Copts in the 16C and 17C), and the Ethiopians now occupy small cells built in the ruins of the 12C Canon's Cloister, over the ruined aisles of the 4C basilica. Despite the poverty it is a very peaceful and attractive place. The central dome in the court is that of the Chapel of St. Helena. On the west is the east end of the Greek cathedral. In the ruined south and west walls are the remains of the 12C arcades with numerous fragments of carving, including elbow brackets from which the arcades spring, and carved voussoirs. Just south of the cathedral the back of the Chapel of Melchizedek above Calvary is visible; and on the south of the cloister are parts of the 12C refectory. A door in the southwest corner leads down to the Chapel of the Ethiopians, and then to the Coptic Chapel of St. Michael, from which it is possible to exit to the Parvis.

The Muristan

Retracing your steps either through the little door in the southeast corner of the Parvis, or back through Khan al-Zait St and Harat al-Dabbaghin, this time walk to the area of the Muristan, which occupies the whole block south of the Church of the Holy Sepulchre, and was the location of the headquarters of the Crusader Knights of St. John, the Hospitallers (see plan). The area has an interesting history, but few remains survived the major redevelopment carried out at the end of the 19C. The modern name is derived from the Persian word for hospital and dates from the 13C. It now contains on the east the German Evangelical Church; in the centre, the New Bazaar; on the north side a Greek monastery and a mosque (see above, p 165); on the southwest the Church of St. John the Baptist (see above, p 164); and on the south the shops along David St.

History

Excavations have shown that the area was quarried in the 7C BC and was presumably outside the town until the time of Hadrian (2C), when a great fill was employed to level the surface prior to the building of Aelia Capitolina. Some 2C and Byzantine remains were uncovered. A hospice built by Pope Gregory I in 603 is recorded. At the beginning of the 9C, in the time of the Abbasid Caliph Harun al-Rashid, the Emperor Charlemagne built a church and hospice for pilgrims here, which was served by the Benedictine order. It was visited by Bernard the Monk in 870, who describes the hospice standing beside the Church of St. Mary, with its library and endowment of land in the Valley of Jehoshaphat. It was destroyed in the persecution by al-Hakim in 1009.

The merchants of Amalfi, established in Jerusalem in the 11C, received from the Fatimid Caliph some land in this area; probably between 1036 and 1070 they built a monastery in honour of St. Mary, perhaps on the older ruins, served by an abbot and monks from Italy. This church was called St. Mary of the Latins and was almost certainly on the northeast corner of the area. A daughter convent adjacent (probably that near the centre of the Muristan) was built by 1080 for women pilgrims, first called St. Mary Magdalene, later St. Mary Major. The Amalfitans also founded c 1070 a hospital and church for poor and sick pilgrims dedicated to St. John (Almoner, according to William of Tyre), but it is not clear whether this was a separate foundation to the ancient church of St. John Baptist in the southwest corner of the area. At an early date both dedications appear to exist. A 12C tradition held that Zechariah, the father of St. John the Baptist, had governed the hospital in its earliest days. By 1099 there were at least three Benedictine foundations south of the church of the Holy Sepulchre: St. Mary of the Latins with its hospice; St. Mary Major and its hospice for women; and the hospital for sick pilgrims, perhaps with another chapel dedicated to St. John Almoner. The administrator of the hospital, dependant on the Abbot of St. Mary's, was Gerard, who remained in the city during the Frankish siege of 1099. The relationship between the early hospital and the Order of the Knights of St. John is obscure. After the capture of the city the hospital received generous gifts from Godfrey of Bouillon and in particular from Baldwin I, and became independent of the Benedictine Order by 1113. By this time the Order of the Knights of St. John and the Hospital in Jerusalem was an international organisation governed from Jerusalem. Gerard died in 1120 and was succeeded by Raymond du Puy, under whom the Order developed its characteristic form and Augustinian rule. He was noted for his piety, but was also an able politician and negotiator. By the time of his death (c 1158–60) the Order had received many gifts, eventually becoming one of the richest of the medieval orders, and had begun to take on a military role which almost overshadowed its primary charitable purpose.

A Papal Bull of 1154 made the Order independent of the local church, responsible directly to the Pope. Stupid quarrels developed in this invidious situation; the Hospitallers rang the bells of the Hospital during the Patriarch's sermons, and actually fired flights of arrows into the Church of the Holy Sepulchre which were collected and hung up in Calvary by the angry Patriarch. At the same time, the hospital's treatment of the sick was in

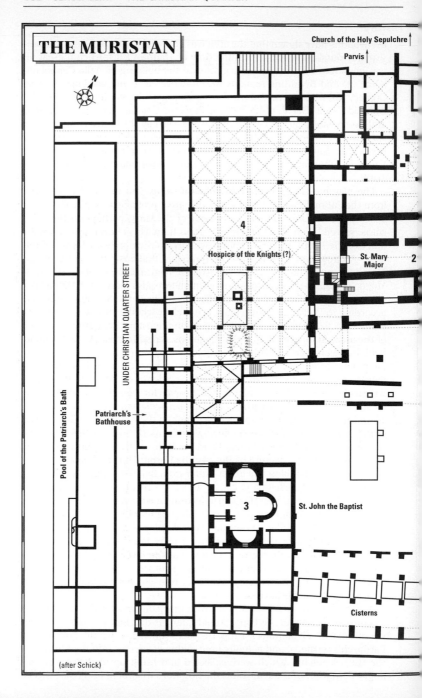

THE MURISTAN

Church of the Holy Sepulchre

Parvis

4

Hospice of the Knights (?)

St. Mary Major

2

UNDER CHRISTIAN QUARTER STREET

Pool of the Patriarch's Bath

Patriarch's Bathhouse

3

St. John the Baptist

Cisterns

(after Schick)

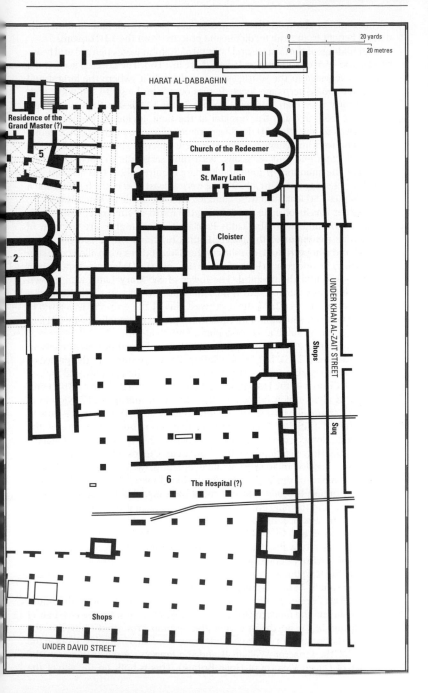

HARAT AL-DABBAGHIN

Residence of the
Grand Master (?)

5

Church of the Redeemer

1

St. Mary Latin

Cloister

2

UNDER KHAN AL-ZAIT STREET

Shops

Suq

6   The Hospital (?)

Shops

UNDER DAVID STREET

0   20 yards
0   20 metres

advance of anything in the contemporary West, and had undoubtedly derived benefit from Arab medicine and practice from the 11C onward.

The buildings of the hospice and hospital of St. John were enlarged and beautified in the 1150s; 400 knights lodged there in 1163. The hospital itself, if the remains excavated in the southeast area belong to it (where the largest and most numerous cisterns are located), was over 70m long, 36.5m wide, with arches nearly 5.5m high. John of Würzburg in the 1160s says there were 2000 patients of both sexes in the hospital at the time, including gynaecological cases; it was so busy that 50 dead were removed in one night (see Aceldama, p 273), and were immediately replaced by new patients. They were looked after by four doctors and four surgeons, with nine sergeants to each ward; the records of the quantities of food and bedding required show this account was probably not exaggerated. In 1179 there were at least 900 in the hospital and a few days later 750 wounded were admitted after the Battle of Montgisard.

The Order was involved in formulating the terms of surrender to Salah al-Din in 1187, and, with the Latin Patriarch, the Knights are accused of ungenerous treatment of the poorer Latin Christians whose ransoms were not paid and who were sold into slavery. Ten Hospitallers were allowed to stay in Jerusalem for one year to look after the sick, but the Order was dispossessed of the church and the hospital. The tower of St. Mary Latin was thrown down, the church turned into a mosque, and the adjacent hospice into a Shafiite College. In 1192/93 the northwest part of the property was given to Salah al-Din's son who built a mosque. A hospital was established in 1216 in the old hospital by Salah al-Din's nephew, Shihab al-Din.

When pilgrimage recommenced, Latin pilgrims lodged outside the city in the Asnerie (see p 245), but Frederick II of Germany stayed in the palace or hospice of the Knights opposite the Holy Sepulchre when he crowned himself king in the Church of the Holy Sepulchre on 18 March 1229. In 1336 a Latin nun was in charge of a hospice in the Muristan; and in 1347 Niccolo of Poggibonsi recorded a hospice 'above John Baptist'; in 1384 a hospice close to the Church of the Holy Sepulchre may have been under the care of the Franciscans. Nompar de Caumont stayed there in 1418–20, and was made a Knight of the Holy Sepulchre by the Franciscan Custos. In 1483 Felix Faber described a hospice in a large vaulted building, which was squalid and ruinous, in a part of the ancient hospital which looked like a monastic refectory. It contained 400 pilgrims, but could have held 1000. Not long after it was so dirty, and the pilgrims so pestered by the local inhabitants, that they had begun to seek accommodation elsewhere. By c 1524 it seems to have been abandoned, and in 1537–41 some of the ruins were quarried for the building of the city walls. The Greek Orthodox built a hospice in the southwest c 1660. Le Bruyn could still see the ruins of the 'House of the Knights of Malta' (as the Hospitallers later became) in 1674. Later the site fell into further decay, and in 1868 was mostly ploughland.

On the visit of Crown Prince Frederick William of Prussia in 1869, the Sultan gave Prussia and the modern Order of the Knights of St. John the east half of the Muristan. In the northeast corner, the German Protestant Church of the Redeemer (Erlöserkirche) was built, and consecrated on 31 October 1898 in the presence of the Emperor William II and the Empress Augusta Victoria (the daughter of Queen Victoria of Great Britain). This is built on the site of the church which was probably that of St. Mary of the Latins, and follows its plan closely. On the south side the old cloisters and refectory were preserved.

The Church of the Redeemer and tower

The Church of the Redeemer and tower (**no. 1 on the plan of the Muristan**) is open Sat–Thur 09.00–13.00, 13.30–17.00; closed Sun. The late 19C building was restored in the 1970s, and the original scuplture on the north door (the principal Benedictine entrance of the 12C St. Mary of the Latins) on Harat al-Dabbaghin has been carefully restored. The main series of reliefs on the arch depict battered and mostly headless figures representing the months, which were named but are now very difficult to distinguish. The series begins at the bottom left with January and is capped by the sun (a half-figure with disc above the head) and moon (a female with crescent) at top centre between June and July. The most easily discerned figure is August, a thresher. The full series included February, a man pruning a tree; April, a seated figure; May, a kneeling man cultivating; July, a reaper; August, a thresher; September, a grape gatherer; October, a man with a cask; November, a standing woman. Above, a frieze of rosettes and modillions with grotesque faces supports a cornice. The lively figural art is reminiscent of the sculptures on the nearby façade of the Church of the Holy Sepulchre. Heraldic shields occupy the corners.

The modern entrance is from the west in Frederick William St. The church was consecrated in 1898. The belfry at the southwest corner is the highest tower in the vicinity and there is a fine prospect of the Old City from it. By previous arrangment only it is possible to visit the deep excavations under the church, the foundations of which are placed on bedrock nearly 14m below. The remains of a 7C BC quarry, a wall of the Hadrianic period and evidence of the Roman forum were discovered. The entrance is from the cloister. On the south side of the church and entered by the door to the Evangelical Hospice in Frederick William St, are the cloisters and refectory belonging to the 12C hospice. They were altered when the buildings were converted to use as a Muslim law school in the 13C–14C; the rebuilt cloisters, with two storeys surrounding a square court, have the refectory on the south side. On the west is an Ayyubid staircase moved from the north side to its present site during the reconstructions in 1898. Fragments of the Crusader church have been preserved.

To the south of this complex is land belonging to the Knights of St. John of Jerusalem, where excavations were carried out in 1961–63. Clearance at the end of the 19C was so drastic that only the foundations of the massive medieval piers were discovered (perhaps part of the hospital, see **no. 6** on the plan). Fragments of the south façade of this building, with vaulted shops and corbels above at first floor level, survive fronting David St. On the opposite side of Frederick William St is the New Bazaar built in 1901 and belonging to the Greek Patriarchate: its elaborate diagonal layout and central fountain have a strong 19C European orientalising character. It stands over the site of the 11C/12C Church of St. Mary Major (**no. 2**), a church with three aisles and three apses which was uncovered briefly during the construction of the bazaar. The Greek Church of St. John the Baptist lies to the southwest (**no. 3**), the Greek Convent of Gethsemane to the north, built in the 19C (allegedly on the site of the residence of the Grand Master of the Knights of St. John; **no. 5**). It requires considerable imagination to visualise the area as the well-built and organised 12C headquarters of a great hospital and military order in the present busy scene of shops and cafés.

Continuing to the south end of Frederick William St, and turning left onto David St brings you down to the great **covered markets** (suqs, main bazaar) of Jerusalem. Daunting in their dimness and size and in the massed quantity of goods in small shops, they epitomise the market of an oriental town. They are made up of three parallel streets interconnected by small alleys. These were Crusader streets, built over the Roman and Byzantine *cardo maximus* at the heart of the city. On the west is the Suq al-Lahhamin (Street of the Meat Sellers), in Crusader times the vegetable market. In the centre is the Suq al-Attarin (Street of the Spice Sellers): in the 12C it was the covered market for the drapers and was the property of St. Anne's Church (see p 138). Some of the shops, set in arched recesses covered by vaults with pointed arches, still have the monogram 'SA' incised in the masonry. When St. Anne's was converted into a mosque and school by Salah al-Din after 1187, he endowed it with this property. The streets on either side were then endowments of the Aqsa Mosque. On the east is the Suq al-Khawajat (Street of the Merchants), in Crusader times called Malcuisinat St. In the 12C at the north and south ends of the markets, the streets running to the east contained that other necessary adjunct to a busy market, the shops of the money changers; that of the Syrians lay to the north, and that of the Franks to the south (in the modern Tariq Bab al-Silsila). Nearby were at least two caravanserais, the Khan al-Zait and the Khan al-Sultan. The atmosphere of these markets can have changed relatively little in the last 2000 years. A short stroll southwards brings one into the excavated section of the Byzantine *cardo maximus* (see p 209). Here the ancient site contrasts with the living market just left; both contribute important images to the historical picture of Jerusalem.

Off the beaten track

At this point you can walk north from the bazaar to the Damascus Gate, or return up David St to the Jaffa Gate having seen the principal monuments of the Christian Quarter. Alternatively you could take a walk through the more distant streets of the quarter. To do this, return up David St and, just beyond the Petra Hostel, turn right into the Harat al-Istambuliyya, opposite the corner of the citadel. About 35m up the street on the left, a covered passage leads into a little circular crossing. A lamp at the centre is placed on a column with Latin inscription dating to the beginning of the 3C. It reads: M(ARCO) IUNIO MAXIMO LEG(ATO) AUG(USTORUM) LEG(IONIS) X FR(ETENSIS)—ANTONINIANAE—C. DOM(ITIUS) SERG(IUS) STR(ATOR) EIUS. It honours a prefect of Judaea and was erected by one of his staff. Another inscription of the Tenth Legion with the names of Vespasian and Titus was found in the excavations south of the Haram.

Returning to the street, opposite to the left is the Greek Catholic Patriarchate; go directly opposite into Muezzin St which twists its way past first, on the left, the Coptic Monastery of St. George or Mar Jirias, a convent and hospice with an old, dark church, in which the insane were said to be cured by the healing powers of St. George. Crusader maps of the 12C mark the Church of St. George infunda (in the market), probably on this site; a Church of St. George served by two clergy is mentioned in the 9C Commemoratorium (see also St. Demetrius, below). Continuing a further 70m, into Aqabat al-Khadr (St. George St) the **Coptic Khan** is on the right. The Khan was built by the Copts in 1836/37 on the site of a sesame oil mill and a garden with olive trees, with voluntary Coptic labour at a cost of

500,000 piastres, for use by Coptic pilgrims from Egypt. Its rear wall overlooks the Pool of the Patriarch's Bath. It is occupied by workshops and rather dingy.

Opposite the khan is the Greek Orthodox Monastery of the Most Holy Virgin, Megale Panagia, 'the Great All-Holy', the Dair al-Banat, or Nunnery, a 12C church and once possibly the site of the Church of the Spoudaioi ('zealous'). The latter was built by the Patriarch Elias c 494 for the society of monks who had attached themselves to the Church of the Anastasis. The church was completely rebuilt in the late 19C. The street then debouches on to Christian Quarter St just before the turning to the Church of the Holy Sepulchre. Continuing to the left up Christian Quarter St, past numerous shops, look for 2C–7C paving stones with ridges polished by long use, which were discovered several metres below the present street level during recent relaying of the drains. Part of a fine gadrooned archway can be seen on the right. It was a Crusader entrance to the Church of St. Mary on the north side of the Rotunda of the Church of the Holy Sepulchre.

At 90m on the left, Greek Orthodox Patriarchate Road (Aqabat Dair al-Rum) leads to the entrance of the Great Greek Monastery, a very large Orthodox complex mentioned c 1400 as the Monastery of St. Thecla, to whom the main 12C church is dedicated. The monastery is probably older, and is a labyrinth of houses and courts, steps and lanes extending to join the Church of the Holy Sepulchre on the east. The chapel of Constantine abuts the Rotunda. Another chapel is dedicated to St. Helena. It has a large library, including manuscripts of 10C date. On the opposite (north) side of this street is the Greek Orthodox Patriarchate. The Greek Orthodox are an important and ancient Christian community in Jerusalem. Tradition notes the first bishop in Jerusalem in the 1C AD, at first subordinate to Caesarea, but his status raised to Patriarch from AD 451. The Patriarch is one of the four Orthodox Patriarchs of the East and has charge of the community, including many monasteries and churches. In 1922 it was estimated that there were nearly 33,000 Greek Orthodox in Palestine, of whom 6000 lived in Jerusalem.

A few metres further up the road, on the right, is the **Greek Orthodox Patriarchate Museum** (open 09.30–13.30; closed Sun), in part of the lower area of a Crusader building over which the Greek Monastery of St. Nicolas was rebuilt in the 17C. It contains objects from the Patriarchate archive, many found on land owned by the Patriarchate. Large Corinthian capitals at the outer entrance came from the Crusader church of St. Mary Magdalen. As well as pottery, glass and a hoard of Umayyad gold dinars from Capernaum, the display includes two sarcophagi (1C AD) from Herod's Family Tomb (see p 263) and a fragmentary lead sarcophagus, possibly from Tyre. Architectural fragments come from the 12C monastery above the Tomb of St. Mary at Gethsemane; a number of busts from Caesarea; and two unfinished but majestic bearded heads of prophets (Moses and Aaron?) from the 12C Church of the Annunciation, discovered in Nazareth in 1867. The fragments of the tomb of Baldwin V (who died aged 8 in 1186), which was destroyed during the fire of 1808 and removed from the Church of the Holy Sepulchre, can also be seen. The fragments include a box base, twisted columns and elaborate capitals above, and on top Christ with angels. There are examples of fine 16C–17C vestments and a Georgian patriarchal stole and embroidery, copies of some important manuscripts, icons, and other church furniture, including the superb reliquary found in the Church of St. John the Baptist (see above). This is a large piece of rock crystal in the shape of a mitre, bound with gilded copper bands with filigree work and set with semi-precious stones. It contains a wooden panel encrusted with relics on both faces; these include a fragment of the True Cross; relics of St. Peter and St. John the Baptist, of almost all the apostles and of some other saints, including St. Oswald, a 7C king of the Anglo-Saxons. The latter suggests the reliquary was originally intended for use in Britain but had to be hidden hastily in 1187. It is a splendid testimony of the importance of relics to the medieval pilgrim.

Next door on the west is the Greek Orthodox Church of St. Nicholas, acquired by the Greeks when the Georgians left in 1685. It stands on 12C foundations.

Returning to Christian Quarter St, and continuing to its north end, on the right in al-Khanqah St, is the **al-Khanqah Mosque**, the Salahiyya Khanqah. Built c 1120 as the palace of the Latin Patriarch in Crusader Jerusalem (it lies just northwest of the Church of the Holy Sepulchre), the property was confiscated after the Latins left in 1187. It was endowed by Salah al-Din as a khanqah (convent for Sufi mystics) in 1189. The assembly hall with mihrab was restored in 1341, and the minaret and portal were constructed before 1417–18. The minaret is a square tower with four storeys, and gallery, lantern, drum and dome above.

You can now continue down St. Francis St towards Khan al-Zait St, passing the Greek Orthodox Monastery of St. Caralambos with the **Eighth Station of the Cross**, and turn left for the Damascus Gate; or walk through the Christian Quarter to the New or the Jaffa Gate.

Opposite the Khanqah Mosque, a street to the north (Harat Dair al-Tuffah) contains, to the left, the Greek Orthodox Mikra Panagia ('Little St. Mary'), or Saidnaya (St. Anne), a 12C church completely rebuilt in the late 19C; adjacent on the north is the Greek Orthodox Church of St. Euthymius. The present church of St. Euthymius existed in the 12C. Southwest on Haddadin St is the Greek Orthodox Church of St. Catherine; a 12C church on this site was acquired from the Georgians in 1685. Little of the Crusader structure seems to have survived. Alternatively, from the Khanqah Mosque, continue west on St. Francis St (formerly the Street of the Franks). Turn right, and at the next angle of the road, on the right is first the Greek Orthodox Church of St. Michael the Archangel, a surviving domed church of the 12C. Just beyond is the large establishment of the Friars Minor or Order of St. Francis and the Custodia Terrae Sanctae with the **Church of St. Saviour** and monastery.

History of the Franciscan church

The Franciscans returned to Jerusalem in 1335 and were granted the right of custodianship of the Christian Holy Places for the Latins. They settled at first on Mount Zion (see p 212). Boniface of Ragusa who was the Franciscan Custos after 1555, bought the 12C/13C Church of St. John the Theologian from the Georgians in 1559, and called it St. Saviour. In the 19C the church was small, with four pillars supporting a low vaulted roof with a dome in front of the high altar. It was inadequate for the large congregation. The monastic complex was fortress-like, and contained cisterns, gardens, courts, stables, cellars, storehouses for food, wood and charcoal, horse-mills, ovens, forges, carpenters' shops, turners, cobblers, candlers, dispensary and printing press, as well as monks' cells, infirmary, library and treasury. Between 1559 and the 19C a large collection of Italian Savona maiolica pharmacy jars was built up in the dispensary, and can now be seen in the Museum at the

Flagellation. The present church on the site is modern, a three-aisled basilica with barrel-vaulted ceiling and a large square 19C tower and spire.

Following the road to the right towards New Gate, at a short distance a cul-de-sac to the right leads to the Greek Orthodox Church of St. Basil. The church is noted in the 12C and the 16C, and was acquired by the Greeks from the Georgians in 1685. Little of the older structure survives.

New Gate St leads north to the New Gate. A small early Ottoman mosque, Masjid al-Qaymari, is adjacent to the city wall, and in the northwest angle of the walls is Christian Brothers College. Continuing by one of the various streets running to the south, on Harat al-Wariyya is the Latin Patriarchate and Seminary begun in 1859, adjacent to the west wall of the Old City. To the east, on Istambuliyya St, is the Spanish hospice, the Casa Nova. Just north of the Casa Nova is the small Greek Orthodox Church of the two St. Theodores on two levels; a 6C church probably on this site is mentioned by Cyril of Scythopolis. South of the Casa Nova, on the east of the street and now part of the Greek School, is the Chapel of St. Demetrius, a church mentioned in the 14C. It is said to stand on Byzantine foundations, and has a dome supported by four piers. As you return in the direction of the Citadel and the Jaffa Gate, you pass through the area which was the Grain Market in Crusader times.

5 • The Citadel

The *Citadel of Jerusalem (A. al-Qal'a) stands on the south side of the Jaffa Gate on one of the highest points of the Old City overlooking the steep-sided Valley of Hinnom to the west. The site was strategically located against attack from both inside and outside the city. Herod the Great built three great towers over earlier foundations to defend his adjacent palace, and these became the basis of citadels at later periods. Probably the site of the Praetorium at which Jesus was condemned to death, and the scene of a massacre of the Roman garrison by the Jews during the First Revolt, the Citadel was called the Tower of David in Crusader times and was restored by both Mamluk and Ottoman rulers. It is now the **Tower of David Museum of the History of Jerusalem**.

• Open Sun–Thur 09.00–17.00 (winter 10.00–16.00); Fri, Sat, hol 09.00–14.00 (winter 10.00–14.00). Sound and light show in the courtyard in English, Apr–Oct on Mon, Wed at 21.30, Sat at 21.00. Guided tours in English, Sun–Fri at 11.00. Information ☎ 02 627 4111; admission charged.

History

The earliest remains recovered in archaeological excavations on the site are of 7C BC date when the area was quarried for stone for the city walls. The area appears to have been outside the city then though there was a considerable build-up of 7C BC debris. The earliest defensive wall (which formed the northwest angle of the city) has been variously dated to the Early Hellenistic period, to the Hasmonean period and to the period of Herod the Great, and may date to the reign of the Hasmonean John Hyrcanus (134–104 BC). There is general agreement with Josephus (War V:161–176) that Herod the Great constructed three great towers on the site, which he named after Phasael (his brother), Hippicus (his friend) and Mariamne (his wife). Immediately abutting the towers to the south, Herod the Great built his palace, which is also described by Josephus (War V:177–183) as notable for its large rooms and porticoes, its fine groves, dovecotes and streams of water. The excavations have shown that this was constructed on a podium which raised the ground level by 3m–4m and covered most of the area from the Citadel south to the present south wall of the Old City, being perhaps 300m–350m in length. Very little of the palace remains, apart from a few wall stubs on top of the podium, and some fragments of painted wall plaster.

The palace continued to be used following the death of Herod the Great, first by his successors, then by the Roman prefects and procurators on official visits from the capital at Caesarea and it seems likely that this was the Praetorium in which Jesus was condemned by Pontius Pilate c AD 30. The palace was attacked and one of its towers was mined by the insurgents in the course of the First Jewish Revolt in AD 66 (Josephus, War II:431–56). The Roman garrison took refuge in the Herodian towers, but were treacherously slaughtered by the Jews after agreeing to surrender. After the revolt the area was used for the camp of the Tenth Legion (of which very few traces remain, though the towers were preserved and presumably used as part of the fortifications of the Roman camp), and very little else survives until the Crusader period, although at least one of the Herodian towers continued to stand and there is some evidence to suggest there was an Umayyad palace on the site. The Fatimid garrison made its last stand in the Citadel in the face of the Crusader onslaught in 1099 and negotiated its surrender from there. It was rebuilt on its present line by the Crusaders. The Turres David was a major landmark of the Crusader town, built on the great tower base usually identified with the Phasael tower of Herod. The association with David is a late tradition. The Crusader king Baldwin II chose the site as his palace (the curia regis) in 1118. Queen Melisande was besieged in this palace-citadel in 1152 by her son Baldwin III. Parts of the palace, including two vaulted ground-floor storage chambers, 17m long, have been found c 125m south of the Citadel. Great rock-cut cisterns were found beneath them.

The Citadel continued to be used, restored and added to in the Islamic period. The Ayyubids added a tower, the Mamluks under al-Nasir Muhammad in 1310–11 built extensively and added a mosque. The mosque was a 'Friday Mosque' to allow the soldiers to attend Friday prayers without leaving the Citadel unguarded, and is the only mosque built in the Mamluk period known in the city. The Ottoman rulers also restored the Citadel, in particular Sulaiman II in 1531–32, who also added a minaret. The barracks of the Turkish garrison adjoined the Citadel to the south. The British General Allenby proclaimed the liberation of the city from the steps in front of the entrance in 1917. The Citadel was a police post and barracks until 1967, and has now been restored as a museum.

Access is by the footbridge to the main entrance on the east side; the dry ditch once surrounded the medieval Citadel, but is now partly filled in. The outer barbican was built by the Ottoman Sulaiman II over part of the Crusader gate system. His inscriptions can be seen on the outer gate, at the open-air mosque south of the bridge and on the north side of the bridge itself. The bridge leads to the fine

Crusader and Ottoman entrance gate built by the Crusaders and restored by the Mamluks (1310–11). The iron-plated doors are Ottoman. Within it is a 12C complex consisting of guardroom with benches, inner gate with a right-angled turn, and portcullis, and this leads in turn to a fine 14C Mamluk hexagonal chamber. Turning right towards the restored Herodian tower, ascend to the viewing point on the roof of the tower for a splendid prospect over the Old City. This great tower of **Herod the Great** rises direct from the grass. Very large stones with flat dressed edges and low but rough bosses are characteristic of his work. The preserved top of the Herodian work in the tower is 21.4m x 17.1m, and wider at the base (22.6m x 18.3m) with eight courses remaining which are founded on bedrock. The preserved height is 18.95m. Although it is usually identified with Herod's Phasael Tower for which the dimensions given by Josephus are closest, there are also grounds for suggesting it is the tower of Hippicus, with those of Phasael and Mariamne yet undiscovered to the east. The smaller masonry in the upper tower is the work of al-Nasir Muhammad in the 14C.

Abutting the tower on the north side is the remnant of a **city wall of the Byzantine period**, thought by some to be part of the Third North Wall of the period of Herod Agrippa. The present Citadel wall is built above it.

On the floor below the observation point a short film can be viewed before visiting the rooms along the east side of the Citadel, where reconstructions illustrate the history of Jerusalem from the days of the Canaanites, to the Late Roman and Byzantine periods. The Mamluk mosque provides an authentic background for the Islamic period. The history is carried right through to Ottoman and Mandate times with a 'moving parts' exhibition in the northwest tower.

The east tower of the citadel is probably Mamluk, built over Crusader foundations. The archaeological excavations in the court can be seen from above. It is possible to walk round the Citadel ramparts and then to descend to the interior to view the remains of the older Citadel. A numbered series of descriptive panels provides a detailed guide. In a beautifully designed garden with lawns and some interesting plants, including papyrus and cactus, the remains of the **Hasmonean and Herodian wall and towers** can be seen lying right across the centre of the present Citadel. The Hasmonean wall with two towers lies to the west of the Herodian tower. The Hasmonean masonry is typically of smaller blocks, with wide drafted edges and low pecked bosses. The Hasmonean city wall was up to 5.4m in width, and Herod the Great increased the size of the central tower and thickened the wall to about 8m. On the south side of the wall and towers, excavations which descended nearly 11m beneath the surface of the medieval courtyard showed rooms abutting the Hasmonean wall. These remains were covered by the construction of the podium for Herod the Great's palace, 3m–4m high, retained by a network of walls on a different alignment. On the podium a few low fragments of house walls were preserved from the destructions in AD 66–70. Other additions were made to these defences in the 1C AD and in the Byzantine and medieval periods.

At the south end of the court is a wall with attached round tower in the style of the Umayyads, with fragments of stone window grilles. It could be part of an 8C Umayyad palace in the Citadel. The Crusaders constructed a castle straddling the old Jewish wall on the present lines; this was first refurbished with the addition of a tower by al-'Adil I in 1213–14 and then dismantled a few years later by al-Mu'azzam.

The Mamluk and Ottoman work on the Citadel can be admired in the southwest area. The Citadel gained its present appearance under the Mamluk al-Nasir Muhammad in 1310–11. He built the mosque in the southwest corner above a Crusader vaulted hall which had a postern gate at its northwest corner (now blocked) and entrance at the southeast corner. He also built the southeast tower and the upper part of the Herodian tower. Sulaiman II made a general restoration in 1531–32. The inscription over the minbar in the mosque records his repair of the mosque, and the adjacent minaret was probably built at this time and restored in 1655.

The fine northwestern gate complex is Mamluk and Ottoman. Two towers that flank the gate—the northwest with fine machicolations—and the inner wall are all Mamluk. Below the southwest tower were Crusader stables and a postern. The gate itself was built by Sulaiman II as was the outer barbican.

6 • The Armenian Quarter

The Armenian Quarter occupies some 10.5 hectares of the southwest part of the Old City. It is divided by Armenian Patriarchate Rd, with various buildings in the 'Armenian Garden' on the west, and the densely built up convent and residential section on the east. Just outside the city walls to the south are the Armenian Church of the Holy Saviour and the Armenian cemetery. The north and east fringes of the quarter are occupied by other groups, including Anglican Protestant Christians, Syrian and Greek Orthodox Christians, Muslims and Jews (for the last-mentioned, see Jerusalem, section 7).

History

The Armenian Christians come from the areas of modern southeast Turkey and northwest Iran which were occupied in ancient times by the Kingdom of Urartu. Armenian merchants and mercenaries are mentioned in Palestine in the Roman period; their kingdom was early converted to Christianity and pilgrims came to Jerusalem as early as the beginning of the 4C. By the 7C an Armenian doctor named Haratoun listed 70 Armenian convents in Jerusalem, mostly founded during the Patriarchate of St. Gregory the Illuminator, of which few traces remain apart from the Armenian mosaic not far from the Damascus Gate (see p 249) and another found on the Mount of Olives (see p 231). These convents suffered during the Persian and Islamic invasions of the 7C and the list of establishments was reduced to 15.

Nearly half the Armenian population of the Araxes Valley and Van migrated southwest to the mid-Euphrates, Taurus and Cilician areas in the 11C due to pressure from the Seljuq Turks, and by c 1077 were establishing small states there. They profited by the scramble for territory among the Byzantines, Turks and Crusaders, establishing the Kingdom of Armenia c 1098, which endured until 1375 in Cilicia. Baldwin became Count of Armenian Edessa in 1098, before succeeding Godfrey as ruler of Jerusalem in 1099. Revival of Armenian fortunes in Jerusalem began in the 12C when the Armenians bought the Church of St. James from the Georgians (also Orthodox Christians, from the Caucasus area of modern Russia). Some expansion is recorded in the 14C, and the 17C and mid-18C were also pros-

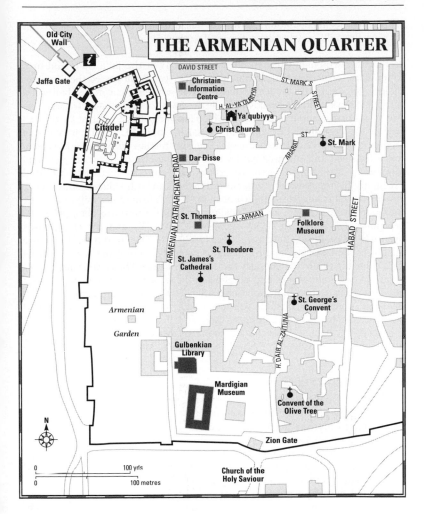

THE ARMENIAN QUARTER

Old City Wall

i

Jaffa Gate

DAVID STREET

ST. MARK'S

Christain Information Centre

H. AL-YA'QUBIYYA

Ya'qubiyya

Christ Church

ARBAT ST.

St. Mark

Citadel

Dar Disse

ARMENIAN PATRIARCHATE ROAD

St. Thomas

H. AL-ARMAN

Folklore Museum

HABAD STREET

St. Theodore

St. James's Cathedral

St. George's Convent

H. DAIR AL-ZAITUNA

Armenian

Garden

Gulbenkian Library

Mardigian Museum

Convent of the Olive Tree

N

Zion Gate

0   100 yds

0   100 metres

Church of the Holy Saviour

perous periods for the Armenians, when they extended their rights in the Church of the Holy Sepulchre. The Armenian Patriarch in Jerusalem was linked by close cultural and hierarchical ties with the Patriarchs in Constantinople and Etchmiadzin (in Armenia), and most higher clerical appointments were filled by Armenians born in the north.

In 1880 the Armenians were few in number, but a thriving community occupying one of the pleasanter quarters of Jerusalem, with a seminary and educated clergy; the convent of St. James was the largest and richest in the Old City. Some survivors of the grim massacres of Armenians in the north by the Turks at the beginning of the 20C came to Jerusalem. The convent retains many of the splendours of the past despite impoverishment and 20C emigration. The local population is now tiny, but Jerusalem is a religious centre for some five million Armenians dispersed worldwide.

To tour the Armenian Quarter, enter the Old City at the Jaffa Gate, and turn south along Armenian Patriarchate Road. After you have passed the Christian Information Centre on the left, where times of services etc. can be obtained, a turning to the left almost directly opposite the entrance to the Citadel leads to the Anglican Christ Church and hospice which is principally of interest for the history of the Protestant Christians in Jerusalem. In 1841, on the initiative of Frederick William IV of Prussia, a joint English/Prussian bishopric in Jerusalem was established and endowed, partly under the impulse of historical piety and missionary intentions, partly to relieve and support distressed Oriental Christians. Bishop Alexander was consecrated at Lambeth Palace, London, on 7 November 1841; he arrived in Jerusalem in 1842. A firman (permit) granted by the Ottoman government for the building of Christ Church was obtained on 10 September 1845. Bishop Gobat succeeded (1846–79) and the church was opened in 1849; Bishop Barclay followed (1879–81). The church was the centre for the London Society for Promoting Christianity among the Jews (founded 1820) and the Church Missionary Society (from 1851). The various missionary organisations built schools and hospitals to the west and south of the Old City (see Jerusalem, section 8: Bishop Gobat's School; the Protestant Cemetery). The Prussian/Anglican partnership was dissolved in 1887. (See also the Church of the Redeemer, p 185 and St. George's Cathedral, p 248.)

Immediately behind Christ Church, to the northeast and approached by Harat al-Ya'qubiyya opposite the Citadel, is the small Muslim shrine called the **Ya'qubiyya**.

History of the Ya'qubiyya site

It may originally have been the site of the monastery founded by Peter the Iberian after his arrival in Jerusalem c 430, to whom were brought the relics of St. James Intercisus (or St. James the Cut-up) who was a Persian martyred under Varahran V in 422. Later, either before or after Peter left Jerusalem, taking the relics with him to Behnasa in Egypt, it became the Church of St. James. A church of St. James with one clergyman is listed in the 9C Commemoratorium. There was a small Crusader church of the same dedication, but after the expulsion of the Latin Christians in 1187 it was little mentioned; in documents of 1394 it is called the Zawiya of Shaikh Ya'qub al-'Ajami (James the Foreigner) and is mentioned as such in 1495 by Mujir al-Din, but became delapidated thereafter. At one time it was used as a prayer hall for the soldiers garrisoning the Citadel, and at the time of the Crimean War it was used as a barracks. It is sometimes also identified as the Church of St. James the Less.

The present building is largely of 12C date with some later alterations. The west end of the mosque has a large pointed 12C arch partly blocked by a smaller portal. Inside, a nave narrowing at the choir has 12C masonry, a cavetto cornice and pointed vaults to the windows and blocked apse. A mihrab is built in the south wall.

It is worth making a diversion to the northeast part of the Quarter to visit the Syrian **Church of St. Mark**, a Syrian Orthodox or Jacobite (also called

Assyrian) convent, on the traditional site of the 'House of Mark'. Continue to the end of Harat al-Ya'qubiyya, turn right into Harat al-Risha (St. Mark's St) and right into Ararat St. The church is 12C on older foundations and is linked with a number of traditions. The Jacobites (or Monophysites) practise an eastern form of Orthodox Christianity which became separated from the mainstream of Orthodoxy at the Council of Chalcedon in 451 after a theological definition of the nature of Christ. The ancient Syriac language is still employed in the liturgy of this church. Open daily 08.00–17.00 (–16.00 in winter); closed Sun and hols.

History of St. Mark's Church

Mark, author of the second and probably the oldest Gospel, is often identified with John Mark, son of Mary of Jerusalem, who had a large house. Tradition links the Last Supper, the site of Pentecost, and the place to which Peter went on his release from prison by the Angel (Acts 12:12) with this house. The church is also believed to be the place where the Virgin Mary was baptised. A Byzantine church is mentioned from the 4C. The present church has a portal and interior vaults of the 12C but the builders are uncertain. The Jacobites fled to Egypt before the Crusader capture of Jerusalem in 1099, and their properties were granted to Gauffier, a Frankish knight. He in turn was captured in Egypt in 1103, and believed dead. The Jacobites were given back their property and there was a problem when Gauffier returned in 1137. A settlement allowing the Jacobites to retain their property was reached only after the intervention of Queen Melisande. It has been suggested that the Crusaders rebuilt the church in the 12C, and it reverted to the Jacobites when the Latins departed in 1187. The convent became the seat of the Syrian bishops in the 15C, and numerous rebuilds are noted in the 18C–20C.

The 12C entrance portal of the convent, with gadrooned voussoirs in a pointed arch, leads to a much restored court. The church opposite is largely 12C with a fine old stone font against the south wall in which the Virgin Mary is said to have been baptised. Above it is a portrait of the Virgin, allegedly painted by St. Luke, which is probably Byzantine in origin. An inscription said to date from the 6C is located on the west pillar inside the entrance. The wall to the left of the altar has a fine variety of blue on-white Kütahya tiles identical to some in the Armenian Convent of St. James (see below). The monk Elia, who did so much work in the Armenian convent between 1726–37, records that he worked on this Syrian church and presumably also installed the tiles.

A visit can be made at this point to the Folklore Museum (for location see map on p 193, for description, see p 207).

You can follow a twisting route southwest along Harat al-Arman through the area behind Christ Church to the remnant of what is probably the Byzantine and Crusader Church of St. Thomas. It lies on the north side of the lane just before reaching Armenian Patriarchate Rd, opposite the southeast corner of the old citadel barracks. The building, 12C on older foundations, is identified as the house of St. Thomas converted into the Church of St. Thomas of the Germans. In 1674 it was a mosque. By the 1960s it was a ruin with a few remnants, including a cornice, and remnants of a chevet, which attested its Crusader origins.

Continuing to Armenian Patriarchate Rd, turn right, pass beneath a vaulted section, and on the left is the entrance to the Armenian Convent of St. James.

Armenian Convent of St. James

The **Convent is a complex built at different times on various levels, entered by a single gate through a high 18C wall. As well as the Cathedral of St. James it contains two other churches, the residence of the Patriarch, accommodation for monks, nuns and pilgrims, a refectory, seminary, library, museum, printing press, administration buildings, school, dwellings and shops.

• The only part of the complex open to visitors is the cathedral, and then only during services: Mon–Fri, Sun 06.30–07.30, 15.00–15.40, Sat 06.30–09.30. Dress must be appropriate—no shorts or sleeveless garments.

History

The church is dedicated to St. James the Great, the son of Zebedee, one of the first of the apostles. He was beheaded by order of Herod Agrippa I in AD 44 during a time of persecution of Christians, when Peter also was arrested (Acts 12:1–3). The site of St. James' tomb was located in Jerusalem by the 4C, but various later confusions included the 6C–7C legend that he preached in Spain, where his body was discovered at Compostela in the 9C. There is no evidence that the present church of St. James is earlier than the 11C–12C, but the chapel building on the northwest side is older and may have been the 5C/6C martyrium of St. Minas.

After the sack of Jerusalem in 1071 by the Seljuq Turks, the Georgian Christians were permitted to build a church and monastery on the site which was dedicated to St. James the Great (between 1072 and 1088); that building forms the central part of the present cathedral. The Georgians became impoverished in the 12C and the Armenians bought the church from them. The earliest Armenian inscription is dated 1151; another mentions Abraham, Patriarch of Jerusalem who died in 1192. Other inscriptions date to the 13C and 14C.

The Armenians made some alterations including the rededication of the chapel on the northwest side to St. Sargis as well as St. Minas. Later the east end of the cathedral was extended and two more chapels were built above the altar, dedicated to St. Peter and St. Paul. The principal relic, however, was the head of St. James the Great; the rest of the body was reputed to be in the church of St. James at Compostela, and other relics in Constantinople. Contacts with the Spanish church were at times close, and included Spanish subsidies in the 15C.

The main entrance was originally on the south side where the 12C doorway is still in use. An arcade along the exterior south wall was blocked, either in 1651 or 1670, to create the Etchmiadzin Chapel. The work was done either by Philip, Catholicos of Etchmiadzin in Armenia, while on a pilgrimage to Jerusalem (he was also responsible for repaving the floor of the cathedral), or by Eliazar, previously Patriarch of Constantinople, then of Jerusalem, who claimed that communications with his superior in Etchmiadzin were too difficult, and had himself proclaimed supreme Patriarch in his own Chapel of Etchmiadzin in 1670.

The Patriarchal throne was donated in 1680. The convent prospered in the 17C, receiving many gifts from pilgrims. It fell into serious debt by the beginning of the 18C. The debts were repaid by the efforts of two Armenians from Bitlis: John the Patriarch in Constantinople and Gregory the Chainbearer, appointed Patriarch of Jerusalem in 1719. Gregory gained his soubriquet by begging with a chain around his neck in the doorway of the Church of the Holy Mother of God in Constantinople for three years, until the debts (variously described as 400 or 800 purses of gold) were repaid.

The financial problems of the Armenians in Jerusalem were pressing at this time, for not only was the Convent of St. James in debt, but repairs to the Church of the Holy Sepulchre were urgently needed, and support for this cause was also sought among the Armenians in the north. Permits from the Ottoman government to restore the Dome of the Holy Sepulchre were granted in 1718–19, and the Armenians were very desirous of joining with the Greeks and Latins in the task. Fine tiles for the Church of the Holy Sepulchre were made and donated by Armenians at Kütahya in Turkey, but for some reason were not used in the repairs. Gregory arrived in Jerusalem in 1721, paid off the debts and initiated another period of Armenian prosperity. He built the wall around the convent; the altar of the Holy Cross in the cathedral; repaired the Church of the Holy Archangels; and in 1727 he repaired St. James' and added many of the decorations—gold and silver ornaments, gold-spun brocades, precious stones and pearls. Fine pottery and the pictorial tiles from Kütahya made for the Church of the Holy Sepulchre were placed in various parts of the convent, probably between 1727 and 1737. Nearly 10,000 fine blue-on-white tiles, mostly from Kütahya, were placed in the various churches and chapels at various times and form an unparalleled collection. Among many interesting objects, the treasury contains sceptres of ancient kings, a staff made from a single large piece of amber, and a fragment of the True Cross in a jewelled casket.

In the following description, the numbers in square brackets refer to chapels at upper levels. The entrance lies between two vaulted sections of the road and leads into a vestibule (**1**). A double-angled entry leads to the courtyard (**2**) which contains a 19C fountain; there are Armenian inscriptions on the west wall, the earliest of which dates to 1151; others refer to Abraham, Patriarch of Jerusalem who died 1192; and Bishop Vartan of Kars (died 1238). In the porch are the wooden bars which were struck like gongs in Turkish times when the use of church bells was prohibited.

The interior of the church is very dim except during festivals on fine days, when sunlight from the high windows and the lights of all the lamps create a dazzling and memorable reflection on the rich vestments, ornaments, tiles and other treasures of the cathedral. Maundrell (1697) describes the 'rich mitres, embroider'd copes, crosses both silver and gold, crowns, chalices and other church utensils without number ... the tortoise-shell and mother-of-pearl are so exquisitely intermingled and inlaid in each other that the work far exceeds the materials ...' which are still so vivid today. The **church** (**3**) has a wide nave and narrow lateral aisles, separated by four squared piers supporting vaulting and a dome. There are three apses to the east with raised altar platforms. The present west entrance dates to the 17C. The marble floor, with inlaid geometric patterns (1651), is usually covered with rugs. The lower piers and walls of the church and those of all the adjacent chapels are tiled mainly in blue-on-white 18C Kütahya tiles with floral and geometric abstract designs. The middle zones of the walls and piers are covered with paintings of saints on canvas mostly of 18C and later date.

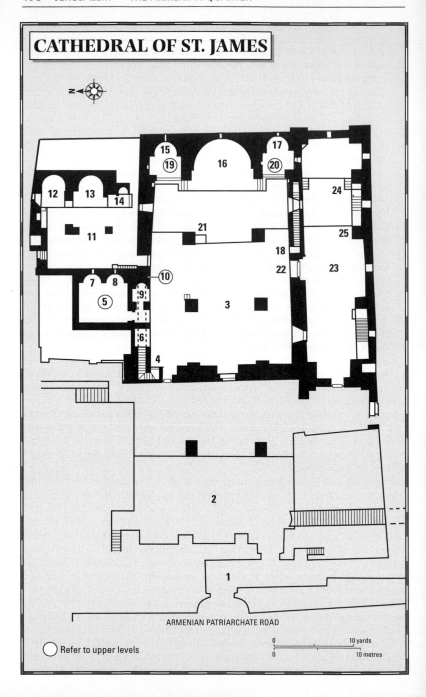

CATHEDRAL OF ST. JAMES

ARMENIAN PATRIARCHATE ROAD

Refer to upper levels

| 0 | 10 yards |
| 0 | 10 metres |

some of which hide earlier frescoes; the piers have medieval pilaster capitals which belong to the cruciform piers that exist under the 18C tiling. On the west face of the southeast pillar is an unusual 12C capital with kneeling lambs among foliage. The low dome, its design deriving from 10C Georgian and Armenian churches, rests on a tall arcaded drum with six lights and 18 blind arcades. The space beneath the vaults is hung with ornaments and lamps making a glittering image of the heavens, and with massive chandeliers. Note the fine egg-shaped hanging ornaments in the church, usually painted in green and yellow on a white ground, sometimes with the winged heads of angels. To the left on entry (in the northwest corner) is a hidden staircase in the west wall (**4**) which ascends to chapels at the upper level to the north, notably the Chapel of the Apostles [**5**]. It has a raised altar, marble floor, and tiles, some of which are concealed by cupboards built against the south wall.

Close to the west end of the north wall of the church is the small 12C Chapel of St. Makarios, Bishop of Jerusalem from 311/12 to c 334. It has some Chinese porcelain tiles set into the Kütahya tiles above the altar, and an 18C inlaid wooden door. Adjacent to it is the entrance to the oldest part of the cathedral, containing the altars of St. Minas (**7**) and St. Sargis (**8**). Between them is the altar of St. Haratoun. There are many lamps and hanging ornaments. The next entry is to the most important shrine, the small 12C **Chapel of St. James the Great** (**9**) on the reputed site of his beheading. A piece of red marble with a circular cavity lies beneath the altar. The chapel also contains Chinese porcelain as well as 18C Kütahya tiles. In the vaulting above is the little chapel dedicated to St. Nishan [**10**].

Further east is the entrance to the **Church of St. Stephen** (**11**), the sacristy and baptistery of the cathedral, with two central piers and three raised altars in apses at the east end dedicated respectively to St. Cyril, Bishop of Jerusalem from c 351 (**12**), to St. Stephen (**13**) and to St. Gregory the Illuminator (**14**). The font in the northeast corner has on the wall above it the chain worn by the Patriarch Gregory in 1719–21 (see History above). This church is also tiled with predominantly blue-on-white tiles. In the cathedral itself, the northeast apse contains an altar dedicated to St. John the Baptist (**15**), the inscribed main apse (**16**) and the southeast altar dedicated to the Virgin Mary (**17**). The south wall contains another hidden staircase (**18**) leading to the chapels of St. Paul [**19**] and St. Peter [**20**] above the main lateral apses. These are also tiled, predominantly with blue-on-white tiles. The entrance to the staircase has a fine carved wooden door inscribed and dated 1355/56, but remodelled for its present situation.

Adjacent to the northeast pier are two patriarchal thrones (**21**). That next to the pier was donated in 1680, and is inlaid with tortoiseshell and ivory in Turkish style. It is said to be the patriarchal throne of St. James the Less, of the family of Jesus and first Bishop of Jerusalem, martyred c 62 at the instigation of the Sadducees. The smaller patriarchal throne to its right is more commonly used, the other being reserved for important occasions.

The doorway (**22**) near the centre of the south wall was the original entrance to the church in the 12C and leads to the *****Etchmiadzin Chapel** (**23**) usually closed. The south side of the doorway has a pointed arch with gadrooned voussoirs (cf. the 12C entrance to the Church of the Holy Sepulchre and the Syrian Convent of St. Mark), and small marble rebated columns. The vaulting in the chapel is supported by 12C elbow brackets. The chapel, built in 1651 or 1670 by blocking in an earlier portico, is long and narrow and contains the Altar of Sinai (**24**) at the top of five steps near the southeast corner. This contains stones from Mount Sinai, Mount Tabor and the place of baptism at Jordan for the consolation of pilgrims who failed to reach these more distant places. The most notable features in the chapel are the delightful and colourful series of pictorial tiles which ornament the north wall on either side of the door, and a section of the south wall (**25**).

The vertical rows of tiles on the north and south walls located beneath capitals were installed by the monk Elia in 1727–37; the horizontal bands by the entrance on the north wall were collected from various places in the convent and placed in position in the mid-20C. Originally made in Kütahya in Turkey in 1718–19 for repairs to the Church of the Holy Sepulchre, they formed sets of scenes (at least 165, of which 52 survive) from the Old and New Testaments which were linked by a description in Armenian on their lower borders. Those for the Old Testament have uncial (unjoined) characters, for the New Testament, cursive; but they are not installed in sequence. There was also a more varied set, which included pictures of saints. The inscriptions mention the names of at least 52 Armenians in Kütahya who donated the tiles, as well as the name of the painter. They are part of a tradition reaching back to the 15C in Turkey, and bear comparison with tiles in the Armenian Church at New Julfa in Isfahan (Iran). The scenes are drawn in brownish black on a white ground with painting in blue, green and yellow, with added red dots in the background. The edicule of the Holy Sepulchre is depicted on one. They are placed among blue-on-white tiles of more abstract design, between which are also interspersed a few Italian majolica tiles.

In 1835 a women's gallery was built at the west end of the church, entered by a staircase from the Etchmiadzin Chapel.

Two other churches lie within the convent walls. The small **Church of St. Theodore** lies just northeast of the cathedral. Entrance is by a tiled porch on the south side containing altars of St. Thaddaeus and St. Sanduxt, with another door on the west. The interior is a single vaulted nave with a raised altar platform. There is a tiny sacristy to the northeast in the Chapel of St. John the Baptist. In the southeast side of the apse is a tiny chapel of St. Mercurius. The walls are covered in mostly blue-on-white Kütahya tiles installed in the 18C. Tradition says the church was built in memory of Theodore, son of Hethum I, who died fighting the Mamluks in 1266. Since 1897 the church has been used as a manuscript library. It contains one of the largest collections of Armenian manuscripts in the world with 4000 items, second to that of Erevan which has 10,000. The collection includes some documents in Syriac, Coptic, Ethiopic, Arabic and Turkish. The oldest manuscripts are Gospels of the 11C, which were not written in Jerusalem. The oldest manuscript actually written in Jerusalem (in the Church of the Holy Archangels) dates to 1316.

The larger **church and convent of the Holy Archangels** lies at a distance to the southeast of the cathedral, in the southeast corner of the convent, just east of the Mardigian Museum (see below) from which it can also be approached. Since the 14C the church has been venerated as the site of the House of Annas, to whom Jesus was taken after his arrest (John 18:12–24) before being sent bound to the House of the High Priest Caiaphas, the son-in-law of Annas (see House of Caiaphas, p 213). It is also called (since the 15C) the Convent of the Olive Tree (A. Dair al-Zaituna), as an olive tree in the courtyard is said to mark the site of the scourging of Jesus. A stone in the exterior northeast corner of the church is reputed to be one of those that would shout aloud if the disciples kept silent (Luke 19:40). The church has a large narthex at the west end, with entrances to north and south, and contains the Chapel of the Flagellation in the northeast angle. The church itself, similar in plan to St. James', has four piers dividing a wide central nave from narrow lateral aisles, with three raised altars in apses at the east end. The lateral altars are also dedicated to John the Baptist and the Virgin Mary. To the left of the entrance is the Chapel of the First Prison of Christ which has an inlaid wooden screen. The main tiling scheme is 18C in uniform blue-on-white, with some polychrome tiles and a few Italian majolica tiles in the west wall.

A chapel at the southeast angle of the complex is dedicated to St. Hrip'sime. It has a carved wooden door inscribed with its date of 1649. Porcelain hanging ornaments, with white ground painted with six winged angels in yellow, blue and green within blackish brown outlines, inscribed in memory of pilgrims in 1739, hang above the main altar and the main nave. The church also contains fine incense-holders. The church probably dates to the second half of the 13C, but a church of the same name is mentioned before the 8C. An inscription on the north wall mentions a restoration in 1377; another inscription is dated 1362. The Patriarch Gregory repaired the convent after 1721 and added the altar of Hrip'sime.

Leaving the Armenian convent and continuing along Armenian Patriarchate Rd, the area behind the wall and buildings to the right is called the **Armenian Garden**. It contains various buildings of the Armenian community, including a seminary, a prospect of the Ottoman wall, and was the site of archaeological excavations in 1961–67 of which nothing can be seen. The land was aquired by the Armenians in the late 14C, and a garden was created here in 1533/34, hence the name.

Just beyond the second vaulted section of Armenian Patriarchate Rd on the left is the entrance to the **Armenian or Mardigian Museum** which occupies an old Armenian seminary (built 1843). Open Mon–Sat 10.00–16.30; closed Sun. The museum has two floors with objects, manuscripts and books illustrating the history and culture of the Armenians and the community in Jerusalem. The adjacent Gulbenkian Library, built in 1929, for printed books, magazines and newspapers relevant to Armenia, is open daily to 17.00.

The Church of the Holy Saviour and the Armenian cemetery (see Jerusalem, section 8) lie just outside the Zion Gate and the tour of the Armenian Quarter can be completed by walking out through the Zion Gate to this church and then round the outside of the city walls to the Jaffa Gate; or by returning along Armenian Patriarchate Rd to the starting point.

7 • The Jewish Quarter

Between the 16C and 19C the south central area of the Old City, c 9 hectares in extent, became known as the Jewish Quarter. Prior to that date, from the destruction of AD 70, the areas of Jewish settlement were less well defined and sometimes non-existent. In the Late Roman period Jews were forbidden to live in the city, and the south area was occupied by the camp of the Tenth Legion. There is sparse evidence for Jewish occupation in the Byzantine period. In the Fatimid period the Jewish population was located in the northeast quarter of the Old City

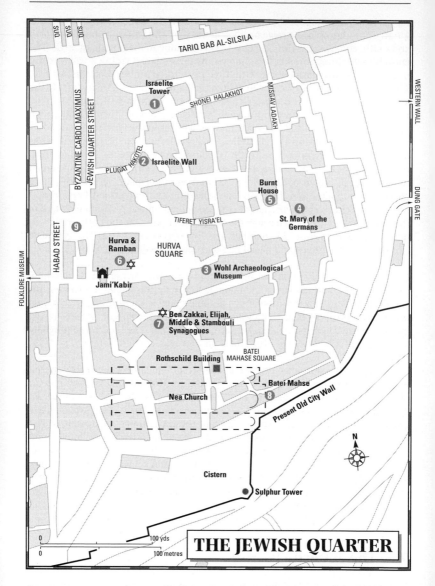

THE JEWISH QUARTER

but it was massacred or expelled in 1099 and resettlement was again proscribed in the early Crusader period. Rabbi Moses ben Nachman, who settled for about a year in the city in 1267, described the wretched conditions of the few Jews then living in the town. A small community developed in the present quarter and he is credited with building the first medieval synagogue. By the 16C there was a strong tradition of pilgrimage and prayer at the Wailing Wall, and in the Ottoman registers of 1525/26 a total of 199 Jewish households were listed in the Old City. By the end of the 17C there were thought to be 300 Jewish families in the city, of whom nearly a quarter were scholars and rabbis.

During Ottoman times taxes were heavy for Jews as well as for Christians. Around 1880 the Jewish population of Jerusalem was estimated at 9000 in three principal divisions: the Sephardi (Spanish) Jews who had been established in Jerusalem since the end of the 15C; the Ashkenazi (European) Jews, a group of whom arrived c 1700, mainly from Germany, Austria, Poland, Hungary and Russia and which included the Hassidim or 'pious' Jews; and the Karaites, a separate and long-established (8C) small community rejecting the authority of the Misnah and the Talmud.

From c 1860 attempts were made by wealthy Jews in Europe (Montefiore, Rothschild and others) to improve the dreadful condition of the Jewish community by establishing hospitals, schools and accommodation for immigrants. Various proposals were made to buy the prayer area in front of the Wailing Wall, but these were aborted by disputes within the local Jewish community. Friction between the Jewish and Muslim communities in Palestine increased from 1929, and culminated in the abandonment of the quarter during the fighting of 1948, when the Old City lay to the east of the eventual armistice line. The quarter was badly damaged during the war, and then occupied by impoverished Arab refugees until 1967.

Following the June War in 1967 and the annexation of East Jerusalem, the quarter was taken over by Israel, and in addition the houses and mosque in the Moors' Quarter on the east side were demolished. Since the 1970s, excavation, restoration and rebuilding throughout the quarter has taken place, followed by the settlement of immigrant Jews during the 1980s.

The great open area before the Wailing Wall, officially called the Western Wall, has become the focus of Jewish religious and national ceremonies and celebrations. Climbing up the steps linking the new plaza and the Jewish Quarter there are contrasts between old masonry and traditional buildings, and modern structures of concrete with local stone facings, including Jewish religious schools, shops for tourists, artists' centres and apartment blocks interspersed with pleasant small open plazas and children's play areas.

The central part of the quarter was the most ruinous after 1948 and most of this has been rebuilt. Restoration work in the quarter was begun by the Ministry of Housing in 1968; then the government established a Company for the Reconstruction and Development of the Old City of Jerusalem Ltd, 1969–1983. The modern quality and input of funds distinguishes it from the rest of the city, and, as so often in Jerusalem, it is the contrasts that reward exploration. Archaeological excavation prior to building has uncovered numerous remains of interest, and it is no longer possible to say—as in guide books written early in the 20C—that there is nothing of interest to be seen in the Jewish quarter. The principal sights are the Herodian Suburb in the Wohl Archaeological Museum and the great main street of Byzantine times, the *cardo maximus*.

On foot the quarter can be reached from the Jaffa or Damascus Gates. Bus 38 takes you to the south side where there is also a crowded car park. The quarter is best avoided on Saturday (the Sabbath) when everything is closed and no refreshments are available. The following tour offers a route with some historical perspective (numbers in brackets refer to the map opposite, on p 202). Note that for a number of sites (Herodian Suburb, the Burnt House, Israelite tower, 'One Last Day Museum' and the City of David site including Warren's Shaft—see Jerusalem, section 9) a combined admission ticket is available; the main ticket office is at the Wohl Archaeological Museum on the east side of Hurva Square. Open Sun–Thur 09.00–17.00; Fri 09.00–13.00; closed Sat.

Enter the Old City by the Jaffa Gate and descend David St to the Street of the Chain; take the first turning to the right into the Jewish Quarter at Plugat Hakotel St. On the corner of Bonei Hahoma St and Plugat Hakotel is the Center for Jerusalem in the First Temple Period with models and child-focused activities, open Sun–Thur 09.00–16.00 (–18.00 in summer), Fri and eve of hols 09.00–13.00. At the junction of Plugat Hakotel with Shonei Halakhot St, several flights of steps lead down beneath the street to the remains of the **Israelite Tower and Hasmonean defences* (**1**). These impressive remains are carefully preserved and beautifully displayed and explained beneath the modern buildings. A massive tower, with walls over 4m thick, still standing 8m high, is dated to the 7C BC. It may have been built by the ruler of Judah, Manasseh, and be part of a gate tower in the Israelite city wall. Against the corner, amid signs of burning, arrowheads were found which probably date to the Babylonian sack of Jerusalem in 586 BC. Following this destruction, the area was abandoned until the 2C BC when another city wall was built (the First North Wall of Josephus). A Hasmonean tower and city wall, which abuts and partly incorporates the earlier Israelite one, has dressed stones with broad drafted edges. Its continuation can be seen beneath the *cardo maximus* to the west (**9**).

Immediately south in Plugat Hakotel St, you can view c 40m of another Israelite city wall (**2**) in an open cutting. Known as the 'Broad Wall', it is 7m in width, and between two and seven courses survive to a maximum height of 3.3m. These are only the foundations of a city wall, built of large, partly hewn stones laid without mortar, perhaps by Hezekiah in the late 8C BC. It is earlier than the Israelite tower (**1**), and on a different alignment.

Continuing south along Plugat Hakotel St, turn left into Teferet Isael and continue to the east side of Hurva Square; on the left in Ha-Karaïm Rd, is the entrance to the Wohl Archaeological Museum (**3**), with The Herodian Suburb.

Wohl Archaeological Museum

Here remains of six houses (mainly the basements) belonging to wealthy residents of Jerusalem between 37 BC and AD 70 are preserved as they were excavated, 3m below the present pavement. They include the so-called Palatial Mansion, and give a detailed picture of life in one of the richest sections of Jerusalem in the time of Christ. The museum exit is onto the stepped passage (Ma'alot Rabbi Yehuda ha-Levi) which leads down to the Western Wall just below Misgav Ladakh St.

In the **Western Building** are baths, with small but fine mosaics, a cistern, and ashlar barrel vaulting in the basement of the house of a wealthy family. They illustrate the requirements of Jewish ritual concerning the laws of purity. There is a photographic display of the state of the quarter during excavation and some remains of an 8C–7C BC house which was not preserved. The **Middle Complex** contains two houses with fine mosaics (one is cut by a massive Byzantine drain), and has an excellent display of whole utensils and objects, including painted bowls and a stone sundial. A cul-de-sac leads to the **Peristyle Building**, perhaps a colonnaded court (partly reconstructed) with *opus sectile* floor. The corner columns have heart-shaped cross sections. There are fragments of an Ionic fluted column (the flutes are mostly cut in plaster) and of painted wall plaster.

The most important building, the **Palatial Mansion**, stood on the east edge of the Western Hill overlooking the Temple and the Lower City. It covered an area of c 600 square metres with rooms around a central court, on two, perhaps originally three, levels. The central court was paved, with cisterns beneath it. To the west, the best preserved wing of the building contained living and guest quarters. Two rows of rooms survived to ceiling height at 3m with the sockets of cypress ceiling beams preserved. Traces of fresco on the plastered walls survived in all rooms. The entrance room to the west wing had a damaged mosaic floor with fret and guilloche patterns in the borders, pomegranate motifs in the corners, and possibly a rosette at the damaged centre. The room to the south had painted plaster in red and yellow panels on the south wall which survived to a height of 2.5m. The painting showed architectural features, such as windows, cornice and acroteria. To the north was a very large reception hall, 6.5m x 11m, mostly destroyed in the modern building process, but decorated in stucco panels imitating ashlar masonry. Moulded fragments found in the debris had fallen from the ceiling. This type of decoration is paralleled in the 1C BC in Asia Minor and Italy. An earlier phase of plastering was painted rather than moulded, with a very attractive floral frieze. The southwest room off this hall contained an architectural fresco dating to an early phase of its decoration.

The east wing of the building was less well preserved. A small bathroom with a mosaic with rosette motif was located near the centre. Stairs descended on the south to the service area at a lower level, where there was a rock-cut corridor, with two doorways and steps descending to a large pool with a barrel-vaulted roof. On the north, other steps led down to a small court and mosaic and to another very large stepped immersion bath with two entrances and a barrel-vaulted roof. A little of the fine furniture of the house survived, some of which is displayed; it included small stone tables, some very expensive glassware and delicate painted ceramic bowls, gaming pieces and lamps. Despite the strong Hellenistic influence, the wealth shown in the furnishing and the number of immersion baths suggested that this was the house of the High Priest of Jerusalem. An alternative view suggests the earlier phase of the building was the Hasmonean and early Herodian (37–23 BC) palace.

The Southern Building, not restored, has a row of small rooms, with, notably, ceiling slots preserved in the back wall.

On leaving the museum, opposite is **St. Mary of the Germans (4)**, a carefully preserved ruin which is combined as a monument and garden on several levels. You enter from Misgav Ladakh St. A notice on the west wall and a plan on an interior wall give the history of this building. It was the 12C Crusader church, hospice and hospital of the Order of the German Knights of the Hospitallers, established in 1128 to serve the German-speaking pilgrims coming to Jerusalem. This area was part of the German quarter of the Crusader town, when Misgav Ladakh was called the Street of the Germans. In 1190 the German Knights established a separate military order, the Teutonic Knights. In the later 13C the buildings were partly destroyed by the Mamluks and subsequently used for other purposes. Part of the complex was in use as a stable in 1967. A programme of excavation and conservation was undertaken in 1968.

As you enter by the main west door of the church on Misgav Ladakh St, opposite is the restored remnant of three apses. On the left a doorway gave onto the hospice, and on the right another doorway led to the hospital at a lower level, which is now mainly occupied by a small garden. A view of the exterior east wall of the church may be had from the garden.

On the west side of Misgav Ladakh, slightly to the north on the left is Tiferet Israel St and just beyond the junction on the right are the remains of the *****Burnt House** (5). The exhibition is in the basement of the Arches House, with audiovisual presentation in a number of languages.

The Burnt House was part of another complex (excavated in 1970) which had been destroyed in the Roman sack of Jerusalem in AD 70. The building may have belonged to the wealthy but oppressive priestly family of Kathros, and is particularly interesting for the fine collection of furniture and everyday objects illustrating the life of a well-to-do Jewish family in the 1C AD. The house, built with plastered blocks of soft limestone, and its contents are displayed just as they were when the fire destroyed them. The exhibition also includes several display cases with objects found in the excavations.

Between Tiferet Israel St and Ha-Karaim Road towards Hurva Square, with the entrance just east of the Wohl Museum, is the Tiferet Israel Synagogue, or 'Glory of Israel', also called the Nisan Bak after its founder. The principal synagogue of the Hassidic Jews, it was built between 1862 and 1872 on land purchased in 1843, and destroyed in 1948. You can see a row of four round arches and the ritual bath in the cellar, restored since 1967.

Opposite is the Court of the Karaites, a sect of Judaism founded by Anan Ben David in Baghdad in the mid-8C, which rejects the authority of the Talmud. The Karaite community, which existed in Jerusalem between the 8C/9C and 11C, was presumably destroyed when the city fell to the Crusaders in 1099. They apparently returned c 1400, and in 1642 there were said to be 27 Karaites living in Jerusalem, but in the mid-18C there were none. The synagogue, named for the founder of the sect and belonging to the small 19C Karaite community in the Jewish quarter, was dedicated in 1864, damaged in 1948, and the ruins removed in the 1970s. A restored synagogue was dedicated in 1981 on what is said to be the foundations of an ancient Karaite synagogue in the cellar. The Karaite community today is located principally in Ramla, Ashdod and Beersheva.

Returning west, in Hurva Square is a complex of synagogues and a mosque. The **Ramban and Hurva synagogues** (6) are complex and poorly preserved remains which stand on the ruins of the Crusader Church of St. Martin. A copy of the letter written by the scholar Rabbi Moses ben Nachman (1194–1270, called the Ramban or Nachmanides) in 1267 is displayed here. He describes the miserable conditions of the city at the time, the presence of just two Jewish brothers, impoverished dyers in a population of 2000, and how he converted a ruin into a synagogue. The Torah scrolls were brought from Nablus: they had been removed for safe keeping in 1244 at the time of the Khwarizmian invasion. The new synagogue attracted more Jews to Jerusalem, and provided for the needs of the tiny community and Jewish pilgrims to Jerusalem. The ruins appear to show a two-aisled hall which was converted into a synagogue towards the end of the 14C. The synagogue collapsed after heavy rain in 1474; a dispute that followed led to its demolition, and the dispute was only resolved by the intervention of Sultan Qa'it Bay. The synagogue was rebuilt by 1523 when it was said to be the only synagogue in Jerusalem. It was closed by order of the Turkish governor of Jerusalem in 1586. A group of Ashkenazi Jews settled in Jerusalem in 1700, but their project to buy land and build a synagogue foundered on internal dissent, debt and the death of their rabbi (Judah he-Hasid), and the land and partly-built synagogue were seized for non-payment. This, the Hurva or 'Ruin', was returned to the Ashkenazi community by Ibrahim Pasha in 1836. A large quadrangular synagogue with central dome was at last built, and dedicated in 1864; it was destroyed in 1948 and its conservation begun in 1977.

Close by the Ramban is the small mosque and minaret of Sidi Umar or the Jami' Kabir, built before 1473–74. The original name of the mosque is unknown but it has also been associated with the ruins of the Crusader Church of St. Martin because of the columns inside. According to Mujir al-Din (1495) the mosque was renewed after 1397. The minaret is a square tower of Syrian type, with octagonal muezzin's gallery. The upper part is typical of 15C minarets in Jerusalem. The mosque (closed) was damaged in 1967 and repaired in 1974.

Before proceeding to view other synagogues in the quarter, you could visit the **Old Yishuv Court Museum**, or Folklore Museum, at 6 Rehov Or-HaHayyim, located on the west side of the central section of Habad St on the flanks of the Armenian quarter in the section called the 'Ari Quarter'. It is established in a complex including the Ha'Ari synagogue (Sephardi, 19C to 1936), the Or Hachaim synagogue (Askenazi, abandoned in 1948) and the Bet Weingarten, refurbished and opened in 1976 to illustrate the folklore and life of the Jewish community from the 19C to 1948. Open Sun–Thur 09.00–16.00, except the eve of holidays. Admission charged.

Returning to Hurva Square, take the street leading south opposite the ruined synagogue and you will see to the left a complex of four synagogues. The **ben Zakkai, Elijah, Middle and Stambouli Synagogues** (**7**) cover approximately 800 square metres and have undergone extensive restoration. They are open 09.00–16.00, Fri 09.00–14.00; closed Sat during services.

Entrance to the Four Sephardic Synagogues.

History of the synagogues

The synagogues are the focus of the Sephardi community, who built the complex with limited funding over an extended period following their ejection from Spain under Ferdinand and Isabella at the end of the 15C. The earliest surviving synagogue, the ben Zakkai, was built c 1606–10 at a time when the Sephardi community was the largest of the Jewish communities in Jerusalem, and named in honour of Yohanan ben Zakkai. (A rabbi in AD 70, he was a moderate, horrified by the hideous strife among the Jewish insurgents in the First Revolt, and escaped to the Roman camp. He led the council of rabbis at Jamnia, which defined the conservation and interpretation of the Law following the destruction of the Temple.) The building was extended by a study and meeting hall on the northwest side c 1625; this was converted to another synagogue c 1702 and named for Elijah. In the mid-18C a courtyard on the northeast side of the ben Zakkai was converted into the Middle Synagogue, and in 1764 the large Stambouli synagogue was completed on the northeast side of the complex. Repairs were carried out in 1835.

The ben Zakkai and Middle synagogues are long halls with cross vaulting; the Elijah and Stambouli buildings have the traditional cross on a square pattern. The seating was, as in all Sephardi synagogues, around a high bimah at the centre of the hall. The Arks of the Law (double in the ben Zakkai) were in the east wall. Abandoned in 1948, the structures survived virtually intact, though lacking all woodwork and furnishings and in a damp condition, until restoration in 1968–72 when they were rededicated. The bimah used for the reading of the Torah, has been lowered from six steps to one to make space for a larger congregation. The doors are designed by various modern artists; the Arks in the Elijah and Stambouli Synagogues are Italian of 15C or 16C date, donated after the rededication.

At the south end of the Jewish Quarter reached via Batei Mahse or Gal'ed Sts is a large complex of buildings around a paved plaza, Batei Mahse Square, which contains sculpted fragments, including a huge Attic base, column drums and Ionic capital found in a Herodian or Hasmonean context in excavations 100m north to the east of the Hurva. They were not found *in situ* and what building they decorated is unknown; it is estimated that the column was originally 10m high (see p 210). The Rothschild Building is on the west side of the square. On the south side is the **Batei Mahse** (**8**). It was built in 1862 to house poor immigrant Jews from Europe.

The most important structure discovered in the recent excavations and which underlies much of this area, though little can be seen, is the **Nea or New Church of Justinian**. The northeast apse of the church is preserved below the Batei Mahse. Open daily 09.00–17.00.

Reconstructed column found in excavations in the Jewish Quarter (N. Avigad, Discovering Jerusalem, p. 163, fig. 180, Oxford, 1984)

History of the Nea Church

The 'New Church of St. Mary, Mother of God' was built by the Emperor Justinian and dedicated in 543. This, the largest basilica known in Palestine, was built, like the south extension of the *cardo maximus*, as part of a fine new layout for the Mount Zion area which became particularly important to the Christians of the Byzantine and Crusader periods. The church was famous for its size and magnificence, but before the recent excavations it was only known from Procopius and other literary sources and from the 6C Madaba Map (see p 71) which indicated its probable location. Its actual location was lost.

In 1970 parts of its foundation were identified in the courtyard of the Batei Mahse. Other fragments identified in the years to 1982 have led to a complete reconstruction of the plan. The basilica's length, including the narthex, was 116m, internal dimensions were 100 x 52m, with two aisles and a central nave, and three apses facing east. The interior was flagged with marble. As well as the church, the complex included a hospital, a hostel, a monastery and a library, none of which have been identified. Part of the northeast apse, the tremendous cistern in the vaults to the south, and the external southeast corner which extends below the Ottoman city wall into the adjacent garden can still be seen.

In the court of the Batei Mahse (with your back to the Rothschild Building) take the steps descending to the right, turn left at the bottom, and descend by more steps to an entrance with grille where part of the northern apse can be viewed.

Much of the great 5C cistern is visible adjacent to the small open-air theatre recently built inside the Sulphur Tower to the south. The cistern was 10m in depth and is built of compacted rubble faced with strong pinkish plaster. There are six interlinked chambers oriented north–south with niches in the north face. The complex measures 9.5–17m x 33m and is supported by pillars 3.5–5m square. It was entered from the northeast corner by a stepped passage, also plastered and vaulted, which leads into the cisterns at the third vault from the west. Opposite the entrance and 8m above the floor, a moulded plaster inscription in Greek on a panel 1.58m long records that it was the work of Justinian carried out by Constantinus, Priest and Abbot 'in the 13th (year of the) indiction', after the dedication of the church itself. Part of the southeast corner of the church can be seen 50m to the northeast outside the next angle of the city wall (see p 76).

The area north of the Batei Mahse, along the east flanks and steep slopes of the Jewish Quarter, has been extensively rebuilt with two yeshivas (centres for study of the Torah) above the Dung Gate (the Porat Yosef Yeshiva, dedicated 1923, rebuilt and rededicated 1977, on the lower road, and the Yeshivat Hakotel above). The effect of the rebuilding, which includes the Nebenzahl House with its five storeys east of the Batei Mahse, has been to create a new skyline on the ridge of the Western Hill which towers with stark modern lines over the Western Wall and the Haram.

The Byzantine Cardo

Recrossing the Jewish Quarter to the west, brings you to the Street of the Jews or Jewish Quarter St. Under this street and Habad St running parallel to the west is the older *Byzantine cardo maximus (9), the scene of much excavation and restoration. Some 180m of this Byzantine street were traced, approximately

2.5m below the modern ground surface. It was probably built by Justinian (AD 527–65) and formed the monumental south extension of the *cardo maximus* of the Roman Aelia Capitolina built in the 2C. It led to the Nea Gate, inside which Justinian built the Nea Church.

The Byzantine *cardo maximus* was a monumental street, with porticoes for pedestrians, c 22.5m wide, bordered on the west by a wall and on the east by an arcade resting on square pillars. The road itself was 12.5m wide. The columns of the portico were monolithic, and stood on bases of Attic type which were not uniform in size; the Byzantine capitals were of Corinthian type; the total height of columns was c 5m. In the south section can be seen traces of small shops, which were cut back into the rock face on the west side behind the portico; one arch is preserved.

Continuing through the tunnel to the north under the new buildings further sections of the *cardo maximus* are preserved, mostly on the west side. Excellent explanations and reconstruction drawings of the remains are displayed. Further north, modern boutiques line the street, preserved ruins and deep shafts with glazed covers permit a view of sections of the deeply buried city walls of earlier periods. Two sections are said to be the west continuation of the Hasmonean wall (2C–1C BC) and one the west continuation of the 7C BC Israelite wall seen on Plugat Hakotel St. The depth of these shafts gives a clear idea of the amount of debris built up over the centuries in this part of Jerusalem. Much of this deposit derives from the sack of Jerusalem in AD 70, which was followed by massive levelling operations for Aelia Capitolina in the 2C. No better testimony to the turmoil of the various sackings of Jerusalem can be given than the sight of the battered walls of the *cardo maximus* itself. At the north end of the cardo maximus are the beginnings of the great medieval suqs and the busy markets (see Jerusalem, section 4) which overlie the Roman-Byzantine *cardo maximus* to the north. Among the gift shops is the entrance to the **One Last Day Museum**, with a photographic exhibition recording the abandonment of the Jewish Quarter in 1948. Open Sun–Thur 09.00–17.00, Fri 09.00–13.00. Admission charged, combined ticket available.

From here the choice is either to continue north through the market to the Damascus Gate or to return by David St to the Jaffa Gate.

8 • Mount Zion

The area now called Mount Zion lies outside the Ottoman city walls on a plateau at the south end of the Upper City. This area was enclosed within the Herodian and Byzantine city walls, and in the 4C was identified by Christians with the place of the Last Supper, with Jesus' imprisonment in the House of Caiaphas, with the Descent of the Holy Spirit at Pentecost, and with the site of the earliest Christian church. Other traditions located here are the Tomb of King David, and the place where the Virgin Mary died, or 'fell asleep' (the Dormition).

Mount Zion can be approached by road and a car park just below the Zion Gate; from within the Old City by the Zion Gate; or by paths and road from the west. Buses 1, 2, 38 pass the south side.

History

The name Zion is of uncertain etymology, perhaps related to the H. sayon ('dry place'), or A. sahwa'(mountainous ridge'). Mount Zion is mentioned in poetic parallelism with the heights of Zaphon, the northern mountain of the Canaanite deity Baal in Ps. 48:2. It is first referred to in the Old Testament in II Sam. 5:6–10 and I Chr. 11:4–9 as the stronghold of Jerusalem captured by David, which was on the southeast hill (see Jerusalem, section 9). Later the name achieved a poetic equivalence with the Temple, and with the city of Jerusalem as a religious capital. The concepts of Zion as the heavenly Jerusalem and as a holy mountain where the Messiah would appear were also deep-rooted. The Davidic and the Christian traditions became merged especially as remembrance of the real location of the ruined city of David on the southeast ridge was lost after the 1C AD, and the name Zion was attached to the southwest hill by Christians by the 4C. The southwest hill was identified with Christian traditions as the place of the house with an upper room in which the Last Supper was held at the time of Passover (Mark 14:15); of the house of Caiaphas the High Priest where Jesus was taken after his arrest at Gethsemane and Peter denied him three times (Mark 14:53–72); and of the house in which the disciples gathered at the time of Pentecost or the Descent of the Holy Ghost (Acts 2:1). Here also was the house of Mary, the mother of John surnamed Mark, where Peter came after his miraculous release from prison (Acts 12:12) and here, by the 5C, was located the tradition that the Virgin Mary died in the House of John. In the 4C Mount Zion was also associated with James the Less, the brother of the Lord and first Bishop of Jerusalem, thus the place of his patriarchal throne. From this tradition grew the title 'Mother of all the Churches' for the great church on Zion.

The earliest defensive walls around the plateau are probably of the 2C BC and survived to AD 70. This area was therefore part of the walled city in the time of Jesus. The New Testament gives no indication of the location of the venerated places, thus the Byzantine Christian locations are plausible but uncertain. The 4C Byzantine city wall enclosed this upper part of Zion, but not the Tyropoeon Valley below. According to the Bordeaux Pilgrim in 333, inside the walls at Zion was the site of the palace of David and one remaining synagogue. Outside the walls on the east were the ruins of the House of Caiaphas.

The first Church of the Apostles was built by Bishop Maximus between 336 and 349. According to Egeria in 384 the church was at the site of Pentecost, but she makes no reference to the chamber of the Last Supper. It was, wrote Epiphanius of Salamis (c 374–94) 'the Church of God, a small building, on the place where the disciples on their return from the Mount of Olives, after the Saviour's Ascension, assembled in an upper chamber' in a part of Mount Zion which had escaped destruction in AD 70. He also records that a synagogue building (one of seven originally located here) had survived to the time of Constantine. He implies that this synagogue was another building, which had disappeared by his time. Not long after, between 397 and 417, the church was rebuilt by Bishop John II of Jerusalem. In the mid-5C it was called Holy Zion, the Mother of all the Churches.

After 450 Empress Eudocia (who extended the wall of the city to enclose the Tyropoeon Valley) built a new Church of the Visitation of the Holy Spirit at Pentecost and one dedicated to St. Peter on the site of the House of Caiaphas. These churches are shown on the 6C Madaba Map. By the 6C the Upper Chamber of the Last Supper had been identified with the Upper Room of Pentecost. It is probable that by the 6C a monastery marked the site where Peter went outside the House of Caiaphas and wept.

The churches were destroyed in the Persian sack of 614. The plan given by the pilgrim Arculf in 680 is presumably of the building restored by Modestus after 614. Arculf notes it was large and the Commemoratorium in the early 9C records it was marginally larger (at 39 x 26 dexteri) than the Church of the Nativity at Bethlehem and was served by 17 presbyters and clergy. Arculf describes a broad-room building with similarities to the much smaller rectangular building we visit today, with entrance near the corner in one of the long walls. Traditions concerning Mary's death in the House of John on Mount Zion seem to date from the 5C, and in 451 Jerusalem was decreed to be the location of this tradition, and not the rival Ephesus in Turkey.

The tradition of the Tomb of David appears to be a late one. Apart from the 4C mention by the Bordeaux Pilgrim and later references to a Palace of David on Mount Zion, the first Christian reference to a tomb of David on Mount Zion occurs in the 11C. The area was in ruins when the Crusaders took the city in 1099.

Although the site was outside the city walls in the 12C, the Crusaders lavished much care on it. They refurbished the holy sites, and built the Monastery and Church of St. Mary on Mount Zion, which were served by the Augustinian order. This 12C church was also large with three aisles. It had a crenellated roof, towers and other defensive features because of its situation outside the walls. The Abbot of Mount Zion owed 150 sergeants in service to the crown, a rating or ranking that can be compared to that of the Patriarch and Chapter of the Holy Sepulchre who owed 500 each. What remains of the church is on two levels, the upper containing the room of the Last Supper (the Cenacle), while in the lower level tradition began to locate David's tomb. Not far away was the Church of the House of Caiaphas.

Following the capture of Jerusalem, in 1192 Salah al-Din rebuilt the city wall to enclose Mount Zion. Local Christians seem to have taken over the service of the church and convent, which may have been affected by al-Mu'azzam's dismantling of the defences in 1219. Work on the restoration ceased in 1244, after which it was a ruin. The chamber of the Dormition and the double chapel of the Cenacle were still frequented by pilgrims, albeit with difficulty. Pilgrims in the 13C and early 14C mention the Tomb of David near the lower chapel, and the tombs of the Kings of Judah in an adjacent rubble-filled crypt. In 1335 and 1337 the Franciscans managed to negotiate the purchase of some land on the south side of the Cenacle; by c 1342 they had a hospice serving the members of monastic orders; and by 1346 they had obtained the Cenacle, Pentecost, and the place of Christ's appearance to Thomas. The Hall of the Last Supper was restored with modifications to the 12C building. By the 1350s the Sisters of St. Mary of Mount Zion had a hospice with 200 beds for female pilgrims in a convent on the site of the Dormition which was under the supervision of the Franciscans by 1373. The Franciscans built a cloister against the south side of the Cenacle c 1377.

Jews and Muslims became convinced of the authenticity of the Tomb of David in the lower storey, and disputed the Christian right to it. After several attacks on the place between 1368–72, the Muslims succeeded in gaining rights over the tomb and by c 1450 had built a mosque in the lower storey, with a marble cenotaph that destroyed the altars and paintings there. They blocked it off from the rest of the building and prohibited access. The custodianship was placed in the care of a Muslim family. The Franciscans were permitted to rebuild the church, but were expelled from it in 1523 by a decree of Sulaiman II, whose inscription of 1524 in the east wall of the mosque at the Tomb of David forbade access. The Franciscans were finally expelled from their convent also in 1551 under the pretext that they were armed and constituted a threat to the defence of the city and the nearby city walls which had been recently rebuilt by Sulaiman. From the mid-16C only very limited access to any part of the complex was permitted to Christians and Jews.

There has been little alteration to the building since that date, mainly the addition in the mid-16C of a superior cenotaph, a leaded dome and a minaret. The area around was used extensively for Christian burial. Near the Ottoman city wall are the cemeteries of the Latins, Armenians and Greeks; the Protestant Cemetery lower down near Bishop Gobat's School dates from 1870. The Dormition was built from 1898. The Muslims were unable to retain their rights in 1948, and the Tomb of David became a major Jewish shrine surrounded by a number of Jewish religious schools and prayer rooms.

From the Zion Gate, if you first turn right, you see on the left the Armenian **Church of the Holy Saviour**. One tradition holds this to be the site of the House of the High Priest Caiaphas, where Jesus was imprisoned and Peter denied him three times. The location of the House of Caiaphas is quite uncertain, but this may be the 5C site of the church built by Eudocia.

The north end of the garden contains a part-built Armenian church. The present church at the south end of the garden probably dates from the 12C; it was acquired by the Armenians in the 14C, and church and cloister were rebuilt c 1480. From 1948 to 1967 the church lay on the armistice line and was badly damaged. It is a simple, vaulted structure (c 14m x 8m). The narrow west door with window above leads to a single nave narrowed at narthex and choir, with raised altar in the apse. The apse originally had a single window, now blocked. Groined vaulting supports the roof. At the southeast corner is the tiny Chapel of the Second Prison of Christ (for the First Prison, see House of Annas, p 201). At the southwest corner is the sacristy. The lower walls of the church have blue-on-white 18C Turkish tiles. Outside are the cells of the monastery, and the tombs of the Armenian Patriarchs who were buried here up to 1948. The earliest extant gravestone in the cemetery is of a monk who died in 1636.

Returning to the Zion Gate, turn right (south), then bear right at the next two forks to the **Dormition Church**, the Dormitio Sanctae Mariae, the place where Mary fell asleep. Open 08.30 (Sun 09.30)–12.00, 12.30–18.00. The land was presented by William II of Prussia to the German Catholic Society of the Holy Land in 1898; the Church of the Virgin was built 1901–10 in Romanesque style (architect H. Renard). Its great circular tower with conical roof and four tall turrets make it is a notable landmark on the south side of the city. The interior is lavishly decorated with mosaics on the floor, walls and dome, depicting mainly the prophets and apostles. The Byzantinesque Madonna and Child on the ceiling was made in 1939. The crypt, a circular pillared hall with ambulatories, is the traditional location of Mary's home and death. It contains the Chapel of the Dormition, with statue of the sleeping Mary surrounded by six columns under a

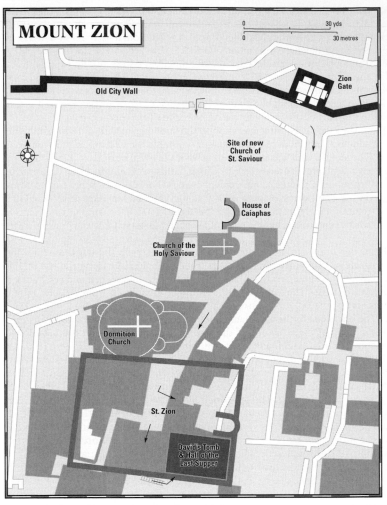

dome mosaic of Christ receiving her soul. The tall tower of the Dormition Abbey to the southwest, setting back in stages from a rectangular base to a balcony and elongated dome with clock, is another landmark dating to the early 20C.

The Cenacle and the Tomb of David

Returning to the main lane, turn right (south) for c 30m; on the left is the entrance to the ***Hall of the Last Supper**, the Coenaculum or Cenacle. This is the traditional site of the Last Supper of Jesus and the disciples in an Upper Room before the Crucifixion, and the site of Pentecost (the descent of the Holy Spirit to the disciples after the Resurrection). Open 08.00–17.00, Fri 08.00–13.00.

Entrance from the lane is by a pointed-arched entrance with chevron and fret design (16C). Ascend the stairs immediately to the left in the courtyard of what was an old pilgrim hospice, then an Ottoman house and leads now to a Jewish yeshiva. Follow an open passage around to the left at first floor level and enter a rectangular hall, 'the Upper Room'. The hall was constructed in the 12C as part of the southern gallery in the upper level of the Crusader Church of St. Mary of Zion. The roof was restored and refurbished by Latin architects in the 14C. Two free-standing columns (that at the east is granite), and a third against the west wall, support the roof. Originally the altar and choir lay to the east but were destroyed in the building of the dome over the Tomb of David in the lower storey. The capitals are of varied type (mainly 12C and Gothic) and from them springs fine groined vaulting. Traces of 14C painted heraldry remain on the wall just inside to the right of the door. The Franciscan entrance from the upper level of the cloister was formerly located in the southwest corner where steps (no entry) descend to the antechamber of the Tomb of David. A dome above the stairs is supported on little marble columns with a noteworthy small capital depicting pelicans pecking their parent's breast, with feet resting on grotesque heads. The pelican is a symbol of charity in Christian art; the popular fallacy that the parent bird restored its young to life with its own blood made it a symbol of parental devotion. A sculpted mihrab (16C) and attractive restored Ottoman coloured glass windows can be seen in the south wall. Returning by the same route, a good view of the Dormition can be obtained from the open passage, and as the descent of the courtyard staircase is made, note the star, bird and other designs in relief (16C/17C?) reused on the wall above to the south.

Return to the lane, turn left and go up a few steps and through the high 16C pointed arch with gadrooned archivolt; turn left into a passage and the 14C Franciscan cloister leading to the **Tomb of David**. Open 08.00–sunset. Men should cover their heads.

Variously claimed as the site of a 1C/4C AD synagogue and of a 4C church, the site is certainly not that of the tomb of David, who was buried in his city on the southeast hill (see Jerusalem, section 9). The Tomb of David was first located near here in the 11C, and only became a matter of contention in the 14C. In the 15C it was taken by the Muslims as the shrine of the Tomb of David, when the whole complex of vaulted passages and buildings was called al-Nabi Da'ud (the Prophet David); the Jews took it in the war in 1948, since when it has been in their custody. Entrance at the southwest corner leads to a hall, formerly part of the 12C Lower Church of St. Mary of Zion which was blocked off in the 15C and modified for use as a mosque. The larger west part forms a low, rectangular antechamber with piers and vaulting; the east wall has fine tiles (18C?), which frame the two square doorways leading to the second antechamber and the tomb. The older tiles, with floral designs in blue, green and red, are patched with green and black geometric tiles of the same make used in 16C repairs to the Dome of the Rock. The same mixture of tiles is employed on the mihrab of the south wall of the second antechamber and on the east half of the screen wall before the tomb. The mihrab was probably first inserted c 1452. Three small windows in the east wall light the chamber.

The screen wall contains three square-framed doors and windows which give onto the very large cloth-draped cenotaph venerated as the Tomb of David but probably dating to the 16C. Behind it is a north-oriented niche in blackened and ruined masonry. which is probably of 4C date. Its origins are uncertain. The argument that this is part of an earlier synagogue incorporated in the 4C church depends on the orientation of the niche. Early synagogues were oriented towards the Temple in Jerusalem (but generally the façade rather than a niche or apse). This niche is oriented to the north rather than to the Temple. It is also unlikely to be the apse of the 4C church, which should face towards the east (unless, like the Martyrium of Constantine, it was oriented on the Tomb of Christ). It has been reconstructed as a niche in the exterior south side of an inscribed east-oriented apse of the 4C/5C church. The burning on the wall may be attributed to the sack of the church by the Persians in 614 or by the Muslims in 965.

You may return from here to the lane and continue to the south for the view and to visit the Protestant Cemetery. Or turn left through the 14C Franciscan cloister and a garden (adjacent to which is now housed the modern Chamber of Martyrs, a memorial—including gas ovens—to the Jews who died under the Nazi regime), then left to the car park, and descend to the east to visit the Church of St. Peter in Gallicantu (see below).

Bishop Gobat's School and the Protestant cemetery are located low on the southwest flanks of Mount Zion, south of the Institute for Holy Land Studies, and can be approached by steps descending to the west of the open ground south of the Tomb of David. Ring for admission. The School was a boys' school built by Bishop Gobat (1846–79) during the period of the Joint Protestant Bishopric. The Church Missionary Society ran the school. A rectangular scarp was discovered when the school was under construction, which formed the base of a tower on the city wall probably of the 2C BC.

The **Protestant cemetery** (since 1869/70) lies to the southeast.

Flinders Petrie

Near the centre of the Protestant cemetery is the grave of the great British archaeologist, Sir W.M. Flinders Petrie (1853–1942), who, after a distinguished career in Egypt, turned his attention in 1928 to the excavation of sites in Palestine, including Jemmeh, Ajjul and Fara. He died in Jerusalem in 1942. His work was significant in advancing archaeological technique, but he had a mathematical and logical genius for assessing his finds, as well as immense energy. He found at Luxor in Egypt the Stele of Merenptah, c 1230 BC which mentions the 'people Israel' for the first time in an historical document. He remarked, 'This stele will be better known in the world than anything else I have found'. Also buried here is Leslie Starkey, who was the British excavator of Lachish in the 1930s, murdered on the Hebron road in 1937; C.S. Fisher, the American excavator of Beth Shan (1921–23) and Megiddo (from 1925). Of more recent fame, Oskar Schindler, hero of the Spielberg film dramatising his rescue of Jews in Germany in the Second World War, is also buried here.

On the east flank of Mount Zion is the modern **Church of St. Peter in Gallicantu** (St. Peter at the place where the cock crew). It was built by the Augustin Assumptionist Fathers, and stands on older remains. A tradition holds that this is also the site of the House of the High Priest Caiaphas where Jesus was taken after his arrest, and outside which Peter wept bitterly after denying his Lord three times before the cock crew (Matt. 26:75).

Open Mon–Sat 08.30–12.00, 14.00–17.00; closed Sun. Guided tours and explanations available. Small shop. Approached from the road around Mount Zion which leads to the Dung Gate. Buses 1, 38.

History of the Church of St. Peter in Gallicantu

The early history of this place is conjectural. The archaeological and textual evidence indicate that the remains in the vicinity date to the 1C AD and later. The site was inside the walls at the time of the Crucifixion. The site of the house of the High Priest Caiaphas is unknown, but in 333 the Bordeaux Pilgrim saw the ruins of the 'House of Caiaphas' on the east slope of Zion outside the then walls. There appears to have been no church here in the 4C, when no dedication to St. Peter is mentioned, perhaps because this site was then outside the walls. The House of Caiaphas and Peter's Denial of Christ seems to have been localised to the north of the Cenacle by the 5C–6C and continued to be venerated there. There may have been a church at this site marking St. Peter's Repentance. There are fragmentary remains which could be those of an early 6C Armenian monastery with Byzantine mosaics and sculpture over a deep cistern-like cave. These might be linked to a 9C mention of a Greek church of St. Peter 'where the glorious apostle wept', which was served by five priests according to the Commemoratorium. That church seems to have survived the difficulties of the 11C and was important in the 12C when almost all pilgrims visited the 'Church of St. Peter in Gallicantu' which was down from the House of Caiaphas towards the Pool of Siloam. It passed into Armenian hands c 1165 but was in ruins by 1323. Records of pilgrims still visiting a cave exist thereafter, but by the mid-15C there seems to have been no trace surviving. The excavation of the ruins on the Assumptionist Fathers' property in the early 20C revealed complex and fragmentary remains of mosaic, walls, steps and street, tombs and rock-cuttings, some of which are preserved in, under and beside the church.

The church, built in 1928–32, is cruciform in plan, with four large and four small apses, an inlaid stone floor, a coloured glass cross in the dome, and contemporary mosaics on the walls. On the east side is a terrace with a fine view over the southeast hill with the ancient city, and over the excavations in the garden revealing an old stepped street, probably Byzantine, which led from the lower city on the east hill up to the upper city on the west hill. It is suggested that it may be part of an older route along which Jesus was taken from Gethsemane to the House of Caiaphas. The church is built on different levels to accommodate the ancient rock-cuttings.

Taking the inside stairs to the left of the entrance to the church, descend to the crypt where there is a chapel; from here you can view the rectangular mouth of an ancient cistern, on which ancient crosses are carved. A pair of high windows are cut into the upper part. Nearby are various fragments of mosaic. Modern steps lead down into the cistern itself. On the wall of the cistern to the right of the steps is a blurred image of a figure with outstretched arms. This is also ancient and said to show the crucified Christ. On the wall opposite, three red crosses are painted. This site is venerated as the site of Jesus' imprisonment in the house of the High Priest Caiaphas on the night before his Crucifixion (Luke 22:54–65).

From the road above, either return in the direction of the Zion Gate and the Old City, or descend by the road towards the northeast to the Dung Gate and the Tyropoeon Valley (see Jerusalem, section 9).

9 • The Ancient City and surroundings

The Ancient City on the Southeast Ridge

The southeast ridge of Jerusalem is the site of the ancient city, occupied from c 4000 BC more or less continuously until the present day, though outside the city walls since about the 11C AD. Today it is usually called 'The City of David'—King David is recorded in the Bible as capturing the city, perhaps around 1000 BC. The ridge is bounded by the steep-sided valleys of the Kidron to the east, and the Tyropoeon to the west. The extent and nature of the occupation has been summarised in the History section. Few remains of the ancient city are visible except in the Archaeological Garden of the City of David and in the vicinity of the Gihon Spring. A circular pedestrian route starting and ending at the Dung Gate is given here, but it is demanding. The tombs in the upper Kidron are described in Jerusalem, section 10; like those in Silwan, which are described here, they can best be approached from Gethsemane. The principal sites described here are in and around the Archaeological Garden.

The City of David Archaeological Garden

• Open Sun–Thur 09.00–17.00, Fri 09.00–13.00; closed Sat.
  The main access route is by a footpath from the ring road south of the Haram; another footpath leads east opposite the car park entrance near the top of the road down the Tyropoeon Valley. There is a viewing platform at the top of the slope. The paths lead to the archaeological zone where each feature is identified by a numbered panel, to which the numbers in brackets here refer; see also the map opposite.

From the viewing platform, note the steep sides of the Kidron valley, and the village of Silwan opposite. The Silwan area was used as a burial ground in the Iron Age.

The 5C BC city wall (**1**) is at the crest of the slope. It was built in the time of Nehemiah and was reused in Hasmonean times. Two Hasmonean (Maccabean) towers abut it. The larger south tower (**2**) is c 17.4m x 5.5m and the smaller north tower (**3**) is c 5.5m x 1.2m. They are constructed of roughly coursed masonry with massive, dressed corner stones. The foundations of the larger tower still stand to a height of nearly 10m. The earlier city walls lay further down the slope.

The archaeological evidence in this area shows that c 1800 BC houses were built on the natural slopes and rock scarps but by the 12C BC a stone podium was built up to widen the flat area at the top. This was done by building stone compartments on the first terrace of the slope, most clearly visible at the northeast foot of the south Hasmonean tower (**8**). These compartments were filled with stone rubble, and built up the level to a height of at least 10m above the bedrock. Above this very impressive podium it is likely that the citadel of the Jebusites was built, but no trace of it has been recovered. It was this citadel that was captured by David early in the 10C BC. During the reigns of David and Solomon the podium was extensively repaired and faced with large stones (perhaps the Millo of II Sam. 5:9). This massive stone ramp (**4**), which is visible from the top down to the first natural terrace of the slope, is the most impressive feature of the site today and dates mostly to the 10C–9C BC.

In the 7C BC terraces were cut into the ramp, and houses built on them. One of these, now called the 'House of Ahiel', has been preserved under a roof on a platform supported by iron girders. These houses are about a third of the way up the

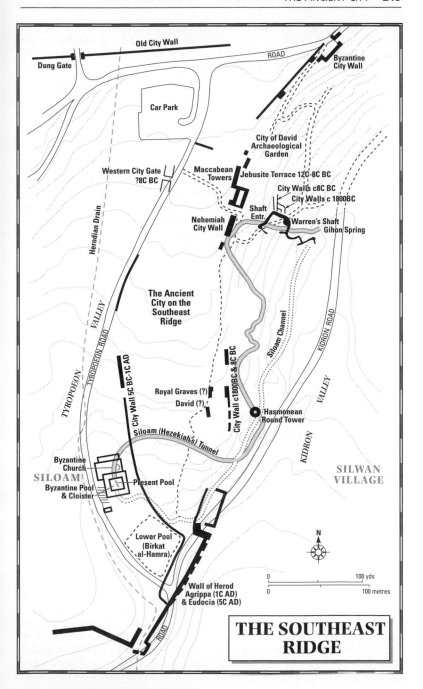

Dung Gate

Old City Wall

ROAD

Byzantine
City Wall

Car Park

City of David
Archaeological
Garden

Western City Gate
?8C BC

Maccabean
Towers

Jebusite Terrace 12C-8C BC

City Walls c8C BC

City Walls c 1800BC

Shaft
Entr.

Nehemiah
City Wall

Warren's Shaft

Gihon Spring

**The Ancient
City on the
Southeast
Ridge**

Siloam Channel

TYROPOEON ROAD

Herodian Drain

TYROPOEON VALLEY

City Wall 5C BC-1C AD

City Wall c1800BC & 8C BC

Royal Graves (?)

David (?)

Hasmonean
Round Tower

KIDRON ROAD

KIDRON VALLEY

Siloam (Hezekiah's) Tunnel

Byzantine
Church

SILOAM

Byzantine Pool
& Cloister

Present Pool

SILWAN
VILLAGE

Lower Pool
(Birkat
al-Hamra)

N

Wall of Herod
Agrippa (1C AD)
& Eudocia (5C AD)

ROAD

0   100 yds
0   100 metres

**THE SOUTHEAST
RIDGE**

slope, and typically for Israelite houses have monolithic stone pillars as parts of the walls and roof supports. Some notable finds were made in the destruction debris of these houses, which were set on fire by the Babylonians in 586 BC. As well as pottery of the period, a fine set of stamped clay seals (from the 'House of the Bullae') and some ostraka were recovered, with wood carvings and other small objects, especially in the 'Burnt Room'. One house contained a lavatory with a shaped stone seat. Much of the rubble which overlay the excavation zone is debris of the Babylonian destruction, and erosion debris following the destructions in the Roman and Byzantine periods.

Warren's Shaft

Leaving the Archaeological Garden by the south gate, further down the slope is the entrance to *Warren's Shaft (open Sun–Thur 09.00–17.00, Fri 09.00–13.00; closed Sat; admission charged; combined ticket available). An impressive tunnel was part of the early water system of Jerusalem by which the inhabitants had safe access from inside the town to the Gihon spring in the Kidron valley below. The water system has been made accessible by inserting metal stairways, but the descent currently includes 82 steps and some steep areas and a return by the same route.

The water system was discovered by Charles Warren in 1867; recent work suggests that a tunnel was first cut in the Middle Bronze Age from inside the walls to a reservoir, which stored water from the Gihon spring (outside the walls). A major new system was begun in the Iron Age, but abandoned, perhaps when Hezekiah's tunnel was constructed. It may be that Warren's Shaft was a natural feature only discovered at that time.

The present entrance to the system is through an Ottoman building, with a small exhibition and a tunnel. The system consists of several sections. The first, upper section is a tunnel with rubble walls and pitched corbel roof. Next is a very steep section in which the top part is Roman and is built with a barrel-vaulted ashlar roof. At the bottom of the first flight of steps the rock-cut entrance of the Iron Age tunnel is reached. The original steps are very worn, and descend steeply for 8m. Chisel marks are visible on the walls. The passage then widens to a system of double steps leading to a platform; and then becomes rather smooth and much less steep for 28m curving down to a natural cave, the outer entrance of which was blocked in antiquity. An additional natural shaft which does not give access to water is also located here. Near the end of the tunnel, and slightly to the side, a natural vertical shaft (Warren's Shaft) in the karst limestone, descends 12.3m to a natural fissure extending 22m east to the spring from the base of the shaft. The water is not visible from the top of the shaft, and it may be difficult, if not impossible, to obtain water by dropping buckets down and hauling them up by rope.

The lower part of the system is cut in the hard rock and may be Iron Age; the upper part, cut in softer rock, and about 3m above the top of Warren's Shaft to the south, is now seen to have led to a reservoir, protected by towers, which lay next to the spring and dates to the Middle Bronze Age. Currently the only access to the reservoir and towers is from the building just above the Gihon Spring.

Climbing back to the entrance, and returning to the path, you can then descend to the floor of the Kidron Valley. A short distance down on the left is the late 8C BC City Wall, still standing to a height of over 3m, which overlies a short right-angled segment of the Middle Bronze Age City Wall (18C BC) just below to the east. The latter, of massive, roughly cut masonry, is 2m wide. These walls were uncovered

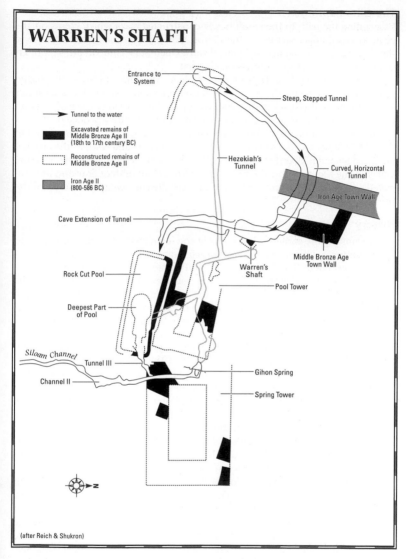

WARREN'S SHAFT

Entrance to System

Steep, Stepped Tunnel

→ Tunnel to the water

■ Excavated remains of Middle Bronze Age II (18th to 17th century BC)

⬚ Reconstructed remains of Middle Bronze Age II

▨ Iron Age II (800-586 BC)

Hezekiah's Tunnel

Curved, Horizontal Tunnel

Iron Age Town Wall

Cave Extension of Tunnel

Middle Bronze Age Town Wall

Rock Cut Pool

Warren's Shaft

Pool Tower

Deepest Part of Pool

Siloam Channel

Tunnel III

Gihon Spring

Channel II

Spring Tower

⊕►s

(after Reich & Shukron)

in the Kenyon excavations in the 1960s. The Middle Bronze Age wall may be part of a tower adjacent to the water gate of the city, giving access directly from the town to the spring below. Note the strategic placing of these walls, which control the present valley floor and the entrance to the spring, and enclose the upper entrance to the water system. The walls higher on the slope are modern retaining walls. More recently an outer Iron Age city wall has been discovered at the bottom of the slope, further to the south, which appears to have enclosed an outer suburb of the town, and perhaps also the spring and its overflow channel.

The Gihon Spring

Descending the path to the small newly constructed plaza which closes off the pedestrianised upper section of the Kidron Valley, you arrive at the entrance to the Gihon Spring (road access is by Silwan). Open Sun–Thur 08.30–15.00, Fri 08.30–13.00; closed Sat. Admission charged.

The Gihon Spring (from H. 'to gush forth', A. Ain Umm al-Daraj—the Spring of the Mother of Steps, the Virgin's Fountain or Well) was the sole good water source for ancient Jerusalem and the reason for the location of the early city on the southeast ridge. It gushes forth strongly but intermittently once or twice a day in the dry season, more frequently after a wet winter. It is first mentioned in the Old Testament as the site at which Zadok the priest and Nathan the prophet anointed Solomon king (I Kings 1:33, 38, 45). Its vulnerable location low in the valley of the Kidron below the city along with its intermittent flow and its associated natural karst fissures and caves have resulted in a complex history for the use of the spring.

History

Presumably the earliest inhabitants of the town above brought containers to the spring to fill and carry back to their houses on the hill above. How soon the intermittent flow was canalised and stored in pools for irrigation of the valley floor to the south, and for other purposes, is not known. In the Middle Bronze Age massive defence and conservation efforts were directed to the water. Below the Middle Bronze Wall, at least two massive towers were constructed beside a large rock-cut pool, which was reached by tunnel from within the city. The pool was fed from the east side by a short tunnel off the Siloam Channel which led the waters of the spring through a rock-hewn and built channel/tunnel down the west side of the Kidron Valley to the Silwan area. South of the pool, its waters could be utilised through sluice-like apertures to irrigate the gardens on the valley floor (probably rather lower in ancient times) and any excess could be held in reservoirs at the bottom of the Tyropoeon Valley (see Lower Pool, below). The channel was also used for collecting rainwater run-off from the slopes of the ridge above.

At the end of the 8C BC Hezekiah built another water system, the famous Siloam or Hezekiah's Tunnel which largely replaced the Siloam Channel and still functions today. This also starts at the Gihon Spring, is 533m in length and pursues a very irregular course beneath the southeast ridge to the Siloam Pool in the lower Tyropoeon Valley (see map on p 219). The gradient is very slight; the height of the rock-cut tunnel is generally about 2m, though towards the south end it reaches 5m, presumably the result of adjusting the gradient downwards. Its sinuous course is variously attributed to inadequate ancient surveying methods; an attempt to avoid the burial places of the kings, which some scholars locate towards the south end of the southeast ridge (see below); and avoidance of hard bands of rock and employment of natural fissures. The last view is gaining increasing acceptance.

The attribution of this tunnel to Hezekiah is generally accepted (II Kings 20:20; II Chr. 32:30) and agrees with the evidence of the inscription found near the south end of the tunnel in 1880, which is now in the Museum in Istanbul. The inscription tells us that the tunnel was cut from both ends, and of the excitement when the stonecutters finally met about 300m from the south end, where there is an especially hectic twist in the tunnel's course. Some assume that as Hezekiah was bringing the waters of the spring within the protection of the walls, therefore the lower Tyropoeon Valley where the Pool of Siloam is located was within the line of the walls at that time. Others think that the valley was not yet enclosed, but that Hezekiah's storage pool was a hidden underground reservoir just outside but protected by the west wall of the city.

Two flights (17 + 16) of stone steps, of uncertain date (Byzantine to modern), give access to an irregular, partly artificial cave containing the spring. Above the steps, the barrel-vaulted stone roof was built in two stages. The inner section was constructed in the Herodian period to prevent the debris on the slope above from blocking the access to the spring. Off this cave open a series of partly natural galleries: to the west they connect with Warren's Shaft and Hezekiah's Tunnel, and to the south with the Siloam Channels and other galleries. It is possible to walk through Hezekiah's Tunnel, but you will need to bring lights, and be prepared to walk through shallow water (up to 50cm deep) in a narrow and occasionally rather low tunnel for 533m. The tunnel emerges at the Pool of Siloam, see below.

Above the spring, a new building houses the recently discovered Middle Bronze Age towers and pool, which can be viewed from a platform constructed over the remains. Low down on the east side of the preserved area is the megalithic south wall of a tower, constructed of huge local stones, with a small Iron Age II wall south of it. In the south centre is a small part of the great rock-cut pool, the north edge being 15m long, and the pool having a depth in one area of 10m. It was fed by a tunnel feeder from the Siloam Channel in its northeast corner. Access (currently closed) to the Warren's Shaft area is to the west. Above to the northwest, the scarped bedrock has another massive tower immediately adjacent to the pool. On the north side of the tower is a smaller Iron Age II wall.

From here the choice is to walk up the Kidron Valley to visit the funerary monuments (about 400m, see Jerusalem, section 10) and then to Gethsemane; or to continue down the Valley to view further excavation areas below the village of Silwan and then return up the very steep Tyropoeon Valley to the Dung Gate.

The Lower Kidron Valley

Continuing south down the Kidron Road for some 150m you arrive at the second area of excavation where remains are still visible on the southeast ridge. Here a further section of the 8C BC City Wall (c 90m in length) overlies a stretch of the 18C BC City Wall about midway up the slope. To the west of the wall, against the inner face, structures of nearly all periods from the Early Bronze Age (c 3000 BC) have been uncovered. Access is by a steep path up the slope at the south end of the large dump created by the excavations, and thence by a track north through the excavations. The line of an outer Iron Age wall at the bottom of the slope has also recently been uncovered further south.

In the area immediately to the south of these remains, which was cleared to bedrock, are numerous cuttings in bedrock mostly of Hadrianic date, but including some long narrow cuttings of uncertain date and purpose. These were thought to be the Tombs of the Israelite kings, including David and his sons and successors, who were buried within the walls of the city (I Kings 2:10) up to the time of Manasseh, after which the 'Garden of Uzza' (perhaps near Silwan) was employed. The most impressive tomb was entered by a shaft which led to a vaulted tunnel 16.5m long and 4m high. At the end is a stone bench with a niche, perhaps intended for a sarcophagus. Another tomb also seemed to reflect a Phoenician influence. These tombs had been looted anciently as well as quarried in the Roman period. Josephus writes that the Hasmonean ruler Hyrcanus I took 3000 talents from the Tomb of David, which he used partly to buy off Antiochus VII Sidetes and partly to pay a mercenary force (War I:61).

On the left of the descent, approximately 20m above the road are the remains of a round tower, probably a dovecote of Hellenistic or Herodian date. The area adjacent to the round tower was certainly used in the Iron Age for burial and the location of the royal tombs in the area just above is therefore not impossible. This area is at least a more likely site than the traditional Tomb of David on the west hill, which was not inside the walls in the time of David.

The Silwan tombs

The extensive modern village of **Silwan** (from the ancient name of Siloam) occupies the east side of Kidron overlooking the gardens of Silwan. The villagers were notorious in the 19C for their aggressive behaviour to foreigners, but they provided most of the workforce for the foreign archaeological expeditions which have worked on the site of the ancient city.

The village contains remarkable but very destroyed tombs of Iron Age date. At the north end of the village (access from the Gethsemane area is easiest), at the edge of the rock-scarp in a prominent position is the monument variously known as the **Monolith of Silwan** or the Tomb of Pharaoh's Wife or Daughter. Because it now has a flat top it can be mistaken for a small village house. It is however a funerary monument of great antiquity, probably to be dated to the

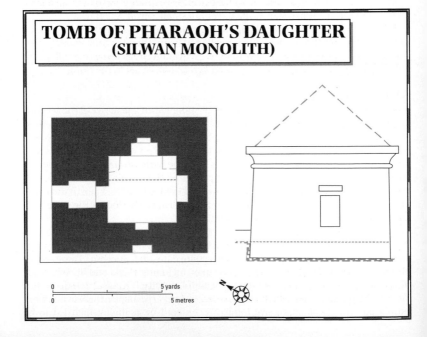

TOMB OF PHARAOH'S DAUGHTER
(SILWAN MONOLITH)

0   5 yards
0   5 metres

9C–7C BC and constructed under Phoenician-Egyptian influence. It has the remnants of an old Hebrew inscription. The tomb's style clearly influenced the later monument of Zechariah.

The monument is entirely hewn from the rock scarp as a free-standing cube (c 5.5m x 4.8m) once capped by a square-based pyramid. The walls of the cube, unlike those of the tombs of Absalom and Zechariah, slope slightly outwards to the base. At the top of the façade, a pronounced roll and a deeply undercut cavetto or Egyptian cornice project. The original doorway was small and was set high in the façade. Above it was a slightly recessed panel wider than the door, with a single-line inscription, perhaps originally of 20 characters. In later (Roman?) times the pyramid was quarried from the roof, and a Byzantine hermit enlarged the door removing most of the inscription in the process. Only a fragment survives at the top left corner of the doorway. Inside, a passage leads to a small squarish chamber; traces of a projecting rock-cut bench survive against the left side, the rest of which was probably cut away by the hermit. Probably at the same time the niches in all three walls were added and the entrance passage enlarged. The gabled roof, cut at approximately 130° on either side of the apex, seems to be typical of other tombs of the Iron Age in the Silwan necropolis.

Two other tombs of this type and date were found slightly further south in the village. Following the same street from the north into Silwan, c 50m further on the left are the remnants of two more monolithic tombs. The first is hard to see, being partly covered by a house and steps; the opening is blocked and the tomb chamber in use as a cistern. It was also partly destroyed during Roman-Byzantine quarrying. In the centre of the façade, a deep niche had a small opening cut at a higher level than the hewn entrance porch. The stone was very smoothly dressed. Of the inscription above the niche nothing survives—it may have been worded like that of the tomb immediately to the south. Above the inscription are traces of a projecting cornice, but the upper part of the monument is destroyed. It was perhaps the tomb of a high official in the court of Judah who had his tomb constructed in Phoenician style at a prominent spot.

The last of these tombs is located immediately south on the left. The inscription is better preserved. The façade is flush with the modern street, c 8m wide, and had a rectangular door and window (subsequently enlarged) in a perfectly dressed surface. The small door was set high in a recessed niche, and had a recessed panel with a three-line inscription in Old Hebrew above it. It was translated by N. Avigad: '(the tomb of)[...]yahu who is over the house. There is no silver or gold here but rather (his bones) and the bones of his wife(?) with him. Cursed be the man who should open this'. It seems to be the tomb of a high steward or chamberlain of the Judaean period perhaps that of the Shebna mentioned in Isaiah 22:15–25. Shebna was a high official, the palace governor who was denounced by Isaiah because of his preoccupation with the building of his tomb 'cutting out your grave on a height and carving yourself a resting place in the rock'. He is often identified with the Shebna who was adjutant-general in the court of Hezekiah, one of the officials sent by Hezekiah to negotiate with the Assyrian army in 701 BC (II Kings 18:18–19:7; Isaiah 36:3). A defaced single-line inscription of the same length was located in a panel over the window. Both inscriptions were removed to the British Museum. The north wall was at least 6m in length and a return seems to indicate that this was also a monolithic tomb. The trapezoidal chamber had a flat ceiling but a rough cornice projecting 0.60m below the ceiling of the south side may be reminiscent of Iron Age practices elsewhere.

Along the scarp below Silwan, south from the Silwan Monolith, are 40 or 50 small square cuttings in the rock. They open onto small chamber tombs: some have gabled ceilings and all are probably part of the extensive Iron Age necropolis of Jerusalem. They are mostly used for storage by the modern villagers.

A diversion can be made further down the Kidron Valley, to the Aceldama Monastery (see p 273). Or you could venture c 250m south of the southeast hill, on the west side of Kidron just beyond the junction with the Hinnom Valley, to the other ancient water supply of Jerusalem, **Bir Ayyub** (Job's Well), traditionally associated with the en-Rogel of I Kings 1:9. Near there was the stone Zoheleth where Adonijah the half-brother of Solomon held a sacrifice of sheep, oxen and buffaloes and declared himself king. It was a point on the border between Benjamin and Judah (Jos. 15:7) and perhaps is also the Dragon Spring of Neh. 2:13.

A well more than 38m deep, with stone-lined upper shaft (small stone lining in the upper 12m, huge blocks in the lower 9.5m), has a rock-cut lower shaft and collecting cave at the bottom. The water supply is directly linked to the winter rainfall, and in a wet January the water used to well up and overflow the shaft; in summer it had to be drawn up, and in modern times pumped up. The water collects from the adjacent limestone strata underlying the Kidron and Hinnom valleys, but had a mixed reputation probably linked to a degree of surface contamination. The lower part may date to the Iron Age, when the valley floor was 10m lower than today, and may have been damaged by an earthquake in the days of King Uzziah (Zech. 14:5). The large masonry lining the lower part of the upper shaft may be of Roman date. About 1880, a ruinous stone building with low dome covered the well, which was one of the principal water supplies for Ottoman Jerusalem. The water was carried up to the city in goatskins by the Silwan villagers who sold it for up to sixpence a skin. They also recounted a legend that the well was a miraculous creation resulting from the healing of Job in a nearby cave and pool. The well was supplanted by the new British pipelines which supplied Jerusalem after 1918.

Further down the Kidron other caves and tombs of the Herodian and Byzantine periods have been noted.

The Tyropoeon Valley

At the lower end of the Tyropoeon (Cheesemakers') Valley is a complex of ancient pools fed by the Gihon Spring, which includes the Siloam Pool and the Birkat al-Hamra. The low minaret of a small mosque on the east side of the Tyropoeon road marks the site of the **Pool of Siloam** (Latin: Siloë; A. Silwan). The mosque is a rectangular stone building with a court and minaret in the northwest corner. It was built by the Silwan villagers on the debris of the underlying Byzantine church in 1894–97. Below the mosque a passage to the left leads to the modern pool of Siloam.

History of the Pool of Siloam

No trace of the pool or covered cistern originally constructed by Hezekiah in the late 8C BC has been found; this may have been the pool referred to by Isaiah (Isaiah 22:9–11) as the pool between the two walls, and referred to elsewhere as the Upper Pool. It was fed by Hezekiah's Tunnel from the Gihon Spring, and was part of a defensive water system built in the face of the Assyrian invasion by Sennacherib in 701 BC.

The water from the pool was used by Jews for purification ceremonies, as the water derived from the actual spring of the City of David. The pool still existed in Jesus' time and was the location of the miracle that cured the man blind from birth (John 9:1–12). Possibly it was the site of the Shrine of the Four Nymphs built by Hadrian in the 2C, and some of the masonry used in the Byzantine pool may be Roman in origin. There seems also to have been a Roman bath house at the bottom of the Tyropoeon Valley which would indicate a fairly extensive use of the pool and its waters in Roman times.

The Byzantine Pool of Siloam was nearly square, was rock-cut on its north and west sides, and probably had an arcade on all four sides. It was approached by a flight of steps descending round the west and south sides to a paved and columned court 1.75m above the level of the pool. A rock-cut tunnel on the south side took the overflow from the pool. A Byzantine church overhung the north arcade of the pool, and appears to have had three aisles. This was probably the church built by Empress Eudocia in the mid-5C to commemorate Jesus' miracle and described c 570 by the Piacenza Pilgrim.

The present pool lies deep in a narrow stone-lined pit, occupying only the central part of the Byzantine pool. It receives the water from Hezekiah's tunnel under an arch at its north end, with an overflow channel at the south. During the building of the mosque the upper part of the north wall of the Byzantine pool was exposed, including a moulded course which is still visible and may have originated in the Roman period.

At the bottom of the Tyropoeon Valley, the overflow channel from the pool is exposed in the rock-scarp at the south end of the southeast ridge. It was originally a hidden tunnel, the end of which utilised the south end of the earlier Kidron channel or Siloam Channel and led into the Lower Pool (also called the Old Pool, today the Birkat al-Hamra'. This ancient pool may well have existed in the Middle Bronze Age. It is now a garden in a walled enclosure in the angle of the Tyropoeon and Kidron Roads.

The road up the Tyropoeon is very steep, although the original floor of the valley is under many metres of debris, and was once very much deeper and steeper. In the 1C AD and the Byzantine periods the street plan included a large drainage system which is preserved right down to the Kidron Valley. Though no ancient remains are visible, the road forms a good point for observing the strategic position of the ancient city on the southeast ridge to the east, and that of the later, upper city on the Western Hill to the right. Above, to the west, is the Church of St. Peter in Gallicantu (see p 216).

10 • The Mount of Olives, Bethany and the Upper Kidron Valley

The principal place of interest is the Chapel of the Ascension and the fine view to be had from the top of the Mount of Olives over Jerusalem. However there are many other worthwhile sights, particularly for Christian pilgrims. Many of them can be visited by car, or accessed from the bus; the full tour on foot is lengthy. Diversions to Bethany and to the ancient Jewish tombs in the Upper Kidron can be made.

The Mount of Olives

The Mount of Olives, the hill opposite Jerusalem on the east above the Kidron Valley, is also called Olivet in the King James Version of the Bible (II Sam. 15:30, Acts 1:12). It is mentioned in the New Testament as the location of many events in the week before the Crucifixion, and as the Place of the Ascension. On Palm Sunday the Franciscans and pilgrims walk from Beth Phage on the Mount of Olives to Jerusalem to commemorate Jesus' entry into Jerusalem. Zechariah (Zech. 14:4) foretold the coming of the Messiah to the Mount of Olives, and some Christians following this text saw it as the place of the Second Coming of Christ. It has many olive groves, now giving place to new housing, and very extensive Jewish cemeteries, for it is the desire of many Jews to be buried in Jerusalem.

The Mount of Olives is a ridge of soft limestone just over 4km long, with three main peaks. The higher northwest part of the ridge is properly called Mount Scopus (903m) and is the location of the Hebrew University and the Augusta Victoria Hospital (see Jerusalem, section 11). The central area, the Mount of Olives proper, is 806m high and is called Jabal al-Tur (from the Syriac *Turo Qedisho*, the Holy Mountain). The south area, Jabal Batn al-Hawa, which is the lowest peak and stands above the village of Silwan, is identified with the Mountain of Corruption (II Kings 23:13).

History

Apart from a Palaeolithic site, the earliest traces of man on this ridge are of the late third millennium when shaft-grave burials were located on the central ridge. The slopes were used for burial in the Middle Bronze Age, and the west slope also formed part of the cemetery of Jerusalem in the Late Bronze Age. The Bible refers to high places dedicated to foreign gods built by Solomon on the right hand of the Mount of Corruption (II Kings 23.13); the west slopes of the south peak were also used for burial in the Iron Age.

The Mount of Olives continued to be used as one of the major cemeteries of Jerusalem in later periods. In Roman times the road to Jericho crossed the saddle between the north and central peaks, and according to the New Testament a path led by Gethsemane up the central peak and on towards Bethany.

Many of the events of the last days of Jesus' life were enacted here: the route of his triumphal entry into Jerusalem before the Feast of the Passover started from the Mount of Olives; his arrest in the Garden of Gethsemane took place low down on the east side of Kidron; and the place of his Ascension is located on the top of the central peak. The sites of most of these events were commemorated by churches from the 4C onwards.

Between 370 and 378 St. Basil founded a monastery here in which were relics of St. John the Baptist. Theodosius (c 518) records 24 churches on the Mount of Olives, and c 570 the Piacenza Pilgrim notes vast numbers of monks and nuns. Many buildings were destroyed by the Persians in 614, and hundreds massacred; some churches were rebuilt by Modestus, and later by the Crusaders. By the 19C little except ruins and gardens remained, but in the second half of that century a reflorescence of building took place.

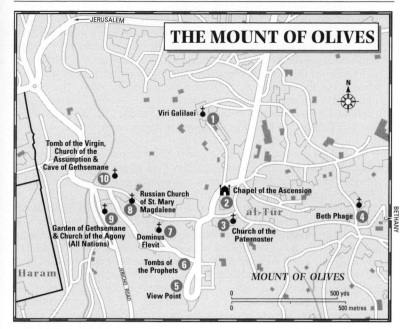

THE MOUNT OF OLIVES

To avoid a steep climb, go by bus 37 or taxi to the top of the Mount of Olives (c 2km), and return on foot down the steep path to Gethsemane. The sites (numbered in brackets) are marked on the map above. It is best to go first to the Chapel of the Ascension at the end of the bus route.

The road passes the Greek Orthodox church of the Viri Galilaei (**1**) established in 1887 (usually closed). This is one of the traditional sites, where the disciples were called 'Men of Galilee' by two men in white immediately after the Ascension (Acts 1:11).

The location of the ***Chapel of the Ascension (2)** is marked by a small minaret and a mosque and is the traditional site of the Ascension of Christ (Luke 24:50–52) which occurred 40 days after the Resurrection (Acts 1:2–9). According to the Old Testament (II Kings 2:11), Elijah ascended in a whirlwind with chariots and horses of fire; in the New Testament, Jesus was lifted up and hidden by a cloud as he blessed the disciples.

History of the Chapel of the Ascension

Tradition maintained that the site of the Ascension of Christ was first venerated in a cave on the Mount of Olives, but c 384 Egeria records that the place of the Ascension was located at the place called Imbomon (Greek bomon = altar) higher up the mountain above the cave and church of the Eleona.

The first church at the Imbomon was built before 392, by Poimenia, a pious Roman lady. It was sacked by the Persians in 614, restored afterwards by Modestus, and described by Arculf in 680. His description is of a circular building with three porticoes entered from the south. Inside, it was open to the sky, with a central edicule which contained the indestructible footprints of Christ in the dust inside a railing. Eight lamps shone brilliantly every night through windows facing west towards Jerusalem. In the 9C the Commemoratorium notes that it was served by three clergy and presbyters. This church was rebuilt as a roofed octagon by the Crusaders c 1150. The central octagonal edicule was rebuilt c 1170. The exterior was fortified. In 1198 Salah al-Din gave the site to two pious followers (Wali al-Din and Abu'l Hasan), for the Ascension of Jesus is recognised in Islam. The church remained in use as a mosque for over 300 years.

The building became more ruinous by the end of the 15C, and the east section was walled off to form the asymmetrical shrine we see now.

Ring the bell for admission. On the right of the entrance is a small mosque (Zawiyat al-Adawiyya), with court and gallery from where there is a good view of both the Chapel of the Ascension and the surrounding countryside. On the left is a small octagonal minaret. Mosque and minaret date to 1620.

The central entrance gives directly onto an open court with paved path to the small Chapel of the Ascension of Christ. The Crusader shrine has a stone dome on an octagonal drum both of which are later Muslim additions. The octagonal walls, with fretted cornice, have piers flanked by small marble columns at the angles. The columns support a fine series of ***12C Crusader marble capitals**, some with elaborately entwined and deeply cut foliage, two with fantastic animal motifs depicting winged quadrupeds with the heads of birds. Entering the chapel from the west, the interior contains a mihrab in the south wall, and, in an asymmetrically placed frame on the floor, the imprint in the rock of the right footprint of Christ. Outside, the west side of the court is enclosed by a much rebuilt octagonal wall of varied masonry; a wall of the 15C reducing the earlier octagon bounds the east side. Bases of columns are visible in the ground which probably belong to the 12C Crusader church, as do some trefoil half-bases against the wall itself. The rings set high in the walls are used to attach tents and awnings at the Feast of the Ascension when Arab Christians come, especially from Bethlehem and Ramallah.

Turning left (south), the **Church of the Paternoster** or **Eleona (3)** is at the junction of the lane to Beth Phage. Open 08.30–11.45, 15.00–16.45; closed Sun.

History of the Church of the Paternoster

A cave on this site was venerated as the site where Christ taught the disciples, and also at first as the Place of the Ascension. Eusebius and the Bordeaux Pilgrim (333) record that a church was built here by the order of Constantine, called the Church of the Disciples and the Ascension, or the Eleona (the church of the Olive Groves). It was one of three churches that Constantine constructed over a cave: that of Christ's birth at Bethlehem, of his death and Resurrection at the Holy Sepulchre, and of his teaching and Ascension here. The site of the Ascension was moved up the hill by 384. The church was destroyed by the Persians in 614, and not specifically mentioned in the restorations of Modestus.

After 614, pilgrims seem to have visited the Church of the Ascension, not mentioning the Eleona, but the Commemoratorium (early 9C) lists 'The Church where Christ Taught his Disciples' with three monks and one presbyter, next to that called 'The Ascension of Christ'. It may have been in ruins by the Crusader period, when the cave was associated in particular with the teaching of the Lord's Prayer, and with the place where Jesus spent the nights during his last days in Jerusalem (Luke 21:37). In 1102–06 a modest oratory was built, and a church was rebuilt in 1152 with funds from the Bishop of Viborg (Denmark) and his butler who were buried in it. The church was damaged in 1187, repaired following the treaty of 1229, still existed at the end of the 13C but was destroyed by 1345; traditions concerning it shifted in the following years. The church of the Credo (where, it was said, the disciples composed the Creed) was also located here.

In 1851 the stones of the 4C church were being taken down to the Valley of Jehoshaphat and sold for tombstones to the Jews. In 1857 the Princesse de la Tour d'Auvergne bought land and started a search for the site of the cave; in 1868 she built a cloister modelled on the Campo Santo at Pisa, and founded a Carmelite convent to the east in 1872. The inner wall of the cloister commemorated the teaching of the Lord's Prayer in the cave with 32 copies of the prayer in different languages. The Byzantine foundations over a cave were discovered in 1910 partly beneath the cloister, which was then moved; and from 1915 an attempt was made to rebuild a basilica on the ancient foundations over the ruined cave: the half-built enclosure today marks this endeavour.

As you enter from the north, on the left of the door is a plaque with the Lord's Prayer written in Aramaic and Hebrew. The large court opposite is the unroofed, partly reconstructed Byzantine basilica built above the cave, with steps down to the place of the Lord's teaching. The cave was partly collapsed when discovered in 1910, and is now a curious combination of ancient rock cuttings, concrete supports and marble furnishing difficult to associate with the ancient place of prayer and teaching. The cave cuts part of a 1C AD rock-cut kokhim tomb.

Continuing up the steps opposite, turn left at the top to the cloister containing 68 copies of the Lord's Prayer in as many languages, inscribed on Palestinian tiles set in the walls. The tomb of the Princesse de la Tour d'Auvergne is located on the south side of the cloister.

The lane to the right of the entrance to the Paternoster leads left to the Russian Orthodox Convent and Russian Church of the Ascension on the Mount of Olives, established 1887 (open Tues and Thur 10.00–13.00 in summer, 09.00–12.00 in winter). Its prominent tower can be seen from the Jordan Valley on a clear day. Byzantine tomb chapels with some fine Armenian mosaics are preserved in the small museum. The finest has a splendid border enclosing elaborate designs with fish, fruit, birds, animals and an inscription in Armenian at the edge 'Susannah, mother of Artaban'; another, less elaborate mosaic, mentions the Armenian Bishop Jacob, and a third names St. Isaiah.

A right turn leads in 500m to **Beth Phage** (**4**), the site mentioned in Mark 11:1 as the beginning of the triumphal procession of Jesus into Jerusalem commemorated on Palm Sunday. The precise location of Beth Phage is uncertain but the modern Palm Sunday procession begins from the Latin Church here (open 08.00–11.30, 14.00–17.00 or –16.45 in winter; ring the bell for entry). The Franciscan monastery was built in 1883 on the medieval ruins of a church found in 1876. The simple church contains a large stone, said to be the mounting block seen by Bernard the Monk in 870 at which Jesus began the procession. It has paintings on all four sides showing: Jesus greeting Martha and Mary (John

11:20–30); the raising of Lazarus; the start of the procession; and the entry into Jerusalem. The painting probably dates to the later 12C, but has been restored. A new Greek Orthodox Church has been built nearby, and a footpath on its north side leads (c 1km) to Bethany (see p 236).

To return to the main route, continue around to the left from the Paternoster, and the road leads to the *Seven Arches Hotel*; opposite, on the right is a famous *viewpoint overlooking the Old City (5)*. To the southwest can be seen the site of the ancient city on the southeast hill. A little to the north and west of the ancient city, you see Mount Zion with the dome and tower of the Dormition church; in front, the south end of the Haram platform with the dome of the Aqsa Mosque, and a view over the recent excavations south of the Temple Mount; further north on the Haram platform is the golden Dome of the Rock; and behind it, at a distance and more difficult to see in the midst of the Old City, slightly to the northwest, is the grey dome of the Church of the Holy Sepulchre, with the high square tower of the Lutheran Church of the Redeemer just south of it. An excellent view of the east walls of the city, including the Golden Gate (the closed east gate of the Haram), can be had from this point; and below on the slopes of the Mount of Olives, the golden onion-shaped domes of the Russian Church at Gethsemane. Returning a few metres in the direction of the Paternoster, a steep lane descends on the left towards Gethsemane.

On the left at the top of the lane are the so-called **Tombs of the Prophets Haggai**, **Zechariah** and **Malachi** (6C–5C BC) of the three last books of the Old Testament (**6**) (open Mon–Fri 09.00–15.30; torch useful). Though venerated as such by Christians and Jews, this is in fact a catacomb of 1C BC/AD date of unusual plan with central circular chamber and radiating fan-shaped corridors with burial places (kokhim). It was used for the burial of foreign Christians in the 4C–5C as shown by inscriptions above the burial places.

Continuing down the steep lane, on the right is the Franciscan property with the **Church of Dominus Flevit (7)**, where pilgrims marked the place where Jesus wept over the city as he rode towards it on Palm Sunday (Luke 19:41). Open 08.00–11.45, 14.30–17.00.

Excavations revealed a cemetery here, used in the Middle and Late Bronze Ages (c 1600–1300 BC), and again from the 1C BC to the 4C AD. A 5C monastery was built here, and a chapel of the 14C was superseded by a 17C mosque (al-Mansuriyya). The Franciscans built a chapel in 1891, and a new church was built over the 5C chapel in 1955. Some of the 18 tomb complexes of the 1C BC–2C AD excavated on this plot are preserved at the side of the path near the entrance. All contained sarcophagi and ossuaries, and some were reused in the 3C–4C. The later burials were placed in trough arcosolia in which the rock was carved to form a sarcophagus, rather than placing the collected bones for secondary burial in a separate sarcophagus on a rock-cut bench as in the earlier kokhim tombs. The pressure for space in the 1C AD tombs was such that sarcophagi were piled up to 3m deep in some chambers. The Bronze Age burial place is not preserved. It contained over 2000 objects, including pottery imported from Cyprus. The modern church is built over a 5C Byzantine monastic chapel, incorporating part of the apse. A Greek inscription on a partially preserved mosaic records the name of the 5C founder; other Byzantine fragments can be seen. The windows frame the view of the city over which Jesus wept.

Lower down the hill on the right is the **Russian Orthodox Church of St.**

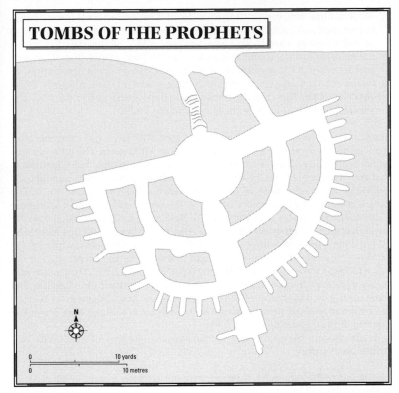

TOMBS OF THE PROPHETS

N

| 0 | | 10 yards |
| 0 | | 10 metres |

Mary Magdalene at Gethsemane (A. al-Moscobiyya) (**8**) set in a garden. This picturesque church with its newly regilded seven golden domes reminiscent of the Kremlin was built by Czar Alexander III in 1888. The yellow stonework and fretted lead barge boarding lend a stolid 19C tone to the architecture, but the agreeable series of shallow round arches at the top of the façade make a bridge for the eye between the building and the delightful domes. The church has iconastasis, icons and paintings. Open Tues and Thur 10.00–12.00.

Descending the lane you arrive at the entrance on the left to the **Garden of Gethsemane** (from Aramaic words meaning 'oil vat') and the **Church of All Nations** or Church of the Agony (**9**). It can also be reached by bus 43 from the Damascus Gate; *Egged* buses 1and 2 both turn south some distance short of the churches. Open Apr–Oct 08.00–12.00, 14.30–18.00 (–17.00 in winter).

History of the Church of All Nations

The site, by early tradition, is that where Christ prayed, was betrayed by Judas, and was arrested by the soldiers sent by the chief priests and elders on the night before his Crucifixion (Matt. 26:36–56). The Bordeaux Pilgrim (333) says that in the Valley of Jehoshaphat there was a vineyard with the rock where Judas betrayed Christ, and a palm tree connected with Palm Sunday; Egeria (384) says there was a graceful church at the place of Jesus' prayer above Gethsemane. This church of Jesus' prayer at Gethsemane is probably the Byzantine structure with three aisles and curious external towers flanking an open portico found beneath the present Church of All Nations. It was probably built by Theodosius I and dedicated c 385. All the churches on the site incorporated the traditional rock on which Jesus prayed. The 4C church was destroyed in the earthquake of 749. The Crusaders built first an oratory on the site, then another church with three apses c 1170 on a slightly different orientation. This church seems to have been abandoned in the 14C. The present church was built by the Franciscans in 1924.

The Franciscan walled garden is a pleasant spot, with large and venerable olive trees, estimates of whose age range from 300 to 1000 years. The olive is a tree which bears fruit only after some years, and lives a long time, but it is unlikely that any here survive from the time of Christ. Although olives were undoubtedly cultivated in this area, many of the groves were cut down by Titus in AD 70. The garden is planted with rosemary and other flowers. A walk around it brings the visitor to the west end of the Church of All Nations. A porch with mosaics on the façade representing Jesus offering his suffering to God fronts a basilica covered by 12 low domes. Inside, the three aisles and three apses are decorated with mosaics on blue and green backgrounds; the light is dimmed by the purple glass in the side windows ('the hour when darkness reigns' of Luke 22:53). The church preserves sections of Byzantine mosaics, the outline of the Byzantine basilica, and some cuttings and fragments of the Crusader church. Small fragments of a fresco of Christ and an angel from the Crusader church are now in the Museum of the Convent of the Flagellation (see p 144).

In the vicinity there are also commemorative gardens of the Greek and Armenian churches.

Descending to the main road, turn right. On the left is the reputed Tomb of Mujir al-Din (1456–1522), an Arab writer who is best known for his book on the history of Jerusalem and Hebron (1495). It is marked by a 20C dome in a square enclosure at the bend of the main road.

A few metres further, on the left, is the ***Tomb of the Virgin Mary (10)**, the Armenian, Greek, Ethiopian and partly Latin Church of the Assumption. Open daily 06.00–12.00, 14.30–17.00.

History of the Tomb of the Virgin Mary

Traditions about the death of Mary in Jerusalem, her burial and Assumption ('*Transitus Mariae*') in the Valley of Jehoshaphat may go back as far as the 2C–3C and were stronger by the 5C, when the claims of Ephesus (in modern Turkey) to this honour were hotly disputed. A church may have been built c 455, when an early tomb with kokhim and arcosolia was isolated by quarrying, to leave the kokhim chamber partly destroyed at an upper level, and a lower chamber with bench arcosolium to be venerated as the Tomb of Mary. This quarrying process was similar to that carried out around the Tomb of Christ in the Church of the Holy Sepulchre. An upper round church which surpassed the lower for grandeur was built by Mauritius Tiberius (582–602) and destroyed in 614 by the Persians.

By the 7C the place of Mary's death had been localised on Mount Zion (see p 213). The Church of St. Mary in the Valley of Jehoshaphat was described by the pilgrim Arculf in 680. He says this was on two levels: the upper contained four altars, and like the lower was round. In the lower level at the east end was an altar, and on the right was the empty rock-cut tomb of Mary. The Commemoratorium (9C) says it was served by 13 presbyters and clergy, 6 monks and 15 nuns. The ruins of this church were rebuilt by the Benedictines c 1130, and Queen Melisande was buried here in 1161.

This 12C Abbey Church of St. Mary of Jehoshaphat had an adjacent monastery which had a court and porticoes, halls with early Gothic columns, and frescoes in red on a green background. The complex, being outside the city walls, was fortified by three towers. Most of the superstructure but only part of the lower storey of the church were destroyed by Salah al-Din after 1187 when the stones were used to repair the city walls (see Bab al-Asbat, p 99). The lower 12C church on Byzantine foundations has survived virtually intact.

As you descend steps from the road to an open square courtyard, the only part of the church visible is the portal of c 1130 with a pointed arch supported on eight marble columns. Inside, a wide staircase of 47 steps descends to the lower storey of the Byzantine church. In the upper section of the stairs the walls are of 12C date, and contain 12C windows blocked to keep out the Kidron floods to which the site has been vulnerable. At the seventh step on the right is the Tomb of Queen Melisande (died 11 September 1161). An arch over the step is carved with a lily-bud motif, and the tomb was once protected by iron bars. The body was moved in the 14C to a place at the foot of the stairway and is not mentioned after 1483. Since the 14C Melisande's tomb has been identified with Joachim and Anne, the parents of the Virgin.

A few steps lower, on the left, were the tombs of some other members of the Crusader royal family, later identified as the tomb of Joseph. Towards the bottom of the stairs the masonry is Byzantine, as is that of most of the church itself. The floor is 10.6m below the level of the entrance. It has a built apse to the west and a longer rock-cut apse to the east. Various cuttings and passages on the north side relate to truncated tombs of the 1C BC/AD. The Tomb of the Virgin is marked by a small square chapel in the centre of the east apse. In Crusader times it had an edicule with arcade supported by 16 columns on a marble socle, and still has a medieval lintel over the north door. The present altar inside the Tomb hides the remnants of a bench arcosolium tomb of perhaps the 1C AD. The niche south of the tomb is a mihrab, installed when the Muslims had joint rights to the church (in Muslim tradition and according to Mujir al-Din, Muhammad saw a light over the tomb of Mary, and Umar prayed at Gethsemane in 638). There are altars of the Armenians and the Greeks in the east apse, and one belonging to the Ethiopians in the west apse with a cistern adjacent. The dimness and the blackened walls add to the formidable sense of antiquity within the church.

Returning to the courtyard, to the left is a passage leading to the **Cave of Gethsemane** or the **Grotto of the Agony**—probably originally a natural cave which may have had many uses and has been several times recut. The channels in the floor, the traces of mosaic and of 12C wall paintings, and the hole in the roof all suggest it may have been used as a burial cave, as a workshop for processing olives, and as a Byzantine shrine. The latter would have been connected with the location of the place where the disciples slept while Jesus prayed, with the place of his prayers or of his arrest, or where he spent the night before his

Crucifixion. A Crusader Church at Gethsemane was located in this cave. Like the Church of All Nations, the chapel is cared for by the Franciscans. Open 08.30–12.00, 14.30–17.00 (Sun and Thur–15.40).

Returning to the road, to the right on the opposite bank of the Kidron valley is the modern Greek Orthodox Church of St. Stephen, which marks one traditional site of the stoning or burial of St. Stephen, the first martyr, outside the city gate (Acts 7:58). In Crusader times it was the north, not the east, gate of the town which was named for St. Stephen.

You can descend further down the Kidron Valley from this point to visit the fine rock-cut tombs (see pp 239–241), or return up the hill to the northeast corner of the Old City.

Bethany

The village of Bethany may be reached by walking c 1km east from Beth Phage (see p 231), by Bus 43 from the Damascus Gate bus station, and by car following the Jericho road 3km southeast, or by minor roads over the Mount of Olives, from the village of al-Tur. Bethany (A. al-Azariyya from the name of Lazarus) is a Muslim and Christian Arab village, population 3600, located on the southeast slopes of the Mount of Olives. Bethany was by tradition the home of Lazarus—whom Jesus raised from the dead (John 11:38–44)—and his sisters Martha and Mary, where Jesus often stayed. Here too lived Simon the Leper, at whose house Jesus was anointed (Mark 14:3). It was also where he returned after his triumphal entry into Jerusalem (Mark 11:11); and near Bethany, according to the New Testament (Luke 24:50), was the place of his Ascension—though no other tradition supports this.

History

Remains in the vicinity of the modern village suggest that a village stood here at least from Roman times and that there was an earlier settlement of the Iron Age nearby. This is equated with Ananiah in the territory of Benjamin (Neh. 11:32) from which the New Testament name is derived (Beth Ananiah = Bethany). There seems to have been no church here in the early 4C, though Eusebius and the Bordeaux Pilgrim (333) mention the tomb in a vault or crypt. St. Jerome c 390 records visiting the Tomb of Lazarus and the guest room of Mary and Martha, which is the Lazarium mentioned by Egeria in the liturgy on Saturday in the seventh week of Lent: 'Just on one o'clock every-one arrives at the Lazarium, which is Bethany ... by the time they arrive there, so many people have collected that they fill not only the Lazarium itself, but all the fields around' (trans J. Wilkinson); at the end of the service, the start of Easter was announced. This late 4C structure was destroyed in an earthquake and a larger one was built probably in the 6C. Theodosius (not later than 518) mentions the place, as does Arculf in c 680. This church of St. Lazarus sur-vived until Crusader times.

King Fulk and Queen Melisande, whose youngest sister was a nun in the Convent of St. Anne in Jerusalem, purchased the village of Bethany from the Patriarch of the Holy Sepulchre in 1143 in exchange for estates near Hebron. She built at Bethany a large Benedictine convent dedicated to Sts Mary and Martha, and the old church was strengthened, extensively repaired and rededicated to Sts Mary and Martha. A large new west church of St. Lazarus was built above the tomb of Lazarus. As the site of the tomb in the rock was small, the whole east end was supported on barrel vaults. The monastic complex was fortified with a tower, and endowed with the large estates of the village of Jericho. Not long afterwards, Melisande's sister Joveta was elected abbess, thus becoming at the age of 24 the head of one of the richest convents in the Kingdom of Jerusalem. Joveta died c 1173/78, and the nuns went into exile at Acre following the fall of the Crusader kingdom in 1187. The west church may have been destroyed at this time, with only the tomb and lower vaulting surviving, but the old east church fared better. The village seems to have been abandoned in the 14C; the ruins are mentioned in 1347 by Niccolo of Poggibonsi, who notes Greek monks attending the tomb chapel. The tomb was also the focus of Muslim veneration, and by 1384 a mosque is mentioned. When the Mosque of al-Uzair (Ezra) was built in the 16C in the Crusader vault below the Lazarus church, Christian access to the tomb became more difficult. The Franciscans were permitted to cut a new entrance from the road on the north side of the tomb; and at some point the original entrance to the tomb from the mosque was blocked. In 1697 Maundrell noted the ruins of 'the Castle of Lazarus' at Bethany (the old tower of Melisande remained a prominent ruin in the 19C village). By 1955 a Franciscan church was built over the ruins of the old east church, and from 1965 a Greek church was built just west of the tomb.

The modern **Franciscan Church dedicated to St. Lazarus**, built 1952–55 (architect A. Barluzzi), contains the remains of the Byzantine church of St. Lazarus, of the Crusader east church dedicated to Sts Mary and Martha and a little of the Crusader monastery which existed to the south. Open March–October 08.00–11.45, 14.00–18.00 (–17.00 in winter).

The forecourt is entered from the north and is located in the west end of the earlier churches, of which parts of the mosaic floor are preserved. The modern church is cruciform in plan, has a mosaic of Mary, Martha and Lazarus on the façade and the interior decorated in polished stone and mosaic work. It is built over the remains of the east end of the earlier churches. The 6C church was a three-aisled basilica repaired and strengthened in the 12C when buttresses and stone roof vaults were added and the floor level raised. Under trapdoors just inside the church can be seen parts of the apse of the 4C church, which was c 12.5m shorter than that of the 6C. The modern apse is located in the same place as the apse of the 6C/12C church. The west wall of the forecourt contains the west façade of the 6C basilica, with three doorways. Passing through the south doorway, the angle opposite to the right contains a pillar of the 6C atrium.

On the south is a long room, part of a 6C room reused in the 12C Benedictine convent. This walled monastic complex south of the church, at least 45m x 57m in area, was later occupied by the houses of the modern village. The room, with rough vaulted masonry, contains an old olive press and mill, and at the east end a pilgrims' dining room. At the west end the stairs lead to the upper part of the Crusader convent, which included the cloister. Leaving the courtyard of the Franciscan church, on either side of the entrance is some 12C buttressing of the 6C wall.

Turning left up the hill, the first entrance on the left is that to the Mosque of al-Uzair, the courtyard of which is located in the Byzantine atrium; the 16C mosque (not usually accessible) is built in the vault which formerly supported the west end of the 12C church of St. Lazarus, and in front of the entrance to the Tomb of Lazarus. This entrance was blocked sometime after the 16C.

A further 25m up the hill on the left is the small modern entrance to the **Tomb of Lazarus** cut by the Franciscans in the late 16C or early 17C. A flight of 24 very uneven stone steps descends to the antechamber of the tomb. Probably originally a rock-cut tomb, very little trace of its original form remains. It is assumed that the rather rotten rock has collapsed, perhaps at the time the large Crusader Church of St. Lazarus was built above it in the 12C. The present sides are of masonry, and even the floor levels may not be original. The original blocked entrance is visible in the east wall of the antechamber (towards the mosque). The alignment suggests the tomb pre-dated the Byzantine churches. The small tomb chamber itself can only be entered by a very low passage.

Continuing up the hill, on the left is the modern Greek Orthodox Church, built from1965, which incorporates a wall of the Crusader church built over the Lazarus tomb. Turning left at the crossroads beyond brings you to substantial ruins which belong to the Greek Orthodox Patriarchate. One tradition identifies them with the House of Simon the Leper, another with the House or Castle of Lazarus. The podium contains drafted masonry of the Roman period reused from some earlier structure, but the remains of a tower belong to the fortified Crusader Monastery of c 1144. The tower is 14.40m x 14.80m, the walls are 4m thick, with a door and stair in the east wall and a rock-cut cistern beneath its floor. Back at the crossroads, the track ahead (on the right as you ascend) leads up to Beth Phage.

The Upper Kidron Valley

The Kidron Valley bounds the east side of the city of Jerusalem. It starts to the north of the city, where it is comparatively broad and open, and is today called the Wadi Jauz. The valley narrows and deepens opposite the Old City, where it becomes known as the Valley of Jehoshaphat, and south of the Haram deepens to a shallow gorge with steep Turonian limestone scarps on either side. At the points where it is joined by the Tyropoeon and Hinnom valleys the floor widens, and alluvial soils and plentiful water create a garden area. Above the east bank is the village of Silwan (see p 224). Below Silwan the valley turns to the east and continues a steep descent through the Judaean wilderness past the monastery of Mar Saba to the Dead Sea.

History

The Kidron is mentioned in the Old Testament, mainly for its springs and its use as a cemetery. Absalom, son of David, is said to have set up his memorial pillar in the King's Valley (II Sam. 18:18) which, like the King's Garden, is identified with Kidron. The destruction in the Kidron of the paraphernalia of foreign gods by the kings of Judah is also recorded (e.g. I Kings 15:13). Monumental tombs were located here from the Iron Age onwards. Following texts such as Jer. 31:40 and Joel 3:2 and 12, the Kidron was identified with the Valley of Jehoshaphat (literally 'Yahweh judges'), and with the site of the Last Judgement, a tradition accepted by both Jews and Christians and one reason for the location of the modern Jewish cemeteries here. The Kidron Valley was occupied extensively by Byzantine hermits.

A short walk in the Upper Kidron Valley provides an interesting view of the city, with a number of ancient monuments along the way. You also get a good view of the principal monuments from the ring road below the Golden Gate. The Lower Kidron is described in Jerusalem, section 9. From Gethsemane take the path that leads southwest from the Jericho Road at a point just south of the Church of All Nations and leads in a few minutes to the Tombs of Jehoshaphat and Absalom.

The ***Tomb of Absalom** is the most prominent monument in the Kidron and—depending on the eye of the beholder—a graceful addition to the landscape, or a monument in decadent late Hellenistic style. The limestone scarp steepens on the left of the path, and the tomb and its rock-cut courtyard is hewn from it. The traditional association with Absalom (who built himself a memorial pillar in the King's Valley) is false but of long standing; de Tollot (a visitor in 1731) records that passers-by threw stones at this tomb because of Absalom's disobedience to his father David. Its construction probably dates to the last half of the 1C BC and it is undoubtedly part of a Jewish burial complex belonging to a wealthy family, perhaps priestly or Sadducee, in the early Roman period. It contains a small tomb chamber but is also part of the complex called the Tomb of Jehoshaphat (see below), which leads off the court at the northeast corner. The Tomb of Absalom may have contained the principal burials, and thereafter acted

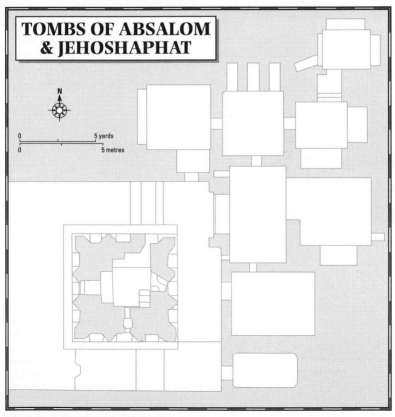

TOMBS OF ABSALOM & JEHOSHAPHAT

N

0   5 yards
0   5 metres

as a memorial cenotaph for succeeding generations of the family buried in the adjacent hypogeum.

The square open court is quarried from the rock-scarp. The monument, pseudo-peripteral and composite in style, has the lower section as far as the cornice cut from the rock, and the upper part built of masonry. The monument stands on a podium. Each corner has an angular quarter-engaged pilaster ending in quarter-columns, and each side two semi-engaged columns. The capitals are Ionic, with egg and dart motifs, and on them rests an architrave with Doric frieze of triglyphs with late triangular guttae, and metopes with paterae. Above is a roll and cavetto cornice which are clearly close copies of those on the Tomb of Zechariah (see below) and the Monolith of Silwan (see p 224). The upper built cubical base, tholos drum and concave pyramid are all developed late Hellenistic features, which, allied with Roman style mouldings, indicate a date into the Roman period in Jerusalem. The pyramid is topped by a rope moulding and a circlet or cup of leaves. The total height is c 16.50m. The holes hacked in the sides are those of looters, except for the original entrance high on the south side (accessible only by ladder) which leads to the burial chamber. Steep steps descend internally from this entrance to a small squarish chamber, with relief ornament of circles and discs on the ceiling and two bench arcosolia. One bench has a ledge above it, possibly for lamps. The tomb was looted in ancient times.

The Tomb of Jehoshaphat

At the north end of the east side of the court is an entrance leading to a burial complex. The portal has a finely carved pediment. The tympanum contains an acanthus and running scroll growing from a vase. The foliage contains flowers and fruits, with carving and motifs similar to Herodian ornament on ossuaries and Herod's temple. Leaf acroteria survive at the corners of the pediment, but that at the centre has been cut away in later work. Inside the hypogeum is a complex of eight rectangular burial chambers. The plan is cruciform with some later chambers added to the east which have bench arcosolia.

A few metres south, the height of the rock-scarp increases, and a further complex of tomb chambers is revealed.

The **Tomb of the Bene Hezir** (traditionally the Tomb of St. James) probably dates to the late 2C BC or the early 1C BC. It is earlier than that of Absalom and in purer Hellenistic style. In the 12C it was believed to be the tomb of St. James the Less. The tomb is rock-cut, with a Doric façade. Two free-standing and two engaged columns without bases have straight Doric capitals supporting a Doric frieze with triglyphs and diglyphs and conical early guttae (cf. the Tomb of Jason, p 260) with cornice above. At the south end of the architrave is an inscription in square Hebrew characters which may have been added at the time of some of the later Herodian period burials in the tomb. The inscription is translated: 'This is the tomb and the memorial of Eleazar, Haniah, Jo'azar, Jehudah, Simeon, Johannan, the sons of Joseph son of 'Oreb; also of Joseph and Eleazar the sons of Haniah, priests of the family of the Bene Hezir'. This family is associated with the Hezir of I Chr. 24:15 who, being of the descent of Aaron, were among those who drew lots for taking charge of the service in the temple. Behind the façade is a portico with steps leading off at a high level to the north and a rough-cut passage to the south which are of uncertain date and purpose. At the back of the portico, a rectangular doorway leads to a hypogeum with cruciform plan, in which bench chambers have unusually shaped kokhim which may also be of early date. The rear chambers have bench arcosolia and may be later additions. Like most family tombs, the hypogeum was probably used for at least three generations.

The **Tomb of Zechariah**, usually identified as the memorial or *nefesh* of the Bene Hezir tomb, and not associated with Zechariah, lies c 10m south of the tomb of the Bene Hezir, in a square rock-cut court connected to the tomb by a rough passage. The solid cubical monument stands on three steps and a podium. The roughly cut chamber below the steps is probably not part of the original plan. Like the tomb of Absalom, the monument has angular quarter-engaged pilasters at the corners which end in quarter-columns; each side has semi-engaged columns with Ionic capitals with egg and dart motifs and good profile. Unlike the tomb of Absalom, the tops of the columns have the beginnings of Ionic fluting, and the capitals of the north, east and south sides are unfinished. The architrave is much plainer, with no triglyphs or metopes, and above is the roll and cavetto cornice which seems to be particularly popular in these Kidron tombs. The monument is capped by a plain high pyramid with square base, again probably copied from the Monolith of Silwan. The detail of the tomb design is early and appears to complement that of the adjacent Bene Hezir hypogeum.

Immediately to the south is a very crudely cut façade with two columns which is not connected with the Bene Hezir-Zechariah complex.

From this point either return to Gethsemane, or continue further down to Gihon and the Lower Kidron or up to Silwan village (see Jerusalem, section 9).

11 • The northern suburbs

The north suburbs beyond the walls of the Old City were only developed during the late 19C. Pierotti (one of the earliest to explore this area in 1864) notes that from the Muslim cemetery on Karm al-Shaikh (near Herod's Gate) to the Tombs of the Kings there was earth, vegetation and bare rock, with no trace of an ancient city. From the 1870s small settlements grew up, and from the 1880s various foreign institutions were established, such as the American Colony in 1881, the Dominican Convent of St. Stephen in 1884 and the German Catholic Hospice and College in 1886. The rate of building increased in the 20C, and especially from the 1950s. Today, as well as various institutions, there are hotels, consulates and hospitals situated here, and it is a populous suburb with the main shopping area along Salah al-Din St. It is mainly inhabited by Christian and Muslim Arabs. Further out, new Jewish suburbs link the western city with Mount Scopus. The principal places of interest are the Rockefeller Museum, and some fine rock-cut tombs including those of the Sanhedrin.

Places of interest close to the Old City

The Rockefeller Museum

Formerly the museum of the Department of Antiquities of Palestine, the **Rockefeller Museum (or Palestine Archaeological Museum) is on the north side of Sulaiman St, opposite the northeast corner of the Old City, two minutes' walk east of Herod's Gate. Buses 1, 2, 23, 37 take you there. Open Sun–Thur, 10.00–17.00, Fri–Sat, 10.00–14.00; closed on Jewish holidays. Admission charged; combined ticket with Israel Museum available.

History

The Department of Antiquities of the British Mandate Government was set up in 1920, and the objects inherited from the Ottoman government collection, supplemented by objects from excavations in Palestine from 1920 to 1967 are housed in this museum. The Palestine Archaeological Museum was built with funds from American philanthropist John Davison Rockefeller, and was formally opened in 1938. It was designed by the architect Austin Harrison (1881–1976) who combined ideas drawn from Byzantine and Islamic palaces and caravanserais with his Lutyens training (see also the main Post Office, p 264 and the old Government House, p 266), and was built of local stone. After 1948 the museum was administered by an international committee of trustees until nationalised by Jordan in 1966. It was annexed by Israel in 1967 and now houses departments of the Israel Antiquities Authority, temporary exhibitions, as well as the excellent systematic display of antiquities largely unchanged since Mandate times.

The vestibule leads to a hall under the central tower, and the building is arranged symmetrically around a rectangular pool in a cloistered court. Study rooms were designed adjacent to the long exhibition galleries, one of which was the home for the Dead Sea Scrolls found in Jordan. There is a lecture theatre and library located in the front wings.

The Tower Hall is used for temporary exhibitions. The permanent display begins in the **South Octagon** to the left of the entrance (*basalt stele of Seti I, another depicting the Canaanite goddess Anat, basalt statue of Ramses III, all from Beth Shean) and continues into the South Gallery. Here the objects illustrate the archaeological assemblages in stone, pottery, metalwork and other materials from the Palaeolithic to the Iron Age. Most of the sites represented are those of the major excavations in Palestine up to 1948, and include the caves at Mount Carmel (Garrod and Bate), Jericho (Garstang; note the Middle Bronze Age face jug), 'Ai (Marquet-Krause), Megiddo (Fisher, Guy, Loud), Tell Beit Mirsim (Albright), Lachish (Starkey), Ajjul, Fara and Jemmeh (Petrie) and Beth Shan (Rowe and Fitzgerald). Particularly notable are the 13C/12C BC 'Philistine' anthropomorphic clay sarcophagi. In the South Room are some of the *great wooden beams and **panels from the Aqsa Mosque** (see Aqsa Mosque and Islamic Museum, see Jerusalem, section 2) which were removed during the 1938–42 restorations. Finely carved, and with important graffiti, they date mostly from the 7C–8C.

In the **West Hall** are *stucco relief and **sculpture from Khirbat al-Mafjar** near Jericho. This Umayyad palace was built by the caliphs Hisham and al-Walid II after c 724 and destroyed, still unfinished, in the earthquake of 749. Notice the delightful and rare Islamic depictions of the human figure, including a statue probably of al-Walid himself in Persian costume; the reconstructed ornament from the bath house porch, including a whole arch and pendentive; and a lively procession of painted quail. Complex geometric and floral patterns cover the entire surfaces, and reflect developing early Islamic art influenced both by Sassanian traditions and those of the local schools of craftsmen. It was the first time in Palestine that carved stucco was used extensively as a surface ornament.

Continuing beyond the hall, a small room to the left contains a fine display of jewellery from the Hellenistic to later periods.

In the **North Room**, among other important pieces of 12C Crusader sculp-

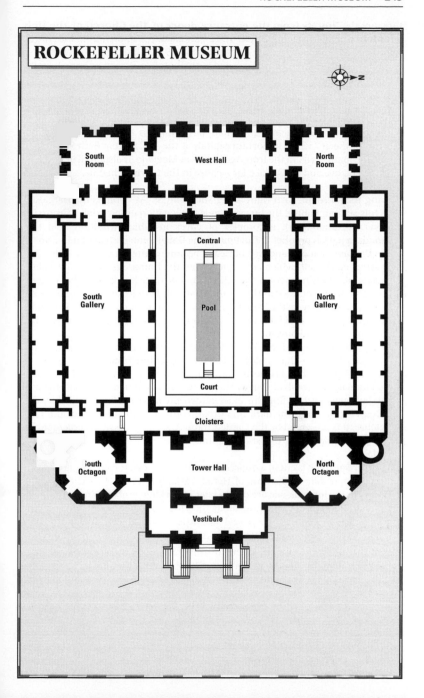

ture, are the *lintels from the entrance doors of the Church of the Holy Sepulchre** (see Jerusalem, section 4). The lintels were removed from the church to preserve them following the earthquake of 1927. One (from the west doorway) shows scenes from Holy Week and is attributed to Tuscan or French craftsmen; the other, depicting naked men and monsters in scrolls of foliage, fruit and flowers, belongs to the 'tree of life' style and is thought to come from a workshop in Abruzzi (Italy) c 1150–80.

In the **North Gallery** is pottery and sculpture of the Roman and Islamic periods. More sculpture, including Roman sarcophagi, a basalt tomb door from Tiberias of the 2C/3C AD, important capitals of the 15C BC from Beth Shean, and one of the mangers from the Iron Age stables at Megiddo, is displayed in the cloister, an attractive and quiet place for a pause in the tourist schedule.

Leaving the museum, turn right along Sulaiman St. At 200m is the Damascus Gate bus station. Behind the bus station is the location of Jeremiah's Grotto (A. Zawiyat al-Adhamiyya), a complex of caves in which tradition held that Jeremiah (a Jewish prophet at the time of the Babylonian destruction in 586 BC) wrote his Lamentations and was buried. It became a Muslim shrine c 1361. The next street on the left, which runs north from the Damascus Gate is the Nablus Rd (also called the Shechem or Ramallah Rd). The large building on the corner is Schmidt's College, founded as the German Catholic Hospice and College in 1886, and used temporarily as the British governorate immediately after the surrender of the city in 1917, and later as the British Royal Air Force Headquarters. The Church of St. Paul adjoins it.

Just up the Nablus Rd is the East Jerusalem Bus Station on the left, and on the right, a lane between high walls leads up to the **Garden Tomb**. This was discovered c 1867, and in 1883 General Gordon (of Khartoum) suggested it as a possible location for the Tomb of Christ. There is no early tradition to support the proposal, but many visitors find this quiet garden site more readily identifiable with the Gospel scene than the dark and urban context of the Church of the Holy Sepulchre. It is preserved by the Garden Tomb Association as an interdenominational place of prayer for Christian pilgrims. Open 08.30–12.00; 14.00–17.30; closed Sun.

The Garden Tomb is cut in a quarried scarp approached through a garden. The quarrying may date to the time of Herod Agrippa I (AD 37–44). The door and windows in the tomb façade are due to later reworking, probably in Byzantine or Crusader times. The deep channel along the ground, sometimes identified as the groove for a giant rolling stone to seal the entrance, is of uncertain date and purpose. The square tomb chamber inside, with three much-destroyed projecting benches with troughs but no arcosolia (which would be typical of the late Roman period), may well date to the 8C–6C BC as part of a nearby cemetery (see St. Stephen, below). The idea of locating the Tomb of Christ in this area was current in the 19C when the knoll immediately to the east and above the garden was identified with Golgotha, the Place of the Skull. This was a popular belief, based on the resemblance of the prominent knoll to the shape of a skull when viewed from the east, with bare rounded top and two caves marking the eyes, and also drew on a Jewish tradition that this was the place of stoning just outside the city on the road to Damascus. This identification of Golgotha was adopted by many scholars; and thus in 1883 Gordon's suggestion of this as the site of the Tomb of

Christ had ready followers and it became known as 'Gordon's Tomb of Christ'. In 1881 Conder (who mapped Palestine) found a 'remarkable' tomb 100m further west, on the west side of the Nablus Road (later covered by the Convent of the White Sisters), which duly became known as 'Conder's Tomb of Christ'. In 1892 Conrad Schick (who contributed to the exploration of Jerusalem) wrote of this spate of proposals that 'everyone may choose which he likes from the three we now have'.

The **Dominican Convent and Church of St. Stephen** is entered a little higher up the Nablus Road.

History of the Convent and Church of St. Stephen

About 415 a village priest discovered the bones of Stephen, the first martyr of the Christian church, and in 438 Empress Eudocia was present when the relics were deposited in their first shrine. She built a church to house the relics c 455–60, on the traditional site of Stephen's death by stoning (Acts 6:5–8:1), and later was herself buried here. A large monastery occupied the site in the 6C, but was destroyed in the Persian sack of 614. A chapel was built in the 7C, and the site belonged to the Benedictine Monastery of St. Mary Latin in the 12C. This complex was pulled down for strategic reasons in the face of Salah al-Din's advance in 1187. A hospice was created in the nearby 'Asnerie' (the stables of the Knights of the Hospital) after 1192 for Christian pilgrims who were not permitted by the Ayyubids to lodge within the walls. This rule was relaxed in 1229 but re-established after 1244. In 1881 part of the 12C stable complex and a chapel with an altar painted with saints were uncovered near the road; and to the east the Byzantine church was discovered. The present Convent of St. Stephen was built on the site in 1884; the École Biblique et Archéologique Française de St. Étienne (with fine library) was established in 1890. The present church of St. Stephen was built in 1900.

Ring the bell for admission to the church, which is built on the foundations and preserves some of the mosaic floors of the 5C Byzantine church. The court contains ancient cisterns and tombs. Entrance to the tombs is by previous permission only. They include one previously sealed by a Byzantine tombstone inscribed: 'Tomb of the deacon Nonnus Onesimus of the Holy Sepulchre of Christ and this monastery.' One tomb had a round blocking stone. There are two monumental tomb complexes originating in the Iron Age, with central rectangular halls leading to burial chambers with benches. The chambers are very well cut (cf. the Iron Age necropolis at Silwan village, see p 224), and were designed to take up to 20 primary burials with small lower chambers for secondary burials. The features which support an early date are the cornice and panel mouldings on the walls, the square chambers with projecting benches, some with troughs but without arcosolia, the headrests carved on the benches (cf. the tombs below the Church of Scotland, p 262) and small parapets along the edge of the benches. Both tombs were reused in the Byzantine period. The first is at the southeast angle of the church, discovered during construction work in 1885; the second, found a few years after, is incorporated in a building used as a cemetery by the monastery since the 19C and is about 50m south of the church. If the tombs are Iron Age, they are the largest tombs of that date known in Judah, and their style and size have suggested to some that they should be identified with the Royal Caverns mentioned by Josephus (War V:147; see also Solomon's Quarries, p 77).

The remnants of an **ancient defensive wall** can be seen 150m north in rough ground on the north side of Umar Ibn al-As St (opposite the garage). It was c 4.3m wide, constructed of varied, mostly reused masonry. More parts are preserved in a small park on the northwest side of the crossroads just to the west. These form part of a wall which stretches parallel to and opposite the central part of the present north wall of the Old City for c 600m, lying c 450m to the north of it. The most easterly point discovered lies in the garden of the Albright Institute (see below), and other sections can be seen west of the Nablus Road. The foundations of seven north-facing towers have been found. Probably the wall was never finished, and it has been robbed since for building materials.

There are now four theories about its origins. Some say it is the Third North Wall of the city of Herod Agrippa I (AD 41–44) described by Josephus (War V:142–160), which Agrippa left unfinished but was later hurriedly improved by the Jews during the First Revolt. It was built to enclose the houses that had begun to extend beyond the Second North Wall, including the new suburb of Bezetha. Others believe it was a forward defence barrier at the time of the First Revolt (AD 66); others that it was a siege wall built by Titus in AD 70; and finally that it was built by Hadrian for Aelia Capitolina.

The *Jerusalem Pottery*, just up the Nablus Rd on the right, has been on this site since 1922, manufacturing colourful ceramics with designs based on old Turkish patterns (Kütahya pottery); made originally by Armenians who came to Jerusalem in 1919 to make tiles for the repair of the Dome of the Rock.

Continuing to the east end of Umar Ibn al-As St, opposite in Salah al-Din St is the Albright Institute of Archaeological Research, founded as the American School of Oriental Research in 1900.

The Tombs of the Kings

The burial complex called the *Tombs of the Kings, on Salah al-Din St just before the junction with the Nablus Rd, is identified as the Tomb of Queen Helena of Adiabene, who died c AD 65. Cut c AD 50, the complex is a large and interesting example of a monumental Jewish family tomb in the Graeco-Roman tradition. Open 08.30–17.00; admission charged. A torch is needed if visiting the burial chambers.

History

The tomb is identified with that described by Josephus (Antiq. XX:17–96, 101; War V:147) as the tomb with three pyramids built by Helena of Adiabene three stadia from the town. Adiabene was in the northeast of modern Iraq, where members of a Jewish merchant community had converted the royal family to Judaism. Following the death of her husband, and the accession to the throne of her son Izates in AD 41, Helena came to Jerusalem, arriving at the time of the famine in AD 44. Her generous gifts to relieve the famine endeared her to the people of Jerusalem, and she stayed on, built a palace in the southeast part of Jerusalem, and a tomb for her eventual burial. She returned to Adiabene on the death of her son in AD 65 and died shortly after. Another son, Monobazes, became king, and sent the bodies of Helena and Izates to Jerusalem for burial, which must have taken place shortly before the beginning of the First Revolt. The disturbed times may have been a factor in placing the principal burial, in a sarcophagus inscribed 'Queen Saddan' in Aramaic (thought to be her Aramaic rather than Greek name), in a concealed lower chamber. The fortunate effect was that it escaped the attentions of the looters who devastated the upper burials.

The tomb seems also to have been used for burial after the First Revolt, as de Saulcy (the French explorer of the tomb) found an urn with ashes in the tomb in 1863, perhaps the ashes of a Roman, as cremation is forbidden in Jewish law. The tomb was probably looted again c 1483 during the reign of al-Ashraf Qa'it Bay and a number of sarcophagi may then have been taken to be used as fountain troughs. One of these is now placed outside the Islamic Museum in

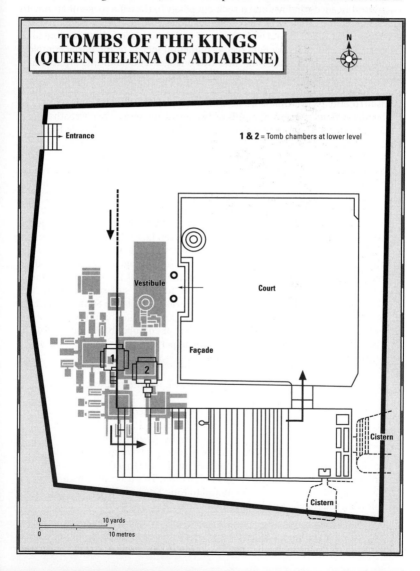

TOMBS OF THE KINGS
(QUEEN HELENA OF ADIABENE)

N

Entrance

1 & 2 = Tomb chambers at lower level

Vestibule

Court

Façade

1

2

Cistern

Cistern

0   10 yards

0   10 metres

the Haram (see p 133). The monument was wrongly identified by de Saulcy in 1863 as the Tombs of the Kings of Judah (the origin of the present name). The tomb was bought as such by a wealthy French Jewish family in 1878, and in 1886 given by them to the French Republic, by which it is still administered.

Entering from Salah al-Din St, turn right to the top of 24 broad descending rock-cut steps. Channels at the side and centre collect rainwater to fill two cisterns located at the bottom of the stairs. That on the right is smaller; that ahead has two round-headed windows and a rock-cut pillar. To the left a rock-cut arch with a single incised moulding leads to an enormous, almost square court. It measures nearly 26m a side, and both the court and the steps may have originated as a quarry. To the west is the damaged ornamental façade of the burial complex. The columns, two free-standing, and two engaged end-columns, are missing. Several fragments of Corinthian capitals were found in the excavation of the court. Above, a flat architrave has a frieze of leaves, citrus and almonds with a central rosette. Above that a frieze with triglyphs, dentils and round metopes with paterae flank the central motifs of two acanthus sprays, two wreaths and a bunch of grapes. The frieze is capped by a cornice. Above, the façade has been reconstructed (on paper) as crowned with three pyramids or memorial monuments, which have not survived. Behind the façade is a vestibule.

On the left side of the vestibule are steps leading down to the burial chambers. At the top, and also just outside the vestibule on the right side of the façade, are two rock-cut basins, probably used for ablution in the funerary ritual. The entrance steps were once blocked by a large round stone (cf. Convent of St. Stephen, above, and Herod's Family Tomb, p 263). They lead to a large square hall off which four doors lead to a complex of seven large chambers with numerous kokhim; smaller passages exist at various levels. The two chambers on the south lead to chambers on a lower level. A fine sarcophagus, now in the Louvre in Paris, was located in the first chamber on the right of the entrance. It has a curved lid carved with leaves, flowers and fruits in rather stiff, stylised forms. The sarcophagus of Saddan (also in the Louvre), was found by de Saulcy in a lower chamber near the centre of the complex. The corners had been knocked off in order to get it into the burial chamber. This burial chamber had bench arcosolia and may have been cut a little later than the upper chambers. Many of the stone sealing doors had relief carved panelling.

Opposite the entrance is the rear of **St. George's Anglican Cathedral**, college and hospice, which is entered from the Nablus Road. The church was built in 1898. The Protestant interests in Palestine were first served under a joint Anglo-Prussian agreement (for details, see Christ Church, p 194), which was dissolved in 1887. Bishop Blyth was then appointed to the Anglican see. The new establishment included the collegiate church of St. George, boys' and girls' schools, an episcopal residence and a clergy house all on the north side of the town. The cathedral, stone-built, with an English character, has a hospice with pleasant garden adjacent. The tower is a memorial to King Edward VII, dedicated 1910.

Following the Nablus Road down the hill to the north is the *American Colony Hotel*. Originally settled by Swedish Protestants and American missionaries in 1881, the American Colony is one of the historic entities of 19C Jerusalem. The hotel remains in the ownership of the family. The central building is a fine example of a princely late Ottoman house with courtyard and many details lovingly preserved. The decorations include tiles made in Jerusalem by craftsmen from Turkey in 1919–20. An upstairs room contains a fine Ottoman ceiling. The Colony has an archive of photographs (showing, among many interesting events, locust devastion and the 1927 earthquake) and news clippings relating particularly to the events of 1917.

North of the hotel is a small mosque of Shaykh Jarrah, a domed tomb of the Amir Husam al-Din al-Jarrahi (c 1201) which used to be specially venerated by country people for the granting of prosperous expeditions, good harvests and good luck, especially with hens and egg production. The mosque was added in 1895–96. The unfinished Muslim building next to it has been caught in Israeli planning controls for some years. From here the road descends into a valley, and then climbs the hill of Shaikh Jarrah, a Muslim quarter established c 1900, now with many institutional buildings, including consulates, the Council for British Research in the Levant and St. Joseph's Hospital. St. John's Ophthalmic Hospital is also located here. Originally founded in 1882 by the revived English Order of the Knights of St. John for research on the endemic Palestinian problems of trachoma, it formerly occupied a building just south of the Sultan's Pool on the Bethlehem Road; the present site was developed after 1948.

Below the south side of the hill of Shaikh Jarrah is located the so-called **Tomb of Simon the Just**. Descending the hill from the American Colony, take the first right turn, then fork left and turn left to the end of the road. A tomb set among other rock-cut tombs on the north side of the Wadi Jauz was identified in Jewish tradition as that of Simon the Just (H. Shimon ha-Zaddiq), who was High Priest in Jerusalem in the late 4C BC and renowned for piety and goodness to his people (Josephus, War XII:ii:5 and Ecclesiaticus 50:1–21). It had a Roman inscription on the rear wall of the antechamber above the low doorway. Though much damaged, it named Julia Sabina, a Roman lady, perhaps related to a Julius Sabinus who was a first centurion of the Tenth Roman Legion. The tomb must date well into the Roman period, and is therefore not the tomb of the High Priest Simon. The site was bought by the Jews in 1876 and is a place of pilgrimage, currently closed except to Jews.

Returning towards the Old City, opposite the American Colony take St. George St to the Kikkar Pikud Hamerkaz. Opposite the north end of Hel Handasa is the Mandelbaum Gate. This was the only crossing point between East and West Jerusalem between 1948 and 1967. It was named for the owner of a nearby house, and a plaque now marks the site. A fortnightly convoy starting here was permitted through Jordanian territory under UN supervision to maintain the Israeli enclave on Mount Scopus.

The Tourjeman Post Museum at the north end of Hel Handasa has an exhibition on the 'Reunification of Jerusalem' in a house belonging to the Baramki family until 1948, which was used as an Israeli frontier post on the edge of No-Man's Land between 1948 and 1967. Open Sun–Thur, 09.00–17.00; Fri 09.00–13.00. Admission charged. Buses 2, 13.

From here turn south along Hanevim (Prophet St), and c 200m from the Damascus Gate can be found the ***Armenian Mosaic**, in a house at the corner of a short street on the right (open 07.00–17.00). The 5C–6C mosaic was found in July 1894. The mosaic is elaborate, with tesserae of many colours. Within a guilloche border is a vase from which springs a vine with many branches and grape clusters. Peacocks, ducks, storks, pigeons, fowls, an eagle, a partridge and a parrot in a cage are depicted in the branches. Under the southwest corner a small natural cave contained human bones and lamps of the 5C–6C. That the room was a mortuary chapel is indicated by the inscription at the east end which reads: 'For the memory and salvation of all those Armenians whose name the Lord knows.' The building is identified by some with the church of St. Polyeucht.

Notre Dame de France, on Hazanhanim St opposite the Old City, another Jerusalem landmark, is now a hotel. It was founded by the Augustinian Fathers of the Assumption as a pilgrim's hospice in 1887; being on the front line, it was badly damaged during and after the 1948 war. It now belongs to the Vatican.

Sites on the more distant northern fringes of Jerusalem

To the northwest (c 2.2km northwest of the Damascus Gate), in the new suburb of Sanhedriyya, is a large burial complex including the **Tombs of the Sanhedrin**. The tombs are now mostly preserved in a small park (open daily 09.00 until sunset) just north of Shmuel Hanavi St (Samuel the Prophet St), reached by buses 2, 10, 16, 39 and 40.

These tombs are part of a large cemetery stretching across the outer edges of the north side of the city. All those known were pillaged in ancient times. The best known of this group of about 20 Jewish family tombs of the first half of the 1C AD is the monument called the Tombs of the Sanhedrin or Judges (Tomb 14 towards the northwest of the group), which was discovered at the beginning of the 17C. The tomb is falsely associated with the 70 judges who maintained Jewish religious law and met in the Temple Area, because of the number of burial places it contains (actually only 55 kokhim, 4 arcosolia and 2 cave/ossuaries). Nothing is known of its real ownership, and there is no evidence that it was used for other than family burial over several generations.

That the site was an ancient limestone quarry is attested by the marks in the floor of the forecourt. The court was used in medieval times as a caravanserai. On the east is a rectangular door with a triangular pediment with dentils. The acroteria at the sides are rather rigid palmettes or acanthus; the central acroterium has gone. The tympanum contains a rather flatly carved all-over design of acanthus scroll, with fruits (no grapes) restricted to the central area. The ornament is copied on the doorway of the hypogeum inside the vestibule, on a reduced scale. The entrances to the burial chambers themselves were generally small, with a rebated edge into which the blocking stone fitted fairly precisely. Inside, this tomb is even larger than that of Helena of Adiabene (see above, p 247). The first great chamber has two storeys (which is a unique feature), with very dense alignments of straight and long kokhim. The openings are arched, with rectangular rebates for the blocking slabs. The upper levels of kokhim are set back in pairs within arcosolia. There are six chambers behind the vestibule, three on the upper level, and three at a lower level reached by stairs.

Tomb 8, to the east, is a fine rock-cut tomb. It has a court with benches and columns which are distyle in antis with pilasters as wall ends. The capitals are late Doric with concave profiles. The pilaster capitals have very degenerate late mouldings. Inside is a central hall with three chambers leading off, one containing four kokhim beneath three arcosolia.

Other tombs are located in the park, and a few outside in nearby buildings.

The **Grapes Tomb** is c 200m northeast of the Tombs of the Sanhedrin, in the Doris Weiler Garden in Yam Suf St. This has a very large court (6.7m), again probably originally created by quarrying. The tomb entrance has a triangular pediment with dentils, and three large, rather stiff acroteria over an Ionic T-framed doorway; the tympanum is very flatly carved with a central rosette and a running vine scroll with grapes. The soffit of the entrance has relief carving of rosettes and foliage in coffer-like panels. The vestibule is large with a cavetto cornice and Doric-type capitals and with ornament in more local style on the pilasters. The interior has a fairly regular plan with three chambers leading off a central hall, each with six kokhim, except that the middle kokh on the south side forms a passage to a further chamber which has three arcosolia and a sunk circular panel on the ceiling containing a star rosette in relief. It probably dates to the beginning of the 1C AD.

Approximately halfway between Sanhedriyya and Shaikh Jarrah is **Ammunition Hill**, the main Israeli War Memorial commemorating the Six Day War, dating from 1975. There is a park and a museum on the south side of Sederot Levi Eshkol, open Sun–Thur 08.30–17.00, Fri and the eve of hols 09.00–13.00; closed Sat and Jewish holidays.

Mount Scopus, the north and higher end (903m) of the ridge which includes the Mount of Olives (Jerusalem, section 10) lies to the northeast of the Old City, and is approached by several roads and by buses 9, 23, 26, 28, and 46. It has various institutions established in the 20C, including the original section of the Hebrew University and some modern and ancient tombs.

Mount Scopus is a strategic high point from which there is an overview of the city—the name itself means lookout or watchtower. It is mentioned by Josephus as the place where Cestius pitched camp in AD 66 (War II:528) before setting fire to the suburb of Bezetha and very nearly taking the Temple from the north before making his disastrous retreat. Titus also pitched camp here in AD 70 (War V:67) at the beginning of the siege of Jerusalem. The Crusaders camped here too in 1099; and the British forces after the taking of Jerusalem in 1917. It contained an Israeli enclave around the Hadassah Hospital and the Hebrew University in 1948–67.

On the south side is the **Augusta Victoria Hospital** at the lower end of the hill. The tall tower (60m) is a landmark providing good views. Built by Wilhelm II and the Empress Augusta Victoria of Germany in 1898, the hospice and hospital were opened in 1910, and it was at first under the protection of the German Protestant Order of St. John. Today it is sponsored by the Lutheran World Federation and the United Nations. The Evangelical Church of the Ascension here is open 09.00–17.30; closed Sun. Bronze statues of the founders (by A. Wolf) have been set up in the courtyard.

Up the hill to the northwest is the **Hebrew University (Mt Scopus campus)**.

History of the Hebrew University

Proposals for a Jewish university in Jerusalem were first made in the 19C and plans were formulated in 1902. The house of Sir John Gray Hill with 20 hectares of land was purchased in 1913, and foundation stones laid in 1918. The first part of the university was officially opened in 1925, with Institutes of Chemistry, Microbiology and Jewish Studies. It expanded up to 1948. Cut off from its staff and 1027 students in 1948, the university and hospital were maintained by a caretaker force until 1967. A new campus was set up at Giv'at Ram.

After 1967 the Mount Scopus campus was reopened, extensively renovated, and expanded. The modern Mount Scopus Synagogue (architect Ram Karmi) is a central feature.

Free tours of the University are available from the Bronfman Family Reception Centre, daily at 11.30.

12 • The western and southern suburbs

The greater part of modern Jerusalem lies west of the Old City and few remains of earlier times can be seen there, apart from some tombs of the Roman and medieval periods and the Monastery of the Holy Cross.

Before the 19C the population lived within the walls for safety and the rocky land outside was used for grazing, gardens and burial. By the mid-19C occupation was beginning to extend west and south along the routes to Jaffa, Gaza and Bethlehem. The Greek Orthodox Clerical Seminary was established in the Monastery of the Holy Cross in 1852; various houses were built in 1855 when Anglo-Jewish philanthropist Sir Moses Montefiore bought land southwest of the city, and the British Consul, J. Finn and Bishop Gobat built summer homes southwest and northwest of the city; Bishop Gobat's house lay north of the Jaffa road, but conditions were still unsafe and the adjacent house was abandoned in 1860 because of bandits.

Building, particularly for institutional use and with a somewhat defensive architectural style, was much more extensive in the 1860s. The Montefiore houses (see below) were put up in 1860, as was the German (or Schneller) Orphanage; the Russian Compound was opened in 1864, the Talitha Kumi Girls' School (German) in 1865, and the Lepers' Hospital in 1867; the carriage road to Jaffa was finished in 1868 and the Nahalat Shiva Jewish Quarter established in 1869. The following 20 years saw a torrent of building, and by 1914 much of the area around the Jaffa Road was built up, the more westerly sections occupied predominantly by new Jewish quarters, with a number of Christian and Muslim Arab quarters to the north, east and south. During the Mandate period many more administrative buildings and services were located in this area, such as the Romema Reservoir and new water pipelines in 1918, the Electric Power Station in 1926, Government House and the Palestine Post Building in 1931, the Palestine Broadcasting Service in 1936, and the Central Post Office in 1938, as well as cinemas and hotels. Considerable thought was given to the planning and development of the entire city, as exemplified in the Zoning Plan of 1922 which incorporated a large area of parkland around the Old City itself. The war of 1948 created havoc between the various ethnic quarters, and many Arabs abandoned their homes west of the armistice line. Since 1948 the expansion of building activity has been considerable, and the Parliament or Knesset and National Museum, have been located here.

The following tour of the western suburbs is divided into four: the central area;

the northern area; the southern area; and the outskirts. Most of the places of interest are located in the central area.

The central area of the western suburbs

This section is bounded approximately by the Jaffa Road, the Hebrew University (Giv'at Ram campus) and the railway station.

The heart of the northeast part is **Independence Park**, located at the old Mamilla Pool and Muslim Cemetery. Numerous buses pass the park, including 19 and 22.

History of the Mamilla Pool and Muslim cemetery

The oldest feature is the Mamilla Pool, a great cemented open tank. Its original date is uncertain, but it may well have started as a rain-fed pool in a quarry at the head of the Hinnom Valley in the time of Herod the Great, and in the 1C AD have been incorporated in the Upper Aqueduct system from Solomon's Pools. It was certainly incorporated in the Mamluk water system in the 15C and later, when a channel linked it to the Pool of the Patriarch's Bath (Hezekiah's Pool, see p 163). It may have been the site of a massacre of Christian captives in 614 whose bodies were said to have been collected by St. Mamilla and placed in a cave.

The cemetery was also used by Christians, in particular as the burial place of the Canons of the Church of the Holy Sepulchre. A Church of St. Mamilla was located here in the 12C.

In the 13C it became the largest Muslim cemetery in Jerusalem, mentioned by Mujir al-Din in c 1495 and in use up to the 20C. According to Mujir al-Din, it 'contains the graves of men who were illustrious for their learning or their piety, or who fell in battle against the infidels'. The ancient church of Mamilla was identified with the Zawiyat al-Qalandariyya which still stood in ruined state in the middle of the cemetery c 1495 when tradition held it had been a Byzantine church. The cemetery has been largely ruined since 1948, and the Independence Park established more recently.

View of the Mamilla Pool and Cemetery in the late 19C (C.W. Wilson, Picturesque Palestine, Vol. I, p 102: Virtue & Co., London, 1880)

The great pool (88.5m x 58.5m x 5.8m deep), normally empty, is located near the centre of the park. In a grove c 50m east of the pool is the **Zawiya Kubakiyya**, an elegant Muslim tomb of c 1289. It is the burial place of the Amir Aidughdi al-Kubaki, who was the Governor of Safad under the Mamluk ruler Baybars, but who was later banished to Jerusalem where he died on 22 September 1289, aged about 60. The original building may have been a mortuary chapel of the Canons of the Church of the Holy Sepulchre, as it incorporates a number of typical 12C Crusader features reused by the Muslims in the 13C.

Its form is essentially a cube supporting a cylindrical drum surmounted by a dome. The entrance on the northwest side has a trefoil horseshoe arch, and on either side of the recess, reused Crusader elbow consoles of different sizes support an arch with voussoirs which are also reused Crusader work. The dated Mamluk dedicatory inscription is placed above the lintel. The drum also contains a series of brackets supporting a cavetto cornice that are probably of Crusader origin. The interior is lit by windows in three walls. The southeast wall contains the mihrab. The interior contains niches with stalactite ornament.

In the centre of the mausoleum is a fine Romanesque Crusader sarcophagus with gabled lid and blind arcading on the sides. It may have once belonged to a dignitary of the Church of the Holy Sepulchre. The tomb was restored in the late 19C; the doorway has been blocked to prevent vandalism.

On the north side of the Mamilla Cemetery and south of Ben Yehuda Road, at 27 Rehov Hillel, is the Nahon Museum of Jewish Art from Italy, also called the Italian Museum or the Italian synagogue. It contains the interior and objects from an Italian synagogue dated 1701. Open Sun 10.00–13.00, Wed 14.00–19.00. Admission charged. Free guided tour sometimes available. Numerous city buses.

On the west side of the Mamilla Cemetery, nearing the south end of King George St, is the building of the **Jewish Agency**, head office of the World Zionist Organisation and containing the Zionist archives, the Golden Books recording donations for land purchase, the Jewish National Fund and the United Jewish Agencies. From 1921 the Jewish National Council, and from 1929 the Jewish Agency, were set up to establish a Jewish national home in Palestine. The building, designed by Y. Ratner in 1927, is regarded as one of the earliest in the modern architectural movement in Palestine, and the design reflects the architect's German training. Thirteen Jews were killed in a terrorist attack here on 11 March 1948. Further south, near the junction of King George St with Gershon Agron, are located the Chief Rabbinate (H. Hekhal Shelomo) at 58 King George St, named for Shelomo Wolfson, father of Sir Isaac Wolfson who donated the building. It has a museum of Jewish liturgical art and folklore and a Torah library; adjacent is the Jerusalem Great Synagogue, which is used mainly for festivals. Free daily tours are available; Sun–Thur 09.00–13.00; Fri 09.00–12.00. Bus 4, 7–9, 14, 17, 31, 32.

To the northwest along the south side of the Jaffa Rd and just over 1km west of the Old City is the Mahane Yehuda (Jewish) quarter, founded in 1887, which has an oriental style market on the south side of the Jaffa Road, busiest on Wednesday and Thursday (buses includes 6–8, 11, 13, 14, 18, 20).

At the south end of the Sacher Park the **Israel Parliament** or **Knesset** building is located off Rehov Ruppin (reached by buses 9, 24). Open Sun and Thur 08.30–14.30. Passports are required if visiting.

Opposite the entrance is a very large bronze menorah (seven-branched ritual candlestick) with scenes from Jewish history, presented by the British Government. Inside the building, opened in 1966, are tapestries, and wall and floor mosaics all designed by Marc Chagall.

A little over 0.5km to the west is the **Hebrew University** (Giv'at Ram campus—for early history, see Mount Scopus, p 251). In 1958 a new campus was established at Giv'at Ram; in 1963 a new medical school was opened at Ein Kerem (see below, Hadassah Hospital). After the 1967 war and the renewed access to Mount Scopus, the faculties of the University were reorganised, and an intensive programme of rebuilding, restoration and expansion began. The Jewish National and University Library has a collection of Hebrew manuscript codices from the 10C onwards, and also some in Arabic, Samaritan, Syriac, Persian, Armenian and Latin; it also houses about 16,000 rare books. Guided tours are available Sun–Fri 09.00–11.00, starting from the administration building. Buses 9, 24, 28.

As well as the university buildings and synagogue, the campus contains the Williams Planetarium, the Wise Auditorium, and the Botanical Garden. Open Sun–Thur 09.00–07.00, Fri 09.00–14.00, Sat 10.00–17.00.

The **Bible Lands Museum Jerusalem** is located across the car park from the entrance to the Israel Museum (see below), at Museum Row, 25 Granot St.

• Open Sun–Tues 09.30–17.30, Wed (Apr–Oct 09.30–21.30, Nov–Mar 13.30–21.30), Fri and eve of hols 09.30–14.00, Sat and hols 11.00–15.00. Admission charged. Free guided tours in English Sun–Fri 10.15, Wed 17.30; for other language tours, current events such as concerts and lectures, ☎ 02 561 1066. Buses 9, 17, 24, 99. Facilities include wheel chair access and restaurant.

Displayed on one floor in a modern building is a permanent exhibition of archaeological material from the Borowski Collection that illustrates the Bible. Items range in provenance from Egypt to Iran, and the collection is divided into 20 sections from biblical beginnings to Roman times. The museum also houses temporary exhibitions.

Israel Museum

On Rehov Ruppin, and south of the Knesset is the ****Israel Museum**, which has housed the national archaeological collection since *1948. As well as antiquities of Israel and neighbouring cultures, the museum contains ethnography and Judaica, period rooms, contemporary art and design, sections on distant cultures, and a youth wing.

• Open Sun, Mon, Wed, Thur 10.00–17.00; Tues 16.00–22.00, Shrine of the Book and Billy Rose Art Garden 10.00–22.00; Fri and hol. eves 10.00–14.00; Sat and eve of hol. 10.00–16.00. For tours, lectures, current exhibitions, concerts and activities, information and monthly programme leaflet ask at the information desk or ☎ 02 670 8811. Admission charged. Combined tickets for Rockefeller Museum available. Bus 9, 24, 17.

The museum has been planned to house the growing national art and antiquities collections in an expandable complex of low, interconnected buildings and pavilions in a pleasant and relatively informal setting. The large area of hillside contains a number of separately housed collections, and sculpture in a garden. The displays also utilise some items from the collections of the Rockefeller

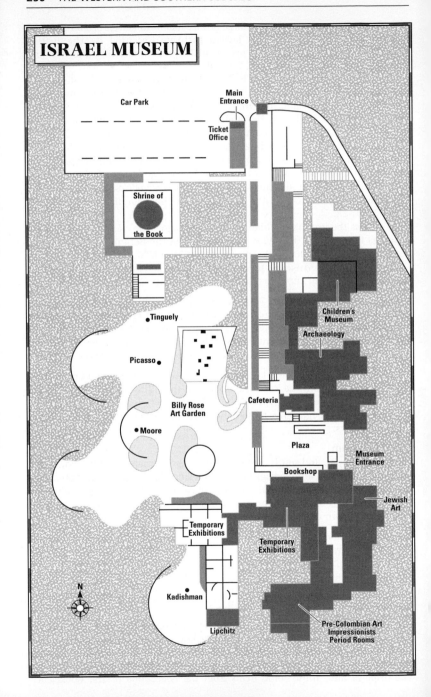

ISRAEL MUSEUM

Car Park

Main Entrance

Ticket Office

Shrine of the Book

Tinguely

Picasso

Billy Rose Art Garden

Cafeteria

Moore

Plaza

Museum Entrance

Bookshop

Jewish Art

Children's Museum

Archaeology

Temporary Exhibitions

Temporary Exhibitions

Kadishman

Lipchitz

Pre-Colombian Art
Impressionists
Period Rooms

N

Museum from excavations before 1967. The museum was opened on 11 May 1965; the Youth Wing was completed in 1979, the Impressionist and Pre-Columbian wings in 1980. The main museum complex was designed by Mansfeld and Gad.

The Samuel Bronfman Biblical and Archaeological Museum At the top of the main approach, cross the plaza to the left past the cafeteria; from the terrace in front of the entrance there is a fine view of the Monastery of the Holy Cross in the valley to the east (see below). The entrance foyer contains a bookshop as well as cloakroom and information desk. The central stair descends to the archaeological exhibition halls.

The first hall contains temporary archaeological exhibitions, some relate to current excavations; the collections of the Bezalel Art Museum lie ahead and to the right (see below).

On the left the permanent archaeological exhibition begins with the **earliest traces of man in Israel**, with displays relating to environment and chronology. Sites, their ancient climatic conditions, flint tools, flora and fauna, many of the latter exhibiting species long extinct in Israel, are shown. They include finds from Ubaidiya in the upper Jordan Valley, around one million years old, as well as from Middle and Upper Palaeolithic sites. This hall also contains Mesolithic material of the Natufian culture (c 15,000–9000 BC), from sites such as Eynan, the Hayonim Cave in west Galilee, and the Mount Carmel caves, with evidence for the earliest beginnings of agriculture and more complex food-processing. The bone and shell beads and pendants are beautifully polished.

Of the **Neolithic material** (eighth to sixth millennia BC), the plastered skull from Beisamun is of interest, and compares with those found at Jericho (see p 445). The increasing social complexity attested is matched by the progress in agriculture, at a time when various cereals and food animals were domesticated. A model of early Neolithic stone hut-circles at Nahal Oren illustrates a small village of the period.

At the lower end of the gallery are notable finds of the **Chalcolithic period** (fifth to early fourth millennia BC). These include stone and pottery ossuaries from Azor, Ben Shemen and Givatayim. Many of the pottery ossuaries seem to be models of the houses of the living and have interesting details in the doors and gable ends. An enormous storage jar of this period, of unique size c 1.6m high, testifies to the need to produce and the capability to store food in optimum conditions.

Finely worked basalt, flint, ivory and haematite objects prepare you for the magnificent ***copper treasure from Nahal Mishmar**, found in a cave west of the Dead Sea. Most of the 429 objects discovered are on display; they include copper axes and adzes, maceheads, sceptres and 'crowns', many cast by a sophisticated lost wax process using copper alloys, indicating high technological achievement as well as fine craftsmanship. Abandoned in a cave, the hoard with its enormous weight of copper and fine ivory may represent the treasure and offerings associated with a contemporary temple.

The **Early Bronze Age** (late fourth to third millennia BC) is represented by finds from Khirbat Karak, Kfar Monash, Arad, Gath (Tell Shaikh Ahmad al-Araini) and other sites, when sizeable towns were normally defended by stone or mud-brick walls. A rather dark mezzanine gallery exhibits pottery from the succeeding non-urban interlude (c 2350–1900 BC), the most interesting object being a silver cup from a tomb at Ain Samiya (in the hill country north of

Jerusalem) with crude relief and incised scenes, the iconography of which derives somewhat remotely from Mesopotamian mythology. Some bone beads from Beth Shean, and a range of copper (occasionally bronze) weapons often deposited in the tombs of this period are exhibited from various sites.

A range of pottery and other artefacts from the **Middle and Late Bronze Ages** (second millennium BC), the period of the Canaanites, includes votive offerings from a seaside temple at Nahariyya on the extreme north coast. Some of the finer pottery of this period is imported from Cyprus, and notable finds from Tell Nagila include a Black-on-Red Ware Cypriot jug probably imported during the 17C–16C BC. Of slightly later date is a fine Cypriote Base Ring Ware pottery model of a bull. Both indicate an increase in mercantile contacts between Canaan and the adjoining countries.

A small mezzanine gallery has an exhibition of artefacts from Hazor, Megiddo, Beth Shean, Lachish and Tel Mevorakh illustrating Canaanite cult and religion. Evidence of Egyptian influence is strong.

At the north end of the galleries is a more monumental display of *Iron Age architecture; this includes the restored 8C–6C window balustrade from Ramat Rahel, sculpture from the gates at Hazor, and a proto-Aeolic capital from Jerusalem.

The next gallery contains a display of objects from later periods, in particular an exhibition of alphabets and inscriptions, and sculpture of various periods. Noteworthy is a **bronze head of Hadrian**, part of a life-size statue found at Tel Shalem near Beth Shean. From this gallery you may either return to the entrance through a gallery with a fine exhibition of glass, Islamic lamps and a hoard of early Islamic jewellery, or continue to the Children's Museum.

The **Children's Museum** in the Youth Wing has lively and much-used displays relating to the past, using a variety of subjects and means to convey ideas. There are also workrooms and a playground. The visitor may leave at a point midway down the main central path, and either return up the hill towards the Bezalel Art Museum and the Billy Rose Art Garden, or continue down towards the entrance and turn left for the Shrine of the Book.

The **Bezalel National Art Museum** has a permanent exhibition of works by Israeli artists as well as works by Cézanne, Chagall, Gauguin, Picasso and van Gogh; there are also period rooms of Old Masters from France, Italy and Britain. A large gallery of Jewish Art includes a collection of Jewish liturgical objects mainly from countries outside Israel, including the ark of the synagogue of Old Cairo. There is also a gallery of pre-Columbian art and temporary exhibitions.

In the **Billy Rose Art Garden**, sculptures donated by Billy Rose are displayed in a terraced garden exhibition designed by Isamu Noguchi. Included are works by Lipschitz, Maillol, Henry Moore, Picasso, Rodin, David Smith, Tinguely and others.

The **Library**, opened in 1968, contains c 50,000 books (open Sun, Mon, Wed, Thur 10.00–17.00, Tues 16.00–20.00).

The Shrine of the Book The Shrine of the Book is mainly dedicated to the famous manuscripts called the **Dead Sea Scrolls (see Qumran, p 453). Located in the lower north part of the complex, to the right of the entrance, it is easily recognised by the gleaming white tiled roof designed (by the building's architects, F. Kiesler and A. Bartos) to resemble the lid of a jar of the type associated with the storage of the scrolls.

The Dead Sea Scrolls

The scrolls were discovered between 1947 and 1956 in caves near the shore of the Dead Sea, preserved in the extremely dry conditions. They were owned by a community of Essenes, a Jewish sect, living at and around the site of Qumran, which was destroyed c AD 69 by the Romans during the suppression of the First Jewish Revolt. The manuscripts include complete (Isaiah) or very fragmentary pieces of all the books of the Old Testament on prepared skins, written mainly in Hebrew and Aramaic between c 225 BC and c AD 69, and are important for comparison with the books of the Old Testament, being copied at the time when the Old Testament was receiving its final written form. Altogether, fragments of nearly 500 manuscripts were discovered, and in addition to the books of the Old Testament, the finds included commentaries, and apocryphal (i.e. not part of the accepted biblical canon) and sectarian works, among which is an order of battle for an apocalyptic war between the Children of Light and the Children of Darkness. They are important for the light they shed on sectarian Jewish beliefs in the time of Christ.

The period of the Second Jewish Revolt (AD 132–35) is also well represented in the Shrine of the Book. Led by Bar Kochba, a second attempt at Jewish revival and independence from Rome was suppressed by the Roman army by 135. A group of refugees hid in a cave in the Nahal Hever above the west shores of the Dead Sea, taking their most important possessions and documents with them, including deeds of land ownership and marriage contracts, but their place of refuge became their tomb. The state of preservation of the organic remains, including textiles, makes a poignant and superb display of contemporary life.

Descending through the forecourt, the entrance to the Shrine of the Book leads to a corridor in which the display cases contain documents, and fragments of manuscripts from the Psalms, the Temple Scroll and apocalyptic works, as well as scroll jars. The principal display area, in a circular gallery under the 'jar lid' is on two levels. On the upper level, in the round central case, is a copy of the great Isaiah scroll. The wall cases, from the left of the entrance, contain parts of the Habbakuk Commentary, apocryphal works and psalms, letters of the time of Bar Kochba, the Habbakuk Commentary, *tefillin* (phylacteries containing set texts from Scripture) from Qumran, parts of the manuscripts of the War of the Children of Light against the Children of Darkness, and the Qumran Manual of Discipline (some manuscripts are copies of the originals). Stairs descend to a lower level, where objects from the cave in the Nahal Hever (Wadi Murabba'at) of the time of Bar Kochba are displayed. Notable for their fine state of preservation, baskets, metalwork, tools with wooden handles, cosmetics, textiles, door keys, jugs and a magnificent glass dish are on display, all deposited in the cave c 135.

The Monastery of the Holy Cross is approximately 400m east of the Israel Museum, on the west side of Sederot Hayyim Hazaz. Entered from a footpath reached from the southeast or northeast corner of the enclosing park, the picturesque monastery is where, according to tradition, the tree grew from which the cross of the Crucifixion was made. Just under 2km from the City Walls it is a

Tower of the Monastery of the Cross

medieval building strong enough to protect the monks from brigandage. Open 10.00–18.00 in summer, 09.00–16.00 in winter.

Built by the Lazes, a kindred people of the Georgians (in modern south Russia) under the encouragement of Peter the Iberian (Georgian, not Spanish) in the mid-5C, the present building was constructed on the site in the 11C by the Georgians under King Bagrat. As the Georgian fortunes declined in the 16C under the Ottomans (when they no longer occupied the favourable position enjoyed under the Mamluks), the monastery was sold to the Greeks and repaired in 1644. From 1852 it was used as a clerical seminary.

Entrance is by a tiny door in the east wall. Ring the bell. Built as an irregular rectangle, the complex contains several tree- and flower-filled courtyards, with monastery, library and church. The **church** at the centre of the monastery dates mainly from the 11C and has nave and side aisles with pointed vaulting, and a dome supported by four pillars. A section of the floor with mosaics dates to the original 5C church. The much repainted late medieval frescoes on the walls tell the story of the Tree used for the Crucifixion. Behind the high altar is a round opening which marks the site where the tree grew. There is a small treasury containing some embroidered stoles. The bell tower is 19C. The library of the seminary is incorporated with that of the library of the Greek Orthodox Patriarchate in the Old City. The **monastery** is mostly now a museum, and can be toured by going up the stairs to the first level on the west side. The scale of the equipment illustrates the once thriving monastery and seminary. An antechamber with fine limestone fountain and basins leads into the refectory. This is a long, cross-vaulted chamber, with three limestone refectory tables, with red limestone edges, wall niches and well. The kitchen opens off the refectory, a suite of paved rooms with a display of vast copper cauldrons—the largest, with four handles, would certainly need four men to lift it—and a bread oven. The upper gallery provides a view of the court below, and has a broad walkway giving access to a suite of rooms. There are marble and red limestone wall fountains, and on the east side a later two-storey addition. A wooden bar and iron hoop hang on the south side. Two great cypresses rise from the lower court. There is a pleasant walk around the parapet, with a view.

Approximately 500m east-northeast of the Monastery of the Cross is the **Tomb of Jason** (open Mon, Thur 10.00–13.00. Buses 9, 17, 22) in a small park on the north side of Alfasi St in the Rehavia suburb. This Hasmonean tomb was cut c 100 BC, about the time of the ruler Alexander Jannaeus, for one Jason, who may have been involved in the Jewish naval exploits recorded by the Greek historian Strabo. The pottery found in the tomb implies that it was in use for two or three generations, with c 25 burials of persons aged between three and fifty. It was robbed, perhaps at the time the Hasmonean dynasty was ousted by Herod the Great in 37 BC; damaged in an earthquake, probably that of 31 BC; and used for a final burial c AD 30.

The tomb has a rock-cut forecourt divided into three, the inner section being entered through a built round-arched portal, with a vestibule on the north side. The tomb itself is restored with a single column in antis (which is unique in Jerusalem at this period). The Doric capital has a straight profile, an early feature. The tomb is topped by a pyramid (restored on the evidence of a few fragments found in the excavations). The plastered walls of the vestibule are decorated with drawings, graffiti and inscriptions. The drawings, in charcoal, show three ships: on the right is a swift warship with ram, 14/15 oars and a rudder, pursuing a fishing vessel, and on the left is a smaller warship. On the north wall is a stag, on the west wall a palm branch; and scratched on the east wall are a chalice and a seven-branched menorah, which are probably later than the charcoal drawings. Aramaic and Greek inscriptions are placed near the ships, of which the principal is a funeral lament in Aramaic: 'A powerful lament make for Jason, son of P ... Peace. Who hast built thyself a tomb ...'

The burial chamber to the left has eight rather irregular kokhim in the walls with stones to close them, and two others, partly cut and partly built, in the floor; opposite is a roughly and irregularly cut ossuary chamber, also with ship drawings in charcoal.

Approximately 400m to the south, at 2 Hapalmah and the corner of Hanasi St, is the ***Mayer Institute for Islamic Art**. Named after Professor L.A. Mayer, the noted orientalist and archaeologist, its museum has a fine and varied collection of Islamic art, which fills a gap in the displays at the Israel Museum. Open Sun–Mon, Wed–Thur 10.00–17.00, Tues 16.00–20.00, Fri–Sat and eve of hols 10.00–14.00. Admission charged. Bus 15.

The terrace has a 13C basalt lintel from the diwan in the City Wall of Tiberias, carved in relief with two confronted animals of uncertain species attacked by lions. Inside, there are displays on three floors, with a library and archive on the top floor.

The **basement** contains books, paintings, tiles, printing, clocks, puppets and the Salomon Collection of Turkish shadow figures.

Main ground floor: room 1 (left) contains Sassanian and Early Islamic Art, including some beautiful pottery and metalwork; chessmen and ivories; textiles from 7C–10C Egypt and from 10C Yemen; and Kufic inscriptions from 11C Iran. Also displayed are three sculptures from Khirbat al-Mafjar, the 8C Umayyad palace at Jericho (cf. Rockefeller Museum). **Room 2** contains exhibits of the high period of Islamic art. To the right is the **Treasury room 3** which contains glass vessels from the 7C onwards, some goldwork and textiles, including objects from Iran and India dating to the 19C and earlier.

First floor: room 1 (left) contains Late Iranian art, including calligraphy, textiles, tiles, metal, leatherwork, some very fine illuminated manuscripts; textiles decorated with wax colours; armour; and blue-and-white lustreware. In the centre, **room 2** contains Ottoman art with coins, illuminated manuscripts, textiles, leather, mostly of the 18C–19C; some fine tiles and bowls, guns, armour and astronomical survey instruments. **Room 3** (right) has Moghul art: fine Moghul jade inlaid with gold and rubies used for dagger handles, cups and other objects. The exhibition also includes silk and textiles from 17C Turkey; inlaid jewelled and enamelled work; laquer-decorated papier mâché work; a large brass astrolabe; horse harness, elaborately inlaid with turquoise and coral; fine armour; inlaid wood; a fine teak window from India; a shawl from Kashmir; brasswork; 17C–19C Indian miniatures; and 19C embroidered cloth from India.

Approximately 250m to the east along Chopin St is the Jerusalem Theatre. The **Museum of Natural History** is on Rehov Mohilever. The exhibition is devoted to local wildlife, mammals, birds, dinosaur models. Open Sun–Thur 08.30–13.30; Mon and Wed 15.00–18.00; Sat 10.00–14.00; closed Fri and eve of hols. Admission charged. Buses 4, 14,18.

Emeq Refaim was the quarter established as the German or 'Templers' colony in the Valley of Refaim, founded by south German Protestant Christians from Württemberg in 1871. A religious community of 'the Temple' or 'Friends of Jerusalem', founded in 1860 to establish the ideal Christian community in the Holy Land, their first colony was established at Haifa in 1868 (see p 290), and the second shortly after in Jaffa. The community was evacuated in the Second World War.

South of the junction of the Emeq Refaim and the Bethlehem Road, is the Jerusalem railway station. The line to Jaffa (Tel Aviv) was opened in 1892. In 1999 the line was closed as it needs major repair.

North of the station is the Khan Theatre. Formerly an Ottoman khan or inn for travellers staying outside the town, or arriving after the city gates were locked for the night, it is now used as an entertainment centre (buses 4, 8, 14, 18, 21).

North of the Khan Theatre at the main intersection of roads to north, east and south and on the crest of the watershed, is St. Andrew's Church of Scotland and Scottish Hospice, built in 1927 to the design of Clifford Holliday. It reflects his interest in Armenian monastic architecture.

Below the church on the east side, was the old road to Hebron and Bethlehem, still in use in Mandate times; now there is a busy road with new development. In the rock scarp below the steps up to the church are some **Iron Age rock-cut tombs** dating to the 8C–6C BC. The tombs were robbed anciently. The chambers have rock-cut benches on two or three sides at waist height or higher. The benches are flat, well-dressed and have carved headrests showing the position in which the bodies were laid, some singly, others up to four in a row, and sometimes alternately head to foot. Below the benches deep caves were cut for use as ossuaries.

On the east side of **Bloomfield Park**, facing Mount Zion and the walls of the Old City, are the **Montefiore Windmill and Houses** (buses 4, 7, 8, 14, 15, 38). Among the earliest structures to be built outside the city, they were founded by Sir Moses Montefiore who attempted to relieve the poverty of poor immigrant Jews in the 19C. The land was purchased in 1855, and the houses, called Mishkenot Sha'ananim, were built in 1860, designed by the British architect William Edmund Smith as two long rows of attached housing with entrance porches. The houses were damaged in the war of 1948, and remained in the front line until 1967 after which they were reconstructed (1973) by the Jerusalem Foundation as a music centre and guest house for visiting artists, musicians and scholars. The windmill itself is now a museum and memorial to Sir Moses Montefiore. To the north of the windmill is the Yemin Moshe Quarter, established in 1891 with 130 houses which were rehabilitated in 1969.

In the north end of the Bloomfield Park, east of the *King David Hotel*, is the **Tomb of Herod's Family**. From the outside this is a much destroyed and rather insignificant-looking monument, though the interior is worth a visit and the site is interesting for its associations. Herod the Great was buried at his fortress at Herodion to the south of Jerusalem, but members of his family may have been buried here. The attribution is circumstantial, depending partly on references in Josephus to the location of Herod's Monuments and Herod's Tomb in this area (War V:108; War V:507; partly to the traces of its former grandeur; and partly to its position on the east side of the Hinnom Valley directly opposite to and visible from the palace built by Herod the Great, 400m to the east.

> ### Family deaths
> Josephus records the deaths of many members of Herod's family: War I:228 records that when Antipater was poisoned by Malichus, Herod 'performed the funeral rites for his father with magnificent ceremonial'; War I:581, on Herod's brother Pheroras, says 'Herod had loved him till his dying day, but for all that it was rumoured that he had poisoned him' ... 'and honoured him with a most magnificent funeral' in Jerusalem. Other possibilities include Herod's wife Mariamne I whom he executed; and his brother Phasael who died at the hands of Antigonus in Jerusalem during Herod's flight.

The date of the tomb is uncertain: it could be of the second half of the 1C BC (Herod's father Antipater died c 43 BC) but some features seem later and it might have been intended for the later Herods. It was robbed in antiquity, and entered again by a breach in the south entrance in 1891.

On the northwest side of the forecourt are traces of a massive podium constructed of high quality masonry set 2m deep into the rock, which may be the base of a nefesh (memorial monument), perhaps with a pyramid similar to that of the Tomb of Absalom (see p 239). The entrance corridor to the tomb leads down fairly steeply from the southwest corner of the forecourt and was blocked by an enormous round blocking stone. This gives access to an antechamber, and on the south side to another corridor with blocking slabs which leads to a small rectangular chamber with asymmetrically placed doors in each wall. This chamber is built with four massive masonry piers, and vaulted. An unusual feature of the tomb is the ceiling of hard limestone which has been left rough. The internal walls of the tomb chambers were then constructed of finely cut, flat-dressed and polished white masonry.

The complex consists of four main chambers. Another long chamber to the south gives access to a thin chamber with another entrance to the south. The north entrance was for mourners, that on the south for the dead. When entered in 1891 the tomb contained only two sarcophagi and some ossuaries, the former in the long south chamber. They are well carved in fine stone, one with a modest moulded panel, the other with an acanthus vase, vine scroll and rosettes. These are in the Museum of the Greek Orthodox Patriarchate (see p 187), and the site itself is owned by the Greek Orthodox church.

Returning to King David St, and continuing north, on the left at a short distance is the *YMCA*, now a hotel. Built in 1933, the tall tower with cupola is one of the Jerusalem landmarks. The tower is open Mon–Fri 09.00–15.00, Sat 09.00–13.00; closed Sun. Admission charged. Buses 15, 18, 21.

Opposite, the *King David Hotel*, another Jerusalem landmark, was built in 1930. It was damaged and 90 people killed in a Jewish terrorist attack on 22 July 1946.

A short distance to the north, on the right is the Hebrew Union College with the Nelson Glueck School of Biblical Archaeology; it contains the Skirball Museum with a small archaeological exhibition, including finds from the recent excavations at Tel Dan (see p 417). At the top of King David St, on the left at 32 Agron St, is the Taxation Museum, which illustrates the history of the taxation of the Jews in Palestine and in the Diaspora. Open Sun, Tues, Thur 13.00–16.00, Mon, Wed, Fri 10.00–14.00. Free admission. Buses 15, 19, 22.

The area north of the Jaffa Road

The north section of the new city, north of the Jaffa Road, contains some places of interest for the history of Jerusalem in the late 19C and early 20C. It also houses many of the most Orthodox Jews, and cars should avoid the area around Mea Shearim on the Sabbath.

At the east end of the Jaffa Road, on the north side, is the Town Hall. At 250m on the left is the Central Post Office (architect, A. Harrison, 1938). The area opposite is part of the old **Russian Compound**, which was established in the 19C for the care of the pilgrims from Christian Imperial Russia, and today contains the Russian Cathedral, the Municipality Information Office, the Police District Headquarters, the Law Courts—and an ancient column.

History of the Russian Compound

In the early 19C when the numbers of Russian pilgrims coming to Jerusalem each Easter were relatively small, they were accommodated in the Greek Orthodox hospices and monasteries of the Old City. By the mid-19C the numbers were increasing, and the Grand Duke Constantine Nicholaevitch visited Jerusalem in 1859 to assess the situation. With a grant from the Imperial Treasury, and private donations, 4 hectares of land were bought on the north side of the Jaffa Road, just outside the city walls, and building commenced. In 1864 Trinity Cathedral was consecrated, and hostels for monks, priests and 800 lay pilgrims, men and women, were provided. A hospital and consulate were also located inside the walled compound. Within 20 years 2000 pilgrims were coming annually to visit the holy places, mostly poor peasants travelling by ship from the Black Sea to Jaffa.

In 1881 further action was taken by the Imperial family, and Grand Duke Sergei Alexandrovitch founded the Imperial Orthodox Palestine Society which built the great Sergievsky hostel in 1889. This contained a refectory and bath house, with drainage, cisterns, ventilation, stoves and heating, and at the same time some much-needed repairs were carried out. By the early 20C up to 9000 pilgrims were coming every Easter (see also the Russian Chapel, p 177). The mass pilgrimages and the need for the hostel ceased at the time of the Russian

Revolution. The compound was used as police headquarters and prison during the Mandate, was purchased by the Israeli government in 1955 and continues in use as a police headquarters and Law Courts.

The Cathedral of the Holy Trinity (open Mon–Fri 09.00–13.00; closed Sat and Sun) lies at the centre of the compound. Its cluster of domes evokes the Russian church at Gethsemane, but they lack the charm and elegance of the latter. In a fenced area of an old quarry in front of the Police building, is a great monolithic column which was found during building work in 1871. Measuring 12.15m, with mean diameter c 1.75m (but greater at base than head), it still lies in the quarry bed, abandoned because it cracked near one end. Its size suggests it was intended for the Royal Portico of the temple of Herod the Great (1C BC). The Police District Headquarters and the Law Courts are in the former men's hospices northwest and southwest of the cathedral. A museum to the east, commemorating Jewish terrorists, is in the building which in Mandate times acted as the central prison and in the 19C was the Women's Hospice.

North of the Police Headquarters, on the opposite side of the road at 13 Queen Helena St is the **Agricultural Museum**, on the site of the Russian Palestine Society Hospice. There is an open-air display of ancient farm tools, including a fine series of olive presses brought from various sites in the Palestinian hills. Open Sun–Fri 08.00–13.00 in summer, Sun–Thur 08.00–14.00, Fri 08.00–13.00 in winter. Buses 6, 8.

Turning left up Monbaz St, left into Prophet St, and right into Ethiopian St, brings you to the domed Ethiopian Church and monastery built 1896–1904. This is located at the south edge of the **Mea Shearim Quarter**, a quarter for strictly Orthodox Jews, built in 1874 and of local architectural interest. The name means '100 gates' and is also a play on the words of Gen. 26:12 'Isaac sowed seed in that land, and that year he reaped a hundredfold ...'. Like the Montefiore houses (see above) the Mea Shearim houses were constructed as row houses, but enclosing common courts, with the outer walls forming a continuous protective façade. The main court leads to semi-private courts which in turn lead to the houses. The courts contained communal kitchen and toilet facilities. The thick masonry, with decorative features (especially to the doorways), the outside stairs, and the European red tile roofs all bear some resemblance to the ghettoes of Europe.

At the time, this formed the largest private building project in Jerusalem. It is now a centre for religious items, books, and scribal work, with many synagogues and Torah schools. The costume of the medieval ghettoes of Europe is retained, with black garments and round fur-bordered hats.

A Muslim shrine of Ayyubid origins is located in Strauss St, 50m southwest of the Mitchell Cinema. This is the **Qubba Qaymariyya**, a walled sanctuary or shrine with a dome, built before 1251 in rather sober style but with good proportions. This Muslim burial chamber was built to house the tombs of five princes of the al-Qaymari family of Damascus, who were martyred between 1250 and 1267, according to Mujir al-Din. Later tombs were added to the shrine, as were the dwelling house and tomb of Shaikh Ukasha, and a minaret. Other rooms were added perhaps to shelter pious visitors, and the enclosure wall was fitted with tethering holes for horses. The monument was still maintained in the first quarter of the 20C, with the five tombs parallel to each other, each with a headstone and green coverings.

The tomb is a cube with dome, with a projection in the centre of each wall containing a narrow window. The drum also has four windows, with concave moulding at the base of a rather flat dome. The entrance is on the north side. The structure is now badly damaged, but the bases of the five tombs remain.

To the south is the suburb of Romema, established in 1921. On the north side of the Jaffa Rd, a little before the junction with Sederot Herzl, the Romema (meaning 'elevation') Reservoir was installed on high ground in 1918 as part of the new Mandate system to provide Jerusalem with a good water supply. Around 1,273,000 litres of water per day were piped from Solomon's Pools south of Bethlehem to the Romema Reservoir, and then distributed by pipe to the Old and New City, and as far as Mount Scopus and Bethany. From 1934 the water was pumped from Ras al-Ain down on the edge of the coastal plain to the Romema Reservoir. The Central Bus Station is rebuilt on the north side of the Jaffa Rd. Just to the northeast at Kikkar Allenby at the end of Romema Road, is the Allenby Memorial commemorating the entry of General Allenby into Jerusalem in 1917.

The southern section of the New City

The southern section of the New City contains relatively few places of interest. The first suburbs were established here in the later part of the 19C, including the Arab quarters of Katamon, established 1875, and Abu Tor also founded in the 1870s. The Beit Josef Jewish suburb was established in 1888, and other Jewish suburbs such as Talpiot from 1922 onwards. Some of these were attacked during the height of Muslim-Jewish tension in 1929. Government House was built to the southeast in 1931. The buildings in the east part of this area were much damaged in the fighting in 1948, when the Arab occupants fled eastwards. From 1949 to 1967 the border between Jordan and Israel ran through the east part, with the old Government House in a demilitarised zone used as the UN Headquarters. There has been much development of new Jewish suburbs in recent years.

The British Mandate Government House was built 2km south of the Old City in 1931, as the High Commissioner's Residence; the architect was Austin Harrison who, as in his design for the Rockefeller Museum (see p 241), employed concepts drawn from local styles of architecture. The building was taken over in 1949 by the United Nations Truce Supervision Organisation, and is now UN Headquarters. In the suburb of Talpiot, 1.3km to the southwest at 16 Klausner St off the Betar Road, is the Bet Agnon. This is the house of Shmuel Yosef Agnon, winner of the Nobel Prize for Literature in 1966, where his study, books and pictures are preserved. Open Sun–Thur 09.00–12.00. Buses 7, 44.

The Betar Rd continues south 0.9km to **Ramat Rahel** (the Hill of Rachel), site of a modern kibbutz (a Jewish collective settlement) occupying a high and strategic position (818m above sea level), with a view of Jerusalem and Bethlehem. It contains a recreation centre and swimming pool, and is the site of an ancient Judaean palace. Bus 7.

History of Ramat Rahel

Excavations showed that the site was first settled in the 9C–8C BC when a royal citadel within a casemate wall was built and surrounded by gardens and farmhouses. It has been identified with the biblical Beth-hakkerem. This first settlement was followed by a larger one, with a massive enclosure c 186 x 165m containing a palace c 75 x 50m. Fragments of at least six proto-Aeolic capitals were found on the site, and a stone window balustrade (now in the Israel Museum). The palace may have been built for King Jehoiakim at the end of the 7C BC, and destroyed not long after in the Babylonian destruction of 586 BC. Another citadel on the site existed in the 4C BC and a poorer domestic settlement in Herodian times. Burial caves of the 1C and 3C AD were found in the vicinity. A villa and a bath house built by the Tenth Roman Legion c 250 were also found on the northwest and central parts of the site, which were reused in the Byzantine period. Also of the Byzantine period, built c 450, were the Church of Kathisma and a monastery. The basilica church with patterned mosaic floor lies at the northeast of the site. The name of the church is preserved in the name of the well of Bir Qadismu, c 400m to the west. According to a Christian tradition, Mary rested here on her way to Bethlehem. There was a poorer settlement in the early Arab period (7C–8C), after which the site was abandoned.

The kibbutz at Ramat Rahel was founded by the Jewish 'Labour Legion' in 1926. It was attacked in 1929 and largely destroyed. Rebuilding by Russian Jewish immigrants began in 1930, and more immigrants from Germany and East Europe came in 1934. Attacked again in 1936–39 and destroyed in 1948, it was then just on the Israeli side of the border. Rebuilding began in 1949. It came under fire in 1956 when four archaeologists working on the site were killed, and being on the border was damaged again in 1967.

The ruins are preserved in the grounds of the kibbutz, a Jewish settlement within the municipal borders of Jerusalem producing fruit, vegetables and meat, and offering guest house, hostel, camping and other facilities.

The suburb of Gonen, formerly Katamon (Greek meaning 'near the monastery'), is 2.2km to the northwest. A Christian and Muslim Arab quarter founded in 1875, it was abandoned when captured by Israel in the 1948 war. The area of **St. Simeon** is at its heart. A Greek Orthodox church and monastery marks the supposed site of the tomb of the upright and devout Simeon of Jerusalem who recognised the child Jesus as the Messiah when Mary and Joseph came to present him in the Temple and make the customary offering. Simeon had been told by the Holy Spirit that he would not die until he had seen the Lord's Messiah. 'Lord, now lettest thou thy servant depart in peace, according to thy word. For mine eyes have seen thy salvation, which thou has prepared before the face of all people; to be a light to lighten the Gentiles and to be the glory of thy people Israel' (*Nunc dimittis*, Luke 2:29–32).

The site of the Tomb of Simeon was located in the 4C, but it was principally in the 14C that tradition located the house of Simeon here. The ruins were bought by the Greek Orthodox Patriarchate in 1859, and the Patriarch built his summer residence here in 1870, 2.5km from the walls of the Old City. The ruins of Simeon's house were incorporated in the present church in 1881. In the northeast part of the interior a rock-cut tomb with rebates for a covering slab is venerated as the Tomb of Simeon. Bus 22, 24.

At the south end of the suburb of Bayit WeGan, 1.6km to the southwest, is the *Holy Land Hotel*, in the grounds of which is a large **model of ancient**

Jerusalem in the time of Herod the Great. It is updated as excavations reveal new insights into the ancient history and topography of Jerusalem, and the model is well worth a visit if you wish to visualise the ancient city and the temple of Herod the Great. Open 08.00–22.00. Admission charged. Bus 21.

Other places of interest on the outskirts of the city

Mount Herzl

Approximately 5km west of the Old City off Sederot Herzl (buses 12, 17, 18, 20, 23, 27) is Mount Herzl. At the east end of the hill is the **Tomb of Theodore Herzl** (1860–1904), founder of the modern state of Israel. In 1897 in Basel, Switzerland, he summoned the first Zionist Congress, which established the political ideal to found a national home for the Jews in Palestine. His remains were brought here in 1949. A museum contains documents relating to his life and work. Open April–Oct 09.00–18.30, Nov–March 09.00–16.00; Fri 09.00–13.00; closed Sat. The Military Cemetery to the north is open daily until sunset.

At 600m to the west (access on south side of Mt Herzl) is **Yad VaShem**, the Holocaust Memorial. If arriving on foot, walk along the upper road, and descend by the steps in front of the entrance to the car park. Open Sun–Thur 09.00–16.45; Fri 09.00–13.00; closed Sat. ☎ 02 675 1611. Full guidance, refreshments and souvenirs are available at the complex.

The main Israeli memorial to the six million Jews who died under the Nazi regime in Europe was established in 1953. The complex built since 1957 contains a darkened Hall of Remembrance with a mosaic floor bearing the names of 21 concentration camps, and a flame of remembrance. Behind is the Museum of History, with exhibition and archival photographs of the history of the Jews in Europe from 1917, with the events leading to and detailed illustration of the Nazi holocaust. Further west is a Holocaust Art Museum containing modern works. In 1993 the Valley of the Communities, which commemorates destroyed European Jewish communities, was completed on a saddle to the southwest. Massive quarried blocks of local stone were used to create piers in a symbolic labyrinth. Many sculptures are also placed in the gardens on the hill top, and near the exit is the Memorial to the Children, with a symbolic descent into darkness. Yad VaShem is usually crowded, and still expanding.

To the west is the extensive Jerusalem Forest.

Ain Karim

The Ain Karim road descends southwest from Kikkar Holland for c 2km to the village of Ain Karim (bus 17). This was once an attractive traditional Palestinian village set amid terraces with vines, the latter now neglected, and increasingly hemmed in by suburban expansion. Christian tradition (but not a more positive identification) regards the village as the birthplace of St. John the Baptist, the home of his parents Zechariah and Elizabeth, and the site of the meeting between the Virgin Mary and Elizabeth (Luke 1:5–25, 39–66). The village contains a number of churches commemorating these events. Like Ramat Rahel (see above) it is identified with the biblical site of Beth-hakkerem (Jer. 6:1), but this is doubtful. There is a modern Jewish suburb (founded in 1923) nearly 3km to the northeast also called Bet HaKerem after the biblical site.

History

Pottery of the late third millennium was discovered in the vicinity of Ain Karim. There was occupation here in the Middle Bronze Age and the Iron Age, and numerous remains of the Herodian, Roman, Byzantine and early Arab periods indicate almost continuous settlement. Pagan objects give hints of a shrine or temple in Roman times before the development of the Byzantine traditions. There are references to a church here in the 6C–8C and 10C. From the time of the Russian Abbot Daniel (1106–07) there were references to two churches at Ain Karim, but both existed earlier. In 1166 King Anselm confirmed Ain Karim as the property of the Augustin Canons of the Templum Domini in Jerusalem. The place was abandoned in 1187, though the churches survived. A Muslim shrine was built in 1242 by Abu Yusuf, 200m west-northwest of the Church of St. John. In 1336 Jacobus di Verona found Armenian monks at the Church of the Visitation, and Muslims at St. John's, but by 1480 Muslims occupied both sites. The Franciscans eventually re-established themselves at St. John's (see below), and in 1681 they persuaded four Christian families from Bethlehem to settle at the village.

The Sisters of Our Lady of Sion arrived in 1860 and built their convent between 1862 and 1890 at the west end of the village. In 1871 the Russian Orthodox came and converted the south ridge above the village into a community for nuns with a church. Ten years later Ain Karim was a flourishing village with about 600 inhabitants, of whom 100 were Latin Christians and the rest Muslim.

In 1894 the Orthodox community also built a church dedicated to St. John the Baptist, and at the turn of the last century Ain Karim's population of around 2000 included 200 Orthodox Russians and Greeks; there were 300 Latin Christians and the rest of the population was Muslim. In 1911 the Sisters of the Rosary opened a house near the Church of the Visitation. On 7 July 1948 Israeli forces captured the town from the Egyptian army who had been holding it for the Arabs, and the town was abandoned. There is now a Jewish artists' colony in the village, with commercial development, attracted by the setting.

Near the centre of the village is the Franciscan **Church of St. John the Baptist**, the reputed home of St. Elizabeth and St. Zechariah, and birthplace of St. John the Baptist. Open Mon–Fri 08.00–12.00, 14.30–18.00, Sun 09.00–12.00, 14.30–17.00 (closes 1 hour earlier in winter); closed Sat.

History of the Church of St. John the Baptist

Fragments of a marble statue of Venus dating to the Roman period discovered in the foundations of the church suggest there may have been an earlier shrine of Venus near this site perhaps in Hadrianic times. A 5C–6C church underlies the present building, which was rebuilt in the 11C. The Augustin Canons were granted it before 1166 and the present building is mainly 11C–12C. It was abandoned by the Latins in 1187, and the Muslims were occupying it by the 14C. The Franciscans managed to secure access by 1485, and got possession and repaired it in 1621. By 1638 there was renewed pilgrimage to it, but by 1672 the wall behind the high altar had collapsed. In 1674 the Franciscans finally managed to return and repair the church. The monastery around the church was also rebuilt on Byzantine and Crusader foundations in 1694–97. In 1895 a new bell-tower was built on the site of the previous one of 1857 which itself had an earlier predecessor.

The west façade, mostly hidden behind a 19C porch, preserves the north Byzantine doorway. The main doorway was rebuilt in 1885. Inside is a nave with side aisles divided by piers which support groin vaulting and galleries above. Except for the dome and east end (17C), most of the structure is 11C–12C. The high altar is dedicated to St. John; the altar on the right is dedicated to St. Elizabeth, his mother.

Steps descend from the north aisle to the rock-cut Grotto of St. John, traditionally his birthplace, where the decoration post-dates 1673 and includes reliefs with scenes from his life. The altar was made in Livorno and donated by Isabella of Spain. The floor is of multi-coloured *opus sectile* of the 11C–12C; parts of a similar floor survive in the nave of the church.

17C and 19C building operations as well as archaeological work in the 1940s revealed fragments of the earlier structure, including two 6C chapels southwest of the church. Some of the surrounding convent buildings also have ground level rooms dating to the 11C–12C.

To the south (at c 400m) is the **Spring of the Virgin** (A. Ain Sitti Maryam) which rises in a cave. Over it is built a small mosque, mentioned as a vaulted place of prayer in 1881; it was abandoned in 1948, but is attractive despite its dereliction. From the 14C tradition held that Mary, on her visit to Elizabeth her cousin, drew water from the spring.

Continuing west along the hillside from the spring, the road leads past the buildings of the Russian Convent (1871) which include two churches. One is dedicated to St. John the Baptist.

Further west is the Franciscan **Church of the Visitatio Mariae** on another traditional site of the home (or summer residence) of St. Elizabeth (or of Zechariah), where Mary visited for about three months. Open 08.00–11.45, 14.30–18.00 (–17.00 in winter); Sat closed.

It contains Byzantine remains and a cave where a legend found in the mid-2C *Proto-Gospel of James* is commemorated. Tradition located here the place in which Elizabeth hid John from Herod during the Massacre of the Innocents. The church is not mentioned before the visit of Abbot Daniel in the 12C. It has been identified as the Cistercian Abbey of St. John in the Woods, mentioned in 1169. A church on two levels is cut into the hillside. The lower church contains two apses, one with a well, and a niche containing the 'Rock of Concealment' which split to conceal the infant John. In the upper church, which served the monastery, the lower part of the 12C apse survives. Abandoned in 1187, by the 14C it was served by the Armenians. By the end of the 14C it was associated with the Visitation, and pilgrims sang the *Magnificat* and the *Benedictus*. The site was purchased in 1679 by the Franciscans who rebuilt it in 1861.

The present church was built from 1938 to the design of architect A. Barluzzi and consecrated in 1946. It has a mosaic on the façade depicting Mary's arrival at the home of Elizabeth. The interior has frescoes and mosaics, with lines from the *Magnificat* on the pilasters ('My soul doth magnify the Lord, and my spirit hath rejoiced in God my Saviour. For he hath regarded the lowliness of his handmaiden...' Luke 1:46–55). The lower church is decorated in similar fashion.

Approximately 3km to the west of Ain Karim at Even Sapir is the small Franciscan Monastery of St. John in the Wilderness or First Desert of St. John. A spring, a grotto and a chapel mark the supposed site of John the Baptist's sojourn and preparation in the wilderness (Luke 1:80). The church and monastery were built in 1922 on a pilgrimage site first mentioned in the late 15C. Open 08.00–12.00, 14.00–17.00.

Southwest of Ain Karim (1.2km)—nearly 8km southwest of the Old City—lies the **Hadassah Hospital** and the Hadassah Hebrew University Medical Centre at Ein Kerem. This modern teaching hospital was built with funding from the Hadassah Women's Zionist Organization and opened in 1963. The modern synagogue here contains magnificent *windows by **Marc Chagall**. These depict the 12 eponymous brothers of the 12 tribes of Israel, with symbolic objects and animals, and particularly colours. Tours of site and synagogue at Tannenbaum Tourist Centre, audio-visual presentation, Sun–Thur each hour 08.30–12.30; Fri 09.30–11.30. Synagogue also open 14.00–16.00. Admission charged. Buses 19, 27.

*Tisch Family Zoological Gardens in Jerusalem** (the **Biblical Zoo**) are at Manhat in the Valley of Refaim on the southern edge of Jerusalem. The site overlooks a stretch of the now closed Ottoman railway line, and a deserted station built specially for the zoo. Open Sun–Thur 09.00–19.30; Fri and eve of hols 09.00–16.30, Sat and hols 10.00–18.00, shorter hours in winter. ☎ 02 675 0111. Admission charged. Buses 26, 33, 99.

The zoo has a beautifully laid out garden with many local plants, landscaped on a south-facing limestone slope over 25 hectares, and adapted to the pre-existing agricultural terraces. It has excellent displays and information on local and imported birds and animals. Species mentioned in the Bible, even locally extinct species, such as bears, lions, leopards, cheetahs and ostrich, are a special feature; the bird houses are particularly good. The zoo also contains one of the most important archaeological sites of the late third and early second millennia within its grounds, discovered only when the site was surveyed prior to the building of the zoo. It is hard to find the notice describing these remains, which are preserved in fenced enclosures mainly in the lower central zone of the zoo. Stone-built houses of a farming community living c 2000 BC stretch over a large area of the hillside, proving that sedentary inhabitants of the central hills existed at that time—something previously doubted. They are probably the only structural remains of this period to be seen in Israel, with walls made of large local boulders. There was also an extensive village of the Middle Bronze Age whose inhabitants, as well as farming, mined the local sand to make pottery. The people appear to have buried their dead mainly in shaft graves on the hillside above the settlement. The remains of an Iron Age farm and olive press are also preserved across the road to the east of the car park. The hillsides around still preserve much of the vegetation native to the terra rossa soils, with many wild flowers in spring.

13 • The Hinnom Valley and the Bethlehem Road

The Hinnom Valley

The Hinnom Valley (Valley of the Sons of Hinnom, A. Wadi al-Rababi) begins in the vicinity of the Mamilla Pool (see p 253) and descends steeply from a height of c 770m above sea level at the northeast end of the Old City, to c 600m where it joins the Kidron Valley. The steep-sided valley formed the defensive west and south boundary of the city in Herodian and Byzantine times.

History

From the period of the Judges the valley marked the boundary between the territory of Benjamin and that of Judah (Jos. 15:8; 18:16). The Old Testament has frequent references to the cults of non-Israelite gods during the period of the Kings, worshipped here by some of the inhabitants of Jerusalem: Baal, and Molech to whom cremation offerings of children were made at Topheth, at the bottom of the Hinnom (II Kings 23:10; Jer. 32:35). According to Jeremiah, it was to be the 'Valley of Slaughter' on the 'Day of Vengeance' (Jer. 7:32). In this tradition lies the origin of the Jewish Gehenna, the hell of fire (gehenna being the Greek and Latin form of Hinnom Valley), symbolism which developed in Roman times under Persian influence. The south section of the valley was used for burial in Iron Age, Roman and Byzantine times, and the tradition developed of the Potter's Field, bought as a foreigner's burial ground by the chief priests with the 30 silver coins for which Judas betrayed Jesus (Matt. 27:3–10). Alternatively it is associated with the Aceldama or 'Field of Blood', which Judas bought with the silver after the betrayal (Acts 1:18–19), and where he fell and burst open (though probably 'Field of Sleeping' is a more correct rendering of the Aramaic). Many incidents seem to be confused in the background to these traditions. The south part of the valley certainly became a place to bury strangers (Matt.27:7). It was given to the Knights of the Hospital of St. John in 1143 for the burial of those who died while on pilgrimage, and some time after 1187 to the Armenians. The traditional location of this field has remained constant for centuries at the southeast end of the valley, and it was used for burial at least until the 17C.

The road descends south from the Jaffa Gate into the Hinnom Valley, with the walls of Sulaiman above to the left, and the totally redeveloped area which formed the border from 1948 to 1967 down on the right. A few Ottoman buildings still survive. The road crosses a strong masonry dam above which is **Sultan's Pool** (A. Birkat al-Sultan). It was c 178m x 80m, up to 12m deep and the solid dam wall over 18m high. Its original date is uncertain. It may have been an early rain-fed pool in the valley, or more probably part of the Herodian low-level aqueduct system from Solomon's Pools which ended at the Temple. It was the 'Germain's Pool' of Crusader days, named after a benevolent inhabitant of Mount Zion. The pool was probably restored by al-Nasir Muhammad late in the 13C when he restored the aqueduct, and again in 1399 and, probably, in the late 15C when more work is mentioned by Felix Faber. Yet again restored in the 16C by Sultan Sulaiman, after whom it is called today, it was already ruinous by 1723, and by the 19C only a muddy pool in the wet season remained.

Continuous work must have been required to clear the debris and silt washed down in winter. In the early 20C a cattle market was held by the pool on Fridays. It now contains the Merrill Hasenfeld Amphitheatre (1980–85), converting one of the great pools or reservoirs of Jerusalem into a modern park-like public place.

A fine Ottoman fountain on the north side of the road bridge was built by Sulaiman II in 1537, with ornately carved pointed arch, muqarnas semi-dome and inscription.

Where the valley curves east, St. Andrew's Church of Scotland stands above to the right (see p 262). The hill to the south, Abu Tor probably had a 6C church of St. Procopius at the top. It was called in Crusader times the 'Hill of Evil Counsel', as a tradition located another house of Caiaphas here, where the decision to kill Jesus was taken. The site was given to one of Salah al-Din's warriors in 1187. He was noted for riding into battle on the back of a bull, whence derives the present name of Abu Tor ('Father of the bull'). He was buried there and the tomb became a place of Muslim pilgrimage. From the **Abu Tor Observation Point** there is a fine view over the Hinnom Valley, the southeast ridge and the Old City.

A road leads further down the Hinnom Valley. Many ancient rock-cut tombs, principally of Hellenistic, Roman and Byzantine date, are located in this area. Towards the lower end of the valley, above the rock-scarp to the right, is the **Greek Convent of St. Onuphrius** which most clearly marks the site of **Aceldama**. Dedicated to a Byzantine hermit, the convent contains the 'Apostles's Cave' now used as a chapel. Like most of the caves in the vicinity, it was a Jewish rock-cut tomb of the Roman period, reused in Byzantine times. It has a frieze (1C BC/AD) above the entrance, carved with eight panels with rosettes and grapes similar to that on the Tombs of the Kings (see p 246). A 16C tradition says eight of the apostles hid here during the arrest and crucifixion of Jesus. The convent site overlooks the junction of the Hinnom with the Kidron Valley, and the gardens of Silwan (see Jerusalem, section 9). Adjacent to the convent are two burial places which the Orthodox associate with Aceldama. Above, and outside the convent to the west, is the complex associated in western tradition with Aceldama.

In 1143 the Patriarch of Jerusalem gave the church and some land at Aceldama to the Order of the Knights of the Hospital of St. John for the burial of pilgrims. A 13C map marks '*carnel(ium) Johannis ubi sepeliuntur Anglici*' (the first word comes from old French into modern English as 'charnel house'). Later the site was given to the Armenians, whose ownership is preserved in the Arabic name of the site—al-Firdaws (al-Armani), 'the (Armenian) paradise'. Descriptions exist in late 19C books of a deep chamber, partly rock-cut, partly masonry, with a massive central pillar supporting a domed masonry roof. A deep layer of bones survived into the early 20C.

Much Crusader masonry and a great pointed arch survive of what was the pilgrims' charnel house of the Knights of St. John. On the west wall are crosses and Armenian inscriptions. Further west are many more rock-cut tombs in the cliff, mostly Jewish but reused in the Byzantine period.

The Bethlehem Road

Following the Bethlehem (Hebron) Road, which runs south passing the Sultan's Pool and the railway station, continue past the turning to Talpiot. The housing at this end of the town contains many poor modern apartment blocks and some ruins. At c 6km from Jerusalem, the road passes the site of Bir al-Qadismu, a well and pool on the left of the road at which tradition placed the site where Mary rested halfway to Bethlehem. The commemoration of this event included the building of a church called the Kathisma, or Seat, by a wealthy matron of Jerusalem, named Ikelia, c 451–58, the name of which is preserved in the present Arabic place name. The Kathisma is usually identified with the Byzantine church and monastery 400m to the east at Ramat Rahel (see p 266).

Approximately 600m further up on the left, 6.5km from Jerusalem, is the Greek Orthodox Monastery of Mar Elias, a semi-fortified three-storey building with square bell tower capped by a tiny dome. The Cretan John Phocas made a pilgrimage to Jerusalem (c 1185) and notes that in 1160 the Emperor Manuel Comnenos rebuilt the monastery from its foundations on the site of the 6C monastery of St. Anastasius; its name (Mar Elias, St. Elijah) only dates from this time. A 12C tradition identified the site with the spot where the prophet Elijah paused on his flight to Beersheba after defeating the priests of Baal at Mount Carmel (I Kings 19:3).

The monastery was restored in the 14C and renovated in the 17C. On the opposite side of the road a stone seat was placed by his wife for Holman Hunt, the Pre-Raphaelite painter (1827–1910): he is particularly noted for scenes with a strong religious inspiration. At a short distance on the right is the road to Tantur, a Christian Arab village, with the Ecumenical Centre for Advanced Theological Studies founded in 1972 on the initiative of Pope Paul VI. There is a Biblical Garden, open 08.30–17.30 (winter 16.30); closed Sun. The town had an old church dedicated to St. Sergius, later incorporated in the Tantur Monastery where the Knights of Malta founded a hospital.

At nearly 8km from Jerusalem, on the right just beyond the Bethlehem check point is the **Tomb of Rachel** (A. Qubbat Rahil), an open cupola possibly of 12C date, modified in the 19C, and completely enclosed as a Jewish shrine in the late 20C. Open 08.00–18.00 in summer, 08.00–17.00 in winter; 08.00–13.00 Fri and Jewish hols; closed Sat. Bus 62 from the Central Bus Station.

History of the Tomb of Rachel

Rachel was the younger daughter of Laban of Haran (in north Syria), for whom the patriarch Jacob laboured 14 years before receiving her as his second wife; the mother of Joseph and Benjamin, she died giving birth to Benjamin between Bethel and Ephrath (Gen. 35:16–21) and was buried near Ephrath in the territory of Benjamin (I Sam. 10:2), probably somewhere in the vicinity of al-Ram (north of Jerusalem). A late gloss on Gen. 35:19 put the site of Ephrath near Bethlehem, and this was accepted by the early Christians.

Various pilgrims mention the tomb at the present site, marked by a heap of stones, and perhaps an altar, up to Crusader times.

The tomb is venerated by Christians, Muslims and Jews, but in the 19C was visited particularly by the latter. It was purchased by Sir Moses Montefiore in 1841, who added an antechamber with a mihrab for Muslims on the east side.

The small square shrine with whitewashed dome, and cenotaph of no great antiquity, was restored in 1967 and completely fortified in recent years. It is much visited by Jewish pilgrims, especially women.

Beyond, the roads to the west offer a diversion to the Christian Arab village of

Bait Jala (1km). It is identified with the Giloh of Jos. 15:51 and II Sam. 15:12. In 1873 it was described as a flourishing stone-built village, depending for water on cisterns and a well in the adjacent valley, with a population of 3000 of whom 420 were Catholic, the rest Greek Orthodox, and was served by a Greek and a Latin church.

Above Bait Jala to the west at 2km is a hill with viewpoint. The observation point is at 923m. Below it a road leads northwest for just over 1km to the Cremisan Convent (Salesian Order) which is noted for its wine production. At 1.4km to the northwest of the convent is the site of the **Fountain of Philip**, (Ain Hanniyya). The tradition which associated the spring and ruined church on this site with the baptism by the apostle Philip of the eunuch who was a high official of the Queen of Ethiopia (Acts 8:26–39) only dates to the 15C. (The Byzantine tradition linked Philip with a more likely spot on a route to Gaza, at 29km on the Jerusalem to Hebron road, at Ain al-Dhirwa.)

THE REGIONS

Flora and fauna

The region of Israel and Palestine has a rich flora and fauna considering its relatively small size. Situated between Africa and Asia and set between mountain and desert, it has a wide variety of soils—limestone, sandstone, basalt and alluvial—in which both African and Asian species are found. The natural abundance was even richer in the 19C, when scientific recording began, notably with such travellers as H.B. Tristram, whose entertaining writings are full of interest. He records a visit to En Gedi in 1872 where 'a host of strange semi-tropical plants send our botanist into an ecstasy of delight'. Agricultural developments, particularly in Israel over the last 50 years, have taken their toll of the wildlife. The drainage of swamps and lakes, such as Lake Hula (1951), and the diversion of the sources of the Jordan to agricultural projects in the south have affected the distribution of many species. Today there are strict conservation measures which go hand in hand with the creation of nature reserves and the development of old and new biblical and regional gardens that provide a focus for education and research as well as conservation.

Over 2800 plant species are listed for the region and many are now protected—you can see them at various nature reserves and in many parks and wild corners. Do not be tempted to pick wild flowers. Large reafforestation schemes are replacing long-depleted woodlands of oak, pine and pistachio. You will also see olives and date palms, which have been cultivated in the region for around six millennia. Native trees included a wide variety of oaks (*Quercus ithaburensis* and *calliprinos*, Tabor oaks), Aleppo pine, willow, poplar, tamarisk, hawthorn, sycamore, laurel, the Judas tree, the plane tree and the carob.

Extinct animals include the Asiatic lion (since the 12C); the cheetah and the Persian fallow deer (since the 19C); the Syrian bear (since 1917); and the Galilee sub-species of the Persian leopard (since 1965). Extinct species such as ostrich and oryx are being imported, raised and eventually reintroduced to appropriate locations. In the 19C crocodiles were still found in the marshes of Lake Hula, since extinct but now reintroduced at a crocodile farm on the Yarmuk river.

Lions and saints

That there used to be lions is illustrated by the number of early Christian saints in the Palestine area who are associated with them. St. Jerome's lion, so often depicted in religious art, was probably cribbed from that of St. Gerasimus, who established a group of monks at a monastery beyond Jericho near the Jordan River. Gerasimus pulled a thorn from the paw of a lion which became devoted to him. A strict man, Gerasimus told the lion that if it stayed with him at the monastery it also had to work and its duty would be to guard the ass that carried the water daily from the spring. This the lion did until one day thieves stole the ass. When the lion returned dejected to the monastery, it was suspected of having eaten the ass and was given the penance of carrying the water itself. The lion carried out this task until one day it saw the thieves coming, attacked them, and rescued the ass, bringing it back to the monastery. After Gerasimus died, the lion was inconsolable, refused to eat, lay by the grave and died.

Gerasimus and Jerome were not alone in keeping large felines. St. Sabas in the same wilderness east of Jerusalem chose a cave in which to be solitary. Unfortunately, the cave was the den of a lion. When it returned and found Sabas sleeping, it dragged the hermit from the cave. Sabas, apparently unperturbed, made friends with it. However, this lion proved a troublesome companion, and finally Sabas told it to behave or leave. It left.

In the early 1960s a leopard was shot in the area east of Jerusalem, and a desperate effort was made to preserve the last ones living in the vicinity of the En Gedi oasis in the 1980s. There are today large herds of ibex and and gazelle, as well as large numbers of hyrax. Wild boar still exist in the jungles along the Jordan. Hunting all these animals for food goes back to the dawn of time. Hunting for sport in the manner of the great kings of Egypt and Assyria seems to have been the practice of the Umayyad Caliph Walid. A poet, and a great marksman, he had a game park for hunting around his palace at Mafjar near Jericho in the 8C AD. The Mamluk rulers had a hunting preserve on Mt Tabor.

The area is famous for the number of birds migrating along the fertile strip between sea and desert in and from Africa in March and October (see Elat), and many find the fishponds established in former lake and swamp areas attractive; 380 bird species are listed. Many stories in folklore involve birds. The hoopoe, still often seen, even in Jerusalem, has a delightful story which was told to J.S. Buckingham travelling in Syria in the early 19C. 'They are called in arabic Hedhed, with the appellation of Beni-Suliman, or children of Solomon; from a prevalent opinion, that in the splendid age of this Jewish monarch, these birds were among the number brought to him, with the peacocks and monkeys from Ophir and other distant lands. It is currently believed by the people of the country that its crest was then a crown of gold; but that the avidity of mankind for this precious metal occasioning the birds to be often killed for their crowns, they assembled together and represented their case to Solomon himself. This monarch, in his great wisdom, understood the languages of all animals as well as of all people, on the face of the earth; and hearing and pitying their case, he prayed to their Creator to ameliorate their destiny, when the crown of gold was instantly changed to a crest of feathers, of equal if not of still greater beauty.' Another distinctive bird is the Tristram's grackle, which can be seen and heard around the date palms of the En Gedi oasis and especially around the rubbish bins at Masada. Shiny black, with flash of russet beneath the wings, its high whistle is a characteristic sound in the wilderness areas.

The *Israel Nature and National Parks Protection Authority* has more than 100 nature reserves, about 20 of which have been developed for public use with Visitor Centres and trails. The **Carmel Wildlife Preserve** actively promotes the re-establishment of wild sheep and goats, and fallow and roe deer, as well as Griffon vultures, Egyptian vultures and Bonelli's eagle (☎ 04 984 1750, visits must be arranged in advance). The **Hula Valley Nature Reserve** (on Highway 90, ☎ 06 6937069) comprises 325 hectares of preserved swamp which attracts many birds. The *Society for the Protection of Nature in Israel (SPNI)* organises walks and nature trails (see www.spni.org) and a number of environmental agencies exist in the Palestinian Territories. The **Biblical Zoo** in Jerusalem is excellent for local species.

The Mediterranean coast

Almost the only feature on the long, straight coastline of Israel and Palestine is the ridge of Mt Carmel projecting into the sea on the south side of Haifa bay.

The prevailing north-westerly winds driving on-shore, and currents flowing from the southwest, made this a difficult coast for sailors, and the lack of good harbours hampered marine commerce in the past. The strength of the wind and current coming up from Egypt meant that the early sailors in the eastern Mediterranean Sea probably followed a circular route, coming north along the coast, then sailing westwards to Cyprus, and from there south again to Egypt. Seafaring was easier in the summer months, and voyages were undertaken seasonally even in medieval times. The modern map shows only two commercial ports, at Ashdod and at Haifa, both developed in the 20C. Archaeological evidence however makes it likely that seafarers were navigating along the coast and crossing to Cyprus at least as early as the eighth millennium. Because the sea level was lower between the sixth and fourth millennia, some coastal settlement at this period is now beneath the sea, which means that the archaeological evidence for the oldest harbours may also be submerged. By c 2600 BC sizeable Egyptian ships were trading north along the coast to Lebanon, and in the Sixth Dynasty (c 2300 BC), a sea-backed military campaign in Palestine is recorded, when an Egyptian army was taken by sea and landed at a place called 'Nose of the Gazelle'. The name suggests a prominent landmark, doubtfully identified with Mt Carmel. Sea-borne trade between Palestine and Cyprus only began to reach commercial levels in the Middle Bronze Age, perhaps starting early in the second millennium. A number of sites along the coast have revealed that harbours and channels were dug, utilising inland lagoons and river estuaries, and the protection of islands and reefs was used to provide safe havens for shipping. Thereafter seaborne trading networks developed rapidly in the hands of the Mycenaeans after c 1400, when the principal ports appear to have been at Akko, Dor, Joppa, Ashdod, Ascalon and Gaza; later, from the 10C BC, the Phoenicians dominated the seas.

The situation changed late in the first millennium (the Hellenistic and early Roman periods), when major artificial harbours began to be constructed for the needs of larger ships and cargoes and a greater volume of trade at places like Akko, Caesarea and Gaza. Underwater excavation at Caesarea has revealed a ship dated to the Roman period, more than 40m in length and with a lead-sheathed hull, which may have originated in France or Italy. These harbours continued to be used, through the Byzantine, and Early Islamic periods and in the Crusader period, when the lifeline for defence and trade lay to the west in Europe. Other small artificial harbours were constructed to serve, provision or act as escape routes for the many Crusader fortresses built along the coast.

Inland from the southern coastline, a broad belt of sand dunes, up to 7km wide and rising to 69m above sea level, runs all the way north to Tel Aviv; further north the coastline is backed by ancient marine sandstones called kurkar ridges, which in past times contributed to the silting of river mouths, and created marshes behind them to the east, many of which were malarial. However, those parts of the coastal strip without sand dunes and swamps provided the best-watered agricultural and horticultural land in the region, with alluvial soils, good rainfall, and many perennial streams coming from the numerous springs in the foothills to the east.

Most of the coast is now intensively cultivated and built up. The **Sharon National Park** (at Hadera junction) provides a small area of reserve with some few remaining vestiges of native trees and pools. The fruits of this land (famously the Palestinian production of Jaffa oranges in the 19C–early 20C), and the wealth engendered by the land and sea routes along the coast, made this the most prosperous and populous region, and it was here that the major adminis-trative centres in historical times were situated—at Caesarea, at Ramla, at Tel Aviv/Jaffa and at Gaza. Today it is densely built up and over half the population of Israel lives in the coastal region.

AKKO ~ ACRE

Akko (A. Akka, H. Akko), the walled Crusader port city on the north coast, retains much of its splendour, even in decay. The town was the gateway to trade and to Western travellers and invaders, and from 1191 to 1291 it was the capi-tal of the Crusader kingdom in the Holy Land. Here you can readily relate to the life and times of the 13C and all the drama of the fall of Crusader Acre to the Muslim army in 1291. Akko lies north of Haifa, off Highway 4, 182km from Jerusalem.

Practical information

Information office

The *Tourist Information Office* is in al-Jazzar St, opposite the Mosque (☎ 04 991 1764). Train and bus services at Rehov David Remez, c 1km from the Old Town

Where to stay

Akko has relatively few hotels; best known is *Palm Beach Hotel* (☎ 04 991 0434) at a good beach south of the old town; hostels (*HI Akko Youth*

Hostel, and *Paul's*, near the lighthouse and the Khan al-Umdan in the old city) offer cheaper accommodation.

Eating out

Abu Christo's on the harbour in the old town is the best known fish restaurant (☎ 04 991 0065). There are several more along the sea front and in the Old Town.

History

The earliest settlement lies under Tell Akko 700m to the east of the present coastline. The history of the early town was linked to the anchorage provided by the rather swampy mouth of a river in the shelter of a promontory, which offered a safe harbour near the junction of two important land routes. The silting up of the river mouth was the probable reason that the settlement gradually moved westwards to the present site on the sea. The ancient tell was occupied late in the fourth millennium BC, and again from early in the second millennium until late in the first millennium BC. Its importance is witnessed by the number of times ancient Akka is mentioned in ancient documents from the early second millennium onwards (Execration Texts, Amarna Letters, Ugaritic texts, Assyrian documents). An important city of the Canaanites, of the 'Sea Peoples', of Phoenicians and pagans, it was not part of early Israel, but may have been one of the cities of Galilee given by Solomon to Hiram of Tyre (I Kings 9:11) if Hiram did not already own it. Pliny claimed that glass-making was invented here, and there is some archaeological evidence for the manufacture of glass and of purple dye. Excellent sand for glass-making was available in the mouth of the Belus River (Nahal Na'aman) to the south.

Akka was an important centre in the Persian Empire. The first evidence for the building of harbour works may date as early as the late 6C or early 5C BC. The city was still prosperous when it surrendered to Alexander the Great in 332 BC. The city was renamed Ptolemais under the Ptolemies, and Antiochia Ptolemais under the Seleucids, and at that time expanded over a large area. In the harbour, the base of the Tower of the Flies has been dated to this period. The inhabitants stood out against the Hasmoneans, but the city was taken into Roman hands under Pompey (63 BC). Julius Caesar visited in 47 BC, and the city counted its dates from the beginning of Caesar's reign. In 39 BC it was the landfall from which Herod the Great on his return from Rome set out to consolidate his rule over Palestine. It became Colonia Claudia Ptolemais in the time of Nero, though the old name of Akka was maintained locally. Major strengthening and heightening of the southern breakwater occurred in the Roman period, to combat a slight rise in sea level. Although pagan, the town had a Jewish minority living and trading there, many of whom were massacred by the inhabitants during the First Revolt. Vespasian made it the base from which he set out to retake Galilee.

The Roman city became an early centre of Christianity, visited by St. Paul, and its bishop is recorded in AD 190. It remained a prosperous port with shipyards during the Byzantine period, then following its surrender to the Muslim armies in 636, reverted to its ancient name and was a base for the first Islamic navy (and the invasion of Cyprus under the Umayyad caliph Mu'awiya). Between AD 868 and 884 Ibn Tulun rebuilt the port; and his work forms the foundation of the Crusader and later work. This included the massive eastern breakwater which connected the Tower of the Flies to the shore to the north, enclosing the outer harbour. In 1104 King Baldwin I captured the town, with the help of the ships of Genoa. The sea level appears to have fallen again in the Crusader period, when massive defence towers were built at the north end of the southern breakwater. In 1187 Salah al-Din recaptured the city. In 1191 Richard Lionheart of England and Philip Augustus of France regained it. As Crusader capital the city expanded greatly to the north and east.

In the Crusader period the city was divided into the 'quarters' of the many orders based here: the Order of St. John of Jerusalem (the Hospitallers) at the centre, the Poor Knights of Christ and of the Temple (the Templars) at the south, the Teutonic Knights in the east, and the Order of St. Lazarus in the northern suburb of Montmusard. The population was typical of a busy port. The 'quarters' of the merchants of the Italian cities of Genoa, Venice and Pisa, whose ships and trade were crucial to the Crusades, were located around the port. Merchants of Amalfi and Marseilles also traded here. The great philosopher Rabbi Moses ben Maimon (the Rambam or Maimonides), spent five months here in 1165, and toured the Holy Land before returning to North Africa. In 1267 Rabbi Moses ben Nachman (the Ramban) came from Spain, and after a brief period in Jerusalem became the spiritual leader of the Jewish community in Acre from 1268 until his death in 1270. The population of the city grew to around 50,000, but each group had its own area of the city, with its own fortifications and narrow streets, and street fighting between the groups is recorded. The Muslim writer Abu al-Fida, writing of the fall of Acre in 1291, says: 'During the Muslim onslaught, one group of its population managed to flee in ships. Within the city were a number of fortified towers, like citadels, in each of which a vast company of Franks had barricaded itself. When the Muslims had killed and sacked so vast a part of Acre as to defy calculation, the sultan commanded those still putting up a resistance from within the towers to come out and to leave no one inside. He then ordered that they be decapitated outside Acre, right up to the last one. Finally he ordered that Acre be razed to the ground.' Despite this destruction, the remains of the Crusader civil, military and religious buildings provide a rich illustration of their former presence.

At this time Acre's wealth was based on trade—woollen products from the west, and a huge array of luxuries from the east: condiments such as sugar, pepper and many spices; dyes; ivory and silks. But Acre also served as a local market for the produce of the hinterland—wine, oil, meat, cereals, fruits, vegetables, cheese—and for the local sea trade, with flax and dried fish from Egypt and goods from Antioch. Caravans paid 4 per cent on the value of merchandise to the customs at Acre, where the market court regulated the trade. Following the destruction of the city in 1291 by al-Ashraf the town was mostly abandoned.

Under the Ottomans in the early 17C, Fakhr al-Din, a Druze amir, began to rebuild over the 13C ruins. Dahir al-Umar (1749–75), a Bedouin shaikh who ousted and replaced the Ottoman governor, rebuilt the city and region; under his rule cotton growing underpinned the economy. His successor, Ahmad al-Jazzar (Jazzar Pasha, 'the Butcher', a Bosniak adventurer, 1775–1804) built the Great Mosque and the Hammam al-Basha. It was these two rulers and Sulaiman Pasha (al-Jazzar's successor) who built the citadel in the city, and also repaired the harbour works, reusing marble and porphyry columns (perhaps from Caesarea). Al-Jazzar, with the help of the English fleet under Sir Sidney Smith, successfully resisted a two-month siege by Napoleon Bonaparte in 1799, and halted the French military expedition to the East, thus again giving Acre an important place in history. Napoleon's base during the siege was on 'Napoleon's Hill', the ancient tell to the east which covers the original town of Akka. Ibrahim Pasha, who took the city from the Turks with an Egyptian army and ruled it 1832–40, repaired the battlements along the south sea front using sandstone from Atlit for the gun ports. The port is too small for modern shipping, and Acre declined as Haifa took its place. Under the British Mandate there was a prison in the Citadel, in which both Arab and Zionist fighters were imprisoned. Today the old town is mainly inhabited by Arabs and the modern town by Jews.

It is the city as it evolved from the 12C that you can explore today; its visual character is shaped by its bold stance on the shore and by the buildings of local coarse, darkish-yellow stone. It still has lively and interesting bazaars.

To see all the remains of interest in Akko requires some time and you can easily spend a whole day here; note that many of the main sites have strict opening hours, and close early on Friday. If time is limited, the 'Underground City' and the port are the most important sights. Arriving by car, the usual approach is along Haim Weizmann St to a tourist car park almost immediately on the right inside the city walls. You can also drive around the north side of the medieval walls (Napoleon Bonaparte St) and find parking along the sea front. However, Akko is best explored on foot. The old town, especially along the main bazaar, has some pleasant small cafés, a fine spice shop and bakeries selling excellent refreshments (such as herb breads, cheese pastries and sweets like nougat).

The walls
As you approach Akko, the high and well-preserved walls are surprisingly well hidden behind the modern town. There are two visible city walls. The outer wall was built by al-Jazzar. The slightly earlier inner northern rampart of Dahir al-Umar is based on the inner 12C–13C Crusader town wall; the Crusader wall had a ditch, and extended further to the east than the present east wall which was rebuilt after 1799. Most of the visible sea walls are based on Crusader lines. It is possible to walk around most of the ramparts. You can either do this as a separate tour, or visit the 'Land Wall Promenade' on the east after seeing the 'Underground City', and the 'Sea Wall Promenade' and port after visiting the Khan al-Umdan.

The north and east (land wall) is accessible on the east side of Weizmann St where the road cuts through the wall, and also by the double ramp inside the central section of the east wall; cannon of various periods decorate the gun ports there. The tower at the northeast angle, the **Commander's Tower** was strategically vital to the land defences and provides a good view of the city. The Land Gate is located near the shore; south of it on the eastern sea wall, the Burj al-Sultan is a surviving Crusader (Venetian) tower at the northeast end of the former Venetian quarter.

The sea walls and mole provide one of the pleasantest walks; the rebuilt mole provides shelter for small pleasure craft and fishing boats and the area is always busy. A short cruise from the port can be made to view the city from the sea. Continuing west from the port is the small inlet called the Pisan Harbour; the promenade continues to the lighthouse, passing St. John's Church. Northwest of the lighthouse is the area of quarried rock, now under water, which was the site of the great fortress of the Templars, 'the palace under the sea'. A focus of the siege in 1291, it has completely vanished, partly in the various destructions and finally when the port walls were rebuilt in the 18C (and see Templar Tunnel, below). It is possible to continue along the road to the Burj al-Kurayim (Vine Tower), a large, partly restored viewpoint. If you carry on further along the line of the north wall, to the east, the Museum of Underground Prisoners (signposted), is entered from the road running between the two city walls. The Burj al-Khazna (Treasury Tower) probably incorporates the Tower of the Hospital; the latter underlies the whole area of the 18C citadel.

Continue into the medieval town on Weizmann St and turn right into al-Jazzar St to reach the core of the town.

The **Great Mosque**, built by al-Jazzar in 1781, is a well-maintained example of the style of the Ottoman period. Enter past a fine kiosk into a courtyard full of flowering plants and, in summer, a rich scent of frangipane; a domed portico with rooms for attendants and students surrounds it. The court has an attractive ablution fountain with pinnacled gold dome, and a notable marble sundial. Near the typically Ottoman thin cylindrical minaret are the tombs of al-Jazzar and his successor, Sulaiman Pasha. To the left of the entrance is the descent to the fine vaulted cistern which can be toured by a walkway. The cistern is built in the ground floor or basement of an earlier, Crusader building, sometimes said to be the Cathedral of the Holy Cross (but the site of the cathedral is now thought to have been further to the east). The mosque itself, with its many green domes and some agreeable tiled panels and decorative multicoloured inlaid stonework, is light and pleasant. Visitors should dress appropriately and not wear shoes inside the mosque. During prayer times, especially on Friday, the mosque is closed to visitors.

The ablution fountain at the Great Mosque

The **Okashi Museum** (closes early on Fri) is opposite the al-Jazzar Mosque. It contains the work of Jewish abstract painter Avshalom Okashi (1916–80) who lived in Akko from 1948 until his death; Akko was frequently included in his subject matter.

The Citadel lies to the west. It was built in the 18C over the 12C–13C remains of the Hospitallers' buildings, the ground floor level was infilled and the new buildings constructed at first-floor level. The complex served as citadel, barracks, arsenal and finally prison. The grand doorway can be viewed from near the Mosque entrance.

The Crusader 'Underground City'.

The entrance to the *Crusader 'Underground City' is opposite the al-Jazzar Mosque. Open Sat–Thur 08.30–18.30 (Sat 09.00–18.00 in summer), Fri 08.30–14.30; may close earlier in winter. Admission charged.

This vast and splendid complex was built by the Hospitaller Knights of St. John. Large areas beneath the 18C citadel buildings have been cleared of fill in recent years. The complex is generally Crusader at base and Ottoman above. The tour begins in the great halls (the Knights' Halls) on the north. The row of connected halls at ground level between towers adjacent to the city wall may well have served as barracks and stables for the knights. Beneath one of the towers is a remarkable sewage system running to the city ditch. These halls adjoin the recently cleared and restored great courtyard and cloister of the Hospitallers' headquarters. A row of Crusader corbels survives on the cloister wall, with a reconstructed staircase on the east side leading to the main rooms on the first floor of a building that stood four storeys high until the 17C. The ground floor contains the vast remains called the Grand Manoir, variously identified as part of the Hospice of the Knights or as part of the Hospital. Across the court to the south is the hall sometimes called the Refectory of the Knights, or more usually the Crypt as it probably had another hall above it. It is a fine two-aisled hall with a groin-vaulted ceiling supported on three massive columns on the central long axis, with three chimneys in the east wall. Fleur-de-lys carved on the consoles suggested an association with the French. In the far corner you exit to a narrow tunnel, long referred to as 'the secret passage' (over 350m have been cleared), now found to be part of the monumental drain which led to the ditch beyond the city wall in the north and to the sea in the south. It runs beneath the Refectory and provides access to a further complex of six adjoining halls, with cross-vaulted roofs, called the Bosta Halls. In the past these were doubtfully identified as part of a caravanserai, perhaps dating from the Fatimid period, but are now seen to be the undercroft of the 13C Church of St. John the Baptist. The remains of the west door of the church can be seen from outside the Underground City, opposite the entrance to the bath house. On the north of the Bosta Halls, another fine hall, known as the 'Beautiful Hall', may also be visited. Recently cleared halls to the south of the Bosta Halls could have belonged to the Hospital. Various Crusader fragments, including a fine tombstone (possibly that of Archbishop William of Nazareth, died 1290), can be seen near the exit from the complex, which is opposite the entrance to the bath house.

The attractive ***Hammam al-Basha** (the Bath house of the Pasha), built by al-Jazzar in the 18C, was in use until 1947. Al-Jazzar also rebuilt the aqueduct bringing water to the town from the north. The bath house is well worth visiting, especially as the main reception room with its central fountain and the hot room with its wash vats, domed roofs and marble floors, are all decorated with very fine 18C tiles.

The west entrance to the **Turkish bazaar**, a covered market selling craft items, is to the right opposite the bath house. A short distance from its east end is the covered **Suq al-Abiad** (White Market) located to the left of the crossing of Weizmann and Salah al-Din Sts. It was built by Dahir al-Umar, and restored by Sulaiman Pasha in 1817/18. It is a fruit and vegetable market.

Across on the south side of the square is the north entrance to the **Khan al-**

Shuwarda, a caravanserai restored in the 18C by Dahir al-Umar, with the surviving 13C Venetian sea tower (Burj al-Sultan) on the right side of the south entrance. The khan, dilapidated but still in use, has a ground floor portico with rectangular masonry pillars and very slightly pointed arches. The upper floors are almost completely missing. A very battered fountain survives in the courtyard.

Marco Polo St, the main shopping area of the old town, runs from the southwest corner of the square and passes on the right the al-Raml Mosque (Sand Mosque) built in 1704–05.

As you continue through the bazaar, a turning on the left approaches the entrance to the **Khan al-Faranj** (Franks' Inn) which is entered from the south. It was built on the foundations of a Venetian 13C warehouse, which served as an inn for French merchants who had a commercial concession in the 16C. The old entrance doors, wooden with nailed metalled strips, have long been immobile; still set in the upper stone hinge, they sag against the gate passage wall. Inside, one portico on the ground floor survives. To the south is the **Khan al-Umdan** (Inn of the Columns) with a large Ottoman clock tower above the main entrance built to celebrate the anniversary of Sultan Abd al-Hamid in 1906. The khan itself was built by al-Jazzar in 1784 on the foundations of the royal customs house (Cour de la Chaine); he brought the reused granite Roman columns in the lower portico from Caesarea and Atlit. The court has a well at the centre, and is surrounded by a portico at ground and upper level with stone vaulted roofs. Pleasant chambers on the upper floor provide shade and a cool breeze in the summer, especially in the rooms overlooking the harbour. The large courtyard is used for concerts and rallies. A passage in the southwest corner leads out to Pisa Square.

On the far side of Pisa Square, on the right, is a fine Crusader doorway, with rebated pilasters and trefoil arch. Opposite is the entrance to the **Khan al-Shuna** (the Grain Inn) built on 12C–13C foundations of the Pisan Square; the entrance archway and passage lead to a court occupied by workshops and other activities. Although run down it is interesting for its complex architectural history. The exit from the Templar Tunnel is located here. The entrance is opposite the sea wall to the west. The **Templar Tunnel**, another section of the 'secret passage' you can visit in the Underground City, was discovered in 1994 and opened to the public in 1999 (admission charged, combined ticket and hours as Underground City). The lower part is cut in bedrock, the upper part built as a barrel vault; this section of the tunnel runs under the Pisan Square to the former fortress of the Templars.

At this point you can go on to visit the port and breakwater, the former lighthouse known as the Tower of the Flies, the sea wall promenade and the present-day working lighthouse.

Alternatively there are other places of interest in the town—many ruinous areas indicate how much of medieval Acre has survived. To the west of the Khan al-Shuna, opposite the western sea wall, is the Greek Catholic **Church of St. Andrew**, a Crusader church rebuilt in the 18C–19C. A little east of Genoa Square is the Greek Orthodox **Church of St. George**, on the site of the Genoese Crusader Church of St. Lawrence. An attractive small church with 18C–19C icons, painted wooden columns and an archbishop's throne; it has a high pulpit for reading the gospel and some attractive marble relief scenes of St. George and of the Nativity. In the northwest angle of the city is a building belonging to the Bahai sect, a large Crusader building called the **Dayr al-Mustapha**.

Entered from outside the north wall of the old city is the **Museum of the Underground Prisoners during the British Mandate**, located in buildings adjacent to the north side of the citadel. An exhibition in the cells commemorates where members of the Jewish Zionist movement who resisted the British Mandate government before 1948 were imprisoned and executed, and also the escape of Zionists in 1947. Open Sat–Thur 09.00–16.00, Fri and eves of hols 09.00–13.00. Admission charged.

Three kilometres northeast of Akko on the road to Nahariyya is the **Bahai Persian Garden** at Bahji, with the house and tomb of the founder of the Bahai faith, Mirza Hussain Ali or Baha Ulla (see also p 292). He was exiled to Akko in 1868 and died at Bahji in 1892. The Shrine of Baha Ulla is surrounded by wonderful gardens. Open Fri, Sat, Sun and Mon 09.00–12.00.

HAIFA AND MT CARMEL

Haifa is the main port and third largest town in Israel. Located on a wide bay at the mouth of the Qishon River, it is sheltered by the northern end of the ridge of Mt Carmel, which drops dramatically into the sea. The town is mainly a modern development, replacing the older ports of Akko and Caesarea. There is evidence on Mt Carmel of prehistoric cave occupation, and it is the setting for the story of the triumph of the prophet Elijah over the priests of Baal. The Mt Carmel National Park is extensive with important nature reserves. There are a number of beaches near Haifa, both at the promontory and along the coast to the south.

Practical information

Information offices

Tourist information offices are located at the port (☎ 04 853 5606), the *IGTO* is at 18 Rehov Herzl (☎ 04 866 6521), near the City Hall, and at 106 Sderot Hanassi (☎ 04 837 4010).

Getting around

The central **bus terminal** (information office ☎ 04 851 2208) is located at the northwestern end of the lower town on Sederot HaHagana, and many sites can be reached by bus. The **Carmelit subway** provides efficient transport up the steep climb between the lower town around the port and the upper town on Mt Carmel; and a **cable** car with more limited hours operates between the Bat Galim Promenade and Stella Maris.

Where to stay

Haifa's many hotels include *Dan Panorama*, 107 HaNassi, Carmel (☎ 04 835 2222; 📠 04 835 2235) and *Hotel Dvir*, 124 Yeve Nof, *Carmel* (☎ 04 838 9131; 📠 04 838 1068) above the town with views, and in the lower town, the *Haifa Tower*, 63 Herzl, Haifa (☎ 04 867 7111; 📠 04 862 1863). The *Carmel Youth Hostel* (☎ 04 853 1944, off Highway 4; beach, tennis; bus 43) is 4km south of Haifa.

Eating out

Places to eat in Haifa are generally cheaper than up in Carmel. The range of cafés and restaurants is wide— Arab, Ashkenazi, Iraqi, Romanian—and prices range from expensive French (*Voilà*, 21 Nordau St, ☎ 04 866 4529) and seafood (at *Dolphin*, 13 Bet Galim, ☎ 04 852 3837), to moderate fish/vegetarian Ashkenazi (*Zimhonia*, 130 Herzl St, day/early evening; *Abu Yousef*, 1 Kikkar Paris for grilled meats and mezze, Palestinian style).

History

The excavated sites of Tell Abu Hawam (Late Bronze Age, Iron Age, Persian and later occupation), on the east side of town in the industrial zone near the Qishon River, and Tel Shiqmona (Iron Age, Persian, Roman periods, Byzantine church, mosaic floors, industrial installation), by the sea at the western edge of the promontory, are predecessors of Haifa. Old Haifa itself was a small town with a mixed Jewish and Muslim population, whose history is a close reflection of that of its larger neighbour Akko. In the 11C AD it was no more than a village close to the Qishon estuary, located at or very near Tell Abu Hawam and the nearby site of a 4C way station. By the 12C this village had been abandoned and the new town, possibly founded under the Fatimids around the end of the 11C, lay a little to the east, in the southeastern part of lower modern Haifa. It had a Fatimid garrison, a port and a ship-building industry, but fell to the Crusaders in July 1100. Most of its Jewish and Muslim inhabitants were massacred.

Unlike Akko, Haifa was captured by Napoleon in 1799. It grew steadily by immigration from the beginning of the 19C when Shephardi Jews from North Africa settled here. In 1868 German Templers established the German Colony at Haifa. This was a religious movement which began in Württemberg in Germany in 1860, aiming at an ideal Christian community in the 'Land of Promise' and from there the regeneration of the church and the social life of Europe. Haifa was the Templers' first colony and houses of the community can be seen in the vicinity of Ben Gurion Avenue near the centre of the lower town. In 1870 Askenazi Jews settled. The construction of the Haifa–Damascus Railway, which opened in 1905, changed the economic role of the city and eventually Haifa displaced Akko in importance. In 1918 the town was captured by the British. The modern port was established in 1936, and its role in Mandate times as the Mediterranean outlet of the oil pipeline from Mosul in Iraq was significant. By 1948 the Jewish and Arab inhabitants were fairly evenly balanced, but only 3000 Arabs remained after the battles with the Haganah (the Zionist militia). Today it is one of the largest container ports on the Mediterranean, and a passenger terminal.

Haifa's fame until modern times was related to the ridge of Mt Carmel, a striking mountain which appears to have been a focus of pagan, then Jewish, Christian and Muslim veneration. Mt Carmel is famous for the competition between Yahweh and Baal instigated by the prophet Elijah (the site is traditionally located at al-Muhraqa c 20km to the southwest of Haifa); the cave in which Elijah (and later the Holy Family) is said to have rested, lies in the lower part of the promontory facing the sea. In Byzantine times it was the location of a cave shrine, churches and monasteries, many of which were rebuilt in Crusader times, and then again in the 19C.

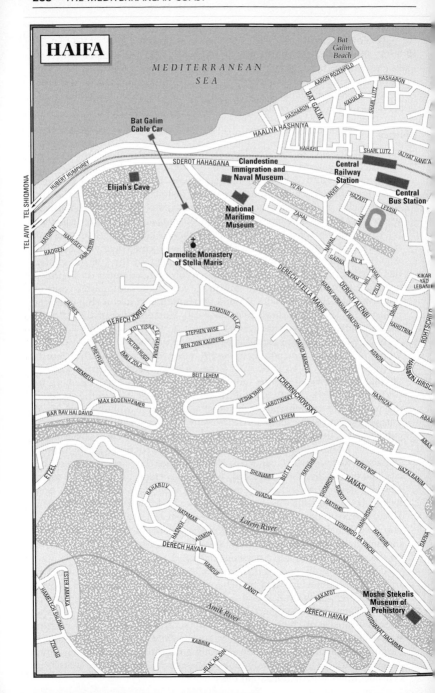

HAIFA

MEDITERRANEAN SEA

Bat Galim Beach

Bat Galim Cable Car

Elijah's Cave

Clandestine Immigration and Naval Museum

Central Railway Station

Central Bus Station

National Maritime Museum

Carmelite Monastery of Stella Maris

Moshe Stekelis Museum of Prehistory

TEL AVIV TEL SHLOMONA

HUBERT HUMPHREY

SDEROT HAHAGANA

HAALIYA HASHNIYA

HASHARON

BAT GALIM

HAHAYIL

AARON ROZENFELD

HASHARON

NAHALAL

SHARL LUTZ

SHARL LUTZ

ALIYAT HANO'A

YO'AV

ANVER

HAZAVIT

AMAL

LESSIN

ZAHAL

NAFAL

GADNA

BIL'A

ZILPAH

ZAHAL

LITZA

KIKAR YAD LEBANII

HATOREN

HAHEGEH

VAN STERN

HAOGEN

DERECH STELLA MARIS

HABAV ABRAHAM HALFON

DERECH ALENBI

DROR

HAHOTRIM

ROHTSCHII

JAURES

DERECH ZORFAT

EDMOND PELEG

KOL YISRA 'EL HAVERIM

STEPHEN WISE

BEN ZION KAUDERS

DAVID MARCUS

AGNON

HABRON HIRSC

DREIFUS

VICTOR HUGO

EMILE ZOLA

BEIT LEHEM

TCHERNICHOWSKY

HASHIZAF

CREMIEUX

MAX BODENHEIMER

YESHAYAHU

JABOTINSKY

ABAS

BAR RAV HAI DAVID

BEIT LEHEM

ABAS

ETZEL

SHUNAMIT

BEIT EL

HATSIBI

YEFEH NOF

HAZALBANIM

BAHARUV

OVADIA

SHIMRON

SUKKOT

HANASI

HARHUSHA

DAFNA

HATAMAR

HASNEF

ASMON

HATSIBI

LEONARDO DA VINCHI

HATSIBI

ESTER AMALKA

HAMELECH SHLOMO

DERECH HAYAM

HARDUF

Lotem River

TZIKAG

KABRIM

JELAL AD-DIN

Amik River

ILANDT

RAKAFOT

DERECH HAYAM

SHOSHANAT HACARMEL

Moshe Stekelis Museum of Prehistory

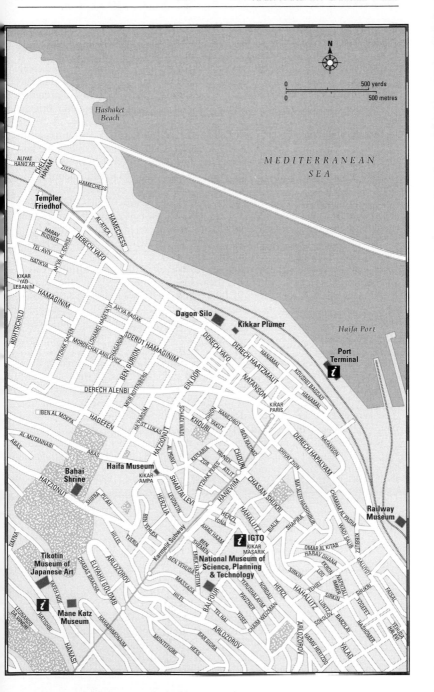

N

0   500 yards
0   500 metres

Hashaket Beach

MEDITERRANEAN SEA

CHELL HANAM
ALIYAT HANO'AR
ZISSU
HAMECHESS
Templer Friedhof
AL ATICA
HAMECHESS
HARAV RUDNER
AHVA AL-EBRISI
TEL-AVIV
DEREH YAFO
RATIKVA
KIKAR YAD LEBANIM
ROTHSCHILD
HAMAGINIM
OHAMEI HAGETA'OT
AH'VA RADAK
YITZHAK SADEH
SDEROT HAMAGINIM
MORDECHAI ANILEVICZ
BEN GURION
DEREH YAFO
Dagon Silo
Kikkar Plümer
Haifa Port
DEREH HAATZMAUT
MEIR ROTENBERG
EIN DOR
HANAMAL
Port Terminal
KOUSIEI BAGDAD
DEREH ALENBI
NATANSON
HANAMAL
IBEN AL MOKPA
HAGEFEN
ST. LUKAS
HAPASIM
TOYWA YOSHES
HANEZIBOT
PRION
YAKUT
IBEN BASRAD
KIKAR PARIS
AL-MUTANNABI
ABAS
ABAS
HATZIONUT
HERZLIA
LEVONTIN
KERSABIA
IZOR
YAINEX
ATLIT
IL PRAVI
YITZHAK'P'RES
Bahai Shrine
HATZIONUT
Haifa Museum
KIKAR AMPA
SHABTAI LEVI
HANEVIIM
CHOUN
DEREH HAPALYAM
SHIVAT ZION
NATANSON
SHIFRA PUAL
BEN YEHUDA
TVERIA
HILLEL
CHASAN SHUKRI
MA'ALEH HASHIHRUR
CHAMAM AL-PASHA
DARNA
Karmelit Subway
HERZL
YONA
HAHALUTZ
BIALIK
SHAPIRA
WADI SALIB
Railway Museum
Tikotin Museum of Japanese Art
ELIYAHU GOLOMB
CHABAS BRACHA
ARLOZOROV
AHAD HA'AM
BEN SIEMEN
EMEK REFAIM
BEN YEHUDA
i IGTO
KIKAR MASARIK
National Museum of Science, Planning & Technology
OMAR AL KITAB
HARAV OHANA
SIRKIN
LOD
IMBER
PKRON
SIRKIN
KIBBUTZ
GALVKOT
LEONARDO DA VINCHI
i
Mane Katz Museum
HATSIBI
YAFEH NOF
MASSADA
HILEL
BALFOUR
TEL HAI
TERUSHALAYIM
NORDAU
PAYZNER
CHAIM WEIZMANN
YOSEF
YEHIEL
HERZL
HAHALUTZ
LUNTZ
BARZILAY
SHUKRI
YODEFET
FAISAL
HAVASI
MONTEFIORE
HESS
BAR GIORA
ARLOZOROV
ARLOZOROV
BALFOUR
SOKOLOV
JARAV HERTZOG
YALAG
YEHUDA HALEVI

The northwestern section of the town

Just east of the junction of the Jaffa Rd with Chel HaYam is the **Templer Friedhof**, the Templer cemetery. In use for expatriate burials since 1865, it encapsulates much of the history of the region in the last century. The cemetery contains the graves of Europeans from the 19C onward; many of the Mandate officials including a section devoted to the Palestine Police; and a well maintained War Grave for the dead of the First and Second World Wars, with British, Australians and Indians of various faiths.

Further west, below the promontory and off Sederot HaHagana, is the **National Maritime Museum** at 198 Derekh Allenby, which exhibits the history of shipping in the Middle East (open Sun–Thur 10.00–17.00, Sat 10.00–14.00; closed Fri). Next to it at the road junction at 204 Derekh Allenby is the **Clandestine Immigration and Naval Museum** (open Sun, Tues 09.00–16.00; Mon, Wed, Thur 09.00–15.00, Fri and eves of hols 09.00–13.00; closed Sat and hol.), with displays and information on sea-borne Jewish immigration before and after the establishment of the State of Israel in 1948. Further southeast along Derekh Allenby is the German Colony, where houses built by the German Templers are to be seen in the vicinity.

Just west and above the junction at 230 Derekh Allenby is **Elijah's Cave**, approached by a stepped path above the road (open: summer Sun–Thur 08.00–18.00; winter Sun–Thur 08.00–17.00; Fri and eves of hols 08.00–13.00, closed Sat and hol). Orthodox Jews maintain the sanctity of the site (headgear is provided).

History of Elijah's Cave

A venerated site, very prominent as a maritime landmark, was perhaps originally a cave associated with the pagan cult of Helios in Hellenistic and Roman times. By the 4C Christian tradition claimed it was the place where Elijah (Elias) lodged on his way to his encounter with the priests of Baal, and also the cave where he was fed by ravens, so a Byzantine monastery dedicated to St. Elias was built around it. During succeeding centuries, the cave continued to be visited by pilgrims, and when the Latin Carmelites returned to the Carmel in 1633 they established themselves by it. In the 18C when the cave was turned into a mosque, the Carmelites moved further uphill (see Stella Maris, below).

The cave is rectangular with modern closure wall. There is a niche on the east side where the Holy Family is said to have rested on the return from Egypt. A niche in the south wall was perhaps cut for a statue and subsequently made into a mihrab. Nothing early survives, apart from the rock-cut cave itself.

Reached by cable car from the Bat Galim Promenade, or by continuing east on Derekh Allenby and turning uphill into Derekh Stella Maris, or from upper Haifa, is the **Carmelite Monastery of Stella Maris** (open 08.00–13.30, 15.00–18.00). The Carmelite Order began with the establishment c 1200 of Latin hermits near Elijah's spring in the narrow, deep Wadi Ain al-Siyah c 4km south of Elijah's Cave (between the modern suburbs of Kababir and Carmeliya). It was a wealthy international order by the 13C. This place was the site of a Byzantine monastery dedicated to St. Margaret. It had important relics, presumably including some of St. Margaret who was martyred at Antioch in Pisidia in the 3C. There was a Greek Orthodox Abbey Church of St. Margaret, possibly established around 1192, but first mentioned in 1217. The monastery was assigned to the Franks in 1283 and abandoned in 1291. It was still visited and served by the Greek Orthodox in the early 17C. The site was redeveloped by the Carmelites in the 18C, and soldiers injured in the Napoleonic campaign in 1799 were nursed in the convent. Any earlier remains were destroyed when the present Stella Maris convent was built between 1831 and 1836; nothing survives of the older St. Margaret, but a small museum contains some architectural fragments from buildings in the area.

The base of the prominent lighthouse nearby are the remains of St. Margaret's Castle, a Templar castle of the Crusaders, built before 1169–72, which may have replaced a Muslim fort and mosque of Sa'ad al-Dawla. The castle was destroyed in 1821.

Central lower town
The docks and railway line occupy the waterfront in the central area. The area is dominated by the **Dagon Silo**, a huge granary that is the area's principal landmark. Its **Grain Museum** in Plumer Square is a small archaeological and documentary exhibition of the history of wheat (guided tours daily at 10.30 except Sat and hols; groups by previous arrangement only). There is a **Railway Museum** further to the east off Derekh Haatzmaut, which houses some rolling stock and exhibits concerned with the arrival of the railway in Haifa. This was an economic factor of importance after the First World War.

Haifa Museum, at 26 Shabtai Levy St, houses the Museums of Ancient Art, of Modern Art, and of Music and Ethnology (open Sun, Mon, Wed, Thur 10.00–17.00; Tues 16.00–20.00; Fri 10.00–13.00, Sat 10.00–14.00; admission charged). The archaeological collections (upstairs) include a fine small collection of objects mostly of the Late Bronze Age and later date. An interesting assemblage of objects recovered from the sea off Haifa includes a Hittite axe and other flat axes of Late Bronze Age date; tin ingots of the 16C–11C BC marked in Cypro-Minoan script; finds of the Persian period; collections of lamps and sculpture of Persian through Byzantine periods; Coptic textiles and Egyptian mummy portraits of the Roman period; Greek pots; terracottas; finds from the excavations at Shiqmona. The modern art collections are principally the work of Israeli artists; the ethnographic displays are mainly African and objects of Jewish ceremonial and folk art.

To the south is the old campus of the Technion, the Institute of Technology, founded in 1925, which now houses the National Museum of Science, Planning and Technology (open Mon, Wed, Thur 09.00–17.00, Tues 09.00–19.00, Fri 09.00–13.00, Sat 10.00–14.00). The Technion campus is now on the Carmel Ridge.

Continuing steeply up Hazionut Blvd for c 1km you come to the **Bahai Shrine**, the world centre of the Bahai faith, often called the Persian Garden. A lovely garden surrounds the Shrine of the Bab, the herald of the Bahai faith (see box). His tomb is in a white marble Neo-classical building topped by a golden dome. The gardens are open daily 08.00–17.00; shrine daily 09.00–12.00. Tourist access is limited to parts of the garden and to one room in the shrine; visitors to the shrine should dress modestly; no smoking, eating or photography permitted.

The shrine and garden have magnificent views down to the port. By day and night it is the aesthetic focus of Haifa, the garden providing a preserved green zone around the shrine by day and the illuminated shrine contrasting with the darkness of the surrounding garden by night.

Bahai

The Bahai faith teaches that religious truth is progressive and that God, through a series of prophets—Moses, Zoroaster, Buddha, Christ and Muhammad—progressively reveals guidance suited to the times. The latest of these prophets was Baha Ullah, the founder of this independent religion, who died in 1892 at Bahji near Akko to which place he was exiled by the Sultan of Turkey after previous exile from Persia by the Shah of Persia. The Bab, or Martyr-Herald of the Bahai faith, who proclaimed Baha Ullah's mission in 1844, was executed in Tabriz (Persia) in 1850. His remains were brought to Haifa and entombed in the shrine in March 1909 by Baha Ullah's son.

The shrine consists of an inner structure built in local masonry and style in the early 1900s; the outer facing and the domed superstructure, built of imported Italian stone, was designed by W. Sutherland Maxwell and built between 1948 and 1953. The dome is faced with glazed, gilded tiles made in Holland. Other buildings, monuments and gardens are located across the road up the hill, and are not open to the public. The structures include the International Bahai Archives building, a monumental Greek-style temple faced with Italian marble and Dutch roof tiles, completed in 1957; and four white Carrara marble temple monuments which form the tombstones of the immediate family of Baha Ullah.

Upper Haifa, on the Carmel Ridge

Adjacent to the top of the subway, at Gan Ha'em, are a Zoo, the Botanical Gardens and the **Moshe Stekelis Museum of Prehistory** (open Sun–Thur 08.00–15.00, Fri 08.00–13.00; Sat 10.00–14.00). The museum has a display of prehistoric dioramas, with models of early man engaged in various activities. The Mesolithic burial of a man and his dog found at Eynan in the Upper Jordan Valley is also displayed here, with representative displays of flint tools. At 89 Hanassi Ave is the Tikotin Museum of Japanese Art with 19C prints and traditional furniture. To the north, Yefeh Nof Rd (Panorama Rd) with observation points, has another fine view over Haifa and the bay; at no. 89 is the Mane Katz Museum housing the works of this Expressionist artist and collections of Judaica, antique furniture and rugs (open Sun, Wed, Thur 10.00–16.00; Tues 14.00–18.00; Fri, Sat 10.00–13.00, shorter hours in winter).

Further south along the Carmel ridge,

Near Kikkar Elizabeth in Ramot Ben-Gurion in the southern part of upper Haifa, c 5 km south of Haifa, is the site of **Rushmiya**. Ruins of a Byzantine way station, with later Crusader hall and tower, were reused by Dahir al-Umar in the 18C.

The Haifa University, with the **Reuben and Edith Hecht Museum** located in the main building, is 7km south of Haifa. There is a regular programme of archaeological exhibitions on the people and land of Israel; art collections. Open Sun, Mon, Wed, Thur 10.00–16.00, Tues 10.00–19.00, Fri 10.00–13.00, Sat 10.00–14.00.

At the top of Mt Carmel is the **Mount Carmel Park** (National Parks Authority, ☎ 04 832 1452 /984 1750), near Highways 2, 4 and 70. If travelling on Highway 4, turn east at Oren Junction; from Highway 70, turn west to the Eliakim interchange, to Nesher, take direction of University of Haifa. There are numerous parks and nature reserves, with footpaths and the remains of settlements, churches and monasteries, ancient and modern. The latter include the ruins of St. Mary of Carmel, which is best approached from below.

Highway 672 runs along the Carmel Ridge to places at a greater distance from Haifa. The **Druze villages of Isfiya and Daliyat al-Karmil** (c 11km and 14km respectively southeast) are noted for handicrafts. Isfiya was settled c 1600 from Lebanon, and Daliyat al-Karmil in the 18C from Syria.

The Druze

The Druze are a branch of the Isma'ili Muslim faith, who separated from mainstream Islam after the disappearance of the Fatimid Caliph al-Hakim in Egypt in 1021. It is a closed religion which is led by the wise or 'initiated' among them; their beliefs include the return of al-Hakim; they venerate Jethro, the father-in-law of Moses who is known in Arabic as Shu'aib. Most Druze live in southern Lebanon, Jabal Druze and the Hauran of Syria.

Al-Muhraqa, c 20km southeast of Haifa, is the traditional site on Mount Carmel where Elijah challenged Ahab, the King of Israel (871–852 BC) and the priests of Baal to a confrontation. When God proved more powerful, Elijah slaughtered all the discredited prophets of Baal (I Kings 18). Jezebel, the Phoenician Baal-worshipping wife of Ahab, threatened vengeance, and Elijah fled south to Beersheba (I Kings 19:3). There is a Carmelite monastery here, 4km beyond Daliyat; no public transport (open Mon–Sat 08.00–13.00, 14.30–17.00, Sun 08.00–13.30).

The **Carmel Caves** are located in the Nahal Me'arot Nature Reserve (☎ 04 984 1750/52), 8km north of Faradis and 17km south of Haifa. These natural caves in the cliffs to the west of Highway 4 are among the most important early prehistoric sites in Israel. Prehistoric man used the caves from around 200,000 to 12,000 years ago, and remains of both Homo sapiens and Neanderthal man were discovered here. You can see a film and tour the caves, including the Tabun Cave and the Mugharat al-Wad, where a model illustrates Mesolithic burial practices. The nature reserve illustrates the modern Mediterranean environment, which was very different in prehistoric times.

To reach the **Ein Afek Nature Reserve** (☎ 04 877 8226) take a turning east off Highway 4 between Haifa and Akko at Kurdani Junction, near Kiryat Bialik. It preserves swampland which has visiting migrant birds in winter and spring, wild flowers, and a two-storey fortified building of the Crusader period, associated with a mill, now used as a visitor centre.

ATLIT

••••••

This ruined Crusader castle, also known as Castrum Peregrinorum (Pilgrims' Castle) stands on a rocky promontory. The castle is occupied by the Israeli navy and is not open to visitors, but it can be viewed from the road. You can find it c 15km south of Haifa, approached by a minor road off Highway 4, either to the modern town of Atlit or to Newe Yam. Khirbat Dustray and quarries can be visited.

History

The castle was built by the Knights Templars from AD 1217 on a promontory just above sea level, which provided some shelter to a wide bay on the south side. It replaced a 12C tower or way station with stables and cisterns just to the northeast at Khirbat Dustray. Like Safad, it became one of the Templars' main bases outside Acre (Akko). The town was sacked by Baybars in 1265 but he did not attempt to take the castle, which was abandoned after the fall of Acre in 1291. The fortifications were then destroyed by the Mamluks, but even more damage was done by the earthquake of 1837 following which much of the stone was taken to repair Acre.

The site has two major components, the castle and the outer suburb. The castle has a series of linear defences across the neck of the promontory, which barred the approach from the landward side; an attacker faced first a rock-cut ditch at sea level with counterscarp wall; then a low forward wall with three rectangular towers containing postern gates; beyond this barrier, a high wall with two massive towers controlled the field of fire over the forward defence wall and ditch; a single entrance gate lay at the north side of the north tower, and led into a narrow passage running almost the full length of the promontory. Within the castle, the outer walls of halls and vaults formed a ring defence, enclosing outer courts and passages; an inner ring of buildings enclosed a large courtyard. One of the inner ring of buildings was a unique polygonal church (mid-13C) which was described in the 18C and early 19C before it became totally ruined.

The *faubourg* or suburb on the flat coastal strip east of the castle was an outer defended unit, with an east rampart 645m long and a south rampart 230m long, with three gates, a ditch and counterscarp. Structures found in this area included the town church, a bath house and attached bakery, stables and a tower.

About 700m to the south of the castle, a moated tower stood near a rampart at the castle boundary and guarded the land and the nearby saltings. Ancient quarries at the edge of the sea and just east of the east rampart ('the narrow ways') were the source of the calcareous sandstone of which the castle is constructed. New villas with architectural pretensions have been built adjacent to the site; one was recently described as 'Organised as a set of cubic volumes, this modernistic house enjoys its proximity to a Crusader quarry.'

CAESAREA
• • • • • • • • • • •

Caesarea Maritima (A. Qaisariya) is the great port city built by Herod the Great which became a provincial capital during the Roman period. The well-preserved ruins include a Roman theatre and a magnificent Crusader fortification.

The site is on the coast: you leave Highway 2 at the Caesarea Junction, or Highway 4 west at Or Aqiva; bus from Hadera. The National Parks Authority (☎ 06 636 1358) administers it. There are shops, restaurants, galleries and a beach inside the site, and a café outside the south entrance.

Where to stay

Caesarea has a number of new luxury hotels including the *Hotel Dan Caesarea* (☎ 06 626 9111) just east of the antiquity site and nearby golf course; otherwise the *Kibbutz Sedot Yam* (☎ 06 636 4453; 📠 06 626 9122) has a hostel and rooms.

History

The origins of the city lie in the Hellenistic period around the 4C–3C BC, in a small Phoenician port settlement of the Sidonians called Strato's Tower. It was captured by Alexander Jannaeus c 103 BC and was part of the Hasmonean kingdom until Pompey took it in 63 BC and included it in the Roman province of Syria. Mark Antony gave it to Cleopatra, and after Antony and Cleopatra lost the battle of Actium, Rome gave it to Herod the Great c 30 BC. He renamed it Caesarea in honour of Augustus. It is usually called Caesarea Maritima to distinguish it from other cities named in honour of that emperor. Herod rebuilt the city between 22 and 9 BC as another of his great pagan centres of Hellenism: it had all the facilities of a great city of the time, with city walls, temples, public buildings, baths, amphitheatre, fine roads in a planned regular Hippodamian network, and main drains which flushed out to sea; in particular he built a deep water port and commodious warehouses to make it the principal harbour of his kingdom. The construction work was in concrete and stone. A great celebration was held to mark its completion, and every five years the city had a great games festival. It became the Roman headquarters in Palestine from c AD 6 and was from that time the capital of the region for 600 years.

Roman Caesarea became a thriving pagan cultural and economic centre, attracting many immigrants and scholars, and must have been a place of great intellectual vigour. A Jewish community became established, but the Hellenised pagan citizens refused them citizenship; the internecine strife was resolved in favour of the citizens by Nero, and one of the causes of the First Jewish Revolt was a massacre of the Jews of Caesarea by its citizens. After the Revolt was suppressed, Caesarea became the capital of the Roman province and the place of residence of the Roman procurators. Vespasian made it a colonia. Jews, who were forbidden to live in Jerusalem after the Revolt, came increasingly to live at Caesarea. Also in the 1C AD Christianity began to be established in the city. According to the New Testament, the centurion Cornelius invited the apostle Peter to Caesarea (Acts 10) where he preached and converted the first gentiles to Christianity. Paul was brought before the Roman procurator in Caesarea but, demanding his rights as a Roman citizen to be tried before the Emperor, he was duly sent to Rome in AD 59, tried and put to death; some of his letters to the Christian communities abroad were written here. In the 2C AD a Jewish scholar who supported the Second Jewish Revolt, the Rabbi Akiva, was tortured and executed by the Romans in Caesarea. In the 3C AD other important scholars were established in the city: the Jewish Rabbi Hosheya and his students, and the Christian scholar Origen, who made Greek translations of the Hebrew bible and other books. Origen arrived in Caesarea AD 231 and established a great library in the city. Eusebius, who became bishop of Caesarea (315–330) wrote the *History of the Church* and his *Onomasticon* (which has been a fundamental tool for modern scholars in identifying ancient biblical sites). Eusebius also describes the martyrdom of St. Procopius, who was beheaded in Caesarea in AD 303. Procopius was an ascetic and scholar, a man full of divine grace, born in Jerusalem, living in Beth Shean, then arrested in Caesarea. When ordered by the Roman authorities to sacrifice to the pagan gods, he refused, and affirmed the existence of the one god. He was the first Christian martyr in Caesarea during the persecution by Diocletian. Religious strife continued in the Byzantine period, when the Samaritan community in Caesarea revolted against the Byzantine government in AD 548.

Byzantine Caesarea occupied an even greater area than the Roman city, some 160 hectares, with city walls, baths, churches, administrative buildings, shops, amphitheatre, new hippodrome and theatre, and still laid out on a regular grid pattern, of which many remains can be seen. The Byzantine walls were probably built under Justinian. Either at the end of the Byzantine period or soon after the Islamic conquest, the southern half of the city was abandoned and laid out as irrigated agricultural plots; garden terraces, watered by wells, are found over the older remains.

The city was captured by the Muslims in AD 640. The much smaller walled city of the early Islamic period lies beneath the later Crusader town. The harbour was repaired and deepened, and in the Abbasid period rectangular courtyard houses and streets were laid out on the edge of the harbour, with many square stone-lined wells being dug. The ceramics indicate a lively commerce with Egypt. The town continued to be occupied through the Fatimid period right up to the arrival of the Crusaders; many cisterns and cesspits date to the Fatimid period, and store rooms again attest to a lively commerce. Fatimid remains have also been found on the great podium fronting the harbour, and in graves south of the medieval city. A remarkable treasure hidden in a well attests both to the prosperity of the Fatimid town, and to the increasing lack of security at the end of the period.

On the arrival of the Crusaders, the inhabitants submitted to Godfrey de Bouillon and paid tribute, but a revolt in 1101 led to the city being sacked and the inhabitants slaughtered or sold into slavery by Baldwin I. The town declined, even though it was the seat of an archbishop and had a cathedral and other churches. It was the lordship of Eustace Garnier from 1105/10–23 and of his brother Hugh in 1160. The Hospitallers and the Teutonic Knights owned property here, and there may have been a Genoese quarter. The city was captured in 1187 by Salah al-Din, who reduced its defences but abandoned it again to the Crusaders in 1191. Some refortification began in 1217, but this was dismantled by al-Mu'azzam Isa in 1219/20; it was started again in 1228 and completed in 1251/52 by Louis IX (St. Louis). The city fell to Baybars in 1265, and was destroyed by al-Ashraf in 1291.

Various medieval accounts suggest that in turn the Temple of Augustus, the principal Byzantine church, the Early Islamic Great Mosque and the Crusader cathedral all stood on the Herodian podium fronting the harbour, where the apses of the 12C cathedral church of St. Peter have been found.

A small village existed on the site in the 16C–19C. Because it was easily accessible from the sea, the ruined city was further despoiled of building materials for the rebuilding of Akko and Jaffa in the 18C–19C. In the 19C a Circassian settlement was attempted and in the 1880s a Bosnian village was established as these Muslim peoples fled from the Russian Christians. The Crusader fortress was rebuilt as their administrative centre, and the inner harbour area contained the market place and mosques. The inhabitants fled from the Israelis in 1948. The Bosnian mosque is now a shop and the Crusader fortress a restaurant.

The site is large, with many features conserved or reconstructed and excellent facilities. It can be approached via three entrances from the coast road: from the theatre at the south end of the site; south of the Crusader city wall in the centre of the site; or through the east Crusader Gate. There is a large car park between the first two entrances, and you will need to work out the route that best suits the time you have available and the distance you want to walk. Private transport between entrances or the more distant part of the site, such as the aqueducts, makes access easier. The description below mainly follows the National Park's suggested route; the most important sights are the Roman theatre, the Byzantine city, the Crusader walls, and the Roman aqueducts, but the waterfront walks are very pleasant and offer numerous places of interest along the way. If walking from the theatre to the port, take the beach promenade in one direction and the *cardo maximus* (the main north–south road) in the other. Between 4 to 6 hours are needed to see the whole site.

The *theatre lies c 70m inside the south wall of the Byzantine city, reconstructed except for the *scaenae frons*, which originally cut off the view of the sea. Its 3500 seats are frequently used for performances. Originating in the time of Herod, the theatre was continuously maintained throughout the Roman and much of the Byzantine period. It contains many granite columns from Aswan. The two-tiered *cavea* now gives a fine view towards the sea. Near the path to the theatre, look for the replica of the inscription naming the Roman procurator Pontius Pilate, whose official residence was in Caesarea and who is principally famous for his appearance at the trial of Jesus in Jerusalem as described in the New Testament. The inscription was found in 1961, reused in the stairway of the theatre; it records Pilate's dedication of a temple to the Emperor Tiberias c AD 26–36. The original is in the Israel Museum. The surviving fortifications around the theatre are of a Byzantine citadel guarding the south end of the city.

Walking along the north side of the fortification to a rocky promontory jutting into the sea, the rectangular foundation rock cuttings of a Herodian **palace** can be seen in a splendid marine setting. On the landward side some reconstruction work has been carried out.

Turning north along the seashore, much of the Herodian **amphitheatre** or stadium can be seen parallel to the beach promenade, although its west side has disappeared into the sea. Built in the late 1C BC, it measures c 265m x 50m, and has 12 rows of seats providing space for 10,000 spectators of horse and chariot racing and other entertainment (athletics, wrestling, gladiatorial fights) in the Roman period. Its main entrance was at the centre of the curved south end, with another on the east side through an ascending vault. The amphitheatre was remodelled on various occasions during its two centuries of use. The amphitheatre went out of use, and houses were built within its structure in the 2C AD. After the 7C the area was used for agriculture, and the stones were robbed.

Inland from the amphitheatre are the remains of a vast public **bath house** complex, built in the 4C AD and occupying the whole south half of an *insula*, which was repaired during the later Byzantine period. The main entrance is at the centre of the east side. The hot and cold baths with lavatory were in the southwest quarter of the building and the palaestra (gymnasium) was on the north side. Pavings of white and figured mosaic and marble, ceramic waterpipes, and frescoes were all parts of the fittings. The bath house was out of use before the end of the Byzantine period.

Southeast of the amphitheatre part of a badly robbed **church** was excavated, perhaps dating to the early Byzantine period. It had an atrium, narthex, three-aisled basilica with an inscription 'for the salvation of Sylvanus and Nunias' in a mosaic in the north aisle.

Above the eastern side of the amphitheatre, built over the fill which sealed it, was a later **palatial building** with courtyards and fine *opus sectile* and mosaic floors on an upper eastern level; a lower western level had a fountain in an exedra above a pavilion which probably descended to a garden facing the sea, laid out over the old amphitheatre.

Towards the north of the beach area are the great **warehouse vaults** originally built in the Herodian period and modified in the Late Roman period. In all there were perhaps four or five *insulae* of 20 vaults along the waterfront. In one of the vaults to the northwest was a Mithraeum, the focus of the cult of the god Mithras which was widespread among the soldiers of the Roman army. In the south side of the *insula* lying south of the medieval city wall, a series of vaults included one with a fresco of Christ with 12 haloed disciples. A complex of Byzantine administrative and commercial buildings, with mosaics, square wells and latrines, were subsequently built over the vaults in this central area, but most of the columns from the great colonnaded streets of Caesarea were used in the building of the Crusader harbour.

A promontory on the site of the Herodian south breakwater juts out and shelters the ***port**, which has a long and intricate history.

History of the port

Originally a natural bay was sheltered by rocks and reefs to the southwest. A round tower in the middle of the bay protected the original harbour of Strato's Tower in Hellenistic times. This harbour silted up so that the Hellenistic tower now lies only c 25m out from the modern beach. The harbour built by Herod the Great greatly enlarged the Hellenistic port. A 400m long curving breakwater on the south and west was built with an entrance gap at the northwest with a shorter breakwater on the north. The outer breakwater was located nearly 400m west of the modern beach. It was built by sinking great wooden box frames loaded with mixtures of marine cement and stones to create an immense 'outer harbour'. An inner harbour (c 250m north/south) had quays on north, east and south. The outer part of the Herodian breakwater had been destroyed in Roman times, probably around the end of the 1C AD (it can be seen as a dark area below the surface of the sea). Some work was done on the middle section of the harbour by the Emperor Anastasius (AD 491–518), by which time the Hellenistic inner harbour had probably silted up. In the later Byzantine period the inner harbour had houses built over it. They continued to be occupied in the Umayyad period and were probably destroyed in the earthquake of AD 749. The 'middle harbour' was again restored and deepened in the 8C–9C. The Crusaders built a new mole around the 'middle harbour', using more than 100 columns of reused Aswan and Troad granite and marble columns taken from the ruined city, many of which can still be seen in the water.

The Crusader citadel, the 'central keep' of the city was a separately fortified strong place. At Caesarea, this was built on the great rock which forms the base of the Hellenistic and Roman work on the promontory above the south side of the harbour. It is more than 100m from the shore and was then islanded from the city by a sea ditch 20m wide. The Crusader citadel was built either in the 12C or early 13C, with a gate facing the harbour on the northeast and two strong towers on the west. Great chunks of fallen masonry from the citadel can be seen under the restaurant, from which an excellent view may be had over the harbour. The 'middle harbour' today has a modern fishing dock.

The **Roman wall** lies a little to the north of the medieval fortifications; a tower, and a gate with a round tower were probably built over the fortification of the earlier port.

The **Temple of Augustus** was built high on the massive podium overlooking the Roman harbour. A huge rectangular podium, on a different alignment to the streets, was constructed in the Roman period of large ashlar blocks. It fronted the harbour, and the west front was recessed, bounding the east side of a piazza, across the centre of which a monumental staircase ascended to the temple from the piazza and the harbour. On the north side of the staircase was a nymphaeum (shrine of the nymphs) with large statues set in niches. On the south side was a luxurious bath house with mosaics. No trace of the temple itself has been located, except for a possible outline of the foundation. The first clear remains surviving on the top of the podium are of an octagonal church, identified as the martyrium of St. Procopius, built in the late 5C; this existed until the end of the Byzantine period but was destroyed by the 9C. The west part of the podium appears to have been used for processing building materials in the 8C, but the northern vaults collapsed in the early Islamic period; the location of the Great Mosque referred to in the 10C–11C is uncertain. In the Crusader period the cathedral was constructed on the southwest part of the podium. The apses and part of the west wall of the 12C **Cathedral Church of St. Peter** survive. It had three apses with sanctuaries, three aisles of five bays, an *opus sectile* floor, and was by tradition located on the site of the house of Cornelius who was visited by St. Peter. A second apse west of the earlier one may be repair work after 1191 or 1220. Whether the work had been completed by the time the city fell in 1265 is unknown, and it is uncertain whether the final phase of the cathedral was completed.

The *city walls, gate and moat** of the **Crusader town** replaced a Fatimid town, and incorporated parts of the older early (9C?) Islamic wall on the same lines as well as reusing many houses. The Crusader town covered just 450m x 250m,

surrounded by ramparts 13m high, a notable glacis (sloping bank) 8m in length, and a moat 7–8m wide and 4–6m deep with a vertical counter-scarp. The fortifications included nine towers on the east, four on the south and three on the north, though the sea wall of Caesarea has virtually disappeared. The main gateways had bent entrances and fine rib vaulting, with a hidden postern exit leading into the moat near each gate, that on the south being well preserved. There is a fine view of the east wall and of the east city gate from outside the walls. The wall built by Louis IX in 1250/51 widened the Islamic wall and in turn overlies a Byzantine wall which was 3.8m wide and which may have been part of the 4C–5C repairs to the harbour.

The moat and bastions of the Crusader town, east side

Excavation of six houses south of the east gate against the inside of the city wall showed the houses had a second storey which extended over a roofed street, and were constructed after the city wall had been built in 1250/51. They also reused parts of older Fatimid structures. They contained rectangular rooms arranged around courtyards, with wall cupboards, cisterns, wells, and evidence that animals were tethered and kept in the lower storeys. The preserved postern gate/tunnel complex lies just south of these houses in the southeast angle of the city wall.

The **Byzantine city** was larger than the Roman city and much larger than the medieval one. The Byzantine wall was 2,600m long, with many gates and square towers. Its south gate lies within Kibbutz Sedot Yam (see below). Just across the road from the Crusader east gate, at the back of modern buildings among trees, is an excavated area of the Byzantine **street**, called 'Statues Square', which illustrates how much bigger the city was in the earlier period. Two vast headless statues survive, one of marble and one of porphyry (a heavy purple-red igneous rock imported from Egypt). The size of the statues makes it likely that they were of Roman emperors, and it has been suggested that the porphyry statue is of Hadrian. They once flanked the entrance to a public building. A mosaic inscription records that the square was renovated in the 6C AD, in the time of the magistrate Flavius Stratigius. It probably lay on the *decumanus maximus* of the city.

The **amphitheatre** which lies in the northeast sector of the site probably dated to the 2C AD and may have been used for gladiatorial and wild beast displays.

The **hippodrome** for chariot racing, and with seating for 30,000, lies in the southeast sector; columns marked the *spina* with a porphyry obelisk 27m high.

There were two *aqueducts**, at high and low level. The seaside town, on the flat and sandy coastal plain, had no fresh water supply, and water was brought by a **high level aqueduct** 7.5km from the springs at Shuni in the north, and later from other sources. The high level aqueduct had first one, and finally three channels, as more water was needed. Running on high round arches in low-lying areas, and in a 442m-long rock-cut tunnel through ridges, the remains of this aqueduct make a fine sight along the beach north of Caesarea. It seems likely that the eastern channel was first built in the Herodian period, but many features of the building style are typical of the mid-1C AD; the western channel was added in the 2C AD. It was repaired by the Roman legions stationed here during the Second Jewish Revolt (AD 131/32–135), the Leg II Traiana Fortis and the Leg X Fretensis, when the town was the headquarters of the Roman army in the province. The aqueduct continued in use until the Late Byzantine period. Part has been eroded by the sea. The **low level aqueduct** brought five times the quantity of water from a reservoir on the Crocodile River; it is 5km long, and can be seen crossing the fields to the north of the city. It was in use until the 5C. Both high and low level aqueducts came together just north of the city. A repair in the Crusader period is noted. The city also depended on wells and rain-fed cisterns within its walls. A public beach is adjacent to the high level aqueduct.

There is a **museum** of finds from Caesarea at Kibbutz Sedot Yam, where the Byzantine south gate of the city was discovered. The kibbutz (which also offers accommodation) was founded in 1940 just south of Caesarea. Some mosaics from the site can also be seen in the Museum of Ancient Art in Haifa and there are other finds in the Israel Museum in Jerusalem.

ARSUF

• • • • • • • •

At Arsuf (H. Tel Arshaf, Byzantine Apollonia, Crusader Arsur) are the ruins of a large town of the Byzantine and early Islamic periods, with a Crusader fortress, walled town and harbour. These are located on the coast, 2km north of the Herzliyya turning, off Highway 2 to Herzliyya Pituach; you turn west towards the coast to find the car park on the cliffs north of the prominent mosque of Sidna 'Ali. The site is run by the National Parks Authority.

History

A Phoenician trading port (?Arshof) was founded on a natural haven in the late 6C BC and is noted in the Persian and Hellenistic periods for dye-making. It expanded greatly to c 60 hectares in the Byzantine period when it was an unfortified city called Apollonia. It did not have a natural water supply, and depended on rainwater storage in cisterns and reservoirs. Excavations revealed evidence for glass-making in the 6C–7C AD in an industrial northern quarter as well as for oil and wine production. Captured by the Persians in AD 614, and then by the Arabs, a town (called Arsuf), approximately one-third the size of its predecessor, was fortified in the Early Islamic period by a wall and a rock-cut ditch on the landward side, and by a wall and kurkar cliff above the beach. Its comprehensive town planning may originate in the early Islamic period, under the caliph Abd al-Malik. It was one of the 13 major early Arab cities of Palestine, with a fine market street lined with food stalls

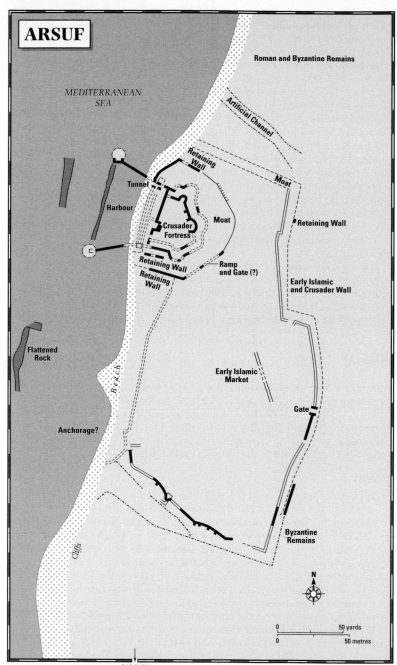

ARSUF

MEDITERRANEAN SEA

Roman and Byzantine Remains

Artificial Channel

Retaining Wall

Moat

Tunnel

Harbour

Retaining Wall

Crusader Fortress

Moat

Early Islamic and Crusader Wall

Retaining Wall

Retaining Wall

Ramp and Gate (?)

Beach

Flattened Rock

Early Islamic Market

Gate

Anchorage?

Byzantine Remains

Cliffs

N

0   50 yards
0   50 metres

CAR PARK
HARAM SIDNA ALI

and shops which continued in use from the 7C to the 13C, and shows no sign of destruction in the earthquake of 749. It was a city of ransom for Byzantine captives, and a beacon site on the main road from Egypt to Mesopotamia.

The army of the First Crusade coming south along the coast in 1099 reached the port of Arsuf, which had a Muslim garrison dependent on the Fatimid administration in Egypt. Arsuf offered to surrender to Raymond of Toulouse, but Godfrey of Bouillon jealously refused to honour any agreement made by Raymond. In 1100 the men of Arsuf, still hoping to agree terms, sent hostages; in return they admitted a Crusader guarantor, Gerard of Avesnes. However, Godfrey wanted more direct control, as the inhabitants were in touch with Egypt by sea. So he attacked the town. The men of Arsuf promptly suspended Gerard of Avesnes outside the walls, and although Gerard begged Godfrey not to shoot, by the time the men of Arsuf generously hauled him back into the town the unfortunate hostage was riddled with 12 of his compatriots' arrows. After the Arsuf garrison had destroyed the Crusader siege towers with Greek fire, Godfrey abandoned the siege. But he left half his army at Ramla with orders to ravage the country around Arsuf, and prevent the people from tilling their fields. Three months later Arsuf sent an embassy to Godfrey, who accepted their submission. Amazingly, Gerard reappeared having recovered from his injuries, and Godfrey—presumably feeling a little guilty—presented him with the fief of St. Abraham (Hebron). Godfrey however still wanted Arsuf to be taken outright, and in 1101 with the help of the Genoese the town was captured. The Muslim garrison left, and was replaced by a Frankish garrison.

Arsuf was owned by the Frankish king until 1163, when it became the seat of an independent Crusader lordship; but it was lost in 1187. Though the Battle of Arsuf in 1191 (Richard of England against Salah al-Din) was not decisive, the outcome favoured Richard, and Arsuf was again in Crusader hands between 1191 and 1265. Sources suggest there was a Church of St. Mary in Arsuf in 1191. In 1261 Balian of Ibelin leased his lordship of Arsuf to the Knights of the Hospital as he could not afford its defence. In 1265 there were 270 knights defending the castle of Arsuf against the Mamluk sultan Baybars, and it was well provisioned; but the siege engines broke the outer walls and the lower town fell. Three days later the citadel surrendered on condition that the survivors went free, but Baybars broke his promise.

Entrance is from the car park on the south side of the site on the cliffs above the beach. The ruins stretch c 400m north–south along the coast in sandy scrub, c 150m east–west, but the scattered and slightly excavated remains of the Byzantine town are found over a greater area to the east. The outline of a defensive wall and a rock-cut ditch on the landward side, and a wall on the *kurkar* cliff above the beach can be clearly seen; the fortifications were built in the early Islamic period and repaired by the Crusaders. A section of the southeast wall, 1m wide with buttresses, a tower and the moat, can be seen to the right; to the left are some of the excavated remains of a villa of the Early Roman period. The citadel in the northwest has been almost completely cleared. The remains of a very strongly fortified Crusader fortress have been excavated, revealing an irregular concentric plan with projecting rounded towers and a 13C gatehouse on a natural hill surrounded by a rock-cut ditch. At the edge of the ditch is a good view down to the harbour. Two rock-hewn tunnels have been located, one of which connected the citadel to the moat, and the other the citadel to the harbour. It is unclear whether they are defensive, or were constructed during a siege. Inside the citadel, the base of steps leading up to the massive donjon have been revealed, with a round feature beneath them.

Descending from the car park to the beach, spectacular lumps of fallen masonry lie fallen from the sea walls on the cliffs above the beach. The citadel overlooks a built harbour with two moles and a breakwater (34m x 94m). An anchorage sheltered by reefs lies to the south.

South of the car park, 800m south of ancient Arsuf, lies a striking walled enclosure. The Muslim **shrine of Haram Sidna Ali** (Sayyidna Ali, Sayyiduna Ali or al-Haram) on the cliffs overlooking the sea marks the venerated tomb (wali) of Ali ibn Alim, a descendant of the Caliph Umar. According to the inscription he died in 1081. The core of the present structure may date to the time of Shams al-Din Abu'l Awn, the custodian in 1481. He is said to have dug the well, and built a tower in 1485. The venerated tomb was the focus of a popular annual Muslim pilgrimage, and ranked with other Muslim festivals at Nabi Musa and Nabi Rubin south of Tel Aviv. A Palestinian village called al-Haram was built around the shrine, but both it and the shrine were captured in 1948 and the village has since disappeared. The entrance on the north side of the shrine leads into a small outer court, with ablutions fountain and rooms, thence into the main court. The minaret stands beside the inner gate. The main court is lined by porticoes with upper rooms (of Ottoman date) to east and west. The tomb, open to the sky, stands before the mihrab. The inscription appears to be of Ottoman date. The octagonal minaret replaces the minaret destroyed by naval bombardment during the First World War. The shrine has seen a number of repairs in the 19C and 20C. A cemetery lies adjacent.

TEL AVIV AND JAFFA/YAFO

The largest city in Israel, Tel Aviv was declared the capital in 1948 and, although Jerusalem was declared capital in 1949, is still the location of most embassies. It is also the country's business centre. The city spreads along the central coastline from north of the mouth of the Yarkon River and includes, to the south, the old town of Jaffa. Tel Aviv is backed by major highways connecting the north and south of the country and to Jerusalem, 62km to the east. The modern city is built mainly on the coastal sand dunes and kurkar ridges and extends into the fertile plain behind. The temperature in January ranges from 9° to 17° C, and in August from 22° to 29° C, and the humidity on the coast is high. The mean annual rainfall is 539mm, most of it falling in winter. It has numerous hotels and is an organised tourist centre, with all the amenities of city life as well as good beaches. Tel Aviv/Jaffa is the centre of Israel's night life with more restaurants, more cafés, more bars, more night clubs and more concerts (outdoor in summer) than anywhere else in Israel. Jaffa is the old Palestinian port town on the site of the ancient Canaanite Joppa, and was included within the city of Tel Aviv in 1950. In 1995 the total population was 356,000 including 15,000 Arabs and other non-Jewish communities.

Practical information

Getting there

The international Ben Gurion Airport is 18km southeast of Tel Aviv. For details of the airport and travel into the city from there, see p 16.

Many companies offer package tours to Tel Aviv, and public transport makes it a good centre for touring. **Central Bus Terminal** at Rehov Levinsky near the centre of town (☎ 03 638 4040). Regular fast *Egged* **buses** connect the North Bus Station on Rehov Arlosoroff, with the main bus station in Jerusalem (*Egged* bus information, ☎ 03 537 5555; for *Dan Bus Lines*, ☎ 03 639 4444). The **Central Railway Station** (☎ 03 577 4000), is nearby; however, the daily railway service to Jerusalem no longer runs, and the train services along the coast from Tel Aviv are mainly used for freight. sharut taxi services offer a good alternative.

Information offices

Government Tourist Office, Entrance Hall, 69 Rehov ibn Gavirol, ☎ 03 521 8500; open Sun–Thur 08.30–17.00, Fri 08.30–14.00. *IGTO* at the Central Bus Station, ☎ 03 639 5660, ▤ 03 639 5659. *International Phone Center*, 13 Rehov Frishman, open Sun–Thur 08.00–23.00, Fri 08.00–14.30, Sat 06.30–midnight.

Where to stay

Dan Panorama, 10 Koifman, near the beach (☎ 03 519 0190; fax 03 517 1777), *Hilton*, Independence Park, beach front (☎ 03 520 2222; ▤ 03 527 2711),

Sheraton, 115 Hayarkon, (☎ 03 521 1111; ▤ 03 523 3322) and *Holiday Inn*, 145 Hayarkon (☎ 03 520 1111; ▤ 03 520 1122). Tel Aviv has the appropriate to a major city. Prices of more moderate hotels are also generally higher than other towns: *Ami*, 152 Hayarkon (☎ 03 524 9141; ▤ 03 523 1151); *Moss*, 6 Nes Ziona (☎/▤ 03 517 1655); cheaper hotels *Bell*, 12 Allenby, near beach (☎ 03 517 4291; ▤ 03 517 4352); *HaGalil*, 23 Bet Yosef, Kerem Hataymanim (☎ 03 517 5036); *Maxim*, 86 Hayarkon, sea front; and many hostels (*Gordon Hostel*, 2 Gordon, ☎ 03 522 9870; ▤ 03 523 7419) including two in Jaffa (*Old Jaffa Hostel*, 8 Olei Tziyon, ☎ 03 682 2370; ▤ 03 682 2316).

Eating out

Tel Aviv/Haifa is the centre of Israel's night life, has more restaurants, more cafés, more bars, more night clubs and concerts (outdoor in summer) and more choice on non-kosher places than anywhere else in the country. Food stalls, markets and ice cream places abound. There are some very expensive and good restaurants, and many well-established and popular local places, many are located around the main squares and streets: *Batya*, serving Jewish food, 197 Dizengoff; *Vienna*, with Ashkenazi dishes, midday, 48 Ben Yehuda; *Zion*, Yemeni menu, not Shabbat, 28 Peduyim, Kerem Hataymanim. In Jaffa, *Dr Shakshuka*, North African food, at 3 Bet Eshel. There are some expensive but good fish restaurants, at the port, *Taboon* (☎ 03 681 1176) and *Turquoise*, Bat Galim, Jaffa.

History of Jaffa

Jaffa (H. Yafo), ancient Joppa, was sited on one of the few promontories on the coast—probably a navigational focus in ancient times, and where limited shelter was provided by offshore reefs. The reefs offered quite good anchorage in the summer months, but otherwise the harbour of Jaffa was treacherous. Jaffa nonetheless developed as a port, but in very ancient times the estuary of the Yarkon River to the north was probably a safer haven for small boats. Settlement of the region dates from at least the sixth millennium. Early in the second millennium the coastal area seems to have been more densely settled, and part of a rampart dating to the 18C BC has been excavated at Jaffa. Joppa was a port frequently mentioned in Egyptian documents of the Late Bronze Age. A story recounts its capture, using an Ali Baba type trick, by an official of Tuthmosis III in the 15C BC, when 200 Egyptian soldiers were smuggled into the town in baskets; in the Amarna Letters of the 14C BC it is recorded as an Egyptian centre. Archaeological excavations have recovered part of the threshold of the citadel gateway with a bronze door hinge and a passage within; below this gate were the remains of an earlier gateway which had been destroyed by fire in the late 13C BC, its door jambs were inscribed with the titles and name of Ramses II. This gate cut into still earlier levels dating to the 18C–14C BC.

Afterwards Joppa was part of the Philistine kingdom, a dependency of Sidqa, King of Ashkelon. Fragmentary remains of the 11C have been excavated, in particular characteristic Philistine painted pottery and the remains of what was probably a Philistine temple. Joppa features in many stories. In the Old Testament, the Yarkon River may be the place to which the cedar logs used for the building of Solomon's Temple (10C BC?) and for Herod's Temple (1C BC) in Jerusalem were floated from the Lebanon. Remains of the 8C BC include evidence of the sloped revetment for a rampart. It was captured by Sennacherib in 701 BC. In the 5C the ruler of Sidon claims Jaffa was given to him by his Persian overlord, and evidence of a Sidonian occupation has been found. It is the location of the story (perhaps developed in the 4C BC) of Jonah and the whale.

The city was colonised by the Greeks, and in Greek mythology it was linked with Jopa, daughter of Aeolus, god of the winds. It was also associated with the story of Andromeda, chained to the rock to be eaten by a dragon and rescued by Perseus (the north end of the Jaffa Reef is known as Andromeda's Rock). Parts of a fortress dating from the 3C BC were uncovered, as well as other remains of the Hellenistic period. Agricultural estates from the time of Ptolemy II in the 3C BC and from the 2C–1C BC were located in the region. Mainly pagan with a Jewish community, the town was captured from the Seleucids by the Hasmoneans, and became the port of Judaea. Archaeological evidence for Jewish and Samaritan occupation has been uncovered.

In the New Testament Joppa is the location of the house of Simon the Tanner (Acts 10:6–9), and where Peter brought Tabitha back to life (Acts 9:36–43). In Roman times it was a less important port than Caesarea, and during the First Jewish Revolt (AD 66–73) it was destroyed, first by Gallus and then by Vespasian in AD 67, and was then romanised as Flavia Ioppa; its continued occupation is illustrated by cemeteries, and by buildings of the Roman, Byzantine and Early Islamic periods in the west part of the Old City. Jaffa became the main port again in early Islamic times, when the Umayyads made Ramla (see p 315) their capital city; it was fortified in the Abbasid period.

Jaffa was occupied unopposed in June 1099 by the Crusaders, and promptly refortified. Its importance continued under the Crusaders when it was the port for Jerusalem, and the principal anchorage on the coast south of Acre. The County of Jaffa lay under the lordship of Hugh Le Puiset, and was later combined with Ascalon, Ramla, Mirabel and Ibelin. Jaffa in the 12C had a citadel (located on the ancient tell) and a lower walled town. The principal church of St. Peter was a dependency of the Church of the Holy Sepulchre in Jerusalem, built probably c 1102 in the citadel, perhaps on the site of an earlier church. The citadel also held the house of the Patriarch of Jerusalem, that of the Count of Jaffa, and one belonging to the Templars; the Teutonic Order and the Hospitallers also had land in the town, as did the Pisans. The existence of other churches and chapels in Jaffa is also variously recorded, but none are known to have survived. The lower town had a sea gate and two land gates.

The town changed hands between Christians and Muslims in 1187, 1191, 1197 and 1204; it was desolate by 1217, restored under Frederick II between 1228 and 1229, but then there were quarrels between Patriarch and Count, and the latter was excommunicated in 1244. Despite a considerable investment in the fortifications, in 1268 Jaffa fell to Baybars, who slighted the walls and mined the town for building materials for his mosque in Cairo. Very few traces of the Crusader period have been found in excavation, apart from some pottery, and some vaults and a bread oven in the centre of the town, and it seems likely that the Church of St. Peter was destroyed at this time.

Some improvement in conditions is described in the early 14C, but in 1344–46 the town's buildings and harbour were destroyed by the Mamluks to prevent further use by the Crusaders. It remained however the port of entry for pilgrims going via Ramla to Jerusalem until modern times. Franciscans from Ramla used to meet pilgrims at the port in the 15C, and a Franciscan house was re-established in Jaffa in 1654. A round tower, which may date to the 16C and belong to a Turkish fort noted in the 17C–18C, is built into the northeast corner of the Franciscan convent (built 1881–91). Aga Mahmud, who ruled Jaffa between 1803 and 1819, fortified the town, and it is particularly his work that can be seen in the old city today.

As large steamships were developed in the 19C, they had to anchor off Jaffa while the passengers and goods were off-loaded in small boats. Jaffa oranges, cultivated extensively in the coastal plain by the Palestinians, were among the principal exports. The port, its small harbour protected by a breakwater, played a role in the 19C economic and demographic growth of Palestine. By the end of the 19C the expansion of the town beyond the walls provided the impetus for the development of Tel Aviv, and in 1906 in the jubilee celebrations for Sultan Abd al-Hamid II, the old town walls were demolished, and a clock tower built. Increasing tension existed between the inhabitants of the Arab town and the adjacent new Jewish settlement of Tel Aviv (which achieved municipal autonomy from 1923), and following Arab riots in 1936, the British Mandate authorities blew up part of the old town. Most of its Arab inhabitants and those of the coastal villages fled in the war of 1948, and the old town of Jaffa was merged with the new town of Tel Aviv in 1950. Since

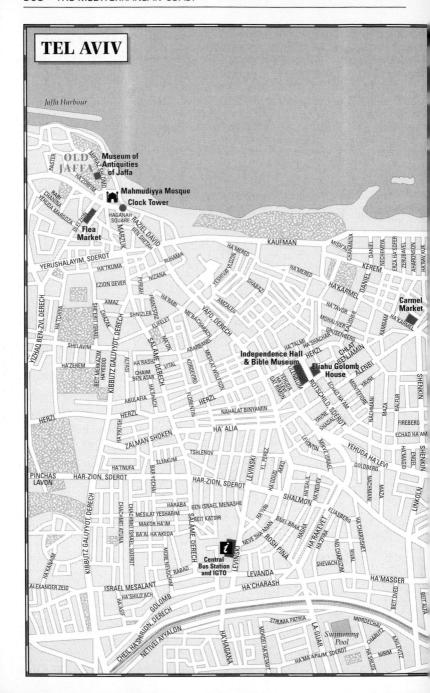

TEL AVIV

Jaffa Harbour

OLD JAFFA

PASTER

MIFRAZ SHLOMO

HA'ZORFIM

Museum of Antiquities of Jaffa

Mahmudiyya Mosque

Clock Tower

RABI CHANINA

YEHUDA MARGOZA

OLEI ZION

MARZUK

HAGANAH SQUARE

RAZIEL DAVID

BEN SHETAN

Flea Market

YERUSHALAYIM, SDEROT

HA'TKUMA

EZION GEVER

RUHAMA

NIZANA

PORIAH

KAUFMAN

HA'MERED

HA'MERED

MISH'A

CHANANIYA

DANIEL

SHECHEMIYA

ERZA HA'SOFER

ZERUBAVEL

AHARONSON

DANIEL

KEREM

HATAVI KUK

YESHIVAT VOLOZIN

SHABAZI

HA'KARMEL

Carmel Market

YIZHAQ BEN-ZVI, DERECH

HATCHVIA

SHERIT ISRAEL

CAZAK

AMAZ

HA'RABI

SHNIZLER

ELFELET

MA'ON

AMZALEG

YAFO, DERECH

ME'BACHARACH

ABARBANEL

MESILAT WOLFSON

HA'TAVOR

MOHALIVER

KALISHER

GRUSENBERG

RAMBAM

HA'KARMEL

SHELAVIM

HA'ZEREM

BEIT MERKAZIM HAYESOD

KIBBUTZ GALUYYOT, DERECH

HA'RASHIT

ALFASI

VITAL

CHAIM BEN ATAR

HA'SHACH

KORDEVRO

FLORENTIN

HATALMI

HA'SHACHAR

YEHUDA HALEVON

CAP'EMON

NACHLIELI

ROTSCHILD, SDEROT

ECHAD HA'AM

Independence Hall & Bible Museum

Eliahu Golomb House

CHLAT

BENJAMIN

ALENBI

MONTEFIORE

YAVNE

MAZA

BALFUR

SHENKIN

HERZL

HERZL

HERZL

ABULAFIA

HA'PLATELET

HERZL

ZALMAN SHOKEN

NAHALAT BINYAMIN

HA' ALIA

YAVNE SDEROT

MIKVE ISRAEL

LEVANTIN

YEHUDA HA'LEVI

SHADADATI

NACHMANI

GOLDBERG

FIREBERG

ECHAD HA'AM

HA'MAGID

ENGEL

HA'TNUFA

ELYAKUM

TSHLENOV

BAR YOCHAI

PINCHAS LAVON

HAR-ZION, SDEROT

HARABA

MESILAT YESHARIM

MAKOR HA'IM

BA'AL HA'AKEDA

BEN ISRAEL MENASHE

BEIT KATSIR

LEVINSKI

Y.L. PEREZ

HABDUD

AKKO

HA'GAUL

HA'NEGEV

HA'YRI

BNEI-BRAK

HABRA

SHALMON

NEVE SHA'NAN

ROSH PINA

HA'RAKEVET

HA'ZRIA

ELUASBERG

YAD CHARUZIM

HA'CHARUSHET

RIVAL

HXYMAGID

NIXONNT

KIBBUTZ GALUYYOT, DERECH

CHACHMEI ATUNA

CHACHMEI ISRAEL SDEROT

MORE NEVOCHIM

RABAD

i

Central Bus Station and IGTO

LEVINSKI

LEVANDA

HA'CHARASH

SHEVACH

HA'MASGER

BEIT OVED

BEIT ALFA

ALEXANDER ZEID

HA'KANAM

ISRAEL MESALANT

HA'SHILO'ACH

HA'ASIF

GOLOMB

GOLOMB, DERECH

CHEIL HASHIRION, DERECH

NETIVEI AYALON

HA'HAGANA

STRUMA PATRIA

MORDEI HA'GETAOT

LA GUAR

HA'MA'APILIM, SDEROT

MORDECHAI

Swimming Pool

CHARLUTZ

ANILEVITZ

NIRIM

HA'SHLUS

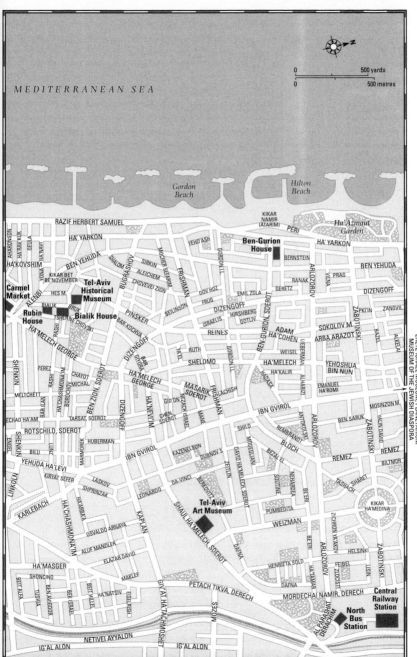

MEDITERRANEAN SEA

Gordon Beach

Hilton Beach

Ha'Azmaut Garden

KIKAR NAMIR (ATARIM)

Ben-Gurion House

Carmel Market

Rubin House

Tel-Aviv Historical Museum

Bialik House

Tel-Aviv Art Museum

North Bus Station

Central Railway Station

KIKAR HA'MEDINA

ERETZ ISRAEL MUSEUM, PLANETARIUM
MUSEUM OF THE JEWISH DIASPORA

0   500 yards
0   500 metres

the 1930s Jaffa's history has been largely that of Tel Aviv. Its port has been a fishing and pleasure base since 1968, and the old city has been developed for leisure and tourism. Its restored 19C buildings and alleys provide a contrast to the intensive modern development of the coastal plain. Today the Palestinian population lives mostly south of Jaffa.

Old Jaffa

Old Jaffa contains a number of places of interest as well as many modern craft and souvenir shops, and is noted for its artists' quarter, clubs and nightlife. In and around the hill of Jaffa are many churches and mosques, as well as the 19C buildings which mark its historical character.

At the north end of Jaffa, the **Clock Tower** in Haganah Square was built in 1906 (with more recent decorations) to celebrate the 30th jubilee of Sultan Abd al-Hamid II, then ruler of Palestine. The **flea market** (Shuq Hapishpeshim) for crafts and junk can be found one block to the south. To the west of Haganah Square in Rehov Mifratz Shlomo, on the right is the **Mahmudiyya** or Great Mosque with minaret and porticoes, built by Aga Mahmud in 1812 incorporating material from older sites. The fountain in the south wall of the mosque is also his work. On the left at 10 Rehov Mifratz Shlomo, is the *Museum of Antiquities of Tel Aviv-Jaffa**, on the site of Aga Mahmud's palace (open Sun–Thur 09.00–14.00, Wed 09.00–13.00 and 14.00–19.00, Sat 10.00–14.00). The displays include archaeological finds from Jaffa from the Neolithic period onwards, the most spectacular of which are the inscribed stone door jambs of the Egyptian ruler, Ramses II, which in the 13C were part of an imposing entrance to the Egyptian citadel of Jaffa, and were excavated under the bath house next to the museum. The restaurant next door to the museum lies on the 19C bath house. Further along, you get a view of the harbour and of the breakwater and reefs, of which the northern is Andromeda's Rock (see History of Jaffa, above). A flight of steps descends to the port; beyond them is the Franciscan **Church of St. Peter**, marked by its bell tower (open 08.00–12.00, 15.00–18.00 or –17.00 in winter). Opposite, more steps ascend to Kikkar Kedumim, the main square: in its centre you can view some 2C BC and later fragments of ancient Jaffa.

Descending to the southwest, you will see a small mosque near the lighthouse in Rehov Shimon Haburski: the **Jami al-Tayiba** (Mosque of the Bastion) is the traditional location of the House of Simon the Tanner. The ablutions fountain incorporates an old well and a reused Roman sarcophagus. The tradition that this was the location of the house of Simon may be at least as early as the 13C.

History of Tel Aviv

The separate development of Tel Aviv dates from 1906, although it includes several earlier enclaves, Arab and Jewish, within the modern boundaries. These include the German Templer Colony (see also p 290) which was established in 1869; some of its buildings (including the Immanuel Church) still exist about 700m northeast of the old city of Jaffa, east of Jerusalem Boulevard and south of Elat Road.

The history of Tel Aviv is closely associated with the history of modern Israel; many events marking the progress to statehood took place here, and are marked by heritage sites. Many streets are named for the major figures of 19C–20C Jewish history: Rehov Herzl, the main street, was named for the founder of Zionism (Theodore Herzl, 1860–1904), as was the first secular high school in the country in which Hebrew was the language employed for teaching. With increased Jewish immigration after the First World War, Tel Aviv was made a separate township with its own administration and culture, which was increasingly influenced by Western Jewry. When tensions between Arab and Jewish communities increased in the 1930s, with Arab riots and closure of the port of Jaffa to Jewish trade in 1936, a small alternative port was developed off the north suburbs of Tel Aviv. As the Mandate troops withdrew, on Friday, 14 May 1948, Ben-Gurion declared the State of Israel in the hall of the Tel Aviv Museum, with Tel Aviv as the capital. The Knesset (Parliament) was established in a hall at 1 Rehov Allenby. War broke out on 15 May, and was followed by the flight of most of the Arab inhabitants of Jaffa; their houses were taken by the massive influx of Jewish immigrants that followed. The seat of government was moved to Jerusalem in 1949. In 1950 the two towns were merged under one administration. Since then the town has continued to grow, spreading north across the Yarkon in the 1960s. The port facilities were superseded by those of Ashdod in 1968, and Tel Aviv is now a harbour for fishing boats and yachts, with good beaches. Prime Minister Y. Rabin was murdered in Tel Aviv in 1995 by a Jewish assassin.

What to see in Tel Aviv

Rehov Dizengoff is the main shopping area, and has a pedestrianised section for cafés and restaurants near Kikkar Dizengoff (Dizengoff Square) with its Fountain of Fire and Water, at the junction with George HaMelech. Kikkar Magen David at the south end of George HaMelech used to be the arterial pivot of the city. In the 1930s a distinctive architectural style deriving from the German Bauhaus genre developed in Tel Aviv, and the houses in this style add character to the modern city. As well as the Philharmonic Orchestra, concert hall and theatres, there are many small museums and libraries relating to the history, activities and personalities of the 20C city. Tel Aviv has excellent beaches stretching along most of the waterfront.

Northern area

North of the Yarkon River in the suburb of Ramat-Aviv, on HaUniversita off Derekh Haifa, is the ***Eretz Israel Museum** (☎ 03 641 5244; formerly the Haaretz Museum). It houses the Alphabet Museum, the Glass Museum, the Kadman Numismatic Museum, Museum of Ceramics, and Museum of Science and Technology, Mining, Ethnography, and is a storehouse of finds from the region with excellent displays showing craft processes such as weaving. Open Sun–Thur 09.00–14.00, Tues 09.00–14.00 and 16.00–19.00, Sat 10.00–14.00; closed Fri. Beside the museum is the site of **Tel Qasile**. Here on the north bank of the Yarkon River, was an important Philistine settlement. Finds from the site (dating from the 13C BC to the 15C AD) are displayed in the museum. Near the main entrance of the museum is part of a mosaic with an inscription in Samaritan script, in the remains of a church or synagogue of the late 6C to early 7C AD, which was probably located outside the settlement of Tel Qasile. Nearby is the **Planetarium** with hourly shows from 10.00 (admission charged). Further along the road is the University of Tel Aviv (guided tours available), with the Nahum Goldmann **Museum of the Jewish Diaspora** (the Beit Hatefutzot, established in 1978). This has interactive displays and information on worldwide

Jewry after the destruction of the Solomonic Temple; its exhibits deal with many aspects of philosophical and cultural life in Judaism. Open Sun, Mon, Tues, Thur 10.00–16.00, Wed 10.00–18.00, Fri 09.00–13.00; closed Sat. Admission charged.

North-central area

The **Ben-Gurion House** is at 17 Sederot Ben-Gurion (☎ 03 522 1010), where the home of David Ben-Gurion (1884–1974), Israel's first prime minister, is preserved with its contents. It is also a study centre. Open Sun–Thur 08.00–15.00, Mon 08.00–17.00, Fri 08.00–13.00. (See also his home and monument at Sede Boqer in the Negev, p 411.) **Tel-Aviv Art Museum** at 27 Sederot Shaul HaMelech has an international collection of fine art (Israeli, European and American) and is a venue for concerts and lectures. Open Sun, Mon, Wed, Thur 10.00–18.00, Tues 10.00–10.00, Fri, Sat 10.00–14.00. Admission charged.

South-central area

There are several musuems in this area, three of them in Rehov Bialik. The **Bialik House** at no. 22 is the one-time home of the poet Haim Nahman Bialik (d. 1934), with archive. Open Sun–Thur 09.00–17.00, Sat 11.00–14.00. At the **Rubin House**, 14 Rehov Bialik (☎ 03 525 5961), home of the painter Reuven Rubin (1893–1974), you can see his studio and paintings especially of local scenery. Open Sun, Mon, Wed, Thur 10.00–14.00, Tues 10.00–13.00 and 16.00–20.00, Sat 11.00–14.00. The **Tel Aviv Historical Museum** at no. 27 displays archive material relating to the history of Tel Aviv.

The **Independence Hall and Bible Museum** at 16 Sederot Rothschild, is the former home of Meir Dizengoff, the first mayor of Tel Aviv. It was in the ground floor hall, when it was part of the Tel Aviv Museum, that Ben-Gurion declared the State of Israel in 1948. It is now a museum of the history of Zionism and a Bible Museum with many old and fine texts of the bible. Open Sun–Thur 09.00–13.30.

At 23 Sederot Rothschild, in the **Eliahu Golomb House**, is the **Haganah Museum** devoted to the history of the Haganah, the Zionist militia that fought against British and Arabs pre-1948. Open Sun–Thur 09.00–16.00, Fri 08.00–12.30. Admission charged. The Palmach History Museum also offers information on the pre-1948 Jewish underground.

The **Carmel Market** (fresh food and clothing), at Rehov Allenby and Hacarmel is Israel's largest open-air market.

LYDDA
• • • • • • • •

Lydda (H. Lod), 4km north of Ramla, was the Byzantine city of Diospolis, later associated with the cult of St. George. It is reached on Highway 434, immediately south of Ben Gurion airport. The present church and mosque, which incorporate parts of the Byzantine and Crusader Church of St. George, are in the old town. Parking is available next to the mosque. The bus station is in the old town, c 100m from the church. The area around the church is now largely derelict, and surrounded by modern apartment blocks. In 1995 Lydda's population was over 52,000, which included about 11,000 Arabs.

History

Remains of the Neolithic, Chalcolithic, Early Bronze 1 and Iron Age periods have been excavated in the ancient tell over which the modern town is built, as well as later remains of the Roman, Byzantine, early Islamic, Crusader and Mamluk periods. Lydda lies south of a river (H. Nahal Ayalon, A. Wadi al-Kabir/Musrara). Egyptian records mention a place which may be Lydda as having been conquered by Tuthmosis III in the 15C BC; it is mentioned in the Old Testament, and in Hellenistic and Roman times.

Granted the status of a city by Septimius Severus, Diospolis later became particularly noted for its association with the cult of St. George, the origins of which are obscure. George is said to have been a soldier martyred in Lydda c AD 303 during the persecutions of Christians under the Emperors Diocletian and Maximian, and his cult spread very widely. His cult at Lydda is first mentioned in AD 618; he was already known in England in the 7C–8C, and became immensely popular during the Crusades (as patron of soldiers, he is said to have appeared in a vision to the Franks before their conquest of Antioch in 1098); Richard I claimed he and his army were under the protection of St. George. The saint's cult reached its apogee in the late Middle Ages, when St. George was patron saint of England, Venice, Genoa, Portugal and Catalonia, but through the centuries Lydda continued to be recognised as the centre of his cult. In the reform of the Roman calendar of saints in 1969, the veneration of St. George was reduced to a local cult, but he remains patron saint of England, his feast celebrated on 23 April. The story of the dragon arose through confusion with that of St. George of Cappodocia.

A church must have existed at Lydda by AD 325 when its bishop attended one of the great church councils, but the church depicted on the Madaba Map (see p 71) in the later 6C and again at Umm al-Rasas in central Jordan in the 8C may have been built by Justinian in the 6C. It appears to have been substantial and a remarkable survivor: of the Arab conquest in 636, of a destruction by al-Hakim in 1010, of earthquakes, and of all the complex battles of the Crusader period, until the Crusaders built a new church on its ancient walls probably between 1150 and 1170. Despite the appointment of a Latin bishop (who had a fortified palace nearby), Orthodox priests appear to have maintained service in the church both during the Latin Kingdom and after the conquests by Salah al-Din and Baybars. In both the Byzantine and Crusader churches, the cave-tomb of St. George the Martyr was located beneath the main altar. It may have been visible from the church in the Byzantine period, but in the Crusader church, with its pavement at a higher level, it was in a crypt approached by stairs on either side. Pilgrims record visiting the shrine in the ruins of the church in the 14C. In the 15C the present mosque was constructed in a subsidiary, less ruinous 6C church on the southwest side of the main church, which may have been part of a Byzantine and then Crusader baptistery complex. The mosque courtyard was placed over the nave of the former church. In 1870 the Greek Orthodox regained rights to the church, where parts of the east end still stood to above the level of the cornice, and they rebuilt the present church over the ruins.

The town was bypassed by the Ottoman Railway of 1892 which linked Jerusalem and Jaffa, but a Turkish military railway linked Lydda to Damascus in 1915, and the British coastal railway from Egypt reached it in 1918. Most

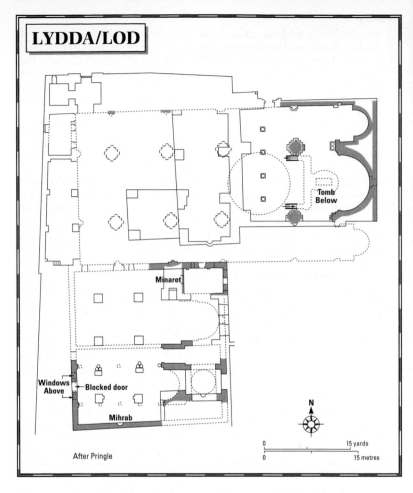

LYDDA/LOD

Tomb Below

Minaret

Windows Above — Blocked door

Mihrab

N

0   15 yards
0   15 metres

After Pringle

of its 17,000 Muslim and Christian inhabitants were expelled in 1948 and the old village was abandoned.

The Greek Orthodox Church of St. George was built from 1870, a plain handsome building, incorporating the main and northern apses and the four northeastern bays of the 12C church (which was a larger three-aisled structure with five bays and three apses), and also some of the underlying Byzantine structure. Four courses of the Byzantine wall can be seen in the north wall and north apse of the present church: its masonry has holes probably used for attaching marble veneer. The 12C work is of limestone with diagonal tooling, with white grey-veined marble used for the capitals, and white marble for the bases. A number of the pilasters, piers, column bases and capitals survive. Note the double bases on the north arcade of the first bay (see below). The central apse including a little of the semi-dome is 12C, with a strong upper cornice with a thick-leaved frieze. The crypt (with plain grey plaster) may be a feature of the 12C when the floor level was raised; the steps leading down to it were rebuilt for the 19C church. It is the site of the tomb of St. George. High in the north exterior wall of the church, east of the modern north door, is a lion gargoyle, probably of medieval date. If the church is locked, the key is with the priest across the street.

The **mosque** built by Baybars lies over the west end of the Crusader church, and is also entered from the north. The minaret in the pleasant mosque court-yard lies against the south side of the Crusader south aisle. The mosque occupies a smaller three-aisled basilica to the southwest, with three surviving Byzantine round-arched windows above a blocked later door in the west wall; a domed chamber to the east was part of the Byzantine complex, but in its present form probably dates to the 11C or 12C. This complex may have been a baptistery in the Byzantine church, and survived the destruction of 1010 better than the main church. Double columns in the mosque with fine Corinthian capitals were prob-ably taken from the first bay of the north nave arcade in the 12C main church where appropriate bases exist (see above), and were originally part of the 5C–6C Byzantine church. One is of red granite. The mosque was renovated in 1980–82.

Across the road a small complex of older buildings survives, and some 100m to the northeast a derelict caravanserai awaits conservation.

The **bridge** (A. Jisr Jindas), spanning the river just north of the town on the old road north from Lydda, is a fine Mamluk structure, built in 1273, as recorded on the west and east sides in inscriptions flanked by splendid heraldic lions in low relief; thin marble columns project from the masonry beneath the lions. The most famous of the bridges built by Baybars, it is over 30m long and 10m wide, with two piers with triangular cutwaters on the west side, and three arches, now largely obscured by silting. The bridge appears to rest on a still older buried bridge. Stones from the ruined church in Lydda and from older sources were used in its construction.

RAMLA
● ● ● ● ● ● ● ●

Founded as the capital of the province of Filastin by the Umayyads in AD 712, Ramla was strategically sited on the ancient crossing of the roads from Jaffa to Jerusalem and from Egypt to Damascus. Although almost nothing survives from the early Islamic period, it has the ruins of the White Mosque founded in the 8C, with its fine 14C minaret, and a well-preserved 12C church which was converted into the Great Mosque in 1190–91. Old Ramla is much ruined, and now part of a vastly expanding new settlement, but the town is nevertheless of considerable historical interest. Close to Lydda, it is c 40km northwest of Jerusalem, at the junction of Highways 40 and 44. Bus and sharut services.

History

Ramla was founded on the sandy coastal plain in AD 712 by Sulaiman ibn Abd al-Malik, who was then the governor of the province of Filastin and resided at the old town of Lydda 4km to the north. Ramla was a strategic loca-tion, but dusty in summer and muddy in winter, and reliant on water from an aqueduct and from cisterns and wells. Sulaiman built his palace and the

'House of the Dyers' at Ramla, and began building the White Mosque here before he succeeded to the caliphate in 715. The inhabitants of Lydda, mainly Christian, were forcibly resettled in the new city. His successor, Umar, completed the building of the White Mosque. The town, as the provincial capital, was probably designed as a large fortified rectangle on the plain, and in the 10C it was described as a fine city with walls, town gates, markets, khans, baths and stone-built houses. The Jewish Academy was temporarily transferred here from Jerusalem in the 10C, when there were Karaite (see p 203) and rabbinical communities. A Bedouin raid inflicted great damage in 1025. Much of the city was damaged or destroyed in earthquakes in 1033–34, 1068 and 1070; it fell to the Seljuks in 1071 and afterwards was depopulated. The remaining inhabitants fled in 1099 at the approach of the Crusaders, who took the abandoned city unopposed and resettled it.

The Crusaders occupied only the eastern part of the former city, and built a moated stronghold. A church was built but little is known of any new Latin settlers, although there were indigenous (Syrian) Christians. Benjamin of Tudela, visiting in 1170, speaks of just three Jewish dyers living in an area of cemeteries. The Hospitallers, the Teutonic Knights and ecclesiastical establishments owned property here, but generally the town was either a dependency of Jaffa or had a royal garrison; and in the church hierarchy it was dependent on the Cathedral Church of St. George at Lydda. It continued to be of strategic significance, and three battles were fought near it in 1101, 1102 and 1105.

The town was captured in 1187 by Saladin. In 1191 he destroyed the castle of Ramla to prevent it being used by Richard I; in the Treaty of Jaffa of 1192 it was agreed that Ramla and Lydda should be divided evenly between Christians and Muslims. In 1211–12 Ramla was described as destroyed and inhabited by Muslims, and was still ruined in 1225; it was ceded to the German Emperor Frederick II in 1229, and it must have been lost in 1244. Baybars took possession in 1266, rebuilt the White Mosque in the form in which it exists today, and established the shrine of Nabi Salih, which is still located in the northwest corner of the White Mosque. It was one of the Muslim pilgrimage centres established by Baybars in reaction to the Crusades, so located as to ensure the presence of large numbers of Muslims at strategic points, particularly at Orthodox Easter when large numbers of Christian pilgrims gathered to visit Jerusalem. The Muslim feast at Ramla was established in the week before Easter. Salih is listed in the Koran as an Islamic prophet sent to the tribe of Tamud, is one of the most important saints for Palestinians, and had other shrines in Palestine.

In 1296 Ramla was prosperous and in 1346–50 it was described as beautiful, by which time the Sultan al-Nasir Muhammad had replaced the old minaret on the White Mosque with the present one. The style of this minaret led several Western travellers from the late 16C to believe that the White Mosque was a former church dedicated to the Forty Martyrs of Sebastia (perhaps because of a Muslim tradition extant in the 15C that the mosque contained the bodies of 40 companions of the Prophet).

During the Mamluk period Ramla seems to have regained importance, and in the early 14C it was described as the most populous town in Palestine. It depended on cotton, agriculture and trade; the Venetians had a colony here;

but it was also still an important point on the Christian pilgrim route from Jaffa to Jerusalem, and pilgrims lodged in the inn in the centre of the town. Between 1395 and 1402 the Franciscans established a pilgrim hospice in Ramla, which was described in the late 15C by the German Dominican Brother Felix Faber. Brother Felix refers to the 27 Articles which pilgrims were asked to observe in the hospice at Ramla at the start of their pilgrimage, all designed to ensure the safe conduct and seemly behaviour of pilgrims at the holy places. They included the following good advice, which often went unheeded:

Article 6: Pilgrims of noble birth must not deface walls by drawing their coats of arms thereon, or by writing their names ... to make marks of their having visited them; for such conduct gives great offence to the Saracens, and they think those who do so to be fools.

Article 7: Pilgrims must proceed to visit the holy places in an orderly manner without disorder and disagreement and one must not try to outrun another, because much disorder often occurs at these places and the devotion of many is hindered thereby.

But Ramla suffered following the Ottoman conquest, and the Jewish community which was re-established in the town in the prosperous 14C again disappeared. The town recovered, only to be hit by another earthquake in 1546. It became a prosperous market town, with an extensive olive oil industry in the later Ottoman period, but increasingly lost its prominence to Jaffa. The rights of Christian pilgrims to stay at the hospice were confirmed under Ottoman rule, by Sulaiman in 1547 and 1549, and again in the 18C. Gradually the hospice too acquired its own biblical traditions. In 1577 it was claimed as the House of Nicodemus; and in 1616 as the House of Joseph of Arimathea, and by the 19C this latter tradition was established. In the 1860s the room in which Napoleon Bonaparte was said to have spent the night in 1799 was shown—Ramla was on his route during his eastern campaign.

In 1922 the town had a largely Muslim population of just over 7000 inhabitants. Some Jewish settlements were briefly established up to 1939, and the town was a centre of Arab resistance in 1948; it was captured by the Israel Defence Forces in July 1948 after it had been abandoned by the majority of its Arab inhabitants, most of the rest being expelled. It became a Jewish immigrant development town and a municipality in 1950. By 1995, it had a population of c 58,000, of whom c 10,000 were Arabs, and was the focus of greatly increased immigrant settlement.

Although no standing Umayyad monuments remain today, some medieval and 13 Mamluk and Ottoman buildings survive in the old town, including mosques, tombs and houses. Before 1948, there were 17 mosques in Ramla of which at least 11 were still in use, but by 1992 only 10 remained; of these, three still have a religious function. Many are very ruinous and do not merit a visit.

The prominent tower of the ***White Mosque** (A. Jami' al-Abiad) lies to the west of the main road in the old town, but was probably located in the centre of the Umayyad town. Little of the original foundation survives. It was described as having floors, columns and panelling of white marble, and doors of cypress wood and cedar. Three Umayyad cisterns lie beneath the court of the mosque; each has two or three aisles of barrel-vaulted bays, the largest being c 30m in

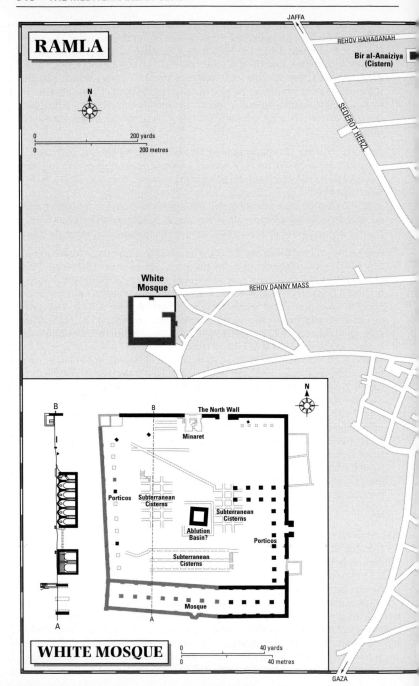

JAFFA

REHOV HAHAGANAH

RAMLA

Bir al-Anaiziya
(Cistern)

SEDEROT HERZL

N

0 ——————— 200 yards
0 ——————— 200 metres

White
Mosque

REHOV DANNY MASS

N

B | B | The North Wall

Minaret

Porticos

Subterranean
Cisterns

Subterranean
Cisterns

Ablution
Basin?

Porticos

Subterranean
Cisterns

Mosque

A | A

WHITE MOSQUE

0 ——————— 40 yards
0 ——————— 40 metres

GAZA

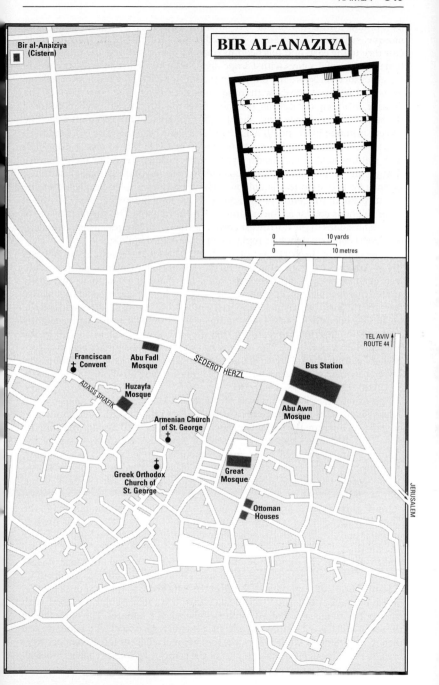

Bir al-Anaziya
(Cistern)

BIR AL-ANAZIYA

0   10 yards
0   10 metres

TEL AVIV
ROUTE 44

Franciscan
Convent

Abu Fadl
Mosque

SEDEROT HERZL

Bus Station

ADASS SHAFIK

Huzayfa
Mosque

Abu Awn
Mosque

Armenian Church
of St. George

Great
Mosque

Greek Orthodox
Church of
St. George

Ottoman
Houses

JERUSALEM

length, and with two aisles of ten bays; the others are c 20m in length. The mosque enclosure, 93 x 84m, is oriented to the cardinal points, with the main entrance to the east, and has been in ruins for over a century; the prayer room had two aisles of 13 bays with 13 openings in the north façade; some arcades of the aisles survive; before the mihrab in the south wall are the remains of a dome supported by pendentives with muqarnas decoration. The west part of the mosque, including the mihrab, probably dates to c 1268 when Baybars restored the building; the east side (with slightly different orientation) is slightly later. The present **minaret** in the north wall, which has long been the principal landmark of Ramla, was built by al-Nasir Muhammad in 1318; it is square, c 30m high with features similar to Crusader architecture, including window niches on five storeys, the upper ones being particularly ornamental. Its spiral staircase ascends by 119 steps to the balcony, which provides a splendid view over the coastal plain. In the centre of the courtyard are foundations variously identified as an ablutions pool or as the original site of the minaret. The shrine (*maqam*) of Nabi Salih stands in the northwest corner of the White Mosque, where a modern flat-roofed concrete structure replaces an older domed building.

Some 600m to the northeast of the White Mosque is the impressive Abbasid **Bir al-Anaziya**, a cistern which lay on the old Jaffa to Jerusalem Road. It is a subterranean excavation, an irregular four-sided shape, lined with strong, finely jointed masonry heavily cemented and paved; it has six aisles separated by five rows of cruciform piers which support a vaulted roof. A staircase descends on the north side; opposite the first landing is a large rectangular frame with a slightly sunken Kufic inscription recording that the cistern was built in AD 789 in the time of Harun al-Rashid. The cistern has architectural significance as a rare Abbasid monument in Palestine, and as the earliest known example of the exclusive employment of free-standing pointed arches. Open Sun–Thur 08.00–15.00, Fri 08.00–12.00, Sat 08.00–16.00.

Approximately 450m southeast of the White Mosque, off the main road in Adass Shafik, is the **Franciscan Convent**. Its Church of St. Nicodemus was built in 1901–02, on the site of the much older hospice used by pilgrims from the end of the 14C. The Chapel of St. Joseph of Arimathea on the west side of the church is a much restored, rectangular structure, with a dome on four columns, probably built a little before 1894 next to an older chapel identified as the House of Nicodemus; the latter is likely to have been the chapel recorded in the 15C, but may not be much older.

Jami' al-Huzayfa is an Ottoman mosque located in Adass Shafik, next to the Church of St. Nicodemus. As you enter from the south, on the right is the rectangular prayer hall, with two bays, heavily restored, and to the left the tomb of Shaikh Huzayfa and the minaret. The tomb is contained in a small, square domed chamber. The minaret, of standard type for the period and place, has an octagonal shaft on a square base, with spiral staircase ascending to a balcony.

Jami' Abu Fadl is on the south side of the Jaffa Road, to the west of Detroit St. and at the back of the Amal Technical College. It is a rectangular enclosure with three prayer rooms, two domed tomb chambers and a minaret. The outer face of the south wall has a decorated façade; the minaret is decorated with windows and niches. According to Mujir al-Din, the minaret and adjacent tomb chamber were built in 1450, though the eastern part of the complex is later, probably Ottoman.

Also on the south side of the Jaffa Rd, 200m further east, is **Jami' Abu al Awn**. It is a medieval mosque with six domes over six bays; the prayer hall is entered from the north. The mihrab is lined with marble, and on either side are engaged marble columns with reused Crusader 12C capitals; a marble minbar existed before 1950, but has been removed; the northwest bay of the prayer hall is partitioned off and contains two tombs, one inscribed as that of Abu al-'Awn; both tombs, now ruined, have large marble cenotaphs. At the northeast corner is a minaret on a square platform.

In the centre of the old town, one block south of the Jaffa Road, is the ***Great Mosque** (A. Jami' al-Kabir), which is built in the former Crusader Parish Church (of St. John?), the principal 12C church in Ramla. In 1191 Saladin seems to have left the Latin church in Ramla intact, but it may have been converted to a mosque almost immediately, perhaps with more work carried out in 1297 when an inscription claims the building was constructed by al-Adil Kitbugha. A minaret over the northwest bay was constructed in 1314–15 but was replaced by the present cylindrical minaret by 1922 (probably between 1881 and 1909). The church is a three-aisled basilica of seven bays, with three semicircular apses; the nave has a slightly pointed barrel vault, and the aisles are groin-vaulted. Constructed of sandstone with limestone detail, the exterior has been badly resurfaced. The interior is still in relatively good condition, apart from some concrete and marble facings on the lower parts of the piers and some repairs to the vaulting. Antique marble was used for the capitals, many of which are older *spolia*. Many of them are linked by a heavy-leaved Romanesque marble frieze (cf. St. George in Lydda, p 315). The original design of the columns and piers is preserved at the east and west ends of the building. To either side of the apse are aumbries (recesses), now only c 20cm above floor level. Similar aumbries/doors are located in the side apses. The west door of the church was restored by Sultan Abd al-Hamid II in 1876–1909. The arch has a hood-mould with three orders supported on six restored columns. Above the west door is a pointed-arched window, flanked by colonnettes on the inside and with a hood-mould outside. The gallery opposite the mihrab probably dates from the 13C.

In the courtyard on the north side of the mosque is the **Tomb of Shihab al-Din**, the largest of the surviving once-numerous shaikhs' tombs in Ramla. It is a tall square building with a dome resting on an octagonal drum supported by squinches decorated with muqarnas, possibly early Ottoman (16C).

The Greek **Church and Convent of St. George** lies c 150m west of the Great Mosque. Almost completely rebuilt in the 19C, it is a three-aisled church with five bays and three apses, of which only the western three bays may rest on 12C work, visible in the lower courses of the external walls with reused through columns. The plain and rather heavy west door appears to be a late- or post-medieval addition. There are references to churches in Ramla from c 784, and there must have been a church built on the site at an early date to serve the native Christian population. References to other dedications of Orthodox churches exist: in 1485 there were many ruined churches, only one then being still in use.

One block southeast of the Great Mosque are two of the surviving houses of old Ramla: the **Qasr Waqf Abu al-Huda**, begun 1713, with a decorative north façade; and the **Dar al-Shaykh Sulaiman al-Taji** (Ottoman) on the opposite side of the lane, but with a common entrance to the upper part, now ruinous.

Further south in the old town are the locations of other mosques: Jami' al-Maghrabi, medieval and Ottoman, with a court prayer hall and octagonal minaret; Jami' Shaikh Raslan, a Mamluk and Ottoman mosque and tomb, now derelict; and Jami' Shaikh Muhammad al-Qubbi (Ottoman).

From at least the 14C Ramla has been famous for its **shaikhs' tombs and shrines**. The standard form is a square chamber covered by a dome, usually with a large rectangular sarcophagus or cenotaph; of the 20 identified in Mandate times ten survive, but only three were still tended in 1992. They include those of Shaikh Hammar and Shaikh 'Antar (1701).

All sizeable Islamic towns had at least one bath house, but of the **Hammam al-Ridwan**, 100m south of Jami' al-Huzayfa, Ottoman in date, only derelict fragments survive. The **Khan al-Azzam**, on the southeast of the city, was used as a pottery factory during the Mandate. Now abandoned and collapsing, it was a large rectangular structure with a central courtyard, a large stable on the east side and tall barrel-vaulted chambers on the south side. The date is unknown, but it may be Mamluk. A ruinous large medieval cistern, the Birkat al-Jammus, lies 300m northeast.

ASHDOD

There is a complex of ancient and modern towns and ports at various locations in the vicinity of the modern city of Ashdod (A. Isdud). The new city and deep water port were established from 1957 and the port inaugurated in 1966. It is named after the ancient Philistine site which lies inland. The modern port city is at the end of Highway 41, 67km from Jerusalem, and the ancient port c 3km south along the coast road. The ancient tell is on the west side of Highway 41, c 7km south of the intersection with Highway 41. Tourist Information Office: 4 Haim Moshe Shapira St, Rova Daled, ☎ 08 864 0090.

History

Like most ancient cities in this region, Tell Ashdod lies inland to the east of the sand dunes. It consists of an acropolis of 8 hectares. and a lower city of at least 28 hectares and was fortified in the Middle Bronze IIC; it was an important textile centre and Canaanite trading city in the Late Bronze Age and was probably destroyed late in the 13C during the invasions of the Sea Peoples. From the 12C it became one of the principal cities of the Philistines. When the Philistines captured the Ark of the Covenant from the Israelites, they brought it to the Temple of Dagon at Ashdod (I Sam. 5). Excavations have uncovered a mudbrick fortress, houses, shrines and cult figures in a Philistine town that expanded during the 11C and continued to be inhabited during the Iron Age when the town was sacked by Sargon. It revolted against the Assyrians in 712 and also in 711 when it was again sacked. In Hellenistic times, when it was captured by the Hasmoneans, the town was called Azotus Mesogaeus. Herod was granted it by Augustus, and as a royal estate willed it to Salome, who in turn left it to the Empress Livia. During the First Jewish Revolt it surrendered to Titus, but by the 4C AD the town was of little importance. It was the site of a battle between Franks and Muslims in the Crusader period. Until 1948 the Arab village of Isdud was located here, but the inhabitants, who grew wheat and fruit, were expelled in October of that year, and there is now little to be seen.

Ashdod Yam (A. Minat al-Qal'a) on the coast was the port of ancient Ashdod. The site has a large, semicircular rampart, an inner and outer earthen glacis supporting a mudbrick wall 3.1m thick, assumed to have been built by Iamani of Ashdod in his rebellion against Sargon of Assyria in 711 BC, but there is evidence of Late Bronze Age occupation on the site also. As Azotus Paralius it became more important than the parent city inland in the Byzantine period.

To the north of the Iron Age site is a castle (40 x 60m) probably Abbasid or even Umayyad in origin, in use during the Fatimid period. It was possibly also a Crusader castle, but the only evidence for this is a reference to its occupation in 1169 by Nicolas de Beroard, a knight of Hugh, lord of Ramla. The castle has a trapezoidal plan, solid rounded corner turrets on the west side facing the sea, and rectangular ones on the east; the gates are located in the centre of the east and west walls between shallow rounded turrets; the external wall has rectangular buttresses. Vaulted cells can be seen on the interior.

ASHKELON

The ancient cities of Ascalon (A. 'Asqalan. H. Ashkelon) lie within great ramparts which protect the site from land and sea. The modern town of Ashkelon lies to the north, and includes the port for tankers and fuel for the power station at Hadera. There are sandy beaches along this stretch of the coast.

Practical information

 Getting there
Ascalon is on the coast, off Highway 4, 77km southwest of Jerusalem. Modern Ashkelon is approached by a spur to Sederot Ben Gurion leading from the main coast road. To reach ancient Ascalon drive west through the town until the coast is reached, and turn south at the T-junction to the park, car parks and beach. Ashkelon is served by Bus 437 from Jerusalem. Bus 6 runs from the Bus Station on Sederot Ben Gurion in Ashkelon to the site, or it is about 30 minutes' walk.

 Information offices
Tourist information office is located at the Afridar Center, 2 Hanasi St, Kikkar Tzefania, ☎ 07 673 2412; open Sun–Thur 08.00–19.00, Fri 08.00–12.00.

 Where to stay
Holiday Inn, P.O.B. 944 (☎ 07 674 8888; 🖷 07 671 8823); *Shulamit Gardens* (☎ 07 671 1261. All the hotels are located along the beach area. Rooms in private houses are available through the Tourist Information Center in Kikkar Tzefania.

Eating out
There is a reasonable small café near the Antiquities Courtyard, and others in the market area in Migdal. There is also a restaurant in the National Park.

The site
The extensive ruins of the ancient city are preserved in a large public park with restaurant and facilities, around which the great semicircular ramparts are the most prominent feature. The site is run by the National Parks Authority, in the charge of the Municipality of Ashkelon. There is free access to the park and beach. The site is regularly patrolled as theft is a problem.

History

The site of Ascalon was a fortified town and port on the coast road to Egypt from the beginning of the second millennium. Set on the long, sandy coastal strip, it had early sea trading links that included Cyprus and Egypt. The city was already large and prosperous by c 2000 BC, with great ramparts enclosing at least 60 hectares. The Late Bronze Age town was smaller, and was destroyed when Merenptah of Egypt reconquered it c 1230 BC. The Sea Peoples, whom he allowed to settle here, turned it into one of the five leading Philistine cities, when large public buildings and substantial houses were built. The Philistine town was at first prosperous and independent (c 1185–734 BC), then came in turn under Assyrian, Babylonian, Persian (when it belonged to Tyre) and Egyptian rule—punctuated by a Scythian attack in 610. In the 2C–1C BC it is suggested that the grandfather of Herod the Great had a priestly position in the Temple of Apollo at Ascalon. It was a profoundly Hellenised small city in which Herod the Great built a basilica and stoas late in the 1C BC. It reached the peak of its prosperity in the late 2C/early 3C AD, with a fine basilica which is mentioned along with the temple, the theatre and the odeon in the early 4C. It was a pagan city until Christianised in the Byzantine period, when new city walls were built. Two basilical churches have been found, and a synagogue, for many Jews resided here too. The city was captured by Umar in AD 636, and it was rebuilt in 968 as a fine Islamic stronghold. The Crusaders captured it twice but only held it for short periods, 1153–87 and 1192–1265. They rebuilt the city walls with at least 14 towers, several churches and a hospital. They reused columns as ties strengthening walls of the city and castle. The castle was concentric in plan, with rock-cut ditch on south and east.

Salah al-Din took Ascalon in 1187 and destroyed it so that the Crusaders could not retake it and use it as a base. Richard Lionheart saw the flames of the burning city from his camp at Jaffa, regained it in 1192 and rapidly rebuilt the defences, which were as rapidly dismantled by the Muslim forces under the terms of the Treaty of Jaffa, and the site lay derelict until 1239. Baybars levelled it in 1270 when its harbour was destroyed, and thereafter little is known of it until modern times.

Archaeologists have uncovered much information about the ancient city; but the site is also notable for the excavations in 1815 of Lady Hester Stanhope, who (as befitted the niece of William Pitt the Younger) set out in grand style, with the approval of the Ottoman government, with a manuscript giving instructions for locating a huge treasure. Instead, her workmen uncovered first a headless over-life-size marble statue, which she made them smash to fragments in case she should be accused of hunting for antiquities on her own behalf; only its foot survives. Then they unearthed a trough which, she estimated, might have held three million pieces of gold before it was robbed. Her companion in this expedition described the countryside around in that late April of 1815:

It would be difficult to give you an idea of the richness, beauty and fertility of the SW of Palestine, as we saw it going towards Ascalon. The clothing of spring might have shown it off to best advantage, but a Country whose face is diversified with gentle undulations, covered with groves of olive trees, and has populous villages, (even under such a Government) almost within sight of each other cannot but wear at all seasons, a most beautiful appearance. It is much more rural than anything I have yet seen in the East. (C.L. Meryon in I. Bruce, *The Nun of Lebanon*)

In early spring the open land north of the ancient city is still bright with wild poppies and lupins.

To the right after entering the park, the principal feature is the northern **rampart**, constructed in the Middle Bronze Age. Near the top of the great mudbrick and earthern glacis (protected by a shelter) is the earliest (c 2000 BC) preserved arched *city gate known, built in mudbrick with a passage c 25m in length sloping up through the ramparts into the city. The city itself lay at a lower level than the top of the ramparts. The preserved gate is the third in a series of four built one after the other, each on top of its predecessor. The semicircular ramparts lie behind a tremendous ditch, and both protected the Canaanite town on the landward side. A cult place was found on the lower outer approach to the gate. This early rampart forms the base of the fortifications of many later periods, and continued in use in the Late Bronze and Iron Ages. Remains of Philistine towers survive on top of the ramparts, and just to the sides of the Middle Bronze Age gate, parts of the medieval stone glacis are also visible. The Byzantine and Crusader walls were also founded on the older ramparts, and protected a semicircle of land fronting the beach which is nearly 1000m north–south and 500m east–west. The Jaffa Gate lay at the north, the Jerusalem Gate at the east, the Gaza Gate at the south and the Sea Gate on the west. Following the track into the site, the area of the inside of the Middle Bronze gateway can be seen. To the south is the mound on which stood the razed Crusader castle built by Richard of Cornwall in 1244, concentric in plan with chapel and protecting ditch; little except the outline survives. The track descends through the Crusader ditch.

Near the centre of the site is the ancient tell; on the northern slopes an area of houses of the Philistine period have been uncovered. To the east is the **council house** (basilica, 110 x 37m) of the late 2C AD with some fragmentary monolithic columns marking the location. To the south is a semicircular tiered council chamber with sculpture, including pilasters with Atlas supporting Nike on a globe, Isis/Tyche and a priest of Sarapis, which probably once decorated the upper façade of the building. A Byzantine or 12C church is located on the south-east section of the ancient tell; there is another 12C church near the northwest corner of the Byzantine site, probably in the inner ward of the Crusader castle (see above); a third is just south of the Jerusalem Gate, recently excavated (see below). A ruined Muslim saint's shrine (Maqam al-Khidr) on the west edge of the

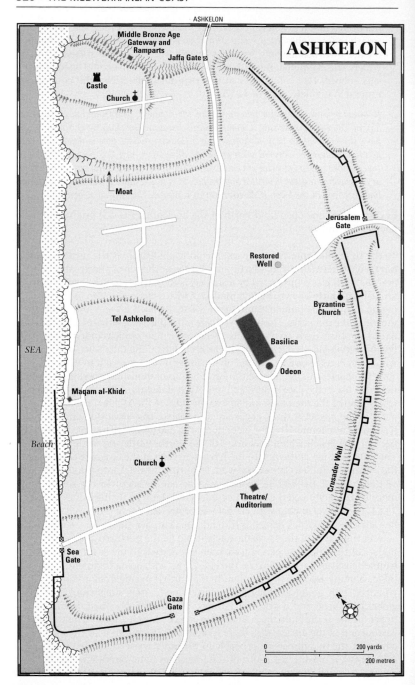

ASHKELON

ASHKELON

Middle Bronze Age
Gateway and
Ramparts

Jaffa Gate

Castle

Church

Moat

Jerusalem
Gate

Restored
Well

Byzantine
Church

Tel Ashkelon

Basilica

SEA

Odeon

Maqam al-Khidr

Beach

Church

Crusader Wall

Theatre/
Auditorium

Sea
Gate

Gaza
Gate

| 0 | | 200 yards |
| 0 | | 200 metres |

ancient tell, by the sea, probably of Ottoman date, may mark the site of a former Fatimid mosque on the site of another Byzantine church (St. Mary the Green).

On the slopes on the south side of the ancient tell, a cemetery—including Late Bronze Age shaft tombs cut in the bedrock above the beach—and a remarkable 5C–4C 'Dog Cemetery' have been excavated. The reason for the ritual burial of over 1000 dogs is still not known. The site of the theatre has also been located at the southeast end of the site. A viewing platform and steps to the beach inside the south ramparts provides an excellent view from the beach of the Islamic/Crusader sea wall fortifications; the built-in reused granite columns originally brought from the Troad and from Aswan in the Roman period can be seen eroding out of the face of the cliff. A view over the sandy level scrub south of the town may be had from the top of the ramparts, and you can walk around the top of the ramparts to the east or Jerusalem Gate. Just south of the gate, a massive round tower is preserved on top of the rampart; and below, cut into its inner face, is a well-preserved church, with an apse and two apsidal niches with four grey granite columns standing, and some remnants of red-painted wall plaster.

A recently rebuilt well and water raising mechanism can also be seen just northeast of the restaurant. It is one of some 37 sweet-water wells supplying reservoirs and the neat patchwork of gardens inside the ramparts which were recorded by Conder and Kitchener in 1883. Palms, tamarisks, cactus, almonds, lemons, olives and oranges were grown, as well as vegetables which included the scallions (spring onions) named for the site of Ascalon.

In the **modern city**, the Kikkar Tzefania with clock tower has several small shops and cafés. In the southeast corner is the **Antiquities Courtyard** (Sun–Thur 08.30–16.00, Fri 08.30–13.30). Sculpture, inscriptions and mosaics are displayed. Two marble sarcophagi of the 3C–4C AD, found in the dunes in 1972, are finely carved with classical scenes and motifs. One depicts the abduction of Persephone and is unfinished; the second is the finer, and depicts the battle between the Greeks and the barbarians. The sarcophagi were brought from Greece or Turkey but probably never used. Between them are the lead fittings of a Hellenistic or Roman anchor found on the beach.

A Late Roman painted tomb adjacent to the beach about 1km north of the ancient site, near the Marina, is one of Ascalon's finer antiquities.

On the east side of the modern town there is a busy Thursday market, and a small museum in the former mosque on Rehov Herzl (Sun–Thur 09.00–13.00, 16.00–18.00, Fri 09.00–13.00, Sat 10.00–13.00). It has the calf shrine discovered in the small temple on the second millennium BC ramparts of Ashkelon.

GAZA

The Gaza Strip

The Gaza Strip occupies the southern section of the coastal plain, and is a semi-autonomous Palestinian region under the Palestine National Authority. Much of the region, 45km long and 5–12km wide, consists of a belt of sand dunes up to

40m high and 6km wide. The average annual rainfall is 150–300mm. As well as Gaza City and a number of smaller towns, it includes eight Palestinian refugee camps housing nearly half a million refugees, and about 19 Israeli settlements, the latter mainly in the southern area. The Jewish settlements create intense pressures in a critically dense population. 'The Strip' combines densely populated areas with limited infrastructure. In 1997 the Palestinian population was 1,020,813 of whom c 2500 were Christian, the rest Muslim; and an estimated 2500 Israelis. Because of the sand the main coast road runs some distance inland, and thus Gaza City itself is located 5km inland from the sea, but its modern and ancient suburbs extended across the sand to the shore. There are no large modern harbours, and in the past the estuary of the Wadi Gaza, further south, and small artificial harbours served the inhabitants. Since 1994, the Palestinian Authority has been developing tourism with hotels, restaurants and craft centres (especially pottery and weaving). The Gaza Strip has had an airport since 1999, east of Rafah near the southern border with Egypt, bombed by Israel in 2001. Palestinian travel agencies and guides are available and local advice is helpful. Tourists should dress modestly as this is a conservative Muslim area, and shorts etc. are not considered polite dress by many of the residents.

For information on border crossing check points, from Israel at Bait Hanun/Erez, and from Egypt at Rafah, see p 14.

Gaza City

The Strip's main city is 104km southwest of Jerusalem; the population was 292,567 in 1997. The centre of the modern town overlies the ancient tell which covers approximately a square kilometre and is marked by its steep sides and the cemeteries which were once outside the medieval walls. The principal streets are Umar al-Muktar (Omar Amokhtar) St and, parallel to the north, al-Wihada St. They connect the two main squares, Shujjaya on the east, and Palestine on the west; between them lies the old city and its markets. Most hotel accommodation, and the fish restaurants, lie along the beach to the west.

Practical information

Getting around

The most convenient transport in and beyond Gaza city is the service taxi. There is no tourist information office.

Where to stay

Accommodation in Gaza is not cheap, and most of the hotels and places to eat are in the beach area or the main road (Sharia Umar al-Mukhtar) between town centre and beach. *Adam Hotel*,

Sharia al-Rashid (☎ 07 282 3519; 🖷 07 286 6976); *al-Amal Hotel*, 33 Sharia Umar al- Mukhtar (☎ 07 284 1317; 🖷 07 286 1832); *Beach Hotel* (☎ 07 282 8800; 🖷 07 282 8604); *Cliff Hotel*, Sharia al-Rashid (☎ 07 282 3450; 🖷 07 282 0742); *al-Hilal al-Ahmar* (☎ 07 205 4261; 🖷 07 205 4621).

Eating out

Abu Nawas (☎ 07 284 5211); *al-Sammak*, Midan al-Mina, fish restaurant in beach area (☎ 07 286 4385); *Salam Beach* (☎ 07 284 4964).

History

The town of Gaza has a long and turbulent history, and is often mentioned because of its strategic location on the coast road to Egypt. It was captured by Thutmosis III in the 15C BC, and thereafter seems to have developed at the expense of the ancient site at Tell al-Ajjul on the edge of the Wadi Gaza, becoming the principal Egyptian administrative centre as well as the residence of the governor of Canaan. It is mentioned in the Amarna Letters (see p 32) and in clay tablets found at Taanach, a site not far from Megiddo. It became the southernmost of the Philistine great cities from the 12C, with a great temple of Dagon. It is this temple which is the setting for the story of Samson who, blinded and goaded, pulled down the columns supporting the temple, killing himself and thousands of Philistines (Judges 16: 21–30). The city was caught up in the wars of Israel, the Assyrians and the Egyptians, and became a royal fortress of the Persian Empire. By the 4C it was becoming important as the Mediterranean terminus of a major land route from Arabia and India, when its port lay 4km to the northwest at Anthedon (the present mound of al-Bilakhiya). Its opposition to Alexander the Great in 332 BC was futile, and he sold its inhabitants into slavery. The city changed hands between the Ptolemies and Seleucids in the 3C–2C BC, and was taken by Alexander Janneus in 96 BC. The silting sand had by this time destroyed the port.

Gaza's fortunes revived under the Romans, particularly under Gabinius the Procurator of Syria, in 57 BC. It became known for its many great pagan temples, the largest dedicated to the principal god of the city, Marnas (a Cretan god); but dedications are known for Zeus, Helios, Aphrodite, Apollo, Athene and the Tyche (guardian goddess) of the city. According to a later source, Hadrian brought Jewish prisoners to Gaza after he defeated Bar Kochba in the Second Jewish Revolt, and sold them in the market there; at this time he instituted a great annual fair. A colossal 2C AD statue of Zeus found near Gaza in the last century is displayed in the Archaeological Museum in Istanbul. Wrestling/boxing contests are recorded in the 2C–4C, games were held in the city in the 2C–3C AD, and chariot racing is attested in the 4C.

Worship of pagan deities remained entrenched in the city after the Edict of Constantine in AD 313. At the time of the arrival of Bishop Porphyry at the end of the 4C/beginning of the 5C, there were eight pagan temples, and only 280 Christians in a population of 50–60,000 people in Gaza. The temple of Marnas was only destroyed in the 5C. Perhaps because of this, the church (the Eudoxiana) erected over its site in the time of Bishop Porphyry was said to be the largest in the region, a magnificent cruciform church with 32 marble columns imported from Euboea (Greece), and quite disproportionate to the size of the local Christian congregation. Other churches were built in the 5C–6C. A theatre and/or hippodrome is referred to, and in the 6C the mime performances were praised. In Roman and Byzantine times, the city was famous for its school of rhetoric, and famous scholars taught there. Its fair continued to be one of the most important in Palestine. A new city (called Constantia Maiumas Neapolis) was built on the harbour which lay 1km south of the older Anthedon and was deeper and larger than its predecessor. Gaza was the greatest port of the region in Byzantine times, the centre of the wine trade and the gateway for the trade routes and cities of the Negev and

Arabia. Its importance is reflected in the 6C and 8C depictions of the city in mosaics from Madaba, Umm al-Rasas and Ma'in in Jordan.

At Dathin near Gaza, in AD 634 the Arab army vanquished the Byzantine army, and the city fell. It became the seat of the Muslim governor of the Nagab (Negev) district. In 1149 it was uninhabited when Baldwin III began to refortify it and then handed it to the Knights Templars. Its history in Crusader times is intimately linked with the fortifications at Dayr al-Balah/Darum along the coast to the south, and to those of Ascalon to the north. The castle, with an outer suburb and port, had achieved some prosperity by 1170, when Salah al-Din destroyed the suburb. In 1187, the Templars surrendered the castle to Salah al-Din, who ordered the destruction of the fortifications. Richard I refortified it, and the Templars were again in occupation in 1192, but under the Treaty of Jaffa the fortifications were dismantled. Later the town was rebuilt and flourished as the capital of a Mamluk administrative district which included the coastal plain as far north as Atlit, and it was an important way station on the Mamluk caravan route from Palestine to Egypt. Surviving Mamluk structures illustrate the redevelopment that took place in the 14C–15C.

Even in the 19C a great annual feast or fair was held at Gaza, at Bab ed-Darûn (the Darum Gate) which was called the Id en-Nasara, 'the Feast of the Christians', which attracted large crowds and was the occasion of a market of considerable size. The city walls still existing in 1915 were probably Mamluk or Ottoman in date. The Christian quarter was located in the south, the Muslim quarter in the north of the town, with the Great Mosque and the Khan al-Zait at the centre. Ottoman rule was only interrupted by Napoleon's campaign in 1799 and the occupation of Muhammad Ali from 1831 to 1840. The city was bombarded by the British army under General Allenby in 1916–17 during the taking of Palestine from the Turks, and the mosque and other public buildings were severely damaged when the munitions being stored inside them exploded. The city was under the British Mandate administration from 1917 to 1948. Under Egyptian control from 1948 to 1967 it expanded enormously, especially in the area between the city and the coast. It came under Israeli occupation after the Six Day War in 1967. The Palestinian uprising, the Intifada, began in Gaza in 1987. The domestic autonomy of the Palestinian areas has been in the hands of the Palestinian National Authority since May 1994, with Gaza City as the seat of government.

Note that visits to some mosques have to be arranged in advance through the Palestinian Ministry of Religious Affairs and that mosques are closed on Fridays and during prayers.

The **'Great Mosque** (A. Jami al-Umari al-Kabir), in part originally the 12C Crusader parish church, lies near the centre of the modern city, just to the north of Umar al-Muktar St. It is not known if this location also marks the site of the Byzantine Eudoxiana church and the Roman Temple of Marnas. The 12C church was a three-aisled basilica of four bays, but presumed apses were suppressed when the building was converted to a mosque. Work was carried out on the mosque by the Mamluk governor, al-Jawili, between 1288 and 1318/19. Damaged in the First World War, the mosque was renovated in 1926. Much of the Crusader structure survives, including the overbuilt west façade with fine decorated marble doorway, porch and marble oculus (which has lost its glazing bars). Large aumbries from either side of the central apse survive. Double-storey engaged columns (mainly older *spolia*) against piers separate the aisles. The nave and aisles are groin-vaulted; north aisle and clerestory windows with pointed arches derive from the original church. Externally the plain walls are buttressed. A menorah is incised high up on one of the columns which was reused from an older building. When the building was converted for use as a mosque, the south wall and mihrab were built further south, and the doors and windows in the north wall were inserted. The minaret on the east side is built on the site of the former sanctuary. Most of the upper structure, like the mosque roof, has been rebuilt since the destruction in 1917. A porticoed court lies on the north side.

The **Mosque of al-Sayyid Hashem**, on Jaffa St off the north side of al-Wihada Street, is named for the great-grandfather of the Prophet Muhammad, who is said to be buried here. It was built in AD 1850 by Abdul Majid using masonry from other ruins. The domed tomb is placed in the northwest corner of the prayer hall. The minaret was rebuilt in 1903.

To the south of the Great Mosque in the old al-Zaitun quarter is a medieval market building, the **Souk al-Qaisariya**; an endowment records its construction in 1476 by Shaikh Shams al-Din Abul-Wafa' Muhammad al-Himsi. A structure with flanking shops c 50m in length, roofed with a barrel vault, it serves today as the **gold market**; its east entrance with typical Mamluk *ablaq* masonry in banded cream and red, illustrates the importance of the market on the main route to Egypt.

A Mamluk bath house, the **al-Samara**, is the only survivor of many that once existed in Gaza. Entered from the north side, a corridor leads to the square, domed chamber paved with marble mosaic in geometric panels; a central fountain is surrounded by platforms with niches used as cupboards for clothing. The hot rooms are to the north.

The **Church of St. Porphyrius** lies c 150m southwest of the Great Mosque in Ras al-Tali St; probably built at the same time as the Latin parish church in the 1150s or 1160s, it was and is the Greek Orthodox church of Gaza. The level of its pavement, now 1.8–3m below street level, attests to its age, and to the possibility that an earlier Byzantine church lies beneath the present building. It is a single-aisled church of two bays in which the marble columns and capitals are older *spolia*. The iconostasis is 20C; the west door and the north door were slightly altered during restoration work on the church in 1856. If the church is locked, the key may be obtained from the priest who lives above the school opposite. The compound is almost surrounded by the Byzantine cemetery of Gaza, where the grave of Porphyrius is located, which is still used today by the Christian community. Just to the north is Katib al-Waliya Jami', a mosque of the mid-16C.

The **Palace of the Pasha**, also called Napoleon's Fort and al-Radwan Castle, is a much altered building at the east end of al-Wihada St; parts may originate in the Mamluk and Ottoman periods. Its history is as varied as its architecture: it has been the residence of the Ottoman governor; associated with Napoleon's campaign in 1799; a police station in Mandate times; and now a girls' school. On the east side of this building is an Ottoman fountain built under Sultan Abd al-Hamid II in 1900, replacing an older one. Nearby is the **Maqam of Shaikh Abu al-Azm**, sometimes called 'Samson's Grave'; it was built in honour of a shaikh who came from Morocco in the 9C AD.

The **Zawiya of Ahmad al-Badawi** near al-Wihada St. commemorates a Sufi shaikh from Egypt with many followers, who died in 1276. In the south part of the prayer hall is the tomb of Qutlu Khatun (d. 1332), the daughter of Bahadur al-Jukundar, a Mamluk amir of Damascus.

On the east side of the old city and of the Sharia Salah al-Din is the al-Shuja'iya Quarter, which has a large market and two 15C mosques. The **Madrasa of Amir Bardabak al-Dawardar** (the Jami al-Mahkama) has an inscription at the entrance which records that it was built in 1455 by the amir. Mamluk decoration includes muqarnas, with geometric and floral designs. A typical court surrounded by halls and rooms and with minaret, it was used as a religious court during Ottoman times, and as a boys' school in the Mandate period. The **Mosque of Ibn Othman**, also a large Mamluk structure, named for Shihab Iddin Ibn Othman who came from Nablus and lived in Gaza, dates in part from 1400 and contains the tomb of a Mamluk governor of Gaza who died in 1446. It has a large court surrounded by porticoes, and the minaret has an octagonal shaft over a square base. The mosque has two entrances with three niched windows, two with muqarnas ornament. The mihrab was built in 1431.

The ancient harbour of **Anthedon** has been located at the northwest corner of the Beach (Shati) refugee camp. Here the mound of al-Bilakhiya, rising 30m above the surrounding coast, has been under excavation since 1995, revealing its massive mudbrick walls. Its remains date at least from the Iron Age, including the 3m wide ramparts of the 7C BC overbuilt by houses of the 5C, a stepped structure of the Roman period, mosaics, and tombs of the Byzantine period which can be seen in the area above the beach. Its harbour had been blocked with sand by the 1C BC and it was finally abandoned in the 7C AD. About 1km to the south can be seen fortifications and quays, probably of the Maiumas harbour, built in the 4C–5C. About 300m south of the modern harbour, a 6C Orpheus mosaic (now in the Israel Museum in Jerusalem) was excavated in a building with one apse and five aisles. An industrial building complex (a dyer's workshop), dated to the 5C AD, was discovered immediately to the west.

Elsewhere in the Gaza Strip

Other sites of interest are located in the Gaza Strip, but if you want to visit them you are advised to take a local guide.

At **Bayt Hanoun**, 8km north of Gaza is the al-Nasr Mosque, built in 1239 by the Amir Shams al-Din Sunqur; nearby are the tombs of Muslim martyrs who died fighting the Crusaders.

Tell al-Ajjul, the great Bronze Age tell on the north side of the Wadi Gaza and 8km south of Gaza City, was excavated by Sir Flinders Petrie from 1930 to 1934. The principal discoveries included important cemeteries and palaces, especially from the late-third to the mid-second millennium; the site is now being re-excavated. Finds made by Petrie can be seen in the Rockefeller Museum in Jerusalem and in many museums in England.

Dayr al-Balah (Crusader Darum, A. al-Darum or Darun) is 16km southwest of Gaza City. An important cemetery was excavated here, in which distinctive anthropoid clay coffins were used c 1400–1200 BC for the burial of Philistine and other incomers who may have served as mercenaries in the Egyptian army before being settled in the region. There is nothing to be seen at the site, but the clay coffins are displayed in the Rockefeller and Israel Museums in Jerusalem. In the 12C this was the southern border of the Kingdom of Jerusalem. A small rectangular castle was built at Dayr al-Balah in the time of Amalric (1162–73) with a village and a church. The village was sacked by Salah al-Din in 1170. The castle held out, but fell in 1187 and was garrisoned by Salah al-Din; it was stormed by Richard I in 1191, but dismantled in 1192. Nothing of it is known to remain.

The modern mosque of al-Khadr (a Muslim saint often identified with St. George) is located c 200m south of the centre of the town. In the 19C the mosque was a small, converted 12C church, possibly on the site of an older Byzantine church as it incorporated some Byzantine *spolia*.

Khan Yunis, a town 24km southwest of Gaza City, was, as its name implies, the site of an important khan or caravanserai, located 4km inland on the coast road leading to al-Arish and Egypt. The khan was built in 1387 by Amir Yunis Ibn Abd Allah al-Nawruzi, whose blazon with the goblet indicating his service as cupbearer to Sultan Barquq appears on the inscription on the surviving façade of the khan, flanking the arched entrance. Constructed of sandstone and limestone, and formerly rectangular with a round tower at each corner, it was intended to protect travellers along the route. Its two storeys provided for living quarters on the upper floor, goods and animals below. Most of the khan has been demolished, but the minaret of its mosque still stands above the gate. The town mosque is on the opposite side of the square at the centre of this market town, which has a museum with recently discovered mosaics from the Gaza area.

Abasan, 5km southeast of Khan Yunis, has a fragment of a 7C Byzantine mosaic pavement and the small shrine of Abraham (Maqam Khalil al-Rahman), a monument (possibly early 20C) marking the journey of Abraham from Hebron to Egypt.

Rafah, 38km south of Gaza City, is the border town and crossing point to Egypt, with the airport to the southeast.

Galilee

The northern region of Israel is called Galilee, from a Hebrew word meaning 'ring' or 'district', mentioned in Isaiah (9:1) as 'Galilee of the nations' and in Matthew (4:15) as 'Galilee of the Gentiles'. It is divided into Upper and Lower Galilee, mostly limestone hill country with volcanic basalts in the east. Settled in Canaanite times and earlier, then divided between Phoenicia and Israel, it became after the Assyrian conquest in the later 8C increasingly an area of gentile (non-Jewish) settlement. In the 1C BC it was conquered by Alexander Jannaeus, who attempted to Judaise it. The region became a major producer of olive oil. Many Jews suffered during the Roman period in the First and Second Revolts, but after the destruction of Jerusalem by the Romans, Galilee became the focus of Jewish settlement, with centres of administration and learning at Beth Shearim, Sepphoris, Safad and Tiberias. In these areas Byzantine Christianity penetrated only slowly, and after the fall of the Byzantine army, from around the 8C–9C the area was increasingly occupied by Muslim settlers and, later, Turcoman tribes (nomads from central Asia) and Druze.

Upper Galilee, the high inland region from the border with Lebanon south to around the level of the north end of the Sea of Galilee, is fragmented by deep valleys and high hills. The highest point is Mt Meron at 1208m, with the town of Safad at 955m. It is a countryside once densely wooded, and still retaining some residual woodland. It has a high annual rainfall, averaging 500mm but can receive as much as 1000mm. Too high and too mountainous for large-scale agriculture, it was a land of generally small settlements depending on olives and grapes. There are no easy routes through these hills, and there were long periods when the land was only lightly settled.

The area to the south, Lower Galilee, stretches roughly between Akko on the northwest and Beth Shean on the southeast. This region includes the very fertile plains of the Jezreel Valley, with the lower range of hills around Nazareth stretching eastwards towards the Horns of Hattin and Tiberias. The prominent hill of Mt Tabor rises to 562m. The good rainfall (average 500–600mm annually), the fertile soil and the main routes that pass through its plains and valleys make this one of the richest parts of the country, and the location of some of the largest cities. The fields and fishing around the Sea of Galilee were also economically important. The most famous inhabitant was Jesus of Nazareth, the Galilean.

Today it has many collective farms, a tourist industry and some light industry in towns and kibbutz. The population is mainly Jewish, including many recent immigrants. There are important Arab and Druze communities.

For tourist information on the many holiday activities available in Upper Galilee, ☎ 06 693 6945; for Lower Galilee, ☎ 06 673 3846. The main centres are served by bus.

YEHIAM
● ● ● ● ● ● ● ● ●

The ruins of the Crusader castle of Judin (A. Qal'at Jiddin), which was refortified and rebuilt as a residence by Dahir al-Umar in the 18C, is at Yehiam, c 12km east of Nahariyya and 16km northeast of Akko. To get to it, take Highway 89 to Ga'aton junction, and turn onto Highway 8833. The site is run by the National Parks Authority (☎ 04 985 6004), and there are park facilities and a kibbutz exhibition.

Byzantine remains are found in and near the Crusader castle of Judin which was built after 1220 by the Order of Teutonic Knights, and destroyed by Baybars around 1268/71. It lies close to two other Crusader castles, being 5km southwest of Mi'iliya (see p 336) and 5.6km south of Montfort (see p 335). It was partially rebuilt by Dahir al-Umar and again destroyed in 1775 on the orders of Ahmad al-Jazzar (see also Akko p 279). Probably the site of a small village in the 19C, it was occupied and partially restored by a kibbutz from 1946 onwards.

The outer and higher elements of the ruins are 18C–20C, and the core is of Crusader date. The surviving 13C elements of the Crusader castle include two towers on a rocky spur with a high enclosure wall (65m x 30m). The east tower has a basement and solar above, with latrine closet in the south wall on both floors, and was perhaps the residence of the castellan. To the left of the west entrance doorway and on the vaulting on the first floor, the masonry is incised and impressed with white lime putty to give the impression of a regular joint, a technique probably imported from Italy in the 12C–13C. A barrel-vaulted chamber (perhaps the undercroft for a castle chapel above) lies between it and the square west tower which had three storeys, the lower two with barrel vaults, the upper residential, perhaps with a groin-vaulted ceiling. This tower may have been the quarters for the knights.

In the 18C the castle was refortified by local rulers, first by Ahmad Husayn Ibn Khaliq and then by Dahir al-Umar. The earliest Ottoman work includes the north gate tower and outer fortifications with round towers and gun slits; the fine gate has an indirect entrance and concealed gun slits. The main work is of Dahir al-Umar, who ruled 1749–75. A large vaulted basement to the westward extension was probably used for storage and access to cisterns and provides a platform for the palatial apartments above, which included a small bath house and mosque. The bath house is an urban facility rarely found in rural areas, but this is a luxury private bath for one or two people. The mosque, with mihrab, was divided into four groin-vaulted bays with a central pier. The old west tower may have contained the shaikh's private quarters.

MONTFORT
● ● ● ● ● ● ● ● ● ● ●

The main castle in Palestine of the Knights of the Teutonic Order, Montfort lies c 205km north of Jerusalem, in western Upper Galilee, some 18km east of Nahariyya. Turn north off Highway 89 at Mi'ilya for c 5km; alternatively turn south off Route 899 through Gornot for 1km for a view of the castle across the valley.

The site is set on a steep ridge controlling a road to Akko. Montfort was built from 1226, and by 1240 had supplanted Mi'iliya (see below) as the central fortress of the Teutonic Knights. The garrison successfully repulsed an attack in 1266, but after a week-long attack in June 1271 the knights surrendered, and were permitted to leave without arms or property. The castle was then abandoned and never resettled.

Montfort is best viewed from the north, but can be approached from either north or south. The route from Mi'iliya passes through the eastern moat and through the eastern outer fortification wall. The very ruined castle on its wooded ridge is concentric in plan, the inner fortification being the first stage in the construction. It was defended on the east by a rock-cut ditch. The outer gate in the northeast corner led to the main entrance to the inner castle on the northwest. The outer fortifications were constructed later, with a postern in the outer bailey to the northwest; semicircular towers projected on the north and southwest, and the outer wall at least in some areas had a crenellated walkway. At the east end of the earlier rectangular inner fortress is a D-shaped keep built of great drafted stones in which a D-shaped hall overlies a cistern. The apartments of the Grand Master were probably in the missing upper floors of the keep. To the west of the keep was an inner bailey, where later a great hall with three rows of Gothic columns was constructed. In the southwest corner of the hall fragments of stained glass and sculpture suggest that the castle chapel was above on the upper floor. A winepress on the north side, and other finds, suggest the ground floor area was devoted to workrooms and kitchens. The apartments of the knights were probably on a missing upper storey. At the west end of the inner bailey, within an impressive outer wall and fine gate tower (17m high), were two halls above which was probably located the impressive great hall of the castle with a central octagonal column.

Below the castle on the north side, are the remains of a dam and of a two-storey building. The lower floor of the building housed a mill, the upper floor has fine groined vaulting, with a tower (which collapsed in the 1940s); the building was converted into a hall house in the 13C and used as a guest house.

Five kilometres to the southeast by road, **Mi'ilya** also has a ruined Crusader castle (Château du Roi, Castrum Regis) with a Christian Arab village inside it. This castle was first mentioned in 1160 and was granted to Count Joscelin III of Courtenay in 1182; it fell to Salah al-Din in 1187. The castle and its lands were bought from Count Joscelin by the Teutonic Order in 1228 and many of the estate records survive. The castle itself was less important than that at Montfort. The Order also owned the castle at Yehiam (see p 334), all three being part of a defence complex guarding the eastern approaches to Acre. Mi'ilya may have fallen in 1266, certainly before Montfort in 1271, and continued afterwards as a prosperous estate in Muslim ownership.

Remains of the castle can be seen among the houses. The castle is square with projecting corner towers. The present Greek Catholic church is on the east side of the inner ward of the castle; it was probably rebuilt in the 1870s over an older Crusader church with monolithic columns. Two capitals in Corinthian style, one with a cross-in-circle, lie next to the church. In the village some of the houses may be 12C–13C in origin and often have crosses over the doors. There is a badly preserved polygonal outer wall.

BARAM

Virtually on the Lebanese border is Baram, where there is a well-preserved synagogue dating to the 4C–5C AD. The village, some 15km northwest of Safad, is reached on Highway 899; alternatively take the side road leading north off Highway 89 which also leads to Baram. The site is run by the National Parks Authority (☎ 06 698 9301).

The synagogue is a rectangular structure with porch, constructed of fine masonry; the façade, which faces towards Jerusalem, is almost completely preserved to the cornice. It has three ornate doorways. Inside is preserved the layout of columns on east, west and north, and the paving. Little remains of a second smaller synagogue in the vicinity, the lintel of which is in the Louvre. The synagogue at Baram lies at the northern limits of the distribution of Galilean synagogues, which are concentrated in eastern Upper Galilee and around the Sea of Galilee. The adjacent Maronite village which stood on the remains of an older village, was destroyed following the removal of the inhabitants in 1948, but the church still serves a local Maronite community who have struggled to retain their rights and access to it. Nearby is the **Baram Oaks Nature Reserve**, which preserves some of the indigenous kermes oak forest, which once covered much of the hill country.

SAFAD

The region's principal town, Safad (Crusader Saphet; H. Zefat) stands high in the hills of Upper Galilee. It is 192km from Jerusalem, on the south side of Highway 89. The area enjoys mild summer temperatures of 18°–29°C in August, while January is cool, ranging from 4° to 9°C; the mean annual rainfall is high at 718mm.

Practical information

 Information office
Tourist Information Office, 50 Jerusalem Street (☎ 06 692 7485). There is a visitors' centre in the old Saray building.

 Where to stay
Safad has a number of hostels and private rooms, as well as a small range of hotels, including the moderately priced *Hadar*, Rehov Yavetz (☎ 06 692 0068) and the higher-rated *Plaza Ruth Rimon Inn*, Old City (☎ 06 076 6706).

History

Little is known of Safad's early history. Tombs of the late third millennium and sherds of Middle Bronze II date indicate an early settlement on the citadel hill. Middle and Late Bronze Age burial caves were found c 500m south of Jerusalem St, on the slopes of Mt Canaan. The town was fortified by Josephus against the Romans in the First Jewish Revolt. From the Roman and Byzantine periods onwards it became one of the four major centres of Judaism, associated especially with religious mysticism and the Kabbala. A Crusader castle, said to have been founded in 1102, was rebuilt from 1140 onwards, apparently in the ownership of the king of Jerusalem (Fulk of Anjou, then Amalric); it was granted to the Templars in 1168 and added much to Frankish security in the upper Galilee region. It was captured by Salah al-Din in 1188; dismantled by al-Mu'azzam Isa in 1220/21; rebuilt by the Templars between 1240 and 1260; and retaken by Baybars in 1266. The castle was rebuilt by Baybars and al-Mansur in the following years, when the huge cylindrical keep was added, three storeys (60m) high with a cistern below. In 1170 according to Benjamin of Tudela, no Jews were living in the town, but a Jewish community is noted in the early 13C and the 14C.

Many Sephardic Jews, who had been exiled from Spain in 1492, settled in Safad and developed it as a centre of religious mysticism. This was a reasonably prosperous period for the town. The region of Safad in 1468 had 1200 villages, but by 1521 only 231 villages were occupied, evidence of a tremendous regional decline in the early 16C. Evliya Celebi travelling in Galilee in 1648–50 found the castle in ruins, and used to pen sheep and goats; but the town had a 'palace' for the pasha, and was a tax-farming centre, with a strong military garrison. The inhabitants, according to Celebi, were poor through oppression. He describes it as inhabited by many Jews and as having many synagogues. There were four shaikhs leading the four Orthodox Muslim rites, with eight main mosques, many smaller ones and six Muslim religious schools; there were three caravanserais, three covered markets (one flourishing, but two were unoccupied and turned into guest houses for travellers) and six public baths in Safad 'three of which are open all the year through'. The gardens of Safad were notable for olive and mulberry plantations.

The castle was refortified in the 17C, and again in the 18C by Dahir al-Umar, who built a citadel on top of the older citadel, and repaired it after the earthquake of 1759. This aided the revival of the town, and attracted the settlement of a group of Jewish Hasidim in 1778. In 1812–14 there was an epidemic and many inhabitants fled. Fighting between Arabs and Druze led to a further decline, and in 1837 an earthquake destroyed the citadel and the town, killing 5000 people. The ruined citadel has been used as a source of building stone for the town over the years, and in the Mandate period the Crusader/Mamluk cistern in the keep was incorporated into the town water system. Settlement fluctuated in the 19C, but by 1948 the population numbered 12,000 Arabs and 2000 Jews. The Arab inhabitants fled the city in 1948.

Though there are no major features to be viewed in the older part of the town, the setting is pleasant for a walking tour. There is an Artists' Colony with galleries of modern Jewish art. The town and its environs contain many synagogues and Jewish tombs. At the southern end of the old town, the Red Mosque (Jami al-Ahmar) was built by Baybars in 1275/76; nearby is a Mamluk tomb (14C).

The **castle** above the town is very much ruined, the site planted with pine trees, but from it you get a good view over town and wooded countryside. The castle was large, oval, concentric in plan on an oval-shaped summit, with steep slopes except on the south where the town occupies a plateau. The great Mamluk cylindrical keep (35m diameter) has been partly excavated. Its outer wall is battered and built of massive stones; the entrance lies on the northwest side, 3m wide, and leads into a small vaulted hall which opened on the right into an ascending spiral passage (the floor is destroyed and it was blocked in the Ottoman period). It once provided access for five horses abreast to the terrace at the top of the tower.

ZIPPORI

Ancient **Sepphoris** (H. Zippori, A. Saffuriya, Crusader le Saforie) was an important Roman and Byzantine city, the centre for Mishnaic and Talmudic studies in the Byzantine period, with fine mosaics and the remains of a Crusader church and fortress. It lies off Highway 79, 6km northwest of Nazareth, between Hamovil junction and Nazareth; entered through Moshav Zippori (the collective farm). The site is run by the National Parks Authority: there are toilets and refreshments and an information centre; ☎ 06 656 8272.

History

The site was mentioned by Josephus as existing in the time of Alexander Jannaeus in the early 1C BC; it was the administrative centre for Galilee in Hasmonean and Roman times. The Romans conquered it and sold its inhabitants into slavery, and then granted it to Herod Antipas who lived at Sepphoris until he founded Tiberias and moved the capital there in AD 23. Herod Antipas fortified Sepphoris and renamed it Autocratoris. Its inhabitants remained loyal to Rome during the First Revolt, but during the time of Hadrian the Jewish council was abolished and a gentile administration replaced it; the city was renamed Diocaesarea. In the 2C AD the renowned Rabbi Judah ha-Nasi moved here from Beth She'arim, completed his redaction of the Mishna, and established the Sanhedrin (the council of 71 scholars who administered Jewish law) here for 17 years. The majority of the population was increasingly Jewish, even after the Sanhedrin was moved to Tiberias c AD 235. A palatial villa excavated on the top of the hill may have been the Roman governor's residence in the 3C. In the time of Constantine, Count Joseph of Tiberias attempted to build a church in Sepphoris despite the presence of a Jewish majority in the population. The remains of a synagogue with a mosaic pavement dating to the 3C–4C were found beneath the Crusader church. Jewish scholars worked on the writing of the Jerusalem Talmud here. Sepphoris had a rich agricultural hinterland, and a large settlement existed 2km north of the site where much of the pottery used by the inhabitants of Sepphoris was manufactured. In AD 351 a Jewish revolt began in Sepphoris, but was crushed. The city was destroyed in the earthquake of 363.

When Sepphoris was restored, its civic centre was shifted to the lower ground on the east side of the hill, and laid out with fine colonnaded *cardo* and *decumanus*. The town may then have been still largely Jewish, but the Christian community grew in the 5C–6C and bishops of Sepphoris attended synods in Jerusalem in 518 and 536. The Piacenza Pilgrim records a church at Sepphoris in the late 6C where there were various objects associated with the Virgin Mary. This may be the source of a later tradition identifying Sepphoris with the home of Mary's parents, Anne and Joachim. Evidence for glassmaking in the 6C has also been found. The town seems to have been burnt, perhaps during the Persian invasion or the Arab conquest in the 7C, and then to have declined, but its Jewish graves were still being visited in the 12C.

In Crusader times there was probably just a 12C village here with fortified keep and parish church. The Frankish army used the springs on various occasions, notably just before the Battle of the Horns of Hattin (see p 341) in 1187. A village in the 13C, which belonged to the archbishop of Nazareth, appears to have been composed of Latin, Orthodox and possibly Muslim inhabitants. The land would have been taken by Baybars between 1263 and 1265, but the castle is still mentioned in the later 13C. The tradition that Sepphoris was the home of Anne and Joachim is mentioned by pilgrims and travellers from the 14C to 17C, some of whom made pilgrimage to the church, which by the 17C was served by a Greek Catholic priest with some support from the Franciscans in Nazareth. The Ottoman government permitted pilgrimage from the mid-17C. The castle was refortified in the 18C by Dahir al-Umar. In 1879 the Franciscans got permission to demolish 39 houses of the Arab village of Saffuriya standing inside the ruins of the church, and cleared and excavated the site. They built a hospice over the east end of the church.

The Roman, Crusader and 18C public buildings are mostly on the summit of the hill, the principal remains of the Byzantine period lie on the lower ground to the east, the Crusader church is to the west, and the cemeteries are mostly located on the slopes of the nearby hills. Long-running excavation projects are in progress at the site, uncovering remains of the Hellenistic to Islamic periods. You start your visit at the ticket office on the upper northeast slope of the hill. The site has good information panels.

Passing an area of Byzantine houses, the **theatre** is cut into the bedrock of the north slope of the hill, c 70m in diameter, with the ends of the *cavea* and the *scaenae frons* constructed in front. Three entrances to the *cavea* are cut into the back wall, which is lined with columns. Most of the stone from the 4500 seats has been looted, and partly now restored. The theatre was built in the late 1C/early 2C AD and continued in use until at least the 5C. Although the sages and rabbis forbade Jewish attendance at games and theatres it is clear that large sections of the Jewish community did visit and indeed occasionally participated in performances and contests.

At the west end of the hill a view point and path overlook the remains of the Crusader church near the foot of the slope, next to the modern Convent of the Sisters of St. Anne. The church is normally locked. The **Crusader Parish Church of St. Anne** probably dates to the second half of the 12C. In the 14C Latin Christians generally believed that Anne and Joachim, the Virgin Mary's parents, lived in Sepphoris and that it was the birthplace of St. Anne. Only the aumbries, sacristies and the outer walls of the first bay of the east end of the church survive fairly intact, with a 19C Franciscan hospice built over them. The arches of the apses are supported on piers with multiple half and quarter columns, making a decorative façade for the hospice. The church was a three-aisled basilica, probably of five bays, which incorporated some Late Roman and Byzantine granite columns and limestone capitals, but also contemporary broad-leaf and derived Corinthian capitals, some of which lie in the garden in front of the hospice. There was a tower above the north chapel or sacristy, reached by a staircase inside the north wall of the first bay.

Down the slope to the north is the so-called Tomb of Jacob's Daughters, once identfied with that of Rabbi Judah ha-Nasi who was probably buried in Beth She'arim. It is a tomb of the 3C AD, now called the Tomb of Rabbi Yodan Nessiya.

At the west end of the summit is a residential area mainly of the Roman period, rebuilt in the Byzantine period. You can see part of a much repaired street, and remains of courtyard houses, many with ritual baths and most with cisterns.

Prominently located at the centre of the summit is the **fortress**, built in the Crusader period on Roman foundations. Only the basement and part of the first floor of a tower-keep survives. The tower, with walls 3.75m thick, is built with *spolia* including sarcophagi; on the south side, the door (rebuilt in the 18C) opens into a barrel-vaulted basement and, on the left, to intramural stairs to the ground floor. The plain windows are replacements from the 1870s. The upper part of the tower was refortified by Dahir al-Umar in the 18C; the house was added to the top of the structure c 1900. Until 1948, the Arab village of Saffuriya was located around the tower. The building was badly restored as a visitor centre in 1994; there is a view point on the roof.

A **palatial villa** excavated just to the east is now excellently displayed and explained under a protective structure. It has a triclinium (dining room) with a very fine ***mosaic**, the central panels (11 of 15 survive) of which illustrate the life and pagan cult of Dionysus, and focus particularly on his role as god of wine and fertility. The small panels, of very high quality, depict in tiny and intricately coloured stones scenes of gift-bearers, grape-treading, merrymakers and drunkenness, as well as the education and the wedding of the god. The panels are framed by a band of wreathed acanthus containing figures, with a particularly notable bust of a woman at the north end perhaps reflecting the importance of the ecstatic Dionysiac cult among women. The white areas of the mosaic mark the position of the dining couches. To the north are bathing rooms and latrines, to the west a two-storey range of rooms, and to the south a courtyard with a pool surrounded by a colonnade. The villa, dating to the early 3C AD, may have been the governor's residence, and was probably destroyed in the earthquake of 363.

Down to the east side of the hill extensive excavations have revealed an orthogonal street plan (i.e. based on right angles) centred on a colonnaded street running southwest–northeast with a colonnaded *decumanus* crossing it; the limestone paved streets were flanked by colonnaded porticoes paved with mosaics. Several Roman structures, some of them with ritual baths were found here. The street plan continued in use in the Byzantine period, with new buildings on top of the earlier ones. The main crossing was renovated by Bishop Eutropius. On the southwest corner of the intersection, at the centre of the new town, a large church was excavated. A Roman **bath house** on its south side, also on the west side of the colonnaded street, continued in use in the Byzantine period. The '**Nile Festival House**' is opposite the bath house on the east side of the street, a large complex built in the early 5C, possibly as the town's public basilica. The ***5C figural mosaic** for which the building is named lies in the west wing: at the centre the Nile river issues from the mouth of a hippopotamus, and separates two scenes, the upper with Nilometer, deities, and animals, the lower showing the city of Alexandria with the Pharos (the lighthouse of Alexandria, one of the wonders of the ancient world) and lively hunting scenes. Other mosaics in the same building depict Amazons hunting and dancing. The contrast between these lively, bright and somewhat naive scenes, still of high quality but carried out with larger stones, and the Dionysus mosaic of the 3C, emphasises the artistic changes that had taken place.

To the northwest is a building which has been identified as the town forum.

The Talmud records that there were 18 synagogues in the late Roman town. A building identified as a **6C synagogue** has been excavated a little distance to the northwest of the centre of the town; its mosaic includes a zodiac at the centre, depictions relating to Temple sacrifices, the Ark, and a menorah.

The higher western part of the site relied on cisterns for water, but the water from two aqueducts reached the lower eastern areas from plentiful springs to the southeast of the town. A huge subterranean water system dating from the 2C–4C AD, which continued to be used up to the 7C as part of the infrastructure of the city, included a reservoir 260m long and c 10m deep which lies 1.5km to the east. It can be visited by marked footpath.

THE HORNS OF HATTIN

This historic site is on the north side of Highway 77, 8km to the west of and above Tiberias.

The **battle of the Horns of Hattin** led to the loss of the Frankish Kingdom of Jerusalem. The final days of the Crusader army were ill-judged and the end of their kingdom was probably foredoomed when they marched against the Muslim army of Salah al-Din. The events from 3 July 1187, when the Frankish army left the springs at Saffuriya (Zippori), until their parched but brave defeat on the hill above Tiberias on 5 July are a well-known story; the heat of summer, the water-less hilltop, the battle fought in smoke generated by grass fires lit by the Arab army, the weight of chain mail and weapons, the exhaustion. The defeat was followed by the execution of Reynald de Chatillon and of the Templar and Hospitaller knights, the captivity of the king of Jerusalem, Guy de Lusignan, and his barons, and the sale into slavery of Frankish soldiers and settlers who were unable to pay ransoms. The battle changed the course of history in the Levant, although the Crusader story continued for the next century in the area. If you are driving from Zippori, you can follow the line of march of the Crusader army to the twin volcanic peaks (the Horns of Hattin) that mark the site of the battle.

The peaks are also of archaeological interest. A volcanic crater is defended by a series of walls, with a Late Bronze Age fortress on the southern summit. A later Iron Age town that extended over the whole area of the crater was probably destroyed in the Assyrian campaign of Tiglath-Pileser III in 733/32 BC. Although small excavations have been carried out on the site, there is little to be seen. The important Druze shrine of **Nabi Shu'aib** lies below the peaks on the north side. It is approached from the east by a minor road 7717.

CANA OF GALILEE

The small village of Kafr Kanna in Lower Galilee, where tradition locates the story of Jesus' first miracle—the changing of water into wine at the wedding feast attended by Jesus and his mother Mary (John 2:1–11)—is c 7km northeast of Nazareth on Highway 154.

The land at Kafr Kanna was sold to the Hospitallers by the lord of Sidon in 1254. By the 14C a Byzantine tradition locating the miracle was established here, and in the 17C travellers identified the remains of a large building with the church built by the Empress Helena in the 4C. The Franciscans were established in Kafr Kanna in 1641, and built the present church over an older church from 1879.

To visit the church (open 08.00–12.00, 14.00–18.00 or –17.00 in winter, Sat 08.00–12.00; closed Sun), park on the side of the highway and walk down the narrow village street to the Franciscan church on the right. A courtyard lies in front of the small church of 1881, with angel figures in the façade between two bell towers over an arcaded narthex. The church is built on two levels. The upper level has the Franciscan chapel of 1881; preserved beneath its floor is a fragment of a 5C–6C Byzantine mosaic which preserves the name of the donor in Aramaic: 'In memory of the pious Joseph, son of Tanhum, son of Bota and of his children who made this table, may it be for them a blessing. Amen.' On the lower floor are a chapel and a small museum with various finds from the site, including a winepress, a plastered cistern and vessels of varied antiquity. Recent excavations have uncovered on the site the remains of dwellings of the 1C–4C AD, of a 5C porticoed atrium; of a Christian funerary building of the 5C–6C; and of a medieval building.

Opposite is the Greek Orthodox church (usually closed); near it, two 13C capitals are displayed. The local shop sells 'Wedding Wine'.

NAZARETH
• • • • • • • • • • •

As the place of the announcement of the birth of Jesus to the Virgin Mary, and the childhood home of Jesus, Nazareth is the most significant town in the north for Christians, who have made it a focus of pilgrimage since the 4C. It lies on the slopes of a hill in Lower Galilee, 157km from Jerusalem, on Highway 79 north of the intersection with Highway 60. There are several important churches, Byzantine ruins and a modern basilica. The town has a population of c 58,000, half of whom are Arab Muslim and half Arab Christian, including Christians of every sect. The new Jewish town of Nazareth Illit lies on the hills above the town.

Practical information

Getting there
The bus station is on John Paul VI St.

Information office
Tourist Information Office, Casanova St (☎ 06 657 3003).

Where to stay
There are large new hotels in modern Nazareth Illit *Marriot Nazareth*, 2 Hermon (☎ 04 602 8200; 🖷 04 601 2238) and *Renaissance*. Below in the old town is the *Nazareth Gardens Hotel* (☎ 06 656 6007; 🖷 04 656 6008) and the more modest *Nazareth* (☎ 06 657 7777), both on John Paul VI St.

Eating out
Various restaurants can be found along John Paul VI St.

History

The town The area around the main churches has produced silos, wine and oil installations and pottery of Middle Bronze II, Iron Age II, Roman and Byzantine date, suggesting that this was the location of the ancient village of Nazareth. One of the many caves that exist here was identified no later than the 4C as the place of the Annunciation. The New Testament gives varying details concerning the lives of Jesus and his family, but is firm in the otherwise rather odd association with Nazareth. According to Eusebius, Nazareth was an entirely Jewish small town in the Roman and Byzantine periods. Some evidence of Jews who had converted to Christianity (Judaeo-Christians) is provided by a 3C historian (Africanus), and pilgrimage to Nazareth is attested by the late 4C. The date of the first church built in Nazareth on the site of the cave or grotto of the Annunciation, is unclear, though perhaps one existed in the time of Constantine or earlier; there was a church from the later 4C onwards. What happened in Nazareth during the difficult period of the Persian invasion in 614, when Jews are said to have allied with the Persians against the Christians, is also unknown. The town continued to be occupied, and was captured by the Crusaders in 1099.

The Crusader town was not fortified, and the activity of the town centred on its Christian devotion. It had become the episcopal seat by 1129, and as well as the cathedral church, had a chapter of regular canons, a hospital for pilgrims, and a library. Salah al-Din expelled the Christian inhabitants in 1187; the town was returned to the Franks in 1229 but they held it only until 1291. The town remained blighted during the Mamluk period, though some Christian pilgrimage is recorded in the 14C. Conditions for Christians improved in the early 17C, in the time of the Druze amir, Fakhr al-Din, when permits were given for monks, monasteries and the establishment of the Franciscans in the town. Orthodox Christians from Transjordan and Lebanese Maronite Christian families settled in the eastern part of the town around the spring, which another tradition also linked with the Annunciation. Conditions again declined following the execution of Fakhr al-Din by the Turks, and Bedouin incursions made the lives of the inhabitants unsettled and impoverished. Under Dahir al-Umar in the mid-18C, conditions again improved in the town: the Franciscans began to restore the Church of the Annunciation; the Greek Orthodox built a church dedicated to the Archangel Gabriel over the spring; the Greek Catholics established themselves in the Church of the Synagogue. More Christians migrated here from Bethlehem. Under Jazzar Pasha conditions for Christians became dramatically worse, and a massacre was only averted by the intervention of Sir Sidney Smith. Since the mid-19C Nazareth has been a central town for Christian pilgrimage and the location of many monasteries.

The Church of the Annunciation There was probably a church on the present site of the Grotto of the Annunciation in the early 4C; an altar is referred to c 384, and a church c 570. Half a metre below the floor of the Crusader church on this site, a Byzantine church was excavated, dating probably to the 4C–5C; it had three aisles, a single projecting apse and a large atrium. A small monastery was built south of the church and extended beyond the line of the later Crusader church. In c 680 Arculf saw two churches in Nazareth, one at Mary's spring and the other at the traditional site of the Annunciation. The latter church certainly survived into the 8C and perhaps as late as the early 9C, when 12 monks, probably associated with the Church of the Annunciation, are mentioned in the Commemoratorium in AD 808. Saewulf refers to a church on the site of the Annunciation in 1102/03. This may have been one built or restored by Tancred, for a detailed account of the church and the grotto of the Annunciation in which the holy family had lived, is given by Abbot Daniel in 1106–08. He refers to the holy place which had been laid waste but had since been thoroughly rebuilt by the Franks; he also refers to the very rich and hospitable Latin bishop. However it seems unlikely that this was the great church whose plan survives.

The Crusader church was larger than the underlying Byzantine church. It had the conventual buildings of the canons on the south side, and probably the bishop's palace on the north side. The church itself was a three-aisled church of six bays, probably with a crossing covered by a dome fronting three apses. The Grotto formed part of a complex below the north aisle containing the House of Mary, with an edicule above. Great effort, time and money went into the adornment of this church, some of which was not completed by 1187, for magnificent capitals, carved with scenes from the lives of the Apostles by French craftsmen, were buried for safekeeping beneath the floor of an adjoining building before they could be installed. It may be that this church dates from a great rebuilding later in the century, perhaps after the earthquake of 1170, and is the church described in 1172. Following the Battle of the Horns of Hattin in 1187, the Christian inhabitants of Nazareth took refuge in the church, but were slaughtered. The church was profaned, but left standing, and Salah al-Din permitted a few clergy to return in 1192. Christian access was permitted, and finally in 1241 Christian control was reasserted. St. Louis made pilgrimage here in 1251. However, in 1263 one of the amirs of Baybars attacked the town and razed the church to the ground. Pilgrims were still permitted access to the Grotto (which was also venerated by Muslims) in 1272, but in 1283 Christians were explicitly forbidden to rebuild the church.

By the 14C Christian pilgrims were charged an entrance fee by the Muslims guarding the Grotto; the site of the church was full of rubbish, and later used for stabling cattle. Parts of it survived. The Franciscans had established a house in the town in the late 14C for a short period, and appear to have controlled the site of the Annunciation for a period in the mid-16C. They started to repair the church in 1620, when they restored and occupied the former bishop's palace on the north side of the church. They were, however, several times expelled in the 17C. In 1730 the Franciscans completed a new church which stood on a north/south axis before the Grotto. Enlarged in 1871, this church was demolished in 1955 for the construction of the present church on the Crusader foundations, which was consecrated in 1969.

Note that parking is impossible in streets in the vicinity of the church; there is a free public car park opposite the *Tourist Information Centre*. Visitors should dress appropriately to visit the churches.

The modern **Church of the Annunciation** (open 08.00–11.45, 14.00–18.00 or –17.00 in winter) is the parish church for 7000 Latin Christians. It is built on two levels above the **cave**, which may date originally from the Iron Age. The cave has been recut and rebuilt many times since the 4C. It may be viewed from the large lower church. To the right of the entrance to the lower church, steps ascend to the upper level, to the vast church decorated with mosaics presented by communities around the world. The shape of the concrete roof is based on that of the flower of the white or Madonna lily, a symbol of the Virgin, and is a landmark 55m high.

In the courtyard on the north side of the church is the baptistery. Some oil presses and silos which are part of the many rock cuttings associated with the old village on the site, are preserved here.

The **Franciscan Museum** (open: 09.00–11.45, 14.00–17.30) is on the east side of the courtyard. It has a model of the Crusader church, which shows three doors on the west, although there was probably only one. Fragments of the sculpture which decorated its arch and tympanum survive. The most important items in the museum are the five *historiated capitals*, which are among the finest examples of 12C Romanesque art to have survived. They were found in 1908, buried under a floor in the old Franciscan convent which was then just outside the north door of the church. Four of the capitals each have six decorated facets with scenes from the lives of the apostles Peter, Thomas, James the Great and Matthew. They were made to be set on engaged fluted polygonal columns. The fifth capital, with a female figure leading an apostle through hell, was designed to fit on a rounded engaged column. All the figures are set below canopies, and all were carved by the same sculptor of the French Romanesque school. It seems likely that the four capitals of the apostles were intended for a new edicule over the Grotto of the Annunciation. The fifth may have been intended as a replacement in the nave for older capitals removed during this work. Other fragments have survived, perhaps from the nave. The fine torso of St. Peter holding the keys and the church was probably designed for the outside of the building, perhaps at an entrance. Another sculpted capital from this site is displayed in the Museum of the Greek Orthodox Patriarchate in Jerusalem (see p 187); and a torso at Chatsworth in England also comes from Nazareth.

The Latin **Church of St. Joseph** (the Church of the Nutrition, built in 1914) lies northeast across the courtyard. It is open 08.00–11.45, 14.00–1800 (–17.00 in winter). Tradition locates here the house of Joseph, where Jesus spent his childhood. The site has extensive archaeological remains beneath it, including many rock-cut caves, and bottle-shaped silos probably of the late Roman period. Above them is a series of tanks with mosaic floors and cellars which are the remains of a Byzantine winepress, though once thought to have been a Judaeo-Christian baptistery. Over this a church was built in the 12C. Its dedication is not clear, but it was certainly identified as the house of Joseph by the 16C–17C. It was a three-aisled basilica of six bays, with three apses. At some points the walls survived to 2.5m in height. The present church was built on these foundations, which can still be seen in the lower walls, as can the lower part of the west door. The present church also has three aisles. Down at the lower level, parts of the 12C apse can be seen, as can the silos and winepress which underlie the church. Looking back from the entrance to the church, you have a good view of the Church of the Annunciation.

The **Church of St. Gabriel** (open Mon–Sat 08.00–17.00, Sun 12.00–14.00) stands 650m to the northeast (take the road above the north side of St. Joseph's) by the spring (see below) and at c 600m, the public fountain known as Mary's Well. The waters of the spring were channelled probably before the 12C. The first mention of a church on the site is that of Abbot Daniel in 1106–08, but its association with the Annunciation is even older, the first encounter between Mary and the archangel Gabriel at the spring being mentioned in the *Proto-Gospel of James*. There may have been a Byzantine church on the site in the 6C–7C, and certainly by 1185; probably it was always an Orthodox church, but there is some uncertainty about the few years following the Crusader conquest when Crusader sources mention a Latin priory of St. Gabriel. From the 14C the superstructure was increasingly ruined, but there was still access to the chapel containing the spring. In 1741 the Greek Orthodox gained permission from Dahir al-Umar allowing them to take over from the Franciscans and Greek Catholics who had earlier been in possession of the site, and in 1750 they built the present church on the south side of the lower chapel. The wooden iconostasis dates from 1767. Seven steps descend to the lower chapel of the spring from the north aisle. A narrow single aisle (which can be very crowded with pilgrims), is roofed by a barrel vault, and the walls are lined with blind arcades ornamented with coloured marble and glazed ceramic of c 1750. At the north end the spring runs beneath an altar. On the right, a blocked stair probably once led up to a convent of nuns according to a 17C account, but its date is unknown. The same account

(Quaresmi) also records that in the 17C there was an altar in the middle of the east wall, now covered by the 18C arcading. The remains of a Byzantine bath house have recently been uncovered and can be seen in a nearby café.

The **Synagogue Church** (open Mon–Sat 08.00–12.00, 14.00–17.00, Sun 10.00–12.00) is 100m west of St. Joseph's, on the street running north from the Church of the Annunciation. It is linked to the traditions that Jesus studied and read from the Book of Isaiah in the synagogue in Nazareth, stories which were current in both Byzantine and medieval times. A church existed by the 12C. The site was ruined and full of rubbish in the early 18C when it was acquired by the Franciscans, who cleared it and made it available to Greek Catholics (Melkites). The Melkites were given the structure in 1771 and built a new church near it in 1882. Little of the surviving structure is certainly medieval, and none appears to be of a church.

MOUNT TABOR

'He was transfigured; his face shone like the sun, and his clothes became white as the light.' So the Gospel describes the Transfiguration of Christ in front of the Apostles Peter, James and John (Matt. 17:1-8). The Bible does not name the setting, but by the 4C the principal location was a rock on the high place of Mount Tabor (the Mount of the Transfiguration). Peter offered to build a shelter there for the Lord, and for Moses and Elijah (Elias) who had also appeared in the vision, so all three were later venerated on the mountain. This strategic hill has also been the site of many battles over the millennia. Its location is off Highway 65, c 15km northeast of Afula.

Eating out
Mizra Grill (☎ 06 642 9214), near Mount Tabor; serves steak meals.

History

The hill rises c 550m above the plain of Jezreel; it was occupied by a Seleucid fortress in the 3C BC, was refortified during the First Jewish Revolt in AD 66 by Josephus, but fell to Vespasian in 67. In 348 St. Cyril of Jerusalem preferred Mt Tabor to Mt Hermon as the site of the Transfiguration, and by the 4C there was a church on the site; by 570 there were three churches (or perhaps a large church with chapels dedicated to Moses and Elias) and by the 7C a fortified monastery with which Armenian monks were associated. A Greek bishop is mentioned in the 9C. It was an important church during the Crusader period, when many hermits lived in cells on the mountain slopes. A Latin abbot was appointed soon after 1099, and the conversion of an Orthodox monastery to a Benedictine house under a bishop 1103–28/29 is recorded; the three Byzantine churches or chapels (of the Saviour, of St. Moses and of St. Elias) were still surviving in 1101–03. A band of Muslims raided the monastery in 1113, but despite the devastation, the monastery was re-established by 1115. During the 12C, the old Byzantine church of the Transfiguration was replaced by a Romanesque three-aisled basilica of six bays, with three apses. This 12C church enclosed the rock which was held to be the site of the Transfiguration. To north and south of the church were the extensive buildings of the Benedictine monastery including a chapel and a small bath house (probably Ayyubid).

In 1183 part of Salah al-Din's army climbed the mountain and sacked the Greek monastery of St. Elias, but failed to take the larger fortified Latin monastery; Salah al-Din was more successful in 1187, but appears not to have demolished the church. From 1212 al-Adil and then al-Mu'azzam Isa built massive fortifications on the whole higher plateau of the mountain to guard the road to Akko; their wall was defended by 13 towers and a rock-cut ditch. Following a Crusader attack in 1217 which was nearly successful, al-Mu'azzam demolished these fortifications; but the main church of the Transfiguration seems to have survived most of this activity, and pilgrims continued to visit it. It was back in Frankish hands from 1229 to 1241; in 1255 it was granted to the Hospitallers as too vulnerable a position for the re-establishment of the monastery. Baybars set up camp at the foot of the hill in 1263 and, negotiations failing, destroyed the church. The hill became a royal hunting park for the Mamluks. In the 14C there is a description of local Christians decking the ruined churches with flags at the feast of the Transfiguration (6 August), a custom which appears to have continued for many centuries. In 1631 Fakhr al-Din granted the Franciscans permission to reside on Mt Tabor, permission confirmed by the Ottoman government on various occasions in the 17C–18C. The Franciscans used principally some of the rooms of the Ayyubid castle bath house but rediscovered the ruined Crusader church in 1858 and began work on it. The work was slow in completion, but by 1924 the present church was erected over the 12C building.

There is a good view from the top of Mt Tabor, which underlines the strategic significance of this hill overlooking the great road running inland from the coast. Coaches are no longer permitted to drive to the top of the hill and there is no public transport. The Ayyubid (13C) walls can be traced around the summit which is divided into Greek Orthodox and Latin Catholic areas. The Latin area is reached through al-Adil's main fortress gate (The Gate of the Winds).

The main **Church of the Saviour** (or Transfiguration) lies at the southeast edge of the plateau, with twin towers flanking the entrance to the basilica (architects F. and A. Barluzzi). Open 08.00–12.00, 14.00–17.00; closed Sat and during services. All three periods of the church (Byzantine, Crusader, 20C) may have been built to roughly the same plan. In the crypt, the west door is now blocked by the new entrance and the lowered floor of the nave. The chapel to south of the west entrance had a 12C wall tomb, and a mosaic floor, which was relaid in 1924.

About 20m west of the Church of the Transfiguration in the old monastery area, on the north side of the entrance path, are the remains of a **small chapel** which may have been the 12C private chapel of the abbot and, like the main church, probably survived to c 1263. The entrance is in the west end of the south wall, a bench lines the walls, and the base of a chancel screen survives. Two steps lead up to the sanctuary, and a projection on the upper step marks the original location of the altar (the altar set further back is modern); there are remains of a window and two aumbries in the apse.

The Greek **Church of St. Elias** lies 230m northwest of the church of the Transfiguration, in the Greek area. Built in 1845, and decorated with wall paintings in 1912, it is a three-aisled basilica of four bays. The lower part of the apses may be early 12C.

Connected with the ascetic hermit tradition on the mountain is the **Cave Church of St. Melchizedek**, located in the northwest angle of the upper plateau. A 4C tradition associated Melchizedek with Mt Tabor, where he was said to have spent seven years as a hermit before meeting and blessing Abraham. Most of the present structure appears to date to the 19C, reusing older masonry.

BET SHE'ARIM

This ancient Jewish city became the central Jewish burial ground in the 2C–4C AD after the Second Jewish Revolt, with a great network of rock-hewn catacombs.

The site is near Highways 75, 722, between Hashomrim and Hatishbi junctions, off Highway 66, c 15km inland from Haifa and c 20km northwest of Megiddo. It is run by the National Parks Authority (☎ 04 983 1643).

History

The site was occupied continuously from the Iron Age II until the Early Islamic period. It is identified with Besara, a village which had belonged to the Hasmoneans from the time of Alexander Jannaeus. According to Josephus (*Life*, 118–19), in the 1C AD Besara was the main village of a royal estate belonging to Queen Berenice (the great-granddaughter of Herod the Great). It passed to the Romans following the First Revolt. After the Second Revolt the Romans forbade Jews to live in Jerusalem, and Galilee became increasingly the focus of Jewish settlement. Rabbi Judah ha-Nassi (c AD 135–217), teacher of the Law and codifier of the Mishnah, who had good relations with the Romans, was given the estate by Marcus Aurelius Antoninus (AD 161–180). Until then it had been a small Herodian town. Rabbi Judah settled in the town, established the Sanhedrin (see p 339) here, and the town expanded enormously, with large buildings and a basilica. Though Rabbi Judah became ill and moved to Sepphoris, he planned to be buried here, and this probably happpened in AD 220. It seems to have led to a desire for other Jews to be buried at Bet She'arim—not just the inhabitants of the town, but Jews from other areas of Palestine and abroad, from Syria, Mesopotamia and Arabia.

A great complex of catacombs developed, consisting of underground courts (some with mosaics) and corridors from which doorways (some with stone doors) open onto burial halls containing sarcophagi, loculi (niches), arcosolia and pits, with both family and public tombs, some holding as many as 400 burials. The tombs were decorated with relief carving, painting and inscriptions. The art depicts the symbols of Jewish ritual, the menorah (the seven-branched candlestick), the Holy Ark of the Law, the *shofar* (ram's horn), *lulav* (palm branch) and *etrog* (citron), as well as showing tolerance of a rich panoply of decorative motifs not specifically Jewish found in the Graeco-Roman art of the time, such as wreaths, eagles, bulls, boats and human figures. The dead were often accompanied by pottery, glass vessels, coins and jewellery. As was also usual at the time, most of the inscriptions are in Greek (the contemporary language of the rich and educated, for many important people were buried here), but also some in Hebrew and Aramaic (the *lingua franca* of the day) and Palmyrene. They often give the name, occupation and sometimes the home of the dead, and end with the word 'Peace' or 'Alas'.

It used to be thought that the cemetery was probably destroyed (and most graves looted) c 351, along with the synagogue and the basilica on the southwest part of the hill, during the Jewish revolt against the Byzantine Emperor Constantius II and his ruler of the East, Gallus Caesar. But more recent excavations suggest that although there may have been a brief decline due to a variety of factors (earthquake, drought and famine) the city continued to be occupied and the catacombs used certainly as late as the Early Islamic period. It is not known if the inhabitants in the 5C–7C were Christian or Jewish, but activity continued even after the catacombs were no longer extensively used for burial, and one cistern has evidence for glass-making (see below). In the settlement there is evidence for olive oil processing in the later period. The catacombs continued to be visited and looted: there are Crusader graffiti, and some evidence for activity in the 13C. After that the cemetery was forgotten, and in the Middle Age Jews revered a grave of Rabbi Judah in Sepphoris.

The National Park has some facilities. A visit can be made to some of the main tombs on the lower slopes of the hill (such as Catacombs 14 and 20, the latter continued to be used in the Byzantine and Early Islamic periods).

Galilean glass

Of particular note at Bet She'arim is a tremendous **block of glass** displayed where it was made and found, in a cave which was a cistern in use until the late Byzantine period. The block, 3.4m x 1.95m x 450mm, is estimated to weigh nine tons.

The coastal region near Akko was famous for glass-making from ancient times, when the sand from the coast was mixed with soda. Recent analysis suggests that this great slab was bulk glass made in a tank on the spot and due to be broken up and used in the manufacture of glass artefacts. However, the batch failed. It appears to have been made at a stage of transition from soda glass to glass made with plant ash; but the mixture resulted in a higher lime content which required a higher temperature. This suggests that it was made when the new plant ash process was being introduced, probably in the 9C AD—and at a time when the Byzantine cistern was out of use. Successful processes of Early Islamic glass-making are known from other sites.

The town occupies the bottle-shaped summit of the hill above the cemetery; at its peak the town probably covered c 10 ha. On the northeast slope of the hill is the site of the synagogue dated to the 3C–4C AD and later; 50m southwest are remains of buildings with mosaic floors which date to the mid-5C to mid-6C AD. The basilica on the west edge of the summit was built in the 2C–3C AD but occupied to the early 7C.

MEGIDDO
• • • • • • • • • •

According to a vision in the New Testament Book of Revelations, the kings of the earth will be assembled at Armageddon (Megiddo), and thunder, lightning, earthquake and giant hailstones will bring the end of the world (Rev.16:16). The ancient site of Megiddo, its mound of ruins rising nearly 60m above the plain, has in the course of its long history probably seen all this—except for the final culmination. The Egyptian ruler Tuthmosis III noted that 'the capture of Megiddo is the capture of a thousand cities', for it played a leading role in Canaan. The archaeological excavations during the 20C have uncovered remains from the Bronze Age to the Iron Age that are well-preserved and easy to visit.

The site lies just off Highway 66, 30km southeast of Haifa, between the Megiddo and Yokne'am junctions. It is managed by the National Parks Authority (☎ 06 652 2167); there is a restaurant, facilities and a site museum.

Where to stay
Megiddo kibbutz hotel (☎ 06 652 5011).

History

Megiddo was one of the most important places in ancient Canaan, set beside the rich plain at the point where the great coast road from Egypt issues northwards from the hills. A strategic location and its place on a major trade route ensured its prosperity. The site has revealed 20 main archaeological strata, beginning at the bottom of the tell with the Neolithic period. Apsidal houses of the Chalcolithic period have been excavated in one area of the slope of the mound, and from the Early Bronze I period, if not before, the site became of major significance. Late in the fourth millennium, near the top of the mound a temple with basalt column bases was built; afterwards, above its foundations, another temple and cult place was set, consisting of a broad-room temple approached from a court, with an altar built against a massive 3m-wide wall. A vast building, probably a temple, discovered in the late 1990s, and dating to the end of the Early Bronze IB period, overlies these. There may be a gap in the occupation in the Early Bronze II period, but by the middle of the third millennium the tell had a great defensive wall which grew to be 8m wide. Within it, first a great round altar in an open court was built near the site of the earlier temples, and then another series of three temples, the so-called 'megaron temples', similar in plan to the old broad-room temple, but much bigger and better built. The sense of continuity of cult over hundreds of years is strong: Megiddo must have been a very important and prominent religious centre for a large and rich area.

Around the 24C BC, when most contemporary cities appear to have come to a violent end, Megiddo seems to have survived a little better than most of the other towns of the country, with settled occupation, one less-impressive temple still surviving and some poorly constructed houses, but no city wall.

As elsewhere in Canaan, early in the second millennium, perhaps c 2000/1900 BC, Megiddo saw a new lease of life. It was newly refortified: excavations have uncovered a fine gate through a city wall which was 1.8m.

thick and protected by towers and a glacis. There was probably a temple, but it was destroyed by later rebuildings. From c 1800 BC Megiddo was a well laid-out town: it had a city wall with glacis, courtyard houses, temple and, late in the Middle Bronze Age, the first of a series of palaces which saw continuous rebuilding and development through the next two or three centuries.

During the Late Bronze Age the city, though prosperous, went through many upheavals which are reflected in its buildings. Historical references to the city begin in the 15C BC when a confederation of Canaanite kings led by the King of Qadesh in Syria revolted against Tuthmosis III of Egypt, and the battle at which they were crushed was fought near Megiddo. The Egyptians captured 924 chariots from the Canaanite kings at the battle, and the siege of the town is said to have lasted for seven months. During the 15C–14C, Megiddo became a base of Egyptian power in Canaan. Biridiya, the Canaanite vassal king of Megiddo, asked the Egyptian king to return the Egyptian garrison that had formerly been stationed in Megiddo to defend his kingdom against his enemies. The Egyptians continued to play a role at Megiddo in the time of Ramses III and Ramses VI, and some of the palace treasures, including fine carved ivory, illustrate the wealth of the time. Around 1130 there was a sudden and total destruction of the city, which was followed by a poor, unfortified settlement.

Megiddo is mentioned in the Old Testament, featuring in the Song of Deborah for example; but it remained a Canaanite town until well into the Iron Age. Many of the Iron Age archaeological features found on the site have been associated with the biblical descriptions of the works of Solomon and Ahab, and some of the building work dated to the 10C reflects a greater sophistication than is usual in cities at the time. According to the Bible (I Kings 9:15) Solomon built Jerusalem, Hazor, Megiddo and Gezer.

In the 11C a rich residential quarter was developed on the site, along with a larger, perhaps public building, that was in turn destroyed. Sometime in the 10C, a planned town or palatial citadel complex was built using fine ashlar masonry, surrounded by a casemate wall entered through a six-chambered gateway. This type of gateway and wall has been associated with the building works of Solomon on the basis of biblical but not contemporary literary evidence. Some fine proto-Aeolic capitals are also said to have decorated the buildings. There was a sophisticated and organised public complex, but it was destroyed and another city replaced it.

The next town was characterised by a four-chambered entrance gateway, a solid wall with offsets, which was 3.6 m thick and 820m long. Inside were large stables or storehouses, and a governor's palace; another five proto-Aeolic capitals were found in this stratum. The great water system was dug at this time too. About half the total area of the mound was occupied by public buildings, and it seems likely that there was a fortified lower town of more residential character in the area where the museum now stands.

The town is listed as conquered by the Egyptian ruler Sheshonq c 925 BC, and by the Assyrian king Tiglath-Pileser III in 732 BC, after which it became the Assyrian provincial capital. Stratum III has been associated with the Assyrian period, with a new orthogonal city plan and a two-chambered gateway. Its administrative role is reflected in the number of large grain silos on the site. It had declined by the 7C, and a fortress was built c 650 BC. After a battle at Megiddo between Necho of Egypt and Josiah of Judaea in 609 BC in which Josiah was killed (II Kings 23:29) the site was almost abandoned, with only slight remains of occupation to c 350 BC.

The settlement of the Roman period lay nearly 1km to the south at Legio (A. Lajjun, H. Kefar 'Othnai), which was the headquarters of the Sixth Roman Legion after the Second Jewish Revolt (AD 131/32–135). In 1918 the British army defeated the Turkish army near Megiddo. The Arab village of Lejjun was completely abandoned and destroyed in 1948.

The site covers c 6 hectares, but during the Early Bronze Age and Iron Age II a lower city extending over the plain to the north made up a far larger town. As at Beth Shean, the large-scale excavation techniques of the early 20C led to the removal of the whole of the upper levels of the tell. The latest features to be seen on the site are of the 8C–7C BC, but with renewed excavation, many structures you can see are much older.

You arrive at the north side of the tell; the ticket office and **museum** are in the former excavation headquarters, and you can see a small display with models. From there a path leads to the tell; about halfway up is a series of **gateways of the Bronze and Iron Age cities**. First on the left is the outer gate of the 10C BC city, with a long flight of steps for pedestrians to approach the main gate above. A little above to the west is the very well-preserved Canaanite city gateway of the 15C; and above it, half of the six-chambered gateway of the 10C (called the Solomonic gate). To the west again is the city gateway of the 18C. Only the stone bases of all these gates are preserved, as the mudbrick superstructure and probably metal-bound wooden doors have disappeared. The gate passages and piers were variously constructed for wheeled transport and defence, with gates being placed at the inner and outer piers.

Arriving on the top of the mound, the most notable feature is a **great round altar** in an open court, built of unhewn stones in the Early Bronze III period and still surviving 8m in diameter, and 1.4 m high. A little flight of steps leads up one side. When it was excavated, great quantities of ash and animal (not human!) bones were found, confirming the sacrificial function of the altar. Beside it on the north are the remains of the three **temples** built in the same period in the middle of the third millennium BC, but slightly later than the altar, which however continued to be used as part of the sacred complex. These temples are of the 'broad-room' type—rectangular rooms with doorway in one of the long sides—which are typical of Palestinian temples of the late fifth through to the third millennium. Recent excavation beneath these temples is revealing a huge earlier building. To the east, in the deeper cut on the present edge of the mound is the series of temples of the Chalcolithic and Early Bronze IB period (late fourth millennium), and lying lower in the cut made during the earlier excavations of the Oriental Institute of Chicago, the city wall of the Early Bronze III period. The excavations by the Tel Aviv Institute of Archaeology in the late 1990s are continuing here, and also a little to the south of the altar, in the area where buildings and tombs of the Middle and Late Bronze Ages were discovered earlier. Remains of the 10C included Building 6000 to the north, which underlies a stable or store building of the time of Ahab.

Continuing across to the south side of the site, a large, circular stone-lined pit was a large **public grain silo** of the 8C; to the left a path leads to an observation point on the southeast side of the tell, on the site of which was a 10C pillared building and further north to Building 338, a fine 10C residence. Returning towards the silo, on the south side is a piered entrance into a large courtyard with a 10C palace; to the west is the remarkable building identified as **stables**, with troughs and mangers for the horses, identified by some with Solomon's chariot cities, and by others as a storeroom used for produce collected as tax. Behind its south wall lies the defensive wall of the citadel in the 10C–9C.

West of it, near the southwest edge of the mound is one of the site's most

Trough and tethering ring in the stables

remarkable features, the ***water system**. The access is good for those who can manage to descend some 180 steps; you can avoid climbing back up the steps by walking along the road for c 600m to the site entrance. In the 10C BC a hidden gallery led to the spring down at the level of the plain below the tell; in the 9C an enormous hidden system was excavated. A large square shaft 25m deep was cut vertically from the surface of the mound, with steps cut in the walls winding downwards; the shaft led to a stepped tunnel, and then to a horizontal rock-cut tunnel which reaches the spring in a cave 35m below the surface of the mound. As the water flowed in a channel from the spring to the inner end of the tunnel, it could be obtained from the bottom of the steps without having to walk the whole distance to the spring. The original access to the spring from outside was blocked. You can exit at the far end of the system beyond the spring cave, seeing the signs of the gate and blocking at the outer access. Then as you walk back by the road around the west side of the tell, you can view the height of the mound and the evidence for the fortifications.

The central hill country

Arab/Palestinian culture is the foundation for many aspects of the hill country—monumental and traditional buildings have influenced modern architectural fashions; Palestinian crafts, such as embroidery and costume, provide much of the colour in the markets and the countryside; many events involve the songs and dances of the Palestinian peasant and pastoralist; traditional methods of cultivation have preserved much of the flora and, where they survive, the old hilltop villages add grace and depth to the countryside, often providing the perspective of medieval paintings. Poverty under the 400 years of Ottoman rule preserved many structures from the ravages of redevelopment.

The hill country broadly encompasses the 'West Bank' (of the Jordan), an area c 130km in length and 40km–60km in width which, since 1967, has been under Israeli military occupation as the biblically-named districts of 'Samaria' and 'Judaea'. It is now a patchwork of small semi-autonomous Palestinian areas surrounded by land still under full military occupation and subject to new Israeli settlement. For the tourist, the military checkpoints may be easier to negotiate in public transport or with a local tour-guide than independently.

In the Palestinian areas, where tourism is being developed, 3 per cent of Palestinians are Christian, 97 per cent Sunni Muslim. There are 19 refugee camps in this region, housing nearly 150,000 Palestinian refugees.

North of Jerusalem

North of Jerusalem is a broad area of limestone hills and valleys, with much fertile land which has a complex history of settlement and politics. Stretching c 85km north–south and c 40km east–west with a ridge extending northwest to Mt Carmel, the hills rise to c 940m above sea level north of Nablus. The fertile terra rossa soils have eroded to the valley floors, and in spring, after good winter rainfall, the countryside is very beautiful with wonderful wild flowers on the rocky hillsides, as well as on the deep terraced soils among the olive trees. It is a country of springs and streams. Occasionally there is snow in winter, but normally a mild, wet Mediterranean winter is followed by pleasant, dry summer temperatures; this climate has made modern Ramallah a favoured summer resort.

The principal towns in the past were mostly located in the region of modern Nablus, a Palestinian administrative centre and market town. It has been the principal town of this area since the Roman period, but before that, in the same area, Tell Far'ah (ancient Tirza) and then Samaria were the capitals of the Kingdom of Israel, and the ancient site of Shechem was the main Canaanite town. The reason for this continuity of location is the crossroads created by the north–south route through the hills, and the strategic east–west route which runs up from the Mediterranean, and down to the Jordan Valley. Nablus is located in a pass through the hills which provides easy access west to the coast and east down the Wadi Far'ah to the Damiya crossing of the Jordan.

The northern hill country was more populous and settled in ancient times than the region south of Jerusalem; according to the Bible (Num. 13:29), the hill country was occupied by the Amorites and other groups, and several Bronze Age towns have been excavated. There was a major breakdown of settlement at the end of the second millennium BC and there is much debate about the origins of the occupants of the new small settlements that appeared early in the 12C in the northern hill country. Whether they were indigenous or foreign, they are generally agreed to represent the beginnings of Israelite settlement, which developed into the historical states of Israel and Judah in the 8C BC.

A major check to this development came in 722 BC with the fall of the northern Kingdom of Israel when Samaria was captured by Sargon II of Assyria. As standard Assyrian practice, he deported a large part of the population to distant regions of his empire, and introduced settlers. This practice, which weakens the potential resistance of subject populations, was also followed by Stalin in the Crimea in more recent times. The vicissitudes of successive conquest continued over the centuries, with armies coming both from east and west. As elsewhere, the population grew to much higher levels in the Roman and Byzantine periods, and much of the terracing of the hillsides may originate at this time, though the process of cultivating the rocky land by terracing to prevent erosion of the soil is much older, and has been shown to begin at least as early as the fourth millennium. The agricultural terraces are one of the most characteristic sights of the hill country. Since the Islamic conquest in the 7C, the region has increasingly become predominantly Muslim. The route from the east made the region vulnerable to raiding and to the ingress of pastoralist tribes in medieval times. The antiquity of this entrance to the hill country is witnessed in the story of Abraham, who in the biblical account came from the lands to the northeast, and first entered the country at Shechem.

SHECHEM ~ TELL BALATA

The site of Tell Balata covers the ancient city of Shechem, a focal point in the hill country from the 19C BC. It lies below Mt Ebal at the eastern end of the pass through the hills, 1km east of Nablus, near the junction of Highways 57 and 60, and 65km north of Jerusalem.

History and monuments

The site was settled in the Chalcolithic and Early Bronze Age I periods; following a gap, nearly continuous occupation is attested from c 1900 to 128/107 BC (with brief periods of abandonment). Egyptian references to the town and territory of Shechem go back to the 19C BC; the Amarna Letters of the 14C BC name Lab'ayu as ruler of a city-state of Canaan. Shechem is frequently referred to in the Old Testament particularly in association with the Patriarch Jacob (Gen. 12:6; 33:18–20; 34; 35:1–4; 37:12–17; 48:22) as a central site for cult and covenant. It was a boundary city between Manasseh and Ephraim, and was Jeroboam's first capital of the Kingdom of Israel (I Kings 12:25). It continued to be occupied after the capital shifted first to Tirzah, then to Samaria; and in Hellenistic times was said to be the chief city of the Samaritans. Its cemetery lies on the slopes of Mt Ebal.

The principal ruins visible originated in the Middle Bronze Age, between c 1750 and 1540 BC. They include massive fortifications eventually 45m wide; a city wall of cyclopean masonry on the west and a multi-chambered northwest gate. A fortress (migdal) temple with stone walls 5.1m wide supporting a brick superstructure was built on the acropolis, also in the northwest. Its entrance is between two towers. Towards the end of this period, the east gate was built; a temple was built against the inner face of the outer defensive wall between the northwest gate and the migdal temple; and in a final stage of the defences, a casemate wall overlay it. Fine houses and objects, possibly part of the administrative or government section, suggested a level of prosperity. Everywhere was evidence of destruction over this city, which is attributed to the Egyptians.

Following a gap in the occupation of the site c 1540–1450, many of these structures were rebuilt, and excavations suggest a rapid return to prosperity. A destruction, c 1350–1300, was followed by a simpler rebuild; there was a massive destruction c 1150. Relatively minor structures are found until the time of Jeroboam I (928–907), when Shechem regained city status. The Assyrians destroyed Shechem c 724 BC. Meagre remains of the 7C were followed by economic improvement in a level characterised by imported Greek pottery, c 331–128/107 BC, when it was once again a fortified city, probably built by the Samaritans after their departure from Samaria. Although Josephus states that the city was destroyed by John Hyrcanus in 128 BC, the coin evidence fits better with a destruction in 107 BC.

Qabr Yusuf (the Tomb of Joseph in a variant Jewish tradition) is on the east side of the village of Balata, and **Jacob's Well** is located a little further east, 2km east-southeast of Nablus. Open 09.00–12.00, 15.00–17.00 (–16.00 in winter); for admission ring the bell at the Greek Orthodox Monastery. Traditionally this was the well on the land bought by Jacob at Shechem (Gen. 33:19). It is a place of Christian pilgrimage based on the New Testament story of Jesus and the Samaritan Woman at Jacob's Well (John 4: 5–42).

History of Joseph's Well

The site had been identified by the 330s and was used for Christian baptisms. By 384 a cruciform church had been built over the well, which was probably destroyed in the Samaritan revolts of 484 or 529 and rebuilt by Justinian. This cruciform church was still standing in the 720s and probably later in the early 9C. The Byzantine church was in ruins by 1099, and only the well was being noted in the early 12C. The church was re-established by Ermengarde, Countess of Brittany, in 1132–35 and 1172. In the Crusader church, steps led from the crossing in front of the altar down to the well (Fons Jacob) in a crypt beneath the sanctuary. The church, dedicated to the Saviour, at this time belonged (with the lands of Balata), to the Benedictine nuns of Bethany. The church had three aisles ending in three apses. In the 13C the church seems to have been again ruined, but the well was still visited. In the 16C the Franciscans said mass annually in the crypt; by the 17C it was difficult to find the well among the ruins. Stones from the ruins around Jacob's Well were removed for the building of the nearby Ottoman barracks in the mid-19C. The site was bought by the Greek Orthodox Patriarchate c 1860, and excavated from 1893 to restore the crypt. Reconstruction of the church began in 1914, in part incorporating the lower walls and column bases of the medieval church, but was halted on the outbreak of war in 1914 still only half built.

Today the steps down to the well and the crypt itself appear to be Crusader work. The well itself in 1877 and 1919 was said to be 22.5m deep, with diameter c 2.25m; the upper part was of masonry, the lower cut in the limestone. Fragments from the Crusader building can be seen in the small museum.

SAMARIA
• • • • • • • • • •

Set on a hill in the fertile northern hill country in distant sight of the sea, Samaria (or Sebaste) was the capital of the northern kingdom of Israel for about 150 years until its destruction in 722/21 BC. Later the city was also famous for its associations with Alexander the Great, Herod the Great and relics of St. John the Baptist.

The site is near Highways 57 and 60, 10km northwest of Nablus. It is maintained by the National Parks Authority.

History

Much of Samaria's early history is described in the Old Testament and has been related to archaeological finds. In c 876 BC, King Omri bought the hill from a man called Shemer (and, oddly, is said to have called it after its former owner), fortified it, and moved his capital city from Tirzah (modern Tell al-Far'ah North). Omri's son Ahab is more widely remembered, notoriously for his marriage to Jezebel, the daughter of King Ethbaal of Tyre, and for his 'Ivory House' (I Kings 22:39). The Bible gives many details of the political and commercial alliances and wars of the kings of Israel, on which some of the fortunes of the kingdom were built; its fortunes were at their highest in the times of Ahab and of Jeroboam II (784–748). The alliance with Tyre was commercially important, and was reflected in the tolerance by the Omride kings of the old Canaanite and Phoenician cults of Baal and Astarte.

Wars with the Aramean kingdom of Damascus were endless conflicts over commercial advantage and territorial gain. Omri was forced to concede a trading quarter to the Arameans in Samaria (I Kings 20:34); Ahab withstood a siege of Samaria by Ben-Hadad II of Damascus (I Kings 20:1–21); a counter-attack by Ahab and victorious battle at Aphek regained cities lost by Omri, and the right to have a trading quarter in Damascus (I Kings 20:34); later Ahab fought to regain control of the territory of Ramoth-Gilead east of the Jordan, but was mortally wounded (I Kings 22:1–38). In the time of Ahab's son, Jehoram, the Arameans again besieged Samaria, which was reduced to famine (II Kings 6:24–25). Jehoram was wounded fighting against Hazael of Damascus when he also tried to regain Ramoth-Gilead from the Arameans (II Kings 8:28); then Jehu, his army commander, led a revolt which ended in the slaughter of the whole royal family. Jehu also lost land east of the Jordan, but Jeroboam II briefly conquered Damascus.

The more significant enemy however was Assyria, which was expanding westwards from the 9C BC onwards. Ahab was a major member of the coalition against the Assyrians at the Battle of Qarqar in 853, where the Assyrians claimed great slaughter; of Ahab's successors on the throne of Israel, Jehu paid tribute to Assyria in 841 as did Menahem in 783. Tiglath Pileser III took a lot of territory from Samaria in 734 and 733; then the Israelite kings Pekah and Hoshea attempted to revolt against Assyria, which precipitated a three-year siege by Shalmaneser III, followed by the conquest and destruction of the city in 722/21 by Sargon II. Many of the people of the northern kingdom were deported to populate remote districts of the Assyrian Empire, and new people were brought to resettle Samaria.

Samaria then became the administrative centre for the successive

Assyrian, Babylonian and Persian governors, and during this time the Samaritan sect became increasingly divergent from that of Judah (see Mt Gerizim, p 363). In 332 BC, the city was captured by Alexander the Great, who settled thousands of Macedonian soldiers and developed a Greek city on the site. Most of the Samaritans appear to have migrated to the site of ancient Shechem at this time (see p 356). Samaria was destroyed and its inhabitants sold into slavery by John Hyrcanus in 108 BC. Pompey annexed the city to Rome in 63 BC and the Roman city began to revive under Gabinius, the pro-consul of Syria. In 30 BC, Octavian (the Emperor Augustus) gave it to Herod the Great, who rebuilt it from c 25 BC and renamed it Sebaste (the Greek for the Latin name Augustus) in honour of the emperor. The city was destroyed during the First Jewish Revolt, but was restored under the Emperor Septimius Severus, raised in status and became a colonia (Colonia Lucia Septimia Sebaste) about AD 196, reaching its peak at this time, with an area of nearly a square kilometre surrounded by a wall. In Byzantine times it declined to quite a small town. By the 4C there was a tradition that the body of John the Baptist had been brought from Machaerus in Jordan (where he had been beheaded at the demand of Salome) and buried in Sebaste alongside those of the prophets Elisha and Obadiah. The remains were taken out and burnt in 361–362 in the persecution of Christians under Julian the Apostate; but the rescued remnants/ashes/relics were still being visited c 384 (along with other relics of John in Jerusalem and Damascus and elsewhere). By the mid-5C Sebaste was the seat of a bishop, and the Cathedral Church of St. John the Baptist had been built over the tombs. All three tombs were still recorded in 723 after the Islamic conquest, and the cathedral is depicted in the 8C mosaic at Umm al-Rasas in Jordan. The great church had fallen by around 808, although the underground tomb was not entirely destroyed. The town was abandoned in the time of the Caliph al-Ma'mun (813–833), but by this time the bishop appears to be located in a second church on the supposed site of John the Baptist's prison and beheading, and this may have survived until the early 11C (see below).

Shortly after the Crusader conquest, and probably before c 1106–08 a Latin religious community was established in the church at Sebaste, and in a separate but nearby structure the tomb was also identified as the prison of John; a Latin Bishop of Sebaste is mentioned in 1129. In 1145 the burnt remains of the three saints and of other prophets and patriarchs were found miraculously in a silver reliquary, and money was raised to rebuild the church enclosing the tomb, on a grander scale on the old Byzantine founda-tions. More funds were still needed in 1169–70, and relics were sold to the West. By 1185 the Prison was also venerated as the site of John's beheading, and the resting place of Zechariah and Elizabeth, John's parents. The relics of John himself were placed in the church above the underground prison. At this time too a Greek monastery and church is mentioned on the site where the head of John was supposed to have been discovered. This Eastern Christian church and monastery appear to have survived the Latin expulsion, and the Greek monks were mentioned in the 13C–14C, finally abandoning the church shortly before 1479. In 1187 however, Sebaste had been sacked by Salah al-Din's nephew, who removed all the rich trappings of the shrine of Zechariah (John's tomb in the Cathedral), and converted it into a mosque.

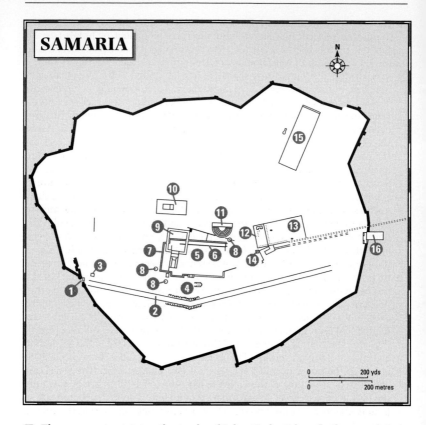

The mosque containing the tombs of John, Zechariah and other prophets is recorded in 1225. Although the cathedral had been converted into a mosque, Christians were still permitted access to John's tomb. In the early 19C as well as the walls and part of the vaulting of the church, the main apse of the ruined church was still standing, but c 1892 the old mosque, which had been built in the west end of the south bay, was moved to the east end of the church, and the Crusader apse was demolished.

The ancient site

The walls of the Roman city of Samaria have been traced round virtually the whole site. The **West Gate** (**1**) was defended by two fine Herodian round towers standing on Hellenistic foundations; the gate itself and the **colonnaded street** inside (**2**) were probably built by Septimius Severus. Inside, to the east, is a shrine of the Roman period (**3**). The street, 12.5m wide, probably ran from near the West Gate to near the East Gate, and was nearly 800m long with around 600 columns supporting porticoes with shops.

Just north of the best preserved section of the street, c 250m to the east of the gate, on the south flanks of the acropolis, are the remains of the excavated **Monastery Church of St. John the Baptist** (**4**), built in the 6C, but destroyed perhaps as late as the time of al-Hakim (1009–14). The ruins are those of the church rebuilt in the mid- to late 11C, a nearly square structure with narthex and projecting main apse, the vault supported on four Roman granite columns; the narthex enclosed a vaulted tomb below the floor at the north end. Eight steps descend to the crypt, the masonry marked by crosses; the crypt itself is groin-vaulted with a small oculus in the centre. The east wall was painted with scenes of the martyrdom of John, the finding of his head and the rescue of his ashes. A niche in the east wall contains an altar slab, and the niche was flanked by kneeling angels (c 1150–75), remnants of which survive. Beneath the floor is an empty tomb in which the head of John was said to have been buried by Herodias. To the west of the church lies the associated monastery dated from the 6C. East of the church was a cemetery.

Towards the centre of the site, the **acropolis** (**5**) contains the **royal enclosure** built by Omri and his successors; Omri's inner wall (**6**) is of the finest smooth-dressed masonry, which probably reflects Phoenician influence. A courtyard house against the south wall was identified with the palace. The fortification of the acropolis was strengthened by Ahab with a **casemate wall** (**7**); all the royal masonry is of high quality, cut and set without mortar. Many beautiful fragments of carved ivories were found (most of which probably once decorated wooden furniture), particularly in a building near the inner north wall of the royal enclosure, the proposed 'Ahab's Ivory House'. However, the ivories (now in the Rockefeller Museum) probably represent an accumulation made by the dynasty through the 9C–8C; the rest of the inhabitants of Samaria dwelt in the large lower city on the flanks of the hill.

The **late Hellenistic inner fortification wall** with square towers (2C BC) generally followed the line of the old Israelite acropolis wall; there are also three magnificent **round towers** (**8**) of the late 3C BC, two at the southwest corner of the acropolis, and one near the northeast. The Hellenistic acropolis was destroyed by John Hyrcanus in 108 BC. Herod the Great later built the **Augusteum** (**9**), a great temple in honour of Augustus, on the acropolis; the temple (rebuilt by Septimius Severus) was constructed with vast forecourt on a great artificial platform. The steps up to the podium, a few column bases and some drafted Herodian masonry survive.

Below the north side of the acropolis is the **Temple of Kore** (**10**) in a temenos; under it was an earlier temple of the 3C BC, dedicated to Serapis-Isis, of which only the foundations remain. To the southeast are some remains of a small **theatre** (**11**), dated to the early 3C AD.

On the plain to the east are the **basilica** (**12**) and **forum** (**13**). The basilica had monolithic columns and at the north end was a bema with semicircular niche and four benches, mostly of the 2C AD. There are no springs on the site, and in early times the inhabitants depended on cisterns. Later an aqueduct beneath the south side of the forum brought water from the hills east of Samaria. Another **shrine** (**14**) of the Roman period lies southeast of the basilica. The site of the **hippodrome** (**15**) is to the north, inside a probable northeast gate. The east gate has not survived.

Other sights

The modern village of **Sebastiyya** lies partly over the east side of the ancient site, and partly over the cemetery outside the walls. In the southeast area of the village was discovered a remarkable **Roman mausoleum** dating to the 2C–3C AD. It is a square, stone building, capped by a dome supported on very early true pendentives. Inside were niches and a number of sarcophagi, two of which are richly decorated. The façade has two rows of four columns and the sides are decorated with pilasters; the entrance has a stone door.

The Mosque (**16**) is located inside the walls of the 12C **Crusader Cathedral Church of St. John the Baptist**, which stands on the foundations of the Byzantine cathedral. The site lies just outside the Roman walls, in part of the cemetery, presumably because a tomb had been identified as that of the prophets Elisha and Obadiah in which, according to tradition, John's body had also been placed. Parts of the paving may belong to a 12C *parvis* (an enclosed area) in front of the church. The west façade is plain, apart from traces of a tower at the north end which may represent 12C or later fortifications. The main west door, with a simple pointed arch, flanked by windows, is a later construction; there is a blocked door to the south. The south wall has buttresses with chamfered tops. The church was constructed of good masonry, incorporating *spolia*. It is a rectangular structure, 48.2 x 22.6m, of three aisles, seven bays and three semicircular apses, which mostly survive to the level of the vaulting. Originally it had rib vaulting in the aisles and quadripartite vaulting in the transept, higher in the crossing. Three corbels, two with grotesques, survive but not in situ; many of the capitals survive, as does most of a varied cornice. The architecture has parallels in the Cathedral of Sens in France—Archbishop William of Sens was a prominent benefactor in the 1170s.

As well as the mosque built c 1892 at the east end of the church, other late structures exist within the ruined Crusader church. The tomb associated with John the Baptist lies under a domed structure in the central nave of the Crusader church, at the fifth bay, and is reached by a narrow flight of 21 steps from another small domed chamber. In the east side of the larger domed structure is a reused Crusader oculus; inside, its west wall is faced with fragments of a marble chancel screen, on which crosses have been partly obliterated. The tomb lies below the domed structure inside a built, niched tomb of the 2C–3C AD which had a hinged stone door.

South and east of the church, traces of other medieval structures, vaults and an olive press have been noted among the modern houses.

MOUNT GERIZIM

Mt Gerizim is the central holy place of the Samaritan community, and the site of a Roman temple and a Byzantine church. It lies above the southwest side of Nablus, 881m above sea level; Mt Ebal opposite is 940m above sea level. According to the Old Testament, Joshua assembled all the people of Israel between Mt Gerizim and Mt Ebal; six tribes recited the blessings (on Gerizim) and six the curses (on Ebal) as decreed by Moses (Deut. 27–28; Jos. 8:30–35). But Mt Gerizim is best known for its association with the Samaritans.

The Samaritans

The origins of the Samaritan sect are debated and obscure. According to Jewish sources, following the fall of the northern kingdom of Israel in 722/21 BC, and the exile of many of its inhabitants, the Assyrians brought in new settlers from other parts of the empire. In adapting to their new surroundings, and seeking to placate the gods of the region, these immigrants adopted the Israelite god. Their descendants became a separate component of Judaism, named Samaritans from their locality, with their principal shrine on Mt Gerizim. The Samaritans themselves hold a different tradition, that their sect is in the true Jewish descent of Joseph, but that it separated from Judaism very early, in the time of Eli the Priest. They believe that the presence of God in the earliest days resided on Mt Gerizim, and that the mountain has primacy over Jerusalem and its Jewish Temple, and is thus the centre of their ritual. They pray facing towards the mountain. The sect recognises only the Pentateuch (the first five books of the Old Testament) as canonical, and rejects all later rabbinical works. Their copies of the Pentateuch indicate a separation from Judaism no later than the time of John Hyrcanus (134–104 BC). When Alexander the Great captured Samaria in 332 BC and settled his Macedonian soldiers there, the Samaritans seem to have moved first to Shechem; and from the 2C AD to Neapolis/Nablus.

Fortified Samaritan towns existed both on Gerizim and at Shechem in the Hellenistic period. Divisions and rivalries between Jerusalem and Gerizim intensified from the 4C BC, when a priest from the Jerusalem temple married into the family of the Samaritan leader Sanballat. According to Josephus, Sanballat built a Samaritan temple on Gerizim, which was destroyed by John Hyrcanus in 128 BC. Samaritan fortunes had varied under the Seleucids and Ptolemies, but improved under Pompey. Ten to twelve thousand Samaritans were slaughtered by the Romans during the First Jewish Revolt, but having changed to the Roman side in the Second Revolt, the Samaritans were permitted by Hadrian to rebuild their temple. A long-drawn-out struggle against Christianity in the 5C–6C AD led to further disasters for the community. After the Samaritan Revolt of AD 484 the Samaritans were driven off Mt Gerizim and a church was built in their sacred enclosure under the Emperor Zeno. It was a constant source of friction between Samaritans and Christians. Further savage revolts led to severe repression. The community declined over the centuries, and the death of the last true High Priest occurred in 1624. By 1874 only 135 Samaritans remained in Nablus itself, though communities existed in other towns in Palestine and to the north. The custom of the Samaritan community to ascend Mt Gerizim for important feasts continued into the 20C. Today the community still celebrates the Passover feast with the sacrifice of a lamb on the evening before the full moon in the month of Nisan.

On the upper north–south ridge of Mt Gerizim excavation has revealed a walled city built in the Hellenistic period, with fortress, towers and four residential quarters as well as extramural habitations. A sacred walled area on the summit was approached by a wide staircase. It may be the site of the late 4C BC Samaritan enclosure/temple built by Sanballat. The archaeological evidence suggests the city itself was occupied from c 200 BC to the destruction by John Hyrcanus c 128 BC or slightly later. The prominent ruins are of the **church complex dedicated**

to Mary Theotokos (Mary, Mother of God) built in AD 484, set in a rectangular fortress. The fortress walls were originally 7m high, and entered by a gate on the north side. Within the wall was a peristyle court with cistern. In the centre of the court the octagonal church itself was a concentric structure of the shrine type. The site continued to be used in the Early Islamic and Crusader periods.

At the northern end of the upper ridge is **Tell al-Ras**, an artificial hill overlooking Nablus. This Roman temple was located on a podium approached from a propylaeum at the east end of the city of Neapolis below by a flight of 1300/1500 steps. Buildings varying in date from the 1C BC to the 3C AD were found beside the stairs, including one which may have been a Samaritan sanctuary. The stairs from the city climbed to a paved plaza, beneath which large cisterns were constructed; above was a stepped podium supporting the temple. Dedicated to Zeus Olympus, the temple probably had two phases—mid-2C AD (reigns of Hadrian and Antoninus Pius) and early 3C AD (reigns of Septimius Severus and Caracalla). It was depicted on coins minted in Neapolis during this period. It probably went out of use not long after the arrival of Christianity, for the Pilgrim of Bordeaux in AD 333 mentions the steps up Mt Gerizim, but not the temple.

NABLUS

The town of Nablus is a Palestinian administrative centre with a population of c 100,400. It lies near the western end of a narrow pass between Mt Gerizim and Mt Ebal, at the junction of several main roads, and has been the principal city of the area since Roman times. Reputed to have 80 springs in the vicinity, it was prosperous in the mid-19C AD. Due to the ravages of time, revolts and earthquakes, very little of the medieval town survives but the street plan in the old town has preserved some of the alignments of the Roman city. A strongly Muslim town since the 13C, and a centre of the Palestinian struggle for independence, it has frequently been under curfew during the military occupation. Advice should be sought before visiting.

Nablus is 64km from Jerusalem, on Highway 60, at the junction with Highways 55 and 57.

Practical information

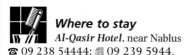
Where to stay
Al-Qasir Hotel, near Nablus
☎ 09 238 54444; ✉ 09 239 5944.

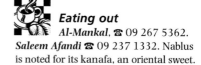
Eating out
Al-Mankal, ☎ 09 267 5362.
Saleem Afandi ☎ 09 237 1332. Nablus is noted for its kanafa, an oriental sweet.

History

Founded AD 72–73 by the Flavian emperors with a core of Roman veterans shortly after the destruction of Jerusalem, on the site of a small earlier settlement, Flavia Neapolis Samariae was probably established to counter the continued resistance of the Samaritans and their efforts to resettle on Mt Gerizim.

In the 2C AD it had a hippodrome and theatre and other public buildings, with an important temple above the city on Tell al-Ras (see Mt Gerizim). The city took the losing side of Roman politics in the time of Septimius Severus, was punished, and eventually pardoned.

In AD 244 Philip the Arab became emperor and raised the status of the city to Colonia Flavia Iulia Sergia Neapolis. Units of the Roman army were stationed in Neapolis in the second half of the 3C AD, when an amphitheatre was built. Christianity was introduced in the 4C and the Byzantine town is depicted in mosaic on the Madaba Map in the 6C.

From Roman times, Neapolis/Nablus was the centre of the Samaritan sect. Great friction developed between Christians and Samaritans, and the Samaritan Revolts of the 5C–6C were cruelly suppressed. The Byzantine cathedral (depicted on the 6C Madaba mosaic map and on an 8C mosaic from Umm al-Rasas in Jordan) was attacked by the Samaritans in 484, 529 and perhaps in 555, and was probably restored by Justinian along with the church on Mt Gerizim. The town fell to the Arabs in AD 636. By the 10C it had a mosque and probably a castle.

Nablus surrendered to the Crusader armies in 1099, and became part of the royal domain. The inhabitants of the town included Samaritans and some Eastern Christians, but were mainly Muslim, and generally hostile to the Franks (Christian immigrants from the West). The town was sacked during an Arab raid from Damascus and a Muslim revolt in 1113. The Crusader town was unwalled, but it had a citadel (probably the former Muslim castle) in the centre of the town; a burgess court, a court of justice and a market were established. The cathedral and bishop were however at Sebaste. Nablus had a parish church and dedications to St. John the Evangelist, St. John the Baptist (with a Hospital), the Passion and Resurrection, and an Armenian Church of St. John are recorded.

Generally the Western Christians settled inside the town rather than in the countryside, but there was some Frankish cultivation of vineyards and sugar production. The area was raided again by the Muslims of Damascus in 1137. The royal estate was settled on Queen Melisande when she was banished to Nablus in 1152 and she lived here until her death in 1161. Many of its Muslim inhabitants fled to Damascus between 1156 and 1173. In 1174 the town was the dower of Queen Maria Comnena, and on her marriage in 1176 passed to her husband Balian II of Ibelin. There was earthquake damage in 1182. Another Muslim raid two years later failed to take the citadel, but Nablus was lost with the rest of the kingdom in 1187, and was not thereafter in the possession of the Franks.

Further earthquakes damaged the town in 1201 and 1202, and it was raided and burnt by the Templars in 1242. Following the fall of Acre and other cities in 1291, a Samaritan chronicle records that the Eastern Christians were evicted and their churches destroyed. The sale of the castle is recorded in 1382, and a possible fragment of it has been identified near the western end of the town. There was another disastrous earthquake in 1546, when a quarter of the town was ruined. Evliya Celebi recorded c 1648–50 that Nablus was a Samaritan town, in a lovely setting among mills and gardens and with a great number of Muslim shrines in and around it, but it was not rich. Another quarter of the town was damaged by an earthquake in

1837. In 1853 Nablus and its countryside saw continuous internal strife between competing Arab factions, who called in the support of the surrounding villagers and of the Arab tribes from east of the Jordan River. In the later 19C it was described as a prosperous and lively town, with a Turkish garrison, producing citrus, fresh and dried fruits—mulberries, pomegranates, grapes and figs, as well as nuts and olives—with the best bazaars in Palestine, full of Manchester cottons, Sheffield cutlery, Damascus and Aleppo silks, Istanbul amber rosaries and tobacco pipes, and Hebron glass bracelets. But its chief trade was in wool, cotton, olive oil and soap—for the latter there were 20 soap factories in the town. Nablus was noted for the production of water carriers from goat skins, and the courtyard of the Khan al-Tujjar on the north side of the city (since destroyed) often had these skins laid out to season.

The town was damaged in the First World War (it was captured by French Cavalry in 1918); in the 1927 earthquake another 300 buildings collapsed, including the only remaining medieval church building (Jami' al-Nasr).

The Roman town

There are few surviving buildings of interest, but excavations in the Roman town have revealed a theatre, hippodrome and amphitheatre. The city is estimated to have extended 1500m x 700m, with its north wall along modern Faisal Street. The main east–west road lay just outside the north wall. The city wall extended westwards to enclose the principal water source at Ras al-Ain; the south wall runs below a line of quarries low on Mt Gerizim to include the theatre, and then east to the propylaeum at the foot of Mt Gerizim. The walls enclosed Ain Dafna to the east and Ain Qaryun in the centre (probably outlets of water channels rather than springs). The main east gate of the city probably lay under the modern military government headquarters. Part of a finely coloured mosaic was found near the centre of the town.

A road ran south to the **theatre** (2C AD) on the south central edge of the city (currently closed, it can be viewed from above). It was one of the largest theatres in the country (diameter c 110m). The middle and upper *cavea*, the *scaenae frons* and stage are missing. The massive supporting back wall, the marble paved orchestra and many seats with their backs carved in the shape of dolphins (which came from the upper level of the lower *cavea*) illustrate the status of the city. Eleven inscriptions with the names of 11 tribes were found on the first row of seats. The theatre remained in use until the Byzantine period, when the orchestra was converted to a pool for nautical games.

The **hippodrome** (76 x 320m), aligned east/west outside the north wall of the city at the west end, was also built in the 2C AD. The east end had 11 entrances into the racetrack for the horses; a vaulted substructure supported the seats along the sides, which were reached by stairs from the vaults. In the mid-3C AD an **amphitheatre** (95 x 76m) was built over the rounded eastern end, reusing stone from the hippodrome, probably at the time Neapolis became a colonia and Roman troops were stationed here.

The town cemeteries lay to both north and south of the town, on the lower flanks of Gerizim and Ebal; the more important tombs were located on Ebal, but because of the poor quality of the rock, the façades and mausolea are usually built rather than carved.

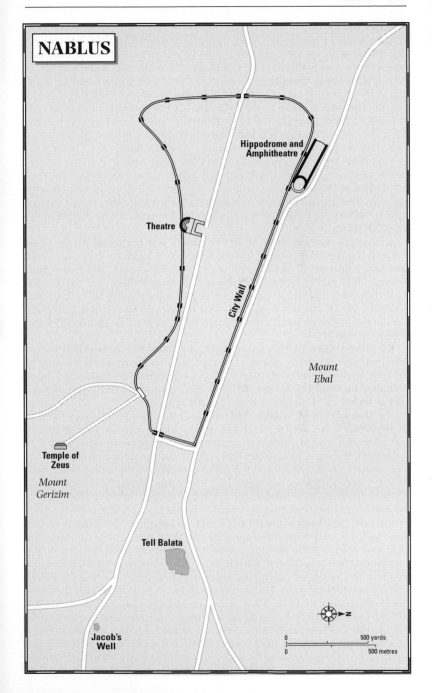

NABLUS

Hippodrome and
Amphitheatre

Theatre

City Wall

Mount
Ebal

Temple of
Zeus

Mount
Gerizim

Tell Balata

Jacob's
Well

| 0 | | 500 yards |
| 0 | | 500 metres |

Nablus today

In normal times a busy market town, Nablus is best explored on foot. Al-Hussein Square lies at the centre of the town with al-Nasir Street and the old town and bazaar to the south. On the corner of al-Nasir Street in the central east end of Nablus is the **Great Mosque** (generally closed to non-Muslims). It may be on the site of the Byzantine cathedral but considerable uncertainty remains about its origins. The Great Mosque is recorded in the 10C but not again mentioned until it was burnt by the Templars in 1242; there were various references to it in the 14C. The present mosque is a long, narrow building, c 60m x 20m, oriented east/west; the prayer hall has three aisles of 14 groin-vaulted bays. The six western bays have reused Roman columns and Corinthian capitals; Frankish capitals in the eastern end may also be reused *spolia*. There is no certainty that the eastern section of the building was originally a three-aisled Crusader church, with the apse now replaced by the entrance to the mosque, but some Crusader masons' marks can be seen. If it was originally a church, it may have been the Frankish parish church.

In Shari' al-Anbiya (Street of the Prophets), just northwest of the Great Mosque (on the other side of the main road in a builder's store), are some masonry fragments of the Hospital of St. John the Baptist, which was built between 1118 and 1131 with an endowment given by Baldwin II to the Hospital of St. John of Jerusalem. It appears to have continued to serve the sick and the poor after the Muslim victory in 1187, later becoming a leper house, and finally the Jami' al-Masakin (Mosque of the Paupers), which was damaged in 1927 and consolidated in 1946.

The **Jami' al-Nasr** (the Mosque of Victory, on Sharia al-Nasr west of the Great Mosque) was completely destroyed in the 1927 earthquake and replaced in 1935, with prayer hall on the first floor over commercial premises and a mausoleum in the southeast corner; in the mosque (normally closed to the public) a pair of reused 12C Crusader capitals flank the mihrab..

The **Mausoleum of Shaikh Badran** (Badr al-Rafiya) lies one block west of Jami' al-Nasr. It is a small squarish building, its dome supported on four granite columns with reused Byzantine capitals; an inscription states that it was renewed by the son of Shaikh Badr in 1273–74, with another date of 1339–40, and a restoration of 1393–94. Other medieval buildings exist in the town, as well as a few surviving soap factories which are worth visiting, and two recently restored Ottoman bath houses, the Hammam al-Shifa (off the south side of Sharia al-Nasr) and Hammam al-Hana (two blocks further south in the old city).

The **Jami' al-Khadra** (the Green Mosque or Mosque of the Sadness of Our Lord Jacob) is located on the lower slopes of Mt Gerizim in the southwestern quarter of the town. The mosque is entered by three doors in the north wall, the central one being the largest. On the outer arch, damaged decoration is surmounted by a decorated cavetto hood-mould which continues across the façade and the two flanking doors. The inscription above the main door dates the building of the mosque to 1288–90. The mosque has three bays of rib vaults. The mihrab has stuccowork in a semi-dome behind a horseshoe arch with marble colonnettes; the short walls have cupboard niches, although the central cupboard on the east wall has been converted into a window. In the west wall, the south niche has been replaced by a door into a small room which tradition says is the place where Jacob wept when told that Joseph was dead. The fine rectangular minaret is 30m to the northeast. It has two string courses, above which are paired windows. The upper stage has white marble colonettes at the angles; above, a projecting parapet rests on corbels; the round top section seems to have been added after c 1880. A Samaritan inscription is built into the base at the southeast corner. Samaritan traditions, an orientation towards Mt Gerizim, and the cupboards suggest it may have been a Samaritan synagogue taken over by the Muslims c 1291. It has features in the doors and minaret which could well be Mamluk, and while the quadripartite rib vaulting inside is similar to Frankish work of 12C date, the structure does not conform to that of a church. It may be a Samaritan synagogue which was rebuilt in the 12C before being converted by the Muslims in 1288–90.

The nearby Samaritan Synagogue is an unadorned building replacing an earlier structure destroyed in the earthquake of 1927; it is noted for its ancient textual versions of the Pentateuch.

APHEK
● ● ● ● ● ● ●

The site of the biblical city of Aphek (ancient Antipatris, A. Ras al-Ain, H. Afek) is in a recreational park at the springs of the Yarkon River (a source tapped for Jerusalem's water supply in Mandate times). The park contains the restored remains of an Ottoman fortress which is built over an important Middle Bronze Age site. It is c 55km from Jerusalem, near Highway 444 and the town of Petah Tikva: the springs of the Yarkon are on the Hod Hasharon–Petah Tikva road, between the Yarkon and Segula junctions; Afek Park is between Ganim junction in Petah Tikva and Rosh Ha'ayin on Highway 483. Yarkon National Park is by the springs just to the east, approached by the Petah Tikva-Kessem junction and is also managed by the National Parks Authority (☎ 03 934 8462).

The strategic significance of the site relates both to the control of the springs and of the crossing of the river fed by the springs. Remains from the Bronze Age have been excavated here, including an important series of palaces dating from early in the second millennium BC. The site is also mentioned in the Bible in connection with the wars between the Philistines and the Israelites and had a nearly continuous history of occupation. Remains of the city built by Herod the Great in 9 BC and named Antipatris for his father, were also partly excavated.

The visible remains are those of the Ottoman fortress of Qal'at Ras al-Ain, built before 1571, measuring 80 x 100m. There are four corner towers—three rectangular and one octagonal; the entrance (badly restored) is on the west side. The fort was already ruinous in the 19C, but parts of the walls still stand c 10m high. A mosque was built in 1573 in the centre of the castle, but its ruins were removed during the 1970s.

EN HEMED ~ AQUA BELLA

The large and well-preserved Crusader manor or monastery building at En Hemed (Crusader Aqua Bella, A. Khirbat 'Iqbala, Dair al-Banat) lies off the south side of Highway 1, c 11km west of Jerusalem, near Kiryat Anavim, the Hemed interchange. It is maintained by the National Parks Authority (☎ 02 534 2741) as a landscaped historic site (with picnic tables).

The large **Crusader building** is set near a group of springs located in a river bed. There was a village here in Crusader times, which is known to have belonged to the Hospitallers by 1163/69. The building has small projecting turrets on west and south; a door on the east leads to a courtyard. Two storeys of rooms existed on all but the entrance side, with external stairs on the south side of the court up to the first floor, and a probable gallery on the west. An olive press of uncertain date can be seen in the ground floor south room; above it is a chapel/hall, which has an apse and aumbry on the east, the base of a chancel screen, several large windows, and a small turret room on the south. The fact that it was groin-vaulted tells us that this was the principal room, as all other rooms in the building are barrel-vaulted. A tower, perhaps a signal tower, rises above the first storey on the northwest side. It may have been built as a manor house then converted to a monastic infirmary for the Hospitallers. Across the stream is a second small building of uncertain function, perhaps a surviving fragment of the village.

The Knights of the Hospital in Jerusalem by 1163–69 owned the lands not just here at Aqua Bella, but also of the castle at Belmont (Suba) and the church at Abu Ghosh. The castellan of Belmont (see below) would have controlled all these places from c 1160.

BELMONT AND ABU GHOSH

The Crusader castle of the Hospitallers at Belmont (A. Suba, H. Zova) is located off Highway 1 at the south entrance to Mivasseret Zion c 12km west of Jerusalem. It was built between 1150 and 1191. A polygonal outer defence surrounds the remains of a courtyard-style structure similar to that at Aqua Bella. There are the ruins of an Arab village which was built inside the castle and destroyed in 1948.

Nearby (signposted from Highway 1) is **Castel** (A. Qastal) the site of an important battle between Arabs and Israelis in 1948. A park with memorial is maintained by the National Parks Authority (☎ 02 533 0476).

Off the north side of Highway 1, c 2km further west, is the village and the Benedictine Abbey at **Abu Ghosh/Qaryat al-Inab** which contains a 12C Crusader church. The place was mistakenly identified as Emmaus in the Crusader period (Castellum Emmaus).

History of the Church of the Resurrection

There is no evidence for a church before the 12C, but the Franks may have been confused by the remains of a Roman reservoir built by the *Legio X Fretensis*, and by an Early Islamic caravanserai (9C–11C) on the road to Jerusalem and decided that this was the village of Emmaus where the risen Christ appeared to Cleopas and a fellow disciple (Luke 24:13–32). Thus by c 1142 the village was considered to be the Emmaus of the New Testament. All its lands were granted to the Hospitallers, who held them until 1187. They built the east end of the **Church of the Resurrection** over the reservoir which became the crypt into which pilgrims descended by the old reservoir stairs; the proportions of the church above were largely dictated by the reservoir beneath.

The church (open 08.30–11.00, 14.30–17.30; closed Thur and Sun; shorter hours on feast days; ring bell for admission) has three apses and three aisles of four bays but is fairly plain. Faint traces of wall paintings at the east end remain: on the central apse, the resurrected Christ and saints; on the north apse, Christ in majesty between the Virgin Mary and John the Baptist; on the south apse, Abraham, Isaac and Jacob; on the north wall, three figures including a mounted soldier, then the Dormition of the Virgin; on the south wall figures like those on the north wall, then the Crucifixion. Other painted areas imitate marble veneer. A few traces remain to show the vault in the crypt had a pattern of stars.

The Abbasid caravanserai, which directly abutted the church on the east end, remained in use to the mid-11C and appears to have been reused by the Crusaders perhaps as a hospice for those visiting the church. It was rebuilt c 1350–1400, and a mosque was built in the east part of the courtyard.

A further 12km to the west, c 24km from Jerusalem, is **Latrun**, a strategic point on the road to Jerusalem and the site of battles ancient and modern. East of the Latrun junction is the Cistercian Abbey of the Trappist order built in 1890 and the source of Latroun wine; on the summit to the south are the ruins of a Templar castle, Toron des Chevaliers.

RAMALLAH

Ramallah is one of the principal Palestinian towns and is not far from the Palestinian university at Bir Zeit. Located 13km north of Jerusalem on Highway 60, Ramallah (population 18,297 in 1999) lies to the west with the historic settlement of al-Bira (population 28,351 in 1999) on the east on the main road to Nablus.

Practical information

Getting there
Ramallah is easily reached by service taxi from the Damascus Gate in Jerusalem, passing the al-Ram checkpoint 6km south of Ramallah into a semi-autonomous Palestinian area. The bus station is just east of Midan Manara around which most taxis operate.

Information
You can learn about both the new town and the old lower town on the excellent website at www.birzeit.edu/ramallah/geninf.html

Where to stay

Grand Park Hotel, with swimming pool (☎ 02 298 6194; 📠 02 295 6950); *al-Bireh Tourist Hotel* (☎/📠 02 240 0803).

Eating out

Ramallah is a busy town and has a number of restaurants and coffee, sweet or ice-cream shops particularly around the Midan Manara, Sharia Rokab and Sharia Yafa which lead off it to the west. Try *Angelo's Restaurant* for pizza (☎ 02-295 6408); *al-Bardounis* garden restaurant, Sharia Yafa (☎ 02 295 1410); *Flamingo's Restaurant* for Mexican food (☎ 02 298 5813); *Caesar's* in the *Grand Park Hotel*.

History

Ramallah has some Crusader remains (a watchtower) but was only established in the 16C, when it was a small agricultural village. During the 1830s Ibrahim Pasha opened up Palestine to European trade and Christian institutions, and many were established at Ramallah; the town expanded greatly from the 1920s despite a steady process of emigration to the USA, and still further with influxes of refugees in 1948. During the 1950s and 1960s Ramallah became the summer resort of Palestine, an attractive town with a pleasant climate, noted for its hotels and garden restaurants; but the town suffered badly under the occupation from 1967 and it is only since becoming a semi-autonomous entity in 1995 that some of the attraction of the town is again becoming visible and tourism increasingly welcomed when political circumstances permit.

Ramallah is a busy market town in process of re-development, with a large modern mosque. It offers shopping—for embroideries, sweets and ice-cream; bakeries, street stalls, cafés and restaurants for traditional Arab food; it is a lively town with a large number of students, and less conservative than Nablus.

Al-Bira (ancient Beeroth, Roman Berea) is to the east, where the al-Bira municipality building and the old al-Ain Mosque are built in the low ground along the main Nablus Road. On al-Ain Street to the east, at c 100m al-Khan St on the right has the remains of a fine but ruined khan (under restoration in 2000). Four bays are almost intact with good ashlar piers and rubble groin-vaulted roofs. Almost opposite is a good example of a traditional working bread oven, in a long vaulted room with floor much lower than the current road level. Continuing to the top of the hill on al-Ain St, the modern al-Umari mosque is on the right, and beyond it, are the remains of a three-aisled **Crusader church** of four bays (dedicated to St. Mary) built by 1128 in what was then the Frankish agricultural village of Magna Mahumeria, destroyed by Saladin in 1187. It was thereafter a Muslim village with a mosque recorded by 1195. Although the vaulting of the church had collapsed by the early 16C, the plan was still traceable until the First World War when the Turkish army used its stones to build a bridge. Much of the plan of the Crusader village survived into the 1930s, and its main street had the church at the top (northern) end and the fortified house of the steward at the bottom (south) end. The remains of the church include the south apse with an aumbry, chancel screen, pier and pilaster bases.

Diagonally across from the church is the building housing the charity In'ash al-Usra Society (a Palestinian women's charity to improve the position of women in the local community) which runs the **Palestinian Folklore Museum**. The museum (open Sat–Wed 08.00–16.00, Thur 08.00–14.00) is entered by a door about 20m down from the crossing. It contains Palestinian costume, pottery, basketry, household and agricultural implements in a small exhibition on the traditional Palestinian house.

Bir Zeit University is an independent Palestinian institution, 20km north of Jerusalem in the West Bank, 7km north of al-Bira on Highway 60. It was founded as an Anglican school in 1924; 4500 students were enrolled in September 1999.

NABI SAMWIL
• • • • • • • • • • • • • •

Eight kilometres northwest of Jerusalem on a hill-top, just north of the checkpoint at the city limits, is the traditional location of the **tomb of the prophet Samuel**. Open summer Sat–Thur 08.00–17.00, Fri 08.00–16.00; winter 08.00–16.00. There is no direct bus but it is walkable (2km) from Bait Hanina (Bus 74 from Nablus Road bus station in East Jerusalem), or from the Jewish settlement of Ramot (*Egged* Bus 36 from the Central Bus Station, Jaffa Rd); if coming by car, the car park is on the east side of the mosque.

History

'Father of the Prophets' and the leading religious personality of Israel in his time (11C BC, see the Old Testament Books of Samuel), the son of Elkanah, an Ephraimite of the town of Ramah, Samuel is linked with the sanctuary of Shiloh and the story of the priest Eli. Samuel anointed both Saul and David kings over Israel. However, there is no evidence that he died or was buried at Nabi Samwil (I Sam. 25:1 records that he died and was buried at Rama). By 553/54 a monastery was built on the site consolidating the tradition, and Justinian added a well and a defensive wall. A village was located here in the 10C and in 1106–08 Abbot Daniel mentions a defensive wall, perhaps that of Justinian.

The site was called Mountjoy (Mons Gaudii, Monjoie) by the Crusaders, because it was from the top of this hill that they first saw Jerusalem on the morning of 7 June 1099 on their way to the conquest of the city. A Premonstratensian abbey may have been built before 1131, but a church certainly existed in 1158/59. It passed between Christian and Muslim ownership between 1187 and 1244, but thereafter the tomb was a site of pilgrimage only, although pottery kilns were again located here in the Mamluk period. In the 17C a mosque existed on the ruins of the church; groined arches supported by brackets were still extant in 1874 and partly incorporated in a mosque built over the aisles, with a minaret in the southeast corner of the south transept and the cenotaph of Samuel in the centre of the earlier nave. The present larger mosque over the nave was begun in 1911/12.

Following almost the same route as the Crusaders, British forces captured Nabi Samwil during their advance in 1917, but the mosque was damaged and the minaret fell in the very fierce battle. A British position here which controlled the road from Jaffa played a strategic part in the capture of

Jerusalem on 9 December 1917. The mosque and minaret were repaired during the Mandate, but the adjacent village was destroyed following its capture by Israeli forces in 1967. The tomb is now a focus of Jewish pilgrimage.

The area around the mosque has been excavated, with a broad expanse of rock cuttings and buildings which include earlier remains of Iron Age, Persian and Hellenistic periods as well as those of the defended enclave of the periods from Justinian to the 12C. The **Crusader remains of church and monastery** include a fortification with vaults around the church and its courtyard, with an unfinished rock-cut moat and quarries. Large Crusader stables, a camping ground, and an inn for pilgrims all existed outside the walls. A village grew outside the walls, and the remains include pottery kilns, including those of the Umayyad period on the left of the approach. Here pottery stamped with the name 'Dayr Samwil' was discovered.

The **mosque** is an attractive building, with the main entrance on the east side

Minaret from the roof

on the site of the former 12C apse. It contains a large hall with groin vaults and a mihrab located on the rebuilt crossing and south transept of the Crusader church. A cornice moulding on the south delimits surviving parts of the older structure. A cenotaph lies on the west side of the mosque; on the northwest steps descend from the former 12C north nave to the crypt of the 12C church with the tomb. A closed chamber with tomb lies to the southwest, and steps to the gallery are on the north. A steep flight of steps on the east side leads to the roof of the mosque, which has shallow domes and a small cupola. There is a fine view from the roof; the Dome of the Rock in Jerusalem can be seen to the southeast.

The exterior of the mosque exhibits reused bossed masonry in the base of the minaret and in the south wall; a Crusader elbow console built into the wall on the southwest corner and a blocked entrance in the west wall, are both probably part of the Crusader cloister. The minaret is octagonal, with two zigzag string courses.

South of Jerusalem

The region south of Jerusalem is dominated by a ridge of limestone, dolomite and chalk hills, rising to just over 1000m near Hebron, declining towards the Beersheba Valley and the coast, and dropping steeply to the Arabah on the east. The main road runs along the crest of the hills, near the watershed between the fertile west and the arid east. The average annual rainfall in the Hebron area is nearly 600mm, dropping to about 200mm at Beersheba, but even less in the region of the eastern wilderness.

The northern section around Bait Jala and Bethlehem is the most fertile, with a landscape characterised by magnificent agricultural terraces on the hillsides, with rich valley bottoms, where fruit, vines, olives and grain are grown. The rocky hilltops are given over to grazing goats, sheep and cattle. To the west, the foothills down to the coast provide some of the richest agricultural land in the region.

History of the area

The Old Testament describes the southern hill country in ancient times as Amorite, including the five Amorite kingdoms of Jerusalem, Hebron, Yarmuth, Lachish and Eglon (Jos.10:5). However, other inhabitants (perhaps tribes or immigrants) are also referred to—the giant Anakim of Hebron, the Perizzites, the Hittites, the Hivites, the Rephaim. And there were the raids of the Amalekites and of the Midianites from the south and the east. Sometime before the first millennium BC the hills south of Jerusalem were occupied by the tribe of Judah, after whom the land has often been called Judah, or the Judaean region, with the wilderness to the east. On the west was the Philistine kingdom occupying the lower fringes of the hills (the Shephelah). In the time of the Iron Age kingdoms (10C–6C BC) the southern fortified border of Judah generally lay in the region of Beersheba. Following the Babylonian conquest at the beginning of the 6C BC, much of the population of Judah was deported and replaced at least in part by Edomites (and perhaps tribal Arabians) from across the Arabah. The region then became Idumea (the Greek word for Edom) and was later incorporated into the Roman, Byzantine and Islamic provinces. At these times also its routes and borders were policed by garrisoned forts, to guard against raiding Arab tribes and threats from Egypt. With so much poor land, its population has been sparse, and in the Late Bronze Age and in the Ottoman period particularly the inhabitants were probably more pastoralist than agricultural, with settlements few and small. In Ottoman and recent times, Hebron and Bethlehem were the principal market towns, and respectively the location of an important mosque and a church, each attracting pilgrimage.

BETHLEHEM
• • • • • • • • • • • •

The market town of Bethlehem, home of King David, is celebrated as the birthplace of Jesus and for the Byzantine Church of the Nativity. The town lies on the east side of the main road from Jerusalem to Hebron (Highway 60), 9km south of Jerusalem.

Bethlehem is a municipality and since 1994 the centre of a governorate of the Palestine National Authority (population c 21,500 in 1997). The town has a number of colleges, schools and hospitals, many founded by religious organisations during the late 19C and early 20C. Bethlehem University was established in 1973, with 2000 students in 1997.

Located on a ridge in the southern hill country, with very steep descents to the wadis below, Bethlehem is set amid fertile land with the wilderness not far to the east. The name means place of meat (classical) or bread, food (colloquial A, and

H.). It has no spring, and originally depended on cisterns, until water was brought by aqueduct from Solomon's Pools probably in the Hasmonean or the Herodian period. It was a mainly Christian market town serving the Bedouin and the surrounding villages, in a region of agricultural, meat and dairy production, of vineyards and wine making. Since the 16C it has had a thriving industry in olive-wood and mother-of-pearl carving (various items of religious significance for Christian pilgrim souvenirs, and jewellery) which can be seen in the many shops.

Practical information

Getting there
By public transport, from Jerusalem, you can take Bus 22 from the Damascus Gate Bus Station; service taxis from the Damascus Gate are very cheap and run more frequently; they go to the west side of Bethlehem, the opposite side of town from the Church of the Nativity. If you are driving, just north of Rachel's Tomb at 8km from Jerusalem is the checkpoint for entering the semi-autonomous Palestinian area of Bethlehem. The road divides, continuing straight ahead to the west side of Bethlehem and to Hebron. Take the left fork into Bethlehem and continue up the hill to Manger Square on the right. Parking and the bus station are just before Manger Square.

Where to stay
Nativity Hotel ☎ 02 277 0650; *Casa Nova Hospice*, Manger Square ☎ 02 274 3981; *Bethlehem Hotel* ☎ 02 277 0702; 📠 02 277 0706; *Orient Palace Hotel*, Manger Square ☎ 02 274 278; 📠 02 274 1562.

Eating out
Bethlehem has a number of restaurants, including the *al-Andalos*, Manger Square ☎ 02 274 3519 and others in or near the square. Coffee may be had in the *Orient Palace Hotel*. A recently renovated old house in Najara St is a coffee house, hostel and small museum.

History

The town may be mentioned in the Egyptian Amarna letters (14C BC), but no settlement of that date has been discovered.

According to the Old Testament, following the Israelite conquest Bethlehem was part of the territory of the tribe of Judah (12C–11C BC). It was also the home of the Levite who became priest for Micah in Ephraim (Judges 17–18), the home of the concubine of the Levite of Ephraim (Judges 19), and the setting for most of the story of Ruth. It was the home of David (c 1004–965 BC), the son of an Ephrathite called Jesse (I Sam. 17:12, 15). Here Samuel anointed David king over Israel (I Sam. 16:1–13). A Philistine garrison occupied the town during the early wars of David (II Sam. 23:14–16) when David longed for a drink of water from the well by the gate of Bethlehem (see David's Well). Later a town of Israel in the time of David and Solomon, and then of Judah during the divided monarchy, it was refortified by Rehoboam (928–911 BC; II Chr. 11:6). The prophet Micah in the days of Jotham, Ahaz and Hezekiah (8C BC) foretold the coming of the Messiah to

Bethlehem (Micah 5:2). Following the Babylonian destruction, in 586 BC many of the town's leading citizens were exiled to Babylon; 123 men returned under the Persian dispensation (Ezra 2:21). Following the depopulation it was settled by Edomites who in turn were expelled by John Hyrcanus. The earliest archaeological discoveries date to the 8C–6C.

The New Testament records two versions of the birth of Jesus in Bethlehem (Matt. 2:1–16 and Luke 1–2), which various authorities think occurred c 4 BC on the basis of the date of the census of Augustus when Quirinius was Governor of Syria (Luke 2:1–2) in the time of Herod the Great, who, according to the story, ordered the Massacre of the Innocents, and following whose death (4 BC) Archelaus succeeded as ruler (Matt. 2:19–22). The New Testament genealogies place Jesus in the descent of Abraham and David. The town certainly acquired greater importance at this time, partly because it overlooked the main roads to Herod the Great's fortress palaces at Herodion and Masada.

Very few remains of the 1C–3C AD have been recovered. Following the suppression of the First Jewish Revolt (AD 70) and the Second Revolt (AD 135) by the Romans, Jews were proscribed from living in the area. Some later writers maintain that from the time of Hadrian there was a grove sacred to Adonis (Tammuz) in the vicinity of the Cave of the Nativity. The tradition of Jesus' birth in a cave at Bethlehem dates back to at least the 2C (Justin Martyr and the *Proto-Gospel of James*), and soon after 246 the Alexandrian theologian Origen noted the cave and the manger.

Constantine's basilica In 325 Constantine built a great basilica with an octagonal shrine over a series of caves identified as Jesus' birthplace, which was dedicated on 31 May 339. Excavations beneath the present church have shown that this was fronted on the west by a flagged court or street, which led to a square court with porticoes on all sides (partly under the present narthex). The porticoes had mosaic floors, with geometric designs, and corner columns with heart-shaped cross-sections. The west wall had three doors and was approached by three steps from the court. The church itself was a square basilica, divided by four rows of nine columns into a 9m-wide nave, and four side aisles. The floor level is 60cm below that of the present church. The floor mosaics, which have a technical similarity to those in the Imperial Byzantine palace in Constantinople, appear to date to the 5C.

To the east an octagon was built over the Cave of the Nativity, approached from the basilica by three stairways. Within the octagon pilgrims were permitted to approach a railing from which the cave could be viewed from above.

From the 4C many Christian pilgrims came to Bethlehem, and the desert on the east became one of the great centres of Byzantine monasticism. The church was visited in 333 by the Bordeaux Pilgrim, whose description includes the traditional cave with manger. The Commemoration of the Holy Innocents (Matt. 2:16) is first noted in the 4C, and a chapel on the south side of the main church is recorded in 417–39. At the end of the 4C St. Jerome (c 342–420), the great scholar of the church, settled in Bethlehem and, with the help of Paula, her daughter Eustochium and other women, founded a monastery, three communities of women, a free school and a hospice. Here also Jerome translated the Bible into Latin, his work becoming the Vulgate, accepted as the authoritative version used by the Latin church at the Council of Trent. His importance within the Western Christian church is reflected in the many depictions of him, including famous ones by Rembrandt, Antonello da Messina and Dürer. The Constantinian basilica was destroyed in or after the Samaritan Revolt of 529.

Justinian's basilica A new basilica was built c 531, usually attributed to Justinian (527–65). Larger, and with a slightly different plan to that of the previous church, it was on the same site and incorporated parts of the previous building. This basilica has survived to the present day.

A legend noted in the writings of Eutychius, patriarch of Alexandria in the 9C, maintains that the architect sent by Justinian to rebuild the church was beheaded on imperial orders for unsatisfactory work. It has been speculated that this was due to a failure to carry through a design involving a dome 33.6m in diameter over the cave. Instead a clover-leaf triple apse was built in the form visible today. At the west end, the atrium was extended; a narthex was constructed above the 4C east portico. The basilica itself was lengthened to 33m, the nave widened and the side aisles narrowed. Justinian's west wall was 2.8 m west of Constantine's, but the north and south walls lie on the same lines. The columns and capitals of the earlier building were reused plus ten new columns, and four new heart-sectioned columns were placed at the crossing beneath the dome.

The church was dedicated to St. Mary Theotokos, and beneath it the cave with the manger was lined with marble. Sophronius (Bishop of Jerusalem) described the church c 614:

And when I see all the glistening gold, the well-fashioned columns and fine workmanship, let me be freed from the gloom of sorrows. I will also look up at the design above, at the coffers studded with stars, for they are a masterpiece, brilliant with heavenly beauty. Let me go down also to the cave, where the Virgin Queen of all bore a Saviour for mankind.

In 570 St. Jerome's tomb was supposed to be near the mouth of the main cave in the church, and though the site moved later, it was still regularly shown in the 12C. His body was moved later to the church of Santa Maria Maggiore in Rome. Jerome also recorded that he buried the matron Paula beside the cave, where she and her daughter Eustochium continued to be remembered.

As well as the church, Justinian rebuilt the walls of Bethlehem. By this time there was clearly an extensive complex of monasteries and guest houses in the town. The Persian sack of 614, which wreaked such havoc on the Christian monuments of Jerusalem, spared the Church of the Nativity, because, it was said, the Byzantine mosaics of the façade showed the Magi worshipping the infant king, and the Persians recognised and respected the familiar dress of Persian holy men. The town was small, principally noted for its shrine, but in Byzantine times was not the seat of a bishophric.

In 634 Bethlehem surrendered to the Arabs, and the church was again spared. In 638 Umar prayed in the south transept and it was given to the Muslims as a place of prayer. In c 675 Epiphanius the Monk on his visit was shown 'the family home of David' to the left of the Church of the Nativity. The town of Bethlehem was clearly badly affected by the earthquake of 749, as it was mostly in ruins in c 750; the Commemoratorium notes that in the early 9C the church was served by 15 priests, clergy and monks. In c 870 Bernard the Monk noted the Church of the Blessed Innocents on the south side. In the 10C when Muslim tolerance of the Christian shrines lessened, the mosaics in the south apse were taken down. The presence of this Muslim shrine again saved the church from destruction by al-Hakim in the 11C.

Just before the capture of Jerusalem in 1099, on 6 June Tancred and Baldwin of le Bourg rode to secure the church at Bethlehem in response to the plea of the mainly Christian population of the town. In 1102 Saewulf found that Bethlehem had been largely destroyed by the Muslims, but the church had survived. On Christmas Day 1101, Baldwin I, the first king of Jerusalem, was crowned in the church, which was richly restored in the time of the Crusaders. In 1110 Bethlehem became the seat of a Latin bishop. The restoration of the church included Byzantine wall mosaics given by the Emperor Manuel Comnenos (1143–80). There was probably a castle adjacent, and an Augustinian monastery was built on the north side of the church. The town itself prospered.

The Latins were forced to leave in 1187, but Salah al-Din allowed two priests and two deacons to return in 1192 as a favour to the Bishop of Salisbury. In 1244 the town was devastated by the raid of the Khwarizmian Turks. In 1263 Baybars destroyed the Latin monastery and in 1266 expelled the Latins. Some repairs were permitted under the Mamluks, and in 1347 the Franciscan Order took over the Augustinian Convent on the north side of the church. In 1350 Ludolf von Suchem described the church as fortified like a castle: the remains of a wall and gatehouse at the west end of the present forecourt have been excavated. The roof was replaced in 1482: Edward IV of England gave the lead; Philip of Burgundy had earlier been granted a permit for repairs, and the wood came via Venice. The progressive narrowing of the west door for defensive purposes, perhaps begun in the 12C, continued from c 1500, and under the Ottoman Turks the looting of stone, marble paving and veneer became almost systematic, and then the removal of roof lead to use for bullets in the 17C. The plan drawn by Amico in 1609 shows a massive walled complex containing church and monastery. In 1670 the Greek patriarch obtained a permit from Constantinople to repair the roof, and also installed the iconostasis, and two years later the Greek Orthodox managed to gain rights to most of the church. The Armenians acquired some rights in 1810, and the Latins were only readmitted to a share through the intervention of Napoleon III in 1852. The present division of the church among the different sects has remained largely in this 19C state. The church and town were damaged in the earthquake of 1834, and the church in a fire of 1869. The aqueduct (see Solomon's Pools, p 392) providing the principal fresh water supply to the town was repaired many times, with clay pipes in 1848 and iron pipes in the 20C. The town grew rapidly from the middle of the 19C, and many monasteries, convents and schools were built. A huge influx of Muslim Palestinian refugees in 1948 completely changed the demographic structure of the town.

During excavations adjacent to the church in 1926, the Franciscans found 13 bells dating to the 14C. Three others had been found buried in the cloister in 1863. They had been removed in the mid-15C when the ringing of Christian church bells was forbidden.

The Church of the Nativity

Approaching the **church (open 05.30–18.00, –17.00 in winter) from the west from Manger Square, the paving in front of the church overlies part of the Constantinian atrium. The wall to the right is part of the Armenian Orthodox monastery, mostly of 18C–19C date over 12C structures which include the so-called Library of St. Jerome, and possibly parts of the Crusader hospital.

Ahead, the large but unimpressive façade with its tiny door is a reminder of the unsettled times through which the great 6C church has survived. Only traces of the original three wide doors and west gable end of the time of Justinian may still be seen, as straight joints, moulded lintels and a baluster capital. Progressively reduced from the great 6C lintel to prevent the ingress of mounted men, and the looting of the fabric, the main central doorway has a blocked pointed arch which may be 12C or later; the smallest blocking may be of Mamluk or Ottoman date. The north door of Justinian is mostly hidden by a buttress of 1775, and the south door by the Armenian monastery; these doors were probably blocked in the 12C. Inside is the dark and partitioned narthex of the 6C church. It extends the full width of the basilica but only a short central section is visible; the partitions are of various dates. On the south a doorway leads through to the entrance to the Armenian convent (not open). The vaulted roof is medieval. The central door to the basilica has the remains of a great carved wooden door presented to the church by two Armenians in 1227, as the inscription in Armenian and Arabic records.

Entering the basilica you are confronted by the splendid wide nave of Justinian. On either side are the double rows of 11 columns (6m high) which separate the side aisles; most of the capitals and columns are reused from the earlier 4C Constantinian basilica (the capitals are Byzantine Corinthian with crosses); the columns themselves are of local white-veined red limestone and 28 have the remnants of 12C and later paintings on their surfaces. These depict the Virgin and Child, a Crucifixion and saints, including King Canute II of Denmark and Olaf of Norway. There are also graffiti representing the crests and mottoes of Frankish knights which mostly date from the 14C to the 17C. The soffits of the architrave have carved timbers some of which probably date to the 6C: some designs are paralleled in the oldest timbers from the Aqsa Mosque in Jerusalem (see pp 134 and 242). The great timber gable roof of the 15C was restored in the 19C. The main lighting comes from the round-arched clerestory windows. The paved floor contains trapdoors, which can be lifted to reveal large sections of the **5C mosaic floor** beneath the present level; those in the central nave are the best preserved.

The walls bear fragments of the splendid series of *12C mosaics which once covered them; they are best seen on the north wall. They were arranged in five registers against a background of gilded tesserae, the lowest illustrating the genealogy of Jesus. The next showed the churches of the towns of the 13 Great Councils of the Church, with texts relating to the decisions made at them; they include, on the north wall, that of the Council of Antioch in 272 which expelled Paul of Samosata as an heretic; of Sardica (Sofia) in 343, which judged the Athanasian heresy; the south wall had Nicaea (325), Constantinople (381), Ephesus (431), Chalcedon (451) and Constantinople (680). The register above has a frieze with jewelled acanthus plants and vases, Byzantine motifs similar to those used by the Umayyads in the Dome of the Rock in Jerusalem in the 7C; the next register shows angels (winged and haloed) between the clerestory windows, with the name of the artist (Basil) at the foot of the third angel from the east on

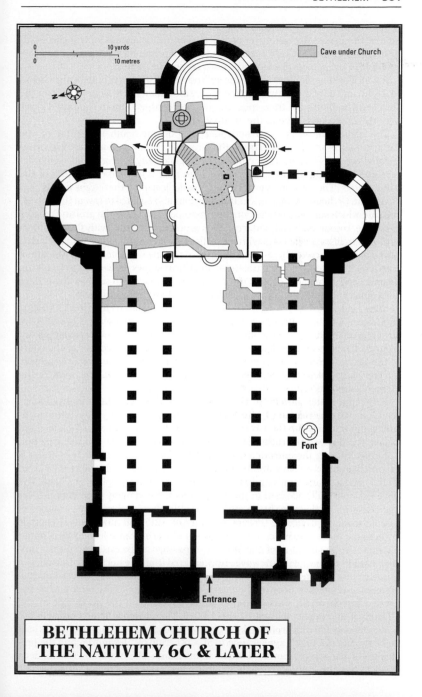

0 10 yards
0 10 metres

Cave under Church

Font

Entrance

**BETHLEHEM CHURCH OF
THE NATIVITY 6C & LATER**

the north wall. At the top was another frieze. The west wall was originally covered with mosaics depicting the prophets. The 6C octagonal font in the south aisle is not in situ. Its Greek inscription reads: 'For the memory, repose and forgiveness of the sinners of whom the Lord knows the names.'

A wall blocking the choir and transept from the basilica was built by the Greeks in 1842, and only the central section was removed in 1918. Doorways from the side aisles lead into the transepts, and thence steps lead up to the raised choir over the grotto, and down to the grotto itself.

The main altar at the east end, and that on the south (the Altar of the Circumcision), are the property of the Greek Orthodox and are lavishly ornamented with a 17C iconostasis crowned with gilded angels, icons, gilded chandeliers and lamps. On the north side of the high altar is the Armenian Altar of the Three Kings. The altar in the north apse is dedicated to the Virgin and is also Armenian Orthodox. Trapdoors in this area can also be lifted to reveal the fine **5C mosaic** which surrounded the Constantinian octagon above the grotto. Complex guilloche, rosette and trail patterns form geometric designs, with floral borders and vine trellises; medallions with birds, flowers, fruits and patterns make a rich and elaborate carpet. There are **12C mosaics** showing scenes from the life of Christ on the east wall: on the north section Christ shows his wounds to Doubting Thomas and a fragment depicts the Ascension; on the south section Christ rides on a donkey through the countryside before the Entry into Jerusalem.

Steps lead up from the south transept to the courtyard of the Greek Othodox monastery. On the south side is the bell tower. On the southeast is the massive tower, possibly 6C at its base, above 12C and at the top 19C; it probably served defence, treasury and residential purposes. In the northeast corner of the court is the Greek Orthodox Chapel of St. George (12C). On its outer wall is a lively carved plaque depicting St. George slaying the dragon. To the west is the Armenian monastery.

Returning to the church, on the south side of the high altar a flight of steps leads down to the **Grotto of the Nativity**. The *6C bronze gates** at the north and south entrances to the Grotto are those of Justinian—have a look at them before you descend the rather steep, dark steps. The rebated pointed arch and columns framing the entrance are 12C. The cave where the birth of Jesus is commemorated is c 12m x 3m. In an apse on the east side a silver star (1717) set in the paving, many lamps and marble lining mark the birthplace of Christ. The cave was splendidly adorned in the 4C but has suffered many depredations over the centuries, and is now hung with painted leather blackened by centuries of candle smoke and incense. Fragments only of 12C wall mosaics and capitals around the manger survive. Steps on the left of the entrance lead to the Roman Catholic Grotto and Altar of the Manger. A passage at the west end of this complex used to connect with the caves now entered from the north (see below).

Ascending the steps on the north side, and continuing northwest past the Armenian altars to a door in the north apse, you come to the west end of the Latin **Church of St. Catherine**, enlarged in 1881 on the north side of the Church of the Nativity (closed 12.00–14.00). The church is first recorded in the 15C, and may have incorporated the chapter house of the 12C convent. It is said to be the site of Christ's appearance to St. Catherine of Alexandria, and the prediction of her matryrdom c 310 (she is buried on Mount Sinai). The modern basilica has three aisles. Built with funds from the Emperor of Austria, this church replaced a smaller one of the same dedication. To the north and west is the Franciscan monastery.

Immediately to the right on entry, steps descend to more of the cave complex beneath the Church of the Nativity. (A guide and map are located on the right side of the steps.) Here **rock cuttings, including ancient tombs**, with various modern additions, chambers and blockings, commemorate various people and traditions. First is the Chapel of the Innocents said to be the tomb of the infants slain by Herod the Great in his attempt to kill the new-born Jesus (Matt. 2:16); there is a chapel dedicated to St. Joseph, the husband of Mary. The tombs are said to be of the devout Roman matron Paula and her daughter Eustochium, who made a pilgrimage with Jerome c 485, later settled in Bethlehem, and were buried near the Cave of the Nativity; to the right is the double cave of St. Jerome, the first containing his tomb, and the further one a chapel marking the site where he is said to have translated the Bible. Another tomb is said to be that of Eusebius, Jerome's successor as head of the monastery at Bethlehem. However, it is unlikely that these locations are authentic. Parts of the Constantinian and Justinian foundations may be seen down here.

Returning to the church of St. Catherine, and leaving by the west door, the **cloister** was restored in 1948 by A. Barluzzi using columns and capitals of the 12C Crusader monastery on the site, where traces of an earlier 5C monastery associated with Jerome also exist. A modern statue of St. Jerome is placed here. Return by the west entrance of the cloister to the courtyard in front of the Church of the Nativity.

Manger Square contains some of the principal buildings of the town, the Post Office, the Municipality and the new Peace Building (intended to house police, car park, small museum and other services), as well as shops. A Byzantine mosaic was discovered while excavating the site of the Peace Building. The Mosque of Umar (late 19C, rebuilt 1954) lies at the northwest corner.

To the west lies the principal section of the modern town, with market place and a number of traditional buildings recently restored, including an Ottoman period building used as an olive oil factory with horse-driven press. Note in particular the narrow passages covered by arches which are characteristic of the town, and many of which have also been recently restored. If you walk 100m along Paul VI St, a right turn leads to the **Old Bethlehem Museum** (open daily except Thur afternoon and Sun), an old Bethlehem house and a reconstruction of its contents.

To the north of the town, c 500m along the road to the Tomb of Rachel (see p 274), on the left are steep steps up to **David's Well**. Various remains on the site, including a well, some tombs, a mosaic (perhaps of the monastery established by Jerome) and references to a 4C church, indicate the Byzantine and later association of the site with the Old Testament story.

On the south side of Manger Square, the street descends steeply to a car park, and a little lower, to the west, to the recently restored Mamluk fountain house, al-Ain. This was served by the Herodian aqueduct, which functioned until 1947. It lies at the south end of the tunnel through which the water continued northwards beneath Bethlehem and then on to Jerusalem.

The street running east from Manger Square along the south side of the Church of the Nativity, passes numerous shops and a workshop for olive-wood

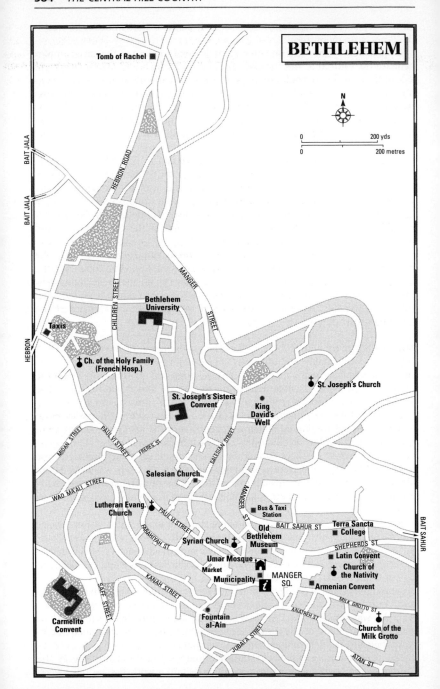

BETHLEHEM

Tomb of Rachel ▪

N

0   200 yds
0   200 metres

BAIT JALA

BAIT JALA

HEBRON ROAD

MANGER STREET

CHILDREN STREET

HEBRON

Taxis ▪

✝ Ch. of the Holy Family
(French Hosp.)

Bethlehem
University

St. Joseph's Sisters
Convent

● King
David's
Well

✝ St. Joseph's Church

MIDAN STREET

PAUL VI STREET

FRERES ST.

SALESIAN STREET

WAD MA'ALI STREET

Salesian Church ▪

Lutheran Evang. ✝
Church

PAUL VI STREET

FARAHIYAH ST.

MANGER ST.

Bus & Taxi
Station ▪

BAIT SAHUR ST.

Terra Sancta ▪
College

SHEPHERDS ST.

Old
Bethlehem
Museum ▪

Syrian Church ▪

Umar Mosque ▪

Market

Municipality

MANGER
SQ.

ℹ

▪ Latin Convent

✝ Church of
the Nativity

● Armenian Convent

KANAH STREET

SAFE STREET

Carmelite
Convent

● Fountain
al-Ain

ANATREH ST.

MILK GROTTO ST.

BAIT SAHUR

JUBALA STREET

ATAN ST.

✝ Church of the
Milk Grotto

carving, and leads to the **Milk Grotto** (at c 250m on the right). The chapel, with small Franciscan Convent, is open 08.00–11.45, 14.00–18.00 (–17.00 in winter). The modern chapel was built in 1838. Steps descend to a cave church where according to legend the Holy Family sheltered on the Flight into Egypt, and where a drop of the Virgin's milk fell on the cave floor as she suckled the infant Jesus. This has given rise to the superstition, shared by Christian and Muslim women, that the rock itself (here rather soft, white and chalky, not uncommon in the Bethlehem region), ground into dust and eaten, will increase the milk of women suckling infants. The first traditions about the Virgin's milk appear to date to the 7C but the dedication of a church on the site is apparently 12C. Above the cave, remnants of a Byzantine mosaic, and a rock-cut Crusader tomb with massive carved cover may be seen in a pleasant garden. The remains have been identified as parts of successive Byzantine and Crusader churches/monasteries, and as a Franciscan custody from 1494.

The Shepherds' Fields

The roads descending to the east of Bethlehem lead through the village of **Bait Sahur**, a mainly Christian village with a number of churches, a fertile area which tradition equates with the home of the shepherds at the Nativity, and with the fields in which Ruth gleaned. A burial cave of the Early Bronze Age was discovered here, and also finds of the later Bronze Age and Iron Age. Just to the east are the sites where the traditions connected with the Shepherds' Fields are localised.

And there were in the same country shepherds abiding in the field, keeping watch over their flock by night. And, lo, the angel of the Lord came upon them, and the glory of the Lord shone round about them, and they were sore afraid. And the angel said unto them, Fear not: for, behold, I bring you good tidings of great joy, which shall be to all people. (Luke 2:8–10)

The Greek Orthodox location of the Shepherds' Fields is at **Kanisat al-Ruwat**, 2km a little to the south of east of Bethlehem in the midst of fields. Open 08.00–11.30, 14.00–17.00. The ruins at al-Ruwat include a cave used as a church in the 4C, of which the barrel-vaulted roof survives and which is approached by a flight of 21 steps. It has three apses with traces of mosaic and old frescoes. The church remained in use to 1955. Above it a Byzantine chapel was built, and was in turn replaced by a larger church, destroyed in 614. It and a monastery were rebuilt in the 7C and survived to the 10C. A new, large church has been built on the east, the 4C lower church restored, and the remains of the upper church and monastery preserved.

At 600m to the north is the site the Franciscans identify with the monastery at the Shepherds' Fields, at **Khirbat Siyar al-Ghanim**. Open 08.00–12.00, 14.00–18.00 (–17.30 in winter). Here, in pleasant surroundings with a fine view towards the hills is a low natural cave or rock shelter with soot-blackened roof, partly enclosed to make a modern chapel. Above is a very modern church designed like a tent, with a sculpted bronze angel; just to the north are ruins of a rectangular monastery, with an early phase dated late 4C to early 5C and a second phase of the 6C–8C. Just the apse of the church survives and a large lintel decorated with crosses. The monastery, with courtyard, had winepresses, bakery, querns, cisterns and animal pens.

At **Khirbat Abu Ghunain** c 3km northeast of Bethlehem is a small walled monastery with a court and cistern. A church with a single apse lies on the north side. This may have been the Monastery of Photinus-Marinus, founded in the 5C by the brothers Marinus and Lukas, disciples of Euthymius. It was one of many Byzantine monasteries in the area; another exists just 2km northeast of Bethlehem at **Bir al-Qutt**. This is a larger complex with a church on the north side, dated to the 6C and with Georgian inscriptions indicating a dedication to St. Theodore.

The Monastery of Mar Saba

Directly east of Bethlehem, and reached by a steep road (c 14km) is the Greek Orthodox Monastery of Mar Saba. The expedition is a pleasant one if you admire views of the wilderness and a fortified medieval monastery, but note that women are not admitted to the monastery. Earlier visitors used to approach on horseback down the Kidron Valley from Jerusalem by a precipitous path; Robert Curzon, who did this in 1834, gives a lively account of being ambushed and captured in the ravine.

At c 8km, just before entering the village of Ubaidiyya, is the Greek **Monastery of St. Theodosius** (or Dair Ibn Ubaid, or Dair Dosi), open 08.00–13.00. A legend says that the Magi stayed in a cave here on their way home from Bethlehem. It housed 400 monks with its founder St. Theodosius died in 529; his tomb lay beneath the church. Modestus, who restored so many of the Jerusalem churches after the Persian invasion in 614, was abbot of St. Theodosius. The Commemoratorium c 808 says there were 70 monks here, but Saracen brigands burnt the monastery and slaughtered many of the monks, the rest fleeing. It was described in 1185 as fortified with towers, but was deserted by 1620. Conder visited the ruins in 1879 when they were used as storehouses by the local Ubaidiyya tribe who also had a maqam or shrine there. The Greeks renegotiated their rights and took possession in 1893. They rebuilt the monastery and uncovered a considerable amount of Byzantine masonry. The present church, partly on 6C foundations, was consecrated in 1955. In a cave on the southwest side are shown the tombs of St. Theodosius, John Moschus and other holy men and women.

Where the road forks in the village, continue to the right for Mar Saba, with views down to the Kidron Valley to the left. The steep descent provides a first sight of the two great towers of the monastery ahead. Only as you arrive can the monastery itself be seen, as it hangs on the near side of the ravine. It is open daily 08.00–16.00 to men only.

History of Monasticism in Palestine

St. Saba or Sabas was one of the most famous monks in Palestine, and is still commemorated by both the Greek and Latin churches. He was born in 439 in Cappadocia (central Turkey), and after an unhappy childhood joined a local community of monks. He came to Jerusalem at the age of 18, and being already attracted to the life of a solitary, he joined Euthymius (376–473), one of the great founders of Byzantine monasticism in Palestine (see p 389). Euthymius sent him as novice to Theoctistus in his monastery east of Jerusalem at Dair al-Mukallik, and eventually Saba settled in a cave in the sides of the Kidron Valley, in the type of wilderness gorge—picturesque, solitary and defensible—that the Byzantine monks of Palestine preferred. There was no water in summer, until a source was excavated near the bed of the wadi. Other monks joined Saba, and the community grew to 150. It needed a priest, and Saba was ordained. The first, or 'God-built' church was consecrated by Sallustius, Bishop of Jerusalem, on 12 December 491. A larger church was built and dedicated on 1 July 501.

Saba was made archimandrite (the superior) over all the hermit monks of Palestine in 493. He was a distinguished theologian, noted for his attacks on the Monophysites whose doctrine was condemned at the Council of Chalcedon in 451. He was twice sent on embassies to the Byzantine Emperor in Constantinople, first in 511 to persuade the Emperor (who supported the Eutychian heresy) to stop persecuting the Orthodox; and again in his 91st year to gain support in putting down the Samaritans, and to seek redress for the Orthodox sufferings during the Samaritan Revolt. He died in 532, and was buried at the monastery, where his relics were venerated. Saba is remembered for the story of the lion that tried to drag him off to eat him. He succeeded in taming it, but it remained a troublesome pet, and finally he told it to be at peace or leave. It left. It is also noted that he vowed never to eat apples because Eve tempted Adam with this fruit; that his date palm still grows at the monastery and its fruit has no stones; and that the monks still feed his birds daily (the Tristram's grackles of the locality). His life was written by Cyril of Scythopolis.

The monastery was plundered by the Persians in 614, and suffered from Bedouin attacks in 796, 809 and 842. Nonetheless in the 8C–9C the monastery was one of the most important in Palestine, notable for the number of its scholars, including St. John Damascene (8C), another distinguished theologian, noted particularly for his attacks on iconoclasm; others were St. John the Silent, St. Aphrodisius, St. Theophanes of Nicaea, St. Cosmas of Majuma and St. Theodore of Edessa. The Commemoratorium c 808 says that there were 150 monks at St. Saba. In 1102, in the early years of the Latin Kingdom, there were more than 300 monks at the monastery. The relics of St. Saba were removed from the monastery by the Venetians, but the monastery survived the upheavals of the 12C.

The monastery was pillaged by the Arabs in 1832 and 1834. When Curzon arrived in 1834 as a captive of the Arabs who had ambushed him, it was to find the Arabs lining the walls of the fortified monastery and clearly in control of the monks and the surrounding area. Having established that they were Franks, the Arab captors appear to have treated Curzon's party with great civility.

Curzon had been attracted by accounts of the fine library which the monastery was said to possess. By scrambling up a ladder in the church to a small door about 3m above the floor, he managed to inspect the library, but was disapppointed to discover that the 1000 manuscripts it contained were all works of divinity, mostly of the 12C, including some enormous folios. He also saw a further 100 manuscripts in the base of the great north tower which included a copy of the *Iliad*. Having purchased three manuscripts, he departed on a visit to the Dead Sea in course of which he used one of the folios he had purchased as a pillow. Curzon returned on two subsequent occasions, and eventually acquired what he deemed to be the most interesting manuscript in the monastery, a 9C–10C copy of the first eight books of the Old Testament.

Severe damage was caused by the earthquake of 1834, and in 1840 the monastery was enlarged and restored by the Russians. In the early 20C there were only about 50 monks at the monastery, who led an austere life, tending their gardens and living mostly on vegetables. The monastery was supported by donations, the small charges for accommodating pilgrims and travellers, and by a few estates, including some near Bethlehem. The library is now housed in the Greek Orthodox Patriarchate in Jerusalem.

There are even fewer monks living there today, but the blue-painted domes give the complex a lived-in look on a human scale, which softens the dramatic situation of the only monastery in Palestine to have had a virtually uninterrupted occupation by its Orthodox monks since it was built in the 5C. It ranks with St. Catherine's in Sinai (Egypt) as being one of the oldest inhabited monasteries in the world.

Saba's return

In 1965 the body of St. Saba was given back to the monastery by Pope Paul, and made the long journey from Venice by way of Jerusalem. A lively, joyous procession met the tiny embalmed body of the saint in the square inside the Jaffa Gate, and priests and monks, bands of musicians, Boy Scouts, and members of the Orthodox community escorted the saint to the Church of the Holy Sepulchre, where he lay in state for some time before venturing on the last stages of the journey Mar Saba. The blackened feet in tiny slippers provided an extraordinary contrast between human fragility and the spiritual triumph and tenacity of the monastery and its founder over the centuries.

The monastery is supported on massive terraces up the cliff-like edge of the ravine. The two great towers are the first visible sections. That on the south, St. Simeon, built in 1612, is detached from the monastery and was used to accommodate women pilgrims, but is rarely open. The great rectangular north tower forms the northwest bastion of the high stone walls. The whole monastic complex dates from the 5C onwards, but much of what is visible was restored c 1840. The entrance is by a low door in the west wall. Within, a stepped passage descends to the main court: in the centre stands the former Tomb of St. Saba. The main church to the east, with large blue dome and adjacent small bell tower, is dedicated to the Annunciation. Five tremendous buttresses support it on the south side. It has five aisles, apse and dome. The frescoes are mostly modern. Parts of an old carved and gilded iconostasis survive in a solid but not very interesting building, now the resting place of the saint.

On the northwest side of the court is the Church of St. Nicholas, built against a grotto in the rock which may be the cave where Saba founded the first church. The royal doors in the iconostasis are 15C. Behind a grille are the skulls of monks slain by the Persians in 614. At a higher level to the north is a chapel with the empty Tomb of St. John Damascene—his relics were also removed during the Crusades but are now lost.

The monastery contains many cells. The terraces, once cultivated as gardens, ascend in steep steps. All around the monastery are the cuttings of many other ancient hermit cells, many of which are or have been in the recent past occupied by Bedouin. On the east side of the wadi, protected by a metal grille, is the cave said to be that of St. Saba. Downstream the approaches to the gorge are further fortified by walls and two towers, the ruins of which can be seen from the monastery.

The cell of St. Sophia, the mother of Saba, who eventually followed him from Cappadocia to Palestine, is 300m to the north, low in the wadi. It has remnants of 12C frescoes.

You can return to Jerusalem via Bethlehem; alternatively turn right at Ubaidiyya, and descend to the crossing of the Kidron. A steep climb up the other side leads to the Palestinian village of Abu Dis and eventually to the Bethany Road, not far from Jerusalem.

Many other monasteries exist in the Judaean wilderness. Three which may be reached from the Jerusalem to Dead Sea Highway 1 are among the more accessible.

The 5C **Monastery of St. Euthymius** (A. Khan al-Ahmar; see plan on next page) is c 14km east of Jerusalem: take the turning to the south to Mishor Adummim (an industrial complex), and the monastery is at 1.5km on the left. It was dedicated on 7 May 428. The founder Euthymius died in 473, and is remembered as one of the major founders of monasticism in Palestine. The monastery was damaged in the earthquake of 749, but seems to be mentioned in the Commemoratorium in the 9C when it contained 30 monks. It was apparently destroyed by Salah al-Din or Baybars in the late 12C or 13C. There is an enclosure with a three-aisled basilica (**1**) in the southeast corner. This church is built over an undercroft with barrel vaults, which according to St. Cyril was the refectory established in the earlier church. The south aisle has a mosaic of c 5C–8C, with geometric and arabesque patterns. To the north near the centre of the enclosure is the tomb/cell of Euthymius (**2**), a chapel with an altar on the east. On the north side of the monastery was a defensive tower (**3**), and outside to the east a very large cistern (**4**), presumably that recorded as built in the 5C. The other rooms contained the domestic facilities of the monastery.

The **Inn of the Good Samaritan** is on the south side of Highway 1, at c 18km east of Jerusalem; the parable (Luke 10:29–37) has been localised here since the 4C as a likely place for travellers to be attacked by robbers. The remains are mainly those of an Ottoman caravanserai, the Khan Hathrurah, which served as a police checkpoint at various times during the 20C.

The **Monastery of St. George of Choziba** is built in the side of the gorge on the north side of the Wadi Kilt. Paths approach it from the Mizpe Jericho road off the Dead Sea Highway 1, or from the south side of Jericho. There is a good view from above the Mizpe Jericho road. A rare Greek Orthodox monastery which by tradition admits women, it is open 09.00–16.00 in summer (–15.00 in winter), Sat 09.00–12.00. It was a hermitage from the 420s, becoming a monastery dedicated to the Mother of God by John of Thebes (St. John of Choziba) c 480–520/30, and is named for St. George of Choziba who died c 620. In the 8C–10C it became associated with St. Joachim and St. Anne, the parents of the Virgin, and the association with Joachim continued in medieval times. The monastery was probably restored c 1179, but fell into ruin after Salah al-Din's conquest in 1187. It was rebuilt by the Greek Orthodox church between 1878 and 1901. The outer entrance is modern; an inner door across the courtyard was the entrance to the smaller medieval monastery. Above it is the Church of St. Mary built against the rock face, dated 1888 but probably based on walls of the

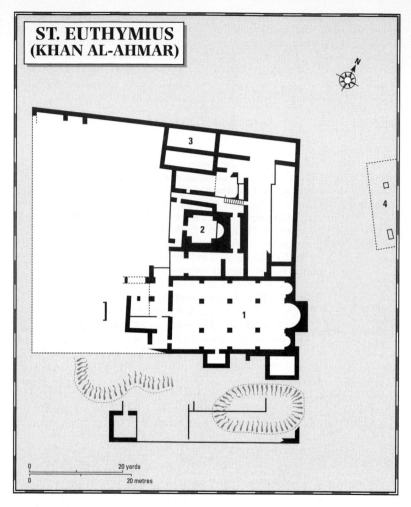

ST. EUTHYMIUS (KHAN AL-AHMAR)

0   20 yards
0   20 metres

5C/6C and 12C; the frescoes are modern, but ancient ones were recorded in the 19C; fragments of a rather crude 12C? geometric patterned mosaic survive. The iconostasis was installed in 1942, but the royal doors are attributed to Emperor Alexius II Comnenus (1180–83). To the northeast is the Chapel of St. John and St. George of Choziba, partly cut in the rock. The right-hand niche in the northeast wall has the skull of St. George of Choziba; his body is interred beneath. Part of a 6C diaper-pattern mosaic floor remains. Above the Church of St. Mary is the Chapel of St. Elias, formerly the Cave Church of St. Joachim.

The valley contains the Herodian and later aqueduct, many other Byzantine hermit cells and some fine scenery.

HERODION
• • • • • • • • • • •

A symmetrical hill towering on the horizon southeast of Bethlehem, marks the spectacular fortress built by Herod the Great; a spacious palace with bath house and pools was built and has been excavated below the north side.

The site, which lies15km from Jerusalem, 5km southeast of Bethlehem, near Highway 356, is maintained by the National Parks Authority (☎ 03 776 2251).

History

Built between 23 and 20 BC by Herod the Great, and named for its builder, Herodion was the capital of a toparchy. It was a remarkable complex of pala-tial summer villas as much as a fortress and administrative centre, and was intended as a burial place and memorial to the king. Josephus describes his funeral procession from Jericho in 4 BC:

Herod was borne upon a golden bier studded with precious stones of various kinds and with a cover of purple over it. The dead man too was wrapped in purple robes and wore a diadem on which a gold crown had been placed, and beside his right hand lay his sceptre. Round the bier were his sons and a host of his relatives, and after them came the army disposed according to the various nationalities and designa-tions ... they were followed by five hundred servants carrying spices. And they went eight stages toward Herodion for it was there that the burial took place by his own order. (Ant. XVII, 196–199)

After Herod's death the site was in the hands of the Romans until the First Jewish Revolt when it became a centre of Zealot resistance. As at Masada (see p 457), the Zealots built a synagogue and ritual baths in the fortress, but it was captured by the Romans following the fall of Jerusalem. The site was abandoned until the Second Revolt when it was occupied in AD 132, perhaps as the head-quarters of Bar Kochba, the leader of the revolt, and again fell to the Romans three years later. It became part of the great network of Byzantine settlement from the 5C to 7C AD, and evidence of four churches has been discovered.

The approach road leads up the west slope of the *fortress of Herodion; the ancient steps were on the northeast side. Josephus also describes Herodion:

At intervals it has round towers, and it has a steep ascent formed of two hundred steps of hewn stone. Within it are costly royal apartments made for security and for ornament at the same time. At the base of the hill there are pleasure grounds built in such a way as to be worth seeing, among other things because of the way in which water, which is lacking in that place, is brought in from a distance and at great expense. The surrounding plain was built up as a city second to none, with the hill serving as an acropolis for the other dwellings. (Antiq. XV, 323–325)

The lower part of the hill is natural, but the artificial upper structure is supported on great foundation walls and an earth fill; cisterns were built into the lower part of the hill and were fed probably by winter rainfall catchment. The **upper fortress** is circular in shape, 63m in diameter with a double wall; it has three semicircular towers and one great circular tower on the east which some suggest was intended as Herod's mausoleum, although the tomb itself has not been found. The entrance on the northeast leads through to a porticoed court which occupies two quadrants; in the northwest quadrant is a small bath house; the southwest quadrant contained a dining area, with an *opus sectile* floor. There were probably living quarters above these two quadrants. The Zealots constructed a synagogue in the dining room. In the Byzantine period, rooms and a bakery were constructed in the bath house. Cisterns and tunnels serving the besieged during the Second Revolt can also be seen in the lower part of the hill.

The **lower palace**, or pleasure gardens for Herod's friends, was equally remarkable. Adjacent to the north slope of the hill is a long rectangular structure which formed an annexe to the palace. It lay parallel to a processional path which may have been part of Herod's funeral ceremonies, and ends at a monument. North of this is a vast layout of pool and garden, with bath house and other nearby buildings.

Herod's work included the construction of a branch aqueduct from the Lower Aqueduct from Solomon's Pools through Artas to bring the large quantity of water required for the town and palace.

SOLOMON'S POOLS

The ancient reservoirs called Solomon's Pools (A. Burak Sulaiman), along with a ruined Ottoman castle, are on Route 60, 3.5km southeast of Bethlehem on the road to Hebron.

The three large rectangular reservoirs are artificial constructions; the two upper pools are probably Hasmonean or Roman in origin; the bottom pool is later, from AD 1483 in the time of Sultan Qa'it Bay. They were refurbished by Sulaiman the Magnificent in the mid-16C, and again in the Mandate period. The pools are part of a major system of aqueducts and tunnels which provided the water supply for Jerusalem from at least the 2C BC. The water came from local springs, and additional water was brought from springs in Wadi Arrub and Wadi Biyar up to 8km to the southeast. The area is slightly higher than Jerusalem, and thus the water could be utilised by gravity.

The aqueduct system was extended at various periods (notably by Pontius Pilate in the 1C AD). The older Lower Aqueduct system passed by Bethlehem to the Temple Area in Jerusalem, and a feeder ran also to Herodion. The Upper Aqueduct more or less follows the line of the main road and reached probably to the Mamilla Pool on the west side of Jerusalem, and thence into the city. The system continued to be used right up to 1948, when the Lower Aqueduct was cut during the war; but by then Jerusalem and Bethlehem had been provided with alternative water supplies.

The **Ottoman fort** (A. Qal'at al-Burak) guarded both the pools and the Muslim pilgrimage route to Mecca. Built by Sultan 'Uthman II in AD 1617 (inscription), it is a rectangular fort, c. 67m x 48 m. with protruding square corner towers (probably for use with cannon), and with a small recessed gateway on the west. It was abandoned in 1917. Some refurbishment took place in the 1930s when for a short time it was a tourist attraction associated with the pools.

MAMRE
• • • • • • • •

The Roman and Byzantine location of Mamre (A. Haram Ramat al-Khalil), the place where Abraham was visited by angels, is 3km north of Hebron to the east of the Hebron Road (Route 60).

'So Abram moved his tent and settled by the terebinths of Mamre at Hebron; and there he built an altar to the Lord.' (Gen.13:18) Although the word 'terebinth' usually refers to the pistachio tree, it is generally an oak that is associated with Mamre, and over the centuries pilgrims visited the oak at this spot. It is the third site with a monumental enclosure of the type built by Herod the Great—the others were for the Temple in Jerusalem and the Cave of Machpelah at Hebron. It also dates to the later 1C BC, but is a much less impressive version, perhaps never finished. In Roman times one of the three great fairs of Palestine was held here at Mamre (others were held at Akko and Gaza), and the place had many pagan associations. Jewish captives were brought here in AD 135 to be sold by the Romans into slavery following the suppression of the Second Revolt. Hadrian perhaps rebuilt the enclosure with a pagan shrine against the east wall. Its pagan activities were so offensive that Constantine was persuaded to cleanse the site and build a church. The Bordeaux Pilgrim and others record in the 4C that Constantine built a basilica at the Terebinth. The church seems to have suffered in the Persian attack in 614, but was restored. Arculf (c 680) says the oak tree was then in dire straits. Thereafter there is no evidence that the shrine was reoccupied, but the site, with a tree surrounded by a marble paving, 'the site of Abraham's tent', was visited by pilgrims in the Crusader period and later.

At Mamre are the remains of the enclosure and the three-aisled Constantinian basilica with a well in the southwest corner of the enclosure by which the terebinth may have stood. It has been excavated on various occasions in the 20C.

HEBRON
• • • • • • • •

Hebron (A. al-Khalil, Crusader: St. Abraham, Ebron, Cariatarba) is the principal market town of the south Palestinian hill country. Here is the great walled enclosure around the Cave of Machpelah, the tomb of the Patriarch Abraham, almost certainly built by Herod the Great (37–4 BC). Part of the Israeli-occupied West Bank since 1967, and now partly under Palestinian administration, it has been the scene of ongoing struggle between Palestinians and Jewish settlers. The town is divided between Palestinian and Jewish areas and is subject to tight Israeli security. You should seek local advice if you want to visit.

Hebron is 30km south of Jerusalem on Route 60, c 900m above sea level.

History

The modern town of Hebron was probably founded in the Roman period and its history is linked with that of the shrine. An earlier site was located on the hill to the south, at Tell al-Rumaida (Tel Hebron), with virtually continuous occupation from the Early Bronze Age to the Iron Age. The finds include a fragment of a cuneiform tablet in which a probable king of Hebron in the 17C BC is mentioned, and there is evidence for a strongly built town of the same date. Rumaida has been proposed as the location of the town of Kiriath-Arba ('four

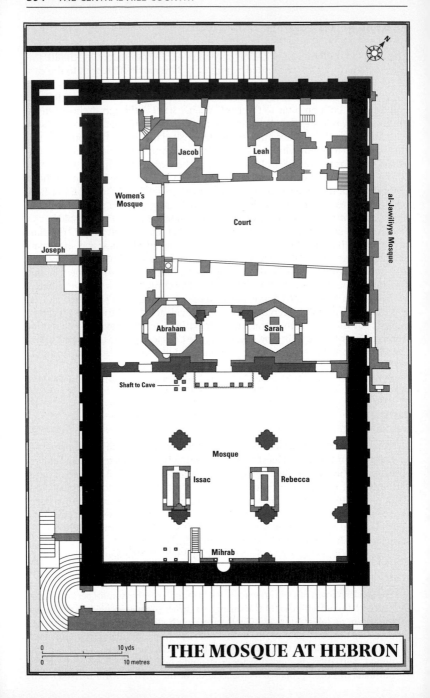

Women's Mosque

Joseph

Jacob

Leah

Court

al-Jawiliyya Mosque

Abraham

Sarah

Shaft to Cave

Mosque

Issac

Rebecca

Mihrab

0   10 yds

0   10 metres

THE MOSQUE AT HEBRON

quarters') (Gen. 23:2), and of the Anakites (?Amorites) (Jos. 14; Jud. 1:10) defeated by Caleb of Judah. It became for seven years David's capital (I Kings 2:11), where he was anointed king (II Sam 2:4), before he moved the capital to Jerusalem. Hebron features in the story of Absalom's revolt (II Sam. 15:7), and as one of Rehoboam's cities of defence (II Chr 11:6-8). It is identified as one of the store cities named on stamp seals of the 8C BC. Judas Maccabeus occupied it during his wars against the Idumeans. It was in the hands of the insurgents during the First Jewish Revolt, but retaken by Vespasian who burnt it.

Eusebius in the 4C describes what is probably the modern site as a large village, and from this time Hebron is likely to have had a continuous history. Its history in the Crusader period is largely that of the mosque (see below); the settlement was destroyed by the Muslims before 1101/03. In the late 19C Hebron was still a small town, dominated by the great mosque with its two tall minarets, set low on a terraced hillside, with well-grown olive trees in the rich valley soils.

By 1918 the old town was primarily Muslim, built around the south and west sides of the mosque, with a small Jewish community further west. In 1922 the population of 16,500 included 430 Jews. Following riots and massacre in 1929 the Jewish community left. In the 1960s about one-third of the Arab old town was razed to clear access to the mosque. Jewish settlement began following the capture of the town by Israel in 1967, partly in the old western quarter, and partly in a new settlement to the east called Qiryat Arba, both under heavy military protection. In 1994 a settler massacred 29 Muslims at prayer in the mosque. By 1997 the population of Hebron had grown to 120,000, including some 5000 Jews in Qiryat Arba.

The Tombs of the Patriarchs

'Abraham buried his wife Sarah in the cave on the plot of land at Machpelah to the east of Mamre, which is Hebron, in Canaan' (Gen 23:19).'His sons, Isaac and Ishmael, buried him in the cave at Machpelah ... with his wife Sarah' (Gen. 25:9, 11). The Patriarch Abraham (the friend/companion of God) is deeply venerated by Jews, Christians and Muslims. The Tombs of the Patriarchs and the Mosque of Abraham (A. Haram al-Khalil or Haram al-Ibrahimi) are what draws visitors to Hebron.

History

The earliest date of Jewish veneration of the site of the tomb is unknown. Although there are no written references to its construction, the great wall surrounding the tombs of the patriarchs, with its fine drafted masonry and upper plinths and pilasters, was certainly built by Herod the Great (31–4 BC) as a rectangular enclosure around the venerated Cave of Machpelah (the Double Cave), the burial place of the Patriarchs Abraham, Isaac and Jacob and their wives (Sarah, Rebecca and Leah). The burial place was at times also identified with the tomb of Adam (see also Church of the Holy Sepulchre in Jerusalem, and of Joseph (see also Nablus). The Herodian complex was very precisely designed, probably with six cenotaphs—rectangular structures with pitched roofs—laid out symmetrically in pairs in an open court, arranged almost as today. Beneath the paving (accessed by a blocked shaft and a flight of 16 steps in medieval times) is an ancient corridor, leading to a subterranean corbelled chamber of excellent masonry. A cavity near the entrance to the chamber descends further to two small rock-cut caves, located slightly east of the cenotaph of Abraham. The entrance to the cave of the burial must have been blocked at an early date. The Herodian entrance to the enclosure and cave may have been at the lower level near the centre of the southwest side near the later Tomb of Joseph.

The Herodian shrine was visited by Christian pilgrims at least from the 4C, when it was described as an open (unroofed) enclosure containing the six tombs; by the 6C it had porticoes around the interior, a basilica, and a screen separating Christian and Jewish pilgrims. There is no trace surviving of a Byzantine church, and it is not known when a mosque was first built, but one is recorded by the 10C, when an entrance was cut at the centre of the northeast wall by the Fatimid caliph (AD 918). The mosque hall for the Friday prayers extended across the width of the enclosure at the southeast end, and the mihrab of the mosque was in the southeast wall. By 985, domes had been built to cover the tombs of Abraham and Sarah, while those of Isaac and of Jacob were respectively in the mosque and in a building at the northwest end. The shrines were decorated with precious carpets on the paving, fine textiles on the walls, and a multitude of lamps and lanterns. A charitable food kitchen lay along the northwest wall, and there were rooms for Muslim pilgrims on the roof above the prayer hall. The tomb of Joseph, under a fine dome, was added against the outer southwest face of the enclosure, and it may be then or earlier that the access to the cave was blocked.

The complex with its great walls, was defensible, and had to be taken by assault by Godfrey of Bouillon in 1100. In Crusader times the shrine was called the Castle of St. Abraham, and lay a short distance east of the town. It was garrisoned and was the centre of the lordship of Hebron, with Galdemar Carpenal as its first lord. A burgess court was established here. Probably following the establishment of a chapter of regular canons (Augustinian), the secular and military establishment may have been housed in a structure abutting the southwest face, which bore an inscription of Sultan Qala'un of 1280. Later it was used as a caravanserai, a religious school (1347–61), and in the 19C as a barracks. Most of this annexe was demolished in the 1960s. In 1119 the location of the tomb cave under the cenotaphs was rediscovered accidentally, and entered by cutting through the Herodian paving of the enclosure to a passage beneath; the bones of the patriarchs were said to have been found in the cave. This discovery was described in a later document of 1136. It was said that the bones found in the cave were brought to the upper court and placed in reliquary boxes. Most were subsequently replaced beneath the court, and labelled with the names of the patriarchs with whom they had been identified. Some bones appear to have been sold to important pilgrims, and taken to the West as relics. It may have been as a result of the discovery of the bones that a new Crusader church was built around this time at the south end of the enclosure on the site of the former mosque, when the cenotaphs of Isaac and Rebecca were displaced slightly to the west to accommodate the vaulting on the southeast side. The church had a rather asymmetrical shape, and unorthodox orientation (to northeast) to fit into the preexisting Herodian wall. The church became the seat of a bishop. During the 12C, access to the caves below appears to have been permitted, and several accounts exist of those who visited the subterranean chambers.

On the fall of the Crusader kingdom in 1187, Salah al-Din converted the church into a mosque which it has remained ever since. Initially, Jewish and Christian pilgrims were still allowed access to the tombs, but Baybars ordered their exclusion in 1266, and recorded building work in the mosque in 1267. Some pilgrims still obtained access in the late 13C. In 1318–20, in the time of al-Nasir Muhmmad, Sanjar al-Jawili, the Superintendent of the Two Harams (see Jerusalem, p 102) constructed a second mosque on the north-east exterior side of the enclosure, called the al-Jawiliyya. In the main mosque, the entrance and the area of the mihrab were decorated with mosaic, and the interior walls were covered with marble panelling in 1331–32. Also at this time the exclusion of Christians was again enforced, but accounts of Muslims descending to the tombs are still extant. Some major changes were implemented (1382–99) to doors, including the cutting of a door in the southwest wall of the enclosure which led to the Tomb of Joseph; porticoes were built along the southwest side of the central courtyard, the 10C dome over the Tomb of Abraham was rebuilt and the four western ceno-taphs all became polygonal domed structures.

By the 1490s access to the subterranean burial caves was closed and has remained closed. For non-Muslims access to the Haram remained forbidden, as in Jerusalem, until the mid-19C and after then only by rare permission. In the 1860s Pierotti visited the shrine, followed in 1882 by Prince Albert Victor and Prince George of Wales, accompanied by Sir Charles Wilson and Captain Claude Conder. Some early plans were published, but the first detailed study took place at the beginning of the Mandate period, although access to the caves was still prohibited. Even in the 1960s non-Muslim visitors to the mosque were not particularly welcome. After the 1967 war Israeli archaeol-ogists inspected the caves and recorded the presence of Iron Age sherds and others of the 12C AD.

The *mosque is open 07.30–11.30, 13.00–14.30, 15.30–17.00; closed Fri and Sat morning. Since the massacre in the mosque in 1994, the Muslim and Jewish areas of the site have been segregated. Access to the Muslim area (south end, with mosque, tombs of Isaac and Rebecca, and remains of the Crusader church) is by a long flight of steps rising along the outer northwest side which turns east and leads past the al-Jawili mosque (1318–20) to the entrance to the courtyard. Access to the Jewish area (north end, with tombs of Jacob and Leah), is by new external steps constructed to the northwest end of the Tomb of Joseph at the northwest corner of the enclosure.

The great rectangular enclosure with two square minarets dominating the town, was built by Herod the Great in the same style as that of the Temple in Jerusalem and of the enclosure at Mamre. Its corners are oriented to the cardinal points of the compass. The splendid Herodian masonry has finely dressed stones with drafted edges, and above the level of the internal court broad pilasters flank recesses with chamfered bases; these are almost completely preserved whereas an identical but much larger system in Jerusalem was almost totally destroyed. The upper rounded crenellations are of more recent date. The minaret on the east prob-ably replaces a 12C bell tower. The entrance in the centre of the northeast wall is variously dated to the Abbasid (Caliph al-Mahdi) and Fatimid (918) periods.

Almost in the centre of the court are the cenotaphs of Abraham (west) and Sarah (east), entered through a groin-vaulted porch (12C–14C). The cenotaphs are 10C–11C, modified in the 14C.

Inside the mosque, in the centre of the southeast wall is the mihrab. The vaulting and supporting piers and capitals derive from the nave of the 12C Crusader church, though the roof is later; the iron gallery was added in the 19C. The upper windows survive from the 12C clerestory. Except for the entrance wall, the side walls belong to the Herodian enclosure. The oculus above the mihrab is probably from the time of al-Nasir Muhammad (14C), as is the marble panelling which hides the bases of the 12C piers. The two cenotaphs inside the mosque were at least rebuilt in the 12C; the one to the west is that of Isaac, that to the east, of Rebecca. Against the qibla wall, to the right of the mihrab, is the fine carved wooden minbar (pulpit) made in 1043 in the reign of the Fatimid caliph al-Mustansir, which Salah al-Din brought from the mosque of al-Husayn at Ascalan when that city was dismantled in 1191; he probably also installed the *dikka* (raised platform) opposite. To the right of the minbar is a fine 12C baldachino (canopy), which was raised over the 12C entrance to the underground passage to the cave tomb, and must have been re-erected later, after the entrance was sealed. Its 14C 'partner', a copy, located to the right of the mosque entrance, is built over a shaft (600mm in diameter), which became the only opening to the ancient chamber overlying the double cave below.

At the northwest side of the courtyard, the tombs of Jacob (west) and Sarah (east) are entered on either side of a chamber, the former Mosque of Jacob. Against the southwest wall is the former Women's Mosque, from which access could be had by two doorways to the upper and lower tomb and cenotaph of Joseph, with the Mosque of Joseph to the north on the upper level. These two-storey rooms now provide access for Jewish pilgrimage.

The town of Hebron, a provincial centre, has markets for local produce (H.B. Tristram, wandering in the bazaars in 1872, bought locally made quince jam) and has for centuries been famous for its production of glass. This is said to be based on production methods and styles of Roman and Byzantine glass workers, but the local industry may derive from Spanish or Italian Jewish immigrants in the 15C. Hebron was probably the major source of glass bracelets, formerly worn by Bedouin women. There are numerous workshops where the manufacturing process can be watched and the products bought, and glass, jewellery and textiles are sold in the market near the mosque. As with most Palestinian towns, the embroidered dresses of the women were decorated with distinctive local designs, in Hebron usually red on a black background. A small municipal museum to the north side of the town contains some illustration of Hebron's past. The dilapidated Sultan's Pool, former reservoir for the market town, lies a short distance from the mosque, slightly south of west, off Sharia Daud.

BET GUVRIN AND TEL MARESHA

Tel Maresha or **ancient Marisa** (A. Tell Sandahannah) was an important city of the Idumeans, and there are some well-preserved and rare remains of the Hellenistic period. Betogabris (Eleutheropolis), 2km north, was its successor in the Roman period, and later became the Crusader Beit Jibelin. Interesting remains ranging in date from the 3C BC to the 20C AD include restored painted tombs and an amphitheatre.

The site is off Highway 35, just west of the junction with Highway 38, opposite Kibbutz Bet Guvrin, c 40km southwest of Jerusalem. The park of Bet Guvrin (A. Bait Jibrin) is run by the National Parks Authority, ☎ 07 681 1020.

History

According to II Chr 11:6–8, Maresha was fortified by Rehoboam after the destructive campaign of the Egyptian pharaoh Sheshonq c 925 BC, but the Iron Age remains so far uncovered date mainly to the 8C–7C BC. In early Hellenistic times, Marisa was the main town of western Idumea, located on the road from Ashkelon on the south coast to Hebron and Jerusalem. In the 3C–2C BC a third town was laid out in a well-organised grid system by a 'Sidonian' community who settled here. This town had a fortified upper town. It appears to have had a temple/administrative block, a commercial block, and blocks of houses. Around it was a lower town, partially walled, covering an area of 32 hectares. Here many of the houses were on three levels: industrial caves cut in the chalk beneath shops; kitchens and storage built at ground level; and the main living quarters on the upper floor(s). Some of the grander houses had evidence of painted plaster decoration. The impressive burial caves of the Sidonians are located below the southeast side of Tel Maresha. They date to the period 196–119 BC. Greek inscriptions include the name of the Edomite god Qos, and indicate the assimiliation of Idumean as well as Hellenic culture by this Sidonian colony. The tombs themselves have parallels in Alexandria and Phoenicia, illustrating the complex cultural links of the period. These are particularly interesting because Antipas, the grandfather of Herod the Great, may have lived in Marisa. Many other caves were cut, and used as living quarters, as cisterns or for wine or olive oil pressing, or as dovecotes. The contents of one excavated dovecote dated from the 3C to the mid-1C BC. The town was captured in the later 2C BC by John Hyrcanus, who forced the inhabitants to convert to Judaism. The city remained in Hasmonean hands until the arrival of Pompey in 63 BC. The city was rebuilt or perhaps just refurbished by Gabinius, and became part of Herod's kingdom in 40 BC. But it was almost immediately destroyed by the Parthians.

After Marisa was destroyed, the Roman town was established at nearby Bet Guvrin. The Roman army was stationed here after the crushing of the Second Jewish Revolt, and there is evidence of not just a large military centre, but a period of intensive urbanisation from the second half of the 2C AD. The military facilities included an amphitheatre and a bath house. Septimius Severus made the city a colony (Eleutheropolis) in AD 200 and granted it very large territories, stretching right across to the Dead Sea. Bet Guvrin was the seat of a bishop in the 4C; and Christian hermits dwelt in the caves around the town.

Beit Jibelin was also a large and important Crusader settlement. In 1134 King Fulk built a fortress which was granted to the Hospitallers in 1136, and a civilian settlement developed around it. The settlement was sacked by the Muslims in 1158, but the castle kept its garrison until 1187 when it was abandoned. The Hospitallers received it back in 1240, but lost it again in 1244; its ruins and that of the Crusader church lie in the northwest corner of the Roman city. The Crusader Church of St. Anne (Sandahannah) is 2km south of Bet Guvrin on the ruins of a Byzantine church.

The houses of the Arab village of Bait Jibelin were semi-fortified and its ruins are also visible; the village was abandoned in 1948.

Because the area of the two settlements is large, several car parks are set along a one-way road system through the park; footpaths connect to the various places of interest. The Crusader fortress of Bait Jibrin and its church are located north of the main road, with the amphitheatre to the west. Tel Maresha is located 2km to the south.

On the north side of the road you can see the ruins of the **Crusader castle** and the north part of the attached Crusader church. It was a concentric castle: the outer ward had a talus and tower on the north; there is a fortified inner ward, c 50m square, with a gate on the south and a projecting rectangular tower on each corner, that of the southeast demolished. The precarious ruins of the **castle church** were partly excavated in 1982. The only remains are the north aisle and adjoining sacristy of a three-aisled church of five bays constructed against the southern outer face of the inner ward of the castle, east of the gate.

A barrel-vaulted medieval building southeast of the castle was used in recent times as the village mosque; it lies just south of the present main road. Beneath the fort are the impressive remains of a Roman bath house. The small but well-preserved **amphitheatre** (late 2C AD), oval, with barrel vaults which supported the missing tiers of seats (maximum capacity 3500), went out of use in the late 4C. It served the Roman army garrison for gladiatorial entertainment

The park, on the south side of the road, is set in undulating countryside. The presence of a soft, chalky rock stratum beneath a harder limestone at the surface encouraged the ancient inhabitants to cut basements for their houses, and the site contains some remarkable caves. Near the second parking lot are an impressive cistern and a columbarium (for pigeons?), and beyond are other caves used for various purposes, including one below the west side of the tell where an olive press has been reconstructed. Nearby, a house of the Hellenistic period has also been reconstructed, and has tremendous cisterns beneath it. The tell stands at the highest point of the park. On its top an almost complete town of the Hellenistic period was excavated early in the 20C, but there is little to see except a tower at the northwest corner.

Just beyond the road junction to the south are the impressive **burial caves** of the Sidonian community who settled in the city in the 3C–2C BC. The long narrow chamber with pitched roof loculi and benches, leading to the urn-flanked doorway is an impressive sight. The important and very rare frescoes in the two principal family tombs, which were in use over a long period, were defaced when first discovered earlier this century, but copies are now on display. They depict a diverse range of people and animals—naive representations of a menagerie by an artist who was not very familiar with all his subjects.

Just to the north is a tremendous range of bell caves where chalk was quarried presumably to make lime between the 7C and 10C AD.

The remains of the Crusader **Church of St. Anne** lie approximately 500m to the north on the hill above the east side of the road. The standing remains are mostly those of the apse of the Byzantine church which was incorporated into the smaller Crusader structure. The Byzantine church was built of fine ashlar courses; holes visible in the masonry were drilled to attach marble veneer. The Crusader church incorporated the round-arched apse of the Byzantine church (which still stands c 13m high) but occupied only part of the earlier central nave. In the Crusader church the three windows in the Byzantine apse were blocked or altered. The Crusader masonry is smaller, with diagonal tooling and has mostly collapsed. Most of the stones of the Crusader church were later used for lime-burning in a nearby lime-kiln, and the ruins have suffered more recent bullet and shrapnel damage.

LACHISH

Lachish (A. Tell al-Duwair), today a large tell covering 12.5 hectares, was the second city of the Kingdom of Judah in the 8C, and the scene of the siege by Sennacherib in 701 BC when the surviving inhabitants were sent into exile. The siege is illustrated in the great Assyrian reliefs from Nineveh which are now in the British Museum.

The site is off Highway 35; approximately halfway between Bet Guvrin and Qiryat Gat, a secondary road leads 2km south to Lachish, The site is managed by the National Parks Authority.

History

Some objects of the later Neolithic period have been found around the site, but the first settlement during the fourth millennium BC was located on the ridge overlooking the Wadi Ghafr (Nahal Lakhish) on the northwest side of the tell. By early in the third millennium a fortified town probably occupied the whole area of the tell, but it was abandoned perhaps in the 24C BC, when again the inhabitants retreated to the northwest ridge to live in caves and some poor buildings. As at Ascalon and many other sites, the city expanded greatly in the Middle Bronze Age, and c 1800 BC or a little later, the tell we see today was shaped. A tremendous artificial glacis, an earthern bank with plastered surface, with a tremendous rock-cut ditch at its foot, provides the structure of the great, almost rectilinear mound which still survives. Within the town there was a central palace and a cult place. This town was destroyed c 1500 BC.

The 14C town was smaller than its predecessor, but remained politically important until its destruction around 1200 BC. The names of three Canaanite kings of Lachish are known, Zimreddah, Shiphti-Ba'al and Yabni-ilu. Probably throughout the Late Bronze Age Lachish was dominated by Egypt. A temple was built down in the great Middle Bronze Age ditch on the west side of the tell. Called the Fosse Temple, it went through three successive rebuilds. Many trappings of the cult were found, but no evidence to say which deity was worshipped there, nor why a rather wealthy and busy temple was relegated to a site in the old ditch. It implies that the cult practised in the temple was offensive to the rulers of the city.

The Canaanite city was rebuilt for the last time early in the 12C BC, and with a rather different plan. At the centre of the mound was a tripartite temple. It had an antechamber preceding a main hall with two central column supports. A flight of steps led up to the sanctuary beyond the hall, flanked by a plastered tank on the right, and on the left, by three columns lining the wall and possibly fronting wall niches. The columns had eight sides, an Egyptian style, and looked a little like the fluted columns of later Greek architecture. The temple walls were decorated with painted plaster. In the ruins was found a thin gold plaque which depicted a naked goddess holding four lotus flowers, standing on the back of a horse. Although details of the iconography are known elsewhere in Canaan and Egypt, the identity of the goddess is not known. This final flourish of Canaanite culture was totally destroyed c 1130 BC, but who the destroyers were is not known either: perhaps the Philistines, perhaps the Israelites (Joshua 10:31–32), but no-one reoccupied the ruins for over a century.

A small settlement was built and destroyed again in the later 10C BC (perhaps in the campaign of the Egyptian pharaoh Sheshonq c 925), but it was only in the time of Rehoboam or one of his successors on the throne of Judah that Lachish rose again. Great concentric inner and outer fortifications were built with a massive gate, a palace and a well. Called by the excavator City IV, it was probably damaged in an earthquake c 760 BC and refurbished as City III when the palace was enlarged. This was the city destroyed by the Assyrian Sennacherib in 701 BC.

Sennacherib was a son of the great Sargon II who had destroyed Samaria and the northern kingdom of Israel less than twenty years earlier. Revolts broke out in the Assyrian Empire when Sargon died, and among the rebels were the kings of Sidon and Ascalon, and Hezekiah, King of Judah (II Kings 18:13–19:36). Lachish met a dreadful fate during the Assyrian campaign to crush the revolt. According to the Assyrian reliefs, a massive attack was launched, with slingers, archers, spearmen, siege engines, ramps and scaling ladders and after a desperate defence, in which fire and arrows were rained down on the Assyrians, the inhabitants of Lachish submitted. Some of the defenders were impaled as a deterrent to other rebels, and the rest led away into exile. Men, women and children are shown carrying what they could in sacks on their backs. Sennacherib's army met what the Israelites understood as divine retribution shortly after on their way to conquer Egypt, an event Byron commemorated in the well-known lines: 'The Assyrian came down like the wolf on the fold ... and the might of the Gentile, unsmote by the sword, Hath melted like snow in the glance of the Lord!'

Not surprisingly the city was abandoned for a while. City II was then built and refortified on a smaller scale and the palace remained in ruins. It was again destroyed by the army of Nebuchadnezzar in 586/87 (Jer. 34:7). The raising of the alarm at the approach of the Babylonian army was recorded in some last letters, written in Hebrew on pottery fragments, discovered in the gate complex, and now called 'The Lachish Letters'. Again the site was abandoned. Some exiles returned to Lachish in the Persian period (Neh. 11:30), when it was a Persian administrative centre. At this time it had new fortifications, a palatial residence for the governor, and a temple (the 'Solar Shrine'). The site was finally abandoned in the 2C BC when Lachish was superseded by the establishment of Marisa (Bet Guvrin) to the east.

Lachish lies on an old route from Gaza and Ascalon to Hebron, in a bend of the Wadi Ghafr which runs around most of three sides, leaving the easiest access from the southwest. The first view is dominated by the defences. The steep slopes

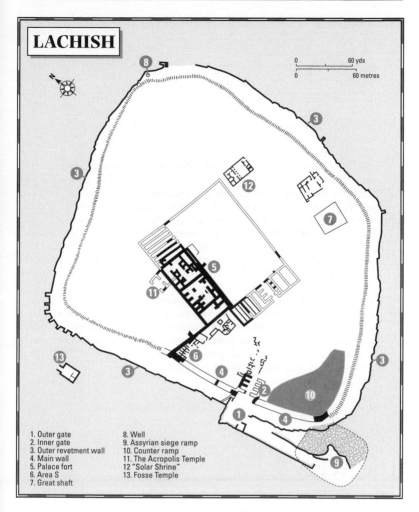

LACHISH

0   60 yds
0   60 metres

1. Outer gate
2. Inner gate
3. Outer revetment wall
4. Main wall
5. Palace fort
6. Area S
7. Great shaft
8. Well
9. Assyrian siege ramp
10. Counter ramp
11. The Acropolis Temple
12. "Solar Shrine"
13. Fosse Temple

were shaped in the first half of the second millennium BC. On these slopes massive fortifications were built in the late 10C or 9C. At mid-slope is a great stone revetment wall (**3**), and above the upper slope a wall 6m wide, stone at the base and originally mudbrick above, which crowned the mound (**4**). The paved approach road leads to a massive gate system (renovated) on the west side, which provides access through the lower and upper walls (**1**) and (**2**).

Although **the defences** were rebuilt many times, the remains visible are particularly notable for the Sennacherib siege in 701 BC (see above). On the right, before reaching the gate, are the remains of the great stone siege ramp built by the Assyrians (**9**), which was countered by a great earthern ramp (**10**) built within the upper wall by the defenders. The paved road led up through the outer gate set on a great bastion, turned at right angles through a court to the inner six-chambered gate which provided access to the city past at least one, perhaps four acacia-wood doors hung on bronze hinges. Within the city the defenders' earthern ramp can be seen to the right. Ahead on the left can be seen the complex where the **palaces** from the Late Bronze Age to the Persian period were built in the centre of the town. The Iron Age palaces of the 9C–8C stood on a series of great stone platforms, built and then extended for City IV (**5**) and (**6**). The platforms still stand to a considerable height, though all the superstructure was destroyed long ago. Adjacent were store houses or stables. On the east side of the podium are the remains of the Late Bronze Age acropolis temple (**11**) built for City VI and destroyed c 1130.

You can also visit some structures on the east side of the tell. At the northeast corner of the central complex is the '**Solar Shrine**' (**12**) of the Persian period but continuing in use into the Hellenistic period. It consists of a court, a hall and a sanctuary at the western end, and mainly because of its orientation has been proposed as the centre for a solar cult. Near the southeast corner of the mound is the '**Great Shaft**' (**7**), a rectangular shaft, nearly 23m deep. It is not known whether this was intended to be a water system like those found at Megiddo, Hazor or Beersheva. If so, it was never completed. It may have been decided that the wells on the site were adequate, for a well (**8**), stone lined at the top and 44m deep, can be seen at the northeast corner of the tell. Both the shaft and well appear to be contemporary with City IV.

The Late Bronze Age **Fosse Temple** (**13**) lies almost at the north end below the west side of the mound. Initially built as a small rectangular hall, it was later almost square, with a raised altar platform at the south end and benches around the other walls, and with auxiliary rooms to north and south. Great quantities of pottery were found inside, including pottery imported from Greece and Cyprus, as well hundreds of little bowls or saucers which probably once contained offerings made in the temple.

The Negev

The area south of Beersheva between the Rift Valley and Sinai, reaching to the Gulf of Aqaba and Elat, is called the Negev (A. Negeb). It is an arid highland area of low winter rainfall and barren but beautiful landscapes.

The occupants of the Negev subsisted mainly on pastoralism, dry farming and trade. The early trade routes focused on the copper mines in Sinai and the Wadi Arabah. Only in the Roman, Byzantine and Early Islamic periods were intensive systems of agriculture and trading patterns linked to camel caravans. The camel caravans were part of the rich trade network established by the Nabataeans.

The Nabataeans were Arabian tribes migrating into the area probably from the 5C BC, developing the trade routes from Arabia to the Mediterranean markets by the 4C BC, and breeding camels and horses. The main route until the mid-1C AD was the Ayla/Elat–Petra–Oboda–Subeita–Elusa–Gaza road, then for a period a more northern route running Petra–Ma'ale Aqrabim/ Scorpion's Pass–Mampsis–Gaza was preferred, and the cities on the old route suffered from the loss of trade. The towns responded to changing circumstances following the Roman annexation, principally by developing local agricultural systems, producing grapes, wine, wheat and barley. A huge increase in population took place in the Byzantine period. As productivity increased, so did the population: as the population increased, so did the need for productivity. A fishing industry developed at Ayla on the Gulf of Aqaba, and dried and salted fish were traded, as far as Ascalon and Jerusalem, from at least the Iron Age to the Crusader period and later.

Three of the best known towns are located at Avdat, Mamshit and Shivta, but others have been excavated. They are of particular importance because in this arid climate, with little or no subsequent rebuilding, the remains of the towns, and even more importantly, their landscape settings, are extraordinarily well preserved and interesting to visit. The inhabitants existed by harvesting the run-off from sparse winter rain into dams and cisterns, and the stored water was used for man, beast and agriculture. The large cisterns are a notable feature in the towns and the countryside. Once the towns were abandoned, these became the routes for Arab pastoralist tribes, who infiltrated the region from the east and migrated between the highlands and lowlands on a seasonal basis.

Today the area south of Beersheva, the region's principal town, is a place of ridges and wadis, undulating and barren, with settlements of Bedouin, dry-farming catch crops of cereals on wadi banks, a place of scrubby tamarisk and eucalyptus clumps. The mobile Bedouin population before 1948 was difficult to count, but it is estimated that there were 57,000, many of whom moved east across the Wadi Arabah in 1948. Further south magnificent desert landscapes can be enjoyed particularly around Maktesh Ramon.

A national nature reserve at the Ramon Park complex at Maktesh Ramon (near Mizpe Ramon, c 20km south of Avdat on Highway 40) provides information on the physical environment, the local flora and fauna (including reintroduced species such as the onager), and the archaeology of the central Negev area, in a visitor centre and campsite (☎ 07 658 8691/8). There is also the *Pundak Ramon Hotel*, 1 Ein Akiv, Mitzpe Ramon, ☎ 08 658 8822; 🖨 08 658 8151.

Most visitors to the Negev come on day trips or longer hiking/camping trips, and arrangements for accommodation are best made locally to suit requirements. In addition to the listed restaurants (see Beersheva and Arad), most major antiquity sites in the area have food available.

BEERSHEVA

Beersheva (biblical Beersheba; A. Bir al-Saba) has been a small market town and gateway to the Negev and to tribal, pastoralist societies for some two millennia. Its climate is arid, cold at nights; in January the temperature ranges from 6° to 16°C, in August from 19° to 33°C; the mean annual rainfall is a mere 204mm.

The town is 84km south of Jerusalem, at a major junction of five routes.

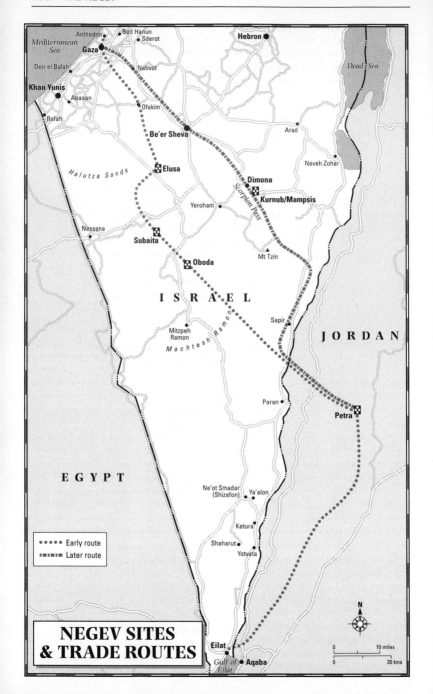

Anthedon
Beit Hanun
Sderot
Mediterranean Sea
Hebron
Gaza
Deir el Balah
Netivot
Dead Sea
Khan Yunis
Abasan
Rafah
Ofakim
Be'er Sheva
Arad
Halutza Sands
Elusa
Neveh Zohar
Dimona
Yeroham
Kurnub/Mampsis
Scorpion Pass
Nessana
Subaita
Oboda
Mt Tzin
I S R A E L
Mitzpeh Ramon
Sapir
Machtesh Ramon
J O R D A N
Paran
Petra
E G Y P T
Ne'ot Smadar (Shizafon)
Ya'alon
Ketura
Shaharut
Yotvata

•••• Early route
▪▪▪▪ Later route

N

0 — 10 miles
0 — 20 kms

NEGEV SITES & TRADE ROUTES

Eilat
Gulf of Eilat
Aqaba

Practical information

Getting there

For drivers, Beersheva is reached on Highway 40. Parking in the town is restricted; the car park just off the highway on the east side of the town is recommended. The Central Bus Station is nearby on Derekh Elat.

Where to stay

Aviv, 48 Mordei Haghe Ha'ot (☎ 07 627 8059⊯ 08 628 1961) in town, or the *Desert Inn* (☎ 07 642 4922), slightly north of Beersheva, offer modest accommodation.

Eating out

The lowest floor of the mall (Kanyon) next to the Central Bus Station has many fairly cheap fast food places which offer falafel, shawarma, pizza, Chinese, Burger-Ranch and more. The upper floors of the mall have more expensive restaurants and cafés, such as *Kapulsky* (☎ 07 623 0425), and *A-propo*. About 10 minutes' walk west on the edge of the old town is *Full Moon*, 2 Rambam, vegetarian, which specialises in ful and humus. In the old town itself near the market is the *Bulgarian Restaurant* at 112 Keren Kayemet St (☎ 07 628 9511). More expensive, about 10 minutes' walk north from the bus station, are *Rigoloto*, an Italian restaurant near the city hall at Heichal Hatarbut (☎ 07 623 7630), and *New York, New York*, American restaurant at the Rasco Center (☎ 07 665 0070).

History

The first evidence for settlement of the site is in the late Roman and Byzantine periods, when it was probably the headquarters of the Roman *limes* (fortified frontier) with a large fortified camp (probably located in the centre of the Byzantine town, but on the northeast edge of the Ottoman town) which was built perhaps for the *Legio X Fretensis* as early as the 3C AD. It remained the military headquarters for southern Palestine in the Byzantine period. At least two churches, a monastery, a bath house, cisterns and some tombs have been found, and the town may then have covered 100–150 hectares.

The modern market town was founded at the beginning of the 20C with wide streets, a mosque and single-storey stone houses, many of which still exist in the old town. The Ottoman railway reached Beersheva in 1915. The town was captured by the 4th Australian Light Horse in October 1917. It grew rapidly during the British Mandate period and by 1945 had a population of 5570 Arabs. It was captured by Israel in October 1948 and all the inhabitants fled or were expelled. Since 1948 Beersheva has been a focus for Jewish immigrant settlement and industry. Its Bedouin market has become a tourist feature in a modern town of many large apartment blocks, which is also the location of the Ben Gurion University of the Negev. In 1995 the population was 152,000.

Beersheva is a busy modern town. The **Bedouin Market** (livestock, jewellery, metalwork, food clothing) is located on the Hebron Road on Thursdays; early morning is best for a visit. The **Negev Museum**, with exhibits of modern art and archaeology, is established in the Ottoman mosque and governor's house on Derekh Ha'atzmaut. Open Sun–Thur 10.00–16.00, Fri–Sat 10.00–13.00; admission charged, except Sat. The archaeological section includes material from the remarkable Chalcolithic settlements of the Beersheba region (fifth to fourth millennia BC). The former home of Arif al-Arif (Palestinian historian) is south of the mosque and is a typical stone structure of local Ottoman urban style.

Abraham's Well is on the south side of town near the market, at the corner of the Hebron road and Rehov Keren Kayemet. According to Gen 21: 25–33 Abraham disputed with Abimelek king of Gerar over a well, where they swore an oath; Isaac built an altar there (Gen. 26:15–33) and Jacob had a vision telling him to take his family to Egypt (Gen. 46: 1–7). Whether the story should be associated with this well at Beersheva or the one at Tel Beersheva—or neither—is equally unknown. The site respects a tradition and tells a story, and is venerated for its association with the patriarchs.

The ancient site of **Tel Beersheva** is c 5 km northeast of Beersheva, on the south side of Highway 60. You can view the ruins on the tell, and some of the finds are displayed in the bungalows of the former excavation camp of the 1950s. The site is maintained by the National Parks Authority (☎ 07 646 7286), and is open daily 08.00–16.00/17.00; admission charged.

The earliest remains date to the fourth millennium BC, but the most important are from the 12C–8C BC. The city was at first unwalled, but had a well; it was fortified in the 10C. The first fortified phase had a solid inset/offset wall, glacis, ditch, four-chamber gate with towers and an outer gate, which was destroyed at the end of 10C, perhaps by the Egyptian pharaoh Sheshonq. The surviving remains are mainly of the 9C–7C, on much the same plan. It was a store city, an administrative and military centre on the southern border of the Israelite kingdom; it reveals a planned, coherent design reflecting the uniform patterns of central organisation.

Much reconstruction work in mudbrick has been done at the site. There is a four-chamber gate and an outer gate, a casemate wall of brick on stone foundations, fronted by a massive glacis with plastered face. Inside the town there are houses of the four-room type with stairs, evidence for an upper storey, and a system of peripheral and radial roads. To the left of the gate is a building that may have been the governor's residence, and behind it is a large four-room building. To the right of gate are three storehouses, each with three aisles separated by two rows of pillars. A number of ostraca were discovered, which record the local taxes. There was a public building with a plaster-lined pool in the centre of the town, and a large water system in the northeast corner where a rectangular shaft was dug 15m down to a large reservoir fed by the subterranean flow of the nearby river. The **well** outside the gate is a remarkable feature; dug 69m down to the water-table, it was in use from the 12C/11C BC until the Hellenistic period. Wood found near the bottom was *Juniperus phoenicia* and probably imported from the other side of the Wadi Arabah. The stones of a great horned altar were found reused in the ruins on the site and have been reconstructed in accordance with the Old Testament as belonging to an unlawful cult of the type condemned by Amos in the 8C; the altar was perhaps broken up following the religious reforms of Josiah. The town may have been destroyed during the Assyrian campaign in 701, but was reoccupied in the 4C BC, when more ostraca indicate a mixed population of Jews, Edomites and Arabs. Later a fortress and bath house were built in the early Roman period; a fortress in the 2C–3C AD continued in use into the Islamic period.

ARAD

Tel Arad is an archaeological site on the edge of the Negev, 30km east-northeast of Beersheva and 10km west of the town of Arad, at Tel Arad Junction on Highway 31, turn north on Route 2808. The site is managed by the National Parks Authority (☎ 07 776 2170).

In the modern town of Arad, a visitor centre at 28 Elazar Ben Yair St (☎ 07 995 4409), near the mall and the community centre, contains artefacts and models of the ancient site, an introduction to the history and geology of the region, and information on trails and other activities.

Practical information

Where to stay

The modern town of Arad has a youth hostel, and several hotels: the *Arad Hotel*, 6 Palmach (☎ 07 995 7040, 📠 07 995 7272) in town; and a little east of town, the *Margoa Arad*, 87 Moav (☎ 07 995 1222, 📠 08 995 5558), or the *Nof Arad*, POB 80, Arad (☎ 08 995 7056, 📠 08 995 4053). The bus station is on Rehov Yehuda in the centre of town.

Eating out

Quick and modest food is available in the lower floor of the mall, about 500m north of the *Egged* bus station, behind the visitors' centre. On the floor above is the more expensive restaurant *Kapulsky* (☎ 07 995 0841). Small and cheap restaurants and cafés can be found in the shopping centre opposite the bus station. A Chinese restaurant, *Mister Shay*, Merkazon Ne'urim (☎ 07 997 1956) is 10 minutes southeast of the bus station, in the rear of a small shopping center; there is a Yemenite restaurant *Ktzat Charif* (☎ 07 9971836) in Arad market just south of the main entrance to Arad from the Beer Sheva–Dead Sea road.

Part of the ancient site of Tel Arad is a **citadel** on a hill with many layers of almost continuous use dating from the 12C BC to the 8C AD. The most important remains here are of a rectangular fortress built in the late 10C and rebuilt and reused to the early 6C BC. It contained the remains of a temple of an unofficial Judaean cult, which appears to have been destroyed during the religious reforms carried through in the reign of King Josiah. In the 5C–4C BC the place served as a way station for cavalry; a tower was built here in the 3C–2C BC, and the site was then abandoned.

Of particular interest however, because of its extent and preservation, is the **town** of the third millennium BC, which covers the area to the southwest of the citadel. In the fourth millennium an unremarkable small settlement gradually developed into an organised town which reached its apogee in the Early Bronze II period. It was then destroyed and thereafter declined, to be abandoned c 2650 BC. This was a town covering an area of 25 hectares, surrounded by defensive walls 1200m long, with gates and a series of round and rectangular projecting towers. Within the town, the central depression appears to have been occupied by a water reservoir which collected the winter run-off from the higher ground. Above this pool, in a central position in a concentric layout, are buildings identified as a palace and temples. The latter are built against a thick wall segregating them from the ordinary houses of the town. Many houses have been excavated, and a walk along the streets of the ancient town provides a real sense of contact with the ancient inhabitants. Living rooms, kitchens, yards and street layout all survive.

The bare loess plains of the region, and the low rainfall (today around 170mm) make this an unexpected location for a town with an estimated population of 2500–3000 people. The finds suggest it depended on agriculture, pastoralism, crafts, and trade with Egypt and Sinai, especially in copper. It may have been changes or competition in trading patterns that led to its failure.

AVDAT
. . . .

The site of Avdat (ancient Oboda/Eboda, A. 'Abda) lies at 619m above sea level, c 45km south of Beersheva on Route 40. Run by the National Parks Authority (☎ 07 658 6391), it has a shop, snack bar and visitor centre.

History

The first traces of occupation (pottery, not architecture) belong to the 4C–3C BC, but development was halted when Alexander Jannaeus sacked Gaza c 100 BC. The first real structures (including a temple) are associated with the time of the Nabataean kings, Obodos II (30–9 BC, for whom the town was named, and who was later deified), and his son Aretas IV (9 BC–AD 40). The town probably consisted of a fort, a few houses and, because Oboda lay on a major road, the services needed to support the trade routes. During the 1C AD there appears to have been a decline in the trade route, paralleled by a greater emphasis on agriculture. After the Roman annexation, Roman garrisons were established in the area and veterans were settled here to counter trouble with Arabian tribes. It was fortified by Diocletian and his successors. During the mid-3C there was a revival and a temple was dedicated to Zeus Obodas and a shrine to Aphrodite. An earthquake in the 5C provided a setback, but the greatest prosperity was in the Byzantine period, with an estimated population of 2000–3000 in the 6C. Most of the visible remains are of this date. The economy was based on a flourishing agriculture, wine production, pottery making and workshops. The town had a bath house and two churches on the acropolis. The Persian sack (618/20) and Arab conquest led to its abandonment. Despite its ups and downs, the site was probably occupied continuously during this long period.

A steep footpath with hairpin bends ascends to the south side of the fortified **acropolis**. The 6C remains incorporated earlier ruins of the Nabataean and Roman periods. Hammer dressed stones are usually of the Nabataean period, and smooth ashlar of later date. The base of the strong retaining walls at the west section of the acropolis are Nabataean. The gateway has been reconstructed; the Nabataean temple of Obodas II was located here.

A fortress built over the east section had nine rectangular towers, an arched gate on the southwest and entrances connecting to the west section of the acropolis. Inside the fortress, a chapel at the northeast end, a central cistern and a single chamber on the south were the main features. It seems to have been built in the 4C AD to replace the extramural fort (see below), and to have served as a defensible refuge for the townspeople.

In the unpaved west section there are two churches. The southeast church, the Martyrium of St. Theodore, is a three-aisled basilica, with the circular base of the pulpit adjacent to the bema in front of the chancel. It has three apses. A colonnaded atrium surrounded by monastic cells lay to the west; graves were found in both church and atrium.

The northwest church, which may be older, is also a three-aisled basilica with a central large apse, but just a vestry on the south; the rooms south of the church contained a marble reliquary; the atrium here too has a central cistern. Beyond a lane to the west is the baptistery with marble lined, cross-shaped immersion font, and a smaller one to the side for infant baptism.

From the top of the acropolis there is a fine view of the surrounding countryside, where field systems of the Nabataean/Roman/Byzantine periods may be seen, and dams across valleys for water conservation have been found.

Below the acropolis the town was surrounded by a wall. To the south of the fortress on a ridge lay the Roman quarter. On terraces around the western slope of the acropolis were 350–400 house/caves, workshops, and wine cellars; some can be visited, and contain features such as cupboard niches, drains, lavatories, benches with hollows for storage jars, and storage bins for domestic and industrial use. Four winepresses, one a substantial structure, have been recorded. A Nabataean potters' workshop was found outside the town on the east, and burial caves below the southeast face of the acropolis; a large burial cave lies c 200m to the south.

The well-preserved bath house is located c 100m west of the acropolis, towards the wadi and near the visitor centre; its water came from a well 60m deep. It had a courtyard and pool, dressing room, and cold, warm and hot rooms, the latter heated by hypocausts and fitted with clay-lined bath tubs.

A great fortified camp lay c 250m northeast of the city, dating from the late 1C BC/early 1C AD. With external towers, barracks, camel sheds, it illustrates well the importance of the well-organised and well-guarded Nabataean caravan route. A monumental Nabataean tomb of the 1C BC lies north of the camp.

David Ben-Gurion's Memorial and Ein Avdat National Park

North of Avdat, off Highway 40, in a park near the Sede Boqer Institute for Desert Research, is a memorial to Israel's first prime minister. Arrangements to see a film of Ben-Gurion's life at the museum can be made on ☎ 07 653 2717.

Ben-Gurion was born in 1886 in Poland, emigrated to Palestine in 1906, and was head of the Jewish Agency when he became the first prime minister of Israel in 1948 and intermittently until his retirement in 1964. He had a home near here as well as in Tel Aviv, and died in Israel in 1974. He was a strong supporter of research on desert agriculture. The simple **monument** in a garden of desert-adapted plants, marking the burial place of both Ben-Gurion and his wife Paula, is a national memorial. There are magnificent views over the Negev from here.

Nearby, 4km north of Avdat, is the lower entrance to the **Ein Avdat National Park** (☎ 07 655 5684); the upper entrance is c 5km to the south. An entrance ticket is available for upper and lower entrances to the park, and you can get a combined ticket for the park and the site at Avdat. No food, dogs, swimming or fires are permitted in the nature reserve (ibex; Euphrates poplar). In the park a spring and a canyon form the top of the Wadi Zin, a major water course for winter rainfall run-off down to the Wadi Arabah. There are paths (demanding climb) to the top of the canyon.

SHIVTA
● ● ● ● ● ● ● ●

The ruins of the old town of Shivta (ancient Sobata/Esbeita, A. Subaita) lie about 16km in a direct line northwest of Oboda/Avdat on the old Gaza caravan route.

The site, near Highway 211, c 40km southwest of Beersheva, is maintained by the National Parks Authority (no telephone). To get there, drivers should take Route 40, turning west at Telalim Junction onto Route 211 towards the Nizzana border crossing point, and turning south after c 12km towards Shivta.

History

Occupation began with the Nabataeans in the late 1C BC, with a small town about a third of the size of the later Byzantine town. Its rather spacious layout suggests sedentarising tribesmen requiring space for their animals. The town may have been abandoned and resettled perhaps in the time of Diocletian. It was probably a civilian agricultural settlement which was adapted for the usual Byzantine development in the 4C, and had no fortress. The town expanded northwards in the 5C and appears not to have been adversely affected by the Islamic conquest, for the Arabs built a mosque near the south church, but did not encroach on it or on the baptistery, suggesting peaceful rural coexistence. At its peak the population may have numbered c 5000, supported by a thriving agriculture and extensive irrigated field system. The remains of the agricultural system surround the town.

The ruins were cleared almost entirely, revealing a rather irregular street plan which emphasises long, winding main streets running roughly north and south over an area c 290m x 390m. The unpaved streets served blocks of houses and two open areas. The spacious, generally courtyard-type houses formed a defensive perimeter, and the nine street ends could be closed by gates. Rainwater run-off was collected inside the town, from roofs and even some streets, and led by channels to the reservoir and cisterns. The Nabataean town and cistern occupied the south section, and the large Nabataean cistern towards the centre was reused in later periods.

The **south church** is a 4C three-aisled basilica with narthex; a square pulpit base is set in front of the bema and chancel; the two side apses are later replacements of earlier diaconicon and prothesis, and were used for reliquaries; the apses were painted. On the north side of the church are court, tower, chapel and baptistery with a monolithic cross-shaped font and a smaller version for infant baptism, with fragments of marble veneer, and steps down inside. Repairs to the church complex are recorded after the Islamic conquest, and the mosque abuts the north side of the baptistery. Another church was excavated near the centre of the town, adjacent to the so-called 'Governor's House'.

The **north church**, with similar plan to the south church, is part of a larger complex including another baptistery, atrium and monastery on the south side. The church was originally decorated with wall paintings, but later marble facings replaced the lower sections; there was marble paving in the church and a mosaic floor in the chapel. The large atrium has the base of a column, probably that of a Stylite (an ascetic who lived on top of a pillar), later buried and venerated (as was the more famous St. Simeon Stylites in northern Syria). The inscriptions, dedicatory and funerary, date to the 6C–7C, but the church may have been founded earlier. A number of winepresses were also found in the monastery and the town, emphasising the importance of grape production in the area.

NIZZANA ~ NESSANA

The site of Nizzana (ancient Nessana/Nisana, A. Auja al-Khafir) is 52km southwest of Beersheva, by Route 211, near the Egyptian border crossing checkpoint at Nizzana, just south of the town on the minor road to Ezuz. In Roman times it lay off the main Elat to Gaza route, on the inland route across Sinai.

A Nabataean settlement was founded in the 2C BC and flourished in the1C BC/AD, the oldest building is a fort (25m x 27m) with round towers at the corners, built on a hill. The settlement declined in the 2C–4C AD, then in the 5C a large fort (35m x 85m) with casemate wall and rectangular corner and median towers was built on the hill; this was the station of the Theodosian Numerus. The army was stationed here till c AD 600, and then the fort became became part of a monastery attached to the church adjacent to the north, also dated to the 5C, and dedicated to St. Sergius and St. Bacchus. The church was built over the early fort; the *opus sectile* pavement was added later. A flight of steps leading down to the town below the hill existed till the 8C. At the end of 7C a church dedicated to St. Mary was built on a hill south of the acropolis.

The fortunes of the town rose and fell with the prosperity of the trade route, which declined in the 2C AD with the opening of the Via Traiana to the east; but improved in the late 6C/early 7C with government support and protection for the Elat–Gaza road. The poll-tax roll for 587–89 shows the town had a population of c 1500. Nearly 152 inscriptions in Greek and Nabataean found on the site date from AD 464–630. Of particular importance are the Nessana Papyri, 195 papyri in Greek and Arabic found near the two churches; dating to AD 512–689, they include business and legal documents, as well as parts of Virgil's *Aeneid* and a life of St. George. The Nessana Papyri also reveal that the fort/village had the same leading family for several generations and that the history of the town continued well into the Umayyad period. The coins, glass and pottery indicate that the site continued to be occupied into the 9C–10C. Remains, principally Byzantine, of the fort, churches, houses and cemetery can be seen.

The modern border town played a part during the First World War and during the 1948 Arab/Israeli war; it was the meeting place of the Israel-Egypt Mixed Armistice Commission between 1949 and 1956.

MAMSHIT
• • • • • • • • • • •

Mamshit (ancient Mampsis, A. Kurnub) is a splendid, well-preserved stone-built ruin, where the sights and atmosphere of the Nabataean and Byzantine town can be readily appreciated. It has all the usual appurtenances of large houses, churches, bath house, fortifications and a caravanserai.

The site lies c 40km southeast of Beersheva, just south of Route 25, 8km southeast of Dimona towards Rotem Junction. It is maintained by the National Parks Authority (☎ 07 655 6478) and the facilities include a restaurant.

History

There is archaeological evidence for settlement in the late 1C BC, but the city is first mentioned in the mid-2C AD and frequently thereafter; it is depicted on the 6C Madaba mosaic map (see p 71). It was located on two routes up from the Wadi Arabah, one from Zoar and one coming from Ayla and Petra via the Scorpion's Pass, and connected with routes to the west—to Beersheba and Gaza, and to Hebron and Jerusalem. The development of the northern caravan route on which the town lay may have been most intense in the early 2C AD, with paved roads protected by fortified way stations, supplied by concrete and stone dams and water systems under the impetus of Roman military organisation linked with the building of the Via Traiana in Transjordan.

The plan of the town was established in the late Nabataean period, with a main street running north–south, having public buildings on the west side and domestic buildings on the east side. A three-aisled building of basilical type was clearly a stable and there is evidence here and in other buildings for a staircase ascending around a rectangular pier. The city walls and gates, and visible street planning date to the 6C–7C AD. It is estimated that Mampsis may have had a permanent population of perhaps 500 in the Byzantine period (see below).

There seems to be little evidence for any extensive occupation of the town in the Early Islamic period, and it is suggested that the town was attacked, taken, but only briefly occupied. Kurnub seems to have been a garrison town on a trade route, with little evidence or land for agriculture. It may therefore have offered little to Arab settlers.

The original section of the city may have been on the highest point to the southeast, where the Byzantine east church was later built. Some Nabataean buildings are preserved to a second storey, with the stairs which lead to them. Much architectural detail is preserved including Nabataean capitals, and typical diagonal tooling of Nabataean masonry can be seen; the walls were often plastered and there is evidence for wall paintings of 3C date with classical themes, including a depiction of the story of Eros and Psyche. Stables reflect the importance of horse-breeding. Reservoirs held the town's drinking water. Many of these buildings served the late Nabataean population too, when the first city wall with towers was constructed, perhaps in the time of Diocletian. A huge coin hoard was found, with coins of the 1C–3C AD, and two cemeteries of this period are also known, one c 800m north of the town, and the other 200m northeast. The former had monuments marking the graves, stepped pyramids, or hollow mausolea. A garrison was stationed here when the Romans established the Province of Arabia, and the burials in the northeast cemetery may date from this period, for they are all cremation burials. The bath house in the northeast near the pool may date from this period, but continued in use in Byzantine times. Fine dams still survive in the nearby wadi, strongly built to retain the water from flash floods.

In the Byzantine period more houses continued to be occupied, often with Christian symbols carved on the lintels, for the expanding population and the insertion of churches added to the pre-existing plan. The old city wall, c 900m in length, was doubled in thickness and the towers strengthened. The main north gate had wooden doors with iron armour plating; a smaller gate was located on the west. On the east, on the highest point of the city, a church was built and dedicated to the Saints and Martyrs. With it were a chapel, a baptistery, a small bath house and perhaps a monastery. The church was notable for the find of reliquaries of saints and martyrs in the diaconicon and prothesis, on either side of the single apse. The side aisles of the church were paved with marble, and the central nave with mosaic laid in simple geometric patterns. As these included two crosses in the design, the church was probably built before AD 427, when this practice was forbidden.

A second church is located to the west, built by Nilus, and with finer mosaics (not open to the public). Papyri were also found. A caravanserai lies outside the city on the northwest. It may date from the Byzantine period, but overlies earlier structures. The probably brief Arab occupation is evidenced by graffiti in the apse of the eastern church.

Nearby is the Iris Yeruham Nature reserve.

The Valley of the Jordan, the Dead Sea and the Wadi Arabah

The African Rift Valley forms a great trough in the crust of the earth which includes in its northern end the Red Sea, the Gulf of Aqaba, the Wadi Arabah, the Dead Sea, and the Jordan Valley and continues on up into Lebanon and Syria. It is formed by a deep fault line between the African and Asian plates and is a zone of permanent tectonic movement, marked by earthquakes, ancient basalt flows, igneous intrusions, and hot springs. Within this trough are the main sources of the Jordan River, three springs which burst out below the slopes of Mt Hermon. The Jordan fed two major freshwater lakes, that of Huleh, a swamp and lake drained in the 20C, and the Sea of Galilee, anciently called the Sea/Lake of Kinnereth/Gennesaret, and later the Lake of Tiberias. The latter was -210m below Mediterranean sea level in 1980; it is now a major Israeli reservoir. Formerly the waters of the Jordan were joined by a major tributary, the Yarmuk River (now a major water source for agriculture), and flowed in a deep-set, ancient, looping course amid a riverine jungle of tamarisk and dense vegetation inhabited by wild boar, to the Dead Sea. It was not a ready source of water for ancient agriculture, because it was lined by saline badlands, and the alluvial soils above them were out of reach of the river. South of Jericho the river flows into the Dead Sea.

The surface of the Dead Sea at -405m below Mediterranean sea level (in 1986) is the lowest point on the surface of the earth. It is c 1150m below Jerusalem which is only 23km distant. The sea was formed around 75,000 years ago when the ancient Mediterranean flooded into the Rift in the area of the modern Valley of Jezreel; eventually this flood formed a vast lake, much bigger than the present Dead Sea, with the top of the sediments deposited near its shores at -185m below present Mediterranean sea level. The cliffs on the west side are formed of limestones deposited 60–90 million years ago; the base of those on the east are of sandstone, formed 500 million years ago. Because there is no outlet for the ancient salt lake, little rainfall and a high rate of evaporation, its waters are full of salts and minerals, such as calcium, bromine, magnesium salts and potassium chlorides, and are 30 per cent heavier than ordinary ocean water. Thus it is easy to float on it, but swimming should not be attempted. Floating in the Dead Sea should only be enjoyed in designated areas. If inhaled, the water can destroy lung tissue; if drunk, it can be toxic. The currents are dangerous, and the sea becomes surprisingly rough very quickly when sudden winds are channelled between the cliffs.

The north basin is 330m deep, but with another 11km of sediment filling the trough beneath. The south basin, south of the Jordanian Lisan peninsula, was very shallow although in the 1960s water still covered the strip between it and the western shore; since then so much water has been extracted from the sources of the Jordan by Israel, that this strip is now dry and the whole southern basin would have evaporated to dry land except that water is pumped to flood the shallow basins for industrial extraction of minerals, such as potassium chloride and magnesium, with salt as a by-product. Thus the level of the Dead Sea has dropped catastrophically since the 1960s, and as the shoreline moved eastwards, it exposed a barren margin which is collapsing as the salts are leached from the soils.

South of the Dead Sea the very barren, dry and sandy expanses of the Wadi Arabah rise very gradually to c 90m above Mediterranean sea level towards the Gulf of Aqabah. Here the surrounding cliffs and wadis gave access to important ancient sources of copper.

The geology of the Rift also cuts aquifers, so fresh water springs erupt and provide many agricultural oases, such as Jericho, Ain Feshka, Engedi and En Boqeq. Where fresh water is available and the ground is not saline, the alluvial soils can be very fertile. In Roman times the region was famous for its balsam and its date palms; and in medieval times for its sugar. Summer temperatures can reach

nearly 50°C, and virtually no rain falls on the western shore which lies in the rain-shadow of the hills of the West Bank. But the winter temperature is mild, and crops of fruits and flowers in the valley ripen much faster than those of the hills. The tropical climate supports unique plants and animals, some being survivals of the African continent, such as the rock hyrax at Engedi, whose nearest zoological relative is the

Hyrax near the spring at Engedi

elephant. The arid wilderness of the sides of the Rift also long provided sanctuary for the leopard and still do for the Nubian ibex. All these and others are now protected species, though protection came too late for the leopard and gazelle, while the crocodile and ostrich are long gone.

The sediments of the Jordan Valley have also revealed some of the earliest traces of man in the region, at the site of Ubaidiya (3km southwest of the Sea of Galilee, see Israel Museum in Jerusalem, p 255); the earliest tools discovered (around one million years old) and the fossil bones also show links with Africa, in particular the African Rift where the oldest ancestors of modern man have been discovered. The history of the valley has been shaped by its unique environment. Some of the earliest evidence for human settlement in built structures from around the 12th millennium (e.g. Eynan, see Israel Museum in Jerusalem), and for the oldest monumental walls and tower—those protecting the town at Jericho in the eighth millennium—have been found in the valley. They were followed not much later by the portrait skulls of the early Neolithic (seventh millennium), the wall paintings of Tulaylat Ghassul (fifth and fourth millennium, in Jordan), the evidence for mining (Timna) and sophisticated metallurgical skills (Nahal Mishmar, see Israel Museum in Jerusalem): all are found in this unique place. A perfume industry may have begun here already in the late fourth millennium (on the north side of the Wadi Daraja), and perfumes and medicines were important industries in the Iron Age and in Roman times. Not least the arid climate has preserved some of the most important ancient documents written on leather and papyrus, the Dead Sea Scrolls found around the site of Qumran.

For tourist information on the Golan, ☎ 06 696 2885.

DAN
• • • • •

According to the Old Testament, the ancient kingdom of Israel stretched from Dan (ancient Laish, A. Tell al-Qadi) to Beersheba (Jud. 20:1), and Tell Dan marks the site both of the biblical and of an older Canaanite city. It lies at the largest of the three sources of the Jordan fed from Mt Hermon. The remains of the Canaanite city of Laish or Leshem (Tel Dan in the Iron Age) include a remarkable brick gateway.

The site is reached via Highway 99, c 11km east of Hamezudot junction, near Kibbutz Dan. A restaurant, facilities and car park are located at the entrance to Tel Dan Nature Reserve (☎ 06 695 1579). The small nature reserve is open 08.00–16.00 (closes 1 hour earlier Fri and eve of holidays).

History

Laish is mentioned in the Execration Texts c 1800 BC (see p 61); it was a Canaanite town captured by Tuthmosis III of Egypt in 1468, and later (c 11C) renamed by the tribe of Dan, who made it their cult centre. Jeroboam I made a shrine of the golden calf here, when he provided his northern half of the kingdom with cult centres to rival Jerusalem (I Kings 12: 28–30). It remained a Semitic cult place for many centuries, and was still active in the 3C–4C AD. In medieval times however, Jews thought Dan was located at Banias.

The nature reserve, with a water-powered flour mill built before 1948, has cool and pleasant trails around the fast-flowing streams and springs, with dense woodland which include the Syrian ash, the Atlantic pistachio, and the jujube. The path leads east to the large, rounded, crater-shaped tell (20 hectares). In the Middle Bronze II the site was surrounded by great sloping earth ramparts, c 50m wide at the base. Set into the southeast side of this rampart is a **mudbrick gate complex**. At the outer end a stepped path climbs to the mudbrick gate which is set back between towers; the gateway, with intact round arch, is c 3m high, and 2.4m wide; inside, the 10.5m long gate passage leads between two chambers through another arch in a central pier, then between two more chambers to the arch at the inner end. Beyond the inner side of the gate, 20 stone steps lead down to the street. The gateway dates to c 1800 BC.

Returning along the path, the formidable **gate complex** built in the 9C–8C BC lies to the southwest of the older Canaanite one. The older part of the complex consists of an outer, middle and inner gate. Between the outer and middle gate was a rubble-paved square and among its stones was found parts of a smashed stele, which mentions 'The House of David', the first time a possible extra-biblical reference to the early royal line of Israel has been found, even if it dates long after the time of King David. Against the outer face of the north tower of the middle gate, a canopied throne was set up as a place of judgement (as II Sam. 19:8). This complex has been restored.

The path then leads on to the northwest corner of the tell, to a casemate enclosure with a great high place or *bamah*, a place of cult and sacrifice, the core of which was built in two phases in the 10C–9C BC. The first, probably open-air enclosure, is assumed to have been built by Jeroboam I, where he dedicated the statue of the golden calf, and the second by Ahab. The latter contained a square structure of very finely cut and set ashlar flat-bossed masonry; the cult area continued in use during the reigns of later kings. A great horned altar (of the type also found at Megiddo and Arad) was built in the 8C and destroyed during the Assyrian conquest. The cult enclosure was refurbished in the Hellenistic and Roman periods.

Finds from the site are displayed in the Skirball Museum of Biblical Archaeology in Jerusalem (see p 264). Nearby on the entrance road is the **Beit Ussishkin Nature Museum** with a display of the archaeology and local fauna and flora; open Sun–Thur 09.00–16.00, Fri 09.00–15.00, Sat 10.00–16.00; a joint admission ticket for the tell is available. The **Hula Valley Museum of Prehistory** is located at Ma'ayan Barukh, 6km west of Tell Dan; open daily 09.00–12.00; admission charged.

BANIAS

An ancient shrine of the god Pan is associated with one of the main sources of the Jordan River, at the lovely springs of Banias, with the fragmentary remains of the Temple of Augustus built by Herod the Great, and later Roman, Byzantine and medieval cities.

The site is c 13km northeast of Qiryat Shemona, reached by Highway 99. It is part of a large nature reserve managed by the National Parks Authority (Hermon National Park, ☎ 06 690 2577).

History

The pagan shrine of Pan is first mentioned c 200 BC when Antiochus III defeated the Egyptians here and took Palestine into the Seleucid territories; but it might orginally have been established by the Ptolemies who identified the cult with that of Dionysos. The shrine was located on a high terrace in a great natural grotto above one of the sources of the Jordan. From 20 BC it belonged to the kingdom of Herod the Great, who built a white marble temple in honour of Augustus before the cave of Pan, and probably a palace. The territory was inherited by his son Philip the Tetrarch who built his capital on the flat ground south of the high terrace in 2/1 BC and called it Caesarea Philippi. Banias is remembered by Christians as the site of Peter's recognition of Jesus as Messiah (Matt. 16:13–20). Christian tradition also lists a bishop in the time of St. Paul.

A palace was built in the time of Agrippa II who refounded the city in AD 61. It remained a predominantly pagan town with a deeply Hellenised Graeco-Roman culture, and Titus enjoyed the amenities of the city after the sack of Jerusalem. After the death of Agrippa II the town was incorporated into the Roman province of Syria in AD 95, and during the 2C–3C AD the Paneion became an important regional sanctuary. By the early 3C the sanctuary included the Augusteum and five temples on the terrace, and housed at least 19 associated sculptural niches. Dedications to Pan, Tyche and Nemesis are attested. Jewish legends attribute a residence of Diocletian to the town. The Roman bath house continued to be used in the Byzantine period and probably later. Christianity was well established here in the early 4C (a bishop is listed in 325). The city grew to cover a much greater extent in the Byzantine period. An aqueduct brought water from the east to serve the needs of the large population.

Banias was the capital of the district of Jaulan in the Early Islamic period and an important supplier of produce for Damascus. Karaite and rabbinic Jewish communities also lived in the city in the 10C–11C. A city with walls, at least nine towers, a defensive ditch and a mosque in the Middle Ages overlay the centre of the Roman town, probably begun in the Fatimid period by the Ismailis (Assassins) c 1126, but after the sect was attacked in Damascus, they handed the town to the Crusaders in 1129, and some of the surviving remains are Crusader work. It was retaken for Damascus in 1132 and had a complex history in the mid-12C almost as a shared Muslim/Frankish town, until it was finally taken by Nur al-Din in 1164. It was rebuilt in the Ayyubid and Mamluk periods (there is evidence for glass-making in the 11C–13C), but was virtually abandoned in the 16C–17C. The roof of the cave of Pan collapsed in the earthquake of 1837. Just a small village of Turcomans, Arabs, Druze and others existed on the site in Ottoman times, and c 200 people in 1967 when the town was taken from Syria.

The shrine of Pan

The ruins of the **Roman shrine of Pan**, including the small remnants of the Temple of Augustus, can be viewed from a trail north of the car park. The caves and the carved niches in the cliff above the spring and beautiful pools form the main focus of a much larger site. In front of the cliff, an elevated terrace formed the temenos. The western source of the springs originally flowed through the lowest west grotto. The white domed building above the cave is the Druze shrine of Nabi Khadir. On a slightly lower terrace and further west is a wall with *opus reticulatum* identified with a palace built by Herod.

Construction of the **Paneion** began at the west end of the main terrace in front of the grotto of Pan in the 1C BC and continued through the 3C AD. Only traces of Herod's temple to Augustus survive, with use of rubble and concrete for *opus quadratum* and *opus reticulatum* walls on east and west, with alternating semicircular and rectangular niches. Following the trail east along the cliff there is first an open-air court of the 1C AD dedicated to Pan and the four nymphs; in the cliff above are two rock-cut niches, each with fluted pilasters flanking a rounded arch with semi-dome decorated as a fluted shell. Greek inscriptions with dedications to Pan are dated to AD 148/49. Next is a large ashlar temple dated to AD 98, dedicated to Zeus and Pan; it has four columns in the façade with Corinthian capitals, then an open-air court of AD 178 dedicated to Nemesis; above, a round column on a square base is also dedicated to Pan, and another high-level niche has geometric decoration in the semi-dome with a pedestal that once formed the base for a statue, and may date to the 1C AD. Then there is a tripartite building of uncertain function, perhaps connected with the sacred goats and Elagabalus; below the central hall, and in the street in front of it, were found the fragments of 28 marble sculptures depicting various Graeco-Roman gods, which had been deposited there in the early Islamic period. Finally there is an apsidal court perhaps dedicated to Pan. Traces of a second temple can be seen below, perhaps dedicated to Tyche, with a damaged niche in a rock-face and a shrine to Nemesis beyond it. The inscription above dates to AD 221. The sanctuary seems to have gone out of use in the 5C. Brilliant blue squill hyacinths brighten the cliff face in spring. A path from the east side of the pools leads to the castle of Nimrod (see p 421).

The city

The centre of the **Roman and later medieval city** is located south of the springs, the car park and road, covering an area of c 300m x 300m. It is approached by a path leading between the river and the souvenir shop northeast of the car park. The trail leads first along the south, then the north bank of the stream. After passing under the modern road bridge, it passes under a fine Roman bridge by a wooden walkway. It once carried the Tyre–Damascus road through the city, and bridges on the site continued to do so in Crusader and Mamluk times. There is access from here to the excavation area south of the road, where a large Roman building with columns, and with stucco and frescoes inside and out, probably dates to the founding of the city by Philip Tetrarch in the 1C AD. A series of about ten vaults or a cryptoporticus in the centre of the town may have formed storage areas in the vicinity of the forum. A large basilica of the late 3C/early 4C AD with mosaics was partly destroyed by the building of the medieval city. Exit by a gate to the north of the ruins to return to the car park.

Alternatively the trail continues along the river to a water-powered flour mill served by an aqueduct. Beyond the mill the trail forks right to continue down to the Banias waterfall (1km), and Kibbutz Snir (2km). A steep channel with massive Roman walling leads the water of the springs and streams to the Banias waterfall, and continues downstream. All along the west side of the site down to Kibbutz Snir are the remains of the city cemetery.

The left fork continues south and another fork to the left leads up to the remains of Agrippa's palace. There is no exit from this area, so return to the trail, which continues south to the southwest corner of the Ayyubid wall. Much of the mostly Ayyubid fortification is visible, covering an area c 250m x 220m with moats to north and east. Some of the eight towers are preserved. The trail leads east along the south edge of the medieval city. Passing another ruined mill which contains part of the medieval wall, the path leads past the Ottoman domed grave of Shaikh Sidi Ibrahim on the left. To the right is the south gatehouse in the Ayyubid wall. An Islamic inscription over the south entrance has the date of 1227; until the 20C it was approached by a bridge across the wadi from the south. Its east side contained a mosque, with mihrab and parts of the south wall constructed in coursed coloured stone typical of the Mamluk period. The trail continues along the impressive moat; at the northeast corner a late Islamic house is built above the medieval wall. This route also brings you back directly to the car park.

NIMROD'S CASTLE

The 13C Muslim castle known as Nimrod's Castle (A. Qal'at al-Subayba) stands on the southern slopes of Mt Hermon, on a high narrow ridge above the Banias spring, which blocked the road to Damascus against the Crusaders. It is splendidly built, and has a fine view.

The castle is c 3km north from Highway 989, c 16km. northeast of Qiryat Shemona. It is maintained by the National Parks Authority (☎ 03 776 2186). The ticket office is below the castle on the southeast; the car park and facilities are adjacent to the west wall.

History

According to the inscriptions, the castle was built in 1230 by the Ayyubid governor, al-Aziz 'Uthman; damaged by the Mongols in 1260, it was repaired and extended under Baybars. Its strategic purpose, entirely related to the Frankish threat of attack against Damascus, disappeared with the fall of Acre in 1291. It depended on its many cisterns to store rainwater. It was damaged in the earthquakes of 1759 or 1837. The later, popular name derives from the biblical son of Cush, Nimrod the mighty hunter (Gen. 10:9).

Approached from the west side, the castle has a long, narrow, heavily fortified, lower enclosure with 16 towers, mainly on its west and south sides, and a strong, rectangular, separately fortified upper keep at the east end. Entrance is usually by the northwest tower, the largest, originally a one-storey gate tower and possibly the main entrance, with portcullis slot and an inscription recording the work of al-Aziz 'Uthman in 1230. The tower was later enlarged on its south and west sides, and two storeys were added above. A fine but fragmentary inscription of 1275 shows this was the work of Baybars; his work is also marked by a carved lion or leopard relief sculpture found on the site. The full height of the tower wall was originally 30m, built of large ashlars some weighing up to 37 tons; a large cistern was constructed in the lower south side, and a well-preserved concealed steep, stepped passage, 27m. long, 1.8m wide led from the tower to a postern gate below the tower. In the first floor is a well-built lavatory next to the passage entrance; next to it a passage and some external stairs led up to the second storey. Ten other towers line the south wall of the castle: note the fine cistern and drinking fountain by the southwest corner tower; the next tower to the east was one of the main entrances. The tower to the east with a rounded external wall was built by Baybars, and is called the 'Beautiful Tower'. The octagonal interior has a great central pier supporting a ribbed vault. Another entrance is located further along the south side, and two additional sally ports existed.

A path leads up to the eastern keep, defended by a ditch once spanned by a wooden drawbridge. Another inscription of al-Aziz 'Uthman can be seen on the southwest corner. Two massive towers overlook its rubble-filled courtyard. This was the residential quarters of the governor; the fortress also has an impressive tower at the northeast corner, with a cistern at base. A steep path leads down from the southeast corner of the keep, past a reservoir pool to the ticket office on the approach road.

HAZOR

The site of the greatest city of the southern Canaanites is situated on the road from the coast up the Jordan Valley to Damascus. With the freshwater Sea of Galilee to the south, the lakes and marshes of Hula to the north, the fertile valley of the Jordan before it and the wooded hills of Galilee behind, the site had rich natural resources. In the Middle Bronze Age it was the gateway for Syrian goods entering southern Canaan.

Hazor lies185km north of Jerusalem; c 25km north of Tiberias on Highway 90. The site is maintained by the National Parks Authority (☎ 06 693 7290). Open daily 08.00–16.00. The museum (☎ 06 693 4855) is located at the entrance to Kibbutz Ayelet Hashahar opposite the entrance to the site, and as it contains many important finds from the site, as well as much information, visiting the museum before the site is recommended. A joint ticket for site and museum is available.

History

Hazor is another of the great tell sites of Israel whose prehistory has been revealed in over 21 levels. The earliest remains, from the Early Bronze Age, are scant, but one large group of pottery dating to the end of the third millennium, and another impressive burial group of the early second millennium suggest that there is still much more to be discovered. Hazor is first mentioned in the later set of Execration Texts (c 1800 BC), as having a ruler called Gt'i.

Its period of greatness was from c 1800–1230 BC, when it was the largest and most important site in southern Canaan, the capital of a city state which had a direct trading relationship with Mari and other kingdoms in northern Syria. The Mari palace archive (c 1800–1750 BC) mentions Hazor and its ruler Ibni-Hadad, records messengers travelling between Hazor and Babylon, and—notably—the sending of 70 minas of tin from Mari to Hazor. Tin was a very expensive commodity imported from the distant east, then mixed with copper to make bronze tools, weapons and artefacts which began to be used regularly in the south Levant at this time. Hazor's control of a large quantity of this material must have been a source of both wealth and power. The finds made on the site, in particular the use of finely dressed basalt slabs for the palaces and temples, illustrate the wealth, craft skills and the investment of labour in developing the city and the state. Egyptian records between the 16C and 13C often mention the city: the pharaohs Tuthmosis III in 1468, Amenophis III and Seti I (c 1303–1290) all claimed to have conquered Hazor. In the Amarna correspondence (c 1350 BC), some letters come from King Abdi-Tirshi of Hazor proclaiming his loyalty to the Egyptian king despite accusations that he has joined the troublesome Habiru. The city of Hazor appears to have been totally destroyed more than a century after this, c 1230 BC.

In the Old Testament, it is claimed that Joshua conquered and burnt Hazor (Joshua 11) and we are also told that Sisera commanded the army of Jabin, King of Hazor (Judges 4). It is speculated that Ibni/Yabni/Jabin was the dynastic name of the kings of Hazor in the Late Bronze Age. The archaeological remains at Hazor between c 1230 and c 1000 are poor and it is suggested that they reflect the period of settlement of the Israelite tribes following the destruction of the Canaanite city.

The Lower City was no longer inhabited after the beginning of the Iron Age, indicating a population decline in contrast to that which marked its expansion about 600 years earlier. According to the Old Testament, Hazor was one of the cities built by Solomon (I Kings 9:15); and the archaeological remains show a citadel occupying just the west section of the acropolis in the 10C. The citadel was surrounded by a casemate wall. As at Megiddo the casemate wall was filled in to make a solid wall, and the area enclosed was extended to include the whole acropolis in the 9C: this phase is attributed to Ahab. Hazor fell to Tiglath-Pileser III in 732 BC. and there was a citadel on the site in the Assyrian, Persian and Hellenistic periods as late as the 2C BC.

The site is divided into two parts. The acropolis site rises c 30–40m above the fields and covers 12 hectares; the lower site or enclosure on the north covers c 80 hectares but is cultivated and closed to the public.

The acropolis At the east end of the acropolis, various remains can be viewed from above, including a section of the fortifications of the 9C–8C BC.

In the central area a sequence of temples and palaces of the Middle and Late Bronze Ages has been partially excavated. The whole acropolis area was occupied in the Late Bronze Age and a long-axis temple existed in Middle Bronze Age II to Late Bronze I. The **royal palace** of the Late Bronze Age occupies the central area of the acropolis (under excavation in the 1990s). There was a great court with a podium opposite the palace entrance. Two columns front the doorway on the west side and appear to lead to a large hall (identified as a throne room), built with walls of mudbrick and cedar, the bases of which are lined with well-cut basalt slabs. It was destroyed in the 13C by a fire which preserved some of the artefacts. A life-size basalt lion couchant in relief has also been found, probably coming from temple or palace (a virtual twin which faces in the opposite direction was found in a Late Bronze Age temple at the opposite end of the site right at the north of the Lower City; these can be seen in the Israel Museum in Jerusalem, see p 255). Massive staircases connected the acropolis to the lower city in the Late Bronze Age, and these can be seen on the north slope of the acropolis.

The remains of the casemate wall of the 10C with a six-chambered gateway also lie in the centre of the acropolis, defending the citadel of the time, which lies further west. To the south of the casemate wall were the foundations of a large storehouse with two rows of pillars which have been dated to the time of Ahab. These buildings have now been moved to a site c 200m to the northwest and rebuilt.

On the south central side of the hill is the *water system. Here a vertical shaft was cut through the accumulated debris from the surface of the acropolis to the bedrock and then its lower section was rock cut to a depth of c 30m. Some 80 steps spiralled down from the surface to the base of the shaft where a sloping, stepped tunnel c 25m long drops another 10m to a pool which taps the groundwater level beneath the site. Attributed to the defensive measures undertaken by Ahab, this system again indicates the manpower at the disposal of the royal house. It can be readily accessed by modern steps.

At the west end of the acropolis is the **citadel**, which was built in the 9C and continued to be used until the destruction of the city in 732 BC, when it was destroyed to its foundations. Proto-Aeolic capitals, though not found in their original position, decorated the entrance to the citadel. It was rebuilt in Assyrian and Hellenistic times. In front of the remains of the citadel, a monolithic slab may be seen, part of an 11C cult place, identified by the standing stone as a high place.

The lower city Overgrown and partly ploughed, this can for the most part be viewed from the acropolis. It is separated from the acropolis by a deep fosse, and on the other sides was surrounded by great man-made ramparts, consisting of banks of earth, stones and mudbrick cores used sometimes to improve an existing natural rise; in other sections a ditch was excavated and the earth built up to create a rampart up to 8m high. Above the rampart were walls and city gates. This was an enormous labour, for the area enclosed is c 1km x 700m; it is the scale which is unusual, but variations on this scheme of defence are found from Qatna, Ebla and Mari in Syria, to Jericho and Egypt. The whole of the area inside the ramparts appears to have been built up with palaces, temples, houses, kilns, cisterns, tunnels and caverns.

An important series of temples were found at Hazor. Their furniture has been removed to museums. A small temple dating to Late Bronze II, with a row of ten stelae (one with a symbol of the crescent moon) and statues of a seated god and of a lion is displayed in the Israel Museum in Jerusalem; copies can be seen in the site museum.

KHIRBAT AL-MINYA

The ruins of a well-preserved palace built by the Umayyad caliph Walid I (705–15) were excavated at Khirbat al-Minya (H. Horvat Minnim) on the shores of the Sea of Galilee. It was reoccupied in the Mamluk period and used as a caravanserai.

To reach it, on Highway 90, c 8.5km north of Tiberias, turn east at the pumping station on the road marked Sappir Site and Kare Deshe for 500m towards the shore of the lake. The ruins of the palace lie amid palm trees and vegetation on the right just beyond a bend in the road.

A building, almost square with three-quarter-round towers at the corners, had semi-round towers at the mid-point of all walls except on the east where the prominent gate is flanked by massive half-round towers capped by a dome. The walls, preserved to nearly the complete height of the ground floor, are constructed of the excellent flat-dressed masonry for which the Umayyads are noted; look for the basalt base courses and a pattern of semi-circles in relief on the interior walls of the gate towers. The plan is typical of the period with a central courtyard surrounded by a portico, which is backed by a range of rooms on all sides. Although the palace was not fully excavated, and mounds of earth still cover large areas, the south wing was identified as the most important, with, from the east, a mosque with mihrab, a throne room, and a suite of five rooms with mosaic-paved floors. Other rooms with mosaic floors (now covered) exist on the west side.

THE CHRISTIAN SITES ON THE SEA OF GALILEE

The Mountain of the Beatitudes with the modern Latin **Church of the Beatitudes** (the Sermon on the Mount) is perhaps the best place to begin a round of visits to the Christian sites on the north shore of the Sea of Galilee. The entrance leads off Highway 90, just north of the lake; open 08.30–12.00, 14.30–17.00 (–16.00 in winter). Standing high on a green hillside, it overlooks the northern shores of the lake, and along with the peaceful setting and a lovely view, it provides the landscape against which to set much of the story of Jesus' ministry. Many of the apostles came from the small towns around the lake shore, such as Capernaum and Bethsaida. It was then a land of fishermen and farmers in small towns and villages. On the slopes descending to the lake are springs, and the remains of reservoirs and channels which fed water-driven grain mills in more recent times. The octagonal church was built in 1938 (architect A. Barluzzi) in Byzantine style with marble veneer casing the lower walls and gold mosaic in the dome; it has cool and quiet gardens, and provides a place to contemplate some of the best-known Christian teachings (Matt. 4:25; 5:1–10; 6:24–29).

*Tabgha, a word derived from Heptapegon or Seven Springs, is the site of the Church of the Loaves and Fishes. It lies down on the shore of the lake, just below the junction of Highways 90 and 87, c 10km north of Tiberias. Open 08.30 (Sun 09.45)–17.00. On this site the Church of the Feeding of the Five Thousand was built c 350 to commemorate the events related in Mark 6: 30–44. The basilica was considerably enlarged c 480, the mosaics were repaired in the 6C, and the church itself destroyed c 685. The site was bought in 1886 by the Deutsche Verein vom Heilige Lande, the site excavated in 1932, and a protective cover built over the mosaics in 1936. The new church was rebuilt in 1982 on the same plan and in the Byzantine architectural style, preserving the magnificent mosaic floor. Under a glass panel can be seen the foundations of the 4C church. Beneath the altar is located the rock on which the loaves and fishes were placed and before it is the charming mosaic (restored) which depicts them. The main mosaic depicts a free-field Nilotic landscape, with pairs of birds in the north aisle, and in the south aisle a Nilometer. (Another Nilotic mosaic can be seen at Sepphoris near Nazareth, see p 338.) Old basalt presses and a font are displayed in the courtyard.

CAPERNAUM
• • • • • • • • • • • • • • •

The site of the finest synagogue of the Byzantine period in Israel (its date the subject of controversy among archaeologists), and also that of the house church of St. Peter, is on the north shore of the Sea of Galilee, on Highway 87. There is a car park and facilities. Open 08.30–16.15; admission charged.

Eating out

Amnon is a moderately priced restaurant on the lakeshore just east of Capernaum, offering fish, salads, wine.

History

Capernaum was a small fishing village on the shore of the lake and was probably inhabited continuously from the 1C BC to the 13C AD.

The excavations have revealed five blocks of rather poor houses in the village, built of the local black basalt stone, each block inhabited by perhaps 100 people. The village developed gradually between the 2C and 4C AD, and changed from a Jewish village in the time of Christ to an increasingly Judaean-Christian population. There are two exceptional structures in the village, the synagogue and the church.

The *synagogue occupies a whole *insula* a little inland from the shore. It is a basilical structure, with a small terrace on the front (south side) and a court on the east side. It is richly decorated, and stands out because, although on a site surrounded by other buildings, it is raised above the adjacent houses and built of imported white limestone. The façade, with three doorways, faces towards Jerusalem. It was originally dated c 200 AD on the basis of the style of the architectural decoration; others suggested the 4C, but a hoard of coins beneath the stone paving also appeared to date its latest stages to the late 5C. Some scholars maintain that the type of synagogue found in Galilee, with façade facing to Jerusalem, is an early type and date the Capernaum synagogue between the 2C and 4C. Others suggest it dates to the late 3C–4C, while a recent radical suggestion attempts to resolve the problems by proposing that as many as four ruined early Galilean synagogues were looted of stone in the 5C, and the Capernaum synagogue was built by Christians, using these varied *spolia*, as a pilgrim shrine on the venerated site of an older house synagogue where Jesus healed the man possessed by a devil (Mark 1:21–28). The proposal attempts to resolve the problems of the many doorways (12 in all instead of the three or four normal in a synagogue), the diverse architectural elements found in the ruins (which are difficult to reconstruct in a coherent system), the late coins and pottery found beneath the floors during the excavations, and the juxtaposition with the prominent church built in the 5C.

The **church** was founded on the traditional site of St. Peter's home in the village (Mark 1: 29–31), closer to the shore, which was venerated as a house shrine by the Judaeo-Christians from the 2C and likely to have been the house church visited by Egeria (AD 381–84). In the 5C the site was levelled and an octagonal church with ambulatory and a mosaic floor with a peacock was built. The church is in the martyrion tradition seen in Jerusalem, and clearly marks a period of increased Christian population and pilgrimage to Capernaum.

This church was destroyed c 636 at the time of the Islamic conquest.

After the conquest the centre of occupation at Capernaum shifted east of the old site; there houses, jetty, fish market and a church dedicated to St. John Theologos existed until the mid-10C. In the Crusader period this village seems to have been little more than seven reused village houses of poor fishermen.

The Franciscan hospice and trees on the lake shore protect a fine array of decorated relief stonework from the excavations, including a depiction of a mobile ark. On the left, olive presses and querns from the site are displayed; beyond are the remains of blocks of ordinary houses built from the Early Roman period onwards. Directly ahead, a large new octagonal church (dedicated 1990) has been built over the preserved remains of the octagonal church of the 5C on the traditional site of the house of St. Peter, which can be viewed below, but is not accessible. To the left are the remains of the **synagogue**, partly reconstructed. The façade has three fine door lintels with palm trees; inside, columns define aisles along the other three sides, with heart-sectioned columns at the corners, both in the synagogue hall and in the adjacent paved courtyard. Note the eight doorways on the east side of the building, set well above the adjacent houses, and the low relief pilasters in the exterior walls.

KORAZIM
• • • • • • • • • •

At Korazim (ancient Chorazin; A. Khirbat Karazah) are the ruins of a Roman-Byzantine town with a synagogue. They lie 4km north of Capernaum and the Sea of Galilee, on Highway 90, between Korazim junction and Almagor, east of Amiad junction. The site is run by the National Parks Authority (☎ 06 693 4982), with some facilities.

The town is mentioned in the Talmud. It is also one of the three cities (with Bethsaida and Capernaum) where Jesus performed most miracles, but whose inhabitants, because they rejected his ministry, were cursed to suffer on the Day of Judgement (Matt. 11:20–24). Chorazin was a town of the 1C–4C AD which flourished especially in the 3C–4C; together with its synagogue at the centre of the town, it was partially destroyed in the early 4C, but rebuilt in the mid-4C and early 5C. The town expanded again in the 8C, but was eventually abandoned. In the 12C–13C a small settlement was established, still surviving in the 16C–17C and, in a small way, to the 20C.

The ruins of the town stand on a low hill, part of an extensive complex of streets and houses forming a large, relatively unplanned, agricultural centre. The remains of several large courtyard buildings lie east of the synagogue. The path from the entrance leads past a stepped ritual bath on the right, and remains of houses on the left. Ahead, the synagogue is similar to those of Capernaum and Baram. Built of the local basalt on a platform, it has steps ascending on the south side from a square in front of the building, leading to three entrances facing Jerusalem. In the prayer hall 12 columns set in a U-shape supported a clerestory. Inside, between the entrances on either side of the main door were the places for the Ark of the Law, and a place for the Torah reading. A basalt throne, with

Aramaic dedication, known as the 'Seat' or 'Cathedra of Moses', found south of the synagogue, has been placed here. Many architectural fragments have been found with relief carving of plants and scenes of rural life, grape-treading, lions, eagle and a bird pecking grapes.

West of the synagogue you can visit a row of partly reconstructed houses, including in the penultimate building a large oil press. The larger, public buildings lay to the east and north of the synagogue.

Dolmens which may date to the late fourth and late third millennia are to be found in the basalt-strewn countryside around; most were robbed in ancient times, and some were reused in later periods.

GAMLA
• • • • • • • • •

Today an archaeological site and a nature reserve in the basalt landscape of the Syrian Golan, Gamla was a city besieged during the First Jewish Revolt, whose inhabitants, according to Josephus, leapt off the precipice rather than face capture by the Romans.

It is in the southern Golan, off Highway 869, 2km north of Daliyot Junction. Check before visiting, as this is a military area which is sometimes closed to the public on weekdays (Nature Reserve, ☎ 06 682 2282). Snack bar.

History

> Mentioned in the time of Alexander Jannaeus c 83/80 BC, and variously in the following years, the town maintained its allegiance to Rome on the outbreak of the First Revolt, but then switched to the Jewish side, when its defence was put under the command of Josephus, who fortified the ridge and later described the Roman campaign in detail. A seven-month siege by the Romans in AD 67 failed, but the city fell shortly after to Vespasian (War IV.3.83). Archaeological finds from the site include Early Bronze Age structures and coins of the 3C BC.

Remains of the ancient settlement on the ridge can be reached by a steep descent (20 minutes) from the plateau. The remains include the city wall and gate, which defended the precipitous ridge with the town on the south flank. Adjacent to the north wall is an early synagogue, a rectangular structure, oriented approximately south towards Jerusalem, with an ambulatory surrounding benches and columns; the corner columns are heart-shaped in section. Adjacent are a court and ritual bath. They were destroyed by the Romans during the First Revolt; many of the slingstones, arrowheads and other evidence of the siege were recovered in the excavations in this area, where the wall was breached in the final assault. To the southwest, near the top of the ridge, high-quality houses were excavated. Other remains include an olive press of the 1C AD (partly restored).

In the nature reserve are some of the many basalt dolmens found in the region, these ones thought to date to the third millennium. The reserve contains the nesting site of griffon vultures, marked trails, and a waterfall.

KURSI
• • • • • •

At Kursi on the shores of the Sea of Galilee are the ruins of a large monastery, which in Byzantine times appears to have commemorated the Miracle of the Gadarene Swine. It lies 5km north of Ein Gev and is reached by Highway 92, on the east shore of the Sea of Galilee. National Parks Authority, ☎ 06 673 1983.

This was a Jewish fishing village in the Roman period, with a built harbour and a fish-holding pond.

A very large monastery was built in the mid-5C in the place where tradition-ally Jesus cast out the demons besetting a madman, changing them into swine that rushed to their doom in the lake (the Miracle of the Gadarene Swine, Mark 5: 1–20). Although Kursi lies at some distance from the town of Gadara, it is at least on the lake shore. The monastery was damaged in the Persian invasion in AD 614, repaired, then abandoned in the 8C. The church contains a large mosaic pavement which depicts many birds, fish and plants; the baptistery mosaic had a Greek inscription. The partly reconstructed church and chapel lie in an attractive setting adjacent to the road.

ARBEL
• • • • • •

An ancient Jewish settlement and the residence of several rabbis and scholars (such as Nittai of Arbela) from the 2C BC to the 8C AD, Arbel is located on a hill on the north side of Nahal Arbel (Wadi al-Hamam) c 9km northwest of Tiberias. To get there, leave Tiberias by the Nazareth road, turning off to the north on Route 7717 through Kfar Hittim and Moshav Arbel, then northeast through the settlement to the top of the cliffs, which provide a panoramic view to the north-ern end of the Sea of Galilee.

Arbel has the remains of an interesting synagogue built, like that at Capernaum, in white limestone in the centre of a black basalt village; it is dated to the 4C AD, with a monolithic T-frame main door on the east side and a mono-lithic chest built into the north wall. The site is also notable for the fortified net-work of caves in the cliffs which served as refuges and were used during Herod's fight against the Galilean Zealots supporting the Hasmoneans, and in later times.

TIBERIAS
• • • • • • • • • •

An important city from Roman to Islamic times, Tiberias (A. Tabariyya) with its springs and fine setting beneath the cliffs on the shores of the Lake of Tiberias, controlled the entrances to Palestine from the north and east. Now the main town on the Sea of Galilee, it is a popular holiday spot.

Tiberias is on Highway 90, on the west shore of the Sea of Galilee, 157km from Jerusalem.

Practical information

Tourist information
The Tourist Information Office (☎ 06 672 5666) is in a medieval building on the east side of HaBanim, beside the archaeological park just inside the south line of the old city walls; open Sun–Thur 08.00–13.00, 14.00–17.00, Fri 08.00–12.00. An excellent map of the town and vicinity can be purchased here.

Getting around
The **bus station** is near the west end of Rehov HaYarden; information on transport in town and the region is available here and at the tourist information office. Boat trips run regularly to Capernaum, Ginosar and EnGev.
Tourist Taxi service, ☎ 06 673 1238.

Where to stay
Scottish Guest House, ☎ 06 672 3769; *Aviv Hostel and Hotel*, ☎ 06 672 0007; *Continental Hotel*, ☎ 06 672 0018; *Panorama Hotel*, ☎ 06 672 0963; *Galei Kinneret Hotel*, ☎ 06 672 8888. At Kibbutz Ginosar, 6km north, are *Nof Ginosar Hotel*, Kibbutz Ginosar, Israel 14980, ☎ 06 679 2161 and *Hostel*, ☎ 06 679 8762.

Eating out
Many fish restaurants line the waterfront in Tiberias. The *Nof Ginosar Hotel* has a restaurant, and at the entrance to Kibbutz Ginosar is a 'chicken in a glove' restaurant.

History

The town was founded as his capital by Herod Antipas c AD 20, and named for the Roman Emperor Tiberias. The Roman city lay north of the springs, but did not extend as far north as the Crusader and medieval Islamic town. Josephus describes the palace of Herod Antipas, the treasury, the archives and the synagogue during that time. From AD 44 the town was under the Roman procurators, and from AD 61 it was included in the kingdom of Agrippa II, whose capital was at Caesarea Philippi (see Banias). The city joined the First Revolt, and its inhabitants built defensive walls which survived the surrender of the city. From AD 96 the town was under direct Roman rule and flourished. A temple was built in honour of Hadrian, and Tiberias became a colonia in the time of Elagabalus. During the early 2C AD it became increasingly a Jewish city, the Sanhedrin was moved here from Sepphoris c AD 235, afterwards also the Jewish patriarchate, and it became the great centre for talmudic studies. A bishop is recorded in AD 451.

Tiberias developed all the facilities of a city in the 4C–6C, in particular the baths around the springs which were regarded as having medicinal and health-restoring properties. The western boundary of the Byzantine city was on Mt Berenice, 200m above the lake, and to the south the walls were extended to enclose the springs of Hammat Tiberias. Parts of the walls, gate, *cardo*, drains, and in the city centre, the theatre, bath house, market place, a basilica (converted into a church certainly by the 5C–6C), exedra and houses have been excavated, mostly now covered by buildings. On Mt Berenice, a 6C church was built in the time of Justinian. Also in the 6C, the Yeshiva (Jewish

Academy) was established as having supreme Jewish religious authority even above the Sanhedrin, and it continued to exist after the Islamic conquest in the 7C.

A later Arab writer (Yaqut c 1225) says that, following the conquest of 634, the Muslims took half the houses and churches, leaving the Christians the remainder. In the 8C there were churches (one being presumably the church on Mt Berenice which was rebuilt in the mid-8C) and synagogues according to a Christian pilgrim (Willibald); and in the early 9C five churches and a community of nuns are mentioned including a church dedicated to St. Peter. Under the Arabs, Tabariya became the principal city in the north of Palestine (supplanting Beth Shean) and nearly all of the main buildings remained in use. In the 10C the Great Mosque stood in the centre of the town with the baths to the south. In the 11C the city began to decline and was then destroyed in an earthquake in 1033.

Godfrey of Bouillon probably found a small town in 1099, and in 1100 it was given to Tancred along with the important principality of Galilee. From before the 11C the region had been vulnerable to tribal incursions, and in the 12C it was a strategically important frontier with Damascus. It faced attacks, and in turn mounted attacks. The city was rebuilt partly to the north of the old location. The Crusaders fortified it. Tancred richly endowed its church, possibly on the site of an old Byzantine Orthodox round church, but in the 12C the archbishop's seat was in Nazareth and only later was a suffragan bishop appointed in Tiberias. The location of the cathedral is not known; but the Church of St. George is located in a rebuilt phase of the old church on Mt. Berenice. In all 12 churches, a castle chapel and two hospitals are mentioned in Crusader Tiberias. The Hospital in Jerusalem owned property here too. In the 12C the population seems to have been mixed; according to a Jewish source (Benjamin of Tudela) there were then some 50 Jewish families and a synagogue in the town.

After it was captured by Salah al-Din in 1187, the wife of the prince of Galilee held out in the castle, but she had to surrender following the disastrous Battle of the Horns of Hattin and received a safe conduct to Tripoli. Salah al-Din dismantled the defences in 1190. In 1240 an agreement was reached that the Franks and Muslims should exercise joint control over Sidon, Safad and Galilee with Tiberias, but the following year Richard of Cornwall gained complete control of Tiberias, and the refortification began soon after. In 1244 the Khwarizmian Turks bypassed it, but in 1247 the Ayyubids captured it and massacred the defenders. It remained in Ayyubid-Egyptian hands in 1283, and was in ruins in the early 14C. A neglected Muslim shrine to Sitt Sukaina, daughter of Husain ibn Ali, dated 1295, stands in the Arab graveyard on high ground to the south of the city. In medieval times the Muslim tombs of Joshua son of Nun, and of Abu Hurairah, companion of the Prophet, were also important. In the mid-14C a Christian monastery and three holy houses are mentioned, probably all maintained by Orthodox native Christians; in the early 15C seven churches are mentioned. In 1560 Sultan Sulaiman (the Magnificent) granted Tiberias to the powerful Jewish-Portuguese banker/diplomat Don Josef Nasi, who rebuilt the town walls and again encouraged the Jewish community. He is also recorded as dismantling and recycling the materials of a ruined church. In 1749 the great Bedouin ruler Dahir al-Umar fortified the city with the walls still visible today. Jewish immigration from the end of the 19C led to a Palestinian revolt in 1938. Zionist forces had taken the town by April 1948 and the town is now entirely Jewish.

The pleasant climate of Tiberias makes it a restful place: the temperature in January ranges from 8° to18°C and in August from 22° to 36°C; mean annual rainfall is 431mm. Its location on the shores of the lake also add to its attractions. As a centre of tourism as well as a regional centre, its shops and promenades are nearly always busy.

The city walls

Parts of the north wall of the Byzantine city are preserved in the Archaeological Park on the east side of HaBannim. The walls were built by Justinian in the mid-6C AD, were 2.5m thick, of well-cut ashlar masonry and with external towers. They ran west from the lake and climbed the steep slopes of Mt Berenice, the summit of which is 600m back from and 200m above the shore, where more sections are preserved. The walls were 2.8km in length and enclosed an area of 77 hectares. A south gate, flanked by round towers but probably not attached to walls until the 6C, was built early in the 1C AD, probably as a monumental entrance at the time of the founding of the city. Many of the structures around it date to the 8C–10C. The line of the Byzantine walls seems to have existed until the 11C.

The 18C town covered c 15 hectares. The substantial remains of its walls, of black basalt masonry, can be seen at various points in the centre of the modern town. The outer wall on the landward side had a castle attached on the inner face of the north wall, with projecting, well-preserved round towers whose upper storeys have gun slits. This so-called 'Crusader Castle' lies c 250m north of the centre, at the corner of Elhadeff and Tajar streets, a four-towered citadel built by Sulaybi/Salibi, the son of Dahir al-Umar in 1745. It now serves as artists' studios and restaurants. A fine basalt lintel from Tiberias is displayed on the terrace of the Mayer Institute in Jerusalem.

Other sights

The **Great Mosque**, now a sadly neglected and locked structure in the northern centre of the town, was built in 1743 by Dahir al-Umar of black basalt, with a porch, domed prayer hall and octagonal minaret. The minaret has darker string courses and gallery. The porch has a triple dome, fronting the *ablaq* (coloured coursed) façade. The central door gives onto the prayer hall, with squinches supporting a drum with traces of plaster muqarnas decoration. The right-hand window gives access to a spiral stair ascending the minaret. The interior walls, the mihrab and the minbar are also faced with *ablaq* stonework. Small columns are missing from the mihrab, and the decoration has been defaced and damaged.

The **Scottish Hospice of St. Andrew** stands on the left at the end of HaYarden overlooking the shore. Established as a Protestant medical mission in 1885, when it was the only hospital in the Tiberias region, it served as a maternity hospital until the end of the 1950s, and has been a hospice since, with garden, chapel and meditation and study rooms. To the left, the lakeside promenade was built during the Mandate Period following a disastrous flood in May 1934 when rainwater from the hills overwhelmed the old houses along the shore.

As you walk along the promenade, at 50m on the right, with an entryway between restaurants, is the unpretentious Franciscan **Church of St. Peter**, formerly the 12C Church of St. Nicholas, built of local black basalt (open daily 08.00–11.45, 14.00–17.00 except Sun and major holidays). The earliest record of this church is in the 14C, and thereafter the building has a very complex history. It became a mosque in the 16C. In 1641 the Franciscans had permission from the Turkish government to visit and live in Tiberias, and by 1649 had bought the property but were prevented by the existence of a mihrab from occupying it. They overcame this problem in the mid-18C, possibly through the good offices of Dahir al-Umar. Greek Catholics thereafter maintained the services. Many repairs and alterations (including the west façade) were made in 1860–70, and the bell tower and hospice added. In 1933 it became the Roman Catholic parish church for Tiberias. It is a small building with single nave; the original single apse exists with pointed chevet, lancet windows and aumbries. A basalt tomb slab of older date is displayed in the garden.

Further south along the promenade the small mosque with short cylindrical minaret is the **Sea Mosque** (A. Jami al-Bahar), partly restored. The mosque was built perhaps in the mid-18C or c 1880, and stands, as its name implies, on the edge of the lake. The mosque itself has an agglomeration of buildings around a courtyard which contains an anonymous tomb. The main entrance was originally on the west, with on the east a sea entrance to the basement which permitted fishermen to moor their boats, and enter for prayers directly. The blocked sea entrance can today just be seen down grilles off the promenade. The prayer hall has four domes supported by a central, monolithic Byzantine column; the mihrab was formerly tiled, and traces of the minbar survive on the wall to its right. On its landward side are some surviving vaults of the Crusader castle of Tiberias.

On the landward side, just west of the *Sheraton Hotel*, is the **Archaeological Park**, with a small modern outdoor theatre attached. It contains a Crusader structure, now the Information Centre, a building identified as a synagogue, and some houses, and is the site for a planned museum. The remains of a large Crusader church, its identification unknown, probably of 12C date, had three aisles of five bays, with three (now missing) apses; in the northwest corner, stairs descend to a crypt. There was a place for a reliquary in the nave. The remains are now preserved under a raised timber floor in the courtyard of the *Jordan River Hotel*, just north of the Archaeological Park, but it is not easy to see them. To the south of the park is a section of the Byzantine city wall. At the south end of the promenade is a Greek Orthodox Monastery on older foundations.

Venerated Jewish tombs are also located in or on the slopes above Tiberias. The **Tomb of Maimonides** (Rabbi Moses ben Maimon, the Rambam, 1135–1204) is c 250 m to the northwest of the 18C castle. Born in Spain, which he left following the fall of Cordoba in 1148, then settled in Fez under forced conversion to Islam, Maimonides became a great Jewish scholar, writer and in 1185 physician to al-Fadil, Salah al-Din's vizier in Cairo. He visited the Holy Land briefly in 1165 and his tomb in Tiberias is a place of pilgrimage. The **tomb of Rabbi Akiva**, who was tortured and executed by the Romans in Caesarea in AD 135 is also traditionally located at Tiberias, at a white domed cave tomb on the slopes above the city.

The eastern summit of **Mt Berenice**, traditionally named for the sister of Agrippa II, rises above Tiberias. Two towers and a section of the city wall of Justinian are well preserved, at this point 3.2m wide; the towers still stand 5m–6m high and were probably originally c 12m high; the wall, built of basalt and cement, was probably originally 8m–10m high. A square gate tower (less well preserved) c 60m east of the northern tower served as a west entrance to the city. Inside the western angle of the city wall a cistern and an oil press were discovered. The wall was extended up the mountain in order to enclose Justinian's newly built church overlooking the scenes of Jesus' miracles. This too was built of basalt, with mosaic and *opus sectile* pavings. It consisted of atrium, narthex and basilical church with three aisles ending in three apses; a bema stood opposite the sanctuary, edged by marble chancel screens. Beneath a marble slab in the centre of the sanctuary a large basalt anchor was found, a suitable relic of safety and hope for Christians. The church had a tiled roof supported on two rows of monolithic columns, which were sawn up and reused in the 8C. A very large vaulted cistern lies beneath the courtyard. The church was again rebuilt in the 12C and was probably dedicated to St. George.

Outside the town

Hammat Tiberias, with hot springs and ancient baths, is 2km beyond the centre, at the south end of the city. The new **Hammam Sulaiman Museum** (the Museum of the History of the Baths of Tiberias) comes under the National Parks Authority (☎ 06 672 5287). The important springs (60°C) were used anciently for their therapeutic qualities, and remains from the 1C BC onwards have been excavated, including baths built by Herod. Medieval baths were also built, and the springs continue to attract visitors today. Two synagogues have been located here, one dating to the 3C AD. There is a 4C mosaic with Jewish symbols including the Ark, a seven-branched candelabra, a central zodiac and a fine lion. Synagogues of the 6C and the 7C–8C were also found. Above the springs are two late 19C synagogues built around the traditional blue-domed tomb of Rabbi Ba'al haNes, a Jewish scholar of the 2C AD.

Kibbutz Ginosar (6km north of Tiberias on Highway 90) contains the *ancient boat in the Yigal Alon Museum, a superb new display of a boat dating to around the 1C AD, recovered from the mud at the edge of the Sea of Galilee. The ancient history of the boat is not known, but it provides information on the types of boats which were used on the lake in the time of Christ. Admission charged.

BELVOIR
• • • • • • • •

This castle of the Knights Hospitaller was built in the 12C on a promontory of the central hills, with a superb view eastwards over the Jordan Valley and to the hills of Ajlun in Jordan. It is 6km west up the steep hillsides by Route 717, off Highway 90, 15km north of Beth Shean. The site is maintained by the National Parks Authority (☎ 06 658 1766).

History

The land on which Belvoir (A. Kawkab al-Hawa, H. Kochav Hayarden) would be built was farmed by a Frankish family called Velos in the time of Fulk of Anjou (1131–43), who sold it to the Hospitallers in 1168. The Knights built the fortress to control the bridges of the upper Jordan Valley and the mouth of the Yarmuk river, and held it successfully against Salah al-Din in 1182/83. The Muslim forces built the castle of Ajlun opposite to it in 1184/85. However, when the Crusader Kingdom fell at the Battle of the Horns of Hattin in 1187, the castle was left isolated. The garrisons at Belvoir and Safad held out, but the Muslim army continued the siege, and in 1189 they mined the east tower of the outer fortifications. The defenders saw the position was hopeless and sued for peace in return for their lives and free passage to Tyre. The castle was repaired by Salah al-Din. Only when the Muslims feared the Crusaders might retake the area did al-Mu'azzam order it to be dismantled in 1219. It was returned to the Franks under the terms of an agreement between al-Salah Ayyub and Richard of Cornwall in 1241, but the Franks were unable to restore it. By the early 19C the ruins were occupied by a small Arab village, whose inhabitants were pushed out in 1948; the ruins were restored in 1966–67.

Although most of the superstructure is missing, the layout of the castle is well preserved, and on the flat plateau edge at Belvoir the builders could produce a 'textbook' plan, without the usual need to adapt it to the contours of the site. The castle had a square version of the normal concentric plan, built of the local basalt stone, but with particular importance given to the outer dry ditch which was the first line of defence. It is 20m wide and 12m deep and surrounds the outer fortifications which have projecting rectangular corner and median towers. The massive barbican controlling the complex main entrance and the approach from the east was mined by the Muslim army in 1191. A second entrance on the west was protected by a drawbridge; and there were additional postern gates concealed at the foot of the west, the southwest, the south, the east and the northeast towers. The extensive ranges of vaults in the outer bailey were used for storage and stabling. Two large vaulted cisterns served respectively the inner and outer bailey. The inner ward, almost square with projecting corner towers, had gates on east and west, the west gate protected by a projecting gate tower with bent entrance and machicolations over the gate. The inner ward had a central court surrounded by kitchen and stables on the ground floor; on the storey above were the refectory and dormitory; the chapel occupied the area above the gate on the west side. Unlike the rest of the castle, the chapel was built of white limestone. Some fine fragments of church sculpture were discovered during excavation, probably deriving from the chapel; they included marble pillars, capitals, a carved head and a relief depicting an angel, dated c 1170–75.

BETH SHEAN
• • • • • • • • • • • • •

The uncovered ruins of Beth Shean (Old Testament Beth-shan, classical Scythopolis, A. Baysan), a great city flattened by the earthquake of AD 749, are a spectacular sight, and the unreconstructed sections are a vivid illustration of the earthquake damage. In an area of great agricultural fertility at the east end of the Jezreel Plain, producing linen and a great variety of other crops, controlling important routes and a crossing of the Jordan River, the inhabitants had great resources, but were still vulnerable to the politics of the neighbouring empires. Important in the Bronze and Iron Ages, but as one of the relatively independent Cities of the Decapolis (a federation of ten city-states in the region), Scythopolis flourished under Roman rule and was very wealthy. Its architecture is characterised by use of the local black basalt stone for much of the substructure, though the surfaces of the public buildings were covered with limestone or more expensive imported marbles and granite. The lower city, lying between a fine theatre and the great looming tell (Tell al-Husn) of the ancient city, can be viewed in a rapid stroll of about one hour, but well rewards a longer visit. The whole ancient city covered an area of c 131 hectares and was enclosed within walls in the Hellenistic, Roman and Byzantine periods. The ancient tell and the main buildings of the Lower City lie approximately at the centre of the city.

The site is 120km north-northeast of Jerusalem, with the entrance off Highway 71 just before its junction with Highway 90. It is managed by the National Parks Authority (☎ 06 658 7189). Excellent facilities and a car park are located at the entrance to the site, with an adjacent park and supermarket. There is a well-organised visitor trail, and transport is available.

History

The history of this great site should be divided into two parts; first the much longer history of the tell where the Bronze and Iron Age city was located; and second that of the classical city on the land below (where remains of the Chalcolithic period have also been found).

The great **tell** or mound of ruins near the centre of Beth Shean rises 50m above a small river. It was occupied from the fifth millennium almost continuously. Following the Egyptian conquest by Tuthmosis III in 1468 BC, the city was a centre of Egyptian administration and cult. The important finds from the series of temples, notably the stelae (particularly those of Seti I and Ramses II), reliefs and inscribed architectural fragments, are now mainly in the Rockefeller Museum in Jerusalem. The dedications include Canaanite deities.

According to the Old Testament, it was a city from which the Canaanites were not driven out by Joshua (Judges I:27). After the Philistines found Saul dead on the battlefield at Mt Gilboa, they cut off his head and nailed the body on the city walls of Beth-shan (I Sam.31:8–10). Only later, in the time of David, is the town said to have been captured by the Israelites. In the 10C Baana son of Ahilud was Solomon's governor of Beth-shan and other cities in the region (I Kings 4:12). Egyptian texts record that the Egyptian pharaoh Sheshonq captured it in 925 BC, and Assyrian texts that it fell to the Assyrian ruler Tiglath-Pileser III in 732 BC.

The **lower city** was established following the campaign of Alexander the Great in 332 BC; it grew into a fully Hellenised city called Scythopolis (City of the Scythians—people of south central Russia, who were settled here) or Nysa (after the nurse of Dionysus, who tradition claimed was buried here) and the cult of Dionysus was important in the city. Houses of the Hellenistic period have been found on the north side, at Tell Iztabba. The city was captured and at least partly destroyed by the Hasmoneans in 107 BC; refusing to convert to Judaism, the inhabitants left.

A pagan city in Roman hands from 63 BC, the city became the only major member of the League of the Decapolis located west of the Jordan River. Its fortunes were at this time linked to the flourishing Roman cities of south Syria and north Jordan and it provided an important trade outlet for those inland regions to the coast. There was a great temple on the upper tell, of which just the basalt foundations were preserved, probably dedicated to Dionysus and probably dating to the 1C–2C AD. It may have been the only structure, apart from a water reservoir, on the mound at this time, and thus a very prominent monument. A marble statue head, possibly also of Dionysus was found nearby. The remaining Jewish inhabitants were killed during the First Revolt, and the pagan status of the city was confirmed after the suppression of the revolt. Scythopolis continued to be a largely pagan city, prospering under Hadrian, Antoninus Pius and Marcus Aurelius; and it was the capital of the province of Second Palestine at the end of the 4C, by which time it was becoming Christian (according to Epiphanius the whole population was Christian by the mid-4C, which is probably an exaggeration).

A great round church with ambulatory around an open court and with a single apse had replaced the temple on top of the great tell by the early 5C AD; it was surrounded by houses, and approached by a paved road from a gate at the northwest edge of the tell. Other churches and monasteries existed in the lower city. During the 6C the city had an estimated population of 30–40,000 people and covered c 131 hectares. It was captured by the Muslims in 636 and then reverted to its old Semitic name, but was destroyed in the great earthquake of 749. The circular church on Tell al-Husn survived to 806, and was succeeded by a maze of streets and rooms within a city or citadel wall which was occupied to at least the 10C and possibly later.

The lower city changed rapidly following the earthquake of 749, with parts of the central area changing from public to residential use, and large parts being given over to industrial use—pottery making and flour-milling—in the Umayyad period; the city declined to a small rural settlement in the Abbasid period and occupation increasingly moved southwards. During the Crusader period a castle was built east of the amphitheatre. A Mamluk mosque served the small town of Baysan during Mamluk, Ottoman and Mandate times. Since 1948 the modern town has received many Jewish immigrants and now has a population of c 15,000.

The line of the eastern city wall is known. It forms the bridge over the Nahal Harod near the northeast corner with, beyond the bridge, a city gate. The line of the north wall of the city follows the high ground, and a church and a monastery mark its line. Only sections of the wall have been identified on the west side, and very little of the southern line is known; it may have enclosed the amphitheatre which lies at the south end, along the modern main road, near the Crusader castle. Most of the outer area would have contained the residential sections of the city, very little of which has been excavated except for Early Bronze Age III and Hellenistic houses on Tell Iztabba.

The lower city

The lower town has been the object of a huge programme of excavation and restoration since about 1980. Excellent information panels with artist's reconstructions decorate the site and generally combine well with the fascinating and visible survival of earthquake destruction; the unreconstructed buildings give a more graphic picture of the city than complete large-scale on-site reconstruction achieves. The layout of the town is not regular, but is successfully adapted to the site; in particular, it is oriented to the central ancient tell which towers over the site, and to the southern hillside into which the theatre is built. The area between was built over a series of structural vaults and terraces to level the ground and permit drainage for the underlying stream, the Nahal Amal, which joined the Nahal Harod northeast of the tell, and served additionally to remove the waste water from the latrines and bath houses. The city we see which was destroyed in the earthquake of AD 749 was based in part on an older Roman layout, with major phases of development in the 2C, 4C and 6C. It is clear that the inhabitants of Scythopolis were proud of the image projected by their city.

Notable for its size, and its construction in basalt and marble, the ***Roman theatre** seated c 7000 in three tiers of seats, of which only the lower tier, the basalt base of the middle tier, and some pilasters from the upper tier are preserved. It was built in the 1C AD and rebuilt in the late 2C AD and probably continued in use for various purposes right up to the 7C. The theatre had sophisticated sounding devices at the level of the second tier; eight passage entrances (*vomitoria*) gave access to the seats, and two entrances beside the stage led to the orchestra, which was marble paved and surrounded by grander seats for important citizens and visitors. The stage was originally paved with stone, and the backdrop, the *scaenae frons*—now reconstructed—decorated with imported marble and granite columns, and relief carving. A portico fronted the street outside the theatre, and on the east side a fine Byzantine stair curved up the rear wall of the theatre, providing access from the city in the later stages of its use.

The grand main street of the city, **Palladius Street**, leads north from the theatre. The modern name derives from a dedicatory inscription of a 4C AD governor. Paved first with basalt in diagonal patterns, and later with marble, with main drain beneath, it had on either side a raised walk with mosaic floor, and a portico with shops. Beneath it is an earlier street of the 2C–3C AD. At the west side of the street opposite the theatre, a propylaeum led up to and was linked by a mosaic paving to the **west bath house**. The large and frequently repaired and modified bath house, was also a major centre of social life in the Byzantine city. It had all the facilities for hot and warm rooms, served by a vast furnace and hypocaust system, while its shady porticoes, stoas and pools were ideal for relaxation and exercise. On the north side of the propylaeum was a latrine. The large halls were roofed with stone vaults and domes, and had painted plastered walls and marble mosaic floors; the late apse at the northwest corner had a glass wall mosaic. The bath house has been carefully conserved.

Immediately north of the bath house, a **Roman odeon** (or *bouleterion*) with c 350 seats belonged to an earlier phase of the city. This small theatre which had various civic purposes, was partly destroyed by the later exedra built above its east side. The exedra (also called the Sigma because of the shape of the Greek letter) is located adjacent to the centre of Palladius Street. A dedication records that it was built by Theosebius, son of Theosebius, governor of Palaestina Secunda in

AD 507. Another grand civic amenity, its semicircular court or plaza was backed by a colonnaded portico and small rooms paved with mosaics; in one, adjacent to the central apse, a medallion representing the guardian goddess of the city, the Tyche, was uncovered: you can see a replica.

Across Palladius Street from the Sigma is a large open area, the location of the **Byzantine agora**. The agora was constructed at around the same time as Palladius Street in the late 4C to early 5C; it was built over a fill, bounded by shops on the west, the theatre on the south, and the east bath house on the east, and had mosaic paved porticoes on these three sides. Some of the mosaics depict large and lively animals. Later in the 6C the agora was reduced in size and areas of *opus sectile* pavement were laid.

The northeast section of the Byzantine agora was built over the **basilica** which was the main civic building of the older Roman town. It was one of the first structures to be built in this area, possibly in the 1C BC, but certainly by the 1C AD. Its foundations are of basalt, with upper walls of soft limestone, coated with stucco and partly lined with marble tiles (*opus sectile*); a second phase dates to the 2C AD. The basilica was decorated with columns and Ionic capitals. At the centre of a central apse at the north end an altar dedicated to Dionysus in AD 141/42 was discovered. The basilica collapsed, perhaps in the 4C, possibly after the earthquake in 363, and was abandoned before the agora was built.

After the Islamic conquest, the whole character of this area changed. The area near the basilica became largely residential under the Umayyads, with an Abbasid mosque being built immediately south of the apse of the basilica. In the Umayyad period the area was crossed by an aqueduct, and flour mills were built over the area of the propylaeum and shops in Palladius Street. A large Umayyad pottery workshop was built over the south end of the Byzantine agora and utilised parts of the theatre. It contained vats for storing and settling clay, and the remains of ten kilns in its courtyard, all of which were destroyed in the earthquake of 749.

Continuing down the street, at the north end on the right, at an angle not aligned to the street, lies a **temple** of the 2C AD fronting a small piazza. The dedication of this small but central temple with semicircular plan, overlooking an important crossroads, is not certain. According to an inscription a statue of Marcus Aurelius stood here; the temple may have been dedicated to the cult of the Roman emperors. Raised on basalt vaults, four large columns stood on pedestals and supported a gabled roof at a height of 15m above the street. Two of the collapsed columns survive. It was destroyed no later than the end of the 4C. Opposite is a spacious propylaeum which lies against the flank of the tell behind; it would be a likely placement for a forecourt leading up to a temple of Dionysus on the top of the tell. To the west the spectacular collapsed ruins of another important colonnaded street ran below the west side of the tell to the west gate of the city. To the east a road bounds the north side of the central section of the city, and a Roman colonnade and Byzantine public building can be seen on the left, with the Antonius monument from which the columns have fallen. A footpath leads up to the top of Tell al-Husn from this point (see below).

On the south side of the road, next to the temple, is the **nymphaeum** or public fountain. An exedra with pool, two tiers of columns and elaborate carving originated in the 2C AD and was remodelled in the 4C. Next to the nymphaeum, and at the top of a major colonnaded street running northeast along the east flank of the tell, is the central monument. This consists of a nearly square platform faced with limestone niches, which supported a decorated column structure which may, like the nymphaeum, have marked the centre of the city.

Valley Street, the bridge and the northern city

The street running northeast along the east side of the tell follows the Nahal Amal, and has the modern name 'Valley Street'. Leading to the northeast gate of the city, it was also paved with basalt in the Roman period, colonnaded, and backed by shops. Street and pavement together were c 24m wide. In the 4C–5C AD its portico too had mosaic flooring.

About 400m northeast along Valley Street, the road with its porticoes crosses the Nahal Harod by a bridge which was also the city wall. The **bridge** is a well-preserved Roman-Byzantine structure, in all c 154m in length. It consists of massive stone embankments (on the south c 73m, on the north c 36m in length) which had two-storey rooms constructed on them; two great stone piers supported three vaults which stood 14m above the river bed; the actual bridge was 45m long. Valley Street then continues up the hill beyond, inside the city wall to the northeast gate. The city wall here is 2.5m wide, and the gate is a single passage gate probably dating to the 2C AD. Twenty Late Byzantine shops, probably built in the late 6C, adjoined the city wall by the gate. The shops had a short life, probably going out of use at the time of the Persian invasion in 614. A workshop for blowing glass of the same date was also found here. The road continued outside the gate, and the city wall runs northwest up Tell Iztabba, where a square tower on the outer face has been recorded.

On the hill to the northwest, remains of houses of the Hellenistic period have been excavated; built in the 2C BC, they lie both inside and outside the line of the later city wall. The line of the Hellenistic city wall seems to have been further north. The houses have small rooms arranged around a central courtyard in an orderly layout. The contents included wine amphorae imported from the islands of Rhodes and Cos, some with Greek graffiti. The quarter was destroyed by fire near the end of the 2C BC, probably due to the Hasmonean attack. Also on Tell Iztabba are the remains of a Martyr's Church (the dedicatee unidentified), with trifoliate apses and colourful mosaic in the nave; the central apse had a reliquary box and an *opus sectile* style pavement, as well as marble chancel screen panels and colonnettes. A large chapel was built at the east end of the north aisle. Between the chapel and the city wall was another room, identified as a refectory with attached kitchen, and 15m away the small Church of the Metropolitan Andreas was excavated; it had one apse and three aisles with two superimposed mosaic floors throughout. The lower floors were of better quality than the upper ones. Built against the inside face of the city wall, 700m west of the northeast gate, is a monastery founded c 567 by a Lady Mary (Kyra Maria), where fine mosaics were discovered, with scrolls and geometric patterns inhabited by human and animal figures.

On the west side of the city a single-spanned Roman bridge existed but was replaced in 1877 by a new bridge, the Jisr al-Khan. The foundations of the Roman bridge, which was c 20m long and c 18m wide, still exist within it. A basalt-paved road ran along the south bank of the Nahal Harod and was carried across the stream at this point. The remains of the west gate appear to be of similar date and appearance to the northeast gate, but more richly decorated. The road continued west towards Caesarea.

The east side of the lower city

Returning to the central monument, to the east there was a Roman and Byzantine street and portico, now called 'Sylvanus Street'. The reconstruction drawing of the Roman portico and reflecting pool brings the ruins to life. Shops were built over the pool area at a later date.

To the south, in the block east of the agora, is the Byzantine **east bath house** which occupied almost the whole length of the block and was nearly as large as that on the west side of the agora. The bath house was originally built in the 2C AD but was considerably modified in the late 4C and then continued in use to the end of the Byzantine period. The hot rooms were on the east side; bordering the street at the south end and thus also serving the nearby theatre is a fine 57-seater latrine, on the west is the frigidarium with apse at the south end which probably contained a fountain, a hall and three pools; the pools had niches containing statues of Graeco-Roman deities, such as Leda and the Swan, Hercules, Hermes and Aphrodite.

On the south side of this bath house was another basalt-paved Byzantine street. On its south side, partly beneath the portico in front of the theatre, is a square Early Roman cult enclosure (originally 1C–2C AD with colonnade and painted plaster), approached by a broad flight of steps, with linked fountain (with relief-carved lion and lioness heads as water spouts) and water installations. In the stylobate area behind, which was constructed with columns and pools, was discovered a dedication to Hygeia, goddess of health. In the Byzantine period there was a fountain house and reservoirs here. The visitor can follow the path around the back of the theatre to the exit.

The upper city

The top five levels of the tell were removed in the excavations between 1921 and 1933, when a deep cut was also made into the lower 15 levels. Renewed excavations have taken place in the 1960s and since the mid-1980s, but apart from some reconstructed brickwork, there is now little to be seen of the seven millennia of Beth Shean. However, the climb is worthwhile for the fine view which can be had from the top over the city and surroundings. A stepped footpath leads up the side of the tell from opposite the nymphaeum in the lower city, although the easiest access is from the northwest.

The **amphitheatre** lies outside the park, adjacent to the highway. In its original 2C AD form it was a hippodrome, which was converted into the visible amphitheatre in the 4C. Walls 3m high around the arena protected up to 6000 spectators from the wild beasts and the gladiatorial events in Roman times. Its use declined after the Christianisation of the city and many of the stones were employed in the construction of the Crusader castle to the east. From being at the edge of the Roman city, the area became part of the residential section of the Byzantine and early Islamic city.

The **Crusader castle**, the 'Old Saray', c 100m east of the amphitheatre, consists of a square two-storey stone keep entered from the north, built partly of stones taken from the nearby ruins. An outer wall has two projecting corner towers on the south side, and was surrounded by a ditch and counter-scarp wall crossed on the north by a wooden bridge on masonry piers. It was taken by Salah al-Din in 1183, and restored to the Franks in 1192. The northern section was utilised in a sugar factory in the late 13C.

The 'New Saray' (government building) across the street was built during the reign of Abdul Hamid II in 1884/85. The Great Mosque of the Forty Martyrs or Warriors lies c 200m along the road running northeast of the tower; a low building of basalt with square limestone minaret, it has an inscription dating its construction to 1403.

BETH ALPHA

This 5C synagogue is outstanding for its 6C mosaic floor depicting the zodiac and other motifs and scenes; the naive style makes it one of the most delightful mosaics in Israel. It is on Highway 669 at Kibbutz HeftziBah c 10km west of Beth Shean off Highway 71 or 90. The National Parks Authority (☎ 06 653 2004) provides facilities, a shop and restaurant; a lively film describes the people who built the synagogue.

The synagogue was found at the kibbutz in 1928; the building, with courtyard, narthex, basilical hall with nave, probably with a women's gallery above, and apse facing Jerusalem with the ark, probably dates to the late 5C AD. The mosaic has two inscriptions by the entrance. The Aramaic inscription says it was laid in the time of Justin I in the early 6C and that the cost was raised by donations in kind from the congregation. The Greek inscription reads: 'May the craftsmen who carried out this work, Marianos and his son Hanina, be held in remembrance.' Beyond the inscription, which is flanked by a guardian lion and buffalo, the first panel of the mosaic depicts Abraham offering Isaac to God, the hand of God, the ram in the bush and two boys with an ass. The central panel of the mosaic has the signs of the zodiac with the names in Hebrew; in the centre is Apollo/Helios with quadriga (four-horse chariot), and in the corners the seasons with their names. The mosaic before the apse shows the ark of the law, religious symbols and lions; in the apse, a pit marks the place where the community chest was deposited—when opened it contained 36 Byzantine coins.

Nearby is the **Gan Hashlosha (Sachne) Park** (National Parks Authority, ☎ 06 658 6219), a recreational park with swimming pools fed by a warm spring (28°C), a rebuilt traditional Arab guest house, and a reconstructed working water-powered flour mill. There is also a replica Jewish settlement of 1936 and audio-visual material on Jewish history in the Mandate period. A museum houses a small archaeological collection. The hills behind are the mountains of Gilboa, where King Saul fought the Philistines and was killed.

JERICHO

Jericho (A. al-Riha; population 13,911 in 1997) lies in the western, arid side of the Jordan Valley, at about -250m below Mediterranean sea level, in an oasis watered by a copious spring which attracted human settlement from very early times and was later the centre of a royal estate with complex irrigation systems and rich revenues.

The modern town of Jericho is the winter resort of Palestine because of its mild climate. A maximum temperature of 48°C in summer can drop to 3°C in winter; the annual rainfall averages 150mm. The main crops are tomatoes, cucumbers, green peppers, citrus fruits, small delicious bananas and dates, which can be bought at splendid fruit stalls. The town has many trees and fine flowering plants, such as orange blossom and bougainvillea, and pools of water, all fed by the waters of the spring. The town and tourism suffered disastrously in the war in 1967 when many of the inhabitants left and many of the houses were made derelict. At that time the large refugee camps established around Jericho since the 1948 war were also abandoned and have since been bulldozed.

Jericho is now under local Palestinian Authority. The area administered by the Palestine Autonomous Authority (1999) is c 6km in diameter, with a corridor northwards to Auja al-Tahta which lies on Highway 90 up the Jordan Valley.

Practical information

Getting there
Jericho is 36km northeast of Jerusalem. Turn north off Highway 1 into Jericho.

Where to stay
The Jericho Resort Village, ☎ 02 232 1255, 📠 02 232 2189; *Hisham*

Palace Hotel, ☎ 02 232 2414; *Dayr Hajlah Monastery*, ☎ 02 994 3038.

Eating out
Green Valley ☎ 02 232 2349; *Jabal Quruntul*, ☎ 02 232 2614.

The hot climate and plentiful water provide Jericho with distinctive environmental conditions, where cereals were domesticated and irrigated crops were produced before the sixth millennium BC; dates were perhaps cultivated in the fourth millennium. Fine aqueducts from the Wadi Kilt on the southwest and from Ain Duk and Nu'aima on the northwest brought more water to Jericho in the Hasmonean and Early Roman periods for the great estates established for the cultivation of balsam, medicinal plants and spices, as well as date palms. Indigo and sugar were grown and processed in the early Islamic period (10C) and bananas in the Crusader period, perhaps earlier.

There is a complex of sites of different periods and purposes around the modern town, the most ancient of which is the tell by the spring, inhabited almost continuously from the ninth to the first millennia BC and famed for its great Neolithic tower. The site of 'New Testament' Jericho, with a palace built by Herod the Great, lies 2km to the southwest. Above it on the hills is the ring of forts built by Herod and his predecessors from the 3/2C BC onwards to guard the great oasis. To the northeast is the palatial hunting lodge and bath house at Khirbat al-Mafjar built by the caliph al-Walid II in the mid-8C AD, with magnificent mosaics. Around Jericho is a series of monasteries, many of which were founded in the Byzantine period and connected to the places of Christian baptism in the Jordan river. There is also a 6C synagogue with interesting mosaics.

The development of modern Jericho

In the Herodian period the town of Jericho was probably spread over the wide area reached by the aqueduct systems. Vespasian arrived in Jericho in June

68 on his way to Jerusalem to crush the First Revolt; the Roman army massacred those inhabitants who had not already fled, and Vespasian was joined there by Trajan with troops of the Tenth Legion.

The modern town lies on the north side of the Wadi Kilt on the edge of the Jericho oasis, on the site of the Byzantine and Islamic towns. Many Byzantine churches were built in and around the town, which is the traditional location of the 'sycomore tree of Zacchaeus' (the tax collector who climbed the tree in order to see Jesus; Luke 19: 1–10). The Bordeaux Pilgrim mentions visiting the tree of Zacchaeus in the early 4C, and by AD 570 a chapel had been built around it. The town was badly damaged in the earthquakes of 749 and 1033, but pilgrims still mentioned the house and tree in the 11C–12C. Jericho was captured by the Crusaders in 1099, was the property shortly afterwards of the Latin Patriarch in Jerusalem, and became the lordship of Eustace Garnier in 1112; these estates were confiscated by King Fulk in 1134, and shortly after, the tithes were granted to the Priory of the Quarantena (see below). In 1143 King Fulk and Queen Melisande granted the lordship and revenues of Jericho to the convent at Bethany but some lands were still held and worked by Orthodox monks in the region. Jericho fell to the Ayyubids in 1187, and from c 1212 was inhabited by Muslims. Felix Faber (c 1480) was shown the House of Zacchaeus, perhaps in a Crusader tower which was rebuilt in Ottoman times and still stood in the mid-19C. Late medieval and 19C accounts tend to describe a miserable village, but the land continued to be cultivated with important crops.

Today, approaching from the south, just before crossing the wadi you see the old British Mandate fort, used in turn by the Jordanian, Israeli and now the Palestinian administration. Opposite is a new large casino. After crossing the wadi, a modern mosque with large blue-tiled dome has been built at the turning of the road into the centre of the town. The main road continues north to the tell, and to the new cable car which connects to the Mount of Temptation. Nowadays '**the tree of Zacchaeus**' is shown a short distance from the centre of town, on the right side of the road leading to the tell.

The ancient tell

The tell (A. Tell Ain al-Sultan) lies on the northern edge of the town, on the road leading northwest out of the town centre. Open daily 08.00–17.00 (longer in summer); ☎ 02 992 1909; admission charged.

It is a high mound of bare compacted earth, much misshapen by the trenching and the heaps of debris of the five archaeological excavations which have taken place since the 1880s. From the car park at the south end of the mound, the path leads up to the view point on the top.

Remains from the first settlers in the ninth millennium, who probably visited the spring seasonally, lie right at the bottom of the nearly 20m of occupation debris which make up the mound. This build-up of debris increased dramatically in the eighth to seventh millennia (Pre-Pottery Neolithic A Period), when a small settlement spread over 3–4 hectares and was fortified by a rock-cut ditch, a stone wall and a great ***round tower** near the centre of the west side. These structures are still unique for this early period. The tower, which can be seen in the deep trench cut by K.M. Kenyon in the 1950s, is a remarkable monument, built of stone, 8.5m in diameter, still surviving 7.75m in height, with an internal flight of c 22 stairs (not accessible; upper end protected by a metal grille) leading from the inside of the town to the top of the tower. The tower and wall were built to protect and defend the closely set, small, round mudbrick houses of the inhabitants and their ownership of the spring, though it has also been understood as a flood defence. The staircase, certainly the most technically advanced feature, would seem to be an unnecessary factor in a flood defence. As well as the remarkable defences, early Jericho (Pre-Pottery Neolithic B period) is also famous for some of the earliest attempts at human portraiture, with a number of plastered skulls and plastered human statues which are usually understood today as associated with a veneration/cult of ancestors. Later in the Neolithic period, as the height of the mound grew, the fortifications went out of use and were buried. The occupation of the site fluctuated during the sixth to fourth millennia, but some of the earliest known pottery was produced here.

The town was again fortified in the Early Bronze Age, and 17 successive phases of mudbrick defence wall around the site have been excavated. Within the walls were small rectangular houses; the height of the mound grew again with the successive builds and rebuilds over nearly a thousand years. Around 2350 BC the town was destroyed leaving evidence of a violent fire, with layers of ash and fallen brick cloaking the ruined houses and filling the outer ditch. After there is only minor evidence for occupation, but many cemeteries are found around the tell, before a small, unfortified village was built. Only around 1800 BC was a fortified town again constructed on the site, and then the development was rapid. In the sides of the great trench, a little to the west of the Neolithic tower, can be seen the sloping line of white plaster which marks the great earthern bank fortification, with massive stone revetment at its foot, once capped by a mudbrick wall, which defended the town until c 1550 BC when it too was destroyed. Much of the Middle Bronze Age town has almost disappeared due to erosion in the succeeding centuries—most of the levels of this period lay above the present top of the mound. There seems to have been only limited settlement, perhaps a fortified manor house, in the 14C.

Where is Joshua's Jericho?

Jericho is most famous in the Old Testament for the story of its capture by Joshua and the Israelites, who processed around the city with the Ark of the Covenant and ram's horn trumpets, and caused the walls of Jericho to fall (Joshua 6). This event, traditionally dated in the later 13C BC, is a period for which there is virtually no evidence at Jericho; the excavations in the 1930s misdated the Early Bronze Age walls to a later period, which fed the stories about the site. Most of the mudbrick which can be seen in the sides of the other trenches on the mound dates to Early Bronze Age walls, not to the supposed time of Joshua.

The **spring**, often called Elisha's Spring (A. Ain al-Sultan) lies on the east side of the tell, across the modern road; open 07.00–17.00. The source has shifted a little over the years; a rounded masonry pool of Roman date was reused in the 12C; the source is now concreted and canalised for distribution to the gardens of the town. It has been suggested that the story of Elisha curing the spring at Jericho, which had in his time caused death and miscarriage among the inhabitants (II

Kings 2:22), may be founded in earthquake disruption and a period of radioactive contamination of the sources of the spring.

New Testament Jericho

The site of New Testament Jericho (A. Tulayl Abu Alaiq) is 2km south of the modern town. It currently (2000) lacks a custodian; no facilities.

Built on both banks of the Wadi Kilt, this was the winter resort of the Hasmonean and Herodian kings—not a town, but a palatial complex at the centre of a royal estate with an industrial complex and with other villas in the area.

An extensive **Hasmonean palace complex** lies in the northwest part of the site. A large palace with wall paintings was established here probably in the time of Hyrcanus 1 in the late 2C BC. The palace was buried under a large artificial mound, most likely in the time of Alexander Jannaeus (c 92–83 BC) and on it was built a fortified palace protected by a large ditch. Twin palaces to the east may have been built by Salome Alexandra (c 76–67 BC). Water for all these palaces was supplied by aqueduct, enough for ritual baths, magnificent swimming pools, pavilions and large gardens as well as daily needs. It was probably in one of the swimming pools on the east side of the complex that Herod the Great had Aristobulus III drowned.

These palaces are matched by the series of **palaces built by Herod the Great**. Three Herodian palaces have been excavated, built of mudbrick on stone and concrete foundations. The first palace (now covered), built 35–30 BC, is rectangular and lies on the south bank of the stream; the second, was built 30–25 BC after the earthquake of 31 BC and overlay the older Hasmonean palace on the north bank; the third palace, built 15–10 BC, was the most impressive (c 200m x 100m), spanning the bed of the Wadi Kilt. The construction is characterised by the use of concrete and of brickwork laid in the styles of *opus reticulatum* and *opus quadratum*. The building on the north bank is the best preserved and has, on the west, a great hall, which was paved with coloured stones and marble (*opus sectile*, almost entirely robbed) and had painted walls. Rows of columns on three sides were plastered to resemble marble and had Corinthian capitals. On the east side of the hall is an enclosed peristyle court (19m x 19m) which had a central garden, and a grand exedra on the north side. To the north and east were suites of rooms and a splendid bath house suite. The latter comprised six rooms, including a circular room with four exedra, walls constructed of *opus reticulatum*, and a round central pool. At the east end of a range of five rooms was another niched room which was one of two hot rooms. A stepped pool was set off to the north. South of the bath suite was another peristyle court, and on the east a large T-shaped reception hall. Most of the south front of the north wing had a portico overlooking the stream towards the palace on the south bank which included a magnificent sunken garden with niched *opus reticulatum* and *opus quadratum* façade, and a large pool. North of the palace are the remains of a service wing; to the northeast, workshops for processing balsam and winepresses were discovered at the edge of the farm lands. The palaces appear to have been abandoned well before the First Jewish Revolt.

The **hippodrome** built by Herod the Great has been located just to the west of the modern town, c 600m southwest of Tell Ain al-Sultan, at Tell al-Samarat. Just before his death, Herod ordered the leading Jews to be taken to the hippodrome at Jericho to be executed when he died, but Salome and Alexas released them. A theatre and gymnasium on a podium adjoin the north end of the rectangular hippodrome. All the structures have been thoroughly robbed for stone. Such places of entertainment are usually assumed to be mainly for pagan use.

Around Jericho

On the hills above, to the west of Jericho, the palace and the estate were protected by the **fortresses** of Threx and Taurus, Cypros and Dok which were also founded in Hasmonean times and rebuilt by Herod. Remains of the last two can be seen.

The **Monastery of the Temptation** (A. Dayr Quruntul) can be reached by cable car from Tell al-Sultan. Open 07.00–13.00, 16.00–17.00 in summer. ☎ 02 992 2827.

One of many churches and monasteries in the region, the Monastery of the

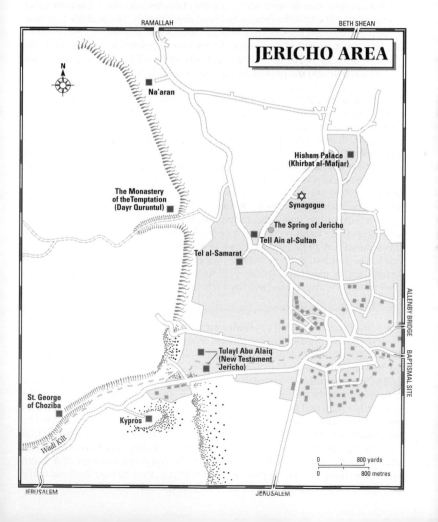

Temptation is built in the side of the mountain northwest and 300m above Jericho, on the site of the older fortress of Dagon (Dok). The monastery commemorates the 40 days' fast by Jesus, followed by his temptation by the devil 'on a very high mountain' (Matt 4: 1–10).

History of the Monastery of the Temptation

St. Chariton founded a monastery c AD 340 in caves cut into the cliff face, which survived at least to the Persian invasion in 614. Another monastery, the Quarentena, had been established here by Latin monks by 1116. It was granted to the canons of the Holy Sepulchre in 1134. A Crusader church was built here in the 12C, and many pilgrims visited the place. The Latin monks were dispossessed in 1187 when the Latin kingdom fell. By the 14C Greek and Georgian monks were occupying the churches and caves, but Felix Faber records c 1480 that the monks had been driven out by the Mamluk governor of Gaza. Pilgrims continued to visit the abandoned monastery and churches (H.B. Tristram in 1872 recorded Abyssinian Christians keeping Lent in the cave) until, in 1874, the site was formally acquired by the Greek Orthodox Patriarchate and the present monastery built in 1895.

The monastery consists of a collection of buildings hanging on the face of the cliff. It includes 19C monks' cells and a number of churches and chapels. The cave Chapel of St. Mary, built c 1175, is today the chapel of St. Elias (rebuilt 1949–65). It has medieval paintings and Greek inscriptions; the paintings include the Pantocrator, the Virgin Mary, St. John the Baptist and, on the north wall, St. Gerasimus pulling a thorn from the paw of his lion (see p 276). The principal church, the Chapel of Our Lord's Fast and the First Temptation, was the main church in the 12C, perhaps on the site of the 4C church, but was rebuilt and reconsecrated in 1904 as the Greek Church of the Annunciation. It preserves a rock cutting which marks the traditional site of the fast.

A steep path leads on to the top of the mountain where is located the Hasmonean and Herodian fortress of Dok, and a Templar fortress of the 12C. Inside the fortress walls, a ruined church (the Chapel of Our Lord's Third Temptation) is mentioned in the 14C, and some Byzantine remains have also been noted. The ruins were destroyed when foundations for a new chapel were laid in the early 20C.

The ruined remains of two **Crusader sugar mills** (A. Tawahin al-Sukkar) can be seen 1km northwest of Ain al-Sultan, on the right of the road to the Mount of Temptation. A mill is mentioned in 1124, when Jericho was reputed to produce the best sugar in the Jordan Valley.

A 6C **synagogue** is preserved in the ground floor of a private house 2km north of Jericho, with Israeli and Palestinian guards. The synagogue was of basilica type with a nave and two aisles separated by square pillars; the apse is oriented towards Jerusalem. The entrance, from the northeast, was originally fronted by two columns. There are fine mosaics. Near the entrance is a six line inscription in Aramaic: 'Remembered for good be the memory of the entire holy community, the old and the young, whom the Lord of the Universe aided and were of strength and made the mosaic. He who knows their names ... may he inscribe them in the Book of Life with all the pious, friend to all Israel. Peace. Amen.' In the nave, the mosaic has a guilloche border, enclosing two panels: on the north, alternating squares and circles; on the south, a pattern of floral lozenges surrounding an Ark of the Law on four legs with a conch above. Below it is a medallion containing Jewish symbols, a menorah, *lulav*, *shofar* (see p 349) and inscription—'Peace upon Israel'. The mosaics in the aisles have simple geometric motifs. The finds suggest the building continued to be used into the 8C.

HISHAM'S PALACE

Located off Highway 90, 3km north of Jericho, is Hisham's Palace (A. Khirbat al-Mafjar), an Umayyad hunting palace. Open daily 08.00–17.00, it is maintained by the Palestine Autonomous (National Parks) Authority, ☎ 02 992 2522. Admission charged.

Set in the open landscape on the north side of the Jericho oasis is a remarkable Umayyad complex of palace, mosque and bath house, which was supplied with water by aqueduct and set in a large walled game park laid out along the bank of a wadi. Such complexes and palaces were built by the Umayyad caliphs in the deserts to the east, and similar buildings existed in Jerusalem and at Khirbat al-Minya on the Sea of Galilee (see p 424). The complex is a rare and well preserved example of very early Islamic art and architecture, influenced by Byzantine and Eastern Sassanian art but creating something quite fresh. The combination of naive figural sculpture, naturalistic and charming animals in the round and in high relief, and intricate relief geometric styles can best be understood by seeing the restored stucco which has almost all been removed from the site and is on display in the Rockefeller Museum in Jerusalem. It was the first time in Palestine that carved stucco was employed extensively for architectural ornament.

The palace was begun during the reign of the Caliph Hisham I, possibly by his nephew Walid, who succeeded him to the caliphate in AD 743. Walid was a great hunter, a great poet but also a great hedonist. The building appears to have suffered considerable damage in the earthquake of 749, but the building programme may have been halted earlier. Later occupation of Abbasid date is also evident from the ceramics found at the site, which was excavated in the 1940s and then partly restored and partly covered for viewing. The complex consists of a walled and gated courtyard on the east side (near the modern site entrance), where pools and fountains were laid out. To the west was a rectangular palace, with central courtyard surrounded by a portico and rooms on two floors, which was probably not completed. The entrance passage was elaborately decorated in carved stucco relief on walls and ceiling; some of the former remains. Probably originally inserted at an upper level on the west side of the court, an elaborate round window, which fell during the earthquake, is reconstructed and displayed in the courtyard. Also on the west side of the courtyard, a small subterranean bath was built. Columns with crosses, marble posts from Byzantine churches, granite columns and other items suggest *spolia* from older sites were used in parts of the building. To the north of this palace was a mosque, and a courtyard.

At the north end of the complex was a magnificent ***bath house**. The façade of the square entrance porch on the east had niches from one of which came a male figure clad in a red robe, bearing a sword and standing on two lions, which may be a representation of Walid II. The porch had a dome supported on pendentives, the whole interior of which was decorated in carved stucco. Male figures were placed in the pendentives with a frieze of sheep above; on the drum the niches were filled alternately with male and female figures, the men in loincloths, the women in skirts and necklaces with breasts exposed; the stucco was brightly painted. Inside the entrance porch is a large hall (30m x 30m) with 16 massive piers which was also elaborately decorated with stucco. In the central apse on the west side was suspended a stone pendant on a stone chain which had been carved from a single stone. A cipher in the mosaic beneath suggests this apse contained the seat of the caliph. On the south side of the room was a large coldwater pool. On the floor is a magnificent complete (if rather damaged), geometric carpet-style mosaic, with a centrally placed fine, circular panel which may be the performer's circle in a room intended for music and song. The mosaic is now protected under sand; the columned piers were rebuilt in concrete to support a roof to shelter the mosaic, but the restoration programme was interrupted by the war in 1948.

At the northeast corner of the complex is first a multi-seater latrine; then the hypocaust and hot rooms in the centre north, entered from cool rooms on the west; and in the northwest corner, originally entered directly from the great hall, a small but beautifully decorated hall, perhaps intended for more private receptions by the caliph. One of the finest mosaics in the region was laid on the floor of the apse at the north end of this room. This **'tree of life'** mosaic is depicted as a fruit (quince?) tree flanked on one side by two gazelles, and on the other by a lion attacking a gazelle. Small, richly coloured tesserae were used to create subtle shading. The walls and ceiling were decorated with carved stucco, the lower areas of which remain *in situ*. There were medallions with flying horses in the pendentives; below the drum over the main area of the room was a frieze of partridges (the latter now in the Citadel Museum in Amman, Jordan); in the drum were eight windows with carved plaster grilles, some of which contained coloured glass. The flattish dome was decorated with a rosette with alternate male and female heads between foliage.

MONASTERY OF ST. JOHN THE BAPTIST
• •

From the centre of Jericho, two roads lead east towards the Jordan River fords, one slightly north of east leads after 9km to the Allenby Bridge (A. Jisr Shaikh Husain; border crossing to Jordan, see p 15); the other runs slightly south of east and reaches after 9km the Baptismal Site and the associated monastery.

The Greek Orthodox Monastery of St. John the Baptist (Mar Yuhanna, A. Qasr al-Yahud, Castle of the Jews) lies 10km southeast of Jericho, with the Place of Baptism (A. al-Maghtas) at the river itself. The monastery is 600m west of the present course of the Jordan, surrounded by marl cliffs.

History of St. John's Monastery

The monastery was built to serve pilgrims coming to the Jordan River, to the place where traditions located the baptism of Jesus by John (John 1:28) and where the Israelites forded the Jordan as they entered the promised land. A small church or chapel also existed on the river bank to mark the place of baptism. Bathing and baptism in the purifying waters of the Jordan was an attraction for pilgrims suffering from leprosy and other illnesses—for the prophet Elisha told Naaman the Aramean to bathe in the Jordan to cure his leprosy (II Kings 5). The monastery was on a road which continued across the Jordan ford to other sacred sites in the Wadi Kharrar, where the tradition of the ascension of Elijah on the east bank of the river may have been localised, and perhaps the Bethany beyond Jordan where John baptised. Many pilgrims then continued east to visit Mount Nebo.

In Byzantine times this was an imperial memorial church on a major pilgrim route from Jerusalem and Jericho, built by the Emperor Anastasius around the beginning of the 6C and provided with an endowment for an attached monastery and community to serve the needs of pilgrims. Enclosed by a defensive wall but in an exposed position above the marl cliffs of the Jordan badlands, it flourished in times favourable to Christian pilgrimage. The Byzantine structure had four great barrel vaults which probably supported a three-aisled basilica. About the middle of the 6C Justinian provided it with a well on the west side. The monks fled in the face of the Persian invasion in 614, but a mass grave discovered nearby in 1983 suggests that many pilgrims, including lepers, from as far away as Egypt and Nubia, were massacred at this time. The church was destroyed in an earthquake in 659, and rebuilt and continued to be mentioned by pilgrims over the succeeding centuries. In the early 9C there were still 35 monks serving the monastery, and 20 in 1114. Perhaps around 1139 when the monastery lay on the edges of the Crusader territories, six monks were killed in a Muslim raid. Sometime after this the Templars built a castle nearby to protect the monastery. Later in the 12C the monastery was again destroyed in an earthquake and rebuilt by the Byzantines (Manuel I Comnenus). The monastery appears to have continued to exist as a Greek establishment into the 13C–14C. In 1335 it boasted a relic of the hand and arm of John the Baptist, which was said to have been brought here from Sebaste. By the 1480s the monk Felix Faber says the church was an Arab robber fortress, its altars destroyed. It became a ruin thereafter, and is not mentioned by Irby and Mangles (English naval officers) who accompanied the pilgrimage to the Jordan in early May 1818. They gave a typical account of the modern pilgrimage:

May 1. After staying more than a month at Jerusalem, we started for the Jordan with all the pilgrims, escorted by the governor and a body of troops. The sight was most impressive. The immense number of Christians, from all quarters, the various costumes of the Greeks, the Copts from Egypt, the Abyssinians from Æthiopia: some of the pilgrims on camels, with double cradles on their backs; some on mules, also with cradles; some on horses; some on asses; in all amounting to about 5000, presented a most curious and interesting scene, winding amongst the hills, in a line as far as the eye could reach ... In the evening we arrived at the camp near Jericho ....
May 2. At two this morning we started by torchlight for the Jordan, which we reached at 7 a.m. Here we found the pilgrims bathing in the river, men, women, and children, all mixed together. They immersed their clothes in the river, gathered boughs off the trees, and filled bottles with the water to take home, in commemoration of their pilgrimage.

The monastery ruins were visited in 1873 and the remains of the Byzantine vaults were recorded, which by 1881 had been incorporated in the Russian-Greek Orthodox monastery which now occupies the site.

Stephen Graham (an English traveller) gives a similar account of a visit with Russian pilgrims to the place of baptism in March 1912, just before the beginning of Holy Week. This time more than a 1000 pilgrims set out from Jerusalem at dawn, in a long straggling crowd, led by a Turkish policeman. There were pilgrims with panniered asses and in vans, but the Russians were mostly on foot, with roughly equal numbers of men and women. At Jericho (which he describes as a miserable hamlet with two grand hotels) there was a Russian shelter where the pilgrims were fed and slept that night. They set off before sunrise next day, to avoid the heat. The sun rose before they reached the St. John Baptist Monastery. They rested in the shade of its high, gleaming, whitewashed walls and were given tea, sugar and bread. There the pilgrimage was joined by many Christian Arabs from beyond Jordan. They processed with the monks through dreadful barren clay banks, and then came to 'a little paradise of green fields and hedges of oleander and tamarisk' at the river. It took an hour for all the pilgrims to bathe. Graham and many others then had a hot walk to St. Gerasimus and were very glad to be given tea (no sugar) and olives (no bread) by the monks there. After a rest, they went on to the Mount of Temptation. Some pilgrims then returned to Jericho, others went to St. George's Monastery in the Wadi Kilt; but Graham himself walked on his own back to Jerusalem, reaching Bethany at 11 pm and then continued on to Jerusalem, reaching his bed around midnight.

The monastery was damaged in the earthquake of 1927; restored in 1952–55; but was reopened after abandonment between 1967 and 1993 when it was on the edge of no man's land. It is still an important place of baptism for Christian pilgrims, with the main pilgrimage in January (at Epiphany). A few fragments of its past survive: medieval and Byzantine carved stones, including capitals and a pair of marble columns, and an old iron-cased door.

DAYR HAJLAH

At 7km from Jericho on the road to the Baptismal Site, a minor road leads south in 3km to Dayr Hajlah, the fortified **Monastery of St. Gerasimus** near the Jordan (it can also be reached from Highway 90). This is the former site of the Monastery Church of Our Lady of Kalamon which was probably founded in the third quarter of the 5C at the same time as a nearby monastery of St. Gerasimus, and occupied until the 12C. An inscription records it was restored in the mid-12C. It was described in 1185 as a fine monastery with walls and towers, with a spacious domed church in the middle, and an adjoining small domed church which had a depiction of the Virgin with Child in the apse, said to have been painted by St. Luke. It was still occupied by Greek monks at the end of the 13C, but was by then being identified as the monastery of St. Gerasimus, which by then was abandoned. The monastery was rebuilt in 1588, destroyed in 1734, and rebuilt in its current form in 1882–85.

The present church appears to be built to the same plan as its predecessor, and some of the outer walls and the east end are medieval. The apse is flanked north and south by rectangular sacristies. There are traces of 15C–16C painting in the apse; and of an 11C–12C mosaic in the north aisle; at the west end an exonarthex may perhaps be built over the western bay of the pre-12C church. The chapel on the south side has been completely rebuilt; the icon of the Virgin noted in the 12C is now in the Chapel of St. Constantine in the Greek Orthodox Patriarchate in Jerusalem (see p 238).

NABI MUSA
• • • • • • • • • • • •

Two kilometres before the turning to Jericho, a minor road (signposted) leads south off Highway 1 and arrives after 1km at Nabi Musa. This is a somewhat confusing location of a pilgrimage shrine of Moses, his supposed burial place.

Open 08.00 to sunset; no entrance fee but donations towards upkeep welcomed; refreshments available.

According to the Old Testament, Moses died before he reached the Promised Land, having been permitted to view it from east of the Jordan, an event which is commemorated by Byzantine Christian tradition at Mt Nebo on the other side of the Jordan. This shrine was established by Baybars c 1269, when the reconquest of Palestine from the Crusaders by the Arabs was being consolidated.

It is a fine place of Muslim pilgrimage, a fortified, stone-built monastery in the wilderness. An arched entrance on the west side leads into an outer bailey or ambulatory with stables and a variety of rooms for the accommodation of pilgrims, and thence into a large courtyard with cisterns and portico; the mosque lies in the northwest part of the court, and has a simple square chamber; a chamber on the northwest contains the cenotaph of Moses. The entrance is decorated by a pair of fine grey marble columns and capitals; a lower chamber for women lies to the west.

On the upper level of the complex is a series of large, square rooms, with windows overlooking the desert, also for the accommodation of pilgrims. Poorer pilgrims lived in tents or in the open around the shrine. The complex is surrounded by the graves of pilgrims and those wishing to be buried in proximity to the shrine. The minaret, and the high ground to the east with a dome over a tomb both provide a viewing point from which Mt Nebo can be seen. The great annual pilgrimage to the shrine in April became a focus of political demonstration in the 1930s and pilgrimage was banned under the Mandate government in 1937. The shrine was used as a fortified base by the Jordanian and Israeli armies until 1973. Pilgrimage began again in 1987, was discontinued during the Intifada, but resumed in 1997.

QUMRAN
• • • • • • • • •

At the foot of the cliffs near the northern end of the Dead Sea lies the site of Qumran and the caves where the Dead Sea Scrolls were discovered (see p 258). It is reached off Highway 90, c 8km south of the intersection with Highway 1. The site is run by the National Parks Authority (☎ 02 994 2235); there are facilities and a very large shop.

History

The discovery The first 'Dead Sea Scroll' was found in 1947 in Mandate Palestine by a local Bedouin looking for a goat in the cliffs west of Qumran, in what was later called Cave I, and was taken to a priest of the Syrian Church in Jerusalem. It was shown to scholars who recognised it as a genuine ancient document. Other scrolls began to appear on the market, and the scholarly world began to investigate the source of the texts in the months leading up to the outbreak of war less than a year later in 1948. Only in 1949, when the site came under Jordanian jurisdiction, were the first proper surveys and excavations begun around Qumran, by a team led by Father R. de Vaux of the Dominican Ecole Biblique in Jerusalem, with G. Lankester Harding of the Department of Antiquities of Jordan and the Palestine Archaeological Museum (the Rockefeller Museum). Around 300 caves were investigated, mainly in the cliffs to the west. Nearly 40 caves showed evidence of ancient use. Cave IV, an artificial cave cut in the marl adjacent to Qumran, contained the most important deposit; originally as many as 400 scrolls were deposited there, but as they had not been stored in jars (perhaps because they had been vandalised by the Roman soldiers during the destruction of Qumran), they had been damaged by damp, salts, white ants and rats, and were mostly in small fragments.

The scrolls discovered during the archaeological investigations were taken to the Rockefeller Museum; the material is displayed in the Shrine of the Book at the Israel Museum in Jerusalem.

The scrolls found around Qumran are said to comprise more than 75,000 fragments belonging to around 500 manuscripts, containing parts of nearly all the books of the Old Testament. They are written on skins and papyrus (apart from the two Copper Scrolls), mainly in Hebrew and Aramaic. There are also commentaries on the biblical books; and there are sectarian works. These include a manual of the creed and conduct of the sect which wrote and copied the texts, who are usually identified with the Essenes, a Jewish sect mentioned by Philo of Alexandria, by Flavius Josephus and by Pliny.

The Qumran documents were written between the 3C BC and the 1C AD, at a time when the final version of the Old Testament was being produced, and in a setting contemporary with the beginnings of Christianity. The importance of the scrolls, is that they provide an early version of the Old Testament with which the later copies of the various versions available to scholars can be compared. In large part they deal with the religious thought and philosophy of the time, which adds to our understanding of Judaism, and of early Christianity.

They were composed at a period of religious sectarianism among the Jews (Pharisees, Saducees, Essenes, Zealots) and of political turmoil, when in turn the Ptolemies, the Seleucids, the Hasmoneans, the Romans and the Herodian Dynasty had provided the fuel for external and internal strife, which culminated in the outbreak of the First Jewish Revolt in AD 66. The site of Qumran appears to be that of a small, sectarian, very conservative Jewish community with strict rules and hierarchy, separating itself from the main orthodox community and the Temple in Jerusalem, with rules relating to ritual baths and communal meals, economic purity and chastity. They lived in the wilderness preparing for a great and holy apocalyptic war, but eventually met their end at the hands of the Romans in AD 68–69 during the suppression of the First Revolt. Generally it is thought that the scrolls were hidden in the caves at the approach of the Roman army.

The settlement was founded on the site of an 8C–7C BC fortress with a round cistern that was probably destroyed in the early 6C BC. The community settled there, probably in the late 2C BC, cleaned out and reused the round cistern, and rebuilt the new settlement with rectangular cisterns. The settlement was modified and enlarged over the next two centuries, showed evidence of defence and destruction probably in AD 68–69, and then perhaps a brief Roman occupation lasting up to the fall of Masada in AD 73.

The community Scholars take many variant views: that the community was or was not Essene; that it was Zealot; that it was early Christian; that the site was a perfume factory and the scrolls are not related to the settlement, but were hidden in the nearby caves by the Zealots (see Masada); none of the many strands fit together completely. None detracts from the excitement and importance of the discovery.

The site is on a low plateau about 2km west of the Dead Sea; a path guides the visitor through the remains, and from the far end there is a view of Cave IV and, to the east, of the cemetery.

The community had a central keep or watchtower with entrance at first floor level, and was bounded on the south by the banks of the wadi, and to north and east by the plateau edge, but was not particularly defensible. The jumble of rough stone walls, with a little mud mortar and brick, covering an area c 100m x 80m, conceals an organised layout of rooms, connecting systems of plastered water channels and 8 main rectangular cisterns and baths. One large cistern is round, and was constructed at the time of the earlier Iron Age settlement. The site has no natural water supply, apart from winter torrents in the wadi below, so a channel brought water from the cliffs to reservoirs on the site. The number of cisterns and baths has been related not just to the need for storage, but also to the requirements of ritual ablution for the community, and the needs of the industrial operations carried out on the site. One large cistern has a major split, perhaps damage from the great earthquake of 31 BC. The function of many of the rooms was indicated by the contents, principally the pottery. Two large rooms are described as assembly rooms, one of which contained a possible inkwell and the debris of plastered tables and benches that fell from an upper room; it is thought that the scrolls may have been assembled, stitched together and written at these tables. Another large room had a small room off it which contained so many serving dishes that it seems likely to have been the community dining room. A large part of the settlement is given over to workshops and storage. Pottery kilns and a basin for cleaning the clay, a milling area and bake oven, and a stable have all been identified; the evidence for workshops underlies the suggestion that this was not the home of a religious community, but an industrial site. However, many medieval and later monasteries have such evidence for industry, as they had in large part to be self-sufficient, and perhaps Qumran should be viewed as one of the precursors of the monastic movement in the Judaean wilderness.

Qumran is clearly not an ordinary village composed of small domestic units; there is little evidence for where the community actually lived, unless all slept in dormitory accommodation in upper storeys, or in the caves, or in tents—there is some evidence for all these solutions. That the community was of some size and duration is also suggested by the cemetery which lies to the east of the buildings and contains over 1000 graves, but little of it has been excavated.

Cave IV in the marl has become dangerously eroded and inaccessible, but can be viewed from the end of the plateau beyond the settlement.

EN GEDI

A remarkable complex of springs, streams, ancient remains, plants and animals make the oasis of En Gedi well worth a visit combined with an opportunity to bathe in the Dead Sea.

The oasis is163km from Jerusalem on Highway 90. The reserve, with facilities, is1km north of the modern resort of En Gedi, where there are hostels, hotels, and many cafés. There are restrictions on access to parts of the reserve.

Information

Nature Reserves Authority, ☎ 07 658 4285.

Where to stay

The *En Gedi Kibbutz Hotel* is 2km to the south, ☎ 07 659 4222, 📠 07 658 4328.

Beaches

There is a public beach with showers on the Dead Sea shore which is very crowded on holidays; a paying beach is nearby. Visitors are encouraged to use the mineral-rich mud said to be good for the skin.

The large **nature reserve** contains four springs, is entered from the road sign-posted Nahal David, and has an excellent leaflet with map. As well as the footpath through the reserve, which leads to a series of waterfalls, there are several other trails through Nahal David, Nahal Arugot or to the plateau, and ibex and hyrax can usually be seen. Between the two valleys and up a steep footpath to a plateau approached from either north or south (but easiest access is from the south side in the Nahal Arugot) is the site of the fourth millennium Chalcolithic temple. Well-preserved foundations of an irregular enclosure with a small passage gate entrance on the south, and a broad-room building opposite. The building has a rounded feature against its rear wall, interpreted from the ash, bones and other materials found on it, including a zoomorphic figurine, as an altar. Benches and pits occupied the rest of the room. In the court is a basin, perhaps intended for libations. Another room, perhaps intended for the custodian or visitors, lies on the east side of the enclosure, adjacent to a second gate on the northeast. It is thought that this temple may have been linked to the same or similar rituals as those con-nected with the Nahal Mishmar treasure (see p 257). The site has a magnificent view over the Dead Sea, and the oasis backed by dramatic cliffs.

Just below the temple on the south is a large colony of rock hyrax living in the canes around the En Gedi spring, whose waters once drove a flour mill (probably Mamluk or Ottoman in date) the well-preserved remains of which survive just below the spring. On the slopes below the mill are the ruins of an extensive set-tlement, with terracing and reservoirs. Several fortresses of Iron Age, Roman and later date existed around the oasis on the south and to the west on the higher plateau. The archaeological remains and documents suggest the oasis was occupied fairly continuously from the 7C BC into at least early Islamic times. In Roman times the Jewish occupants of the settlement grew dates and were famous for the production of perfumes. They were massacred by the Zealots at Masada during the First Revolt.

On the south side of the date grove is the road signposted to Nahal Arugot. At 250m on the right is the modern tent-style roof over the remains of the **En Gedi synagogue** (National Parks Authority; ☎ 03 776 2163). First built in the 3C AD, and subject to modifications and enlargement until the mid-5C, the synagogue appears to have been destroyed by fire in the mid-6C. The fire preserved much of its contents. It had an entrance passage from which three doors gave onto the west side of the synagogue. At the entrance is a long mosaic dedicatory inscription, and in the centre an attractive mosaic with birds. In the north wall, facing Jerusalem, was the place of the Torah scroll and the niche with a repository in which scrolls were found; in front was a raised platform, and to right, a seat for the leader of the congregation. Around the synagogue are the remains of a street, buildings and a ritual bath of the 1C AD.

After a further 300m, on the right just east of the track leading up to the Chalcolithic Temple, is the partly excavated Iron Age mound of **Tel Goren**, with remains dating from the 7C BC and later. After 600m you come to the Nahal Arugot parking lot. As well as the trails and waterfalls, further up the valley there are pools.

MASADA
• • • • • • • • •

Famous for the siege of the Sicarii Zealots by the Roman army in AD 72–73, Masada is also the most impressive of the forts built by Herod the Great in one of the most dramatic landscapes of the region, overlooking the Dead Sea and the wilderness.

From the east, it is c 180km from Jerusalem, west of Highway 90; from the west, 22km from Arad on Highway 3199. The shortest road connection between the east and west entrances is 70km. The site is managed by the National Parks Authority (☎ 07 658 4117/8).

• Open daily throughout the year, except Yom Kippur, from sunrise to one hour before sunset; access from the Dead Sea (eastern side) has large restaurants, shops and facilities. The cable car operates 06.30–16.00/17.00 except Fri and eve of a holidays when it stops at 14.00; eve of Yom Kippur stops at 12.00; the service is at half-hourly intervals (more frequent at busy times). Access for walkers by the steep Snake Path on the east (45–60 minutes). On the west side there is a car park and basic facilities, and an easy 15–20 minute climb by the siege ramp. A sound and light show operates at the west entrance to the site, in the summer, accessible from Arad (tickets ☎ 07 995 9333). There are camping facilities nearby if reserved in advance. Visitors should come prepared with hat, sunglasses and footwear with good soles.

History

Most of what we know about Masada depends on the historian Josephus Flavius, who could offer the experience of one who had served on both sides in the First Jewish Revolt, although he was not present at the siege.

Josephus notes Masada had been fortified on a small scale by Jonathan, who is usually identified with Alexander Janneus. In 40 BC Herod had to escape from the Hasmonean faction and fled southwards from Jerusalem to the protection of the Nabataean king. On his way through the wilderness he paused at the rock of Masada, where he left most of his family in an apparently secure refuge, with a garrison of 800 men to protect them. But it was not a well-stocked refuge, the rock was besieged by his enemies, and the family nearly died of thirst before a violent and unexpected rainstorm saved them—the rainwater collected in pools on the surface.

This episode must surely have remained vivid in the minds of Herod and his family, and after he became king in 37 BC he took steps to put the fortress of Masada in good order. Josephus says he selected this remote spot because it was a secure refuge in the event of his overthrow by the Jews; and because it formed part of a chain of fortresses which protected the south flank of the kingdom against attack from Ptolemaic Egypt, where the queen Cleopatra was hoping to persuade Mark Antony to get rid of Herod.

Herod began building and provisioning Masada on a vast and luxurious scale. The building work continued through a number of years, perhaps starting in 33 or 31, up to his death in 4 BC. Under the administration of the Roman procurators in the 1C AD, a garrison force was maintained in the Herodian fortress, and because of the arid conditions the vast siege supplies laid in by Herod survived—corn, pulses, dates, wine, oil etc.; the rock had huge cisterns fed by run-off in the winter, and by aqueducts.

When the First Jewish Revolt started in 66 AD, Menahem, a Zealot (conservative sectarian Jew) of the extremist Sicarii (meaning 'knife' or 'dagger') group and his men, overwhelmed the Roman garrison at Masada by a stratagem and slew them. The Herodian stores on the rock at Masada made a very secure refuge for the Zealots. Menahem however was murdered in Jerusalem not long after, and was succeeded as leader by a member of his family called Eleazar ben Yair. After the fall of Qumran and Jerusalem to the Romans, the group was probably augmented by other refugees. The remains left by the devout but fanatical Jewish sect found at the rock include not just simple domestic objects of pottery, glass and metal, but also ritual baths for purification, and written documents, on pottery fragments, leather and papyri. The scroll fragments included many biblical fragments including parts of the Books of Psalms and of Leviticus, as well as Qumran sectarian documents and wisdom literature.

Josephus makes these Sicarii Zealots the villains of the story, and as a result exaggerates; but they were certainly responsible for ravaging the local countryside, killing many of the people at En Gedi, and they may also have destroyed the settlement at En Boqeq. Josephus has ben Yair say before the end that defeat is 'God's vengeance for the many wrongs that in our madness we dared to do to our own countrymen'. The Zealots remained in possession of the rock all through the Roman suppression of the First Revolt, including the terrible siege and downfall of Jerusalem in AD 70. Bassus was then appointed Roman legate and set about capturing the fortresses of Herodion and Machaeros, also still in rebel Jewish hands. In AD 72 Flavius Silva was appointed procurator and probably in autumn of that year set a full-scale military operation in train to mop up the last centre of resistance at Masada. Flavius Silva set out from Jerusalem with a large force of the Tenth Legion (the regular Roman troops garrisoning Jerusalem since its fall), plus auxiliary troops, plus thousands of Jewish prisoners-of-war as a workforce to take Masada. Their aim was the reduction of Masada and the capture of its garrison—960 Sicarii Zealots under Eleazer ben Yair, including some women and children.

At Masada we can see most vividly the process of the crushing of a local rebellion within the Roman Empire. Silva built a siege wall right round the site, with 12 straddle towers and eight camps to police it, to ensure nothing and no-one got in or out of the fortress. Once this, and his long supply chain to feed and water his army in the wilderness was established, he set his force to work on building a siege ramp on the more accessible west side of the mountain, but still from a spot c 152m below the fortress walls. Here the Romans raised a platform to a height of c 100m; on top of it they built a pier composed of great stones fitted together, c 25m wide and of the same height; then a tower c 27m high was erected and covered all over with iron plates; on this the Romans mounted a number of spear-throwers and stone-throwers who drove the defenders from the battlements. Then a great ram was constructed, and set to swing continuously against the wall till at last a breach was made. In the spring of AD 73, rather than surrender, the Zealot defenders set fire to their houses and then the men killed the women and children, and drew lots to decide who should slay the rest; Eleazar, the last man, died by his own sword. Only two women and five children were said to have hidden from the carnage and survived.

Afterwards a Roman garrison was maintained on the rock till at least early in the 2C AD. It was then abandoned until in the 5C–6C some monks settled on the site and built a monastery church and cells over and in the ruins.

The site was rediscovered in 1838, since when it has been the focus of much archaeological activity and restoration work, and a major focus of tourism. The defence of the Sicarii Zealots against the Romans became the symbol of Israel's fight for an independent state. Today the story presented by Josephus and so well illuminated by Yigael Yadin (who excavated Masada) is questioned by some. All we know about the defenders of Masada before the siege gives an unpalatable picture of an extremist group who were noted for murdering the High Priest in Jerusalem, and massacring the Jewish inhabitants of En Gedi; the speech of Eleazar ben Yair before the suicide of the defenders of Masada given in such detail by Josephus must have been written by the historian himself, as it is unlikely that the few survivors relayed it. For many years Masada has been the icon of Israel, exemplifying the determination to fight to the end against great odds; now some in Israel suggest such extremists were ultimately more destructive.

Masada rises c 400m above the Dead Sea. As you ascend on the east side of the rock, you obtain a good view of the Roman siege wall and camps around the base of the site, including a partly reconstructed camp next to the car park. Just below the crest, some large cisterns are viewable. On the top, well defined paths lead the visitor around the remains. The short path takes you round the principal remains on the north half of the rock; if you have more time, a second path takes you to the south end of the rock.

The top of the rock (c 600m x 300m) is surrounded by a defensive double wall with compartments (a casemate wall) which were used by the Zealots as living quarters. Their occupation is marked by cooking ovens and ritual pools. The path leads past a quarry on the left and a large residence and then a villa on the right, which may have been the commander's residence, to a street dividing a large administration building (on the left) from (on the right) a very extensive complex of storerooms—the resource of the besieged. The latter have been restored (above the black line) with the stones that fell from their upper walls. Beyond to the north is a large **bath house**, well conserved, which had all the latest Roman mod cons of piped water and hot air. Like most of the buildings at Masada, it had painted wall plaster covering the rough masonry, here in particular providing a luxurious Roman-inspired elegance of vegetal and architectural designs. A view of the surrounding structures may be had from the domed roof. The bath house is aligned to and relates to the palace which lies ahead, but is separated from the private quarters of Herod by a massive wall.

Beyond the dividing wall is the upper terrace of the ***Northern Palace** which provides a dramatic view to the north of the rock and a partial view down to the two lower terraces of the palace. This was the luxurious villa/palace of Herod the Great, virtually hanging in space with graceful curves on three terraces cut in the top of the northern cliff of the rock, with a well-guarded stepped approach. Living quarters with simple black and white mosaics fronted by a semicircular porch were located on the upper terrace. The lower two sections of the palace are well worth visiting, but the visit involves a descent by a modern metal access stair (c 160 steps) down the west side. The two lower terraces were solely for rest and relaxation. A circular columned pavilion and other rooms are located on the middle terrace. The room on the lowest terrace was probably for dining, and remains of wall paintings of the type which imitates panels of veined ornamental stone survive, with pilasters and columns fluted in stucco. The Corinthian capitals here were painted in gold on white (elsewhere at Masada, rather plainer capitals were also painted). There is a small royal bath house on the west, at the lowest point of the lowest terrace.

Returning to the top, the area near the top of the modern stairs is where fragments of pottery inscribed with names, including that of ben Yair, were discovered, and associated with the drawing of lots in the final death pact. Continuing along the west ramparts, built into the casemates are the remains of a synagogue, Zealot in its last phase, oriented towards Jerusalem, with stepped benches lining the walls. Here and just beyond were found scrolls, some relating to those found at the site of Qumran.

The eroded remains of the great Roman siege ramp can be seen towards the centre of the west side, and the part of the rampart which was breached in the final attack lies at its head. This point also provides a dramatic view of the Roman siege wall opposite, running across virtually inaccessible rocks, and to the northeast, Silva's camp. Ahead lies the Western Palace, the Herodian throne/reception room complex of state rooms and courts, with an early style of polychrome mosaic of pleasing design and colour; here too is evidence of the Zealot occupation.

Just north of the palace and opposite the siege ramp lie the remains of the **Byzantine church** and monastery established in the 5C–6C. A walled complex was built in the 1C AD ruins, entered by a gateway incorporating an early pointed arch. The church, with apse with window, was served by courtyard and annexes and may at its peak have contained up to 20 monks. The evidence for some 13 hermit cells was found outside the enclosure scattered over the plateau; there is some evidence that the monks had window glass in their cells.

From here you can return to the cable car past another large building identified as the officers' quarters, or continue on to the south end of the rock where scattered remains can be seen. Below the western side of the summit were great ranges of cisterns which you can visit by descending the ramp path and following the marked path. Immediately south of the Western Palace is a pool and another house, and further south to the right is a columbarium, usually understood as a dovecote or pigeon house. At the south end are a great reservoir and a cistern, and at the extreme end, the Southern Citadel. From here also the siege wall is still plainly visible.

ELAT

• • • • •

In the far south of Israel, Elat lies on the northwest tip of the Gulf of Aqaba, opposite the Jordanian port of Aqaba. Aqaba (ancient Ayla) was the regional port during the last two millennia; Elat (pop. 38,000 in 1995) has been developed as Israel's port on the Red Sea since 1949. It has no ancient remains.

Elat has been intensively developed as a seaside resort and marina between the beach and the mountains. The average January temperature ranges from 9° to 21°C (but in August 25°–39°C); the mean annual rainfall is only 25mm.

Practical information

 Getting there
There is an airport in the centre of the town—its terminal is closer to the centre than the *Egged* bus station which is located further northwest on Hativat Ha Negev Rd.

 Tourist information
The Tourist Information Centre is on Yotam Rd overlooking the Central Park (☎ 07 637 2111; 📠 07 637 6763); opening hours Sun–Thur 08.00–20.00, Fri 08.00–14.00, Sat and hol 10.00–14.00. Leaflet available with up-to-date information on where to stay (hotels in town, local bed and breakfast accommodation, kibbutz fly-drive packages) and what to do. For access to the coast of Sinai, see p 14.

 Where to stay
Elat has huge numbers of hostels and of luxury hotels, many of the latter serving package holiday visitors in winter and local summer holidaymakers. The *Red Mountain Hostel,* (☎/📠 07 637 4263) is near the bus station, the *Adi Hotel,* 6 Topaz (☎ 07 637 6151 , 📠 07 637 6154) near the Tourist Information Centre. The *Taba Hilton*—in Egypt but between the Israeli and Egyptian border posts—requires Israeli passport formalities but has a

desk at the Egyptian frontier and is cheaper if you want a first class hotel (and a casino).

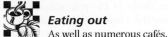

Eating out
As well as numerous cafés, and hotel restaurants, there is *Au Bistro* (French, ☎ 07 637 4333) and *Fisherman's House* at Coral Beach.

The principal attractions of the town and area are desert nature trails and water-sports, particularly underwater training and tours to observe the corals and fish. The **Underwater Observatory** (open Sat–Thur 08.30–16.30, Fri 08.30–15.00) just before the Egyptian border at Taba. The **Coral Beach Nature Reserve**, also south of Elat on the Taba Road (National Nature Reserve, ☎ 07 637 6829; open 09.00–17.00, –18.00 in summer), has stony corals and fish in a reef environment, for swimmers and snorkellers. The coral reefs are subject to careful regulation to avoid pollution and damage.

Elat lies on the bird migration route which follows the coast of the Red Sea southwards, and the Mediterranean littoral northwards. Between February and May the hydroponic farms, salt pans and date plantations in the area attract huge numbers of birds on their way north for the summer (a bird sanctuary is located just north of the salt pans and airport). Nearly a million birds of prey pass by on migration, and as many as 4000 migrating white storks have been seen soaring on the thermals over the Negev. A Birdwatchers' Trail starts from the North Beach, passes the bird ringing station, date grove and the salt pans, and arrives at the bird sanctuary.

Outside Elat

Elat is a centre for tours into the Negev, mainly by jeep, but there are also some walking trails (Amram Pillars and Shehoret Canyon), to view the remarkable desert landscapes.

You can visit the ancient and modern copper mining site of **Timna** some 30km north of Elat off Route 90, set in a large semicircular valley, now Timna Park (facilities). The dramatic rock pillars, including 'Solomon's Pillars', mark the site of mines and smelting camps worked from the fourth millennium onwards, in particular by Egyptian expeditions sent by Ramses III; a mine, walled smelting camp and the remains of an Egyptian shrine or sanctuary (14C–12C BC) dedicated to Hathor, which was also used by the local population, can be seen. The principal site of Roman exploitation lay c 10km to the south at Beer Ora.

The **Yotvata Wildlife Preserve** lies c 35km north of Elat, between Kibbutz Yotvata and Kibbutz Samar on Highway 90 (National Nature Reserve, ☎ 07 637 3057). In an environment of acacia forest, salt marsh and sand dunes are pre-served herds of onagers, ostrich, oryx; there is a predator centre for wolves, foxes, leopards and other felines, as well as hyenas and reptiles; and in the Desert Night Life Exhibition Hall, night conditions are artificially maintained during the day for gerbils, spiny mice, dormice and other nocturnal animals.

Glossary

Note: A. = Arabic; H. = Hebrew

Ambulatory corridor for walking, often covered

Amir (A.) prince, military commander

Aqaba (A.) slope or lane

Architrave the lowest part of the entablature, the beam resting on the capital; ornamental moulding around the exterior of an arch

Archivolt the under curve of an arch from impost (see below) to impost

Arcosolium term used for a rock-cut trough or bench burial with arched opening above it

Ashlar squared stone laid in regular courses

Atrium in early Christian and medieval churches, the colonnaded forecourt

Bab (A.) gate

Basilica Roman hall of justice and commerce; church or synagogue with nave, aisles and clerestory

Bimah (bema) platform in a synagogue for the reading of the Torah (the law); sometimes in churches opposite the chancel

Bir (A.) well

Birkat (A.) pool or reservoir

Broad-room a rectangular room with entrance in one of the long walls

Cavetto a hollowed moulding whose profile is the quadrant of a circle

Chamfer to bevel or channel an edge

Ciborium a canopy raised over the high altar in a church

Corbel projecting or overlapping stone blocks supporting a roof

Cornice projecting upper section of an entablature, or a horizontal moulded projection crowning a building or some part of it

Crenellations indented parapet

Cupola dome, especially a miniature dome on a lantern

Cyma-recta moulding a moulding consisting of a concave and a convex line, an ogee

Dar (A.) house

Dair (A.) Christian monastery

Daraj (A.) steps

Derekh (H.) road

Dentils teeth-like row of small rectangular blocks under a cornice

Diaconicon a sacristy or vestry

Diglyphs a block with two grooves between metopes in a Doric frieze

Dikka (A.) platform for prayer repeater in a mosque

Diwan a room open at one side, often with raised floor, where judgements were given and councils held in Ottoman practice

Dosseret extra stone set above the capital to level columns of varying height

Drafted masonry building stone with flat-dressed edges

Elbow consoles or brackets engaged angled columns supporting a capital

Firman (Persian) royal decree

Gadrooned voussoirs voussoirs(see below) decorated with sets of convex curves at right angles to the architrave

Giv'ah (H.) hill

Guttae stone pegs beneath the triglyphs in a Doric entablature

Hammam (A.) bath house

Hanafi one of the four canonical law schools of Islam.

Hanbali one of the four canonical law schools of Islam.

Har (H.) mount
Haram (A.) a sanctuary, as in Haram al-Sharif, the Noble Sanctuary
Hypogeum an underground chamber or vault
Iconostasis the screen in Orthodox churches separating the sanctuary from the main body of the church, on which icons are hung
Impost upper (projecting) course of a pillar or abutment, often decorated, on which the foot of an arch rests
Iwan vaulted hall with a large arched opening
Jami' (A.) congregational mosque in which the Friday prayers are said (as in Masjid al-Jami')
Joggled voussoirs voussoirs (see below) joined by notches and corresponding projections
Khan (A.) caravanserai, or hostel providing accommodation for merchants and other visitors
Khanqah (A.) Muslim monastery for Sufi mystics
Kikkar (H.) square
Kokhim (H.) term for rock-cut burial places of the Roman period which are roughly oven-shaped
Lantern a structure with (glazed) apertures on top of a dome or room, which admits light and ventilation
Loggia a gallery or arcade having one or more sides open to the air
Long-room a rectangular room with entrance in a short wall
Machicolation opening between the corbels supporting the parapet (often above a gate) through which combustibles, molten lead, stones and other objects were dropped upon attackers
Madfan (A.) a burial place
Madrasa (A.) religious school for teaching the principles of orthodox Islam
Maktab (A.) a Muslim primary school
Maliki one of the four canonical law schools of Islam
Mar (A.) Christian saint
Mastaba a raised platform, particularly an open-air prayer place in the Haram.
Mathara (A.) place of ablution
Mawazin (A.) in Jerusalem specifically the 'scales', or arcades on the platform of the Dome of the Rock
Mazar (A.) a shrine visited by pilgrims
Metope space between two triglyphs in a Doric frieze
Mihrab (A.) niche (normally in a mosque) marking the direction of prayer
Minaret (A. *manara*) tower from which the call to prayer is made
Minbar (A.) stepped pulpit, normally inside the mosque, from which the Friday sermon is given
Misnah Jewish law
Mouldings projecting or recessed bands used to ornament walls, arches etc
Muezzin (A.) official who gives the call to prayer for the mosque
Muqarnas decoration stalactite carving, usually ornamenting the vault of a semi-dome or a corbel and much used in Mamluk times in Jerusalem.
Musalla (A.) open place for performing the Muslim prayer
Orthostat a straight-sided, standing stone
Ostraka (Greek) an inscribed potsherd
Palmette an ornament with narrow radiating divsions, somewhat resembling a palm-leaf
Pendentive a section of masonry forming a spherical triangle supporting a dome above a rectangular base
Pilaster rectangular engaged column
Prothesis a place for the elements before the Eucharist

Qanatir (A.) arcade, especially the arched colonnades on the platform of the Dome of the Rock

Qibla (A.) the direction of prayer

Qubba (A.) dome

Rehov (H.) street

Ribat (A.) in medieval Jerusalem a hospice where pilgrims were given free accommodation

Riwaq (A.) portico, in Jerusalem the arcade around the north and west sides of the Haram

Sabil (A.) fountain founded for the free supply of water for drinking and ablution

Saray (A.) palace

Sederot (H.) boulevard, avenue

Sha'ar (H.) gate

Shafi'i one of the four canonical law schools of islam

Shaikh (A.) elder, tribal chief

Shari'a (A.) street

Shi'a the minority Islamic group, adherents of the cause of the Caliph 'Ali and his descendants

Siqaya (A.) drinking fountain, water for ablutions

Soffit the under surface of a lintel, vault or arch

Spandrel triangular space between two arches, or between an arch and a wall

Springers architecturally, the supports or imposts from which an arch springs

Squinch a straight or arched support constructed across an angle to support a superstructure

String course a horizontal course in a façade, sometimes ornamental

Stucco coating of (ornamental) plaster or cement

Sufi a Muslim mystic

Sunni the mainstream orthodox group of Islam.

Suq (A.) market street or bazaar

Talmud interpretation of the Mishnah

Tariq (A.) road

Temenos (Greek) sacred area around a temple, sacred enclosure or precinct

Tie-beams structural, and often ornamental, beam linking the tops of capitals in an arcade

Triglyph a block with three vertical grooves between metopes on a Doric frieze

Turba(t) (A.) mausoleum

Tympanum in medieval architecture the space between the lintel and the arch above it

Voussoirs wedge-shaped stone blocks forming an arch

Wali (A.) Muslim saint or holy man

Waqf (pl. awqaf)(A.) endowment(s) for pious purposes

Yad (H.) memorial

Yeshiva (H.) rabbinical seminary

Yishuv older Jewish population established in Jerusalem by the early 20th century

Zawiya (A.) 'corner', a place for devotion, often the dwelling and later burial place of a pious Muslim

Zuqaq (A.) alley

Index